FROM CORTÉS TO CASTRO

FROM CORTÉS TO CASTRO

An Introduction to the History of
Latin America, 1492-1973

SIMON COLLIER

Macmillan Publishing Co., Inc.
New York

Macmillan Publishing Co., Inc.
866 Third Avenue, New York, N.Y. 10022

Library of Congress Cataloging in Publication Data

Collier, Simon Daniel White.
  From Cortés to Castro.

  1. Latin America—History. I. Title.
F1410.C7   980   74-3252
ISBN 0-02-527180-6

SECOND PRINTING 1975
Printed in the United States of America

Contents

List of Maps   vii
Acknowledgements   viii
Preface   ix
Postscript – September 1973   xii

Chapter 1   THE STORY—OR PART OF IT AT   1
            LEAST
            Conquest and Settlement, 1492–1580
            The Course of Empire, 1580–1807
            The Wars of Independence, 1807–30
            The Creole States, 1830–1910
            Toward Uncharted Seas, 1910–73

Chapter 2   GEOGRAPHY AND COMMUNICATIONS   75
            Basic Geography
            Transport and Communications

Chapter 3   THE PEOPLES OF LATIN AMERICA   101
            The Amerindians
            The Iberians
            The Africans
            Mestizos, Mulattoes, and the Castes
            The Completion of the Ethnic Pattern

Chapter 4   SOCIAL AND ECONOMIC DEVELOP-
            MENT TO 1860   160
            The European Invasions
            . Aspects of Colonial Life
            Late-Colonial Changes
            Independence

CONTENTS

Chapter 5 SOCIAL AND ECONOMIC DEVELOP-
           MENT SINCE 1860   217
           The International Economy
           Changes and Constants
           Some Contemporary Dilemmas

Chapter 6 POLITICAL TRADITIONS   301
           The Imperial Framework
           The Impact of Liberalism
           Dictators and Dictatorships
           Movements and Programs

Chapter 7 LATIN AMERICA, THE WEST, AND
           THE WORLD   372
           The Colonial Period
           Independence and Balkanization
           The New World and the Old
           The Era of the *Pax Britannica*
           Echoes of War
           The Age of the Superpowers
           Today and Tomorrow

A Note on Further Reading   409

Index   411

List of Maps

War of the Triple Alliance 1865–1869   27

War of the Pacific 1879–1883   30

Mexican Revolution 1913–1914   41

The Main Uses of the Big Stick 1906–1934   44

The Chaco War 1932–1934   50

Ecuador-Peru Conflict 1941   54

Brazil and Brasilia   60

Cuban Revolution 1956–   62

Acknowledgements

The author and publishers would like to offer their thanks to the following: Mrs. George Bambridge and Eyre Methuen & Co., Doubleday & Company, Inc., and the Macmillan Company of Canada for permission to reprint two lines from Rudyard Kipling's poem "The Broken Men", which appears in *The Five Nations*; London Magazine Editions for permission to reprint four lines from their edition of Donald Davie's extended poem "Six Epistles to Eva Hesse".

The verse which appears on p. 66 is taken from *The Tom Lehrer Song Book* by Tom Lehrer, © 1952, 1953, 1954 by Tom Lehrer. Used by permission of Tom Lehrer.

The verse which appears on p. 133 is taken from "The Return of Martin Fierro" from *The Gaucho Martin Fierro* by José Hernández, translated by Walter Owen. Copyright 1936 © 1964 by Holt, Rinehart and Winston, Inc. Reprinted by permission of Holt, Rinehart and Winston, Inc.

Preface

This book provides a historical introduction to Latin America. It is divided into seven chapters, the first of which is devoted to a very simple narrative of the main events in Latin American history since 1492, before which date, properly speaking, no such thing as Latin America existed. I have brought the story as close to the present as possible, but by the time this book appears in print, the developments mentioned in the last few pages of Chapter 1 may look strangely out of date, and the focus of interest may well have shifted to events which have still not occurred at the time of writing. (Last-minute revisions were added in May 1973.)

After the question "*What* happened?" come the questions "How?" and "Why?" The six remaining chapters, therefore, try to sketch something of the geographical, ethnic, social, economic, political, and international aspects of Latin American history. For the most part each topic is treated chronologically. History remains history even when it is broken down into separate themes. It cannot in any convincing way be dealt with backwards; the flow of time cannot be frozen for long.

Latin America is rather a noisy part of the world, its noises being variously interpreted as the dawn chorus for a glittering revolutionary future, as the importunate chink of grasshoppers, or as the clash of ignorant armies. Perhaps nowhere else in the world are so many conflicting claims so stridently advanced. In such an atmosphere I believe it important to stick to the view, neatly expressed by the English poet Donald Davie, that

> Holding the middle ground is harder
> And asks more judgement, no less ardour,
> Than to espouse exclusive themes
> And fly to one of two extremes.

For the benefit of those readers wholly unacquainted with Latin America, there are three technical points that ought to be made:

1. The terms "America," "Latin America," etc., sometimes cause confusion. This springs from the fact that the worthy founders of the United States of America failed to provide the republic with a name

different from that of the continent as a whole. This oversight has meant that in Great Britain and most of Europe the words "America," "American," etc., tend to refer to the U.S. In Spain and Portugal, by contrast, the equivalent words are taken to mean Latin America, while "North America," "North American," etc., refer to the U.S. (even though Canada, and indeed Mexico, are also part of North America). The expression "Latin America" appears to have come first into use in France around 1860, and by the end of the nineteenth century it won a wide degree of acceptance. It is not a term which has always found favor, and several alternative expressions, all of them more or less justifiable, have been proposed at one time or another: Ibero-America, Hispanic America, Indo-America, Eurindia, etc. It is, no doubt, an amusing pastime to invent poetic neologisms like these, but there is something to be said for sticking to convention in such matters, and this I shall do in this book. I therefore adopt the expression "Latin America" without too many pangs of conscience, and use the words "America," "American," etc., to refer to either (*a*) the American continent as a whole, or (*b*) the U.S., or (*c*) Latin America (in quotations from Latin American writers who follow the Spanish and Portuguese convention). The context will always make the meaning plain.

2. In the English-speaking world at least, Latin American surnames often cause bewilderment which (in the mass media especially) results in silly mistakes. The basic rules are really quite simple. Spanish Americans, like Spaniards, have two surnames. The first or principal surname is paternal, the second maternal. In common use, the paternal surname is used on its own to refer to the person in question, e.g., Fidel *Castro* Ruz. Some people, however, use both the surnames all the time, usually where the first surname is fairly common, e.g., Gabriel *González Videla*. (The conjunction *y* ["and"], used to link the two surnames, is less common nowadays than it used to be.) Spanish American *señoritas*, when they become *señoras*, tack their husband's main surname onto their own maiden (main) surname.

In Brazil, as in Portugal, the rule works the other way round. The paternal surname comes second, e.g., Getúlio Dornelles *Vargas*.

There are exceptions, of course, to these basic rules. And since surnames in the Spanish- and Portuguese-speaking worlds, as in the English-speaking world, can be double- and even treble-barreled, a Latin American's full set of surnames *can* be very impressive indeed—though it is rare, these days, for such things to be ostentatiously displayed.

3. The place names mentioned in this book are given in their Spanish or Portuguese forms unless there is an accepted English form. Panama,

for instance, loses its acute accent; Asunción and Bogotá do not. It is a rather pointless affectation to use an expression such as "Río de la Plata" when there is a perfectly good English translation, "River Plate." Spanish-speaking people do not refer to New York and London as such, but to Nueva York and Londres. (Some formerly accepted English equivalents have fallen into disuse. Nobody now refers to Santiago, Chile, as "St. Jago" or São Paulo as "St. Paul.")

Although I am an Englishman, the spelling in this book is American. I ought to make it clear that I have no objection to this at all. It is high time the English-speaking peoples agreed on a common set of spelling conventions.

I take this opportunity of thanking my friends Mr. Richard Ogle, Mr. David Stephen, and Dr. Ronald Hill, who must, between them, have commented on practically the whole of the text. My friends Dr. Richard Southern and M. Christian Anglade have both given me many memorable hours of conversation on Latin American themes, and may unwittingly have sparked off more than one idea to be found in this book. I apologize to any writer I may unconsciously have plagiarized; no author is ever entirely certain as to where all his phrases come from. The responsibility for unintentional errors of fact, foolish interpretations or infelicities of style is, of course, entirely my own. My students at the University of Essex, and (during the tumultuous spring semester of 1970) the University of Wisconsin will, I hope, forgive me for having used them as a sounding board for some sections of this book.

I also wish to thank Mrs. Shirley Aldridge, Miss Leila Dixon, Mrs. Marjorie McGlashan, Mrs. Caroline Davies, Mrs. Doreen Scully, Miss Mary Bonner, and Miss Pauline Cowlin, all of whom dealt with substantial portions of the typescript.

S. D. W. C.

Thorington Cross, Essex
May 1973.

Postscript—September 1973

While this book was going to press, two events occurred which, for their sheer unexpectedness and importance, seemed to require a last-minute addition to the narrative contained in Chapter 1, although it has not been possible to take them into account in the remainder of the text.

Throughout the middle months of 1973, the situation in Chile (see pp. 69–71) grew steadily worse, with the Allende government defending itself against a bitterly and militantly hostile opposition in the midst of economic troubles which were fast proving uncontrollable. The blast of the storm was too strong for the country's deeply cherished traditions of party politics and democracy. On September 11, a military junta seized power in a coup d'état which was far from bloodless. President Allende died, perhaps by his own hand, in a palace already wrecked by a ferocious but accurate airforce bombardment. His supporters fought back but were overwhelmed. The "Chilean way to socialism," which had excited attention far beyond the confines of Latin America, was suddenly and brutally sealed off. The new junta proclaimed its task to be one of national reconstruction; there was to be no role in this for party politicians, at least for the time being, and "foreign doctrines," said the junta, were to be eradicated.

In Argentina (see pp. 72–73), Dr. Héctor Cámpora's presidency was of short duration. He soon gave further proof of his loyalty to Perón by agreeing to resign, thus paving the way for a second presidential election. Although seventy-seven years old, and in indifferent health, Perón himself decided to assume the formal as well as the effective control of the Argentine government. The election was held on September 23, and the old general won sixty-two per cent of the popular vote and a third term of office eighteen years after his second had been cut short. Few twentieth-century politicians, it might be thought, could boast so spectacular a reversal in their personal fortunes. Only a year earlier, most Argentines—not to mention everyone else—would have regarded such a sequence of events as almost inconceivable. The month of September 1973 was a striking lesson, if lesson were needed, that the almost inconceivable should never be discounted in the strange affairs of the human race.

"... the last of the unspoiled continents ..."

> —Description of South America,
> Pan American World Airways advertisement
> (1966)

"Feverish landscapes, tumultuous peoples ..."

> —José Santos Chocano

Chapter 1

THE STORY—OR PART OF IT AT LEAST

In this opening chapter I try to give a simple and inevitably somewhat bare account of some of the main "facts" of Latin American history— to present, in short, a basic narrative which can be referred to in the later sections of the book. My emphasis here, then, is on the heroes, the villains, the dates, the battles, the treaties, the frontiers, the revolts —in other words, the actions, events, and personalities which have marked the story of the twenty Latin American states we know today. It is not, of course, the whole story, although it is certainly the part of it which most people want to know about first.

Conquest and Settlement, 1492–1580

Let my inquisitive readers consider whether . . . there have ever been men on earth who showed such daring.

BERNAL DÍAZ DEL CASTILLO

The birth of Latin America was one of the most momentous features of a period that is often referred to as the Age of Discovery. In the course of the fifteenth and sixteenth centuries the history of the world began to move, for the first time, with a planetary rhythm. Civilizations which had hitherto been largely isolated from each other began to be connected and linked in new and unprecedented ways. Ships began to cross entire oceans; the West became aware of the East, and the East of the West; the impulses of trade pushed to the ends of the earth. The main agents of this enormous change were the nation-states of the western seaboard of Europe, beginning with Spain and Portugal. To Portugal fell the distinction of pioneering the new sea route from Europe to Asia by way of the southern tip of Africa, in explorations culminating in Vasco da Gama's voyage to India and back between 1497 and 1499. Spain, by contrast, attempted to gain direct access to

1

Asia by establishing a route westward around the globe. The globe proved larger than had been supposed, and an immense new continent was disclosed on the far side of the Atlantic. History affords no purer example of the totally unexpected. Christopher Columbus, the Genoese sailor whose persistence finally won financial backing from the Spanish crown, was not himself aware of the surprise: he believed that he had reached the eastern fringes of Asia; nonetheless his landfall in the Bahamas on October 12, 1492 marked the exact beginning of Latin American history—the moment when "Latin" Europe first made contact with America.

At the start, Spain and Portugal were the only serious contenders in the race for further discoveries. In 1493 (soon after Columbus returned from the first of his four voyages) Pope Alexander VI divided the world into zones of Spanish and Portuguese conquest; his longitudinal line of demarcation was subsequently shifted westward by the two countries themselves in the Treaty of Tordesillas (June 1494).[1] Spain, recently united under the Catholic monarchs Ferdinand of Aragon and Isabella of Castile, was well fitted to undertake the subjugation of the newly revealed Western hemisphere. While a number of explorers, not least Columbus himself, reconnoitered the shadowy outlines of the American continent in their fragile naos and caravels, the first Spanish colonies were established on the islands of the Caribbean, starting with Hispaniola. Puerto Rico and Cuba were conquered in 1508 and 1511 respectively. In April 1500, meanwhile, a Portuguese flotilla on its way to India under the command of Pedro Alvares Cabral made what may have been an accidental landfall on the coast of Brazil; this territory lay to the east of the Tordesillas line, and was claimed (though not immediately colonized) by Portugal.

Spain's advancing imperialism did not remain confined for long to the West Indies. The westward urge was strong. A struggling colony was founded on the Panama isthmus; in September 1513 its leader, Vasco Núñez de Balboa, made his way through the jungles of the isthmus to achieve fame as the first European to set eyes on the Pacific Ocean. The original Spanish dream of a direct sea route to Asia still persisted; but the notable expedition (1519–22) initially captained by Ferdinand Magellan, one of whose five vessels became the first to circumnavigate the globe, revealed that there was no easy way into the Pacific (Magellan it was who gave the ocean this name) through the American continent. Spanish ambitions to outbid the Portuguese in Asia were frustrated. This was the more galling, perhaps, since Spain

---

[1] The "Tordesillas Line" was 270 leagues west of the Cape Verde Islands and the Azores.

now bade fair to become a dominant power in Europe. King Charles I, founder of the Hapsburg dynasty in Spain, was elected in 1519 as Holy Roman Emperor, assuming the title by which history knows him best: Charles V. A "world monarchy" seemed within his grasp.

But disappointment in Asia was amply counterbalanced by a staggering series of successes on the American mainland. Up to the time of Magellan's voyage, the Spaniards had encountered relatively backward peoples, notably the Arawaks and Caribs of the Caribbean area. These had been easy to subdue and exploit. In the fifteen years after 1519, however, the two most sophisticated states of the mainland—the Aztec Confederacy in Mexico, and the Inca Empire of Peru—fell before the audacious onslaughts of small bands of *conquistadores*. Two names above all stand out in this extraordinary epic of conquest. In 1519 the well-born and charming Hernán Cortés invaded Mexico with some six hundred followers. Two years later, after a highly dramatic and much-chronicled sequence of adventures, his triumph was finally ratified by the wholesale destruction of Tenochtitlán, the Aztec capital whose temples and flower gardens, lakes, and causeways, had so dazzled the Spaniards on their first arrival. The semiliterate Francisco Pizarro was in many ways a contrast to Cortés, but equaled him in sheer boldness. In 1531, with a force of less than two hundred, he landed in Peru. At Cajamarca, in the Andes, he lured the Inca emperor, Atahualpa, into captivity, compelled him to disgorge an immense ransom, and then had him garroted (February 1533). This treacherous action gave Pizarro the empire. The Spaniards then marched through the Andean highlands to take possession of Cuzco, the Inca capital. Three years later, a massive native revolt failed to dislodge the invaders. They were there to stay. In the course of a mere fifteen years, two notable American civilizations had been overwhelmed by no more than a handful of European adventurers.

Nothing, it seemed, could contain the impetuous and brutal pace of the Spanish conquest. The immense mountain ranges, icy plateaus, impenetrable jungles, arid deserts, and joyless swamps which are such constant features of the American landscape proved no match for the heroism and endurance of the conquerors. From Mexico (as also from Panama) expeditions advanced into Central America. From Peru, Quito (the old "northern kingdom" of the Incas) was quickly overrun; further expeditions added what is now Bolivia and northwestern Argentina to an already enormous territorial empire; in 1541 Pedro de Valdivia began the conquest and settlement of the fertile central valley of Chile. Meanwhile, entirely separate enterprises opened up those territories which had so far escaped the conquering sword. In 1536–37

3

Gonzalo Jiménez de Quesada made his way through the forests of the Magdalena valley and, in the lush highlands of what now became New Granada, overran the two kingdoms of the Chibchas. The adjacent territory of Venezuela was colonized more slowly.

In southern South America, the fierce nomads of the Argentine plains momentarily held back the conquistadores, and forced the early abandonment of the outpost established by Pedro de Mendoza in 1536 at Buenos Aires. The first nucleus of permanent Spanish settlement in the area was the remote, upriver colony in Paraguay which existed from the end of the 1530s. From this colony, in 1580, a handful of men sailed downriver and refounded Buenos Aires, an event which may be taken as marking the effective end of the period of Spanish conquest in the New World.

Well before 1580, of course, the Spanish crown had created appropriate institutions of settled government for its immense new overseas empire. From 1524 transatlantic affairs were supervised by a new Council of the Indies. Territorial divisions were decreed. Mexico became a viceroyalty in 1534. In Peru, however, the immediate aftermath of the conquest was marked by bitter strife, amounting to open civil war, between the surviving conquistadores. Francisco Pizarro was assassinated. The situation was exacerbated by Emperor Charles V's decision, in 1542, to issue a code of laws—the New Laws of the Indies —giving a measure of protection to the conquered native population of the American empire. This was fiercely resented by the Spanish settlers. (In Mexico a serious clash was avoided; the viceroy simply suspended the more contentious sections of the code.) The newly arrived viceroy of Peru, Blasco Núñez de Vela, was greeted by a rebellion captained by Gonzalo Pizarro, brother of the conqueror. Pizarro defeated the viceroy's forces at Añaquitos (January 18, 1546); Núñez de Vela's head was displayed in the main plaza at Quito. A sagacious royal commissioner, Pedro de la Gasca, was hastily dispatched to Peru, where he broke the back of the rebellion and had Pizarro and his accomplices executed (April 1548). The viceroyalty was speedily pacified.

The high (if brutal) drama which accompanied Spain's colonization of Mexico and Peru was almost wholly absent from the Portuguese settlement of Brazil. Cabral's initial discovery in 1500 was followed by three decades of official indifference. In 1533 King John III divided the territory into twelve captaincies, which he granted out to individual proprietors; but only two colonies, Pernambuco in the north and São Vicente in the south, became even moderately well established. The captaincy scheme was abandoned, and in 1549 a governor-general, Tomé de Sousa, was sent to Brazil. He built a capital at Bahia and settled the surrounding area. Six hundred miles down the coast, above the great escarpment behind São Vicente, the township of São Paulo was created in 1554. In 1567, following a French attempt to plant a colony in Guanabara Bay, the town of Rio de Janeiro was added to the slowly enlarging map of the Brazilian colony. For the moment, however, the modest coastal settlements and patriarchally run sugar plantations of the Portuguese hardly bore comparison with the glittering viceregal cities which were now rising in the Spanish-American empire: for the conquerors of Mexico and Peru had struck silver, and their successors were generating prodigious wealth for Spain and the colonies alike.

By 1580 or so, both Spain and Portugal had carved considerable—in the Spanish case, enormous—colonial empires out of a substantial part of the American continent. They were the first colonial empires of the modern world. They were to last longer than any of their later rivals. In the course of the three centuries which followed the great discoveries, European civilization was to be superimposed on a vivid background of native culture which had suffered assault and destruction on an overwhelming scale during the successive waves of Iberian conquest. Two worlds had collided; Latin America was the outcome. By 1580 it was on the map, and it has stayed there ever since.

The Course of Empire, 1580–1807
Westward the course of empire takes its way.

BISHOP BERKELEY

In 1580, the year of the second foundation of Buenos Aires, King Philip II of Spain, taking advantage of the extinction of the Avis dynasty in Portugal, united the Iberian peninsula under one crown. The Spanish and Portuguese empires were thus temporarily combined. They were never properly unified, however, and Philip II's incapable successors on the throne did little but stimulate the Portuguese desire for independence. Portugal's "Babylonian Captivity" was finally brought to an end in 1640, when an anti-Spanish revolt placed the new Braganza dynasty on the Portuguese throne. Thereafter the two countries, and the two empires, went their separate ways. What might have been a great historical opportunity was lost.

By the end of the sixteenth century, it was apparent that neither Spain nor Portugal, whether united or divided, would be permitted to remain in undisturbed possession of the New World. Other maritime nations—notably England, France, and the newly independent Netherlands—were eager for both trade and territory in America. The adventurous forays of English sea-dogs such as John Hawkins and Sir Francis Drake were, perhaps, no more than a nuisance to the Spanish crown, and in any case the Anglo-Spanish treaty of 1604 brought their era to an end. The French, too, were active, especially in Brazil, but won no permanent foothold there. The most serious threat to the territorial integrity of the Iberian empires came from the Dutch, who in 1624 captured Bahia. Though dislodged the following year, they returned in strength in 1630 and entrenched themselves along the northeastern coast of Brazil, eventually controlling a considerable swathe of territory extending from São Luis de Maranhão almost to Bahia. The Dutch colony reached its widest extent during the governorship (1637–44) of Johan Maurits, Count of Nassau-Siegen, known to Brazilians as Maurice of Nassau. Following his departure the Dutch dream of dominion in Brazil gradually faded; the boundaries of the colony contracted; and in 1654 the remaining Dutch surrendered and left.

During approximately the same period, the Caribbean was successfully penetrated by England, France, and the Netherlands; all three nations established colonies on many of the smaller Caribbean islands.[1] Cardinal Richelieu incorporated Guadeloupe and Martinique into the French empire in 1635; the French colony of Saint Domingue grew up at the western end of Hispaniola, though its existence was not recognized by Spain until the Treaty of Ryswick (1697). In England, Oliver Cromwell dreamed of impressive conquests in the Caribbean, but his expeditionary force had to content itself with the capture of Jamaica (1655). Contrary to expectations, Jamaica became a rich colony in its own right and a principal center of buccaneering activities. The buccaneers—men of all nationalities and of none—were a brutal fraternity, usually outside the law, though often encouraged in their bloodthirsty marauding by their respective governments. Henry Morgan, who may have been the most notorious of them, repeatedly raided and sacked Spanish settlements around the Caribbean, but survived to win a knighthood, the governorship of Jamaica, and a respectable old age. By the end of the seventeenth century, the buccaneers as a breed were well on the way to extinction, increasingly frowned on by the major European powers.

Foreign assaults and incursions of the type I have mentioned did little to slow down or to curtail the growth of the Spanish and Portuguese colonies. Even during the time of the Dutch, the remainder of Brazil developed a vigorous capacity for exploration. In the north, Portuguese claims were staked out along the River Amazon. From São Paulo, parties of settlers in pursuit of slaves and minerals spread out across the Brazilian hinterlands. Some of these expeditions (ban-

[1] Even Denmark gained a Caribbean foothold, with the acquisition of St. Thomas in the Virgin Islands in 1672.

deiras, as they were known by the 1630s) performed prodigious journeys: between 1648 and 1652, to take the outstanding example, Antônio Raposo Tavares and his bandeira traveled through at least seven thousand miles of the deep interior of the country. Exploits such as these did much to mark out the limits of modern Brazil, far to the west of the line agreed in the Treaty of Tordesillas. Spain, too, continued to expand her imperial frontiers in the course of the seventeeth century, not least in the north and west of the viceroyalty of New Spain, as Mexico was called. From time to time revolts by the Indian populations interrupted the advance of empire: one of the greatest of such revolts broke out in New Mexico in 1680, when the Pueblo Indians massacred or expelled the Spanish settlers. Not until 1696 was Spanish authority fully reasserted in that remote frontier region.

Foreign attack, internal growth, and occasional rebellion—these themes dominated the history of the Iberian colonial empires. The transition from the seventeenth to the eighteenth century was appropriately provided by the War of the Spanish Succession (which brought flurries of fighting to the Caribbean and Brazil). Its pretext was, as its name suggests, a change of dynasty in Spain, where the House of Bourbon (after years of European war) succeeded in establishing itself in succession to the extinct Hapsburg line. The Bourbons were to rule a country which had manifestly sunk from the high position it enjoyed in the days of Charles V and Philip II. The reforming drive of the new dynasty was to do something to offset this sad decline, especially during the reign of Charles III (1759–88), who deserves to be remembered as one of the greatest of Spanish monarchs.

No such national renewal came to Portugal. But Brazil continued to grow. A typical and turbulent gold rush shifted population southward from the traditional areas of settlement: in 1720 Minas Gerais (the "General Mines") became a separate province. Portuguese settlement now began to move still further south, toward the River Plate—a development which was soon to cause friction between the Spanish and Portuguese empires, for the Spanish colonies in Paraguay, in the Argentine interior, and at Buenos Aires were now closer than ever to Brazil. Spanish settlement on the north shore of the Plate estuary was now proceeding apace; Montevideo was founded in 1724. Spanish attention was also focused on the region by a serious rebellion which broke out in Asunción, the Paraguayan capital, in the 1720s. The *comuneros*, as the Paraguayan rebels came to call themselves,[1] were finally crushed only in 1735.

[1] This had been the name given to supporters of the municipal rebellion against Charles V in Castile in 1520–21.

FROM CORTÉS TO CASTRO

Thanks in part to the menace of Brazilian expansion southward, the River Plate region now began to assume an increasing importance in the Spanish empire. An attempt was made, in the Treaty of Madrid (1750), to regularize the frontier between Brazil and the Spanish colonies. Colonia, the Portuguese foothold in the River Plate, was to be abandoned in exchange for some territory further north, on the eastern shore of the River Uruguay. The area in question contained seven "reductions" —missionary-supervised Indian settlements which were part of a considerable network of such communities built up (since 1609) by the Jesuits in Paraguay. The Guaraní Indians of the reductions resisted their transfer to Brazil, and were not finally repressed until 1756. As it happened, the boundary settlement envisaged in the Treaty of Madrid did not come into effect, and there was further fighting between Spaniards and Portuguese in the area in 1761–62. In 1776 Charles III finally grasped the nettle. The River Plate was raised to the status of a viceroyalty.[1] The Portuguese were evicted from Colonia. The boundary problem was resolved in the Treaty of San Ildefonso (October 1777).

As so often in history, two independent chains of events became briefly linked at this particular point. The supposed complicity of the Society of Jesus in the revolt of the seven Guaraní reductions strengthened official antagonism toward this remarkable religious order, the most influential in the two Iberian empires. Enlightened opinion in Europe detested the order. To the Spanish and Portuguese governments its ubiquitous concerns seemed to make it something approaching a state within a state. The Marquis of Pombal, virtual dictator of Portugal from the early 1750s to his fall in 1777, was the first to act: the Jesuits were expelled from Portugal's dominions in 1759. Eight years later Charles III followed suit. Approximately two thousand Jesuits were deported from Spanish America, an abrupt measure which produced a sharp sense of shock among the Spanish-American populations.

Throughout the eighteenth century, Latin America felt the side-effects of European wars. The peace treaties which ended the War of the Spanish Succession awarded Great Britain a legal entry into Spanish-American commerce by means of the *asiento*, an official contract to ship slaves to the Spanish colonies from Africa. The Anglo-Spanish conflict which began in 1739 as the War of Jenkins' Ear[2] and ended in 1748 as the War of the Austrian Succession saw unsuccessful British attacks on Cartagena in New Granada and Santiago in Cuba.

[1] It was the fourth viceroyalty to be created in the Spanish-American empire; the third, New Granada, had been established in 1739.
[2] Robert Jenkins was a sailor whose ear had been cut off at Havana in 1732, an event which provided a pretext for whipping up English opinion against Spain.

8

It brought no alteration of the status quo in America. Soon afterward, Spain somewhat tardily entered the greatest of the Anglo-French struggles of the period, the Seven Years' War (1756–63), on the side of the French. The British promptly occupied Havana, capital of Cuba (August 1762). Havana was returned under the Treaty of Paris at the end of the war, but Spain was obliged to cede Florida to Great Britain, and was given Louisiana (as a kind of compensation) by France. Both France and Spain now awaited an opportunity for revenge against the triumphant British. It came soon enough. When the thirteen English colonies in North America declared their independence, Spain joined France in lending them support. The Treaty of Versailles (September 1783) duly ratified the independence of the new United States, Great Britain was humiliated, and Spain regained Florida.

Away from the Caribbean, that traditional arena of conflict, the clashes of the European powers produced no more than a faint echo. This did not preserve the colonies from occasional internal convulsions. In the early 1780s, Spain had to face two serious rebellions in South America. The great Indian insurrection which broke out in the Peruvian highlands in November 1780 was, perhaps, the gravest ever to occur in the colonies. Its leader, José Gabriel Condorcanqui, who called himself Túpac Amaru in memory of an Inca chief who had been executed in 1571, spread the revolt throughout the Andes of southern Peru. Betrayed and captured, Túpac Amaru himself was condemned to a horrible death in the main plaza at Cuzco (May 18, 1781), but his brother and nephew took up the cause away to the south, and a further year elapsed before the highlands were duly repressed into peace. This Peruvian revolt was paralleled by a number of movements against high taxation led by Creoles (American Spaniards) rather than Indians: the rebellion of the comuneros of Socorro, in New Granada, was the most serious of these. For a while it assumed menacing proportions, but was speedily suppressed by the Visitor (see pp. 305–06) who had originally imposed the contentious new taxes.

The closing years of the eighteenth century were overshadowed by momentous international developments which were bound to leave their mark even on a somewhat isolated region like Latin America. The American Revolution, whose triumph had owed at least something to Spanish help, was nonetheless viewed with foreboding by the Spanish crown. Might not the anticolonial example of the United States prove contagious further south? The first sign of contagion came not from the Spanish colonies, but from Brazil, where a group of dissident young intellectuals in Minas Gerais began to plot the independence of their country. The leader of the group, Joaquim José da Silva Xavier, was a militia officer and part-time dentist; he is usually known by his nick-name, Tiradentes ("toothpuller"). The conspiracy was discovered, its main protagonists were arrested (May 1789), and Tiradentes himself, after prolonged investigations, was hanged just under three years later. The effect of the plot was negligible, but it was, in a real sense, symptomatic of the times.

And the times were turning critical. In the summer of 1789 France erupted into revolution. The shock waves from that memorable explosion ravaged the whole of Europe and precipitated far-reaching events in Latin America. The eloquent political principles of the revolution seeped through the filter of censorship devised by the Iberian authorities. Antonio Nariño, the New Granadan who printed a translation of the Declaration of the Rights of Man only to be immediately arrested (August 1794), was by no means the only Creole who imbibed the heady draught of liberal ideas. Several revolutionary conspiracies, none of them particularly serious, were uprooted in the years that followed. The most dramatic immediate effect of the French Revolution was experienced in France's own Caribbean colony of Saint Domingue, where a large-scale insurrection of Negro slaves broke out in 1791. Its gifted leader, Toussaint L'Ouverture, was eventually captured by the French (1802), but his lieutenant, Jean Jacques Dessalines, continued the struggle. On the last day of 1803 Saint Domingue became the independent state of Haiti. (Dessalines immediately proclaimed himself emperor.)

Neither Spain nor Portugal had leaders who could rise to the challenge of the era of revolutionary wars that was now dawning in Europe. Under the Treaty of San Ildefonso (of 1796) Spain aligned herself with France against Great Britain, as so often in the past. The immediate result of this was the defeat of the French and Spanish navies at Cape St. Vincent and the loss of the island of Trinidad (1797). Matters became worse with the rise of Napoleon Bonaparte. Under a further Treaty of San Ildefonso (October 1800) Spain was forced to return Louisiana to France on condition that the province should not be transferred to a third party; Napoleon promptly sold Louisiana to the United States for fifteen million dollars (May 1803). The foolishness of Spain's servile attitude toward France was abundantly revealed when, on October 21, 1805, the combined French and Spanish fleets confronted Lord Nelson's warships in calm waters off Cape Trafalgar. The British victory deprived Spain of the means to enforce her influence in the American colonies.

This new powerlessness was thrown into relief the following year, when a British expedition from South Africa suddenly occupied Buenos

Aires. Though ejected after six weeks by a hastily mustered Creole force, the British returned with a larger expedition in 1807 and captured Montevideo. A second British attack on Buenos Aires, however, proved an ignominious failure, and the invaders agreed to leave the River Plate. Meanwhile, at the northern end of South America, a more sinister event had occurred. For many years Francisco de Miranda, a Venezuelan Creole living (for the most part) in Europe, had been the most active plotter against the Spanish empire. In 1806 Miranda tried to liberate Venezuela with an expedition organized in New York. He optimistically supposed that the people of Venezuela would rise in support of his venture. They did not. The expedition was a disaster; Miranda disconsolately returned to England. Spanish America, it seemed, was in no mood to rebel against the Spanish motherland. Brazil was equally quiet. The Iberian empires had lasted three hundred years. Was there any reason to suppose that they would collapse overnight? The question was answered two years later.

The Wars of Independence, 1807–30

. . . the greatest work ever entrusted by heaven to men . . .
SIMÓN BOLÍVAR

On November 21, 1806, in Berlin, Emperor Napoleon signed the first of his decrees setting up the Continental System—the closing of the European mainland to British trade. Portugal, England's oldest ally, refused to join the system. A French army under Marshal Junot was sent to enforce obedience. As the troops neared Lisbon, the Portuguese royal family and several thousand retainers set sail for Brazil, escorted by the Royal Navy. The Court reached Rio de Janeiro, after a brief stay in Bahia, on March 7, 1808. As we shall see presently, this abrupt translation of the Portuguese imperial government was directly responsible for the independence of Brazil some fifteen years later.

Having dealt with Portugal, Napoleon next turned on Spain—his own ally. In March 1808 King Charles IV had abdicated in favor of his son, Ferdinand VII. Napoleon, in a grotesque scene at Bayonne (May 1808) forced father and son alike to renounce the Spanish throne, which he then gave to his brother Joseph. The outraged Spanish people rose almost as one man against the French invaders. Great Britain beamed approval and sent troops. With Ferdinand VII confined to Talleyrand's pleasant chateau among the woods and meadows at Valençay, hastily formed committees—juntas, as they were called—took over the government of Spain, a Central Junta at Seville (and presently Cadiz) quickly rising to the fore. Spanish reformers now took advantage of the king's absence in France to replace the traditional absolute monarchy of the past with a liberal constitution; this was duly approved at Cadiz in 1812. Meanwhile Spanish guerrillas and British regulars (under the greatest British general of the age) embarked on the bloody task of driving the French from the peninsula.

The effect of these catastrophic events across the Atlantic was dramatic. With the king in captivity, should the colonies obey the essentially spontaneous authorities which had now emerged in Spain? Could they not establish juntas themselves, on the Spanish model? To the colonial viceroys and governors—Spaniards nearly all of them—these daring notions smacked of political heresy. The standard of home rule was first raised in the Andes—at Chuquisaca, La Paz, and Quito between May and August 1809—and the movements were severely repressed. But with most of Spain under French occupation, the need for autonomous governments in the colonies—to preserve them for Ferdinand VII—could hardly be denied. In 1810, one of the key dates in Latin American history, it was denied no longer. The governing juntas set up in Ferdinand's name at Caracas in April, Buenos Aires in May, Bogotá in July, and Santiago (Chile) in September swept aside traditional authority and acted from the start as sovereign administrations. For the Creole landowners and lawyers who had led colonial society—while denied political power—this was a moment of triumph. It was they who were now in charge. Most of them wanted home rule; a few saw (and plotted) ahead to full independence. The distinction was ignored by the Spanish government; as early as July 1810 the Venezuelan junta was proclaimed to be in a state of rebellion. The battle lines between Creole "patriots" and Spanish "royalists" were drawn.

The South American revolutions of 1810 were the work of respectable Creole aristocrats operating through the municipal councils (*cabildos*), bodies on which they had always been well represented. There was nothing respectable about the rebellion which broke out in Mexico in September that year. Under the leadership of a humble parish priest, Father Miguel Hidalgo, an irregular army numbering tens of thousands threatened to overthrow not only the Spanish colonial authorities but the rich and powerful in general. The leading Creoles of the viceroyalty were appalled by the social overtones of Father Hidalgo's movement. No patriot junta was installed in Mexico City; and in due course Hidalgo himself was captured, defrocked, and shot (August 1, 1811). The cause of independence and reform was taken up by another priest, Father José María Morelos, whose guerrillas soon controlled a large area of southern Mexico. But Morelos, too, was eventually captured by the viceroy's forces, and, like Hidalgo before him, was defrocked and executed (December 22, 1815). In Mexico, at least, Spanish colonial rule survived intact—for the time being.

In South America, by contrast, a full-scale war of independence was now under way. It was fought in two main theaters, at opposite ends of South America. In the north of the continent, Venezuela moved quickly to a declaration of independence (July 5, 1811), but the infant republic was overwhelmed by local royalist resistance. A Venezuelan army officer, Colonel Simón Bolívar, restored patriot fortunes in a lightning invasion of his native province from neighboring New Granada in mid-1813; in October that year the cabildo of Caracas conferred on him the one title he consistently cherished to the end of his life—the title of Liberator. But Venezuela was far from liberated. A stubborn Spanish officer, José Tomás Boves, now enlisted the support of the *llaneros*, the lawless cowboys of the plains, and the war reached a new pitch of ferocity. By the start of 1815 Venezuela was once again under royalist control. After briefly campaigning in New Granada, Bolívar went into voluntary exile in Jamaica (May 1815).

Still bleaker days awaited the patriots. At the end of the war in Europe in 1814, Ferdinand VII had been restored to the Spanish throne; he was grimly determined to bring the rebellious American colonies to heel. In April 1815 a Spanish expedition of upward of ten thousand men under General Pablo Morillo reached Venezuela. After "pacifying" the province with a good deal of unnecessary brutality, Morillo moved on to New Granada, where the flame of freedom still burned. There, the massively fortified port of Cartagena withstood 180 days of siege before being taken. Bogotá fell in May 1816. In northern South America, as in Mexico, Spain was once again in command.

But there was a second focus of the patriot revolution: Buenos Aires. After 1810 the Argentine patriots found themselves fighting on two main fronts. Across the Plate estuary, in the Banda Oriental,[1] the royalists were entrenched at Montevideo. The city capitulated in June 1814, but soon afterward fell into the hands of the outstanding patriot leader in the Banda Oriental, José Gervasio Artigas, whose "federalist" followers were almost as hostile to Buenos Aires as they were to Spain. These divisions within the patriot ranks gave the Portuguese, in Brazil, a golden opportunity to seize the Banda Oriental; an army under General Lecór captured Montevideo in January 1817.

Far to the northwest, meanwhile, Argentine soldiers were fighting on a second front. On the bleak Upper Peruvian plateau, they came face to face with the entrenched power of the Viceroyalty of Peru, the great

[1] Literally, "eastern side," i.e., of the River Uruguay.

bastion of royalism and colonial tradition in South America. The winds of reform had blown in vain there in 1810. Lima, its proud and opulent capital, had remained quiet. An astute viceroy, José Fernando de Abascal, had declared war on all patriot movements within reach. Upper Peru quickly became a battleground. Three times between 1810 and the end of 1815 patriot offensives struck across the desolate Andean plateau deep into royalist territory; three times, too, the patriot soldiers were driven back into Argentina. To one patriot officer, Colonel José de San Martín, the idea that the road to Lima lay through the interminable serrations of the Andes seemed absurd. The war in Upper Peru had clearly reached a point of stalemate; an alternative strategy was needed if Peru were ever to be defeated. San Martín's scheme was this: an Argentine army was to cross the Andes into Chile, a navy would be assembled with the help of the patriot Chilean government, and a seaborne expedition could then attack the Viceroyalty of Peru at its heart.

The key to San Martín's strategy was, of course, Chile. But patriot Chile had succumbed, at the battle of Rancagua (October 1814), to the last of three expeditions sent against it by the patriot-hating Viceroy Abascal. San Martín's invasion of Peru, therefore, could no longer be mounted without a prior (and no doubt costly) campaign for the liberation of Chile. The moment seemed singularly unfavorable. All over Spanish America, except in the River Plate, the patriot cause lay in ruins; the Spanish flag waved triumphantly over a dozen colonial capitals. But the issue was now in plain view. Spain's behavior toward the colonies made reconciliation impossible. At this gloomiest of moments, the Argentine congress, meeting at Tucumán, nailed its true colors firmly and defiantly to the mast by issuing a declaration of independence (July 9, 1816). By the end of the year San Martín, working quietly in Mendoza, in the shadow of the Andes, was ready to go over to the attack.

San Martín's Army of the Andes was composed of Argentines, exiled Chileans, emancipated Negro slaves, and a handful of European adventurers: in all they numbered more than five thousand. After a perilous crossing of the ten-thousand-foot Andean passes, and a descent through rocky valleys into Chile, the army defeated the royalists at Chacabuco (February 12, 1817) and went on to occupy Santiago. O'Higgins,[1] San Martín's closest Chilean friend, took over the government. The battle of Maipó (April 5, 1818) set the final seal on Chilean

[1] Bernardo O'Higgins was the Chilean son of a brilliant Irishman, Ambrosio O'Higgins, who had risen in the Spanish colonial service to become viceroy of Peru (1796–1801).

independence. Events thereafter moved very much in accordance with San Martín's general plan. A small Chilean navy was created—almost from nothing—and O'Higgins' agent in Europe secured for its command the services of one of the greatest British sailors of the age, Lord Thomas Cochrane. On August 20, 1820 eight Chilean warships, together with sixteen transports carrying over four thousand men, sailed out of Valparaíso Bay toward the north. Eleven months later the royalists evacuated Lima, San Martín declared the independence of Peru (July 28, 1821), and himself became head of the new patriot government with the title of Protector. This was his hour of glory. It did not last long.

In northern South America, Simón Bolívar returned to the fray in 1816 after several months of exile in Jamaica and Haiti. He first concentrated his efforts on the eastern region of Venezuela, gradually building up a base from which to liberate more territory. By the start of 1819 he felt strong enough to summon a congress to the town of Angostura, on the Orinoco River. Later that year, Bolívar took the gamble of conducting a surprise invasion of New Granada, avoiding for the time being the powerful royalist army in Venezuela. He led a two-thousand-strong expeditionary force across the rain-soaked *llanos* and their swollen rivers, and up through the high passes of the Andes into the highlands of New Granada. There, on August 7, 1819, he and his men won a brilliant victory over General Barreiro's royalist troops at Boyacá, the news of which caused the viceroy to flee from Bogotá. With New Granada liberated, Bolívar doubled back to Angostura to persuade his congress (December 17, 1819) to create the Republic of Colombia, a gigantic federation embracing the whole of northern South America. He himself became president of the federation.

Much remained to be done. Quito was still under Spanish rule, while the heartland of Venezuela was controlled by General Morillo. But the royalists' hopes of reinforcements vanished with the outbreak of the liberal revolution of 1820 in Spain. Instructed to negotiate with the patriots, Morillo accepted a six-month suspension of hostilities (November 1820). When the war reopened at the close of this armistice, the patriots took the offensive; the decisive battle of the Venezuelan campaign was fought at Carabobo on June 24, 1821. The Liberator-President now looked to the south, to Quito. A Colombian expedition, under the young Venezuelan general Antonio José de Sucre, was sent to help the port of Guayaquil, which had recently set up a patriot government. From there, Sucre thrust into the highlands and, at the battle of Pichincha (May 24, 1822), added Quito to the republic of Colombia.

By now the two great movements of liberation in South America were beginning to interlock and to compete. In July 1822 San Martín and Bolívar met face to face at Guayaquil. The occasion was something less than a marriage of true minds. The future status of Guayaquil,[1] the form of government for the liberated nations, the best way of destroying the considerable royalist strength in the highlands of Peru—on none of these important questions could the two greatest heroes of Latin American independence agree. The differing characters of the two men did little to help: Bolívar was charming, dazzling, mercurial, while San Martín tended to introspection and taciturnity. On returning from Guayaquil, San Martín resigned as Protector of Peru and set sail for Chile. He later made his way to Europe, where he remained for the rest of his life. Peruvian independence, still only partially secured, now seemed exposed to acute peril from the royalists.

Yet events which occurred elsewhere in Latin America in 1822 confirmed—if confirmation were needed—that the day of the Iberian empires was over. In Mexico, independence came by a somewhat unusual route. In 1820 an ambitious and personable Creole army officer, Agustín de Iturbide, was sent to hunt down the leader of one of the few surviving guerrilla bands in the country. The two men made contact and somewhat unexpectedly agreed on a program for the future settlement of Mexico. This program, the Plan of Iguala (February 24, 1821), provided for an independent Mexican empire, whose monarch (it was hoped) would be Ferdinand VII or a member of his family. In the months following the Plan of Iguala, Iturbide and his "Army of the Three Guarantees"[2] won control of a large area of Mexico. The newly arrived Spanish viceroy, General Juan O'Donojú, in discussions with Iturbide, negotiated what amounted to a confirmation of the Plan—in the Treaty of Córdoba (August 24, 1821)—and a month afterward Iturbide made a triumphal entry into Mexico City. A provisional government was organized (both Iturbide and O'Donojú were members), and the independence of the new Mexican empire was duly proclaimed (September 28). O'Donojú's sudden death ten days later left Iturbide in effective command of the country. Early in 1822 it was learned in Mexico City that the Spanish Cortes had rejected the Treaty of Córdoba. Since no Bourbon prince would now become emperor of Mexico, Iturbide decided to take the job himself (March 1822). No link with Spain, whether real or merely hoped for, now remained. In fact Iturbide's empire lasted less than a year, and Mexico quickly became a republic.

In Brazil, independence was the result of what might almost be

---

[1] Should it go to Colombia or to Peru?
[2] The three guarantees were religion, union, independence.

described as a simple family agreement. The Portuguese royal family had taken to Brazil with enthusiasm after their abrupt arrival there in 1808, and showed no desire to return to Portugal when the end of the Napoleonic wars made this possible. The outbreak of a liberal movement in the homeland in 1820, however, made King John VI's presence there urgently necessary. On saying farewell to Brazil, he left behind his son and heir, Prince Pedro, as regent, frankly advising him to take notice of any independence movement that might develop and to seek to control it if it came.

It came very quickly. Throughout 1821 and 1822, the Portuguese motherland showed very clearly that it intended to undermine the new and favorable status which Brazil had acquired as a result of the royal residence there. Several irritating measures were enacted, and Prince Pedro, then in his early twenties, was ordered back to Europe to complete his education. This he refused to do. "I remain!" he proclaimed. During the middle months of 1822, the prince took the lead in countering Portuguese claims. The climax came on September 7. Prince Pedro was standing on the banks of the Ipiranga, outside São Paulo, when he was delivered a number of arrogant dispatches from the Portuguese Cortes. Trampling the insulting documents into the ground, he proclaimed the freedom of Brazil with a simple shout of "Independence or death!" (There was never a written declaration; it was not needed.) A few weeks later, Pedro was made Constitutional Emperor of Brazil "by the will of God and the unanimous acclaim of the people." His coronation took place in Rio de Janeiro on December 1, 1822. Brazil, unlike Mexico, became a real empire.

The independence of Latin America was now almost complete. The final campaigns of the war in Spanish America took place soon afterward in the Peruvian highlands. After a certain amount of hesitation (during which the royalists greatly improved their position) Bolívar and his Colombian army moved in to fill the vacuum created by the departure of San Martín. The majestic landscapes of the Andes now became the stage where the last act of the drama was played. Bolívar's victory at Junín—fourteen thousand feet above sea level—in August 1824 was decided by the cavalry; this was just as well, since many of the patriot infantrymen were suffering from mountain sickness. For the royalists it was the beginning of the end. In December of that year, at Ayacucho, General Sucre won the second decisive battle of the campaign. The royalist commander, Canterac, told his captor, the English volunteer, General William Miller: "The harassing war is now over, and to tell you the truth, we were all heartily tired of it."[1] Sucre, now

[1] John Miller, ed., *Memoirs of General Miller*, 2 vols. (London, 1828), II, 178.

awarded the resplendent title of Grand Marshal of Ayacucho, next advanced into Upper Peru and on April 9, 1825 declared the war at an end. Four months later a congress meeting at Chuquisaca declared Upper Peru an independent and separate state; it flatteringly took the name Bolivia.

In November 1826 Simón Bolívar returned to Colombia after a triumphant progress through the highlands of Peru and Bolivia. His career as liberator was now over, as was the war of independence. Spain still ruled Cuba and Puerto Rico in the West Indies, but the entire mainland of Latin America was free. Ten independent countries faced the tangled problems of nation-building. By the time Bolívar died, in December 1830, their number had risen to thirteen. In 1825 Argentina went to war with Brazil over the question of the Banda Oriental. Such fighting as there was failed to decide the issue. The outcome, due in large part to British mediation, was the creation of the new republic of Uruguay in the disputed territory (1828). Meanwhile, severe political tensions were wrecking Bolívar's cherished Colombian federation. In January 1830 Venezuela withdrew; in May, Quito followed suit and became the republic of Ecuador. Bolívar, rejected by the squabbling politicians of Bogotá, plunged into the lower depths of disillusionment in the final months of his life. "America is ungovernable," he wrote. Many of the dying Liberator's worst fears were to be amply fulfilled in the difficult years that followed. In Latin America, contrary to the English proverb, the darkest hour came *after* the dawn.

The Creole States, 1830–1910
America can well tolerate seventeen nations . . .

SIMÓN BOLÍVAR

Although Brazil emerged from the independence period intact, the new Spanish-speaking republics were destined to remain separate political units. Simón Bolívar's one serious attempt to organize a loose confederation of the former Spanish colonies—the Congress of Panama (1826)—was a conspicuous failure; only four countries sent delegates and only one (Colombia) subsequently ratified the resulting treaty of confederation. This tendency toward fragmentation was confirmed, as we have seen, by the breakup of Colombia in 1830. The precarious federation which had been created out of the five small provinces of Central America in 1824 broke up, in similar fashion, at the end of the 1830s. By the end of 1840, there were seventeen Latin American states. The number was increased shortly afterward to eighteen. The former

Spanish colony of Santo Domingo, the oldest of all, had been invaded by Haiti (with which it shared the island of Hispaniola) in 1822. A national rising in February 1844 expelled the Haitians and brought into existence the new Dominican Republic.

Complementing this tendency toward fragmentation was a marked pattern of disorder and conflict in the new states. The revolutions for independence had been carried out in the name of liberal and (except in Brazil) republican principles. But it proved far easier to design liberal and republican constitutions than to make them work. Almost everywhere, in the first decades after independence, congresses were dissolved, elected presidents were irregularly removed from office, and rebellious generals vied with each other to rule—or ruin—the state, rising and falling with a regularity that soon became monotonous as well as melancholy. Constitutions were rarely respected for long. In some countries, as we shall see, civil war became endemic.

Not surprisingly, perhaps, "strong men"—*caudillos* as they became known—quickly assumed a commanding place in Latin American history. The nineteenth century was their golden age. Both in and out of power, these caudillos shaped the early development of many of the eighteen states. Some of them deserve to be singled out here. Up till 1846, for instance, Venezuelan politics were almost entirely dominated by the figure of José Antonio Páez, formerly one of Bolívar's most valued lieutenants. He returned for a final appearance as dictator in 1861–63. In Ecuador, General Juan José Flores (the creator of the republic) and Vicente Rocafuerte, an aristocratic liberal, fiercely contended for power until the mid-1840s. Even more striking was the case of Paraguay, where Dr. José Gaspar Rodriguez de Francia, known as El Supremo, ruled alone and unchallenged from 1813 to his death in 1840. Francia deliberately isolated his landlocked country from all save the most minimal contact with the outside world.

In these three countries, as in many others, the first generation of dictators was followed by a second—and there and elsewhere by a third, and a fourth, and so on up till modern times. Venezuela, a peculiarly dictator-prone land until the late 1950s, went through a period of internecine civil conflicts after Páez' final departure, but in 1870 fell into the hands of another caudillo, Antonio Guzmán Blanco, a vain figure who delighted in such titles as "Egregious American," "National Regenerator," etc. Guzmán Blanco ruled the country either directly or—a familiar device—through puppet heads of state for eighteen years. In Ecuador, one of the most extraordinary nineteenth-century Latin American dictators took power in 1861. He was Gabriel García Moreno, an extreme pro-clerical conservative who concluded with the Papacy a Concordat (1862) which, from the Catholic Church's viewpoint, was probably the most favorable of modern times. The Ecuadorian constitution of 1869—the country's eighth and García Moreno's second—made active Catholicism a condition of citizenship. In 1873 García Moreno's congress officially dedicated the republic to the Sacred Heart of Jesus. This theocratically inclined dictator, like many of his counterparts elsewhere, came to a violent end; he was stabbed to death while coming out of Quito Cathedral (August 6, 1875). Dr. Francia's successor as dictator of Paraguay was Carlos Antonio López, an immensely fat and sensual (and relatively easygoing) glutton who ruled from 1844 to 1862, and did much to amend Francia's Tibetan-style policies. He was followed almost immediately by his son Francisco Solano López, an ambitious man with most of his father's vices but little of his amiability. López the younger will reappear in this narrative.

The cases I have mentioned form no more than a part, and a small part, of the long and somber catalogue of Latin American dictators. Their rise and fall occurred against a bloodstained backcloth of civil strife—civil strife in which contesting political principles played a part as well as the base ambitions of unscrupulous power-seekers. Labels like "liberal" and "conservative," "federalist" and "centralist," became pretexts for prolonged political battles—which were all too often physical battles as well. Modern skeptics have cast doubt on the significance of such labels, but they were proudly borne and passionately defended or attacked. In Europe and the United States, Latin America became notorious as a region of perpetual revolutions. In the decades immediately following independence, only two countries succeeded in breaking free from this pattern of disorder and conflict: Chile and Brazil. Chile, the smaller of the two, was the first.

Seven years of rather mild anarchy had followed the downfall of Chile's first head of state, the soldier O'Higgins, in 1823. Then, in the brief civil war of 1829-30, a coalition of conservatives assumed power, suppressed the liberal opposition, and remolded the country in accordance with their own austere ideas. The constitution of 1833, a landmark in Chilean history, gave the nation a framework of institutions which actually held firm. The man behind this transformation was Diego Portales, a sardonic and hardworking merchant who consistently refused the presidency—unlike practically every other Latin American who found himself in the same position in the 1830s. Under a succession of conservative administrations, Chile enjoyed economic progress, internal peace, and an uninterrupted sequence of regular congressional and presidential elections—though the franchise was very small and the elections themselves were to some extent "fixed" by the government. In 1851 and again in 1859, the liberal opposition rose in armed revolt against the dynamic but high-handed President Manuel Montt, but without success. From the 1860s onward, however, politics became altogether more open, the parties competed on more equal terms, and the liberals gradually replaced the conservatives as the main element in government.

The first true test of Chile's newly acquired political stability came as early as 1836, when her northern neighbors, Peru and Bolivia, were forcibly united in a confederation by General Andrés Santa Cruz, a veteran of the wars of independence.[1] Portales, a firm nationalist, believed that the existence of this potentially powerful state threatened Chile's independence, and he pushed his country into war. Ironically enough, he himself was murdered by a mutinous regiment in the early months of the war (June 1837), but his policy held firm; the second of two Chilean expeditions occupied Lima and went on to inflict an irreversible defeat on Santa Cruz' forces at Yungay, in the Andes, on January 20, 1839. Santa Cruz took refuge abroad, and the Peru–Bolivian Confederation was dissolved. (General Gamarra, the new Peruvian president, made a final attempt to reunite the two states, but lost his life at the battle of Ingaví on November 18, 1841, when the Bolivians repulsed his invading army.) Victory on the battlefield greatly added to the mounting prestige of Chile.

The early difficulties of the empire of Brazil were more serious and protracted than those of Chile. Emperor Pedro I's initial popularity with his Brazilian subjects soon wore off; in 1831, tired of petulant disputes with his politicians, he abruptly abdicated and returned to Portugal. His son and heir, also called Pedro, was only five. Under the regencies of the 1830s, the future of the monarchy and (more seriously perhaps) of Brazilian unity seemed increasingly in doubt. Provincial revolts—some of them with a republican and separatist tinge—broke out with unhealthy frequency. The most serious of these by far was the so-called *revoluçao farroupilha* ("ragamuffins' revolution") in the south, where, in September 1836, the rebels proclaimed the independent

---

[1] At the height of his power, Santa Cruz enjoyed a magnificent string of titles: "Andrés Santa Cruz, Great Citizen, Restorer and President of Bolivia, Captain-General of the Army, Brigadier-General of Colombia, Grand Marshal, Pacifier of Peru, Unvanquished Supreme Protector of the North and South Peruvian States, Commissioner of the External Relations of the Three States, Supreme Protector of the Peru-Bolivian Confederation, Decorated with the Medals of the Liberating Army, of the Liberators of Quito, Pichincha, Junín, Cobija, and with the Medal of the Liberator Simón Bolívar and the National Medal of Peru, Grand Officer of the Legion of Honor of France. . . ."

Republic of Rio Grande do Sul.[1] Despite the emergence of a strengthened regency in 1837, there was every chance that the empire of Brazil would fall apart, just as Spanish America had done. It was at this point that a number of politicians conceived the idea of advancing the young Emperor Pedro II's age of majority, due in 1843. After considerable agitation on the part of these "majoritarians" (*maioristas*), regency and Congress alike gave in. In July 1840 sovereignty was transferred to the adolescent emperor.

So began what Brazilian historians refer to as *O Segundo Reinado*, the Second Reign. The hopes of the majoritarians were fully realized, for it lasted almost half a century and gave Brazil internal peace, international prestige, and a fair measure of material progress. In February 1845 the Republic of Rio Grande do Sul took advantage of generous terms and returned to the imperial fold. Thereafter only one armed rising occurred during the rest of the Second Reign: at Recife in 1847–48. The political system as it developed under Pedro II proved resilient and durable. Thanks to the crucial "Moderative Power" exercised by the emperor, liberal and conservative ministries alternated peacefully in office. The emperor himself grew up into a quiet, admirable figure, a model of the domestic virtues, an intellectual with scholarly interests; he could speak eight languages. His task was made easier by the support of several statesmen of high caliber. With the growth of internal stability, Brazil began to play a much more decisive part in the affairs of the South American continent, as we shall see.

The histories of the two largest Spanish-speaking republics, Argentina and Mexico, in the decades after independence were much closer to—indeed, they were good examples of—the common Latin American pattern of disorder and conflict. The United Provinces of the River Plate, as Argentina was known, went through years of bloody civil war. Its fundamental cause was the fierce hostility between Buenos Aires, the capital and richest port, and the provinces of the interior. In the provinces, local caudillos at the head of irregular gaucho[2] cavalry often warred against each other as well as the hated metropolis. The educated liberals of Buenos Aires were centralists; the conservative caudillos naturally took up the banner of federalism. In December 1829, with the

---

[1] The rebels were ragamuffins because they lacked decent uniforms. They were helped by a number of foreign adventurers, one of whom played a major part in the history of Europe. He was Giuseppe Garibaldi. During this period he met his Brazilian wife, Anita.

[2] The gaucho was the seminomadic cowboy of the Argentine plains. He acquired military skills in the wars of independence and briefly became the dominant character n the history of the republic.

appointment of Juan Manuel Rosas as governor of Buenos Aires, the federalist cause scored a decisive triumph. Rosas was one of the richest men in the province of Buenos Aires, but endeared himself to the caudillos and their gaucho followers by his public posture in favor of federalism and (not least) by his extraordinary expertise in riding a horse, in using a knife, and in throwing the lasso; these virtues were much admired at the time. Except for one short interval (December 1832 to April 1835), he retained supreme power in Argentina until 1852.

Rosas' federalist dictatorship was both harsh and thorough. The Illustrious Restorer of the Laws, as he chose to call himself, hounded all known centralists or liberals to death or into exile. His own person became the object of a grotesque national cult; the federalist color, bright red, played an obligatory part in sartorial respectability and public ceremony. To exiled liberals like Domingo Sarmiento, the regime represented the triumph of barbarism over civilization. Rosas was no respecter of persons, Argentine or foreign. His maltreatment of Frenchmen provoked France to blockade Buenos Aires in 1838–40; in 1845 the British joined with the French in a second and more serious blockade, which lasted until 1849. Rosas' greatest enemy nearer home was General Fructuoso Rivera, who in 1839 became president of Uruguay. With the aid of Rivera's domestic opponents, Rosas mounted a full-scale siege of Montevideo (February 1843). It lasted eight years, seven months and twenty-seven days.

By the end of the 1840s the strongest of Rosas' provincial supporters was Justo José de Urquiza, caudillo of Entre Ríos. He became increasingly unhappy about the way in which Rosas, despite his strident professions of federalist faith, nevertheless used his power to reaffirm the privileged economic position of Buenos Aires. In May 1851 Urquiza broke with his master, relieved Montevideo, and, with Uruguayan and Brazilian support, marched on Buenos Aires at the head of an army of twenty-eight thousand men. The battle of Caseros (February 3, 1852) sent Rosas scurrying into exile in England (where he died in 1877) and gave Urquiza an opportunity to unite the country. The extent of Rosas' inability to heal Argentina's self-inflicted wounds now became abundantly revealed. Buenos Aires refused to accept (or even to help draft) Urquiza's notable constitution of 1853. Two states, in fact, emerged from the wreck of the Rosas regime: Urquiza's Argentine Confederation, recognized by the great powers, and the more prosperous and powerful though unrecognized state of Buenos Aires. In October 1859, at the battle of Cepeda, the Confederation defeated the state. But this apparent dawn of unity proved false. Just under two years later, Buenos

Aires rose in opposition to the new order. The battle of Pavón (September 1861) was indecisive, yet it proved to be an important turning point, for Urquiza now retired from politics and the judicious governor of Buenos Aires, Bartolomé Mitre, was able to win control of the country through a policy of reconciliation. From 1862 Argentina enjoyed effective national government for the first time, it is fair to say, since before independence. During the presidencies of Mitre (1862–68), Domingo Sarmiento (1868–74) and Nicolás de Avellaneda (1874–80), the age of the caudillo was left behind for good; in Sarmiento's contest, civilization won. In 1880, after a further tiny spasm of civil war, the city and the province of Buenos Aires—whose weighty combination had so incensed the interior—were finally separated, the city becoming a federal district.

If Rosas can lay claim to have been the evil genius of early post-colonial Argentina,[1] that role in Mexican history was taken by the vainglorious figure of General Antonio López de Santa Anna. Though his periods in power were relatively brief, he was nonetheless the main actor during the long-drawn-out struggle between liberals and conservatives which set in after the fall of Iturbide in 1823. (Santa Anna was both a liberal and a conservative in his time.) His military career was a mixture of the absurd and the disastrous. In 1829 he launched himself as a hero by taking credit for the surrender of a Spanish expeditionary force whose failure to reconquer Mexico had been brought about less by his generalship than by yellow fever. Seven years later, when the largely English-speaking settlers of Texas declared their independence of Mexico, it was Santa Anna who finally lost the province, at the battle of Lynchburg Ferry (April 21, 1836). Prestige flooded back again, however, when a French punitive expedition landed on the Caribbean coast (1838); a French cannonball obligingly blew off one of his legs. The French soon went home, but in 1843, when Santa Anna became president (for the second time), the leg was ceremonially interred in Mexico City. It was disinterred, and most unceremoniously dragged through the streets, when the hero was overthrown by a popular rising the following year.

Santa Anna next found himself implicated in one of the main catastrophes in which nineteenth-century Mexico abounded. The United States, now living through a heady period of territorial expansion, annexed the Republic of Texas, whose loss Mexico had never accepted, in March 1845. War between Mexico and the United States soon

[1] Argentine nationalist writers of the twentieth century would not accept this claim. They regard Rosas as a great nation-builder. This, however, is myth rather than history.

followed. The almost empty province of California soon fell. Santa Anna, recalled from exile, was made acting president, but he and his troops were defeated both by General Zachary Taylor, advancing from the north, and by General Winfield Scott, who moved inland from the coast at Vera Cruz. On September 13, 1847 the Americans entered Mexico City. The subsequent peace settlement, embodied in the Treaty of Guadalupe Hidalgo (February 1848), deprived Mexico of Texas, California, and the land in between—roughly half her total land area—in return for fifteen million dollars. Well before this, Santa Anna had been sent into exile once more.

He was recalled for a final bow in April 1853—a conservative regime's desperate bid to retain power in the face of a new upsurge of liberalism. But the day of His Most Serene Highness, as he now liked to be known, was over. August 1855 saw him sailing into exile again. The liberal movement which now won control of Mexico is known to history simply as *La Reforma*, the Reform. It aimed to introduce fully constitutional government and—a key aspect of liberal hopes—to attack the enormous temporal power of the Catholic Church. It was, indeed, in Mexico that the nineteenth-century struggle between Church and state was most intense. The measures taken by the Reform government, which included the Lerdo Law (1856) dispossessing the Church of its plentiful lands, and which culminated in the liberal constitution of February 1857, were fiercely resisted by the Church and its conservative supporters. There ensued the bloodiest and bitterest of all Mexican civil wars of the nineteenth century: the Three Years' War, sometimes called the War of Reform. While it lasted, Mexico had two presidents: one, a conservative, was based in Mexico City, while the other, the liberal Benito Juárez, made his headquarters at Vera Cruz. A dour and inflexible Zapotec Indian, Juárez was the greatest Mexican of the age. The war itself was fought with great ferocity. In June 1859 Juárez gave free rein to liberal anticlericalism by enacting a set of harsh measures against the Church. All ecclesiastical property was confiscated; monasteries were dissolved; churches were frequently sacked by liberal commanders in the field. The war was over by the end of 1860. Juárez' entry into Mexico City (January, 11, 1861) was singularly unostentatious; Santa Anna had always loved processions, flags, and music.

The triumph of the Reform did not mean an end to Mexican misfortunes. In an effort to straighten out the country's finances, Juárez suspended (July 1861) payments on foreign loans. This provoked Great Britain, France, and Spain to send a punitive expedition to Vera Cruz. The British and the Spaniards merely wanted their money back; the French, on the other hand, had deeper designs. Napoleon III, influenced by Mexican conservative exiles, conceived the harebrained idea of establishing a French-protected Catholic empire in Mexico. He selected Archduke Ferdinand Maximilian, younger brother of the Austrian emperor Franz Josef, as his candidate for the Mexican throne; a French army forced Juárez and the government to retreat to the north; and in the summer of 1864 a Hapsburg ruled over Mexico for the first time since 1700. The United States lent Juárez moral support, but little else—for the Civil War was then raging. Emperor Maximilian turned out to be an eccentric, rather liberal-minded man who speedily disappointed the hopes of Mexican conservatives; but in any case he was kept in power solely by the presence of General Bazaine's French troops. When these were withdrawn, under pressure from the recently re-United States, the Franco-Hapsburg empire collapsed. The unfortunate Maximilian was shot—crying "Viva Mexico!"—at Querétaro on June 19, 1867. Juárez, re-elected president of Mexico that autumn, now bent his back to the task of national reconstruction. If ever a country needed reconstructing, it was the Mexico of 1867.

The crazy French intervention in Mexico in the 1860s was paralleled by a series of episodes which pointed to a revival of the imperial instincts of Spain. Between 1861 and 1865 the Dominican Republic reverted to colonial status at the request of its own leaders; the experiment was not a success. On the west coast of South America, a Spanish naval squadron seized the guano-producing Chincha Islands off the Peruvian coast (April 1864) to punish Peru for alleged (and in some cases real) maltreatment of Spanish subjects. Though the immediate issue was quickly settled and the islands evacuated, the actions of the Spanish squadron drew four of the west coast republics—Chile, Peru, Bolivia, and Ecuador—into a common alliance against Spain. The squadron, depleted by the loss of a schooner to the tiny Chilean navy, was no longer able to provision itself in Pacific waters; but before retiring to the Atlantic, its commander subjected the defenseless Chilean port of Valparaíso to a two-and-a-half-hour bombardment, causing tremendous destruction (March 31, 1866).[1] Callao, the port of the Peruvian capital, was also attacked, but there the Spanish warships were beaten off (May 1866).

By the time this minor war between Spain and the west coast republics had ended, an altogether more devastating conflict was under way in the River Plate region: the War of the Triple Alliance, waged between Brazil, Argentina, and Uruguay on the one hand, and Paraguay

[1] Only two people were killed. The citizens, warned by a Spanish ultimatum, took to the heights surrounding the town.

WAR OF THE TRIPLE ALLIANCE 1865-1869

in solitary isolation on the other. In 1864 the Brazilian empire attacked Uruguay in order to secure a pro-Brazilian government at Montevideo. Paraguay, driven by the ambitions of its Napoleonically inclined dictator Francisco Solano López, intervened on behalf of Uruguay. Argentina, as well as Brazil, was soon drawn in. President Mitre refused to allow López' troops to cross Argentine territory to get to Uruguay; the Paraguayans immediately occupied the town of Corrientes in retaliation. On May 1, 1865 Argentina, Brazil, and Uruguay concluded the Triple Alliance, with the object of bringing the upriver megalomaniac to heel.

"To Corrientes in a fortnight! To Asunción in four months!" Mitre's boastful assertion proved valueless as prophecy; it took the better part of four years, in fact, to reach the Paraguayan capital. López had assembled an army of upward of sixty thousand. Early in 1865 he dispatched two invading expeditions in the direction of Uruguay. Neither got there. The first, down the Paraná River, was an immediate failure; the second reached the Brazilian province of Rio Grande do Sul, but was compelled to surrender to the Allies at Uruguaiana (September 18, 1865). In mid-April 1866, under Mitre's command, the Allied army (forty thousand Brazilians, eighteen thousand Argentines, and around two thousand Uruguayans) crossed the Paraná into Paraguay. Two great battles were fought, to the advantage of the Allies, at Estero Bellaco and Tuyutí (May 2 and 24), but López' extensive fortifications along the Paraguay River prevented the Allies from penetrating into the country. They dug in and waited for a year. In mid-August 1867 a Brazilian flotilla succeeded in moving upriver past the lethal Paraguayan batteries at Curupaití, and approached the main enemy fortress at Humaitá, "the Sebastopol of South America," as some of the more fanciful journalists called it. A second great battle was fought at Tuyutí on November 3, 1867; the Allied victory drove López northward. It was the task of Marshal Caxias, Mitre's Brazilian replacement as commander-in-chief, to storm and capture Humaitá at the cost of two thousand men (July 16, 1868).

The fall of Humaitá allowed the Allies to scent victory. In October 1868 the Brazilian gunboats penetrated upriver to a point close to López' new headquarters, some thirty miles south of Asunción. A Brazilian force of over thirty thousand men followed soon afterward, and, at the battles of Las Lomas Valentinas (December 21–27) the Paraguayan army was destroyed. López fled. Marshal Caxias entered Asunción and declared the war at an end (January 5, 1869). His command of the Allied armies won him a dukedom from Pedro II. López continued to wage guerrilla warfare for several months, but soon became no more than a hunted fugitive. His life was taken, at Cerra Corá in the far north, by a Brazilian corporal (March 1, 1870). His last words are reputed to have been: "I die with my fatherland." It was, of course, an exaggeration, but only just. The consequences of this most tragic of Latin American wars were mind-shattering. Before the war Paraguay's population had been of the order of half a million. This was now halved. *The adult male population had fallen to less than thirty thousand.* Fortunately the Allies' own rivalries prevented Paraguay from losing very much territory. As the Argentine foreign minister observed, lest the Brazilians should misinterpret the situation: "Victory confers no rights!" But quite apart from the appalling loss of life, postwar Paraguay was a sad place, its previous tradition of dictatorship having been replaced by a newer tradition of constant political upheaval.

Misfortunes, it is widely believed, never come singly. Within ten years of the prostration of Paraguay, another international conflict of major proportions broke out in South America: the War of the Pacific. For the second time in the nineteenth century, Chile took on her northern neighbors Peru and Bolivia. An explosive situation had been building up for some time in the Atacama Desert—Bolivian territory lying just across the border from Chile. The rich nitrate deposits of the desert had been opened up, and were largely exploited, by Chilean capital and Chilean talent; thousands of Chileans had flocked into what had previously been a deserted (as well as a desert) region; the port of Antofagasta, founded by and predominantly populated by Chileans, was Bolivian only on paper. When the Bolivian dictator Hilarión Daza attempted to auction off the major Chilean nitrate concern in the Atacama on the grounds that it was disputing a new Bolivian tax,[1] the Chilean government was bound to react. It did. In February 1879 a small Chilean force occupied Antofagasta; in March the Bolivians were forced out of the Atacama; in April, Chile declared war on both Bolivia and Peru, which were linked by a secret treaty of alliance signed in 1873.

The opening phase of the war was dominated by a naval contest between Chile and Peru. As long as there remains a Chilean on earth, the name of Captain Arturo Prat will be held in reverence, yet the battle in which he perished, off Iquique on May 21, 1879,[2] gave the Peruvians temporary command of the sea. This was reversed at Cape Angamos on October 8, when the Peruvian ironclad *Huascar*, on whose deck Prat had died in a heroic boarding operation, was finally hunted down and

A previous treaty between Chile and Bolivia had exempted Chilean nitrate enterprises in the Atacama from increased taxation.

[2] The battle of Iquique was studied for decades afterward in naval colleges all over the world.

WAR OF THE PACIFIC 1879-1883

captured by the Chilean navy. Her gallant commander, Admiral Miguel Grau, was killed in the action. The *Huascar* is nowadays on view to the public in Chile's main naval base at Talcahuano.

Shortly after Cape Angamos, a Chilean army landed in, and quickly overran, the Peruvian desert province of Tarapacá. In Bolivia, Daza was overthrown; a magnificent war leader, Nicolás de Piérola, came to power as dictator in Peru. A second Chilean offensive got under way early in 1880, when an expedition of ten thousand men, under General Manuel Baquedano, landed at Ilo, marched through the desert, and defeated the Allied forces at the battle of Alto de la Alianza, outside Tacna (May 26, 1880). At this point Bolivia effectively withdrew from the war. Overlooking the town of Arica, meanwhile, the Peruvians were entrenched on the strongly fortified clifftop known as the Morro. Authoritative observers considered their position to be impregnable; but the Chileans captured the Morro, in a series of ferocious assaults, on June 7; it took them fifty-five minutes. Colonel Francisco Bolognesi, the commander of the fortress, was shot. "On to Lima!" now became the cry of the Chilean people. The government yielded to public pressure and toward the end of 1880 a Chilean army numbering some thirty thousand men disembarked just south of the Peruvian capital. Piérola's formidable defenses proved no match for the Chileans. The bloody battles of Chorrillos and Miraflores (January 13 and 15, 1881) gave them the city.

The war continued in a lower key for over two years, Peruvian guerrillas skirmishing intermittently with the occupation forces in the mountains. But Chile's triumph was complete, and was eventually recognized as such. In the Treaty of Ancón (October 20, 1883), Peru ceded Tarapacá to Chile forever, and handed over Tacna and Arica for a period of ten years, after which a plebiscite would decide on the fate of those territories. (The plebiscite was never held, and the "Tacna–Arica question" was only finally settled in 1929, when Tacna reverted to Peru, leaving Arica as the northernmost town in Chile.) A truce signed between Chile and Bolivia at Valparaíso in April 1884 allowed Chile to remain in control in the Atacama region, but a full peace treaty was not concluded until a much later date—October 20, 1904. This ceded the Atacama in exchange for a Chilean-financed railway from Arica to La Paz, the Bolivian capital. Bolivia thus became an entirely landlocked nation.

The War of the Pacific left Chile the strongest nation on the west coast of South America and one of the most respected (and, perhaps, feared) republics on the continent. Her long tradition of political stability had remained intact throughout the war—in contrast to the upheavals which had afflicted Bolivia and Peru. But this tradition was briefly and tragically interrupted a mere ten years after the Chilean army entered Lima. One of the principal foundations of Chile's political system since the 1830s had been presidential authority. During the 1880s this was increasingly challenged by those who advocated a "parliamentary" regime, by which they meant the supremacy of congress. The dynamic liberal president, José Manuel Balmaceda, who was elected in 1886, tried to reverse this process. In 1888, for the first time, a Chilean congress contained a majority hostile to the head of state. After months of acute tension, the president and congress alike exceeded their constitutional prerogatives. Civil war broke out. In January 1891 the leaders of the "congressionalist" movement were transported to the northern provinces by the navy, which had come out on their side. Balmaceda retained control of the army. His rule became increasingly dictatorial. In the north, the congressionalists raised an army of their own, brought it south, and devastated the president's forces at the battles of Concón and La Placilla (August 20 and 28, 1891). Balmaceda took refuge in the Argentine legation in Santiago. There, on September 19 that year, as his term of office ended, he shot himself. Days before this, however, the congressionalists had assumed power. As life returned to normal, the legislature became the focal point in Chilean politics. It was a shift of decisive importance.

The end of the nineteenth century saw a more drastic series of changes in the other South American country with a reputation for peace and quiet. During the long years of the Second Reign, the empire of Brazil had won the applause of Latin American statesmen. A great "crowned democracy" was what Mitre of Argentina called it—though by the standards of post-1867 England, for instance, this might be thought something of an exaggeration. As Pedro II grew older, some of the main pillars of the imperial monarchy began to crumble. An undignified tussle in the early 1870s between the government, two ultramontane bishops and the Papacy, over the question of freemasonry,[1] undermined the allegiance of the Church. A second issue was more serious: slavery. Negro slavery survived in Brazil long after its abolition in Spanish America at the time of independence. In 1850, admittedly, the slave trade from Africa was suppressed, while in September 1871 the conservative administration of Viscount Rio Branco put through the "Law of the Free Womb," which provided that all children born to slaves

[1] The Church's opposition to freemasonry was doubtless justified in Spanish-American (and Latin-European) nations, where the movement was uncompromisingly anticlerical. But in Brazil, ironically enough, freemasonry, as in Anglo-Saxon countries, was more tolerant.

thereafter would be free. In 1888, when the emperor was abroad, his heiress, Princess Isabel, as regent, called to power an abolitionist cabinet which abruptly enacted the famous "Golden Law" giving the slaves their freedom. The slave-owners received no compensation. Their support for the monarchy could no longer be counted on. Baron Cotegipe, the conservative prime minister thrust aside in favor of the abolitionists, summed the matter up when he told Princess Isabel: "You have redeemed a race, but you have forfeited a throne."

The empire might have survived the disaffection of Church and landowners had it not been for the fact that the army now began to show symptoms of restlessness. Some of its senior officers, influenced by the fashionable French philosophy of Positivism, came to look upon the monarchy as an obstacle to the progress of Brazil, as well as the immediate source of several real or imagined grievances. On November 15, 1889 an entirely bloodless coup d'état dismissed the conservative cabinet of Viscount Ouro Preto and inaugurated a republic. The emperor's departure was as mild-mannered as his whole life; as he abdicated and sailed into exile, he left his warmest wishes for the future of his country. Contemplating this civilized political upheaval from her retreat in the Scottish highlands, Queen Victoria thought the news "Very dreadful and terrifying."[1]

The first president of the new republic was Marshal Manoel Deodoro da Fonseca, the leader of the coup. He was a veteran of the Paraguayan war. Under his auspices a new constitution was enacted (February 24, 1891) and there was an orgy of republican legislation. "Order and Progress" was the positivist-inspired motto now affixed to the national flag; but in its early years, at least, the republican form of government brought neither. Deodoro was forced out of office by provincial revolts after he had high-handedly dissolved Congress. His successor, Marshal Floriano Peixoto (1891–94), had to face a rebellion by the navy (September 1892), which was only prevented from bombarding Rio de Janeiro by the intervention of foreign warships anchored in the bay. Meanwhile Rio Grande do Sul had erupted into a major rebellion (June 1892) which took some time to suppress; the last important battle of what was in effect a civil war was fought at Campo Osório on June 24, 1894. The next president, Prudente de Morais (1894–98), encountered still further turbulence, including the bloody and tragic "rebellion in the backlands" of the half-crazed religious fanatic Antonio Maciel, "the Counsellor," whose inaccessible headquarters were at Canudos, a small

---

[1] *Letters of Queen Victoria*, 3rd series, Vol. I (London, 1930), p. 534. In a telegram to Lord Salisbury, the old lady wondered whether the Royal Navy ought to take steps to protect the lives of the emperor and his family.

settlement in the hinterland of Bahia. It took four expeditions to crush this obscure messiah. When the army finally overran his pathetic township, on October 5, 1897, not a man, woman, or child was left alive. Canudos was, however, the last serious episode of republican Brazil's time of troubles. As the nineteenth century expired, the clouds gradually lifted; the positivist motto came to seem somewhat more appropriate. The early financial difficulties of the republic were overcome; Rio de Janeiro was greatly improved and adorned; Baron Rio Branco, foreign minister from 1902 to 1912, secured highly advantageous settlements of outstanding boundary questions, his greatest triumph being the transfer of the immense Acre territory from Bolivia to Brazil (1903).

The closing years of the nineteenth century and opening years of the twentieth in Latin America saw a continuation of many of the now traditional patterns of civil strife and petty tyranny which had been etched on the face of the region's history after independence. It would be tedious to give more than the odd example here. In Colombia,[1] where liberal–conservative rivalry had produced a series of civil wars, the conservatives under Rafael Núñez (president from 1880 to 1882 and from 1884 to his death in 1894) succeeded in imposing a semblance of centralized government, but were repeatedly challenged, often by force of arms, by their liberal opponents. Colombia's most serious civil conflict, the Thousand Days' War, lasted from 1899 to 1902 and is estimated to have accounted for about one hundred thousand lives. The conservatives were not dislodged. Toward 1910, however, there were clear signs that Colombia was beginning to outlive her unruly past. In neighboring Ecuador, political commotions remained commonplace, though the pace of politics was increasingly set by the anticlerical Radical Liberal Party rather than the conservatives. Venezuela in the same period maintained her tradition of dictatorship. Guzmán Blanco fell in 1888, but he was succeeded eleven years later by General Cipriano Castro, so-called Lion of the Andes and self-styled Supreme Leader of the Revolutionary Liberal Restoration. An unusually dissolute figure, Castro eventually handed over (in 1908) to his main henchman, vice president Juan Vicente Gómez. Gómez ruled until 1935—one of the most remarkable of the Venezuelan line of dictators, and certainly by far the nastiest.

Yet the persistence of old patterns should not blind us to the fact that, in some parts of Latin America, immense changes were now in

[1] New Granada adopted the name in 1863, although originally it had been only a part of Bolívar's Colombia, which is sometimes referred to by historians as Grancolombia (Greater Colombia) to avoid confusion.

progress. In the economic sphere, as will be seen in Chapter 5, the progress of Europe was creating a profound impact in the region. Nowhere was the impact more profound, or the changes greater, than in Argentina, a country which underwent a genuine economic miracle from the 1870s. The key to this miracle was the opening up of the *pampa*, the great and fertile plain stretching inland from the coast. From earliest colonial times, nomadic Indian tribes had held up permanent settlement on the pampa. In 1879 General Julio Roca and his well-equipped army swept out across the plains; within a few months the nomads had been cleared out of the way; ranches and railways spread across the pampa. What progress! The ports and cities blossomed; foreign immigrants, numbered by the million rather than by the thousand, poured in; Argentine meat and cereals went, in ever-increasing quantities, to the markets of Europe. The first decade of the twentieth century found Argentina closer to the general level of well-being enjoyed by the European nations than any other Latin American country. Buenos Aires was now one of the great cities of the world.

In this epoch of growing prosperity, Argentina was governed by a narrow circle of aristocratic politicians—the political heirs of the generation of liberals that had risen to the fore on the fall of Rosas. The franchise was deliberately limited in the interests of the dominant political party. Not surprisingly, this situation gave rise to opposition, which sometimes spilled over into violence. In July 1890, at a moment of acute financial crisis, a fierce revolt panicked President Juárez Celman into resigning in favor of his deputy. From the main organization behind the insurrection there presently came the Radical Party, which rapidly became a focus for intransigent opposition to the regime. Occasionally participating in armed risings, the radicals systematically boycotted the electoral system on the ground that it was a farce. In this, they were perfectly right; it was. For the moment, however, the radical opposition did not particularly worry the governments of the day, which were more preoccupied with monitoring the prodigious economic growth of the country or with settling outstanding international problems. Of these latter, the question of the boundary with Chile was by far the most contentious; an arms race between the two countries seemed, by the end of 1901, to presage open war. Tension was acute. Fortunately, wise counsels prevailed. In May 1902 an important treaty ended the crisis; a few months later King Edward VII, the arbitrator in the border dispute, gave a verdict which was accepted by both sides; and to immortalize the new-found amity between Chile and Argentina, a great statue of Christ was erected on the frontier, high in the Andes. These events, however, whether political or diplomatic, seemed less important to most Argentines than the signs of economic progress all around them.

Economic progress also seemed to be the main theme of Mexican history at this period. Here, however, the forefront of the stage was occupied by a single figure—General Porfirio Díaz, who first seized power in 1876, four years after the death of Juárez, and who was subsequently "re-elected" president in 1884, 1888, 1892, 1896, 1900, 1904, and 1910 (the term of office was lengthened from four years to six in 1904). Mexican historians refer to this period simply as the *Porfiriato*; during that time his power was unchallenged and perhaps unchallengeable. The general had started out as a liberal, and he never forgot that liberalism demanded the economic development of the country. Under Díaz, railways and telegraph lines spread out across the crumpled landscapes of Mexico; new industries grew up; the country was properly policed; and in 1894 the budget was balanced for the first time since independence. Foreigners, investors and politicians alike, expressed their admiration for this achievement; the investors invested, while the politicians made complimentary speeches.

Under the glittering surface of progress, however, the Díaz regime was directly responsible for much human suffering. It was self-evidently a tough dictatorship. Political opposition or seriously critical journalism were alike inconceivable in Don Porfirio's Mexico. (One famous dissident journalist, Filómeno Matta, was jailed no less than thirty-four times during the Porfiriato.) Díaz encouraged the full implementation of the famous Lerdo Law of 1856, which had prohibited corporations from owning land; the leaders of the Reform had aimed this measure at the Church, but it was equally applicable to the communal lands held by the Indian villages, of which there were many thousands. The enlargement of the great private estates, at the expense of the Indian, was a constant feature of the period. Alongside this often tragic and brutal process there went a wholesale transfer of public lands to private owners, sometimes foreign owners; Díaz may well have given away something like a fifth of the land area of the republic under this system. Many of these developments were viewed with approval by a group of practical intellectuals which in the mid-1890s began to exercise considerable influence in government circles. Like the Brazilian colonels of 1889, these *Científicos* (literally, "scientists") were vaguely affected by Positivist ideas. The cold, ruthless progress they visualized needed a climate of political stability and public order—a climate which Díaz, with his dictum of "less politics, more administration," and his *pan o palo* ("bread or the club") rule of government, seemed more than capable of providing. That he might also be providing the materials for a huge revolutionary catastrophe by way of reaction does not seem to have occurred to the Científicos, or, indeed, to anyone else.

By far the most momentous events in Latin America at the turn of the century occurred in the Caribbean, where the last remaining Spanish possessions in the hemisphere were liberated, and where, too, the growing shadow of the United States began to spread across the shape of Latin American history. The islands of Cuba and Puerto Rico had remained in Spanish hands when the mainland became independent. In Cuba, a large-scale separatist rebellion—the Ten Years' War—preoccupied the colonial authorities between 1868 and 1878. The pact which eventually ended it was unacceptable to a minority of Cubans, who continued to organize on behalf of independence. The heart and soul of this renewed crusade was a visionary poet, José Martí. The inevitable rising broke out in February 1895, in the east of the island; Martí himself was soon killed, but the insurrection gathered force; in desperation, the Spanish government sent out a new and brutal commander, General Valeriano Weyler, known as "the Butcher."[1] He lived up to his nickname.

Meanwhile, considerable anti-Spanish feeling had been whipped up in the United States, where President William McKinley was repeatedly called on to intervene in favor of the Cuban revolutionaries. During the night of February 15, 1898 an American battleship, the *Maine*, anchored in Havana harbor, suddenly blew up. Who blew up the *Maine*? Some said that the Cuban patriots had done it, to bring about American intervention. Others thought the Spaniards had been responsible. The Spaniards suggested that the vessel had simply blown up of its own accord. "Remember the *Maine*!" became the cry in the United States, and in April 1898 war was declared on Spain. It was soon over. A large American force landed near Santiago, at the eastern end of Cuba. On July 3 the Spanish fleet sailed out of Santiago to immediate destruction, its admiral, Cervera, maintaining that it was better to have honor without ships than ships without honor. Puerto Rico and (on the other side of the world) the Philippines were duly wrested from Spain. On January 1, 1899 an American military governor took over Cuba.

At the start of the Spanish-American War, the United States government had rejected the possibility of an outright annexation of Cuba, though, as McKinley himself suggested in his message to Congress on December 5, 1898, the island would inevitably be bound to the United States "by ties of singular intimacy and strength." The American proconsul in Havana, General Leonard Wood, summoned a constituent

---

[1] Among those who observed the Spanish campaign against the rebels was a young English subaltern on leave from his regiment: Winston Churchill.

assembly; by February 1901 the constitution of an independent Cuba was ready and waiting. At this point, the United States sent the Cubans a document known to history as the Platt Amendment,[1] to be incorporated into the constitution. Among other things, this specified that the United States was to have the right to intervene in Cuban affairs in order to preserve Cuban independence or to maintain a government adequate for the protection of life, property, and liberty. When Governor Wood transferred power to the newly elected president, Estrada Palma, on May 20, 1902, it was evident that Cuba had achieved her independence at the cost of becoming, in effect, an American protectorate.

For several decades now, the United States had been particularly interested in building a canal across Central America to link Atlantic and Pacific. In January 1903 Washington negotiated a concession from the Colombian government to build the canal across the Panama isthmus. Unfortunately, the Colombian Senate regarded the amount of money offered by the United States as inadequate, and an impasse was quickly reached. President Theodore Roosevelt wanted his canal; and by a happy coincidence, a number of Panamanians wanted independence from Colombia. In November 1903 the rebels struck for their freedom; an American warship was conveniently on hand to prevent Colombian troops from suppressing the revolt. Three days later Washington recognized the new Republic of Panama, the twentieth and last of the Latin American states to come into existence. One of the little republic's first actions was to conclude (November 18, 1903) a special treaty with the United States, which was to be given sovereignty over a ten-mile-wide Canal Zone across the isthmus in return for an annual rental of two hundred and fifty thousand dollars and a promise to "guarantee" Panamanian independence.

The events in Cuba and Panama helped to spread a deep suspicion of the United States in Latin America. They also did something to undermine the spirit of "inter-American cooperation" which had been growing up since 1889, when representatives of the Western hemisphere republics had met in Washington to establish a somewhat tenuous international organization—the Pan-American Union, as it eventually became known. Now, however, the United States seemed to be assuming a markedly interventionalist role in Latin America. Roosevelt himself confirmed this trend when he told Congress, on December 6, 1904, that the United States was quite prepared to exercise "the international police power" in countries whose behavior fell below what was regarded, in Washington, as a civilized standard. Action followed

---

[1] It was, in fact, an amendment to the U.S. Army Appropriations Bill (1901), which dealt with the withdrawal of U.S. troops from Cuba.

words. In 1905 Roosevelt assumed control of the customs service in the Dominican Republic. Between 1906 and 1909 an American military administration ruled Cuba, called in at the request of President Estrada Palma.

In the course of the year 1910 the various Latin American states which owed their origins to the revolutionary movements of a century earlier held luxurious celebrations in honor of the centenary. Parades, fireworks, speeches, handsome bound albums, commemorative postage stamps abounded. In Mexico, the octagenarian Porfirio Díaz arranged a brilliant program of festivities to recall Father Hidalgo's insurrection. In Buenos Aires, at the opposite end of Latin America, the celebrations were no less spectacular, though the local anarchists tried hard to disrupt them. Much, certainly, had been done in the first century of independence. There was cause for hope. In more than a handful of countries, the old unruliness seemed to be on the wane. But one fact was overwhelmingly clear in 1910. If the first century of independence had begun in the shadow of the Iberian powers, it had ended in the shadow of the United States.

Toward Uncharted Seas, 1910–73

The historic mission of America is to offer to man a land of liberty and a favorable environment for the development of his personality and just aspirations.
CHARTER OF THE ORGANIZATION OF AMERICAN STATES (1948)

Latin American history in its most recent phase is difficult to describe and still more difficult to interpret. Like a river swollen by unexpected rains while crossing a parched desert, it has forced its way into new channels. Where these will lead it, in the end, is anybody's guess; the seas are uncharted, though the would-be navigators are many in number. Nevertheless, the landscapes through which the river passes contain features that are readily identifiable. What are some of these landmarks?

From around 1910 or so—and the date is no more than approximate—what was often referred to as the "social question" began to figure, in lurid characters, on the agenda of Latin American politics. Poverty, malnutrition, illiteracy—these perennial curses were now seen to be more tenacious than nineteenth-century optimism had supposed. Their causes were probed, their consequences deplored. The inefficiency of Latin American agriculture became a source for desperate laments. The gulf which had always separated rich from poor now seemed to gain a new dimension of darkness. Later, the ungainly explosion of the region's cities, unaccompanied by any corresponding increase in industrial enterprise, perplexed and puzzled even the best-intentioned politicians and planners, and provided both the sociologist and the demagogue with rich material. All these ills were, and are, compounded by an insistent upsurge of population.

As if this were not enough, the international scene, too, began to darken. Two world wars, and a devastating depression in between, undermined the precarious edifice of progress built up over the previous fifty years. Partly as a result of these momentous conflicts, Latin America found her economic life increasingly tied, in several important respects, to that of the United States. By 1929, the year of the Great Crash, some $5,500,000,000 of American money was invested in the twenty republics. American capital and American management took over the oil of Venezuela, the copper of the Chilean desert, and the copious bananas of the Central American plantations. Later on, substantial sections of manufacturing industry were created by American rather than by local enterprise. Here was a potent fuel to feed the fires of nationalist emotion. As the United States, in the wake of World War II, rose to become the most powerful nation on earth, these economic links seemed (in the eyes of many influential Latin Americans) to underpin a wider scheme of political predominance. Such external irritants, combined with the urgent and unmistakable need for internal renovation, increasingly set the pace of contemporary Latin American history. It was to be ambiguous and occasionally convulsed.

The first, and in some ways the largest, of the convulsions was the Mexican revolution. In May 1911, following several months of revolt in different parts of the nation, the endlessly "re-elected" dictator Porfirio Díaz finally resigned. In essence, the revolution which overthrew him was political. Its main slogan, not surprisingly, was "Effective suffrage: no re-election!" But Francisco Madero, the vegetarian and teetotal lawyer who now became president, failed to appreciate (or sympathize with) the insistent demands for social reform that were beginning to surface; in the state of Morelos, to take the most notable example, the great agrarian leader Emiliano Zapata and his followers were already expropriating estates on behalf of the landless. Unfortunately, Madero himself aroused hostility from the Right. In February 1913, after ten tragic days of artillery bombardment between loyal and disloyal sections of the army in Mexico City, he was overthrown by General Victoriano Huerta. The American ambassador was incidentally implicated in the rise of this brutal and drunken reactionary. Madero and his vice-president were subsequently murdered, almost certainly on Huerta's orders.

MEXICAN REVOLUTION 1913-1914

Huerta's actions provoked an immediate spasm of revulsion through-out Mexico. The *real* Mexican revolution may be said to have begun at this point. It was, in a sense, a counter-counterrevolution. In the great battle against Huerta four leaders soon stood out. Three of them came from the northernmost provinces of the country: Venustiano Carranza, the elderly governor of Coahuila; Alvaro Obregón, who headed the revolt of Sonora; and Francisco ("Pancho") Villa, who gathered an army of cowboys in Chihuahua and captured Ciudad Juárez in the autumn of 1913. Emiliano Zapata, meanwhile, proclaimed himself "Leader of the Liberating Army of the Center and South." He con-tinued to expropriate haciendas, a habit which was imitated by several of the revolutionary generals advancing from the north. In July 1914 Huerta accepted defeat and fled, leaving the capital to the revolution-aries. Obregón and his men were the first to get there (August 1914). Carranza now became president.

The revolution had triumphed. But its leaders found it impossible to agree among themselves or even to agree to differ. By the end of 1914 a savage civil war was in the making, a civil war between Carranza, Obregón and their Constitutionalist Army on the one hand, and Pancho Villa, loosely allied with Zapata, on the other. Forced to withdraw to Vera Cruz, and to win new allies, Carranza began to lay considerable emphasis on social reform—his plan for land redistribution was revealed in a full-scale decree in January 1915, and shortly afterward an agree-ment with the most active trade union organization in the country yielded six "Red Battalions" for his cause. The test of Carranza's sagacity and, more to the point, of Obregón's generalship came in the middle months of 1915. Four great battles (two at Celaya, one at Silao and León, one at Aguascalientes) finally decided the issue; in scale they were almost comparable to the battles then being waged in the mud of Flanders. Villa retreated to the north, where he remained on the loose until 1920, a romantic but cruel bandit chief whose work for the revolu-tion was over. Zapata, the other principal thorn in Carranza's side, con-tinued to resist until 1919, when he was treacherously lured to his death.

President Carranza was now firmly in the saddle. A constituent convention meeting at Querétaro gave the country a new constitution (February 1917). It was a notable document. Woven into its fabric were many of the social aspirations of the revolutionary movement: agrarian reform, an acceptance of the basic rights of the urban working class, and a renewed emphasis on the separation of Church and state. But constitution or no constitution, politics in Mexico remained violent. When Carranza tried to bar his ally Obregón from the presidency in 1920, there was another flurry of civil war, and he himself was murdered.

By now the revolution had run its course for ten years; hundreds of thousands of Mexicans had lost their lives. Obregón's presidency (1920–24) laid greater stress on reform than Carranza's. More land was redistributed; the trade union movement, such as it was, was fostered; Obregón's secretary of education, José Vasconcelos, put in hand the building of over a thousand *casas del pueblos*, rural schools which were also community centers. Imaginative state patronage bore fruit in the murals of Diego Rivera and José Clemente Orozco, and in the music of Carlos Chávez. By the time Plutarco Elías Calles succeeded Obregón in the presidency—after another serious revolt—it was clear that the bloody cataclysm of the revolution had brought discernible if puzzling changes to Mexican life.

In the very different atmosphere of the "southern cone" of South America, the rather more tranquil political panorama gave, during roughly the same period, the impression that it was both broadening and deepening under the impulse of reform. In the tiny republic of Uruguay, the monotonous nineteenth-century pattern of civil war was finally broken; it was supplanted by a strong tradition of electoral democracy, to which were added, over the years, many of the features of what later became known as the "welfare state." If any one man may be said to have been responsible for this transformation, it was José Batlle y Ordóñez, president from 1903 to 1907 and again from 1911 to 1915. Uruguay gradually acquired a reputation as the Switzerland of South America—a reputation which was reinforced, perhaps, by Batlle's personal interest in the Swiss "collegiate executive."[1]

In Argentina, across the muddy waters of the River Plate from Uruguay, the restricted franchise—for long the main bone of contention between government and opposition—was at long last replaced with universal male suffrage in 1912 by the conservative president Roque Sáenz Peña, a man of attractive character and high ideals. The disaffected Radical Party was now allowed a place in the sun. Its leader, the dour and somewhat puritanical Hipólito Irigoyen, was duly elected to the Argentine presidency in April 1916. For the crowds who unhitched his carriage and drew it down the main avenue of Buenos Aires, Irigoyen's inauguration seemed like the dawn of a new era. In some ways it was. The remarkable "university reform" which occurred at Córdoba in 1918 owed little, perhaps, to Radical inspiration; yet its main principles were incorporated into Irigoyen's important university

---

[1] More than twenty years after Batlle's death, Uruguay did in fact adopt the collegiate executive (1951) in the form of a nine-man National Council of Government; a more orthodox presidential system was restored in 1967.

THE MAIN USES OF THE BIG STICK 1906-34

law of 1919. A few steps were taken in the direction of economic nationalism: Argentina's oil deposits were reserved for the nation. The country's neutrality in World War I was clearly reaffirmed. Irigoyen was less certain in his handling of trade union problems: several hundred people were killed during the suppression of a strike movement in January 1919. Moreover, Irigoyen's tight personal control of the Radical Party led, in the end, to a split between his own following and an "antipersonalist" wing led by Marcelo Alvear, Irigoyen's successor as president. Despite this, Irigoyen's name carried magic with it in the eyes of the electorate. He was returned to power in 1928 by a large majority.

A political shift of similar importance also took place in Chile, where the "parliamentary" system introduced after the 1891 civil war caused increasing popular dissatisfaction after 1910 or so. A champion of social and political reform soon offered himself: he was Arturo Alessandri, a lawyer of spellbinding oratory who won himself the nickname of "the Lion of Tarapacá." Alessandri's narrow victory in the presidential election of 1920 should have been followed by a period of vigorous legislation. It was not; congress either opposed the president or dragged its feet. The events which followed—a military coup (September 1924), the flight of Alessandri, a second military coup (January 1925), the recall of Alessandri, the enactment of a new and more presidentially inclined constitution (September 1925), a second withdrawal by Alessandri, and the emergence of Colonel Carlos Ibáñez as dictator (1927)—seemed to put an end to the time-honored Chilean tradition of political stability. Where was that once proud republic going?

In a much-quoted speech in Minnesota in September 1901, President Theodore Roosevelt of the United States had outlined his attitude to international affairs: "Speak softly and carry a big stick; you will go far." While the revolutionaries in Mexico and the political reformers of southern South America were engaged on their various tasks, the "big stick" was being wielded in no uncertain fashion in the Caribbean. Cuba and Panama were already, in effect, American protectorates. In 1911 U.S. Marines were sent into Nicaragua to bolster up the conservative regime of President Adolfo Díaz; they stayed there, though usually only in small numbers, for nineteen out of the next twenty-one years. In 1914 the high-minded Woodrow Wilson (who once expressed a determination to teach Latin Americans "to elect good men") sent a contingent of Marines to Vera Cruz, to help the Mexican revolutionaries against General Huerta—but without their permission and, in fact, to their considerable annoyance.

In 1915 it was the turn of the chronically chaotic republic of Haiti: the American occupation lasted nineteen years, during which period the country was governed by a series of puppet presidents. A similar fate befell the adjacent Dominican Republic between 1916 and 1924, though here an American military government was installed; its positive achievements were not appreciated by Dominican nationalists. The habit of intervention died hard. In 1925 the Marines were pulled out of Nicaragua, but an immediate outbreak of civil war brought them back again the following year. This time, however, their presence provoked a resistance movement. Its leader was a Nicaraguan army officer, Augusto César Sandino, a clever, fast-moving, romantic adventurer with a belief in social reform.

It is worth mentioning at this point—though somewhat out of chronological order—that the later histories of the countries chastised by the "big stick" present a singularly depressing picture. Haiti, when the Marines went home, quickly reverted to her traditional pattern of chronic instability—an instability only halted, after 1957, by the rise of one of the most grotesque of modern dictators, Dr. François Duvalier. The primitive tyranny of "Papa Doc," as he was known, lasted until his death in 1971. In Nicaragua, the commander of the American-trained National Guard, Anastasio Somoza, established himself as dictator in 1936, having connived, two years earlier, at the murder of Sandino. Somoza's dynasty still retains power in Nicaragua at the time of writing. For the Dominican Republic, too, later events were disastrous. In 1930 the American-trained commander of the army, General Rafael Leonidas Trujillo, assumed the presidency. The "Glorious Era of Generalissimo Trujillo" which now opened lasted for three full decades. The Benefactor of the Fatherland, as Trujillo was styled, renamed the capital city after himself; a province, not to mention the country's highest mountain, also took the dictator's name; the Trujillo family came to own much of the land and most of the lucrative enterprises. There was, of course, no place in the Benefactor's scheme of things for the freedom or democracy so prized in the country whose Marines had given him his start in life. His tyranny was all-embracing.

It was natural, certainly, that American intervention in the Caribbean should be discussed in the various inter-American forums of the period. At the fifth and sixth Pan-American conferences, held at Santiago de Chile (1923) and Havana (1928), the issue caused considerable tension. The United States resolutely resisted any limitation of her right to intervene. By the end of the 1920s, relations between the United States and her southern neighbors were seriously embittered. The need to resist "Yankee Imperialism" was stressed by numerous Latin American writers; it was a theme which found a place in a growing number of political programs. Deriving their inspiration from the Bolshevik revolution, the newly formed (and for the most part very weak) Communist parties of the region denounced the United States as the fortress of international capitalism. Other movements, too, took up the cry.

Of these, none was more remarkable than the Alianza Popular Revolucionaria Americana, best known as APRA (American People's Revolutionary Alliance). It was founded in Mexico City in May 1924 by an exiled Peruvian intellectual, Victor Raúl Haya de la Torre. Haya's brilliant if eclectic mind took Marxism, the Mexican Revolution, and Peruvian history and fused them together in a powerful revolutionary doctrine—no less powerful, perhaps, for being a hybrid. APRA was publicly launched with five aims: (1) joint action of the American peoples against Yankee Imperialism; (2) political and economic unity of the Americas; (3) nationalization of lands and industries; (4) solidarity with the oppressed classes and peoples of the world; (5) internationalization of the Panama Canal. Haya wanted to take action on these points on a continental scale but, although branches of APRA were founded in several different countries, only in Peru did the movement gain ground. The incumbent Peruvian dictator, Augusto Leguía (1919–30), viewed it with implacable hostility; only after his downfall did Haya return home. Failure in the presidential election of October 1931—Haya won 106,000 votes as against the victor's 152,000—determined the men of APRA to try to seize power by force of arms. They launched their revolt in Trujillo, Haya's home town, in July 1932. It was repressed with some savagery by the government; a large number of Haya's followers (perhaps several thousand) were taken to Chan-Chan, a ruined pre-Inca city near Trujillo, and shot. For the remainder of the 1930s APRA concentrated on building up its already considerable strength, while continuing to experience more or less systematic persecution.

The fall of Leguía in Peru in August 1930, which gave Haya and APRA their chance to contend for power, was symptomatic of what was occurring that year throughout Latin America. No republic wholly escaped the consequences of the great economic depression that followed the Wall Street crash of October 1929. Governments everywhere were affected, and many of them fell. Even in Uruguay there was a brief departure from constitutional practices. In Brazil, as we shall see presently, the crisis brought about far-reaching changes. Irigoyen of Argentina, partly incapacitated by old age, was ousted in September 1930 by General José Uriburu; although civilian control of politics returned with the elections of November 1931, the greater part of the Radical Party were rigorously excluded from the game. The conservative government of General Agustin Justo (1932–38) did, however, take several intelligent measures to offset the worst effects of the depression. The Roca-Runciman Pact of 1933, for instance, secured Argentina's place in the all-important British market. The dictatorship of General (as he now was) Carlos Ibáñez in Chile collapsed in July 1931, yet another casualty of the economic crisis. The sixteen months which followed were among the most unusual in Chilean history: one government after another rose, floundered, and fell. Finally, at the end of 1932, the Chilean electorate turned to the Lion of Tarapacá to be led into a more tranquil era. As far as stable politics was concerned, Chilean history was now back on course. No longer the dazzling champion of reform he had been in 1920, Alessandri governed with the support of the Right. The powerful Radical Party, long a main actor in Chilean politics, now joined forces with the Communist and Socialist parties in a Popular Front. The Front's Radical candidate, Pedro Aguirre Cerda, an amiable vineyard-owner, won a narrow majority in the 1938 election.[1] The Radicals, as the main partners in the alliance, soon assumed the predominant role in political life.

During the years of the depression, Colombia underwent what seemed, at first sight, to be a shift in the direction of social reform. Although the world price of coffee (Colombia's main product) plunged by two thirds, the country's constitutional order was not disturbed; stability was a recent growth in Colombia, but it survived; indeed, in 1930 a long line of conservative governments gave way, at the polls, to a liberal regime. A second liberal administration, under President Alfonso López (1934–38), adopted the slogan "Revolution on the March!" and announced a program of reforms in the labor and agrarian spheres. Colombian conservatives—not least a strange, violent aristocrat called Laureano Gómez—reacted strongly to these reforms, modest as they were. The scene was gradually set for a renewed buildup of party rivalry—accompanied, this time, by a massive popular demand for reform which, sooner or later, would find itself a champion.

International conflict, as well as economic distress, preoccupied Latin American attention in the 1930s. The "Leticia Incident" between Peru and Colombia, and the Chaco War between Bolivia and Paraguay, broke out roughly at the same time. In August 1932 a group of Peruvian irredentists occupied the fever-invested Amazon river-port of Leticia, which had recently been transferred by treaty to Colombia. The

[1] With the electoral support of the Chilean Nazi movement; without this support it is doubtful if the Popular Front could have won.

incident brought about preparations for war in both countries. Tempers slowly cooled; the League of Nations took up the affair; talks were held in Brazil; and in May 1934 a settlement was reached. Peru then evacuated Leticia.

No such happy solution was forthcoming in the long-standing territorial quarrel between Bolivia and Paraguay. The sunbaked alluvial plain known as the Northern Chaco, one of the emptiest regions in South America, was thought to contain oil, a precious commodity which had recently been discovered in the foothills of the Bolivian Andes. The ownership of the Chaco was disputed; a number of incidents, notably the one which occurred at Vanguardia in 1928,[1] heightened the tension; and in the middle of 1932 the two countries put the matter to the ultimate test. In both men and material, Bolivian strength was greatly superior to that of Paraguay. But the Paraguayan soldier felt he was fighting on home ground; many Bolivian conscripts were Indians from the high plateau, unused to the low altitude and intolerable temperatures of the Chaco. In desperation after early defeats, the Bolivians summoned Hans Kundt, the German general who had trained their army,[2] and placed him at the head of their troops in the field. Kundt's efforts were fruitless. The Paraguayan positions at Fortín Nanawa—the "Verdun of South America," as journalists soon described it—held out.

In September 1933 the Paraguayan commander, General José Félix Estigarribia, an outstanding soldier, launched a counterattack from Nanawa. In December, using his famous *corralito* (encirclement) tactic, he took eight thousand Bolivian prisoners at Alihuata—an event which cost General Kundt his job. The Paraguayan advance was halted just north of Fortin Ballivián, and a further Bolivian counterattack was mounted from the north under Colonel David Toro. Estigarribia responded with his usual vigor. At El Carmen, a further corralito yielded another eight thousand prisoners; Fortin Ballivián fell on November 17, 1934. On the northern front, at Irendagüe, the Paraguayans cut off the enemy's water supplies and left the Bolivians to die of thirst in the overpowering heat. After this the Paraguayan advance became rapid in the extreme, thrusting well beyond the Bolivian general headquarters at Villa Montes, overwhelming Carandaiti (January 1935), and reaching the line of the River Parapiti, close to the modest Bolivian oilfields. Villa Montes, however, did not fall, and a Bolivian counter-

[1] Notable because on that occasion the Bolivian air force carried out the first air raid in Latin American history.

[2] Kundt's assistant in the training mission was Ernst Roehm, later Hitler's right-hand man in the Nazi Party. He was murdered in the "Blood Purge" of June 30, 1934, when over 70 allegedly dissident Nazis were killed.

THE CHACO WAR 1932-1934

offensive was under way when, in mid-June 1935, international pressure finally managed to bring the war to an end. Bolivia had lost some seventy thousand dead, Paraguay some twenty-five thousand.

The peace negotiations were complex and protracted. Not until July 1938 was a settlement reached. Paraguay gained the greater part of what she had conquered. Judged by any standards, however, the Chaco War, the only major Latin American war so far this century, was one of the most senseless in history. It had little effect on Paraguay,[1] though the humiliation of defeat set off a number of significant reactions in Bolivia.

The events of the 1930s which I have described so far were in large measure overshadowed by highly dramatic political developments in the two largest Latin American nations, Brazil and Mexico. In Brazil a "New State" was founded; in Mexico, the revolution was suddenly renewed.

The two decades preceding the depression in Brazil had witnessed the gradual decay of the "Old Republic," the republic established in 1889. Two states alone, São Paulo and Minas Gerais, exercised the preponderant influence in Brazilian affairs; their political machines held a tight grip on power and patronage; and it was tacitly accepted that *paulista* and *mineiro* candidates should rotate in the presidency. When this unwritten rule was broken, in the election of 1930, the government was seized by Getúlio Vargas, the amiable but shrewd governor of the ranching state of Rio Grande do Sul. The new president proclaimed his determination to reform and modernize Brazilian society. Politically, his path was far from smooth. The irregular character of his regime provoked, in July 1932, an armed insurrection in São Paulo, headed by General Bertholdo Klinger. In the aftermath of its defeat, a new constitution was enacted (July 1934), and Vargas' presidency gained a measure of legality. In November 1935 a Communist revolt had to be suppressed. To some observers, Vargas seemed over-tolerant abroad toward Germany and Italy and at home toward the new and vocal *Integralista* movement, which derived its inspiration from Mussolini's fascism and the *Estado Novo* ("New State") set up in Portugal by Dr. Oliveira Salazar in 1933.

On November 10, 1937 Vargas sent troops to close down Congress. Over the radio, he announced the creation of an Estado Novo for Brazil. Political parties—the green-shirted Integralistas along with the rest—

[1] Estigarribia became president in August 1939, but was killed in an air crash a year later. Since 1940 Paraguayan history has been dominated by two "strong men": Higinio Morínigo (1940–48) and Alfredo Stroessner (1954–   ).

were abolished. A new, fascist-style constitution was introduced—
though never submitted to the verdict of a plebiscite as Vargas had
promised. Nevertheless, while the new regime was openly a dictatorship,
it was in no sense draconian. This enigmatic man, with his un-Brazilian
taciturnity and his private enthusiasms for golf and flying, was no
megalomaniac tyrant on the European pattern. Under his government,
Brazilian industry progressed as never before; enrollment in schools
nearly doubled between 1932 and 1942; the trade unions were built up
in association with (and under the control of) the state. By the 1940s
it was apparent that, whatever the fate of the Estado Novo, Brazil could
never revert to the mold of the "Old Republic."

By the early 1930s the revolution in Mexico was giving clear signs
of having run into the sands of venality and incoherence. Plutarco
Elías Calles, both as president (1924–28) and subsequently as power-
behind-the-throne, was the dominant figure of the period. At the outset,
the Maximum Leader of the Revolution (as he liked to be known) had
pressed social reform with exemplary vigor, but after 1928 (when Alvaro
Obregón was assassinated), he began to reverse many aspects of the
revolutionary program: the redistribution of land slowed down, the
trade union movement was destroyed, and corruption, always widespread,[1] grew in scope. The disease seemed incurable. Nevertheless,
Calles himself had (perhaps unwittingly) bred the necessary antibodies,
by giving the revolution, in 1928, its own political party.[2] For the
presidential period 1934–40 the party selected, as its candidate, General
Lázaro Cárdenas, previously the governor of Michoacán. He was
thirty-nine. Calles' hope that Cárdenas would prove a compliant
puppet was quickly disappointed; in April 1936 the Maximum Leader
was abruptly packed off to the United States.

Cárdenas was the most honest and single-minded Mexican ruler
since Juárez. His government's achievements were well out of the
normal range. It consolidated the revival of the trade unions and made
the new CTM (Mexican Workers' Confederation) a pillar of the
state. It renamed and reorganized the ruling party, giving it the key
place in the political system which was now developing (1938). Above
all, it speeded up the land reform. The previous revolutionary governments, between them, had redistributed approximately twenty million
acres; Cárdenas' total, in six years, was nearly forty-five million. The
system of great estates—so overwhelming a feature of prerevolutionary

[1] It was in fact Obregón who told the Spanish novelist Blasco-Ibáñez: "I know of
no general capable of resisting a cannonade of a million pesos."

[2] From 1928–38 the party was known as the PRN (National Revolutionary Party);
from 1938–46 it was called the PRM (Party of the Mexican Revolution); since 1946 it
has been known as the PRI (Institutional Revolutionary Party).

Mexico—was decisively broken. For many years the oil industry had been the supreme symbol of the presence of foreign capitalism in Mexico. In March 1938, at the end of a long conflict between the government and the American and British companies concerned, Cárdenas expropriated the industry and turned it over to a state corporation. This was unquestionably the most severe measure against foreign capital taken by any Latin American government up to that time.

Ten or twenty years earlier, Cárdenas' striking demonstration of economic nationalism would have provoked a strong reaction in Washington. But times were changing. By 1938 the "big stick" had been put away; the United States, under President Franklin Roosevelt, was attempting to become a "good neighbor," to use Roosevelt's own phrase. In May 1934 a new Cuban–American treaty disposed of the Platt Amendment. At a specially convened inter-American Peace Conference held in Buenos Aires in December 1936, an unconditional ban on intervention was finally accepted—to the delight of the Latin American delegations. Several economic measures, notably the creation of the Export–Import Bank (1934), attempted to offset the stagnation of inter-American trade. Roosevelt's reaction to Cárdenas' action of March 1938 was mild and tactful. By now, of course, the American president was deeply concerned about the deterioration of the international scene, and was eager to rally the Western hemisphere countries behind the United States if it came to war. The Nazi swastika was rising triumphantly over Europe. Would it rise, too, over America? The Declaration of Lima, drawn up at the eighth Pan-American Conference (December 1938), affirmed the "continental solidarity" of the American republics.

The outbreak of World War II in September 1939 sent the Western hemisphere foreign ministers hastening to Panama, where they issued an inter-American declaration of neutrality. After the fall of France in mid-1940, a second conference of foreign ministers, at Havana, drew the cords of "hemisphere solidarity" still tighter. Only two things seemed to mar this picture of increasingly cordial cooperation. One was the attitude of Argentina, which throughout the 1930s viewed American initiatives with decided coolness. The other was a brief outbreak of war between Peru and Ecuador. Peru had long claimed part of the Oriente, Ecuador's Amazon territory, and these claims were pressed more vigorously after the settlement of the Leticia Dispute. In July 1941 Peru invaded the Ecuadorian province of El Oro; her air force bombed several defenseless villages; Machala, the provincial

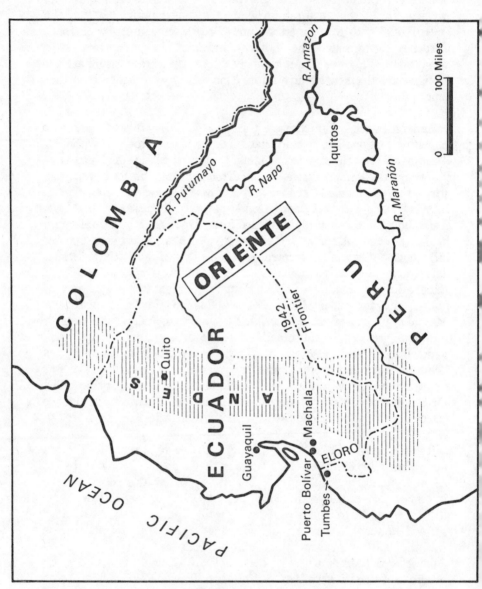

ECUADOR-PERU CONFLICT 1941

54

capital, and nearby Puerto Bolívar soon fell, the latter to Peruvian paratroops. International pressure quickly imposed a cease-fire; but that Ecuador had been disastrously defeated could not be denied. From the viewpoint of "hemisphere solidarity" a settlement had to be negotiated fast—for, following the events at Pearl Harbor in December 1941, the United States was in World War II. At Rio de Janeiro in January 1942, behind the scenes at the third meeting of the American foreign ministers, Ecuador was persuaded to part with roughly seventy thousand square miles of what she believed to be her territory—a sacrifice, many Ecuadorians believed, on the altar of inter-American unity.

By the close of the Rio de Janeiro conference every Latin American state except Chile and Argentina had broken off diplomatic relations with the Axis powers, and nine—the Central American and Caribbean island republics—had declared war alongside the United States. Brazil declared war in May 1942, Mexico three months later, and the remaining nations had all become belligerents by the end of March 1945. The last state to adhere to the general line was Argentina, whose coolness toward the United States was now accentuated by the scarcely concealed pro-Axis sympathies of several successive governments. (In June 1943 a military coup unseated the conservative president, Ramón Castillo.) Apart from Argentina, most Latin American republics supported the Allied war effort against Germany and Japan with enthusiasm. Two countries actually sent men to fight. Mexico's contribution was an air force squadron—Squadron 201—which saw active service in the summer of 1945 in the Philippines and Formosa. Vargas' Brazil sent an expeditionary force of twenty-six thousand men to the European theater; it fought with honor alongside General Mark Clark's Fifth Army in the liberation of Italy.

Hemisphere solidarity, and the increasingly cordial relations between Latin America and the United States, seemed at first sight to bear impressive fruit in the years immediately following the end of the war. The Treaty of Rio de Janeiro, drawn up at a special conference in August and September 1947, provided in essence for a military alliance between the American nations against aggression, whether external or internal.[1] The ninth Pan-American Conference, held at Bogotá from March 30 to May 2, 1948, brought into existence the Organization of American States and gave approval to its Charter. Formally defined as a "regional agency" of the United Nations, the OAS proclaimed representative democracy as the ideal of member nations, and set up a

---

[1] The Korean War was not regarded as a case of aggression against the Western hemisphere and the Rio Treaty did not apply. Colombia, however, sent an infantry battalion to Korea.

coherent system of international consultation and collaboration. By 1948, however, the United States was more concerned with Europe and with the incipient Cold War than with the problems of Latin America. The triumph of inter-American unity was far more apparent than real.

The end of World War II was marked, not surprisingly, by an upsurge of democratic (and even social-democratic) feeling throughout the world. A fair number of political developments in immediate post-war Latin America can be related to this democratic upsurge. In Brazil, for example, Getúlio Vargas lifted censorship and organized presidential elections; lest he should go back on this, the armed forces insisted (October 1945) that he retire, which he did. A new constitution (1946) replaced the Estado Novo with electoral democracy. In Venezuela —where transitional regimes had followed the death, in 1935, of the brutal dictator Gómez—the reforming *Acción Democrática* (Democratic Action), under Rómulo Betancourt, came to power with military help in October 1945. Despite its conscientiously vigorous effort to introduce reforms, and a massive victory in the 1947 presidential election, the movement's lease on power was abruptly terminated by the army in November 1948; for the next ten years Venezuela lived under a military dictatorship.

The Chilean Popular Front had broken up in 1941, but in 1946 the Radical candidate for the presidency attempted to revive his powerful party's alliance with the Left. "The people call him Gabriel"—so ran the haunting refrain of an election ballad contributed by the great Communist poet Pablo Neruda. Duly elected, Gabriel González Videla included three Communist ministers in his first cabinet. The marriage was not a success. In 1948 González Videla turned against his allies and outlawed the Communist Party. In neighboring Peru, the democratic upsurge had the much-persecuted APRA at its center; in return for its support at the polls, President José Luis Bustamante gave the party three cabinet posts (1945). Two years later he felt obliged to jettison APRA; it was too late; he was himself overthrown (October 1947) by General Manuel Odría, who hated APRA with a peculiar intensity. Haya de la Torre was able, in January 1949, to seek asylum in the Colombian embassy in Lima; he remained there *five years*, Odría refusing point-blank to offer him the traditional safe-conduct out of the country. With APRA curbed, the dictatorship was safe. It lasted till 1956.

More tragic still was the course of events in Colombia. In 1946 the conservatives returned to power. The hopes of liberal reformers were centered on the person of Jorge Eliécer Gaitán, a self-made man of working-class origins, a crusading lawyer and former mayor of Bogotá. Gaitán, who split the Liberal Party for the 1946 election, seemed destined to become twentieth-century Colombia's great reforming statesman. But on April 9, 1948—the most tragic date in recent Colombian history —he was shot dead in the center of Bogotá. A paroxysm of popular fury devastated the heart of the capital. In the aftermath of the *bogotazo* (as the orgy of rioting was soon christened) the conservative government stepped up its already vigorous persecution of the liberals. To complete the job, the fanatical Laureano Gómez was given the presidency in 1949. The consequences were hideous. Partisan violence spread through the peasants of the countryside in a terrifying chain-reaction which, in the years that followed, accounted for perhaps as many as three hundred thousand lives. The worst of *la violencia*, as Colombians called this phenomenon, was stanched after 1953, when General Gustavo Rojas Pinilla replaced Gómez' civilian dictatorship with his own more orthodox military variety.

Among the small states of Central America, Costa Rica had long enjoyed a reputation for constitutional order. This tradition came under attack in 1948, when an outgoing government tried to reverse a presidential election in which a coalition of its opponents had clearly won. José ("Pepe") Figueres, the leader of one of the parties thus cheated, organized an Army of National Liberation and advanced on San José, the diminutive capital. Two months of fighting brought victory; the government capitulated, and Figueres took over as chairman of a revolutionary junta. After some emergency legislation, which included the nationalization of the country's banks, the junta handed over to the legally elected president. (Figueres himself, at the head of a new political party, the National Liberation Movement, served as president from 1953 to 1958. He was re-elected in 1970.) For modern Costa Ricans, the civil war of 1948 remains the key moment of recent history.

The most conspicuous landmark of postwar Latin America was to be found in Argentina, a country whose equivocal attitude to the Allied war effort had provoked widespread distrust abroad. The generals with pro-Axis sympathies who seized power in 1943 were soon eclipsed by an ambitious colonel (whose international sympathies were the same as theirs). It was Juan Domingó Perón's particular genius to sense, from his post as secretary of labor, the ways in which Argentina's fast-growing working class could be useful to an ambitious colonel with ideas of national regeneration. By the middle of 1945 his standing with the workers and their trade unions was such that he could enlist their support in time of trouble. Trouble came soon enough. On October 9 he was placed under arrest by his resentful superiors. Eight days later, after tumultuous demonstrations in Buenos Aires, they brought him back, and gave him the balcony of the presidential palace from which to announce his presidential candidacy.

General Perón, a colonel no longer, governed Argentina for nine memorable years. For the workers—the *descamisados*,[1] as Perón called them—the new regime signified an era of unprecedented prosperity. The trade unions gave Perón their complete allegiance, and benefited accordingly. For needier workers, Perón's glamorous wife, Eva, ran a lavish Foundation which dispensed food, clothes, and medicines all over Argentina. State control of the economy developed by leaps and bounds; a Five-Year Plan and a National Economic Council were introduced; great emphasis, long overdue, was now laid on industrial progress. A resonant Declaration of Economic Independence, signed at Tucumán in July 1947, underlined a new determination to shake free from excessively tenacious foreign connections. In 1947-48 the enormous British-owned and British-operated railway network was bought and nationalized: THE RAILWAYS ARE OURS! cried the posters up and down the land.

Abroad, President Perón proclaimed his country's adoption of a "third position" in the Cold War, and (less openly) worked to establish Argentine hegemony in South America. At home, however, his government proved increasingly authoritarian. The General and his wife became the objects of constant national adulation. A new constitution (1949) greatly expanded the president's powers. Education was quickly brought into line; university autonomy became a dead letter. The gradual silencing of the press—culminating in 1951 with the seizure of the right-wing paper *La Prensa*—and the occasional use of descamisado mobs to intimidate the opposition[2] were further sinister signs of this tendency. Mass rallies and balcony speeches were the hallmarks of the new political style.

Perón was re-elected president by a large majority in 1951, but his second term was plagued by bad luck and a deteriorating economic situation. Eva Perón died of cancer in July 1952 at the age of thirty-three; her memory was no substitute for a presence which had been magical for millions of Argentines. Then, toward the end of 1954, Perón clashed with the Church—a bitter clash which ended in the excommunication of his government by the Vatican. When news of the excommunication reached Argentina, aircraft of the navy attacked the

[1] Literally, "shirtless"; in practice, shirtsleeved.
[2] In April 1953, for instance, the aristocratic Jockey Club in Buenos Aires, with its priceless library, was burned to the ground in one such exercise.

presidential palace (June 16, 1955). The revolt was crushed. But two months later, when the General Confederation of Labor called for arms to be issued to the workers in order to defend the regime, the army finally deserted the president. General Eduardo Lonardi, a devout Catholic, called out the provincial garrisons; Admiral Isaac Rojas' warships blockaded the Plate estuary. On September 19, 1955 Perón took refuge on a Paraguayan gunboat in Buenos Aires harbor. Two weeks later he was on his way into an exile which was to last seventeen years. "De-Peronization" was the watchword of the new military government. But the descamisados remained faithful to the memory of the man who had put money in their pockets and dignity in their hearts.

The Indian villages and banana plantations of Guatemala were a world (as well as a subcontinent) away from the ranches and factories of Argentina, but there too, at almost exactly the same period, a tense political drama was being played out. Juan José Arévalo, the attractive idealist who was elected to the presidency in 1945, defined himself as "a spiritual socialist" and embarked on a vigorous program of reform. In 1950 the Guatemalan electorate voted for a second installment; Arévalo's mantle fell on Lieutenant-Colonel Jacobo Arbenz, who took sixty-five percent of the popular vote. To a number of observers, Arbenz seemed unnecessarily close to the small (but well-organized) Guatemalan Communist Party. When his reforming hand reached the extensive banana plantations of the United Fruit Company—the land reform law of June 1952 spoke of creating a "capitalist peasant economy" in place of the great estates—the United States government protested, but to no avail. An appropriate condemnation of Communist interference in the Western hemisphere was wrung from the tenth Pan-American Conference, which met at Caracas in March 1954. Finally, the U.S. Central Intelligence Agency was authorized to help a group of Guatemalan rebels, headed by Colonel Castillo Armas in Honduras, to invade their homeland. The invasion was more ludicrous than serious, but it did the trick. Arbenz, deserted by his army, resigned on June 27, 1954.

For more than a few Latin Americans, this covert intervention in Guatemalan affairs recalled the worst days of the "big stick." In a book published soon afterward, ex-President Arévalo compared the United States to a shark, and the Latin republics to a shoal of defenseless sardines. The parallel found favor in many circles.

In Bolivia—a land whose nineteenth-century history had been a melancholy catalogue of tyrants—social problems were perhaps even

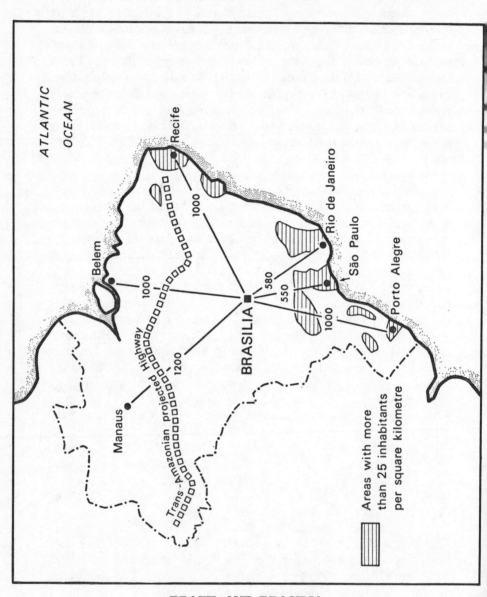

BRAZIL AND BRASILIA

more intractable than in Guatemala. A predominantly Indian population, eighty percent illiterate, lived mostly on the infertile *altiplano*,
twelve thousand feet up in the Andes, in appalling poverty. The mining
of tin, the chief export commodity, was controlled by three rapacious
companies, whose mineworkers suffered atrocious conditions. Could
such misery ever be altered? A bloody insurrection on April 9–11,
1952 brought to power a Nationalist Revolutionary Movement (MNR)
under Victor Paz Estenssoro, a shrewd, pipe-smoking economist with
radical ideas. The MNR immediately nationalized the "Big Three"
mining companies (October 1952), and ratified an agrarian reform
(August 2, 1953) which the peasants themselves were already carrying
out in many provinces. These changes were considerable—and also
irreversible. Paz Estenssoro served two terms as president in the twelve
years that followed, but his election for a third term, in 1964, provoked
widespread discontent, even within the MNR. On November 4, 1964
he was ousted by his vice president, the tough and popular air force
general René Barrientos. The new "strong man" was killed in a heli-
copter accident in 1969, an event which ushered in a renewed period of
political instability, in which the pendulum swung from left to right
with bewildering frequency. But the Bolivian Revolution was a basic
fact, whichever clique of colonels governed Bolivia.

For Brazil, that giant among Latin American nations, the 1950s
brought portents which were both tragic and utopian. Getúlio Vargas
returned to power, properly elected this time, in 1951. He had lost his
old touch. Faced with urgent demands from the army that he should
again retire, he suddenly shot himself (August 24, 1954). "I leave life
to enter history," he wrote. Few would dispute that his place there is
secure. The flamboyant campaign of Dr. Juscelino Kubitschek, presidential candidate of the Social-Democratic Party in 1955, promised
"Fifty Years' Progress in Five!" The doctor-turned-politician from
Minas Gerais, a bundle of energy, promised something else as well:
the transfer of the federal capital from Rio de Janeiro to a brand-new
city to be built in the thinly populated interior. Kubitschek's dynamic
presidency was responsible for many things—impressive industrial
progress, extravagant government spending, unchecked inflation—but
it was the new capital, Brasília, which won the world's attention. It was
a stupendously imaginative idea. As Oscar Niemeyer's graceful modern
buildings rose above the red earth of the Goiás plateau, six hundred
miles from the coast, a mystique of national development and of future
glory took hold of Brazilian hearts. Poverty on a vast scale might still
exist in their enormous land; but for many of the seventy million

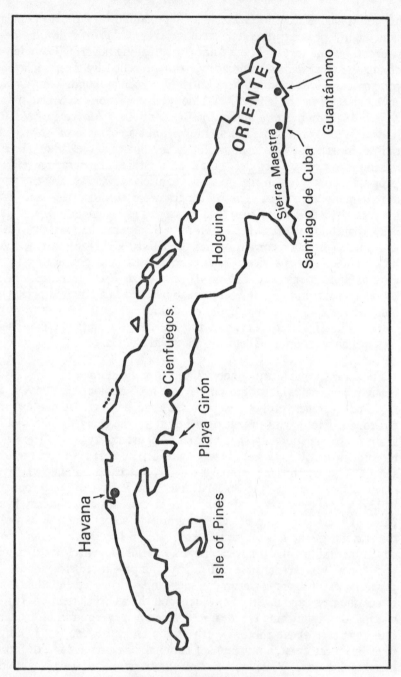

CUBAN REVOLUTION 1956-

Brazilians of the Kubitschek era, the future was all that mattered. Their gleaming new capital beckoned them onward.

Toward the end of the 1950s, a number of political changes in Latin America gave rise to hopes that the upsurge of reform and democracy halted (for the most part) in the postwar period, was about to break through once more. The military dictatorship of Rojas Pinilla in Colombia, for example, was overthrown in May 1957; the Liberal and Conservative parties subsequently agreed to cease their fratricidal strife and to share power, in a National Front, for twelve years.[1] Next door, in Venezuela, the brutal regime of Colonel Marcos Pérez Jiménez— heir to the officers who took over in 1948—was finally toppled in January 1958. A junta headed by Admiral Wolfgang Larrázabal took over, and the way was cleared for Rómulo Betancourt, leader of Acción Democrática, to be elected president. He resumed the task of reform abandoned ten years earlier. A new attachment to electoral democracy took root in the country. Betancourt finished his term of office (1959–64), the first elected Venezuelan president to do so.

Two weeks before Betancourt's inauguration, a third tyrant had fallen. When, in the early hours of January 1, 1959, the Cuban dictator Fulgencio Batista fled from Havana, optimistic observers throughout the world concluded that Latin America was, indeed, on the verge of a great democratic awakening. General Batista, a "strong man" in Cuba since the 1930s, had installed himself in power again in March 1952. His coup provoked several acts of resistance. One of these—a vain assault on the Moncada army barracks in the city of Santiago on July 26, 1953—brought to the fore a young lawyer called Dr. Fidel Castro. His July 26 Movement trained, in Mexico, for a guerrilla campaign against the dictator. On December 2, 1956, at the head of a force of eighty-two revolutionaries, Dr. Castro landed on the Cuban coast with the intention of restoring his country's violated constitution. Only twelve of the eighty-two escaped through Batista's troops to the wooded mountains of the Sierra Maestra; among them were Dr. Castro himself, his brother Raúl, and an asthmatic Argentine doctor and adventurer, Ernesto ("Che") Guevara. The guerrilla army grew slowly; it fought skirmishes rather than battles; but by the end of 1958 Batista's demoralized troops were decisively checkmated. On January 8, 1959, after a triumphal progress along the length of the island, Dr. Castro entered Havana, a bearded hero in a crumpled battledress. He was thirty-two.

It was the first Latin American revolution to take place in the era of television. Dr. Castro was now a world figure, as well as being universally

[1] Later extended to sixteen; the arrangement is due to expire in 1974.

popular at home. How would he wield his tremendous authority? In the first flush of his victory, Dr. Castro spoke of elections within a year to eighteen months, and speedy reorganization of political parties. In the meantime, the pace of reform was brisk, and the atmosphere throughout Cuba one of a joyous recovery of freedom. By the end of 1959, however, Dr. Castro was beginning to lean, as Arbenz in Guatemala had done, toward the Communist Party, whose support for his guerrilla campaign had been at best skeptical and at worst non-existent. In November he excluded a number of moderates from his cabinet; a month later he nullified, in effect, the sweeping victories obtained by his own July 26 Movement in trade union elections, by insisting that union leaderships co-opt a large number of Communists.

Around this time, a new tone of bitter invective crept into Dr. Castro's references to the United States. Some sections of the American press retaliated by accusing Dr. Castro, somewhat prematurely, of being a Communist; events were soon to turn him into one. In the summer of 1960, after a fierce clash with the principal foreign oil companies operating in Cuba, the revolutionary government embarked on a whole-sale program of nationalization. In the course of a month or two, all American investments in Cuba—amounting to one thousand million dollars' worth—were effectively liquidated. A First Declaration of Havana (September 1960) openly identified the United States as the historic enemy of Latin America. There was now no turning back. The drift of the revolution was as unmistakable as it was unprecedented. Agriculture was rapidly collectivized; industry and trade, too, were brought under the direct control of the state. All the country's major institutions were quickly brought in line with the revolution; a new orthodoxy spread to the universities and to the press. People's militias and block-by-block Committees for the Defense of the Revolution were set up throughout the country. All talk of elections was now forgotten. As for political parties—there was to be one, and one only: a fusion of revolutionary movements, notably the July 26 Movement, with the Communist Party. Internationally, Cuba turned with enthusiasm toward the Soviet bloc, from which she soon began to receive massive economic and military aid. In January 1961, well before many of these developments got under way, the United States broke off relations with the island.

By the spring of 1961 there were at least one hundred thousand Cuban exiles in the United States. The new American president, John F. Kennedy, somewhat hesitantly agreed to back an invasion of Cuba by some of the more militant exile groups. Over one thousand men were landed at Playa Girón in the Bay of Pigs (April 17–19, 1961). But Cuba was no Guatemala; it was an embattled island ready to defend its revolution to the last man; and the invasion was an ignominious and ludicrous failure. Dr. Castro now officially defined the Cuban revolution as "socialist," and, on television later that year (December 2, 1961) detailed his development as a fully fledged Marxist–Leninist. The United States, in addition to imposing a complete embargo on trade with Cuba, secured her expulsion from the Organization of American States (February 1962). The Cuban reaction was a Second Declaration of Havana, a passionate affirmation of violent revolution as the only solution to the problems of Latin America. There followed, in October 1962, the most dangerous episode of the quarrel: the installation of Soviet offensive missiles in Cuba, withdrawn by Nikita Khrushchev only after a week of fearsomely agonizing international tension. The outcome of the crisis caused the United States to pursue its policy of isolating Cuba still more earnestly. By the end of 1964, Mexico was the only American republic still maintaining diplomatic relations with Dr. Castro's government.

But whether isolated or not, Cuba could still spread her example. Her drastic revolutionary scheme seemed to strike at the roots of economic backwardness as well as injustice; her crash program to do away with illiteracy, for example, won widespread admiration in the rest of Latin America. Sierra Maestra-style guerrilla movements sprang up in a number of Latin American countries, notably Colombia, Peru, Guatemala, and Venezuela. Nowhere did they win power. During Kennedy's presidency, the United States set up a vigorous counter-insurgency program; Latin American officers were taught how to deal with guerrillas. Proof of the American determination to combat Cuban influence was given, in no uncertain fashion, in the Dominican Republic in April 1965. The assassination there of General Trujillo (May 30, 1961) had been followed by a series of political changes, including a seven-month interlude of democratic rule by Juan Bosch, the country's most famous writer (February–September 1963). Bosch was ousted by a military coup; but on April 24, 1965 an armed insurrection broke out against the ruling junta and called for his return. On the flimsy (and undocumented) pretext that the local Communists were using the revolt to gain power, the United States sent in more than twenty thousand soldiers and Marines to take control of the situation. As that brilliantly sardonic American, Mr. Tom Lehrer, commented in one of his savage little songs:

65

They've got to be protected,
All their rights respected,
Till somebody we *like* can be elected!

The Marines, reinforced by contingents from Brazil and Central America, duly remained on hand in the Dominican Republic until a new round of presidential elections in June 1966.

Cuban-inspired guerrilla movements continued to take to their various mountains and forests throughout the 1960s, though with differing luck. In Peru, the army counterattacked briskly, and with success, in 1965–66. A further guerrilla "front" was detected in the mountains of General Barrientos' Bolivia in March 1967. It soon won worldwide attention, for its leader, Che Guevara, had been Dr. Castro's right-hand man in the Cuban revolution and a persuasive advocate of the guerrilla method of winning power; his mysterious disappearance from Cuba in 1965 had provoked prolonged international speculation as to his whereabouts. All speculation was abruptly ended on October 8, 1967, when "the Che," as he was known to millions of Latin Americans, was killed by Bolivian counterinsurgency forces near the small town of Valle Grande. Despite such reverses, it could safely be assumed that guerrilla movements would continue to make some kind of mark, whether in the countryside or (as occurred later) in the rapidly swelling cities. By the start of the 1970s, it is true, no "second Cuba" had arisen in Latin America. But how will the picture look at the start of the 1980s? Prophecy is a dangerous profession.

"Poverty, the population explosion, and Dr. Fidel Castro"—these, thought a French demographer in 1962, were the combustible materials for a great explosion in Latin America.[1] Poverty was conspicuous enough in the 1960s, and its effects were sharpened by the stark, inescapable fact that the Latin American population was now rising at breakneck speed—from around 162 million in 1950 to around 265 million in 1970. How could economic progress—"development" as it was now called—be assured? From the Economic Commission for Latin America (ECLA; its Spanish acronym is CEPAL), set up by the United Nations in 1948, there came an avalanche of studies and proposals. High on the list of ECLA priorities was the economic integration of the region. The idea bore fruit in the Treaty of Montevideo (February 18, 1960), when seven states[2] agreed to establish a

[1] Alfred Sauvy, "L'Amérique du Sud en éruption," *L'Express*, Paris, September 27, 1962.
[2] Argentina, Brazil, Chile, Mexico, Paraguay, Peru, and Uruguay—later joined by Colombia and Ecuador.

Latin American Free Trade Area (ALALC) as a first step toward an eventual common market. (A meeting of the heads of state of the American nations at Punta del Este, Uruguay, in April 1967, agreed on 1985 as a target date for such a common market.)

The difficulties of organizing such a scheme soon provoked some serious questions. Was ALALC too large? Were smaller groupings of states perhaps desirable, as a halfway house? Already, in December 1960, four of the small Central American nations had joined together to set up a common market (MCCA),[1] with favorable results for international trade in the area. Within ALALC itself, several South American nations (Bolivia, Chile, Colombia, Ecuador, Peru, and Venezuela) agreed, in the mid-1960s, to establish an integrated Andean Group. After intensive negotiations at Cartagena, Colombia, a full-scale agreement on an Andean Common Market was signed in Bogotá on May 26, 1969.[2]

The revolution in Cuba, meanwhile, had (as we have seen) drawn the attention of the United States to the condition of its southern neighbors. In his inaugural address (January 20, 1961), President Kennedy spoke of an "alliance for progress, to assist free men and free governments in casting off the chains of poverty." The American eagle now carried the arrows of war in one talon and a checkbook in the other; twenty thousand million dollars were pledged over a ten-year period for the "Alliance for Progress." The aims of the program were laid down in the Charter of Punta del Este (August 17, 1961); in return for greatly increased American aid, Latin American governments were to push through crash programs of reform in the agrarian, educational, fiscal, and housing spheres. The United States would henceforth give vigorous encouragement to elected governments, while casting a cold eye on military dictatorships. Few of the conditions laid down at Punta del Este were met. With one or two notable exceptions, the reform programs were not pushed hard; often, indeed, they were not pushed at all. American aid did not increase on the scale expected. Nor did Washington's much-vaunted preference for elected governments long survive the tragic death of President Kennedy in November 1963.[3] The early failures of the "Alliance"—noble as its conception was—merely served to illustrate the true dimensions of the problems facing Latin America.

[1] Costa Rica joined the Central American Common Market in 1962.
[2] Venezuela declined to join immediately, but entered in 1973.
[3] Kennedy was extraordinarily popular in Latin America. I was in Quito, Ecuador, on the afternoon of his assassination; rarely have I seen more genuine and universal sorrow.

THE LAST FEW YEARS

In several Latin American countries, the main trends of the early 1960s were maintained to the end of the decade and beyond. In Colombia, for instance, the liberal–conservative alliance of the National Front continued to hold power—although, in the presidential election of 1970, the ex-dictator, General Rojas Pinilla, ran the National Front candidate, Misael Pastrana, very close indeed. The neighboring republic of Venezuela continued to defend her newly acquired reputation for constitutionalism. Raúl Leoni, Betancourt's successor in the presidency, was himself succeeded by a Christian Democrat, Rafael Caldera, in 1969.

Two countries long renowned for their political stability suddenly found themselves in difficulties toward the end of the 1960s. Uruguay, the Switzerland of South America, became somewhat less Swiss than previously. Extreme left-wing "urban guerrillas," calling themselves the *Tupamaros*, continuously embarrassed the government with their audacious robberies and kidnappings, placing the political system under a strain nobody could have foreseen ten years earlier. (A decisive counterattack destroyed most of the movement's strength during 1972.) In Mexico, where the ruling Institutional Revolutionary Party (PRI) had presided over a booming economy for over a quarter of a century, a serious conflict between militant university students and the government of President Gustavo Díaz Ordaz (the fifth "party" president since Cárdenas' retirement in 1940) erupted in the summer of 1968. In October that year, troops called in to maintain law and order massacred over thirty demonstrators—the number may have been very much higher—in the Plaza de las Tres Culturas in Mexico City, at a time when the city was preparing to play host to the Olympic Games. What had gone wrong? Could the PRI continue to resolve Mexican political tensions within its immense and protean framework? Díaz Ordaz' successor, Luis Echeverría, took office in December 1970 surrounded by an aura of reforming zeal. On him were pinned many sincere hopes that the country would recover from the trauma of 1968.

In Cuba, by contrast, the utmost stability prevailed throughout the 1960s. Dr. Castro's supremacy as leader of the revolutionary government seemed totally assured. The drastic reorganization of the island's economy, combined with the redirection of trade as a result of the American commercial embargo, caused considerable difficulties. The entire population was mobilized in an attempt to achieve a ten-million-ton sugar harvest in 1970; the total reached was eight and one half million tons. In an extremely gloomy speech on July 26, 1970, Dr. Castro disclosed a dismal picture of economic failures, and offered to resign; the offer was not taken up. Cuba's close relations with the

Soviet bloc became even more intimate in mid-1972, when she joined COMECON.

From the middle of the 1960s, four Latin American countries in particular attracted international attention. They were Peru, Chile, Brazil, and Argentina, and their varying fortunes were widely interpreted as having more than purely local significance.

PERU

The veteran leader of APRA, Haya de la Torre, won a narrow victory in the Peruvian presidential election of 1962. Triumph at last? He was not allowed to take office. The army intervened, ran the country for nearly a year, and then arranged new elections. This time, the winner was the reform-minded Fernando Beláunde Terry, a youngish architect of considerable personal appeal. His presidency began on a note of public hope and good will. His concerns, not least his interest in the welfare of the country's Indians, were genuine enough. Some of his plans were visionary—notably the great (and unfinished) scheme for an immense highway through the largely unexploited territory to the east of the Andes. But after the halfway mark of his term of office, Beláunde was increasingly beset by troubles; the army lost patience; and in October 1968 tanks once again rolled in to surround the presidential palace. The overthrow of Beláunde was no mere holding operation. This time the generals had come to stay—for thirty years, some of them said—with the resolute intention of succeeding where the previous regime had failed. The radical nationalism of the new government, headed by General Juan Velasco Alvarado, immediately astonished the outside world. Its first step was to expropriate the extensive assets of the American-owned International Petroleum Company, which operated in the northern deserts. In June 1969 a large-scale agrarian reform was decreed; land was to be distributed to the peasants in the form of family holdings or cooperatives. On the first anniversary of the coup, President Velasco Alvarado's speech to the nation emphasized that the aim of the Peruvian revolution was to alter "the established order . . . in a fundamental way, in all its essential respects." Subsequent reforms affecting the press and industry seemed to confirm this tendency. In Havana, Dr. Castro expressed approval as well as interest. (Peru reestablished relations with Cuba in 1972.)

CHILE

Beláunde, despite his subsequent eclipse, had undoubtedly offered Peru a new departure. In Chile this role was assumed, in somewhat different circumstances, by Eduardo Frei Montalva, the idealistic and serious-minded leader of the rising Christian Democrat Party. During the austere, conservative administration of President Jorge Alessandri (1958–64) the Christian Democrats—who stood far to the left of their Western European counterparts of the same name—suddenly broke through to become the largest single political force in the land. They were challenged, further on the left, by a powerful People's Action Front (FRAP) consisting, in the main, of the country's two Marxist parties, the Socialists and the Communists. In the 1964 election, in the absence of a candidate from the right, Frei won fifty-six percent of the popular vote, as against the thirty-nine percent which went to his main opponent, Dr. Salvador Allende, the socialist leader of FRAP. The traditional right was decimated in the congressional elections of March 1965.

"Revolution in Liberty"—this was the slogan of the Christian Democrats. The new government, the first of this complexion in the Americas, moved too slowly for some Chileans, but rather too fast for others. Its measures were concrete enough: the acquisition of controlling stakes in the big American-owned copper companies which were so vital to the economy (April 1966), a singularly comprehensive agrarian reform (mid-1967), and vigorous attempts to encourage "popular participation" at the grass roots of politics. (The agrarian reform struck a heavy blow at the great estates, but had covered only about one fifth or at most a quarter of the families it was supposed to benefit by the time Frei left office.) The main effect of the Christian Democrat program was to provoke a significant revival of the right, while doing little to appease the parties which comprised Dr. Allende's FRAP. For the 1970 presidential election, the right put forward the crusty ex-President Jorge Alessandri, now seventy-four. Dr. Allende returned to the fray at the head of a People's Union (UP) coalition, which, though Marxist-dominated, was wider than the old FRAP. In the event, Dr. Allende won 36.2 percent of the popular vote, as against Alessandri's 34.9 percent and the 27.8 percent which went to Tomic, the Christian Democrat. A right-wing backlash had produced a left-wing triumph.

The democratic election of a Marxist executive was unprecedented in Latin America.[1] Were Marxism and democracy compatible? The UP program spoke of a "regime of transition to socialism," while Dr. Allende, in his first annual message to Congress (May 21, 1971), insisted that Chile would move in this direction in a "pluralist, democratic and libertarian manner." But move she certainly would. Dr.

---

[1] Though not in the world. The Communist leader Klement Gottwald was appointed prime minister of Czechoslovakia as a result of the general elections of May 1946.

Allende, a politician of great skill, took immediate steps to carry out some of his key policies. The largest copper mines were now completely nationalized; relations were re-established with Cuba; the agrarian reform was accelerated, at the cost, in some provinces, of considerable confusion; the state took over the private banking system and tried to embrace a large section of industry. These actions quickly provoked opposition. The Christian Democrats and the right (who between them controlled Congress) repeatedly expressed fears that Chilean democracy was in danger. The rhetoric of violence—and sometimes the real thing—seemed to be growing on all sides. Two years after Dr. Allende's inauguration, the Chilean economy was in serious trouble, and the political climate stormier than it had been for many years, though the congressional elections of March 1973 showed that Dr. Allende enjoyed the confidence of some forty-four percent of the voting public.

BRAZIL

The course of events in the largest Latin American nation was very different. The dynamic Kubitschek, builder of Brasília, had been followed in the presidency by Jânio Quadros, who most unexpectedly resigned after only seven months in office (August 1961). His vice-president, João Goulart, who now succeeded, was a reformer with a demagogic streak in his character; he was bitterly distrusted by the armed forces, as well as by such civilian politicians as the sharp-tongued right-wing governor of Guanabara,[1] Carlos Lacerda. In March 1964 a series of events which seemed (perhaps deceptively) to indicate a drastic move to the left on Goulart's part provoked the armed forces into a decisive intervention. At dawn on March 31, troops from Minas Gerais began to march on Rio de Janeiro; the powerful Second Army, based on São Paulo, joined the revolt the same day. Goulart fled—first to Brasília, in the vain hope of rallying resistance, then to his home state of Rio Grande do Sul, and finally into exile in Uruguay. In the aftermath of the coup, an *Ato Institucional* (Institutional Act)—the first of many—conferred wide powers on the executive, and on April 11, General Humberto de Alencar Castello Branco, the inspirer of the revolt, was elected president by a Congress which had been duly cowed by events.

It soon became clear that 1964 was as important a turning point in Brazilian history as, say, the start of the Estado Novo. Castello Branco began by suspending the constitutional rights of nearly four hundred

[1] The state incorporating Rio de Janeiro, set up when the capital was transferred to Brasilia in 1960.

leading politicians—including ex-presidents Goulart, Quadros, and Kubitschek. In October 1965 a second Institutional Act abolished political parties, replacing them with two completely new and somewhat artificial groupings: ARENA (National Renovation Alliance) and MDB (Brazilian Democratic Movement)—the first of these was supposed to act as a "government" party, the second as a kind of loyal opposition. Castello Branco's successor as president was elected by Congress, the opposition abstaining, in October 1966. He was Marshal Artur Costa e Silva, inaugurated in March 1967. Because of illness, he was relieved of his duties in August 1969 by a military triumvirate; in October the same year the Brazilian high command chose General Emílio Garrastazú Médici as the next president, an appointment duly approved by Congress.

Whichever general was in office, however, the military regime followed an undeviating line. Old-style politicians were firmly prevented from making a come-back—the hostile *Frente Ampla* (Broad Front) formed by Kubitschek, Lacerda, and Goulart in 1967 was immediately declared illegal. The sporadic and violent opposition to the regime mounted by the revolutionaries of the extreme left was repressed with no great concern for squeamishness; ugly rumors of torture began to spread through the world's press. Internationally, a strongly pro-American attitude replaced the tentatively neutralist approach favored by Quadros and Goulart. The economic policies of the regime were austere and orthodox, but a succession of very high growth rates led many observers at the start of the 1970s to talk of a "Brazilian miracle."[1] In 1970 the government launched an immense project for the construction of a Trans-Amazonian Highway, designed to cross the entire Amazon basin from east to west and to link up (at some unspecified date in the future) with roads into Peru, Colombia, and Venezuela. This was a giant among projects—but Brazil had long been a giant among nations; her population passed one hundred million in mid-1972.

ARGENTINA

Two years after the Brazilian coup, civilian government also collapsed in Argentina. Right-wing generals, scornfully called "gorillas" by their more radical opponents, were now in power in both countries. Despite talk of a "Brasília–Buenos Aires axis," however, the two situations were at least as different as they were similar. Ever since the fall of Perón in 1955, Argentine politics had suffered from marked instability, while the

---

[1] According to the more humorous Brazilians, their miracle was unique. The Germans always worked hard, and Japanese discipline was notorious. But the Brazilian miracle—that really *was* miraculous!

nation as a whole, once so prosperously confident, seemed caught in a morass of stagnation. Perón's working-class following remained substantial—as did the determination of the armed forces to deny it a share of power. The intelligent radical president, Arturo Frondizi, elected in 1958, hoped to reincorporate the Peronists into political life, but their electoral success (to the tune of nearly thirty percent in March 1962) brought about his immediate downfall. The avuncular but indecisive Arturo Illía, elected in July 1963, hoped, equally, that the armed forces would now withdraw for good to their barracks, airfields, and warships. He, too, was disappointed. On June 28, 1966 the army removed him from the palace and installed General Juan Carlos Onganía as president.

Immediately after the coup, a Revolutionary Statute cleared the way for the dissolution of Congress and the abolition of political parties. Onganía intervened very heavyhandedly in the universities—many academics left the country—and, over the months which followed, displayed a considerable aversion to nightclubs and miniskirts, which he considered to be signs of the decadence of Western civilization. Both economically and internationally, he followed an orthodox and pro-American line. But the Argentine revolution, as Onganía and his associates styled it, soon ran into trouble. Severe rioting in Córdoba in May 1969 and again in May 1970—as well as sporadic urban terrorism—reflected an increasing public discontent, and in June 1970 Onganía was abruptly replaced as president by General Roberto Levingston.[1] Onganía had lasted forty-seven months; Levingston lasted only ten. In May 1971 he was deposed by General Alejandro Lanusse, the new "strong man" of the armed forces.

With Lanusse's rise to power, it was evident that the military revolution of 1966 had failed in its object of reshaping the country; it was equally evident that the policy of excluding Peronism from political life, pursued intermittently for fifteen years, was unworkable. Lanusse himself sought accommodations with as many political forces as possible, in his quest for a *gran acuerdo nacional* ("great national agreement"). Presidential elections were fixed for March 1973. In November 1972 Perón himself, now seventy-seven, was allowed to leave his comfortable Spanish exile and to return to Buenos Aires. The visit was a short one—something, reporters decided, of a damp squib. Yet when the elections came it was the Peronist candidate who won. Dr. Héctor Cámpora, whose main claim to fame was that he had always been the truest of the true to the old exile, was swept to power with forty percent of the popular vote. His administration began on May 25, 1973, amidst the

[1] The inevitable joke found its way into the headline of the British news-weekly *Latin America* in its issue of June 19, 1970: "General Levingston, I presume."

uncertainty created by a renewed outburst of urban terrorism. Of all the events in the recent history of Latin America, perhaps none was more surprising than this resounding echo of an era many had thought gone forever.

Surprise and uncertainty—they are, I fear, the proper notes on which to end a bald account of Latin American history. We do not know where the river will flow next or whether it is anywhere near the sea; we know only that the sea is uncharted. Will the future—*can* the future—be happier than the past? Inevitably, it is the past which has been my chief concern in this opening chapter, and, when I contemplate the generations of Latin Americans who have lived and died since Columbus' landfall in the Bahamas, a vivid (though differently applied) phrase by Thomas Carlyle springs to the forefront of my mind: "One thing therefore History will do: pity them all; for it went hard with them all."

Chapter 2

GEOGRAPHY AND COMMUNICATIONS

Basic Geography

Geography is able to explain many things in history. The position of a country on the map, its internal configuration, its general suitability for agricultural or industrial development—these factors, along with many others, must always be borne in mind before any truly historical assessment can be made. Geography's underlying influence in shaping long-term historical processes can never be ignored. Some of the ailments which afflict modern Latin America can be seen to have originated in the physical shape, the geographical peculiarities, of the region. Some of these must now be briefly outlined.

DIMENSIONS AND POSITION

The first feature to note is that Latin America is vast. The twenty Western hemisphere republics with which we are here concerned occupy nearly all of South America, most of Central America, a portion of North America, and the two largest islands of the Caribbean Sea.[1] This represents a surface area of just under eight million square miles, to which South America (often considered a continent in its own right) contributes nearly seven million. In all, Latin America accounts for about one fourteenth of the land surface of the globe. It contains, not surprisingly, some very sizable countries. Brazil, the most gigantic, is the fifth largest country in the world, preceded only by the Soviet Union, Canada, China, and the United States (including Alaska). Argentina and Mexico, too, are giants. Even a medium-sized republic like Chile is rather larger than either France or the state of Texas. At the other end of the scale, the Central American and Caribbean island

---

[1] Central America may be said to begin at the isthmus of Tehuentepec in southern Mexico and to terminate where Panama meets Colombia. Mexico thus occupies the southern extension of North America.

countries tend to be small, at any rate by European standards. Cuba, for instance, is less than half the size of Great Britain.

A quick glance at any map of the world will indicate the essential features of the region's geographical position. Latin America covers nearly ninety degrees of latitude, from 32° 40′ N to 56° S. and something like three quarters of its territory falls within the tropics—the only Latin American state to lie wholly outside the torrid zone is Uruguay. But the region is by no means exclusively tropical in its climate. A great deal of settlement has, in fact, taken place in mountain areas: more than a handful of the major cities of the region are to be found at fairly high altitudes.

The South American landmass extends a great deal further east than its North American counterpart. The westernmost point of South America is on more or less the same line of longitude as Pittsburgh. Valparaíso, the main port of Chile, is to the *east* of New York. The easternmost point of South America, in fact, is some twenty degrees further east than the equivalent point in North America. The eastern seaboard of South America is nearer to parts of Africa, and not a great deal further from Europe than from the principal areas of settlement in the United States. From Cape São Roque in Brazil to Freetown (Sierra Leone) is a mere eighteen hundred miles. Such is the shape of South America that points on the east coast to the south of Cape São Roque are actually nearer by sea to some Western European ports than they are to the eastern United States. Buenos Aires, for instance, is about fifty-three hundred miles from Lisbon—some five hundred miles nearer than it is to New York. Until the building of the Panama Canal, the principal west coast ports of South America—Valparaíso, Callao, Guayaquil—were, in effect, similarly placed in relation to Europe and the eastern United States, since the normal approach was through the South Atlantic and around Cape Horn. The completion of the canal in 1914, however, gave the eastern United States an advantage of more than two thousand miles over, for instance, the ports of France or England.

South America is, of all the world's great landmasses, in many ways the most isolated. The west coast republics stare out over the empty expanses of the Pacific, a clear seven thousand miles from Australia. Chile and Argentina thrust southward into latitudes where they are accompanied by no other land on the globe. Brazil, as has been mentioned, is relatively close to Africa, but—the slave trade apart—this has never implied a close commercial connection. It cannot be said that South America is well positioned in relation to the main centers of population and wealth in the rest of the world. The United States, by contrast, occupies what is in many ways the most-favored portion of the American continent. North America is at any rate reasonably close to Europe, and certainly closer to Asia than is the greater part of Latin America.

SURFACE CONFIGURATION

In seeking to summarize the physical configuration of Latin America, it is convenient to take Mexico, Central America, and the Caribbean islands first, and the South American continent second, although, as I have already mentioned, South America accounts for an over-whelming portion of the land area of the region.

Geographically, Mexico is the southernmost extension of North America. Its main feature is an immense highland area stretching from the United States frontier to the isthmus of Tehuentepec. This upland area of ridge, plateau, and valley is flanked by two more or less parallel mountain ranges, the Western Sierra Madre and the somewhat smaller and lower Eastern Sierra Madre. The heartland of the country is situated toward the southern and higher end of these highlands. At this point (approximately 20° N) a volcanic cordillera crosses the country from east to west. Popocatepetl and Ixtaccihuatli, whose eighteen thousand-foot peaks shine magnificently over Mexico City, belong to this chain. Here, too, are the principal intermontane basins (all several thousand feet above sea level) which contain the country's main area of settlement. With the exception of the limestone tableland which forms the Yucatán Peninsula, there are few areas of continuous lowland in Mexico. Hernán Cortés is said to have described the geography of the country he had conquered by crumpling a piece of paper in his hand— an eloquent gesture whose aptness it would be hard to deny.

The six republics of Central America are again predominantly mountainous, and most human settlement has taken place well above sea level. The surface configuration of the area is very complex: the general trend of the mountain ranges is from west to east, and there are two distinct highland areas, broken by a thin belt of lowland which crosses Nicaragua from coast to coast, taking in two sizable lakes— Managua and Nicaragua—on the way. North of this natural divide, the mountains (which begin, in fact, in southern Mexico) reach thirteen thousand feet and more in Guatemala. Further down the isthmus, in Panama, their height gradually drops to around three thousand feet. It is a gap between the two small cordilleras of Talamanca and San Blas that accommodates the Panama Canal, the isthmus at this particular point being no more than forty miles wide. Throughout Central America, lowlands are a relative rarity. Apart from the San Juan, which flows

from Lake Nicaragua into the Caribbean, there are no rivers of importance, a characteristic the isthmian region shares with Mexico.

It is interesting to note that Central America appears to be structurally
connected to the Greater Antilles, which are partly occupied by the
three island republics of Latin America. Cuba and Hispaniola (Santo
Domingo/Haiti) are formed partly by the same mountain system as
Guatemala, Honduras, and Nicaragua. This divides into two ranges:
the northern one appears as the Sierra Maestra in Cuba. (The southern
forms the Blue Mountains in Jamaica.) The two ranges re-emerge as
the two peninsulas of Haiti, and then converge for their short journey
through the Dominican Republic. Hispaniola is very largely mountainous; Cuba, on the other hand, consists mostly of undulating
countryside well suited to modern agriculture. Only a fourth of Cuba
can be said to be mountainous: though the Sierra Maestra rises to eight
thousand feet, the other ranges in the island are much lower and by
mainland standards hardly constitute mountains at all. The high temperatures which Cuba's tropical position would lead one to expect are
modified by the close proximity of the sea to most parts of this long,
straggling island.

South America, with its seven eighths of the surface area of Latin
America as a whole, has a roughly triangular shape whose main features
are arranged very simply. The western side of the continent is dominated by the Cordillera of the Andes. Grouped at intervals along the
Atlantic coast, there is a series of three ancient plateaus. Between these
highland areas—and to some extent enclosed by them—are three major
lowland areas (making up about half the area of South America), each
drained by an important river system. I shall briefly describe these
various features.

Well over four thousand miles long, the Cordillera of the Andes is
in many ways the most stupendous mountain range in the world, and
until the surveying of the Himalayas in the nineteenth century was
generally supposed to be the highest. It contains some forty-nine peaks
of over twenty thousand feet. The progress of the cordillera can best be
followed from south to north. From Tierra del Fuego to northern Chile,
the Andes form a single range, which reaches a considerable height at
the level of central Chile. Aconcagua, at 22,830 feet, is the highest
mountain in the Western hemisphere, and rises seventy miles northeast
of the Chilean capital, Santiago. At around 28 degrees south, the
cordillera splits into two ranges, which enclose a series of intermontane
basins in northern Argentina, Bolivia, and Peru. In Bolivia, a number
of such basins are connected, and form what is known as the altiplano,
a high plateau measuring approximately 450 miles by (on average)

eighty, and containing much of the Bolivian population. The Andes at this point attain their maximum width—four hundred miles, and both the component ranges display high and often spectacularly beautiful summits. Near La Paz, the eastern cordillera (or Royal Cordillera as it is known locally) rises to twenty thousand feet with peaks such as Illampu and Illimani—the latter presiding superbly over La Paz itself. At the northern end of the altiplano, in Peru, the two ranges converge at the "Vilcañota knot," only to split into three soon afterward. The eastern-most of these three descends into the Amazon lowlands and vanishes, while the two remaining ranges meet at the Cerro de Pasco knot. Once again they split into three, and once again the easternmost of the trio forks away to disappear into the lowlands. The central range, breached by the Marañón River, rejoins the western cordillera at Loja, in southern Ecuador. For their passage through Ecuador, the Andes again divide into two, forming an "avenue of volcanoes" which encloses a further series of high intermontane basins. In Colombia, from the "Pasto knot" northward, there are again three separate ranges: the western and central cordilleras end here, while the eastern, on one of whose plateaus Bogotá is situated, eventually divides in two: one fork terminates along the Guajira Peninsula, passing the separate but massive Sierra Nevada de Santa Marta, which itself rises to nineteen thousand feet, on the way. A second fork forms a series of ranges which run along the northern coast of Venezuela, only finally disappearing beyond the Gulf of Paria on the island of Trinidad.

The Andes occupy a quarter of the area of South America, and act as an immense natural barrier between east and west. Except in the south, most passes across the cordillera are more than ten thousand feet high. An obvious parallel here is the chain of the Rockies in North America, which are wider than the Andes but lower and a great deal more passable. On the eastern side of the Andes, a number of deep valleys descend, usually rather gently, to the lowlands. Many of them are extremely fertile and salubrious—for instance, the Bolivian *yungas*. On the west side, however, the descent from the cordillera is abrupt and precipitous. Lowlands between the cordillera and the Pacific Ocean, where they exist at all, are narrow. Nor are the rivers flowing from Andes to sea more than marginally important; with the exception of the Guayas in Ecuador, not one is navigable for more than a few miles inland. From Ecuador to southern Chile there runs a parallel coastal cordillera, though this is not always clearly defined: and the rich and fertile Central Valley of Chile, the heartland of that republic, lies between this coastal range and the main bulk of the Andes. From Copiapó in Chile to the border between Peru and Ecuador the west coast is predominantly desert: in Peru, rivers intersect the coastal zone and form oases; in northern Chile, on the other hand, complete aridity prevails. In the whole expanse of the great desert of Atacama between Arica and Copiapó—a distance of about six hundred miles—only one river, the miserable stream of the Loa, is able to make its way through the desert and the forbidding coastal range to the sea. A coastal city such as Antofagasta needs to bring its water supply by pipeline from the cordillera, two hundred miles away. The Atacama Desert is one of the driest regions on earth: in some areas, no rainfall has ever been recorded.

The Andes, like the mountain ranges of Mexico and Central America, are of relatively recent formation and are still unstable. Active volcanoes still abound, and the whole western side of South America is subject to earthquakes and tremors. Few cities have escaped from the ravages of these frightening phenomena. Santiago was wrecked in 1647, Lima in 1746, Caracas in 1812. Valparaíso was seriously damaged in 1906, and more recently, in May 1960, the southern end of the Central Valley of Chile was devastated: the cities of Concepción and Valdivia were destroyed; over nine thousand people perished. By far the most horrific of recent disasters, however, was the appalling earthquake of May 1970 in the Peruvian Andes; some fifty thousand people lost their lives.

The three eastern highland areas of South America are neither as high nor as dramatic as the Andes. But they are much older. Geologically, they are in fact the oldest portion of the southern landmass, and aeons ago may have formed part of the immense Gondwanaland continent whose existence is posited by some geographers. Of the three, the largest and most important is the Brazilian plateau, which covers nearly one million square miles and has an elevation of between fifteen hundred feet and five thousand feet. In shape, the plateau resembles a right-angled triangle, whose longest side flanks the coast from Cape São Roque to the state of Rio Grande do Sul, creating a massive escarpment, the Serra do Mar. The plateau slopes toward the interior of the continent, a fact which means that rivers are obliged to flow away from the coast for long distances before reaching the sea. The classic example of this is the São Francisco, a river which rises in the Brazilian heartland, not far from Rio de Janeiro, but nevertheless flows for well over a thousand miles through the plateau before curving eastward to meet the Atlantic. The plateau itself consists mainly of rolling hills and tablelands and, more rarely, mountains: its highest summit, the Pico da Bandeira, to the northeast of Rio de Janeiro, is just under 9,500 feet. The interior of the plateau is remote and thinly settled, and the foundation of Brasília, on the planalto of Goiás, was mainly conceived as a means of bringing this area into active use.

Two other highland areas on the eastern side of South America also need to be mentioned though neither is even remotely as well populated as the eastern sections of the Brazilian plateau. The Guiana Massif, which falls partly within Venezuela, partly within Brazil, runs one thousand miles from east to west, and at its widest point, six hundred miles from north to south. It is covered by a mixture of dense forest and savannah, and its mysterious air of inaccessibility has been immortalized in such works of fiction as W. H. Hudson's *Green Mansions* and Sir Arthur Conan Doyle's *The Lost World*. The Patagonian plateau, in the extreme south of the continent, occupies a quarter of the national territory of Argentina. Geologically distinct from the Andes, it is separated from the cordillera in many places by a narrow ribbon of lowland. Its height rises to about five thousand feet towards the west. A number of rivers—notably the Negro and the Chubut—cut grooves through the surface of the plateau to the coast; only in the valleys thus formed is crop cultivation possible. Elsewhere the desolate and windswept grasslands lend themselves almost exclusively to sheep-raising.

The main lowland regions of South America, which take up approximately half the continent, may be considered as three in number. Each is drained by an extensive system of rivers. Two of these systems are actually connected. The smallest of the lowland regions, located in the north of the continent, is the basin of the Orinoco, an area which houses the *llanos* of Venezuela and Colombia. This is a region of coarse grass, brushwood, and tropical forest, of plains which are either sun-scorched or flooded. Despite the hazards, the llanos have proved suitable for cattle-raising and horse-breeding, and the llaneros, the tough, obstinate cowboys of the plains, have displayed their fierce courage in warfare and revolt on more than one occasion in the past. The Orinoco River itself opens up what might have become a major route through the llanos and into the interior of the continent, were it not for the shallowness of the river and a series of rapids some six hundred miles from the sea.

By an extraordinary quirk of geography, the Orinoco is in fact connected to the greatest of South American river systems, the Amazon. The link is the Casiquiare channel; over two hundred miles in length, it diverts some of the water from the main stream of the Orinoco, meanders through the Guiana highlands, and eventually pours into the Rio Negro, which is a tributary of the Amazon.

It is almost impossible to write about the Amazon River without using highly colored superlatives. After the Cordillera of the Andes, it is certainly the most dramatic natural feature in Latin America, and easily the biggest river in the world. The Marañón, in Peru, is generally regarded as its upper section, and the total length of the Amazon–Marañón is around 3,700 miles. The Ucayali, which joins the main river near Iquitos in Peru, could also be considered as an alternative upper section, which would give a length of around 4,500 miles. The Amazon discharges a truly impressive amount of water into the Atlantic —estimated at 3,500,000 cubic feet *per second*—and traces of this can frequently be observed two hundred miles out to sea. There are innumerable tributaries: some of them—the Xingú, Tapajós, Madeira, Purús, and Jarúa to the south, and the Japurá, the Negro, and the Blanco to the north—are enormous rivers in their own right. In all, the Amazon system offers some twenty thousand miles of navigable waterway. In time of flooding, this is nearly doubled.

The lowlands of Amazonia cover more than two million square miles of territory, and contain what is probably the largest region of continuous dense forest in the world. Most of the region is below five hundred feet, and floodplains generally accompany the line of the rivers. The greater part of the basin, however, consists of what is known locally as *terra firme*, and is safe from the swollen waters. On the floodplain, the immense forest undoubtedly merits being described as "jungle." Impenetrable undergrowth covers large areas. On the higher land, on the other hand, there is often less undergrowth, and occasionally stretches of savannah country. An incredible profusion of trees and plants, and a wide variety of exotic animals and reptiles, is the main characteristic of the region. Although average temperatures are not as high as is popularly supposed, the level of humidity tends to be unacceptable to most Europeans. Despite one or two vain attempts at planned and intensive settlement, the whole Amazon basin remains one of the most thinly peopled parts of the world. It may be considered as one of the world's last frontiers.

A low divide, the Chiquitos highlands, separates the Amazon basin from the third and southernmost lowland area, that of the River Plate. Moving southward along the line of the Paraguay River, the traveler first encounters a four-hundred-thousand-square-mile zone known as the Gran Chaco.[1] It is shared by Bolivia, Peru, and Argentina. Partly forest, partly marsh, and, during the dry season, a lethally scorching suntrap, the Chaco would appear to possess considerable agricultural potential, but, like the Amazon basin, its surface has barely been scratched.

The heart of the Platine lowlands is the Argentine pampa, which is drained by the rivers Paraná (whose main tributary is the Paraguay) and Uruguay. These combine to form the estuary known as the River

[1] *Chaco* means "hunting ground."

Plate, a shallow and muddy stretch of water approximately one hundred miles in length. Here is to be found one of the most prosperous main areas of settlement in Latin America. The pampa extends three hundred to four hundred miles north, south and west of the city of Buenos Aires, and covers 250,000 square miles. Its eastern section, the humid pampa, is well watered by rainfall; further west, on the so-called dry pampa, some thought has to be given to irrigation. Nevertheless, the pampa as a whole is marked by three major advantages over the other lowland regions of Latin America. It is easily accessible from the sea. Lying well below the equator, its climate is essentially temperate. And its soils are of high quality; indeed, their quality is almost *too* high, since the general lack of stones in the soil of the pampa has made roadbuilding more difficult than is normal.

NATURAL RESOURCES

It would be impossible to summarize, even superficially, the great variety of soils and climatic features which condition Latin America's capacity for agriculture. But it will be obvious that much of the surface configuration of the region works against large-scale farming. Only one really large expanse of near-perfect soil is to be found: the Argentine lowlands, and even these are not to be compared, as far as size goes, with comparable parts of North America. Elsewhere good soil, if it exists at all, is confined to zones which by their very nature tend to be small and restricted: valleys, intermontane basins, narrow coastal lowland. Over large areas of Latin America, the soil is thin and lacks the elements necessary for sustained crop cultivation. The tropical soils of the Amazon basin, for example, would need to be fertilized and in many places drained before they could be used efficiently for agriculture: the exuberant vegetation of Amazonia is not due to rich soils so much as to other factors like heat and humidity. Much desert or semiarid terrain—northern Mexico, the coastal strip of Peru and Chile, southern Argentina—needs very extensive irrigation before much can be produced. Irrigation *has* become a major characteristic of the agricultural pattern of some countries: in Peru, for instance, nearly two thirds of all arable land is irrigated. Results can, therefore, be achieved; but money and technical skill are prime necessities, and these are very often lacking. Archaic land-tenure systems often form a further barrier to progress. It should not, perhaps, surprise us to learn that only five percent of Latin America is used for crop cultivation; in the United States the percentage is double this.

Having said this, it is nevertheless important to remember that despite all the disadvantages, Latin America does succeed in producing a number of tropical crops on a large scale. Over three quarters of the world's coffee comes from Latin America, together with two thirds of the world's bananas, a quarter of the world's sugar and cacao, and perhaps a tenth of the world's cotton. Temperate crops such as wheat and maize are widely grown, not only in Argentina but also in the mountainous zones further north, where altitude offsets latitude. There are, too, a number of minor crops whose cultivation is almost unique to the region: yerba maté, coca, quebracho, to name but three.

Approximately seventeen percent of Latin America is said to be used for grazing, and the region is rich in horses, cattle, sheep, and pigs. A quarter of the world's cattle are to be found in Latin America, but outside the River Plate basin much remains to be done to promote truly efficient dairy farming. Very nearly half of Latin America is covered by forest of one kind or another; but up to the present, at least, the felling of timber has not been a main activity, though here, plainly, there is much potential for the future. Similarly, very little fishing on a large scale has been done until recently. Before World War II, less than two percent of the total world catch derived from the limited Latin American fishing fleets. By the early 1960s, this situation had changed radically—between ten and twenty percent of the world catch came from the region. This was very largely accounted for by one country, Peru, the development of whose fishmeal industry was one of the more dramatic economic processes of the later 1950s.[1] Chile and Ecuador also increased their catch in the same period.

In general, agriculture and the associated activities I have mentioned are hampered by a number of obstacles, some natural, some man-made. It is clear, however, that there is appreciable potential for development. New lands, more than in most other parts of the world, can be said to await the hand of the pioneer. But a still greater challenge to development lies in consolidating and making efficient use of land where settlement is already concentrated. Here the problems are social and psychological as well as geographical.

As far as mineral resources are concerned, Latin America is at least as well endowed as any other major area of the world. Without attempting a complete catalogue of minerals, some indication of these resources can nevertheless be given. Very considerable deposits of high-grade iron ore are to be found in Brazil and Venezuela, and also (though mostly unexploited) in Bolivia. Chile, Cuba, Mexico, and Peru also contain deposits. Brazil possesses the world's largest reserves of manganese. Tin is produced in large quantities in Bolivia, from the rich veins high

---

[1] Large numbers of anchovies from the Peruvian Current are caught and processed: fishmeal is used as fertilizer or as a component in animal foodstuffs.

in the Eastern Cordillera of the Andes, and although Bolivia is the only major producer in the Americas, other countries—Argentina, Brazil, and Mexico—could eventually join her. Chile is the second copper-producing country in the world—something like half her output is taken from one mine, Chuquicamata in the Atacama Desert. Argentina, Bolivia, Mexico, and Peru also have reserves. Lead and zinc are mined in Mexico, and to a lesser extent in Peru, Bolivia, Argentina, and Guatemala. Silver and gold—the leading mineral exports from Latin America in colonial times—are found in Mexico, Peru, Bolivia, Central America, and Colombia. Colombia produces the only platinum in Latin America, and also accounts for ninety-five percent of the world production of emeralds, though neither of these commodities can be said to be commercially important: in 1964, platinum accounted for 0.3 percent of Colombian exports. (In the same year coffee accounted for 73.4 percent.) Mexico takes her place amongst the world's most important producers of sulfur, while Chile is fortunate in possessing the only substantial deposits of sodium nitrate in the world, though these have lost their importance since the discovery, half a century ago, of the means of elaborating synthetic nitrate.

Against these signs of considerable mineral wealth has to be set the fact that Latin America is seriously deficient in coal. Deposits exist in Argentina, Brazil, Chile, Colombia, and Mexico, but the coal is generally of low quality, and Latin America's total production is less than one percent of the world's. Other sources of energy are, however, more plentiful. Oil is found in every country of South America except Uruguay and Paraguay, and also in Mexico, Cuba, and Costa Rica. Perhaps one fifth of the total world output is taken from Latin America, but between two thirds and three quarters of this comes from a single country—Venezuela. Production began there toward the end of World War I, predominantly in the Lake Maracaibo basin in the west of the country. The population of the town of Maracaibo itself—as good an indicator of the scale of expansion as any—rose from about fifteen thousand at the time oil was discovered to five hundred thousand by the later 1960s. Of the 230 million metric tons of oil produced by Latin American countries in 1965, 172,500,000 tons came from Venezuela. Natural gas, which is often found with oil, is a further alternative source of energy, and in recent years has been increasingly exploited. Argentina, Brazil, and Venezuela have taken the lead here; all three countries have installed major pipelines. Latin America is also believed to have about a quarter of the world's potential waterpower capacity. Brazil has done most to make good use of her potential in this respect: by 1963, Brazilian hydroelectric plants could generate approximately six million kilowatts.

Chile, Mexico, and Peru are also developing hydroelectric power in an impressive way.

On the face of it, therefore, the wealth of Latin America need not be disputed. Nature has provided the region with the means not merely of subsistence, but also of progress. And yet there are problems of a purely geographical nature, as well as those which history has imposed. Many of the areas in which agricultural expansion can be expected to take place are poorly located in relation to the coast. Except in the River Plate basin, the lowlands of South America are difficult to reach. If the region's deficiency in coal can to some extent be offset, the lack of a truly extensive zone of high-quality agricultural land is less remediable. The sheer size of Latin America is a further problem, particularly when coupled with a position on the globe that adds a dimension of inter-continental inaccessability, and a surface configuration that makes communications difficult. The Andes, it is worth repeating, are a much more severe natural barrier than the mountain ranges of Europe or North America.

But it should not be forgotten that the assessment and use of natural resources varies according to historical circumstances. Oil was of no importance until twentieth-century technology made it almost indispensable. In the sixteenth century, when the extraction of silver and gold was deemed a sure means of building up national wealth, no Spanish conquistador could have foreseen that the riches of the Argentine pampa would one day make the fortune of the greatest Spanish-speaking city in the world. It would, of course, be idle to speculate as to how the twenty-first century will evaluate and exploit the natural resources of Latin America. There may well be some interesting surprises. Some of them may even be beneficial.

Transport and Communications

The history of transport and communications in Latin America has gone through three distinct—though overlapping—phases. The first of these, which can properly be described as "archaic" or "traditional," lasted throughout the colonial period and well into the era of the Creole states of the nineteenth century. Its characteristic expressions were the mule-train and the sailing ship. A second phase, which can conveniently be labeled "early modern," began in the mid-nineteenth century with the introduction of the railway, the electric telegraph, and the steamship. The third and most recent phase, the "modern" phase, opened around the year 1920. Its main features have been the advent of the motor vehicle, the airplane, and radio.

THE ARCHAIC PHASE

The carriage of goods and people in the Latin America of the colonial period was almost entirely dependent on animals and human beings. Among pack-animals, the mule was predominant. In the high Andes, it was complemented by the llama, and horses were also used, though much less extensively. It is difficult to exaggerate the impact of the mule on the pattern of Latin American transport, though many a sophisticated modern smile may greet this statement. This stubborn and sturdy creature, introduced from Europe, revolutionized the carriage of minerals and merchandise: in the mountainous terrain of Mexico and Peru, where so much of colonial life was concentrated, it quickly proved indispensable. Other means of transport were naturally employed as well. The oxcart was familiar on the plains of the River Plate, though not in high mountains. In the cities, barouches (two-wheeled carriages) and coaches were by no means uncommon. Horses were often used by travelers, particularly in the lowlands. But by far the commonest sight on the roads of Latin America at this period was the mule-train. The *arriero*, or muleteer, was one of the most enterprising figures on the colonial stage: he frequently grew rich. Mules—needed in the mines as well as on the roads—were big business. As many as sixty thousand a year would be sent from Argentina to the mining communities of Upper Peru. As pack-animals, they had their disadvantages. They were slow. In high altitudes they often died while on a journey; it was common, therefore, for reserves of mules to travel behind the larger trains. But against this had to be set the fact that their sure-footedness eliminated the need to build wide and well-surfaced roads.

With the coming of the European pack-animal, a new network of communications quickly established itself. Roads—often little more than well-defined tracks, and sometimes not even well defined—spread outward from the main centers of Spanish and Portuguese power. Mexico City was connected with Vera Cruz on the Caribbean coast, with Acapulco on the Pacific, with Central America (via Oaxaca), and with the great expanses of the North West (via Guadalajara). A much-frequented route crossed the isthmus from Panama to Nombre de Dios —later Portobelo.[1] In Spanish South America, the old roads of the Inca empire—much admired by the conquistadores—now served the new overlords from Europe, though sometimes the Spaniards preferred alternative routes, as in northwest Argentina. Isolated colonies developed their own rough-and-ready systems of cart tracks and roads—a case in

[1] The idea of driving a canal through the isthmus was mooted more than a few times during the colonial period.

87

point being the old "Frontier Road" through the Central Valley of Chile. By far the most important axis of land travel that developed in South America was the line from Lima, the viceregal capital, to Buenos Aires, by way of Upper Peru. This came into intensive use only in the eighteenth century, with the beginnings of growth in Buenos Aires. A Spanish officer who visited the River Plate in the 1750s has left an excellent description of the oxcarts which made the journey from Buenos Aires to Tucumán at that time:

> The carts used . . . are very big. Their normal load is 200 arrobas each [approximately five thousand pounds], and each of them requires two peons to manage it—one on horseback, and one inside the front of the cart to wield the goad that drives the oxen. . . . Each cart usually takes three pairs of oxen, and is always accompanied by a fair number of horses and by a numerous herd [of oxen]—with lambs mixed in to provide fresh meat daily.[1]

But, for the journey from Tucumán to the altiplano, and the mining communities, and from the mining communities to Lima, such relatively spacious methods of travel no longer served, and the indispensable mule was called into action once more. Rivers, as well as mountains, constituted major obstacles to roadbuilding. Bridges were rare, although some of the old rope bridges of the Incas remained in use in the Andes. Most rivers had to be crossed by canoe or raft. Toward the end of the colonial period, the Spanish dominions in America put in hand an impressive program of road improvements, as did Spain herself. By the early years of the nineteenth century, several important sections of road had been paved. But old habits, and old obstacles, still hampered development, and the general state of the highways was far from good on the eve of independence. Alexander von Humboldt, the most intelligent of European travelers to the Indies at this period, noted the situation in Mexico as follows:

> The central tableland is travelled in four wheel carriages in all directions . . . but in the present bad state of the roads, waggons are not established for the conveyance of goods. They give preference to the employment of beasts of burden; and thousands of horses and mules cover in long files the roads of Mexico.

The descent from tableland to coastal plain was still an uncomfortable experience: "the road . . .," Humboldt reported, "is frequently nothing

[1] Francisco Millau, *Descripción de la provincia del Río de la Plata, 1772* (Buenos Aires, 1947), pp. 65–66.

but a narrow and crooked path."[1] The same was true of most roads in New Granada and Quito. The vast viceroyalty of Brazil was particularly backward. Occasionally, however, a sustained effort could produce results: the high road from Mexico City to Vera Cruz, completed in 1803, was well paved over its whole distance and its ascent from Vera Cruz to Perote, as Humboldt admitted, bore comparison with the best roads across the Alps; stone columns stood at intervals to mark both distance and altitude.

At sea, throughout the colonial period, the sailing ship was the only effective means of communication over long distances, whether on the various coastal routes in the colonies or across the Atlantic. The earliest ships to cross the ocean were predominantly caravels of well under one hundred tons; these immortal craft of the great age of discovery were gradually replaced by larger merchantmen of several hundred tons, and from the mid-sixteenth century the galleon, the standard armed escort of colonial days, became a common sight in American waters. It remains, for most people, the most vivid symbol of Iberian imperial power. Spanish galleons, in addition to providing protection for merchant vessels, also had the function of transporting the royal silver from Mexico and Peru.

The pattern of maritime activity that developed during the colonial period was a direct outcome of imperial policy. Colonial trade was very strictly controlled and directed—though rather less so in the case of Brazil. The Spanish commercial system, as it operated from the sixteenth century to the mid-eighteenth, was based essentially on monopoly ports and convoys of ships. Convoys became standard from the 1560s. Two fleets left Spain each year. The first set off in the spring, and sailed to Mexico, where the monopoly port was Vera Cruz. A second fleet left in the summer, bound for the Panama isthmus, from where it moved on to Cartagena. Both the convoys moved on to Havana at the end of the winter, and, when summer had come round again, made the return journey to Spain together. Described in these terms, the system appears cumbersome. Nevertheless, it had many advantages. It provided protection against Spain's enemies, and it was regular and dependable. Portugal adopted a not dissimilar system in relation to Brazil: until 1765, one fleet a year sailed from Lisbon.

The convoy system, in the Spanish empire, implied that all trade would pass either through Vera Cruz or the isthmus of Panama. The colonies on the Pacific (and even the River Plate) were to import and

[1] Humboldt, *Political Essay on the Kingdom of New Spain*, 4 vols. (London, 1811), IV, 2–3.

export only through Panama. The main ports of the west coast—Guayaquil, Callao, Arica (the outlet for Upper Peruvian silver) and Valparaíso—were therefore served by a separate system of fleets. In the sixteenth century, shipbuilding for this coastal trade developed at Guayaquil and also in Central America. There was, obviously, an element of paradox that the distant southern colonies—Chile and the River Plate—should be required to direct their commerce northward to Panama rather than through Buenos Aires. The silver from the Upper Peruvian mines could more easily be exported by way of the River Plate than by way of Panama. After 1740, the system of convoys and monopoly ports was gradually abandoned. It was replaced by vessels sailing individually under license to a much wider range of colonial ports. This more sensible system helped to bring about a considerable expansion of trade, and also enabled the imperial governments to speed up their postal systems. Communications had never been better in the Spanish and Portuguese empires than at the time of independence. But it was still animal-power and wind-power that made communications possible at all.

THE EARLY MODERN PHASE
The second, or "early modern," phase referred to at the start of this section began at sea. The first sign—and it was no more than a sign—that a technical revolution was about to take place in Latin American transport came in 1822, in Valparaíso. It came, as did so much in the nineteenth century, from England. The steamship *Rising Star* had been built in a Rotherhithe shipyard for Lord Thomas Cochrane, who had intended to use it in his campaign against the Spanish naval forces in the Pacific. Completed in 1821, this 428-tonner with her two 45-h.p. engines became the first steam-powered vessel to sail the Atlantic in a westward direction, and the first too, to enter the Pacific. It is, perhaps, no more than a courtesy to refer to the *Rising Star* as a steamship. In appearance she was a fully rigged sailing ship: her internal paddle-wheels only provided auxiliary power, and were apparently used for less than twenty hours during the entire journey from the Thames to the Bay of Valparaíso. Nevertheless, her arrival in South American waters indicated that a new era in maritime transport was dawning. Less than two decades later, an extraordinary and enterprising American, William Wheelwright, raised capital in England, chartered the Pacific Steam Navigation Company (February 1840), and brought two identical steamers, the *Chile* and the *Peru*, into the Pacific to serve the two countries after which they were named. They reached Valparaíso on October 15, 1840, and the date may be taken as the effective start of

commercial steam navigation in Latin America. After a financial start that was little short of disastrous, the Pacific Steam Navigation Company (PSNC) went on to play an honorable pioneering role in linking the west coast republics to the wider world. Its headquarters were set up at Valparaíso. In 1868 it spread its sphere of operations to the River Plate, though here another British company, the Royal Mail, had opened up regular services in 1853, soon after the fall of Rosas. Before long, steamers were operating in and out of all the major Latin American ports. The 1840s and 1850s saw the beginnings of steam navigation on the great rivers—the Amazon, the Magdalena, the Paraná in particular— which now became arteries of commerce on a far larger scale than ever before.

Steam gradually transformed the merchant marines of the new Latin American republics. These had been developing since independence, though usually on a very small scale. How did a century later find them? In 1910–11, according to *Lloyds Register of Shipping*, the list of the world's first twenty merchant fleets included those of Brazil (16th: 383 ships totaling 251,753 tons), Argentina (18th: 267 ships totaling 163,421 tons), and Chile (19th: 139 ships, totaling 151,218 tons). These fleets were, of course, very small when compared with the largest then operating. (The world's leading maritime nation, Great Britain, then possessed 11,495 merchant vessels totaling nearly twenty million tons.) Since World War II, Latin American merchant fleets have continued to grow in size, and this tendency seems likely to continue. Independent merchant marines save foreign exchange, and guarantee regular services for national trade. In 1964, however, the total gross tonnage of all Latin American merchant ships put together was still equivalent to only one sixth the tonnage of the merchant fleet of the United Kingdom. Most Latin American exports are transported by sea, yet the national fleets do not account for a high proportion of the carrying trade: in the early 1960s perhaps a fifth of Argentina's exports and imports were carried in Argentine vessels, and just over a quarter of Brazil's in Brazilian vessels. Over fifty foreign shipping lines operate cargo and passenger services into the region, though passenger sailings have tended to decline in recent years. The two British pioneering companies, PSNC and Royal Mail, both withdrew their passenger liners from the South American run in the 1960s.

From the start, the chief significance of the steamship lay in its ability to connect Latin America with the rest of the world more speedily and dependably than had been possible before. As far as the transmission of general and commercial information was concerned, this was done in a still more revolutionary fashion by the advent of the electric telegraph. Its first appearances were within countries rather than between countries, and, indeed, this was inevitable. The earliest lines were installed in Mexico (Mexico City to Puebla) and in Chile (Santiago to Valparaíso) and opened in October 1851 and June 1852 respectively. The Chilean telegraph was installed by Wheelwright. Other countries followed fairly rapidly: the first Brazilian telegraph was ready for use in May 1854, and Argentina installed one six years later. Expansion was rapid: by the time of the restoration of the republic in Mexico in 1867, over one thousand miles of line had been installed in that country. At the end of Sarmiento's presidency in Argentina (1874), there were over three thousand miles there—and Brazil, at the time of the fall of the empire in 1889, possessed nearly twelve thousand miles. Politically and commercially, the spread of the telegraph within the Latin American countries was highly important. But the international aspect was perhaps even more so. In 1866 a submarine cable was laid across the River Plate, connecting Buenos Aires and Montevideo. And only eight years after the installation of the first permanent cable under the North Atlantic, the enterprising Brazilian Baron Mauá, sponsored a submarine connection between Recife and Portugal. Emperor Pedro II sent the first messages from South America to Europe on June 23, 1874. After early plans for a submarine cable across the Gulf of Mexico had fallen through, Mexico was eventually linked to Europe via the United States.

If the steamship and the telegraph revolutionized international communications, there can be no real doubt that the railway—introduced very soon after the steamship—had the biggest impact on internal transport since the arrival of the mule in the sixteenth century. Land communications in most of the republics in the first decade after independence remained essentially "colonial" in nature: although a number of roads were improved, the mule-train and the packhorse, the oxcart and (in a very few areas) the diligence, were still the dominant modes of transport and travel in the mid-nineteenth century. All this was now changed. Within ten or fifteen years of the opening of the Stockton-to-Darlington railway in England (1825), Latin American governments were making the first concessions for the construction of tracks on their own territories. The first lines actually to be built came in 1850–51: eight miles of track at Vera Cruz in Mexico (opened on September 16, 1850), the Lima-Callao railway in Peru (April 5, 1851), and, in Chile, the line from Copiapó to Caldera, built by the indefatigable Wheelwright (December 25, 1851). The longest of these was the Chilean line: fifty miles. The first few miles of Baron Mauá's "Petropolis Railway" in Brazil were opened on April 30, 1854 by Emperor

Pedro II.[1] On January 28, 1855 the newly built railway across the isthmus of Panama—it had taken five years to build—came into use.[2] August 1857 saw the opening of the first six miles of the first line in Argentina—running westward out of Buenos Aires.

These beginnings were modest enough, but over the next generation railway-building proceeded apace. In Chile, Santiago was linked with Valparaíso in 1863. The Argentine Central Railroad connecting Córdoba with the river-port of Rosario—yet another achievement of William Wheelwright—was completed in 1870. Mexico was joined to Vera Cruz three years later. Central America—apart from Panama and Costa Rica—had to wait slightly longer, but Guatemala, El Salvador, and Nicaragua all had railways by the end of the 1880s. By the eve of World War I, four areas of Latin America possessed extensive systems of track: the Argentine pampa, the Brazilian heartland, Mexico, and the Central Valley of Chile. Most other countries had at least several lines. Railway-building as a major activity came to an end in the 1920s, and since World War II a number of lines have been closed, though Latin America's experience in this respect is no different from the rest of the world's. Nevertheless, one or two important *new* railways have been built over recent decades: a line across the Andes from Salta to Antofagasta (finished in 1948); the line from Santa Cruz, Bolivia, to the Brazilian border at Corumbá (1953); the Atlantic Railway in Colombia, linking Bogotá and the Caribbean port of Santa Marta by way of the Magdalena Valley (this opened in 1961); and, most recently, the rail link to Brasília (1968).

In 1960, there were nearly eighty-six thousand miles of track in Latin America, although Argentina, Brazil, and Mexico accounted for seventy-seven percent of this total. The great majority of lines were single-track, but in terms of route-mileage, the railways of Latin America represented approximately ten percent of the world total—more or less the same as the U.S.S.R. (The United States and Canada account for thirty percent, Europe for twenty-five percent, and Asia for ten percent.) Nothing like as much freight, however, was carried on railways in Latin America as in either North America or Europe.

Railway-building in Latin America was often an almost heroic process. As might be expected, the construction of the Andean lines presented extraordinary difficulties. That these were overcome at all is perhaps astonishing. (None of the seven major lines that run into the

[1] In fact it was the building of this railway that secured Mauá his barony; his sponsorship of the submarine cable to Europe, already referred to, gained him a viscountcy.

[2] This was not the first railway in Central America; a fourteen-mile section had been built in Costa Rica the previous year.

Andes from the west coast of South America rises to a point *lower* than 10,452 feet.)[1]

The most audacious enterprise was the building of the Central Railway of Peru. The promoter of the railway was a colorful American, Henry Meiggs, who had already taken on the task of completing the Santiago–Valparaíso railway in Chile. The first stone of the first station of the Central Railway was laid on January 1, 1870 by President Balta: the banquet for eight hundred laid on by Meiggs was wholly characteristic of the sumptuous ritual that attended such engineering projects in the nineteenth century, whether in Peru or in England. Half Meiggs' workmen were Chinese, shipped in specially from Macao; the remainder were Peruvians, Chileans, and Bolivians. Many of them died. As the railway rose higher into the mountains, insect bites induced a fatal illness, the *verruga*, which more than decimated the construction gangs. The workmen themselves were often unruly. One episode involving some drunken Chileans—the so-called "Ocatara incident" (1872)—almost provoked a major political crisis. But despite problems such as these, the greater part of the work was completed by the time Meiggs died in 1877, though the final sections of the line did not come into use until the 1890s. The Central Railway, with its sixty-six tunnels, almost as many bridges, and twenty-two switchback sections, was one of the wonders of the nineteenth-century world. It reaches its highest point above sea level—15,688 feet—only a hundred miles from Lima. Meiggs' brilliant achievement should not, however, be allowed to obscure the fact that the building of other Andean railways also represented dazzling feats of engineering. Some of them had to wait many years for completion: the long-planned Guayaquil-Quito[2] line in Ecuador was not finished until 1908; the *transandino* railway from Los Andes (Chile) to Mendoza (Argentina) was only made continuous by the blasting of a tunnel in 1910.

Some of the ways in which the Latin American railway systems developed may fairly be described as deficient. In the first place, relatively few countries succeeded in creating truly "integrated" networks: Argentina, Brazil (in the southeast), Chile (in the Central Valley),

---

[1] The exact heights may be of some interest:
    Guayaquil–Quito: 11,841 ft. (Urbina Pass)
    Lima–Huancayo 15,688 ft. (Galera tunnel)
    Arequipa–Cuzco: 14,688 ft. (Crucero Alto)
    Arica–La Paz: 13,390 ft. (Gen. Lagos)
    Antofagasta–La Paz: 13,000 ft. (Ascotán)
    Salta–Antofagasta: 14,680 ft. (Chorillos Pass)
    Los Andes–Mendoza: 10,452 ft. (tunnel).

[2] In strict fact, Durán to Quito: the line starts on the eastern shore of the River Guayas, opposite Guayaquil itself.

and Mexico perhaps came nearest to this. In general, however, railways were built to link zones of agricultural or mineral production with ports, and it seemed to matter little whether the different lines so built were connected in any way. Partly as a result of this, a bewildering variety of different gauges came into use in Latin America—some ten different gauges, in fact. The commonest were the 5'6" (wide), the standard (4'8½"), and meter gauges.[1] It is also important to remember that the international links established by rail were never of major importance except in one or two isolated instances. Many countries were never joined by rail at all. The southeast of South America was to some extent an exception here: thanks partly to the efforts of a dynamic American entrepreneur, Percival Farquhar, plans were put in hand for a full international system between Brazil, Uruguay, Argentina, Paraguay, and Bolivia. As a result, Rio de Janeiro and Montevideo were linked in 1911. But Farquhar's schemes, which depended on European capital being available, were wrecked by World War I. Interest in setting up international rail links in Latin America has at times run high. Before World War I there was considerable enthusiasm for a Pan-American Railroad to run between the United States and Argentina—an idea which had been approved by the first Pan-American Conference in 1889. In the 1960s, with the creation of the Latin American Free Trade Area (ALALC), further impetus was given to the idea of extending and strengthening international rail connections. A sign of this came in March 1964, when representatives of Argentine, Brazil, Chile, Ecuador, Paraguay, and Uruguay met in Argentina to form the Asociación Latinoamericana de Ferrocarriles (Latin American Railways Association). At present, however, the international connections which exist are relatively little used.

By the 1960s, the state of the railways in many parts of Latin America was run-down. Some countries—Mexico and Chile spring to mind immediately—were making strenuous efforts to revitalize their networks through electrification and the renewal of rolling stock. But in general the situation seemed far from promising. The majority of track was "obsolete, with old and lightweight rails, badly ballasted, with sleepers in poor condition, and with deficient general maintenance."[2] Of the 3,770 steam engines in use in Argentina in 1960, 2,504 were over forty years old, and a similar pattern could be observed in several other countries. Diesel locomotives were gradually replacing steam engines—

[1] In Argentina in 1960, 55.3 percent of the track was wide gauge, 34.8 percent meter gauge; 88.9 percent of Brazilian track was meter gauge; in South America, only Uruguay (standard) and Bolivia (meter) had one-gauge railway systems.

[2] Comisión Económica para América Latina, *El transporte en América Latina* (New York, United Nations, 1965), p. 9.

by 1960 they were more numerous than steam engines on the Mexican system—but it was very clear that vast sums of money would be needed if railways were to play an increased part in transport. The basic reason for the relative decline of the railways was, of course, a simple and obvious one: no sooner had most of the major networks of Latin America been completed, than a new and more flexible form of surface transport began to challenge their predominance.

THE MODERN PHASE

Steam had been the key to the revolution in transport during the nineteenth century. From around 1920 or so, it was the internal combustion engine that ushered in the third and most recent phase of the story. The motor vehicle offered a convenient alternative to the railway train, while the airplane, at any rate for some purposes, challenged the steamship. For the movement of passengers, the motorbus quickly established itself as a rival to the railway; for the conveyance of goods, the truck—though often used at first in journeys to and from the nearest railhead—increasingly became an independent form of transport. In countries like Argentina, where the railway system was extremely well developed, or Chile, where coastal shipping was (and is) an important factor, the motor vehicle took longer to make an impact than elsewhere. By the early 1960s, however, well over half (and in some cases three quarters) of the cargo transported within the Latin American countries was carried by road. (In Western Europe, the railway was generally able to do more to hold its own; in Eastern Europe, as a result of deliberate planning, railways still accounted for an overwhelming proportion of traffic.) The number of private automobiles also increased, though in absolute terms Latin America lagged behind other parts of the world. In 1962 there were 13.4 cars per thousand people in the region; France in the same year had 147.6 per thousand.

In 1920 relatively few Latin American roads were passable in all seasons of the year. With the appearance of the motor vehicle, road-building replaced railway construction as the main "infrastructural" priority. Whereas railways had, by and large, been left to private interests to build, roads tended to be treated as public works, as they had been since colonial times. Dictators (who invariably adore public works programs) sometimes conceived the building of roads as a means of immortalizing themselves. Under Gómez, for instance, Venezuela was provided with an acceptable network of highways well before most other Latin America countries.[1] Leguía, the Peruvian dictator, both

[1] It should be remembered, however, that railways had never had much of an impact in Venezuela.

built and planned: within a few years of his downfall, a Central Highway (following the line of the Central Railway) soared into the Andes; in 1943 it was extended to Pucallpa, a port on the River Ucayali on the eastern side of the range.

The greatest expansion in roadbuilding was registered after World War II. The highway system of Brazil, for instance, doubled in size between 1938 and 1960. Indeed, Brazil's efforts in this sphere were perhaps the most impressive single feature of the general panorama of Latin American transport in the early 1960s. In conjunction with the foundation of Brasília, new highways were planned and built to link the new federal capital with the major cities of the country. This was an enterprise which resembled, in magnitude and drama, the exploits of Meiggs and his contemporaries in the Andes a century before. The road from Brasília to Belem—over a thousand miles long—was carved out of the wilderness at the rate of more than three miles a day. Two major routes through the heart of Amazonia were also planned at this period: one would eventually link up with the Central Highway of Peru, while a second—somewhat more utopian in conception—might one day join Brasília and the Colombian capital, Bogotá (see also p. 72). On the initiative of President Beláunde of Peru, work was begun in the mid-1960s on stretches of the proposed Carretera Marginal de la Selva (Jungle-Edge Highway) to link the eastern areas of Colombia, Ecuador, Peru, and Bolivia. Whether the Brasília–Bogotá highway, or the grandiose scheme sponsored by Beláunde will finally materialize or not is a question the future alone can answer.

Both the Brazilian and Peruvian projects mentioned carried the firm intention of linking different Latin American countries. Roads have, in general, served better than railways in this respect, though a number of connections—e.g., Argentina/Chile—remained tenuous even at the end of the 1960s. With the spread of the motor car in the first twenty years of the century, the idea of a mammoth highway joining North and South America was enthusiastically mooted in various quarters. The fifth Pan-American Conference (Santiago, 1923) gave the go-ahead for the project. Since then the Pan-American Highway, as it was called at first, has changed in conception from a single trunk road to a series of linked highway systems. (Its official title, in fact, is now the Pan-American Highway System.) From Mexico, a main artery passes through Central America. Branches fork east into Colombia and Venezuela, while the southward trunk road passes through Ecuador and along the Peruvian coast. From there one branch goes to Argentina by way of Chile, while another passes through Bolivia and links up with the road systems of Brazil, Paraguay, and Argentina. At the start of 1963, roughly 17,500 miles out of the planned twenty-nine thousand or so were paved, and most of the rest was passable in all weathers. Only one major gap remained in the system—a five hundred mile stretch to join Panama and Colombia. Plans to bridge this were made at the eighth Pan-American Highways Conference in 1960.

In 1962 there were nearly fifty-seven thousand miles of paved road in Latin America. In addition, some two hundred and fifty thousand miles were considered usable in all weathers. One or two comparisons with other regions of the world reveal that Latin America, despite considerable efforts, has so far failed to develop a highway system which can truly be thought adequate to its size or needs. Latin America's paved roads covered only slightly more distance than Africa's in 1962. In all, the paved roads of Latin America accounted for a mere 2.2 percent of the world total.

At a fairly early stage of its history, the internal combustion engine also took to the air. Enthusiasts for aviation history will not need to be reminded that it was a Latin American pioneer, the Brazilian Alberto Santos-Dumont, who made the first airplane flight in Europe (1906). The impact of the airplane in Santos-Dumont's own continent was considerable almost from the start. Remote areas of territory could now be more successfully integrated with their country's heartland. Light aircraft could operate in regions where the railway and the motor road were unlikely to penetrate. But probably the most important effect of the advent of air transport was to be found in the international dimension. Before the establishment of airlines, Latin American statesmen who wished to visit neighboring countries, or Europe or the United States, calculated their journeys in terms of days or weeks. This was doubtless a great improvement on colonial times, when a viceroy might take several months to reach his post; but the airplane, by reducing international journeys to a matter of hours, made Latin America still smaller, and made personal contacts between governments a matter of almost commonplace regularity.

The first airline in Latin America was organized by a group of Germans living in Colombia. SCADTA (Sociedad Colombo–Alemana de Transportes Aéreos) was founded in 1919 and, under its later name, AVIANCA (Aerovias Nacionales de Colombia), can today claim to be the oldest airline in the Americas. SCADTA started regular services in September 1922 between Barranquilla and Girardot, and by 1925 it had carried five thousand passengers. The second airline to take the field[1] was also established by Germans: Lloyd Aéreo Boliviano

[1] Leaving aside two ephemeral ventures, one English and one German, in Argentina (1922 and 1925).

(LAB), which began operations in August 1925 with a flight from Cochabamba to Sucre. SCADTA and LAB were presently joined by others: the year 1927 saw the opening of two foreign airlines in Brazil—the German Kondor Syndikat, and the French Aéropostale—and one indigenous company, VARIG (Viaçao Aerea Rio-Grandense). All three were to play a major part in consolidating air transport over the next decades. The following year witnessed the formation of a Mexican airline (Compañía Mexicana de Aviación), and the setting up of a Peruvian line by the American Elmer J. Faucett. Chile and Venezuela entered the race in 1929. Central America benefited from the establishment of TACA (Transportes Aéreos Centroamericanos) by a pioneering New Zealander, Lowell Yerex; it operated regular services from 1933 onward. Ten years after the specially adapted Junkers W.34s of SCADTA had made their debut down the Magdalena Valley, hundreds of aircraft were regularly plying their various trades through the Latin American skies.

As in the days of steam, foreign companies played an important part in the growth of air transport in Latin America. Foremost among these, beyond all question, was Pan-American Airways, which opened services to and from Havana in 1927. Within three years, Pan-American had encircled the Caribbean and was operating down the eastern side of South America; from 1929, its subsidiary, Panagra, operated from the Panama Canal Zone to Buenos Aires by way of the west coast. European airlines were also active, though on a smaller scale. Kondor and Aéropostale have already been mentioned; KLM ran flights in northern South America from 1936. It was the European airlines that pioneered the first regular services across the South Atlantic, several years before North Atlantic flights became an accomplished fact. From April 1932 until the suspension of airship operations in the summer of 1937, the German *Graf Zeppelin* made regular flights from Friedrichshafen to Brazil. The year 1934 saw the introduction of mail services from Europe to South America by Deutsche Lufthansa;[1] two years later Air France started a similar run from Toulouse to Santiago de Chile; these—and a short-lived Italian service that started in 1939—came to an end with World War II. None of them had ever carried passengers on the crossing of the ocean from West Africa to Brazil. After the war the South Atlantic route was opened up again by British South American Airways (later merged with BOAC), and by the mid-1950s at least eight major airlines used the route.

World War II, as might be expected, brought a number of important changes in the pattern of air transport. The German airlines—which

[1] The journey from Berlin to Buenos Aires, via West Africa, took four days.

had built up impressively in the later 1930s—were taken over by other companies, or dissolved. In some areas, the United States constructed airfields for defense purposes, and these were often left for the use of civil airlines when the war was over. The postwar period, not surprisingly, saw an enormous expansion in air travel. In the decade of the 1940s, the route-mileage of the Latin American airlines showed a twentyfold increase. Some countries—Argentina, Brazil, Colombia, and Mexico in particular—were becoming as "air-minded" as any in the world. Nowhere was growth as dramatic as in Brazil, which for a short period during the 1950s came second only to the United States in terms of passenger journeys undertaken. The merger, in 1961, of the two most substantial Brazilian concerns, VARIG and REAL, brought into existence the largest airline in Latin America. In 1960 there were some nine Latin American airlines flying more than 200 million passenger miles per year; of these, at least six were independent of foreign interests. The latest aircraft were bought with avidity, and, indeed, it was Aerolineas Argentinas (the Argentine state corporation created by Perón) which ran the first commercial jet services across the South Atlantic to Europe and from South America to the United States, in May and June 1959 respectively.

The history of transport, particularly over the last two centuries, has displayed one theme with special prominence: the constant heightening of speed. In the eighteenth century, it still took more than three months, on average, to sail from Cadiz to Buenos Aires. In the nineteenth eentury, steamships cut this to less than three weeks. There is every prospect that sometime during the 1970s the Concorde supersonic airliner will enable the traveler to lunch in London or Paris and dine in Rio de Janeiro or Buenos Aires. It would, though, be an early lunch and a late dinner.

Chapter 3

THE PEOPLES OF LATIN AMERICA

The Amerindians

They were nothing short of us, nor beholding to us for any excellency of naturall wit or perspicuitie, concerning pertinency. The wonderfull, or as I may call it, amazement-breeding magnificence of the never-like seene Cities of Cusco and Mexico . . . shew that they yeelded as little unto us in cunning and industrie. But concerning unfained devotion, unspotted integrity, bounteous liberality, due loyalty and free liberty, it hath greatly availed us, that we had not so much as they: By which advantage, they have lost, cast-away, sold, undone and betraied themselves.

MONTAIGNE

Christopher Columbus' stubborn belief, in 1492, that he was heading toward Asia had an important linguistic consequence. For the following three hundred years, the Spanish and Portuguese dominions in the New World were known as "the Indies." The West *Indies* are still there to remind us of this. Similarly, the pre-Columbian inhabitants of the American continent were given the name "Indians."[1] The term has survived and will doubtless be used for many centuries to come. But it is in many ways an unsatisfactory term, for it disguises the immense variety of cultures that existed and flourished in America before the arrival of the European. Precisely how many Indians inhabited the American continent before 1492 will never be known with any certainty. One widely accepted estimate gives a total population of 13,385,000, more or less equally divided between South America on the one hand, and North and Central America on the other.[2] Alternative calculations

[1] In the Spanish language, in fact, the word *indio* means Amerindian, while Indian (from India) becomes *hindú*. *Indiano* means "of the Indies."

[2] Angel Rosenblat, *La población indígena y el mestizaje en América*, 2 vols. (Buenos Aires, 1954), I, 102.

show a much higher total, but it is unlikely that a truly accurate assessment can be made.

INDIAN CULTURES BEFORE THE CONQUEST

Though it is not known with any final certainty when and how man first entered the New World, this important event probably occurred within measurable distance of 13,000 B.C., and the origins of American man are to be sought in Asia. Men of Mongoloid stock, organized in very rudimentary fashion in small hunting and gathering communities, crossed the Behring Straits and, over the course of the next few thousand years, penetrated the entire length of the American continent. Whatever distinctively Asian characteristics they had possessed on first arriving in their new environment they soon lost. None of the numerous Amerindian languages, living or dead, seems to bear any relation to the tongues of Asia. Over the next few millennia, these newcomers gradually developed their own agriculture: the domestication of maize, the staple American crop until the European conquests, was the crucial event of this long process. It occurred either in central Mexico or in the Andes, probably around 4000 B.C. Other crops—potato, pineapple, avocado pear, chocolate, cocaine, rubber, tobacco, to name but a few of the best known—were domesticated as well. The inevitable consequence of this agricultural revolution, as in the Old World, was the eventual growth of organized cultures and, as a culmination of this process, of city-based civilizations. Three of these developed in the American continent. They developed, it is worth remembering, in isolation from the civilizations of the Old World; their ways of life, though often extremely sophisticated, seemed—and indeed were—irremediably *alien* to the European conqueror and settler of the sixteenth century.

By no means all the Indian peoples had reached the stage of city-based civilizations at the time Columbus discovered America. Some— the primitive peoples of Tierra del Fuego and the nomadic inhabitants of the Argentine pampa, for instance—were still in a wholly pre-agricultural condition, while the immense variety of tribes living in the Amazon rain forest still subsisted mostly by hunting, fishing, and gathering. A rather larger number, perhaps, were typified by the Arawaks of the Caribbean, whom Columbus met on his first voyage. His first impressions of them were favorable. By all accounts, the Arawaks were a gentle and innocent people, living in village communities several hundred (sometimes several thousand) strong. They practiced agriculture, were able to travel from island to island by canoe, and exhibited certain primitive skills in woodcarving and the working of gold. (It was this final attribute that aroused the interest of the Spaniards.) Arawak religion was primitive and animistic, and there existed no political structure over and above the village or, at most, group of villages. Broadly speaking, many American Indians resembled the Arawak tribes on most of these counts. Some, like the innumerable tribes of the Tupí family in Brazil, or the more settled Guaranís of Paraguay, shared the peaceable inclinations of the Arawaks. Others were more warlike: the Caribs (on the smaller Caribbean islands and on the mainland of northern South America) habitually preyed on the Arawaks, and were cannibalistic. In southern Chile, the Araucanians appear to have lived in a state of constant warfare of tribe against tribe.

Despite important differences, which should not be underestimated, peoples such as the Arawaks and the others mentioned all enjoyed a recognizably similar cultural level. More advanced than any of them were the Chibcha communities of what is now Colombia. Of generally peaceful disposition, the Chibchas possessed a well-developed agriculture and a fairly extensive commercial system at the time of the conquest. In one or two spheres—notably the working of gold—they were supreme in America, but they had failed to devise anything approaching a centralized political system, and they had not yet reached the stage of building cities. The Chibchas, in fact, do not bear comparison with the "high cultures" of Mexico and Peru, where the bulk of the Indian population in 1492 was probably to be found, and whose later fate under colonial rule deserves the greater part of our attention here.

The first of the three great civilizations produced in the New World was that of the Mayas of Central America and Yucatán. It originated during the first millennium B.C. and reached a peak sometime around A.D. 500. The Maya civilization appears to have gone through two main periods (sometimes referred to as the first and second empires). In the first of these, the original Mayas reached out from the Caribbean coast of Guatemala, and colonized the adjacent highlands, the isthmus of Tehuentepec, and the peninsula of Yucatán. Around A.D. 800 the first period came to an end, and the main center of Mayan culture became concentrated in the cities of Yucatán, the three most important of which were Chichen-Itzá, Uxmal, and Mayapán. These three cities were leagued together for much of the second period, but after 1200 or so, warfare between them became savage and continuous, and it was this, probably, that provoked the final downfall of this remarkable race. In the mid-fifteenth century, Mayapán was destroyed; the remaining cities were abandoned. The glories of the Maya past had been totally extinguished by the time the Spaniards came on the scene. And glories there had certainly been, in great profusion, as archeologists have now discovered. In astronomy and mathematics, the Mayas had been the undisputed leaders of the New World: in neither field could Europeans of the early medieval period have rivaled them. The sophistication of their architecture and arts was almost unparalleled in America. They had developed a form of pictographic writing, and apparently used books. Maya religion was polytheistic and complex, and was sustained by a numerous priesthood. Politically, the city-states and leagues of city-states that formed the Maya "empires" were subjected to what appears to have been a semitheocratic despotism. A hereditary nobility provided soldiers, priests, and administrators.

Sometime during their second period, the Mayas had been temporarily subdued by a conqueror from the north, from central Mexico. In all probability he was a war-chief of the Toltecs, a fierce race which was then building massive cities in the highlands. The enormous complex of ruins at Teotihuacán (near Mexico City) stands today as the most impressive monument to the dead Toltec civilization. The twelfth-century cross-fertilization which occurred between Toltec and Maya was fruitful: on his return to the highlands the Toltec ruler—who was later immortalized as Quetzalcoatl—introduced Maya learning to his own people: though at the same time, his visit to Yucatán appears to have resulted in the adoption of human sacrifice—a highland practice—by the Maya cities. A century or two later, the Toltec civilization itself crumbled, probably as a result of internal discord. The eventual inheritors of the whole of central Mexico were the Aztecs, an originally nomadic people who established themselves at Tenochtitlán in the Valley of Mexico in 1325. There they assimilated the culture of the highlands, consolidated a strange and notable civilization, and, in the mid-fifteenth century, allied themselves with two neighboring city-states, Tlacopán and Texcoco, to pursue a vigorously expansionist policy: from coast to coast, Mexico was rapidly taken over by the Aztec Confederacy. Advanced cultures like those of the Mixtecs and Zapotecs were incorporated into the rising empire.

The Aztecs never succeeded in imposing a wholly centralized government in Mexico: as Cortés discovered in 1519, the small "republic" of Tlaxcala had successfully preserved its independence of the Confederacy. In theory, the Aztec government was conciliar in nature, although it appears to have been moving toward hereditary monarchy; by 1519 the family of Montezuma II had held the position of war-chief for several generations. Government was underpinned by a powerful nobility of warriors, while religion, which permeated the whole society in a peculiarly pervasive fashion, was served by the large priestly caste.

Agriculture was well regulated; and trade—despite the absence of beasts of burden—was actively encouraged. The Aztecs, like the Mayas before them, kept track of time in a remarkably accurate manner. Their calendar was based on cycles of fifty-two solar years; the world was supposed to be miraculously renewed at the end of each cycle.

These attributes were less impressive to Cortés and his followers than the sheer splendor of Tenochtitlán and other cities—and the sheer horror of the Aztec religion. To the European, the Aztec tradition of human sacrifice seemed to be obviously and directly Satanic in origin. Constant streams of sacrificial victims were hustled up the long flights of steps to the summits of hundreds of Aztec temples, there to have their hearts torn out by the deft motion of a priest's obsidian knife. The motive was a simple one: the propitiation of the capricious and vengeful gods of the well-populated Aztec pantheon. Victims were generally supplied by prisoners taken in warfare—hence the need to wage war constantly, but war, it should be noted, with the aim of *capturing* rather than *killing* the enemy. The conquistadores doubtless exaggerated the numbers of sacrificial victims in Aztec times,[1] but there seems little doubt that the altars were fed continuously and on a large scale.

Very different from the Aztecs and their grim deities were the Incas of Peru. Here was a civilization which had grown up in complete isolation not only from the Old World but also from the other "high cultures" of America. There was, however, one respect in which the Incas resembled the Aztecs: they, too, were inheritors as well as creators. A whole series of previous cultures had flourished in Peru, on the coast and in the highlands, over the preceding millennium. Some of the achievements of these cultures had been striking: the Nazca society, for instance, had produced weaving of a quality unmatched even in Mexico; the Chimus, whose capital, Chan-Chan, occupied more than twelve square miles, were noted for superb ceramics. Tiahuanaco, on the altiplano near Lake Titicaca, had been a city-state whose influence (and perhaps authority) had spread throughout the highlands a thousand years before the Incas, and was already a distant memory when they created their empire.

From their original nucleus in the basin of Cuzco, the Incas[2] had

---

[1] It should not be forgotten that the exaggeration of numbers for rhetorical purposes was still common in Europe at the time of the conquest. Cortés claimed to have had an army of two hundred thousand besieging Tenochtitlán in 1521. Not until Napoleonic times were armies of this size regularly assembled in Europe.

[2] Technically, the "Incas" were the members of the governing caste of the empire, an extended royal family. The state they constructed could more properly be referred to as the Quechua empire. Its own name was *Tahuantinsuyo*—the Empire of the Four Directions.

spread out to occupy most of the Peruvian sierra and coast by 1450 or so. Under the emperor Huayna Capac (1493–1527), their dominion had reached its widest extent: from the southern borderland of Colombia to the Maule River in Central Chile, there was nobody who failed to acknowledge the supremacy of Cuzco. The empire was bound together by skillful diplomacy: districts subdued by the Incas were brought within the framework of the state by the winning over of local chieftains, the occasional transfer of population, respect for local usages and religions, and the imposition of Quechua as a universal language. Warfare was employed only where diplomacy failed.

At the head of the empire, exercising personal rule, was the Sapa-Inca or emperor. He was a lineal descendant of the Sun, and his authority was therefore unquestioned. Beneath him, in the political hierarchy, were four viceroys and a whole host of provincial and local governors; the empire was administratively subdivided down to units of ten households. Everything depended on the will of the state, and the state was the emperor. Land was distributed—one third for the emperor, one third for religion, and one third for the use of the local community —in accordance with a simple but universal scheme. Personal behavior was strictly controlled, though in return the state looked after the welfare of the subject in exemplary fashion. Such a system obviously required excellent communications, and these were made possible by a network of imperial highways stretching from Cuzco to the four corners of the empire. Relays of official runners (*chasquis*) carried messages along these roads; resthouses were regularly spaced along the way. By these means, information could be conveyed from, for instance, Cuzco to Quito in just over a week. No form of writing, however, was ever elaborated by the Incas, although *quipus* (knotted cords in different colors) appear to have enabled the government to keep records of some kind.[1]

The supreme achievements of the Incas lay in their engineering and in their religion. Agricultural terraces, irrigation works, the unexampled masonry of their temples and public buildings—in the construction of these, the Incas displayed a practical genius which has often won for them the title of the Romans of prehistoric America. It is more than a little surprising that this resourceful race should never have made use of the wheel. In religion, the official cult of the empire, though it coexisted tolerantly with an enormous variety of lesser and local cults, came closer to monotheism than its counterparts in Mexico. The sun,

[1] It is clear from the early accounts of the conquerors that the *quipu* was an extremely effective mnemonic device—almost as effective, it seems, as a proper system of writing. Detailed knowledge of how it worked is still lacking.

conceived as an emanation or as an agency of the supreme god Viracocha, was the chief object of Inca worship. Human sacrifice, while not totally unknown, was very rare. Inca religion, in fact, was by no means despised by the Spanish evangelists.

THE INDIAN UNDER COLONIAL RULE

It is tempting, though pointless, to speculate about the kind of progress the great civilizations of Mexico and Peru would have made had they been left alone by Europe. But in any event, the Iberian conquest and settlement of America signified the end of a long and extraordinary chapter in Indian history—and the opening of a chapter that was in most respects tragic. From the point of view of the Indians, the conquest was an act of vandalism without precedent. It destroyed their way of life, deprived them of their rulers, and exposed them to the harsh impact of a ruthless foreign overlordship, an overlordship which proceeded to impose its own religion, and to a lesser extent its language, on the conquered peoples. There were numerous hideous atrocities in the early years of the conquest, including the wholesale murder of Indian populations who stood in the way of the advancing conquistadores. It was said that in the province of Popayán, in southern New Granada, the bones of so many dead Indians lay scattered along the roadsides that it was impossible for a traveler to lose his way.

The first way in which the Indian experienced the impact of the European was in forced labor. Though the actual enslavement of Indians in most cases was formally prohibited at an early stage,[1] the Spanish crown permitted the growth of practices which amounted to something approaching servitude. The institution of the *encomienda* was introduced in the earliest period of Spanish colonization in the Indies, and it remained a major form of exploiting the Indians for much of the first century of imperial rule. What *was* the encomienda? In essence, it was a grant of a number of Indians to a Spanish settler, who was expected to Christianize and civilize his charges, and in return to exact labor services or tribute from them. In no sense was the encomienda a grant of land to the settler—though, as we shall see, land *was* acquired, and usually at the expense of the Indian. It is fair to say that from the very beginning the paternalistic, "civilizing" element in the encomienda system took second place to the exaction of labor and

---

[1] Indians taken in warfare or who rebelled against the Spanish empire *could* be legally enslaved. As a source of labor, slavery was in most areas confined to the early years of the colonial period. In Brazil Indian slavery was more common and lasted longer.

tribute. Tremendous abuses followed, and, to the credit of the invaders, a small group of humanitarian churchmen (particularly within the Dominican Order) put up a resolute opposition to the maltreatment of the Indian. In December 1511 the Dominican friar Antonio de Montesinos, preaching a highly controversial sermon to the settlers of Santo Domingo, let loose a thunderous denunciation of their conduct: "By what right or justice do you keep these Indians in such a cruel and horrible servitude?" he asked. "Are these not men? Have they not rational souls? Are you not bound to love them as you love yourselves?"[1] It was a question that echoed through the three Spanish centuries that followed; and the answer was generally—though not exclusively—negative.

The Spanish crown, by no means unsympathetic to the appeals of the churchmen, made many efforts to regulate the workings of the encomienda system, and to alleviate its harshest effects. The Indians, for their part, had a notable group of stout defenders, nearly all ecclesiastics, the most tireless of whom was Fray Bartolomé de Las Casas (1474–1566). The central point in the attack mounted by men such as Las Casas was that the Indian, as a rational being, had exactly the same rights as any other Spanish subject and ought to be treated accordingly; he should in no way be taken advantage of by the colonizer; the encomienda was therefore unjustifiable. Against this, a number of theorists argued that the Indians were essentially inferior beings, "naturally servile" in the Aristotelian sense. The intellectual debate was prolonged, and ultimately inconclusive. The Papacy, for its part, threw its weight on the side of Las Casas and the Indians. In his Bull *Sublimis Deus* (June 1, 1537), Pope Paul III resonantly affirmed that

> the Indians are truly men and . . . are . . . capable of understanding the Catholic faith. . . . The said Indians are by no means to be deprived of their liberty or the possession of their property, even though they be outside the faith of Jesus Christ . . . nor should they be in any way enslaved.[2]

The Spanish crown took due note of this, and in 1542, as mentioned in Chapter 1, issued its momentous "New Laws." The full title of this code—"Laws and Ordinances newly made by His Majesty for the Government of the Indies and Good Treatment and Preservation of the Indians"—is adequate commentary on its intentions and implications.

---

[1] Quoted in Lewis Hanke, *The Spanish Struggle for Justice in the Conquest of America* (Boston, 1965), p. 17.

[2] *Ibid.*, p. 73.

But the New Laws, as we have seen, were fiercely opposed in the colonies, and the ultimate compromise of a few years later did more to preserve the encomienda than the Indian. Despite this, the crown was by no means wholly defeated on this issue. Encomiendas were to continue to be inheritable, though only for a limited number of generations; the emphasis now was on Indian tribute rather than labor services; and, in fact, the institution slowly ceased to be of importance in the American empire, as more and more Indians came under normal royal government.

It is clear from this that the Indian was viewed in at least two different lights by the Iberian colonizer of the New World: the more rapacious settler looked on him as a convenient source of cheap or forced labor, while the churchman (or at least *some* churchmen) regarded him somewhat paternalistically as someone to be evangelized and, as part of this, to be protected. The Spanish crown—and I am here restricting my remarks to the Spanish empire—had to reconcile these points of view, and the result was a general inclination toward a policy of ethnic trusteeship, combined with an admission of the claims of the settlers. On paper, the Indian village communities—the only real units of the old Mexican and Peruvian civilizations to survive the conquest—were guaranteed lands, were accorded the services of a priest, were isolated from the settler population,[1] and were permitted to preserve their local usages. By the end of the colonial period, each of the thirteen *Audiencias* (see p. 304) had attached to it an attorney specializing in Indian matters, and in Mexico a special high court (*Juzgado General de Indios*) was set up in the 1570s to serve the needs of the Indian population. Indian communities were officially subject to separate magistrates (*corregidores de indios*). Apart from ecclesiastical payments, the only direct tax to which an Indian was liable was the normal tribute, a capitation tax whose scope was gradually reduced. The American branches of the Inquisition were disqualified from dealing with Indians. Moreover, a whole host of decrees from Spain regulated the conduct of the Spanish settler toward the native races: we may take as examples the fact that, in theory at least, the Indian was not to be whipped, used as a beast of burden, or accorded the familiar and unflattering Spanish epithet of "dog."

Implicit in this apparatus of trusteeship was a fair measure of paternalism. No Indian was allowed to be sold either arms or strong liquor. Furthermore, it was Spanish policy to concentrate—in effect, to "regroup" —the native population in communities which were reasonably close to

[1] In theory the movement of Spaniards into and out of the Indian communities was severely restricted.

the main centers of colonial life, and often, of course, close to the mines. This regrouping was carried out with reasonable effectiveness, in both Peru and Mexico, toward the end of the sixteenth century. It appears to have been done with considerable harshness. In the last analysis, the intention was probably beneficent: better protection could be ensured, as well as better control. But its effects were traumatic.

Traumatic—the adjective seems singularly appropriate to describe the long-term impact of the conquest on the Indian peoples. Only a rigorously enforced policy of protection—neither Iberian power was capable of enforcing one—could have prevented the tragedies that followed. The first of these was a drastic decline in population. The wars of the conquest, the destruction of Indian agriculture, the toll of lives exacted by the encomienda, the introduction of fatal European diseases such as smallpox, yellow fever, and malaria—all these factors played some part in reducing the number of Indians. The Arawaks and Caribs of the West Indies were virtually extinct by the mid-sixteenth century. In central Mexico, according to one modern study, the Indian population declined by ninety percent by the early seventeenth century,[1] and it is clear that a similar process occurred in other Indian areas. (The policy of regrouping, already referred to, was due in part to the need to concentrate as much as the population as was left in accessible areas.) At the same time, the mixing of the races which had started with the conquest itself submerged whole peoples: the Chibchas, for instance, slowly began to disappear as a separate race during the colonial period, though plenty of Chibcha blood flows in the veins of the modern Colombian *mestizo*.

Indian lands, as well as Indian lives, were soon attacked. Early Spanish settlers bought lands from—and were occasionally "given" lands by—the Indian, often under extremely dubious circumstances. The holders of encomiendas, and even official magistrates, sometimes made illegal use of their position to build up farms and ranches at the expense of their charges. Indian lands left vacant by the regrouping policy could also be conveniently occupied. Land grants (*mercedes*) from the colonial authorities completed the process. According to one study of the Valley of Mexico, well over half the usable area of the valley had been granted to Spaniards for farming or ranching by 1620.[2] This is not to say that the Indian communities were deprived of *all* their

[1] Sherburne F. Cook and Woodrow Borah, *The Indian Population of Central Mexico 1531–1610* (Berkeley, Calif., 1960). Angel Rosenblat, in his short work *La Población de América en 1492* (Mexico, 1967), considers the findings of Cook and Borah a gross exaggeration.

[2] Charles Gibson, *The Aztecs under Spanish Rule: A History of the Indians of the Valley of Mexico* (Stanford, Calif., 1964), p. 277.

holdings, far from it. But a steady process of usurpation and injustice is certainly observable.

Nor did the decline of the encomienda mean the end of forced labor for the Indian. From the sixteenth century to the end of the colonial period, Indian communities were required to make available one seventh[1] of their menfolk at periodic intervals for work in mines, in textile workshops (obrajes), and on estates. In Peru the system was known as the mita (the name of an analogous institution that had existed under the Incas), in Mexico simply as the repartimiento ("distribution"). Despite numerous royal decrees regulating conditions of work, the institution laid itself open to considerable abuse. In Peru, the harshness of the mita was one of the many factors which provoked the great revolt of Túpac Amaru in 1780–81. Túpac Amaru himself had protested more than once about the effects of the mita. The Indians leaving the villages, he wrote, "make their farewells, to die or never to return to their homelands."[2] It was an accurate description: many thousands—perhaps hundreds of thousands—of Indian mitayos perished in the mines of Potosí.

As a result of the conquest, therefore, the Indian became, in W. H. Prescott's famous phrase, "an alien in the land of his fathers."[3] Only in a few highly favored areas did he escape the lash of the settler. Occasionally, it is true, the Church attempted to intervene on behalf of the Indians by setting up separate, church-controlled native communities with a workable economic base. Such were the "hospital-pueblos" established in Mexico by Vasco de Quiroga, Bishop of Michoacán, in the 1530s. Such, too, were the missions run by the religious orders on the remoter frontiers of the Spanish empire. Such, most notably of all, were the hundred-odd "reductions" organized by the Jesuits in Paraguay between 1610 and 1767.[4] Yet the total number of Indians affected by these expedients was small. For the vast majority of the indigenous peoples, colonial rule spelt diminution, death, and disruption. A few Indians were lucky: some elements of the former Aztec and Inca aristocracies were able to keep their wealth and to some

[1] This was generally true, though unscrupulous Spanish officials often exceeded this proportion. For mining labor, only one twenty-fifth of the menfolk was required.

[2] Jorge Cornejo B., Túpac Amaru: La revolución precursora de la emancipación continental (Cuzco, 1949), pp. 33–37.

[3] Prescott, History of the Conquest of Peru, Book IV, Chap. 6.

[4] The Jesuit Province of Paraguay, constituted in 1607, covered a wider area than the modern republic of the same name. On the eve of the expulsion of the Jesuits in 1767, some forty reductions were functioning, with a total population of more than one hundred thousand Guaranís. There can be little doubt that this was a remarkable experiment; it caught the imagination of more than a few European writers of the Enlightenment.

extent their social position. Other Indians became craftsmen; indeed, Indian craftsmanship soon gained an excellent reputation in the colonial cities. Still others were able to acquire strings of mules and, as muleteers, to make a more than acceptable living. For the immense majority which was unable to adapt in ways such as these, a retreat into profound apathy seemed to be the only answer—an apathy worsened by persistent alcoholism. Antonio de Ulloa, the eighteenth-century Spanish traveler to the Indies, found the Indians of Quito "involved as it were in cimmerian darkness, rude, indocile, and living in a barbarism little better than those who have their dwelling among the wastes, precipices and forests."[1] Apathy was, however, sometimes replaced by revolt. The insurrection of Túpac Amaru in Peru was only the most serious and spectacular of a long series. On the fringes of the Spanish empire, resistance was often successful: the Araucanians of Chile, for instance, may have concluded temporary peace treaties with the Spaniard, but were never subdued by him. At the same time, it can hardly be denied that many Indians took to the religion of the conquerors with a piety that put their masters to shame. Their loyalty to the crown, too, was often attested by visitors to the Indies.

THE INDIAN AFTER INDEPENDENCE

At the time of independence, approximately a third of the Latin American population was composed of Indians. How did the ending of Iberian colonial rule affect them? Many of the Creole leaders of the independence movement adopted a strikingly pro-Indian posture. Deep admiration was expressed, by writers and politicians alike, for the glories of the Aztec and Inca past. The conquest was deplored, on numerous occasions, with highly colored rhetoric. Simón Bolívar, on his visit to the Peruvian highlands in 1825, acclaimed the Inca empire as "a social organization of which we have no conception, no prototype, or imitation anywhere else." Peru, he added, was "unique in the annals of man."[2] The new patriot governments, almost to a man, enacted legislation which gave the Indian full equality of rights with other citizens, in accordance with the liberal principles that animated the independence movements. Some politicians went further in their desire to reverse the results of the Spanish conquest. At the Tucumán Congress of 1816, the Argentine patriot Manuel Belgrano sponsored a

[1] Jorge Juan and Antonio de Ulloa, *A Voyage to South America*, 2 vols. (London, 1758), I, 417.
[2] Bolívar to J. J. Olmedo, Cuzco, June 27, 1825. V. Lecuna and H. A. Bierck, eds., *Selected Writings of Bolívar*, 2 vols. (New York, 1951), II, 501.

scheme for placing a descendant of the Incas on the throne of an independent America, whose capital—some delegates hoped—could be located at Cuzco. The idea did not prosper. (A similar plan for an Aztec "restoration" was briefly mooted in Mexico in 1821.)

Much of this sympathetic attitude toward the Indian seems to have derived from eighteenth-century European ideas about "the noble savage," rather than from genuine concern for the underdog. The Indians themselves tended to remain neutral in the struggle between Creole and European. Only in Mexico, in the insurrections of Hidalgo and Morelos, did they unite in favor of independence. Elsewhere, they were generally to be found in both patriot and royalist armies at the same time.[1] On paper, however, their lot improved appreciably. The payment of tribute, the mita, and numerous other colonial practices were suppressed. Bolívar's decrees of 1824-25 in Peru attempted to favor the restoration of illegally alienated Indian lands. In short, the whole complex of protective (and paternalist) colonial legislation was dismantled or modified.

The effects of this were twofold. In the first place, it *was* now possible for an Indian, with a certain amount of good fortune, to rise in the social scale. Some Indians did. One, Benito Juárez, became the outstanding Mexican of his time. In this sense, the principles of equality proclaimed by the new Creole states proved to be a positive gain for the Indian. It has to be admitted, however, that for all practical purposes the position of the Indian actually *worsened* as a result of independence. In part, this was due to the operation of the very principles of civil equality already mentioned. Since the Indian was now a free man, since his communities were no longer in possession of a special legal status, it was logical to suppose that he could take part in transactions which had hitherto been denied him: above all, he should be allowed to buy and sell land freely.

This new state of affairs presented the traditional Indian communities with their most serious challenge since the conquest. Everywhere, there was a steady encroachment on Indian communal lands. Precedents for this, as we have seen, had been set during the colonial period, but after independence the process may well have been accelerated by the breakdown of the protective element in colonial legislation. The great estates

---

[1] Some Indians, undoubtedly, were conscious that independence was, in part at least, a reversal of the Spanish conquest. A surviving brother of Túpac Amaru, Juan Bautista, wrote to Simón Bolívar (May 15, 1825) to compliment him on the liberation of Peru. "I have been preserved to the age of 86," he wrote, "in order to witness the consummation of the great and just work which will give us the enjoyment of our rights and freedom." (Boleslao Lewin, *La Insurrección de Túpac Amaru* [Buenos Aires, 1963], pp. 110-11.)

enlarged themselves continuously through the nineteenth century, often at the expense of the Indian. In Mexico, the Lerdo Law of 1856, applied most fiercely during the long dictatorship of Porfirio Díaz, deprived many Indian villages of their *ejidos* or common holdings. A similar process occurred in the Peruvian and Ecuadorian highlands. In Bolivia, a half-crazed dictator, Mariano Melgarejo, tried to lay open the Indian communities to the rapacity of the Creole estate-owners; in this case, however, Indian resistance was sufficient to compel an alteration in the law under the next government (Law of August 9, 1871). But throughout the traditional areas of intensive Indian settlement, the communities were subjected to more or less constant assault during this period. The enlargement of the great estates found many more Indians than ever before working as peons—often bound to their bosses' haciendas by long-term debt. Debt-peonage had existed in the colonial period; but the number of Indians who suffered from it greatly increased in the hundred years following independence.

This picture is undoubtedly a somber one, and it indicates that few of the high ideals proclaimed by the leaders of independence were put into practice. As in the colonial period, the Indian peoples were sometimes stirred into revolt—only to meet with harsh repression. The so-called "War of Castes" in Yucatán, starting in 1847, saw the wholesale destruction of Creole haciendas. On its suppression, the Indians of the peninsula were sold into virtual slavery on the plantations of Cuba. After another revolt, during the Porfiriato, the Yaqui Indians of Sonora were sold in similar fashion to the henequén plantations of Yucatán. For many of the Indian peoples on the fringes of "civilization," the nineteenth century held the threat of ultimate extermination. The fierce Charrúas of Uruguay were eliminated altogether in the 1830s, on the orders of General Fructuoso Rivera. The nomadic Indians of the Argentine pampa were either exterminated or herded onto reservations by General Roca's "Desert Campaign" of 1879. A year or two later, a similar fate befell the stubborn Araucanians of Chile. In the backlands of Brazil—in Rio Grande do Sul, Minas Gerais, and the Amazon—expeditions against Indian tribes were a permanent and cruel feature of nineteenth-century life.

A century after independence, therefore, the plight of the Indian seemed considerably more desperate than during the colonial period, even though it was clear that the nineteenth century had merely witnessed an accentuation of colonial trends. Fortunately, the situation in certain areas was partially rectified in the twentieth century. By this time—four hundred years after the initial impact of "Latin" Europe on "Indian" America—the Indian was overwhelmingly outnumbered by

European, mestizo, and Negro elements. In 1950, in fact, Indians made up approximately one tenth of the total population of Latin America.[1] In absolute terms, their numbers were rising, for the Latin American population in general was rising. There seemed little chance that the Indian peoples were on the way to extinction. Indeed, some twentieth-century tendencies favored the Indian in a very pronounced fashion.

The Mexican revolution from 1910 onward was, perhaps, the first sign that the Amerindians who had once controlled the whole of the American continent were about to take their rightful place once again. Nowhere else in Latin America had the process of encroachment on Indian lands gone so far as in Mexico: nearly all of the sixty thousand or so Indian villages there in 1910 relied on the great haciendas for their livelihood. The land reform set in motion by the revolution certainly benefited the Indian communities to an appreciable extent, particularly after President Cárdenas injected new vitality into the process in the 1930s. But still more significantly, perhaps, the revolution made a genuine attempt to reintegrate the Indian into the life of the Mexican nation. The reforms which followed 1910 were publicly interpreted as a final reversal of the Spanish conquest.[2] The Indian past was exalted and glorified by writers and painters alike. Archeologists set out to reconstruct the civilizations of prehistoric Mexico in rigorous detail. In the 1960s the building of a sumptuous new Museum of Anthropology in Mexico City (surely one of the most spectacular museums anywhere in the world) signalized the continuation of the trend, by exhibiting Mexico's past glories with attentive care and in superb style. It is a commonplace observation of the travel writer that, in Mexico today, no statues are raised to Hernán Cortés, while his final Aztec opponent, Cuauhtémoc, is widely honored.

Parallel developments can be observed in other countries with large Indian populations. In Guatemala, during the period of the abortive "October Revolution" (1944–54), attempts were made to follow the Mexican example. The 1952 Bolivian revolution, by conceding full political rights to the Indian and by organizing a far-reaching land

[1] Six of the twenty Latin American republics in 1950 had more than ten percent of their populations made up by Indians: Mexico, Guatemala, El Salvador, Ecuador, Peru, and Bolivia. The remaining fourteen had well below ten percent. See Rosenblat, *La problación indigena y el mestizaje en América*, table opposite I, 20.

[2] There is a sense in which the Spanish conquest of Mexico is still a living issue in that country. A distinguished Mexican scholar who was visiting England in 1966, at the time of the nine hundredth anniversary of the Battle of Hastings, asked me in all seriousness: "What is the position adopted by the youth of England toward the Norman conquest?" I replied, truthfully enough, that the youth of England had no position whatsoever on the subject. My visitor assured me: "It would be very different in Mexico."

reform, had much the same type of psychological consequence. The living standards and the agricultural habits of the Indian may not have altered profoundly in the short term, but the Indian's sense of actively *belonging* to the wider nation was greatly enhanced in both cases, though perhaps more successfully in Bolivia. In those republics where no drastic rearrangements have occurred in the countryside, the Indian has played a part—often, doubtless, without realizing it—in the formulation of distinctive ideological and literary positions. In Peru, for instance, Haya de la Torre and the APRA movement turned to the old Inca traditions of communal landholding for inspiration, and ardently preached the reintegration of the Indian. Latin America, in the *aprista* view, should be termed *Indo*-America instead. "Indianist" intellectuals such as Luis Valcárcel wrote stirring defenses of Indian life. These attitudes plainly influenced the political and philosophical outlook of President Fernando Beláunde Terry (1963–68). In the Peru of the 1960s, however, it still remained true that the Indian communities of the highlands were, in essence, a separate nation.

The renewed interest in the Indian provoked by the Mexican revolution and by the intellectual and political attitudes of other countries was reflected, at the international level, by the convening of the first Inter-American Conference on Indian Life at Patzcuaro (Mexico) in 1940. This meeting recommended (among other things) the renewal and protection of the distinctive Indian way of life, the enactment of land reforms where these were necessary to the well-being of the indigenous communities, and the creation of special departments or ministries of Indian affairs by the American governments. Some governments had already formed such departments. Brazil, for instance, had established its deservedly famous Service for the Protection of the Indian (*Servicio de Proteção aos Indios*) in 1910, under the leadership of a very remarkable man, Colonel (later General) Cândido da Silva Rondon. Rondon had gained experience of the Indian—and a humane and civilized attitude toward him—while constructing telegraph systems throughout the backlands. He himself had Indian blood in him. "Die if you need to, but never kill"—this was Rondon's advice to his subordinates in the Service. Under his wise and expert guidance, a network of remote outposts was established, beginning with the state of Mato Grosso, with the aim of providing practical instruction to those Indian tribesmen who sought it.

In the long history of the Indian in Latin America, one fundamental point is clear. The greatest achievements of the indigenous peoples, and their potential for independent progress, were cut short—and savagely cut short—by the European colonizer. Irreversible changes were set in motion by the settlement of America by the Iberian powers. The mixing of the races, the dislocation of traditional Indian agriculture, the long process of Christianization—none of these things can now be rescinded. A variety of cultures, as we have seen, existed in America before the arrival of the European. A variety of fates would now seem to await those Indian communities which have managed to survive. For some, decline and oblivion may well be all that is left. For others—as in Mexico and Bolivia—the hope of a better life, and integration into a wider community on terms of equality, may not be entirely unjustified. Still others await elementary acts of justice. But, when all is said and done, the balance is indisputably a negative one. The nineteenth-century Ecuadorian writer Juan Montalvo once crystallized the matter in words that should still compel us today: "If my pen had the gift of tears, I would write a book called 'the Indian,' and I would make the whole world weep."

The Iberians

The Roman Empire left more of its essential stuff in Spain than in Italy. The coarseness, solidity, Stoic strength of character of that great Imperial people form the understructure of Spanish life, on top of which has been built an edifice of an entirely different sort—a fretted skyline of Oriental minarets and battlements that make up the tight and well-defended fabric of pride and honour.

GERALD BRENAN

The tremendous impulse that transformed "Indian" America into Latin America came from Europe, from the Iberian peninsula. What factors had prepared the peoples of the peninsula, Spaniards and Portuguese, for their imperial role of conquering and settling the New World? In part, their geographical position—in the southwestern corner of Europe, facing the Atlantic—was responsible. But at the same time, their previous history during the Middle Ages had predisposed both peoples toward such a destiny.

THE MEDIEVAL KINGDOMS

One of the two or three most crucial events in Iberian history occurred in A.D. 711. In that year a mixed army of Arabs and Berbers, Moslem peoples, crossed from North Africa and began a highly successful invasion of the peninsula. Within a few years the intruders had overwhelmed the Visigothic kingdom that had been established in Hispania after the fall of the Roman empire. The defeated remnants of this once-flourishing Christian state were soon confined to small redoubts in the

Pyrenees and Cantabrian Mountains in the north. The next eight centuries were largely spent dislodging the infidel invader from Iberian soil—and this long-drawn-out process, the *reconquista*, must be regarded as the central fact of medieval Spanish and Portuguese history. The reconquest was never quite the straightforward clash of Christian and infidel it seems at first sight. Both Christian and Moorish states fought as often among themselves as they did each other. This helps to explain why it took the Spaniards eight centuries to undo what the Moors had set up in as many years.

The reconquest is traditionally supposed to have begun with the victory of Covadonga (718), which secured the independence of the small Christian kingdom of Asturias. But for many decades it was difficult to make headway against the Moors, who by the end of the eighth century consolidated, in the southern half of the peninsula, a unified state based on Cordova—a city which, under the Ommayad dynasty, became one of the most brilliant centers of a superb Arab civilization. Early in the eleventh century, however, the Ommayad caliphate broke down, giving place to a number of small and disunited Moslem states (*taifas*). These were less capable of resisting the rising Christian kingdoms of the north, of which the most forceful and thrusting was by now Castile. By the mid-eleventh century Castile had assimilated León, the kingdom from which it had won its own independence a hundred years earlier, and was emerging as the most powerful state of the peninsula. Castile it was that took the leading part in the reconquest. In 1085 its king, Alfonso VI, captured Toledo—the first most notable sign that the initiative now lay with the Christians. It is true that a unified Moslem power was twice revived in the south over the next century and a half, but never for more than a season. The decisive victory of the reconquest was won by an alliance of the Christian states at Las Navas de Tolosa in 1212. Thereafter it was only a matter of time before the main Moslem cities of Andalusia fell into Christian hands. Ferdinand III of Castile took Cordova in 1236, and Seville, the richest of the southern cities, twelve years later. After this, Moslem power was confined to the small kingdom of Granada, where it lingered for upward of two centuries; the Christian states could turn with relative impunity to fighting among themselves, at which they were already adept.

After Castile, the most powerful of the Christian kingdoms was Aragon, which had emerged as an independent state in the mid-eleventh century. By uniting (in 1137) with the maritime and trading county of Barcelona, Aragon acquired the wily and industrious genius of the Catalans. Almost from the first, therefore, Aragonese eyes were turned eastward into the Mediterranean rather than southward. King James the Conqueror (1213–76), it is true, played a notable part in liberating Valencia and Murcia, but not before extending Aragonese dominion to the Balearic Islands. Unlike Aragon, the third major Christian state of the peninsula—Portugal—owed its original existence to Castile, and followed a career of reconquest similar to that of the parent-kingdom. Lisbon was captured from the Moors in 1147, and the Portuguese reconquest was over by the middle of the thirteenth century. Portugal showed little inclination to be reincorporated into Castile: the battle of Aljubarrota (August 1385) set the final seal on her independence. Already in 1373 an alliance (still intact after six centuries) had been concluded with England; Portuguese history thus began to diverge fairly markedly from that of the rest of the peninsula.

The fourteenth and fifteenth centuries were dominated by internal strife within the Christian kingdoms. Turbulent military aristocracies attempted to impose their unruly will on the crown—successfully in Castile, less so in Aragon and Portugal. Dynastic feuds shattered the peace at regular intervals. The ambitious municipalities won their traditional *fueros*, their customary rights and liberties, from monarchs who needed their support in the struggle against the magnates. In Castile, the three great military-religious orders of chivalry—those of Alcántara, Calatrava, and Santiago, founded to further the reconquest in the twelfth century—gained colossal power and influence. The feudal struggles of this period did much to perpetuate the old-established "tradition of conquest" which had molded medieval Spanish life, and much, too, to prolong a general cult of military honor.

A new and harsher tone—a tone of revived crusading zeal—was infused into the anarchic behavior of the Iberians by the events of the mid-fifteenth century. In the first place, Portugal, having consolidated itself as a nation, embarked on a career of commercial and missionary expansion with the expeditions down the African coastline organized by Prince Henry the Navigator (1394–1460), an adventure which culminated at the end of the century in the opening of the sea route to Asia by Vasco da Gama. Meanwhile, Castile and Aragon were bringing the rest of the peninsula under a single crown through the marriage of Isabella, heiress to Castile, and Ferdinand, heir to Aragon. Isabella became queen in 1474, Ferdinand king in 1479. Under this remarkable and active couple—*Los Reyes Católicos*, the Catholic Monarchs[1]—royal authority was reasserted and reinforced; religious orthodoxy was enhanced by the establishment of the Inquisition and by the expulsion of the Jews from Spain (1492); and in 1482 Ferdinand

[1] The title was conferred on them by Pope Alexander VI.

and Isabella opened a final campaign to subdue the last Moslem redoubt in the peninsula, the kingdom of Granada. The city of Granada fell ten years later, in the spring of 1492. The following autumn, by dramatic coincidence, saw Columbus in the Indies. Reconquest was to be followed by conquest.

THE IBERIAN CHARACTER

What kind of peoples had emerged from the long travail of the reconquest and the formation of the feudal kingdoms? It is both difficult and unsafe to generalize about something as elusive as "national character"; there are always too many exceptions to be taken into account. Yet it would be hard to deny that the Spaniard and the Portuguese have been marked by a number of specific characteristics which have set them off, historically and psychologically, from the rest of Europe. The rest of Europe feels this instinctively, as do the Iberian peoples themselves. The character of the Spaniard, in particular, seems to stand out in bold relief. The best extended commentary on the subject is to be found in Cervantes' *Don Quixote*, "that book, which contains all other books on Spain."[1] The eternal duality embodied in the book, the profound contrast between the Knight, on the one hand, and the ever-faithful squire, on the other, undoubtedly has a universal significance, but it is an extremely useful starting-point for a consideration of the specifically Spanish character. For some features of the highly complicated Spanish psychology are clearly *quixotic*: its acute individualism, from which stems the whole notorious complex of pride and honor; its disdain (at one level) of material considerations; its love of the grand gesture combined with the capacity to survive making it. On the other hand, the side to the Spanish character exemplified by Sancho Panza is, equally, a constantly observable feature: its stoicism and endurance; its national conservatism; its sobriety and moderation.

The "true juridical ideal" of the Spaniard was once defined by Angel Ganivet, that tormented nineteenth-century writer: "Every Spaniard should carry in his pocket a personal charter with a single article . . . : 'This Spaniard is hereby authorized to do what he jolly well likes.' "[2] A deep consciousness of the value and the efficacy of the individual will permeate the whole of the Spanish conquest of America. The conquistador was, above all else, an individual, leading other individuals by sheer strength of character. Pride—pride in his style and performance—was a key element in his psychological makeup. Indeed,

[1] V. S. Pritchett, *The Spanish Temper* (London, 1954), p. 217.
[2] Angel Ganivet, *Spain*, trans. J. R. Carey (London, 1946), p. 61.

pride often shaded into arrogance and an unreasoning disregard for other people's opinions. Not for nothing is the adjective "haughty" so frequently applied to the Castilian. "I like the Spaniards for not worrying about the rest of the world," once wrote Rudyard Kipling, "but I can't love 'em."[1] This very quality was, however, a useful— indeed indispensable—asset in the colonization of the Indies. In a situation which called for the highest virtues of courage, resilience, and audacity, the Spaniard was not usually found wanting. Yet individualism was invariably subordinated to some high principle or set of principles which would explain and justify its excesses. Religion was one such principle; honor another. The conquest of the Indies was justified very largely on religious grounds, and "the Spaniard's thirst of gold and war," to use Byron's phrase, was never the sole motive of an expedition. A hardened conquistador such as Bernal Díaz could reconcile the two aspects in a statement that, for him at least, had no ironical overtones: he and his contemporaries, he wrote, had come to the Indies "to give light to those that were in darkness, and also to become rich."[2]

For both the conquistador and the churchman, the notion of honor (whether individual honor or the honor of the Church) was highly important. In the greatest of late-medieval Spanish poems, the *Coplas* of Jorge Manrique (1476), the departing hero is informed, by the angel of Death, that there are three distinct levels of existence: first, the ordinary, mortal life of the senses; third, the eternal life of salvation; and, in between, an intermediate life of honor, secured by the perform-ance of noble deeds which win lasting fame on earth. Noble deeds were consistently interpreted to mean fighting. It was the cult of honor, of the intermediate type of immortality poetically described by Manrique, that motivated many of the most typical adventures of the conquest. How otherwise is it possible to explain those fruitless expedi-tions in pursuit of El Dorado, of the City of the Caesars, or any one of a dozen other chimeras, in the years following the conquest of Mexico and Peru? "For what in fact the conqueror sought," a modern Spaniard explains (convincingly enough), "was not wealth, nor even power, but greatness."[3]

Once this important point is grasped, many aspects of Spanish behavior—and not only in the golden age of the conquest—become more easily explicable, though whether they become more excusable depends on the reader's viewpoint. The ferociousness with which the

[1] Charles Carrington, *Rudyard Kipling* (London, 1955), p. 497.
[2] Bernal Díaz del Castillo, *Historia Verdadera de la Conquista de Nueva España*, Chap. 210.
[3] Salvador de Madariaga, *The Fall of the Spanish American Empire* (London, 1947), p. 13.

Spanish soldier fought the Indian (and, almost as often, his fellow Spaniard), his indifference to material hardships, his rejection of compromise as a means of settling disputes, his affection for the grand gesture—these traits are amply documented in the histories of the time. Some of the actions of the conquistadores reached a peak of quixotism which will probably never be excelled. Let us take one case in point. Mancio Serra de Leguísamo, a cavalryman, was a follower of Pizarro in the conquest of Peru. On the occupation of Cuzco, he was awarded the great sun of beaten gold which hung in the greatest of the Inca temples. Presumably the sheer glory of conquest was enough for him, for he was prepared to forfeit this priceless object—perhaps the most priceless in the Indies—in a gambling contest shortly afterward. He lost it.[1]

Underpinning this tendency toward quixotism, with its visionary overtones, a number of other qualities should be noted, and it is not altogether fanciful to associate these with the figure of Sancho Panza. The stoicism of the conqueror—his ability to endure deprivation, hardship, and the prospect of immediate death with relative equanimity —speaks almost for itself. Steadfast loyalty (provided the quality of leadership justifies it) is a further characteristic that shines out in the narratives of the conquest. The Spaniard may be an individualist. His quixotism may lead him to carry his pursuit of a particular vision to extraordinary lengths. But, at the same time, he is equally a restrained and often moderate person—especially in day-to-day life. In many respects he is profoundly conservative. This is notoriously true at the national and regional levels of his psychology. As a nation, Spaniards may be said to be suspicious of foreigners, though never discourteous to them. And within the nation, *regional* differences assume a vital (and sometimes a tragic) role.

It should never be forgotten that the regional differences within Spain are at least as important as the much-vaunted distinctions between Englishmen, Scotsmen, and Welshmen within Great Britain.[2] Catalonia

[1] Serra's love of gambling was apparently very considerable, but he was eventually cured of it. The great mestizo chronicler, Inca Garcilaso de la Vega, who knew Serra, relates the story as follows: "Later the city council, seeing how he was ruining himself by his gambling, elected him one year as *alcalde ordinario*, hoping to reform him. He served his country with such care and attention (for he had all the qualities of a gentleman) that he never touched a playing card the whole year long. Seeing this, the city reappointed him for a further year, and thereafter for many more years to public offices. Occupied in this way, Mancio Serra forgot his passion for gaming and came to hate it ever afterwards." (*Royal Commentaries of the Incas*, trans. Harold V. Livermore, 2 vols. [Austin, Texas, 1966], I, 180.)

[2] Great Britain has never suffered from an issue as contentious as "the Catalan question"—the perennial "Irish" question, in its day, was a good deal *more* contentious. Since 1968, it has been again.

and Euzkadi (the Basque country) have invariably longed for some degree of autonomy—some Catalans and Basques even for full independence. It would be impossible to catalogue the subtle variations of regional character that are to be found within the general Spanish character without writing a whole book. It must suffice to say that such variations do exist, and that they played their part in the conquest. The industrious Catalans, to take one regional group, were generally absent, but men from most of the other regions enacted some role or other: the lively, garrulous Andalusians, the prickly and reserved Basques, the stolid and dependable Galicians—all were present in the New World almost from the first, all with their distinctive outlooks and regional quirks. Extremadura, the arid tableland to the west of Castile, provided many of the most famous conquistadores: Balboa, Cortés, Alvarado, Pizarro, Almagro, Valdivia—to name but six—were all *extremeños*. Many of their followers, not to mention the colonists who went later, were Andalusians—and the American variants of the Spanish language bear the vivid mark of the *andaluz* to this day.

Much of what I have said of the Spaniard could also be applied to the Portuguese character. There can be little dispute as to the strength of regional (in this case amounting to national) feeling that has kept Portugal separate from Spain for so long, though this, as Angel Ganivet speculated, may be due to "the close similarity of their characters."[1] It would be unwise to underestimate the degree of quixotism in the Portuguese. "Here at least, in this small land of Portugal, there will not lack those who will do and dare for Christendom!" Such was Camoens' proud (and justified) boast in the seventh canto of his epic, *The Lusiads*.[2] Yet it is possible to discern a somewhat more relaxed tone in the Portuguese character. Individualism seems more often to be tempered by compromise than in the Spanish case. The political conflicts of Portuguese and Brazilians, as a result, have not usually been pushed to the same extremes. The settlement of Brazil was not by any means a wholly peaceful process: but it lacked the high and intense drama of the Spanish conquests. In part, of course, this was due to circumstances: Portuguese energies were focused elsewhere at the time, and more than one Portuguese conquistador was to be found in sixteenth-century Asia. But in general the cult of honor was neither as acute, nor was it responsible for quite the same effects, as in Spain. Possibly, when all is said and done, Sancho Panza lies closer to the Portuguese heart than Don Quixote.

[1] Ganivet, *Spain*, p. 92.
[2] Luis Vaz de Camoens, *The Lusiads*, trans. William C. Atkinson (Penguin Books, 1952), p. 163.

THE CONSCIENCE OF THE CONQUERORS

Much has been made, and rightly, of the cruelty, devastation, and disruption caused by the Iberian settlement of America. From the middle of the sixteenth century onward the European rivals of the Iberian powers laid stress on this feature of the conquest, and the resultant *leyenda negra*, or Black Legend, has permeated all subsequent interpretation of the initial impact of Iberian on Indian. Its foundations are solid enough. As a distinguished American scholar has put it, "the substantive content of the Black Legend asserts that Indians were exploited by Spaniards, and in empirical fact they were."[1]

But this is not the whole story. It should never be forgotten that most of the materials that went into the creation of the Black Legend were supplied by the Spaniards themselves. They were the fiercest critics of their own actions in the Indies. In essence, the Spaniards (and to a lesser extent the Portuguese) never ceased to ask themselves two fundamental questions: (1) How could the Amerindian peoples be incorporated into the empire in a morally acceptable manner? (2) What, if anything, gave the Iberian powers the right to rule in the Indies at all? Rarely, perhaps, have such questions been posed *from within*, and with such earnestness, in the initial phases of an advancing imperialism. The Papal Bulls of 1493 had enjoined on the Iberian nations the right, and the duty, of evangelizing the newly discovered territories. Thus nobody in sixteenth-century Spain and Portugal doubted for a minute that it was necessary for the American Indian peoples to be taught the Christian revelation. But—and here lay the crux of the problem—should they be *compelled* into conversion or *persuaded* into it, and even if they remained *un*converted, should the conquerors be entitled to make war on them? The Spanish crown quickly came to have doubts about the moral propriety of conquest as a means of Christianization. As we have seen, it prohibited the direct enslavement of Indians (except in special cases) almost from the start. In 1513 it ordered a committee of jurists to draw up a suitable manifesto to be declaimed, formally and publicly, to Indian communities before an offensive could be opened against them. This document, known as the *Requerimiento* (Requirement), gave the Indians a brief summary of the history of the world and of the Spanish intention to Christianize the Indies, and demanded that they acknowledge the supremacy of King and Pope and listen to the preaching of the faith. Only if the Indians failed to accede to these terms were the conquistadores then empowered to make war. The *Requerimiento* was read in the Indies on numerous

[1] Gibson, *The Aztecs under Spanish Rule*, p. 403.

occasions—many of them grotesque and farcical—over the next few decades. It had little practical effect on the course (or the ferocity) of the conquest. But it was a remarkable and significant idea.

The decimation of the Indian population, and the wholesale abuse of the encomienda system, provoked further doubts about the morality of colonization. The struggle over the encomienda has already been recounted, as has its indecisive outcome; and it was an impressive struggle, for it demonstrated that there *were* Spaniards, and more than a handful, who were truly shocked by the maltreatment of the Indians. Fray Bartolomé de Las Casas was their most effective and articulate (not to say passionate) spokesman for over five strenuous decades. He argued from experience. Himself a settler in Santo Domingo and Cuba, he underwent (in 1514) a wave of revulsion at what he saw around him. From then until he died, a nonagenarian, in 1566, Las Casas lost no opportunity to defend the Amerindian and to denounce the way in which Spanish colonization was proceeding. He himself twice experimented in practical fashion with alternative schemes of colonization. His first plan was to settle part of the Venezuelan coast with Spanish farmers and laborers, who would live alongside the Indians and gradually draw them into the orbit of Christian civilization by example and persuasion. The scheme was an abject failure, and as a result Las Casas entered the Dominican Order. A later experiment, which began in 1537 in a hitherto unconquered district of Guatemala, relied exclusively on missionaries to convert the Indians. It lasted for nearly twenty years. The Spanish settlers, chagrined by the success of this plan, were delighted when an Indian revolt brought it to a sudden end.

Las Casas' views on conquest and the Indians greatly influenced official policy. The controversial New Laws of 1542 were the most dramatic instance of this, and their eventual modification did not daunt the fiery Dominican. He kept up the pressure. On April 16, 1550, Charles V decreed the immediate suspension of further conquests while the whole question of "just wars" in the Indies was scrutinized more formally. This was done before a junta of jurists, theologians, and members of the royal councils, which assembled at Valladolid in August–September 1550 and April–May 1551. The main feature of these meetings was the clash between Las Casas and Juan Ginés de Sepúlveda, one of the foremost Spanish intellectuals of the time. Sepúlveda based his justification of conquest on the Aristotelian concept of "natural slavery," which he applied to the Indians.[1] The debate had no practical outcome. Further expeditions of conquest were soon organized, though

[1] See Lewis Hanke, *Aristotle and the American Indians* (London, 1959), pp. 38–73.

in 1573, when the regulations for such expeditions were codified, the word "conquest" was replaced by "pacification." Nevertheless, the spectacle of a powerful empire holding up its expansionist operations in order to discuss rights and wrongs is, to say the least, an unusual one.[1] Furthermore, it is surely significant that Sepúlveda's book *Democrates Alter*, the basis of his argument at Valladolid, was never permitted to appear in printed form.

The problem of whether Spain had a "just title" to the Indies was, of course, part and parcel of the "just war" issue, and it preoccupied thinkers and statesmen throughout the sixteenth century. Here again the Bulls of 1493 were the starting point of most discussions, though the eminent jurist Francisco de Vitoria (1486–1546) denied the Papacy's right to make grants of temporal dominion at all, as did a number of other leading Spanish thinkers of the time. Perhaps the most interesting attempt to demonstrate the justice of Spanish imperial rule was that made by Francisco de Toledo, viceroy of Peru from 1569 to 1581. He arranged for what would nowadays be thought of as an opinion survey to be conducted among suitable Indians to prove that Inca rule had been tyrannical and hence, according to all prevailing notions, unjustified. "Your Majesty," he told Philip II when the investigation was complete, "is the legitimate ruler of this kingdom and the Incas are tyrannical usurpers." This argument failed to win assent from, *inter alia*, the contemporary Jesuit historian Father José de Acosta, who asserted that the fact that somebody was a thief did not give somebody else the right to rob him.[2]

The majority of Spanish settlers, it seems certain, were not unduly concerned by these various debates. While churchmen and intellectuals argued, they vigorously got on with the job. Las Casas' written works were well known in the Indies and indignantly rejected by the colonizers. Nevertheless, the defense of the Indian—however vain in the long term—and the intellectual arguments which went on throughout the first century of the conquest, indicate that the conscience of the conquerors was by no means an easy one. Some individuals came to regret the fact that the conquest had taken place at all, and to regret it bitterly. Mancio Serra, the conquistador who won the golden sun in Cuzco, was one of these. His remorse at the overthrow of the well-organized society of the Incas was poignant in the extreme. Just before he died in 1589, he dictated, to the king, a lengthy preamble to his will, in which he made this abundantly clear.

[1] It may of course be argued that by 1550 the major conquests were already over. As it happened, this was true, but there could be no certainty about it at the time.
[2] Hanke, *The Spanish Struggle for Justice*, pp. 165–67.

The motive which obliges me to make this statement is the discharge of my conscience, as I find myself guilty. For we have destroyed by our evil example the people who had such a government as was enjoyed by these natives. . . . But now they have come to such a pass, in offence of God, owing to the bad example that we have set them in all things, that these natives, from doing no evil have changed into people who now do no good or very little. . . . I pray God to pardon me.[1]

How many former conquistadores came to feel as Serra did can never be known. But his testimony on its own is remarkable enough, and throws an extraordinary light on the complex psychology of the conquerors.

CREOLE AND EUROPEAN

Migration from Europe to the Iberian colonies in the New World was never on a large scale. In the case of the Spanish empire, it seems unlikely that much more than a thousand people emigrated permanently in any year throughout the sixteenth century; more may have done so during the seventeenth and eighteenth centuries, though no detailed records survive to enable the historian to arrive at final conclusions. By the 1570s, the total Spanish population of America stood at between one hundred thousand and one hundred and fifty thousand. At the same period, there were approximately twenty thousand Portuguese in Brazil. The lure of the Indies was doubtless considerable.[2] But migration was fairly strictly controlled. Although Charles V opened the Western hemisphere to non-Spanish subjects of his empire, little advantage was taken of the offer and from the time of Philip II onward foreigners were rigidly excluded. Foreigners *did* sometimes settle in colonial Latin America, but only with special permission or under some illegal arrangement.

It is evident that Spaniards and Portuguese alike took to America their own distinctive psychologies and modes of living, but they were, naturally enough, altered in subtle ways by their new environment. Contact with the Indian peoples gave them new words for their vocabulary, new foods for their kitchens, new climatic and physical conditions with which to cope. But they remained Spaniards and

[1] Sir Clements Markham, *The Incas of Peru* (London, 1910), pp. 300-1.
[2] It is worth mentioning that Cervantes petitioned Philip II (May 1590) for a post in the Indies, with the idea of spending the rest of his life there. His request was turned down. Perhaps this was just as well. Would *Don Quixote* have been written in America?

Portuguese, for their own religion, language, architecture, and domestic customs—to name but four things—accompanied them across the Atlantic. Often, regional rivalries were transported whole from the Iberian peninsula to the New World. In the exuberant mining city of Potosí, for instance, the bloody clashes of Basques, Andalusians, Extremadurans, Portuguese, Castilians, and so forth, were notorious in the sixteenth and seventeenth centuries; they amounted almost to minor civil wars. Yet gradually, as time passed, one much greater (and ultimately more disruptive) rivalry eclipsed all others—the rivalry between the European-born (the "Peninsular") on the one hand and the American-born on the other. It was a tension implicit in any colonial empire administered—as were the Spanish and Portuguese empires— by men from the homeland. It was bound to develop from the moment the first generation of settlers produced the second. The Creoles, as they became known—American-born Spaniards or Portuguese[1]— inevitably developed their own peculiar emphases and outlooks.[2]

In theory and in law, the Creole and the European were equal in the Iberian empires. If anything, Spanish imperial law *favored* the Creole as far as the provision of official and ecclesiastical posts was concerned. In practice, however, Creoles were strictly denied access to the highest positions in Church and state in the Indies. This was plainly official government policy almost from the start. Of the 170 viceroys who ruled in Spanish America, only four were Creoles; of the 602 governors, only fourteen. Preferment in the Church was easier: rather more than a quarter of all archbishops and bishops in the Spanish-American empire were Creoles. Lower magistracies, treasury jobs, and other run-of-the-mill government posts were somewhat more evenly shared out. Nevertheless, Creoles became acutely aware—how quickly it is difficult to say—that they were excluded from the best and most lucrative positions. In trade, too, they were at a distinct disadvantage

[1] The word "Creole" (Port. *crioulo*, Sp. *criollo*, Fr. *créole*) appears to have originated in Portuguese, and probably derived from the verb *criar* (to bring up, to raise). A Creole was thus someone brought up in the Indies. At first the word was applied to Negro slaves born in America, as well as to Europeans.

[2] Some of the names given by American Spaniards and Portuguese to their European counterparts are of significance. In the Spanish empire the European was politely known as a *peninsular*; metropolitan Portuguese were known as *reinóis* (lit. "men from the Kingdom") in Brazil. In Mexico a less complimentary expression for Spaniard was *gachupín* which probably derived from nahuatl words meaning "a man with spurs"; elsewhere in Spanish America, the common term was *chapetón* ("tenderfoot"). In Brazil, Portuguese came to be known as (among other things) *marinheiros* ("sailors") and *pés-de-chumbo* ("leadenfeet"). It is worth mentioning here that the Spanish-American term "Creole" was not used in colonial Brazil to mean the same thing. *Mazombo* was the nearest Brazilian equivalent of *criollo*, though it had pejorative overtones.

compared with the peninsular Spaniard or Portuguese. In the course of time, Creoles found themselves a thwarted colonial aristocracy, as the owners of estates and mines who nevertheless lacked the corresponding mercantile and political influence they might have expected to enjoy. There were always certain compensations open to them. They were able to acquire such "status symbols" as titles of nobility, knighthoods in the ancestral orders of chivalry, and (later) posts in the militia. But their aspirations to high political office and commercial importance remained frustrated.

The rivalry resulting from this situation was expressed in several different ways. It was expressed, first, in competition for those jobs which *were* open to Creoles: especially lucrative, and hence especially contentious, was the elective post of Provincial (district head) in some of the religious orders, where a system of alternation between Creole and European was supposed to operate. Rowdy and indecorous politicking was a constant feature of elections to these Provincialships. In the *cabildos*, the municipal councils of the Spanish Indies, efforts were sometimes made by Creoles to limit the numbers of Europeans allowed to serve as councilors and magistrates.

There seems little doubt that a fairly severe anti-Creole prejudice existed in Spain and Portugal. It was seriously debated in the peninsula as to whether a native-born American Spaniard or Portuguese was fitted for the task of governing, or in fact was much good for anything else. It was even suggested that he might be a congenitally inferior being. Such aspersions were indignantly rejected by both Creoles and pro-Creole Europeans. The eighteenth-century Spanish writer, Fray Benito Jerónimo Feijóo, ardently defended the Spanish-American from such charges, as his predecessor Juan Solórzano Pereira (perhaps the greatest expert on colonial jurisprudence that Spain produced) had done a hundred years earlier. In 1771 the municipal council of Mexico City submitted a bluntly worded memorandum on the subject:

It is claimed that those of us born of European parents on this soil scarcely have sufficient powers of reason to be considered men. . . . The Spanish Americans are capable of the highest offices. They do not yield in intelligence, application, conduct or honour to any of the other nations of the world. So impartial authors whose criticism the literary world respects have confessed. So experience proves each day, except to those who wilfully close their eyes to plain truths.[1]

[1] Peggy S. Korn, "Mexico on the Eve of Independence," in F. B. Pike, ed., *Latin American History: Select Problems. Identity, Integration and Nationhood* (New York, 1969), pp. 108–10.

The tone of this memorandum and of other contemporary documents reveals that by the eighteenth century a proud and distinctive Creole awareness had grown up. A new Spanish regionalism, based on a new set of regions, was now noticeable, and it boded ill for the future of the empire.

In the second half of the eighteenth century, the Spanish government was sufficiently concerned by the rift between Creole and European to contemplate ways and means of overcoming it. At an extraordinary meeting of the Royal Council in March 1768, Count Campomanes and the future Count Floridablanca suggested methods of combating "the spirit of independence and aristocracy" that had arisen among the Creoles. The formation of Creole regiments in Spain and the dispatch of larger numbers of Europeans to America—this seemed one possibility.[1] It appears probable, too, that Count Aranda, another of King Charles III's great ministers, proposed the establishment of three semi-independent vassal-monarchies in America as a way of containing Creole aspirations—which (he quite rightly assumed) would be enlarged by the recent example of the American Revolution. King Charles IV thought in terms of five such kingdoms. There can be little doubt that proposals of this sort, if not exactly a counsel of despair, nevertheless reflected a certain disquiet on the part of the Spanish government.

At the start of the nineteenth century, when Iberian rule in America had run for three hundred years, there were rather more than three million Creoles and European Spaniards in the Indies; the European and European-descended population of Brazil was probably rather less than one million. In all, the "white" element made up approximately one fifth of the total Latin American population. But it was, of course, the vital element. Tension between Creole and European was at as high a level as it had ever been. Alexander von Humboldt, in Mexico, recorded this in his usual acute manner, noting the "jealousy and perpetual hatred" that existed between the two communities, the arrogant superiority complex of the Peninsular Spaniards, and the steady relaxation of the bonds of empire.

> The most miserable European, without education, and without intellectual cultivation, thinks himself superior to the white born in the new continent ... The natives prefer the denomination of *Americans* to that of Creoles. Since the peace of Versailles (1783) and, in particular, since the year 1789, we frequently hear proudly declared

[1] Richard Konetzke, "La condición legal de los criollos y las causas de la independencia," *Estudios Americanos*, II (1950), 45-47.

"I am not a *Spaniard*, I am an *American!*" words which betray the workings of a long resentment.[1]

In 1807–8, the long resentment was at last presented with a golden opportunity to express itself in concrete political fashion. The struggle for independence was the outcome—and it was the Creoles who led the way. It was, in essence, their revolution, and their victory.

THE NEW IBERIAN NATIONS

The wars of independence were a continuation of the oldest of Spanish traditions. By the start of the nineteenth century, Creole Spaniards had discovered a new principle to which they could subordinate the fierce individualism they had inherited from their European forebears. Bolívar, San Martín, O'Higgins, Sucre, Artigas—Creoles such as these formed a new breed of conquistadores, no less mindful of their personal honor, no less adept at making the grand gesture, no less quixotic in their objectives, though here the search for treasure was replaced by a set of immense hopes for the rebirth of society.

By the time the dust had settled, it was already apparent that the long growth of Creole self-awareness had hidden a parallel growth of stubborn regionalism. In Brazil, the institution of monarchy was able to hold the vast and sprawling country together, but nothing could prevent the disintegration of the Spanish-American empire. The Creoles had not only grown apart from Spain; they had grown apart from each other. A Mexican Creole was now almost as different from a Chilean or an Argentine as he was from a Spaniard. The primary allegiance of the Creole shifted to his particular province, which now became his particular *nation*. Even Simón Bolívar, who rarely ceased toying with the idea of confederating the new states, ultimately believed that the specific, local *patria*—in his own case Venezuela—should "take preference," as he put it. "Are there any greater sacred claims upon love and devotion?" he asked General Santa Cruz in 1826. "Yes, General, let each serve his native land as a paramount duty, and let all other things be secondary."[2]

Although the wars of independence brought a whole chain of new nations into existence, these nations were still essentially Iberian in character. For it was the Creoles who inherited the two Iberian empires:

---

[1] Humboldt, *Political Essay on the Kingdom of New Spain*, trans. John Black, 4 vols. (London, 1811), I, 205–6.

[2] Letter of September 14, 1826. Lecuna and Bierck, *op cit.*, II, 639. Bolívar declaring his own intention of doing "all the good I can for Venezuela," tells Santa Cruz: "Substitute a purely Peruvian program for continental American planning, that is, a program designed exclusively to promote the interests of Peru."

it was Creoles, in most cases, who made up the governing classes in the new republics. But the distinctively Spanish and Portuguese character in Latin America was slowly undermined, after independence, by a number of factors. British trade and French cultural influence altered the outlook—and sometimes the habits—of the Creoles. In countries such as Argentina, Uruguay, and Brazil, massive nineteenth-century European migration modified the ethnic pattern very considerably, as we shall see. Gradual rearrangements in the social structure of the republics also helped, in some cases, to produce a situation where mestizo, Indian and Negro influences came into play in determining "national character." Creolism—if we mean by this the distinctive attributes of the old colonial aristocracies—survives to this day, whether in the pronounced interest shown by some aristocratic families in their Iberian family trees, or in a sympathetic fondness for traditional folk music, cuisine, dress, or behavior;[1] but it is more a picturesque curiosity than anything else. The Latin American nations of the 1970s are psychologically as far removed from their Iberian motherlands as the United States is from Britain.

Yet this particular parallel points to a further obvious truth. Just as the United States undoubtedly derives certain crucial features of its civilization from Great Britain, so do the Iberian nations of the New World owe much to those of the Old. The Spanish and Portuguese languages, and the Catholic religion, are the two most outstanding Iberian legacies, and perhaps the most permanent. But it would be impossible to deny that some features of the old Iberian character have remained active in modern Latin America as well. In many of the Spanish-speaking countries, for instance, political passions are still pushed to the point of no return. In Brazil, by contrast, the tendency toward compromise has usually prevented large-scale civil strife. Quixotism, the search for honor, the high function ascribed to the individual will, the role of the commanding personality—these still color Latin American life. They are as much a part of the Iberian heritage as language or religion.

In 1940, during the investigations which followed the murder of Leon Trotsky in Mexico City, the chief of the Mexican secret police had occasion to arrest his compatriot, the painter David Alfaro Siqueiros. After the arrest, the two men talked.

We chatted about things which had no connection with the affair in hand, and I even told him of an episode in my military career when

---

[1] In these contexts, the expression *muy criollo* ("very Creole"), still employed in many parts of Spanish America, means little more than "very traditional."

I was taken prisoner by the enemy during our bloody revolution, in the year 1915. "I was a young man at the time," I added, "and since then I have had a deep respect for human life, unless it is a question of the payment of a debt of honour."[1]

In ways such as this, the spirit of the conquistadores lives on.

The Africans

The white man paints the devil black,
And the black man paints him white;
But a man by his colour ain't influenced,
It doesn't hold for, nor yet against;
The Almighty made only one kind of man,
Though their faces are dark or bright.

JOSÉ HERNÁNDEZ

The presence of the African Negro in Latin America is tragically associated with the institution of slavery. The black component in the Latin American population, it is fair to say, owes its existence to man's inhumanity to man. Slavery as an institution had underpinned the world of classical antiquity, but in most parts of Europe it had been transformed into serfdom or villeinage well before the close of the Middle Ages. Indeed, serfdom itself was becoming a thing of the past in certain countries. In the Iberian peninsula, however, partly as a result of the long process of reconquest, slavery still survived—Moorish and Jewish slaves were not uncommon. Nevertheless, the institution was probably on the decline by the fifteenth century. It cannot be said to have been a major characteristic of Iberian life. Its existence was prolonged—and prolonged for nearly four centuries—by the events of the Age of Discovery. The African Negro was to become its chief victim.

THE SLAVE TRADE

In this renewal of slavery, the Portuguese were the pioneers. Their voyages of discovery to the south brought them into contact with the small Negro kingdoms of West Africa—and in 1442, for the first time, a shipment of slaves was brought back to Lisbon. A hundred years later the trade was so well developed that the city had more than sixty different slave markets. The beginnings of Spanish colonization of the West Indies made the migration of Negro slaves to the New World a distinct possibility within half a century of their arrival in the Iberian

[1] General Leandro A. Sánchez Salazar, *Murder in Mexico* (London, 1950), p. 199.

133

peninsula, although there can be no certainty as to when the first African reached the Indies. The crown had serious doubts about the propriety of such a development. Although Governor Ovando was permitted to take Christian Negroes from the peninsula in his expedition in 1502, the government reversed this decision at least three times over the next eight years. Demands for labor from the Spanish settlers proved sufficient, however, to break down this particular barrier. In 1510 more than a hundred slaves were purchased in Lisbon for dispatch to the Indies, and the following year saw the first direct shipment from Africa to the American colonies. It was the start of a long, merciless story.

The factors which swung the balance of official opinion in favor of further development in the slave trade were the rapid decline of the Indian population of the Caribbean islands, the consequent need of an alternative labor force, and the desire in some circles to defend the Indians who had survived. Early in the reign of Charles V, a number of churchmen, including Bartolomé de Las Casas, recommended the use of Negro slaves as laborers in the Indies. Las Casas, it is fair to point out, very quickly repented of his decision to support this move, believing firmly to the end of his days that Negroes were just as much rational human beings as were Indians.[1] In 1518 the Spanish crown gave a license to one of its Flemish subordinates to supply four thousand Negroes to the colonists. Ten years later, in 1528, the crown concluded a contract (the first asiento) with two Germans at court to ship four thousand Negroes over a four-year period. Negroes, in fact, were very close on the heels of the Iberians in the New World. Either as slaves or as free servants, they were to be found in the conquest of Mexico and Peru, and in the civil wars of the conquerors that followed. The start of regular Portuguese colonization in Brazil in the 1530s opened up a new field for Negro slavery—the institution, in fact, was to prove far more inportant there than in the Spanish dominions. The first direct shipment of slaves from Africa to Brazil occurred in 1538. By the end of the 1580s there were perhaps as many as fifteen thousand Negroes there, mostly on the sugar plantations of the northeast. Within a century of Columbus' first voyage, therefore, the pattern was already clear. The West Indies and Brazil were to remain the main areas of Negro settlement in Latin America, and remain so today.

It is difficult to generalize about the different types of African that were taken to the New World. The slave traders operated along much of the west coast of the African continent, from the Senegal and Gambia rivers in the north to Angola in the south; areas of special importance were those extending from the Ivory Coast to what is now eastern

[1] Las Casas, *Historia de las Indias*, Book III, Chap. 102.

Nigeria, and the coasts (and hinterlands) of the Congo and Angola. But it is certain that the tentacles of the trade reached far inland, and to many corners of the continent. Many Africans transported to America were of Bantu stock, from the southern and central regions of the continent. Many others belonged to the partly or wholly Moslem peoples of the Sudan and West Africa: Hausas, Mandingos, Yorubas, Ashantis, to name but a few. Some of them, it is fair to say, came from a more sophisticated cultural and economic background than the Amerindians of Brazil encountered by the first colonizers.

Although Portugal began the slave trade, several other European nations joined in, particularly after the growth of non-Latin colonies in America. By the end of the seventeenth century, the English, Dutch, French, and Danes were fully implicated. Of the forty or so European "factories" on the African coast at the end of the eighteenth century, ten were British, fifteen Dutch, four Portuguese, four Danish, and three French. Literally hundreds of vessels were involved. The Spanish empire never gained direct access to the African slave markets, and it was forced to buy from foreigners. During the union of Spanish and Portuguese empires, this presented no problem, since the Portuguese were able to conduct the trade on Spain's behalf. Later, however, foreign powers fixed greedy eyes on the prospect of supplying Spain's colonies with slaves. In 1701 the asiento was granted to the French Royal Guinea Company, but at the end of the War of the Spanish Succession, it passed to the English South Sea Company until 1750. It is probably true to say that the trouble the Spanish asiento caused in international diplomacy was out of all proportion to its intrinsic economic value.

How did the slave trade work? It was branded, at each successive stage, with signs of systematic inhumanity. First came the traumatic moment of enslavement. In the interior of Africa, villages were raided, either by Europeans or by their African agents, and Negroes were rounded up and marched—sometimes hundreds of miles—to the nearest port. African rulers, eager for the wide variety of merchandise proffered by European traders, sold their prisoners-of-war into slavery; often it could be doubted as to whether the "wars" in which such prisoners were taken had been genuine.

The worst part of their experience came next, during the second stage. Slave ships were small, and carried less than three hundred Negroes as a general rule, at any rate until toward the end of the eighteenth century. Slaves were consigned in chains to the hold, where they were accommodated ("stored" would be a better word) in narrow galleries. Gross overcrowding, and the lack of even the most rudimentary sanitation, combined with a wholly inadequate diet, exacted a dreadful toll in disease and death. Slaves often spent several months in these surroundings. Quite apart from the crossing of the Atlantic—the dreaded "middle passage"—there were frequently delays on either side of the ocean. No ship left the African shore until it was fully loaded. Again, on arrival in American waters, ships would sometimes call at several ports before disembarking the whole of their human cargo.

Before arriving at their destination—the third stage of the slaves' horrifying odyssey—efforts were usually made to heal (or at any rate to conceal) the injuries sustained by the Negroes on the journey from Africa. Once this had been done, they were ready to be sold for a second time. How much they cost their new owners, on average, is difficult to say. During the eighteenth century at least, an individual slave may have cost between thirty pounds and sixty pounds (seventy dollars and one-hundred-and-forty dollars), and earlier prices seem to have been at much the same level. The trade was immensely profitable: the prices the European traders paid in Africa were very small in comparison with those they received in America.

Statistics on the total number of Africans forcibly transported to Latin America by the slave trade are impossible to compute. Not only are the records incomplete in themselves, but contraband invariably accounted for additional numbers throughout the colonial period. At the start of the nineteenth century, the Negro population of Brazil amounted to around two million, about half the total population of the country. The Spanish-American empire included (according to Humboldt) 776,000 Negroes, over half of whom were concentrated in Cuba and Puerto Rico. A further five hundred thousand or so (perhaps rather less) lived in the former French colony of Saint Domingue. A number of general considerations ought to be borne in mind at this point. Far fewer women were transported than men, and there is plenty of evidence to show that the fertility of female slaves was much reduced. Added to which, it seems certain that the average slave did not have a very long life after his arrival in America. It is reasonable to suppose, therefore, that the total Negro population of Latin America at the end of the colonial period—approximately three and a quarter million—was the outcome of continual renewal by importation rather than natural increase (though this is not to say that there was *no* natural increase). The total number of slaves transported to Latin America, therefore, has to be measured in millions. It was a process of migration (albeit involuntary migration) which was not paralleled until the great movements of population from nineteenth-century Europe. In volume, it far outweighed Spanish and Portuguese migration during the colonial period.

It is all the more important, therefore, that we should remember how it was carried out.

SLAVERY IN THE COLONIES

Slavery in colonial Latin America (including French Saint Domingue) was a cruel institution; this need not be doubted. But the *legal* position of the slave had some bearing on his *practical* condition, and the Iberian legal tradition with respect of slavery had a number of redeeming features. "In effect," Frank Tannenbaum has written, in a famous essay on the American systems of slavery, "slavery under both law and custom had, for all practical purposes, become a contractual arrangement between the master and his bondman. There may have been no written contract between the two parties, but the state behaved, in effect, as if such a contract did exist, and used its powers to enforce it."[1] What this meant in practice was that even a slave had certain recognized *rights*. He had, in the first place, the right to buy his freedom—and this included the purchase of freedom by installments. He also had the right to be spared excessive maltreatment—if his master indulged in sadistic practices with him, he could be compulsorily transferred to another owner by the courts, or, in certain circumstances, emancipated. Furthermore, the Iberian tradition regarded the manumission of slaves as an honorable and Christian act. These facts should be borne in mind when the institution of slavery in Spanish and Portuguese America is considered.[2]

But slavery it was, and slavery it remained. Plantation life was essentially similar throughout the Indies. Though somewhat different conditions prevailed in the mines (particularly in eighteenth-century Brazil), in domestic service, or in any of the other occupations into which Negro slaves were forced, the exaction of sweated labor was a feature common to them all.

The treatment or maltreatment of slaves varied, naturally enough, according to the personal inclinations of the masters. Flogging was the common mode of punishment throughout colonial Latin America, and although the number of strokes of the lash for any given offense was often laid down by law, many slave owners exceeded the limits. A wide variety of sadistic practices is documented by contemporary writers. Outright murder, it would appear, was not uncommon. At the end of the seventeenth century in Brazil, a Jesuit recorded that some plantation

[1] Frank Tannenbaum, *Slave and Citizen* (New York, 1947), p. 55.
[2] French practice in Saint Domingue, which it is necessary to include in this account because it forms the background to the emergence of Haiti, was in part the outcome of *not* having a legal tradition of slavery of this sort.

owners "for trifling offences threw their slaves alive into furnaces, or killed them in various barbarous and inhuman ways."[1] The eighteenth century may have brought slight relief. When a group of slave owners in Minas Gerais proposed the cutting of the Achilles tendons of captured runaway slaves, the Portuguese government rejected the idea.[2] The Spanish empire abolished the branding of slaves in 1784. Five years later, the royal *cédula* of May 31, 1789, which codified the legislation on Negro slave matters, strictly regulated an owner's freedom to mete out punishments, stipulated (not for the first time) that slaves were to be fed and clothed decently, and attempted to humanize the system as far as this was possible.

Revolt and escape (often perforce combined) were two means of combating the harsh conditions of slavery. The first Negro revolt in the Spanish empire occurred in Hispaniola as early as 1522. Over the years that followed, escaped slaves (*cimarrones*, as they were known) became a constant problem to the imperial authorities. In Panama they menaced the safety of the trans-isthmian traveler. Often they set up their own independent communities in the mountains or forests. These *quilombos*, as they were called in Brazil, sometimes endured for many years. The largest, most famous and longest-lasting was the "Republic of Palmares" in the backlands of Alagoas. It holds a notable place in history. There may have been as many as twenty thousand Negroes in this well-organized redoubt, which maintained a separate and highly successful existence for nearly half the seventeenth century, before being reduced to obedience by a sustained military offensive. Palmares was paralleled, on a smaller scale and in a less sophisticated manner, in every area where slaves were concentrated: in Brazil, in the West Indies, and on the fringes of the South and Central American mainland.

Alongside the clearly attested cruelties of slavery there also went those redeeming features which I have mentioned already. The Church, it should be noted here, was always insistent on affirming the slave's status as a Christian soul. It was considered important that the slave should be baptized, should attend Mass regularly, and should be taught the elements of Christian doctrine. From this viewpoint, the slave was never regarded as an *inferior* human being—merely as an *enslaved* human being. The manumission of slaves was straightforward and by no means infrequent: it was often an adjunct to celebrations in the master's family, and slaves would go free at weddings and birthdays. They could also be emancipated under the last will and testament of their master.

[1] C. R. Boxer, *The Golden Age of Brazil, 1695–1750* (Berkeley and Los Angeles, 1962), p. 8.
[2] *Ibid.*, pp. 172–73.

Manumission, then, was an honorable act, highly regarded by the Church. The purchase of freedom was also common. Money for this purpose could be offered at baptism. It could also be paid at any later stage of a slave's life, and if necessary by installments. This latter system—*coartación*, as it was known in the Spanish empire—was well developed by the end of the colonial period. It was possible for a slave to have his value fixed by the courts and to redeem his freedom by a series of payments. In the cities, slaves often worked, in effect, for themselves—either as craftsmen or as laborers—merely paying a proportion of their income to their owner. These *negros de ganho* were a common sight in the towns of colonial Brazil.

At the start of the nineteenth century, Humboldt found that slaves in Spanish America were "somewhat more under the protection of the laws than the negroes of the other European colonies. These laws," he added, "are always interpreted in favour of liberty."[1] Manumission and the purchase of liberty meant, in practice, the emergence of a substantial class of free Negroes in colonial Latin America. In Spanish America, it is true, certain restrictions were placed on free Negroes, but freedom signified greater mobility, and often meant the opportunity to take up craftsmanship or general labor in a town; indeed, once free, Afro-Americans became decidedly urban creatures. By the time of independence freemen outnumbered slaves in the black population of Peru and Venezuela; and even in Cuba, in the final century of colonial rule, freemen never amounted to less than a third of the number of slaves, and were frequently more.

There is some possibility, therefore, however slight, that the system of slavery as it operated in Latin America was somewhat less harsh than in other parts of the New World. In the British colonies both in the West Indies and in North America, manumission was by no means as common. It was frowned on by authority and, in some areas, was subject to special (and heavy) taxation. The churches took relatively little interest in slaves (though the record of the Nonconformists was better in this respect than that of the Anglicans). There were no legal loopholes which enabled a slave to secure his liberty against the consent of his master, as certainly occurred in Brazil and Spanish America. Possibly the fundamental difference between the Latin and Anglo-Saxon systems was that in the latter, the *slave* and the *Negro* were automatically identified; whereas in Latin America, the fact that the slave happened to be of African origin was less important than the fact that he was a slave—once free, he could take his place, and his chances,

[1] Humboldt, *op. cit.*, I, 241.

in a society which did not discriminate against him on grounds of color.

THE END OF SLAVERY

The slave trade and slavery never won the wholehearted support of the Catholic Church. Indeed, they were condemned by the Papacy at least once a century during the colonial period.[1] But although the great Peruvian Jesuit, Alonso de Sandoval, denounced both the trade and the institution in the early seventeenth century, the majority of his ecclesiastical contemporaries confined themselves to denouncing the sins of individual slave owners and trying to alleviate the harshest effects of the trade. Even the heroic Catalan missionary St. Peter Claver, who spent forty years of his life ministering to the slaves who arrived at Cartagena, did not argue in favor of abolishing slavery as such. In the eighteenth century, however, the tide of "enlightened" opinion in Europe swung severely against the evil: more importantly, in practical terms, Nonconformist opinion in England now moved in the direction of abolition. Great Britain controlled over half the slave trade at this period, and her free institutions permitted the growth of a strong campaign in favor of an end to slavery. The movement gathered speed after Lord Mansfield's famous legal decision of 1772, abolishing slavery in the British Isles; and soon, under the leadership of men such as William Wilberforce (1759–1833), it was to win the day.

But before this had occurred, slavery itself had produced its own outcome in one small corner of Latin America. Nowhere in the eighteenth century had the slave population grown so fast as in the French colony of Saint Domingue. To Frenchmen, this "pearl of the Antilles" was the main jewel in their colonial diadem. Nearly half a million African slaves worked the sugar and coffee plantations there in the 1780s, outnumbering the white population by ten to one. Conditions were appalling, and certainly more severe than those which prevailed in Spanish America or Brazil; the provisions of Louis XIV's *Code Noir* (1685) were largely ignored. The French Revolution shattered the colony's artificial stability. In August 1791 the slaves rose against their masters in a spasm of killing and burning. Under the extraordinary leadership of Toussaint L'Ouverture, the Negroes won control of the colony, while in Paris, in January 1794, the National Convention decreed the abolition of slavery. For the next few years the great Negro general was the effective ruler of Saint Domingue. Though Toussaint himself was

---

[1] By Pope Pius II in 1462; by Paul III in 1537; by Urban VIII in 1639; by Benedict XIV in 1741; and by Gregory XVI in 1838.

willing to maintain an association with the French Republic, Napoleon Bonaparte, on becoming First Consul, had different ideas. It was Napoleon's decision to restore slavery, to have Toussaint captured, and to bring back the already decimated slave-owning class that provoked the final, triumphant resistance of the Negroes of Saint Domingue. Renamed Haiti in order to underline the break with France, the former colony emerged as an independent state—the first of the twenty republics of Latin America to do so. It was a convincing demonstration of "black power," and a significant one for the cause of Latin American independence. For it was from Haiti, a dozen years later, that Simón Bolívar sailed to liberate Venezuela.

Meanwhile, the abolitionist campaign in Great Britain had reached a new pitch; and the British government declared the slave trade within its dominions at an end from May 1, 1807.[1] (Slavery itself was abolished in the British Empire in 1833.) The government immediately embarked on a policy of persuading other countries to follow suit. Neither Spain nor Portugal demonstrated excessive eagerness in doing so. In 1815 Portugal agreed with Great Britain to prohibit the slave trade north of the equator; Spain signed two treaties (1817 and 1835) on the subject, but made no great effort to enforce them. In the meantime the wars of independence had transformed the Spanish-American empire into independent republics, most of whose leaders were sympathetic to the antislavery cause. Both Bolívar and San Martín liberated Negro slaves to fight in the patriot armies. The new governments very quickly enacted laws partially or totally abolishing slavery and the slave trade. Slavery was finally abolished in Venezuela in 1821, in Chile in 1823, and in Mexico in 1829, though some other countries waited rather longer: in Peru, for instance, slavery was restored by General Gamarra after having been abolished in 1821 by San Martín; it was again abolished, this time forever, in 1854.

Brazil, and the remaining Spanish colonies of the Caribbean (Cuba and Puerto Rico), maintained slavery intact for several decades after independence. Puerto Rico saw it go in 1873. In Cuba, it survived until 1880, at which time there were one hundred and fifty thousand slaves in this island. Abolition in Brazil formed one of the central issues in the political history of the Second Reign. It is worth remembering that, throughout the long struggle, Emperor Pedro II (who manumitted his own slaves in 1840) was a convinced, if cautious, supporter of abolition.

---

[1] The honor of being the first European nation to do away with the trade goes not to Great Britain but to Denmark, which in 1792 had decreed its abolition as from the end of the year 1802.

Opinions differ as to how harsh Brazilian slavery in the nineteenth century really was. The observant and lyrical English traveler, Sir Richard Burton, believed that "nowhere, even in oriental countries, has the 'bitter draught' so little of gall in it; in the present day the Brazilian negro need not envy the starving liberty of the poor in most parts of the civilized world."[1] The Brazilian abolitionists themselves, however, maintained (logically enough) that this argument hardly justified the continuation of slavery, and they doubted the truth of such assertions. On balance, it would appear that conditions *had* to some extent improved since independence. By the time of the Golden Law of 1888, there were probably at least three times as many free Negroes as slaves in the Brazilian empire. Some seven hundred and fifty thousand now gained their liberty, and, with the Golden Law, slavery disappeared at last from the American continent.

It will be clear from the foregoing account that well before the end of slavery a substantial proportion of the Negro population of Latin America—in contrast to the position in other areas of the New World—consisted of freemen. This undoubtedly helped the emancipated slaves to become more easily integrated into an open society with which they had previously been unfamiliar. It can reasonably be argued that racial discrimination of the type to be found in, for instance, South Africa had never been a feature of the general Latin American scene. In Cuba, before the end of the colonial period, "the fundamental criteria for ranking an individual were not his racial attributes but his cultural and economic background."[2] The same observation could be applied to any other Latin American republic with a large Negro element. In general, any tendencies toward the growth of color discrimination have been combated in twentieth-century Latin America. A vigorous restatement of racial equality was one feature of the Cuban revolution from 1959 onward, at a time when the Negro element in the country amounted to about twelve percent. The idea of "ethnic democracy" is intimately linked to the Brazilian sense of national identity, and in Brazil, just over ten percent of the population was classified as black in 1950. "Uniquely among the large multi-racial societies of the world," a modern English observer has commented, "Latin America is a society where no one is likely to be killed for his colour alone."[3]

---

[1] Quoted in W. L. Schurz, *Brazil, the Infinite Country* (London, 1962), p. 84.

[2] Herbert S. Klein, *Slavery in the Americas: A Comparative Study of Virginia and Cuba* (London, 1967), p. 226.

[3] J. Halcro Ferguson, *Latin America: the Balance of Race Redressed* (London, 1961), p. 88.

Mestizos, Mulattoes, and the Castes

"Pray, be seated, gentlemen,"—a South American President is said to have requested the Minister of a neighbouring republic known for its predominantly mestizo *population. "But, I am alone, Mr. President." "Oh"—smiled the President—"you people of your country, you are always each at least two."*

SALVADOR DE MADARIAGA

So far we have considered what may be described as the three *primary* ethnic elements in Latin American history. They were clearly distinct from each other, and had radically different origins. It is now necessary to mention the process of miscegenation which introduced further racial elements—this time combinations of the three primary ones—into the population of Latin America. Time has been a great mixer in the region; and by mixing, it has perhaps helped to heal some of the injuries caused by the tumultuous collisions of the three founder-races.

SOME DETERMINANTS

Some sort of process of miscegenation was inevitable from the moment of the conquest onward. The mixing of racial stocks has almost invariably been a feature of colonization movements. In the Latin American case, it was undoubtedly rendered easier by the relative absence, in the Iberian peninsula, of ethnic prejudice of a type which might impede intermarriage (and less regular sexual unions) between the conquerors and the conquered. It is noteworthy, too, that illegitimacy did not carry the kind of stigma in medieval Spain and Portugal that it carried elsewhere in Europe: Iberian history is littered with illustrious bastards. Furthermore, it should be remembered that Don Juan, as well as Don Quixote, is a recognizable Iberian prototype. The vulgar slogan of the 1960s, "Make Love, not War!" would have seemed inappropriate to a sixteenth-century Iberian colonizer, whose motto (had he wished to phrase it as crudely) could well have been "Make War *and* Love!" For the conquistador—as is very evident from the chronicles of the conquest—the two things often went hand in hand.

Whether there existed any psychological predisposition in favor of the Amerindian woman on the part of the European newcomers is a matter which can be, and has been, discussed interminably. The great Brazilian writer Gilberto Freyre suggests such an attraction in the case of the Portuguese:

Long contact with the Saracens had left with the Portuguese the idealized figure of the "enchanted Moorish woman," a charming

143

type, brown-skinned, black-eyed, enveloped in sexual mysticism, roseate in hue, and always engaged in combing out her hair or bathing in rivers or in the waters of haunted fountains; and the Brazilian colonizers were to encounter practically a counterpart of this type in the naked Indian women with their loose-flowing hair. These latter also had dark tresses and dark eyes and bodies painted red, and, like the Moorish Nereids, were extravagantly fond of a river bath to refresh their ardent nudity. . . ."[1]

Whatever the truth of Freyre's view, it is clear that a number of more practical reasons helped to determine the pace and scale of miscegenation in the New World. The Spanish conquest was in the nature of things very largely a masculine adventure. In the early days of settlement, relatively few Spanish women went to America, although the crown made fitful attempts to encourage the conquerors to marry their own kind: a hundred suitable Spanish girls, for instance, were dispatched to Mexico after the conquest. (Not all the women who crossed the Atlantic at that period were married or betrothed to the settlers, or even on the lookout for a husband: in 1526 the imperial government gave permission for the establishment of a brothel in San Juan, Puerto Rico—possibly the first regular institution of this sort in Spanish America.)[2] Individual women, it is true, accompanied the major expeditions of conquest as wives, lovers or camp followers, and sometimes won for themselves a special place in the chronicles of the time. Inés de Suárez, a tough and strong-willed Extremaduran widow who became the mistress of Pedro de Valdivia, must rank as one of the foremost. She took part in an extremely active fashion in the conquest of Chile, even lending a hand with the fighting when occasion demanded.

The case of Inés de Suárez[3] was paralleled by many others. But in numerical terms this did not add up to very much. There were often lengthy delays (sometimes amounting to several years) before Spanish or Portuguese women arrived in the newly founded cities of the Indies. Even when they did finally arrive, it was usually only in small numbers; it is—as usual—impossible to compute an exact figure. The conquerors and their Creole successors had ample opportunity, therefore, to indulge

[1] Gilberto Freyre, *The Masters and the Slaves*, trans. S. Putnam, abridged (New York, 1964), p. 19.

[2] This, in the words of the official authorization, was to preserve "the chastity of the city and of the married women thereof, and to excuse other injuries and inconveniences."

[3] Valdivia was in fact married at the time of his association with Doña Inés. Pedro de la Gasca, royal commissioner in Peru, ordered Valdivia to break off the affair, which he did. Doña Inés married one of his fellow conquerors.

their natural inclinations elsewhere, whether they were attracted to what was available elsewhere or not.

MISCEGENATION: THE MESTIZO

From the mixing of Iberian and Indian there came the *mestizo* (in Brazil the *mestiço*, *caboclo*, or *mameluco*), numerically the strongest of the secondary or composite racial strains of Latin America, and today the predominant strain in many parts of the region. Mestization began from the very first moments of Spanish settlement in the West Indies. How did it occur? Most of the conquerors and colonists took Indian women, many of whom were captured and distributed in the campaigns of the conquest. There were more than a few instances of Indian leaders who gave their daughters to the advancing conquerors. A number of women were presented to Cortés during the conquest of Mexico. (Afterward, some of the Indians who had made the gift asked for them back. Most of the girls, it is interesting to note, refused to go.) Although a good deal of coercion must have accompanied many of these early contacts between Spaniards and Indian women, there were plenty of cases of real affection springing up between men and women of the two races: Hernán Cortés' mistress, the justly celebrated Doña Marina, given to him at Tabasco in 1519, served him with complete devotion, and gave him the cleverest of the four mestizo children he recognized[1] —and he was a very long way from being the only conquistador who relied on an Indian mistress as guide and interpreter. In some regions, Indians showed a distinct readiness to mate with the newcomer. One such region was the coast of Brazil. According to Gilbert Freyre:

> The milieu in which Brazilian life began was one of sexual intoxication. No sooner had the European leaped ashore than he found his feet slipping among the native Indian women, and the very fathers of the Society of Jesus had to take care not to sink into the carnal mire. . . . The women were the first to offer themselves to the whites.[2]

The chronicler Pedro Cieza de León noted (from personal experience) the extreme amorousness of the women of various districts in New Granada and Peru. In some areas, however, the conquistadores complained of the ugliness and frigidity of Indian women; and in the long term they probably preferred Negro women.

[1] This was Martín Cortés, whose Spanish half-brother bore the same name; he later fought in North Africa and Germany.
[2] Freyre, *op. cit.*, p. 83.

Marriages between the conquerors and the conquered were by no means uncommon. The Spanish crown, after some initial hesitation, came down in favor of such mixed marriages and a royal cédula of 1514 made the position clear:

> It is our will that Indians and Indian women should have, as they ought to have, entire liberty to marry whom they like, whether Indians, or natives of these our kingdoms, or Spaniards born in the Indies; and let no impediment be placed in their way.

Both state and Church alike were strongly opposed to irregular unions and enthusiastically in favor of holy matrimony. On occasion, marriage could be used as an instrument of colonization. Governor Ovando, in Hispaniola, ordered the settlers to wed the Indian *cacicas* of the island, and nearly half a century later Pedro de la Gasca, the pacifier of Peru, tried to consolidate a series of alliances between conquistadores and ladies of the Inca nobility, not wholly without success.[1] In its considerable zeal to encourage matrimony, the Spanish crown insisted that all holders of encomiendas should either be married or, if single, should get married within a stipulated period. When tied to an economic incentive such as this, moral exhortations proved reasonably effective. The Church, by dint of constant persuasion, sometimes managed to regularize the morals of its flock. The Jesuit missionary Father Manoel de Nóbrega wrote from Pernambuco in 1551 that most of the Portuguese colonists "have had an Indian woman for a long time, by whom they have had children, and they have held it to be a great infamy to marry them. But now they are marrying and setting up the right kind of life."[2]

But for every mestizo child produced by marriage, dozens came from irregular unions of either a casual or a stable type. Some married conquistadores displayed decided dilatoriness in bringing their wives across from Spain, and most of them took Indian concubines in the meantime. Pedro Cieza de León claimed to have known Spaniards in Peru whose mistresses had borne them upward of fifteen mestizo offspring and whose wives had been waiting fifteen or twenty years in Spain for the summons to America. The holders of encomiendas were in a specially favorable position. Bishop Juan de Zumárraga reported to Charles V from Mexico in 1529 that "many of those who have Indians have taken from the chiefs of their villages their daughters,

---

[1] There was at least one case of an Inca prince marrying a Spanish lady: a grandson of Huayna Capac married an Extremaduran.

[2] Freyre, *op. cit.*, p. 83.

sisters, nieces and wives, under pretext of taking them to their homes as servants but in reality for concubines."[1] In 1570 it was reported of one encomendero in Quito that he "is always living in concubinage and normally he has five or six Indian or negro concubines, pregnant or who have given birth."[2] These examples must be regarded as fairly typical.

At the time of the conquest at least, mestizos were sometimes created on an almost heroic scale. Two picturesque cases may be cited here. The first is that of Francisco de Aguirre (1508–81), one of the conquerors of Chile and for a time the governor of Tucumán. Aguirre was a more than life-sized figure. He *recognized* at least fifty mestizo children as his own, and there may have been many more. At one stage of his rumbustious career he was accused by the ecclesiastical authorities of having sustained a large number of heretical propositions, one of which was that "the service rendered to God in engendering *mestizos* is greater than the sin incurred in so doing."[3] The second case that can be mentioned is that of Domingo Martínez de Irala and the founders of Paraguay. Irala, the first governor of the colony, at Asunción, recognized (in his will) the offspring of at least six Indian concubines, mostly his servants. His behavior in this respect was no different from that of his fellow colonizers. A shocked priest reported from Asunción in 1545, less than a decade after the start of the colony, that a number of Spaniards there had "seventy women; unless a man is poor," he added, "he never goes below five or six; and the greater part have fifteen or twenty or twenty to forty."[4] It is scarcely surprising that the Paraguayan colony very soon gained the reputation of being a kind of Moslem paradise on earth. Governor Irala himself is known by Paraguayans as the Father of the Nation; he was certainly the father of a substantial part of it.

Concubinage as a familiar institution persisted throughout the colonial period (and beyond). There is some evidence for supposing that sexual morality was looser in the Indies than it was in the Iberian peninsula. A seventeenth-century president of the Audiencia of Quito was charged with having enjoyed "lewd relations with much publicity with many women after he became President, married, widows, and those enjoying the reputation of virgins, living with them in con-

---

[1] Quoted in C. E. Marshall, "The Birth of the Mestizo in New Spain," *Hispanic American Historical Review*, XIX (1939), 179.

[2] Quoted in Rosenblat, *La población indigena y el mestizaje en América*, II, 81.

[3] Thomás Thayer Ojeda, "Francisco de Aguirre," *Revista chilena de historia y geografía*, No. 64 (1929), p. 31. Aguirre was obliged to retract this and numerous other brash statements in a religious ceremony in 1569.

[4] Quoted in Rosenblat, *La población indigena y el mestizaje en América*, II, 110.

cubinage and thus causing scandal and creating an unfortunate example."[1] His record was a common one. There need be little mystery, then, as to the origins of the numerous race of mestizos. Well before the close of the sixteenth century, their weight of numbers was causing concern to the imperial authorities, and the social and legal status of the mestizo was being lowered. The first generation of mestizos in Spanish America contained several truly illustrious names: Martín Cortés, Diego de Almagro the Younger, Diego Muñoz de Camargo, Father Blas Valera, Juan de Betanzos, Ruy Díaz de Guzmán, and many others achieved well-deserved fame as soldiers or scholars. The most outstanding mestizo of this early period, perhaps, was the Inca Garcilaso de la Vega, the son of a Spanish conquistador and a niece of the Inca emperor Huayna Capac. His *Royal Commentaries of the Incas* and other works placed him in the highest rank of colonial historians.

But the well-born mestizo, legitimized by his Spanish father and perhaps inheriting some of his wealth, was far outnumbered by a great mass of his poorer fellows. By the start of the seventeenth century, the Spanish authorities were expressing fears as to the degree of loyalty to be expected from this growing—and often turbulent—mestizo population. Viceroy Martín Enríquez of Mexico was probably correct, however, when he wrote, in 1574, that "although many of them lead bad lives and have bad customs, when all is said and done they are the sons of Spaniards . . . and must always follow the Spanish party."[2] In many ways the mestizo was indispensable to the advance of Iberian colonization in the New World. The second foundation of Buenos Aires, in 1580, was very largely a mestizo achievement. In the seventeenth century the heroic São Paulo bandeiras which explored the Brazilian hinterland were composed principally of mestiços or mamelucos.

By the end of the colonial period, mestizos already represented a formidable component in Latin American society. In the viceroyalty of New Spain, for instance, they accounted for rather more than a third of the population. Psychologically, they had inherited elements from both their ancestries, as the amusing anecdote placed at the beginning of this section would tend to indicate. Culturally, however, the Iberian element came to predominate. In many areas, mestization amounted in effect to hispanization. The process was to some extent reversed (though only on an insignificant scale) in a few outlying territories: in Chile, for instance, where Araucanian Indians sometimes carried off Spanish women in raids, a few wholly "indianized" mestizos grew up

[1] J. L. Phelan, *The Kingdom of Quito in the Seventeenth Century* (Madison, Wis., 1967), p. 184.
[2] Quoted in Rosenblat, *La población indígena y el mestizaje en América*, II, 65.

behind the Indian "frontier." Elsewhere some distinctive Indian characteristics were able to retain their force even when the process of mestization was complete. The population of Paraguay today is very largely mestizo: but it is a mestizo population that speaks the Guaraní language as well as Spanish.

MISCEGENATION: THE MULATTO

Second only in importance to the mestizo among the composite ethnic strains of Latin America is the mulatto, the result of the mixing of Iberian and African. There is a certain amount of evidence that the attractiveness of the Indian woman was surpassed by that of the African as far as the Iberian colonizer was concerned. The dark-skinned woman seems to have enjoyed an excellent reputation as a source of erotic satisfactions. As a popular jingle from the Mato Grosso has it:

> *Moça morena é quitute,*
> *Moça branca é canja fria.*
> "A dark girl is a delicious tidbit
> A white one like cold chicken soup!"

The mulatto emerged as a distinctive strain as soon as the first Africans reached the New World, and in precisely those regions where Negro slavery was most firmly established as an institution: the Caribbean and Brazil. The pattern of the Iberians' relations with African women was not substantially different from the one outlined in the case of the mestizo. Concubinage applied to the African as well as the Indian, and it appeared almost as early on the stage of colonial life. Writing from Salvador at the end of the 1550s, the indefatigable Father Nóbrega observed that "nearly all" the Portuguese colonists, "married and unmarried alike, are living in concubinage with their Negro women . . . and there are priests who are free with their absolutions and who live in the same manner." On another occasion the Jesuit reported: "The people of the land are living in a state of mortal sin, and there is no one but has many Negro women, who bear them many children, and this is a great evil."[1] Evil or not, it was a fact. The mulatto soon became as familiar a sight as the mestizo.

Several writers have commented on the interesting fact that miscegenation in colonial Brazil proceeded faster, and was more widespread, than in the other overseas colonies of Portugal. The institution of slavery undoubtedly had a great deal to do with this. The connections between the "big house" and the "slave quarters" on the Brazilian

[1] Freyre, *op. cit.,* pp. 376–77.

plantations were not solely economic, but also sexual. Who acted as wet-nurse for the Brazilian planter in his childhood? A slave. Who sexually initiated him? A slave. With whom did he indulge in extra-marital dalliance in later life? Slaves. The standards of morality in colonial Brazil obviously left a great deal to be desired. Priests and members of the religious orders—with the notable exception of the Jesuits—took Negro women. As Freyre puts it, in his usual exuberant fashion, "in place of ascetics austerely concerned with their vows of virginity there flourished formidable stallions in clerical garb." The tale of the Jesuit who asked a congregation for a "Hail Mary for the Bishop's woman, who is in labour" may or may not be apocryphal, but, in this context at least, seems far from incredible.[1]

In the Spanish empire, so Humboldt found, mulattoes were "distinguished for the violence of their passions and a singular volubility of tongue."[2] Nevertheless, at least one mulatto won outstanding renown in colonial times. Father Martín de Porres (1579–1639), a religious of Lima, was recognized in his own lifetime as a man of great holiness of character, and the Catholic Church later confirmed this verdict; he was beatified in 1837 and canonized in 1962. In Brazil, the greatest sculptor and architect of the colonial period was a mulatto: Antonio Francisco Lisboa, known as O Aleijadinho, who overcame the crippling effects of leprosy to produce the fine churches and sculptures still to be seen in the old mining towns of Minas Gerais.

THE CASTE SYSTEM

One further combination of the races should be mentioned at this point. This was the mixing of African and Indian, which produced the *zambo* (in Spanish America) or *cafuso* (in Brazil). The Spanish crown was opposed to this particular mixture, and attempts were made to discourage concubinage. They failed, largely because the African proved extremely attractive to Indian women. But official displeasure meant that the zambo was placed in an unenviable social position. The imperial authorities seem to have been even warier of zambos than of other mixed bloods. As early as the later sixteenth century, López de Velasco described them as "the worst and vilest people there are in these lands," and this was a common reaction. Even so, it was from the ranks of the zambos that there came, in the eighteenth century, the outstanding intellectual of the Presidency of Quito—Francisco Eugenio de Santa Cruz y Espejo (1747–95), a precursor of the independence movement.

[1] *Ibid.*, p. 391.
[2] Humboldt, *op. cit.*, I, 244.

Iberians, Indians, Africans—these, as we have seen, were the three founder-races. Mestizos, mulattoes, zambos—these can be regarded as the three main secondary strains. From these six there came every conceivable mixture, every imaginable variation of bloods and, particularly in the Spanish empire, an exuberant nomenclature was developed to cope with this immense profusion of racial combinations. As many as fifty-three different names, covering almost as many distinctive mixtures, have been identified.[1] Mestizos, mulattoes, and zambos, and the further variations derived from them and from the three primary strains, were known as *castas de mezcla* ("mixed castes") or sometimes just "the castes," even though the three primary strains were also castes. Iberian colonial society attached great importance to these distinctions. I must conclude the present section by mentioning some aspects of this. The discussion is confined to the Spanish empire at this point; for, in practice, the Portuguese empire in Brazil was neither as systematic nor as thorough, nor, indeed, as consistent, although its underlying social principles were similar.

The earliest caste distinctions in the Spanish empire were the obvious ones affecting Spaniards (peninsular or Creole), Indians (the "protected" subject-race) and Africans (the great majority of whom were slaves). Mestizos, in the early decades of colonization, had the same rights as their Spanish fathers. But as the mixed castes grew larger— and since they were nearly all to be found in the lowest social strata— legislation was introduced to regulate the status, the duties, the office-holding opportunities, the tax obligations and (in some instances) even the dress of the different racial elements. Colonial functionaries were told to watch over the conduct of these groups. Royal cédulas at the start of the seventeenth century pointed out that the number of mestizos, mulattoes, and zambos was growing very fast, and that the crown wished the viceregal authorities to ensure that "men of such mixtures, and so vicious most of them, should not cause trouble and damage in the kingdom."[2] The system of castes which operated in the

---

[1] Some of these names were picturesque, but there is space for only a few examples. The son of a zambo and a mulatto, for instance, was known as a *calpanmulato*; if the calpanmulato crossed with another zambo, the child was called a *tente en el aire* ("hold-yourself-in-the-air"), signifying that the racial balance was undisturbed; the offspring of a tente en el aire and a mulatto was styled a *no te entiendo* ("I-don't-understand-you"); if a no te entiendo married an Indian woman, the result was known as an *ahi te estás* ("there-you-are"). A Spaniard and a mulatto produced what was known as a *morisco*; if the morisco then mated with a mulatto, implying a darkening of the offspring, the result was called a *salt-atrás* ("jump-backwards"). These terms seem to have varied considerably as between regions and possibly as between different periods. See Rosenblat, *La población indigena y el mestizaje – América*, II, 168–79.

[2] S de Madariaga, *op. cit.*, p. 123.

Spanish empire was in no sense as rigid or as all-embracing as the Hindu system. Nevertheless, it was assumed in theory and practice alike that a man's place in society could be clearly related to his "color."

In the eighteenth century at Cartagena in New Granada, the travelers Juan and Ulloa found that

> Every person is so jealous of the order of their tribe or caste, that if, through inadvertence, you call them by a degree lower than what they actually are, they are highly offended, never suffering themselves to be deprived of so valuable a gift of fortune.[1]

The uppermost rungs of the caste ladder were occupied by the *blancos* (the whites), the peninsular and Creole Spaniards. The Negro slave occupied the lowest rungs. It was hardly surprising, therefore, that "the greater or less degree of whiteness of skin," as Humboldt put it,[2] decided a man's social status. But this should not lead us into supposing that a South African-style "color bar" existed in the Spanish empire. Although the Spaniard laid great stress on his *limpieza de sangre,* his "cleanliness of blood," this was in some ways as much a *social* as a *racial* emphasis. Many Creoles were really mestizos, even if their Indian blood had become very attenuated; and it was always possible for someone of mixed blood to be certified as "white" by the courts. *Que se tenga por blanco* ("Let him be considered a white") was a common legal verdict in colonial days—and, as Humboldt urbanely observed, "these declaration are not always corroborated by the judgement of the senses."[3]

Despite this, there *were* numerous instances, throughout the colonial era, of racial (or was it social?) prejudice. Two examples must suffice here. In 1763 some Spanish volunteers in the militia at Huancavelica (Peru) objected to having to march alongside mestizos; their protest was upheld. In the reign of King Charles IV, the municipal council of Lima petitioned the king to remove the caste restrictions on a talented *mulato prieto* (i.e., the son of a mulatto and an Indian). The man concerned became a distinguished professor of medicine in the university. Nevertheless, the attempt he subsequently made to enter holy orders was successfully blocked by the local ecclesiastical authorities. Cases of this type were frequent.

Only the coming of independence demolished the kind of legal structure that sanctioned social superiority on racial grounds. The revolutionary governments of Spanish America abolished caste dis-

[1] Juan and Ulloa, *op. cit.*, I, 32.
[2] Humboldt, *op. cit.*, I, 246.
[3] *Ibid.*, I, 247.

tinctions at more or less the same time, and for more or less the same reasons, that they removed the colonial laws relating to the Indians. In economic terms, even in psychological terms, this may have signified relatively little for the groups concerned. But many more mestizos, mulattoes, and zambos—not to mention the more subtle mixtures with their exotic names—were now able to rise in the social scale than had been possible in colonial times. As for the long process of miscegenation, it continued inexorably throughout the nineteenth century, and it continues today. It will continue tomorrow—and this is one of the very few certain statements that can be made about the future of Latin America.

The Completion of the Ethnic Pattern

> God bless the just Republics
> That give a man a home. . . .
> RUDYARD KIPLING

There remained, at the time of independence, one major group of people still to arrive in Latin America: the nineteenth- and twentieth-century immigrants. Three countries in particular were very deeply influenced by mass migration from Europe: Argentina, Brazil, and Uruguay. Most of this migration occurred in the last three decades of the nineteenth century and the first three of the twentieth, after which a period of restrictions and quotas set in, bringing truly large-scale movements of population into the region to a halt.

Between roughly 1830 and 1930 or so, something in the neighborhood of sixty million Europeans migrated from the Old World. About forty million of them stayed permanently in the countries to which they had flocked. Where did the sixty million settle? Thirty-four million went to the booming United States; no other country attracted anything like this amazing total. But Latin America also proved a fairly popular destination. Argentina registered the arrival of no less than 6,405,000 newcomers between 1856 and 1932; Brazil took 4,431,000 between 1821 and 1932; and between 1836 and 1932 modest Uruguay received 713,000. The remaining Latin American states took few in comparison.

Nowhere in the nineteenth-century Latin America was the encouragement of immigration more enthusiastic than in the Argentine Republic. It was a key aspect of the political program of the brilliant generation of liberal exiles that fought the long dictatorship of Rosas. Argentina, the exiles reasoned, was an empty land. Bring in the European, and it could be filled and modernized at one and the same time. Immigration, in short, was the key to national development. In the Argentine case, the main task of any government was to encourage population growth.

"To govern is to *populate*"—so ran the immortal phrase of Juan Bautista Alberdi. "Every European who comes to our shores" wrote Alberdi, "brings us more civilization in the habits which he spreads immediately to our people that many books of philosophy. . . . A hard-working man is the most edifying catechism. . . . The government that does not double the census every ten years has wasted its time on trifles."[1] The Argentine Constitution of 1853, which embodied so many of the ideals of exiles like Alberdi, stated in its preamble that its main purpose was to "assure the benefits of liberty to us, to our posterity, and to *all men on earth who wish to live on Argentine soil.*"[2]

This generous attitude was soon rewarded. What had been a mere trickle of immigrants soon became a stream, and presently swelled into a mighty inundation. In the 1880s, well over six hundred thousand people from overseas settled permanently in Argentina. The 1880s saw a recession, but the first decade of the twentieth century produced over a million new residents, and the total was again high in the 1920s, after a drop caused by World War I. Between 1840 and 1940, it has been estimated, nearly seven and a half million immigrants entered Argentina, and rather more than half of them stayed there. Of those who did not, many were laborers who arrived in time for the harvests and sailed away with their savings at the end of the season: these were known as *golondrinas* ("swallows").

The Argentine population rose from 1,800,000 in 1869 to 8,000,000 in 1914 and 16,000,000 in 1947. Over the period 1840–1940, it has been estimated, the growth in the population was accounted for in the following way: twenty-nine percent of the increase was due to immigration, forty percent to births resulting from immigration, and thirty-one percent to births independent of immigration.[3] Another very careful estimate illustrates the impact of migration even more dramatically: "In the absence of international migration, the population [of Argentina] would have been approximately 27 percent smaller than it actually was in 1895, 46 percent smaller in 1914, and 52 and 55 percent smaller respectively in 1947 and 1960."[4]

[1] Quoted in W. R. Crawford, *A Century of Latin American Thought* (Cambridge, Mass., 1963), p. 23.
[2] Italics added. Art. 20 of the constitution gave foreigners the same civil rights as citizens and allowed them to become naturalized after only two years. Art. 25 gave the federal government the specific task of fomenting "European migration."
[3] Marcel R. Reinhard and André Armengaud, *Histoire générale de la population mondiale* (Paris, 1961), p. 352.
[4] Z. L. Recchini de Larres, "Demographic Consequences of International Migratory Movements in the Argentine Republic 1870-1960," in *Proceedings of the World Population Conference, Belgrade . . . 1965*, Vol. IV (New York, United Nations, 1967), p. 212.

The *speed* at which immigration took place also had some extraordinary consequences. In 1914 three tenths of the Argentine population had been born abroad. Among males aged twenty or over, foreigners accounted for fifty-two percent. In Buenos Aires there were almost three foreigners over twenty for every native-born Argentine of similar age. These proportions were very much higher than the equivalent proportions in the history of the United States, where the numbers of the foreign-born in relation to the total population had reached a peak a little earlier.

Nearly half the total migration to Argentina was Italian in origin. Just under a third was Spanish. The remainder was made up of Russians, Eastern Europeans, and Frenchmen, together with a number of very small groups of "elite migrants." (These groups will be mentioned presently.) The high percentage of "Latin" Europeans in the general stream of migration signified a relatively easy process of assimilation, although by sheer weight of numbers alone the newcomers were bound to alter the Argentine national character even while becoming acclimatized themselves. The Italians, for instance, brought with them their own cuisine. Their intonations influenced the distinctive River Plate variant of Spanish. But the resulting culture was fiercely Argentine rather than Italian. The French statesman Clemenceau, who visited Argentina in the early twentieth century, was impressed by the ease with which the adjustment was made. He wrote: "You ask a child, the son of an immigrant, whether he speaks Italian or Spanish. He answers haughtily, 'At home we all talk Argentine.' "[1]

The pattern of migration to Argentina was repeated across the estuary in Uruguay, though necessarily on a much smaller scale. (At no time since independence, it is worth remembering, has the total population of Uruguay surpassed that of the city of Buenos Aires.) Once again, Italians formed the main component. As we have seen, approximately three quarters of a million foreigners entered Uruguay between 1836 and 1932: the republic's *net* gain was probably rather less than half a million over the same period, though this was more than enough to have a drastic impact on the growth of the population.

In the case of Brazil, the persistence of slavery until a late date acted as an impediment to mass immigration, although the governments of the empire were consistently interested in stimulating this. Once slavery had disappeared, the numbers of migrants entering the country grew very rapidly. Italy supplied the largest contingent: 1,500,000 between 1820 and 1935. The city and state of São Paulo was the principal area of Italian settlement. Second came Portugal, which provided

[1] Georges Clemenceau, *South America Today* (London, 1911), p. 76.

1,400,000 over the same period, and Spanish migration to Brazil was also considerable (approximately 600,000). Of the several numerically smaller groups, the Germans (215,000 in the same span of time) were the most important; they settled extensively as colonists in the states of Paraná, Santa Catarina, and Rio Grande do Sul. Their first colony dated from 1824. The Germans were assimilated less rapidly than the immigrants from Latin Europe. They retained a greater attachment to their mother tongue, and, until forced to desist by the Vargas government in the 1930s, were in some cases eager to maintain a separate educational system for their children. (It is interesting, however, that these characteristics were much more pronounced among German Protestants than among German Catholics.)

The impact of immigration on Brazil was undoubtedly smaller than it was in the Argentine and Uruguayan cases. The Brazilian population was already large at the time immigration began on a massive scale (over seventeen million in 1900). Its chief effect was not so much in building up the numerical strength of the country as in accelerating changes in the ethnic balance *within* the country. The imperial census of 1872 revealed the following racial composition: thirty-eight percent white; twenty percent black; forty-two percent mixed (and Indian). Nearly eighty years later, after the effects of mass immigration had been largely absorbed, the census of 1950 showed a somewhat different combination: 61.6 percent white; 10.9 percent black; 25.6 percent mixed; one percent Indians. From being a minority, the European element had become the majority, and the role of large-scale immigration was an important one in bringing this about.

Outside Argentina, Brazil, and Uruguay, immigration to most Latin American countries since independence has to be measured in tens of thousands rather than hundreds of thousands. Nevertheless, two further countries should be briefly mentioned at this point: Cuba and Venezuela. Cuba received 857,000 immigrants in the years between 1901 and 1932. The vast majority of these were Spaniards, and very many of them sooner or later returned to their native land. Even so, over five hundred thousand residents in Cuba in the mid-1930s were classified as Spaniards, although this may well have been something of an exaggeration. Since World War II, Venezuela has taken active steps to foster immigration. By the close of the 1950s over half a million residents in the country were foreign-born: just under a third of these were Italians, just over a quarter Spaniards. Despite this flurry of migration to Venezuela, and despite the fact that there is still a stream of migrants to Brazil and Argentina, mass migration would appear to be a thing of the past. The most recent large-scale movement of population—

involving several hundreds of thousands of men and women—has been *emigratory*: the Cuban revolution was responsible for the self-exile of many who felt unable to reconcile themselves to the new order in the island.

As we have seen, Italians, Spaniards, and Portuguese made up the great bulk of foreign migration to Latin America in the nineteenth and early twentieth centuries. In general, they went as laborers, share-croppers, small-time traders. Other—very much smaller—European migrant groups went into what would nowadays be termed "managerial" positions, often in enterprises financed by or controlled from the country of their origin. Of these "elite migratory groups," as they have been called, Germans, French, and British were the most significant. Quite apart from those Germans who settled in large numbers as farmers in southern Brazil (or in the south of Chile), there were others who later established themselves in all the major cities of Latin America, though in greatest numbers to the southern South American republics. Small French and British colonies of the same type were to be found all over Latin America well before the close of the nineteenth century. Of these three groups, it is probably fair to say that the British were assimilated least easily into the Latin environment: several thousands of Anglo-Argentines, Anglo-Brazilians, Anglo-Uruguayans, and Anglo-Chileans still survive as a not-so-mute testimony to this fact.[1]

Non-European migration to Latin America (leaving aside the primordial journeys of the Amerindians) has never been very considerable. Chinese laborers were used on railway-building in nineteenth-century Peru; they were also employed in the guano industry. As a result, Chinese-Peruvians of several generations' standing continue to flourish in Lima and other cities. In Cuba, too, there was a small but long-established Chinese colony, amounting to perhaps one percent of the island's population in 1959. This, however, appears to have declined since the 1959 revolution. Japanese migration has been somewhat more extensive. Starting in 1908, there has been an intermittent movement of Japanese to Brazil: by the time of World War II there were perhaps as many as two hundred and fifty thousand there, many of them in agriculture. Japanese colonists have also settled (more recently and in very much smaller numbers) in the eastern lowlands of Bolivia since the 1952 revolution; and in 1959 the Stroessner government in Paraguay

[1] The size of these smaller migratory groups is best indicated in percentage form. Taking gross immigration to Argentina (1857–1926) as the basis: 47.3 percent of all immigrants were Italians, 32.2 percent Spaniards, 4 percent French, 1.9 percent Germans, 1.7 percent British; the remaining 12.9 percent was accounted for very largely by Central and Eastern Europeans and Russians (including many Jews).

agreed to admit a total of eighty-five thousand settlers from Japan over the next thirty years.

One other non-European migrant group which has had particular commercial importance must be mentioned here: the *turcos* ("Turks") as they are generically (though not altogether accurately) styled in Latin America. Most of them were (or are) Syrians and Lebanese, with contingents from other parts of the Levant.[1] Their acumen and drive enabled them to establish highly successful businesses—in general, small retail businesses—throughout the region. After two or three generations some of these businesses are very far from small. Several major industrialists in modern Latin America are turcos; and the Levantine shopkeeper is still a familiar sight in most, if not all, of the twenty republics.

One by one the various ethnic elements which have helped to form the Latin America of today have taken their place. The Indian was there at the start. He was joined by the Iberian, and the Iberian brought the African. From the mixing of these three primary elements came the whole range of the "castes" of colonial days. In the nineteenth and twentieth centuries, mass immigration provided a further important element, mostly Latin, in certain countries. What has been the outcome of these ethnic changes and movements? The panorama is rich—and also varied. It may be helpful to consider, if only briefly, the regional variations in the ethnic pattern of Latin America today.

The twenty republics may be said to fall into four main groups: (1) "Indian" countries; (2) "mestizo" countries; (3) "white" countries; (4) "Negro/mulatto" countries. By an "Indian" country is meant a country where the Indian element is the *single main element* in the pattern of the races. Four republics may properly be classified as preponderantly Indian, with the remainder of their population mostly accounted for by mestizos. These are: Bolivia (fifty-five percent Indians, thirty percent mestizos), Guatemala (roughly the same percentages), Peru (forty percent/thirty-five percent), and Ecuador (forty percent/thirty percent). In all of these countries, the Indian population not only shows no signs of diminishing, but seems likely to survive as a separate element in society.

The second group—of mestizo countries—is by far the largest. In Mexico and Central America (except for Guatemala), mestizos account for well over fifty percent of the population: at least sixty percent in Mexico, and rising to eighty percent in Honduras. Mexico, of course,

[1] Areas which were, at the time this migration began, subject to the Turkish empire, hence, probably, the name by which these groups are known in Latin America.

has a substantial Indian minority. In northern South America, both Colombia and Venezuela have mestizo majorities (amounting to sixty-five percent or so in each case). Chile displays a not dissimilar pattern—though the Negro and mulatto element present in northern South America is missing there. In Paraguay, mestizos account for over seventy percent of the population.

The "white" countries (i.e., those whose people are mostly of pure European stock) fall into two groups: those which are overwhelmingly white, and those which are only preponderantly so. Argentina and Uruguay fall squarely into the first group; indeed, Uruguay is often described as being the "whitest" country in the American continent. In Costa Rica and Cuba, the white element accounts for well over seventy percent of the population. In the Costa Rican case, the remaining minority is mostly mestizo; in Cuba this is replaced by an important Negro and mulatto element. Brazil is more problematic; it could also be considered a "white" country, though nearly forty percent of its population consists of Negroes and mixed bloods (mostly mulattoes), and the sheer *size* of the Brazilian population makes this doubly significant. In many ways Brazil deserves to figure separately in any such classification as the present one, and some writers would unhesitatingly place her in the ranks of the mestizo countries. As one Brazilian scholar has put it:

> Despite the fact that two-thirds of the population is now classified white, Aryanization may not be inferred—that would be an absurdity, for the standard of whiteness is one that would not be used in Europe, North America, or South Africa, including as it does large numbers of light-skinned mestizos. Ethnically and culturally we are a Republic of Mestizos.[1]

It is clear from this that Brazil cannot be unequivocally assigned to the "white" group of countries, and is at least a candidate for membership of the mestizo group.

Finally, the fourth group. It is the smallest, and consists of only two republics. Haiti is overwhelmingly Negro, probably to the extent of ninety-five percent, while the rest of the population is made up of mulattoes. The neighboring Dominican Republic is preponderantly mulatto.

[1] José Honório Rodrigues, *Brazil and Africa*, trans. R. A. Mazzara and S. Hileman, (Berkeley and Los Angeles, 1965), p. 101.

Chapter 4

SOCIAL AND ECONOMIC DEVELOPMENT
TO 1860

The rhythms of social and economic history are frequently rather different from those of political history. That the two sets of rhythms are connected and interdependent seems obvious to most historians, although the precise nature of the connection is a matter of permanent and fascinating debate rather than of hard-and-fast conclusions. In the case of Latin America, there is some reason to suppose that the underlying patterns of social and economic life have proved unusually resilient and tenacious in the four and a half centuries that separate Hernán Cortés from Fidel Castro. It is these underlying social and economic patterns that will concern us in the present chapter and in the chapter that follows. There are, perhaps, some general observations which deserve to be made at the outset.

One or two things strike one immediately in examining the record of continuity and change in Latin American social and economic history. The first is what might be called the persistence of a strongly aristocratic and hierarchical tradition. Nearly everywhere in the region, an aristocracy based on (or at least closely associated with) the ownership of landed property has occupied the key position in the social order right up to the present day or at any rate up till the fairly recent past. This tradition was fixed in a stubborn mold in the colonial period, and it remained intact (indeed, was probably reinforced) in the era of the Creole states that followed; the pressure of twentieth-century social and economic changes has to some extent modified, and in one or two cases actually broken, the original mold, but it survives in one form or another in more than a few of the modern republics. It is in this sense that Latin America can be said to be a profoundly stable and conservative region, despite its long-standing reputation for revolutionary turmoil and political upheaval.

A second consideration that should be borne in mind in reading the account which follows is the way in which the connections between Latin America and the outside world have affected the shape of the social order and the economy in every successive period. Latin America was created, as we have seen, by a powerful and irreversible impulse of conquest and colonization. Iberian imperialism dictated the main social and economic configurations of colonial times; these were conditioned and maintained by the dynamics of colonial dependence as well as by the autonomous, internal development of colonial life. The Spanish and Portuguese empires in the New World lasted three centuries; the effects of imperial rule went deep. Independence brought relatively little change to the underlying Latin American patterns, though more than has sometimes been assumed. Later in the nineteenth century (as will be seen in Chapter 5) the Creole nation-states were incorporated into the new international economic system of the period in a way which permitted external forces and conditions to continue to exert a major influence on the internal development of the region.

This particular feature has led some modern historians to describe the more recent phases of Latin American social and economic history as essentially "neo-colonial" in character. It would be difficult to deny an element of justice to this view, and for that reason it needs to be singled out here. But at the same time it would be wrong (as well as simpleminded) to attribute everything in the shape and form of the Latin American social order to the pressure of external impulses. Such impulses do not work in isolation. They act upon what is already there. In fact, the aristocratic, hierarchical social tradition which has been mentioned—itself the product of the initial imperialist impulse—can be seen to have adapted itself without undue difficulty to many of the outside pressures experienced by the region. An awareness of the fact of colonial or "neo-colonial" dependence is not the only key to Latin American social and economic history. It is one among several. Others will be suggested or at least hinted at in the present chapter: the geographical (and, in colonial times, legal) isolation of Latin America; the ubiquitous and pervasive influences of church and state; the singularly noteworthy domination of the countryside by the city; the way in which ethnic differences can be seen to have sharpened conventional social divisions; and so on. The object of the present chapter (and of Chapter 5) is to present a general impression of the most salient features of the social and economic development of Latin America. If the reader can discover a single, fundamental explanation for all these various features—a single melody above the different rhythms—he is almost certainly wiser or more perceptive than I can claim to be.

The European Invasions

Immediately on landing, Cortés repaired to the house of the governor, to whom he had been personally known in Spain. Ovando was absent on an expedition into the interior, but the young man was kindly received by the secretary, who assured him there would be no doubt of his obtaining a liberal grant of land to settle on. "But I came to get gold," replied Cortés, "not to till the soil, like a peasant."

W. H. PRESCOTT

Spanish imperialism was for the most part Castilian imperialism. Of the two kingdoms linked together by the Catholic Monarchs, Castile was the larger (with a population of around six million as against Aragon's one million) and the more dynamic. It was Castile, not Aragon, which mounted the invasion of America.[1] The dominant themes of Castilian history at the time of Columbus' voyages were the emergence of a confident and powerful central government, and the re-emergence of the age-old "tradition of conquest" referred to in Chapter 3. The Castilian state successfully curbed its turbulent aristocracy and, with equal success, harnessed the tradition of conquest to new and rewarding enterprises overseas. The drive southward into Andalusia during the Reconquest, the subjugation of the Kingdom of Granada, and the colonization of the Canary Islands—these expansionist ventures had taught Castilians some of the methods and techniques of their later imperialism: not least, the carving out of great estates worked by a semi-servile labor force, and (in Granada and the Canaries) the rapid imposition of settled institutions by the central government. These features of the medieval tradition of conquest were soon to be reproduced on an altogether vaster scale in the New World. Castilian imperialism spelled conquest. Portuguese imperialism, by contrast, tended to spell commerce. Ever since the rise of the Avis dynasty in the 1380s, the Portuguese monarchy had been markedly responsive to the powerful merchant interest of Lisbon. The career of Prince Henry the Navigator and the exploration of the African coastline testify to the high regard in which commerce was held by the royal government. As a result, the pattern of Portuguese imperialism in the sixteenth century was strikingly different from that of Spain. Based on a network of trading centers and staging posts in Africa and Asia, the Portuguese empire was territorially insignificant. The Spanish empire was not. Individual Spaniards dreamed of landed fiefs and vassals to underpin an aristocratic way of life. The Spanish state soon came to emphasize the exploitation of

[1] At first, only Castilians were permitted to migrate to the Indies; but the restrictions on Aragonese were modified in 1506 and removed altogether by the close of Philip II's reign.

mineral resources as a means of financing the crown in its various activities in Europe. For these particular purposes, control of territory was obviously vital. The contrast is an important one, and deserves to be stressed. In the earliest period of European colonization in the New World, Portugal's main territorial acquisition was incorporated into the empire in a very half-hearted manner—as the thirty-year gap between Cabral's initial discovery of Brazil and its first formal colonization tends to show rather clearly.

Despite its centralizing ambitions, the Spanish crown on its own was not able to plan, finance, or organize the expeditions of conquest which followed the discovery of the West Indian islands. Such ventures were well beyond its capacities. In general colonization had to be the work of individual enterprise, of individual conquistadores and their small private armies of followers. But it was, of course, individual enterprise regulated and controlled by the central government. The characteristic means of regulation and control was the contract, or *capitulación*, drawn up between the crown and the would-be conqueror. The terms of such capitulaciones varied from case to case; but common to all of them was an insistence that the state had certain basic rights to be recognized and observed by individuals responsible for the expedition of conquest. The spreading of the Christian religion was invariably insisted on, as was the ultimate right of royal control over the territory to be invaded. In return, the conqueror was guaranteed the right to enjoy the spoils of conquest; he was granted the right to exercise the government of the new territory, at least temporarily; and he sometimes qualified for a title or similar honor. Approximately seventy contracts of this type were drawn up.

The first contract to colonize America which concerns us was, of course, awarded to Christopher Columbus. It gave him considerably greater authority, and notably higher status, than was commonly to be the case with his successors. This situation was not allowed to develop. Columbus' powers, and the powers to which his family was entitled, were systematically eroded almost from the beginning. The family campaigned for many years to recover what they considered to be their legal rights; they were eventually bought off in 1536 with titles, an estate in Panama, a healthy annuity, and the island of Jamaica. After the original episode with Columbus, the crown narrowed the scope of the contracts concluded with the conquerors, and made certain that the normal agents of the central government—royal officials, not to mention the Catholic Church—followed as quickly as possible on the heels of the valiant adventurers who opened up the newly discovered territories. This final point is one to which we shall have to return.

The conquistadores themselves were by no means representative of the highest levels of Spanish society. The upper aristocracy had no particular wish (or need) to leave its estates in Spain, though later on it saw advantages in accepting viceregal office in the colonies. For the most part, the conquistadores were drawn from the fairly numerous *hidalgo* class: the Spanish equivalent, in some respects, of the English "gentry." Sometimes they were hidalgos' impecunious younger sons; occasionally their social origins were less exalted. But whatever their peninsular background, these extraordinary men shared a common psychology, a psychology conditioned by the essentially military experience of the Spanish Middle Ages. Merit, honor, wealth, social prestige—these things had traditionally been *won* rather than worked for systematically; the psychology of the conquerors was a non-commercial psychology. This did not mean that it was noneconomic, or that economic motivations played no part in the conquest of America. It certainly did not mean that effort as such was despised; but it was *military* effort, *heroic* effort, the winning of *honor* that was exalted; the hard and continuous grind of manual labor was regarded as beneath the dignity of any sane and right-thinking conqueror. The idea that it was in any sense the duty of the invaders to settle down and themselves to become farmers was alien and unwelcome. This psychological characteristic was to have immense consequences.

Much has been written on the motivations of the conquistadores, a good deal of it fanciful. It is perfectly fair to regard the love of adventure in itself as one of the discernible motives. Loyalty to the crown, and the belief that it was a solemn duty to win territory for Spain, also played a part. Religious zeal—the desire to incorporate the heathen populations of America into the fold of the universal Church—must also have been a more than merely formal consideration for more than a handful of the conquerors. In the opening chapter of his account of the conquest of Mexico, Bernal Díaz del Castillo tells us that he had "always had the zeal of a good soldier, which I was obliged to have in order to serve God and our lord the king, and to try to win honour, which is the way noble men *should* seek life." We can accept the patent sincerity of this vivid chronicler; yet later on in the same book he is perhaps a trifle more revealing, when he defines the purposes for which he and his companions had come to Mexico in the first place (see p. 121). They came, he says, in order to "serve God and His Majesty, to give light to those that were in darkness, and also to become rich, which we all commonly came in order to seek."[1] It would be hard to find a crisper summary of the conquerors' motives than this.

[1] Chap. 210.

It was natural that those who undertook the long and perilous journey from Spain would reasonably expect some return on their adventure. Many of them, perhaps even the vast majority, sought wealth, and it was generally mineral wealth they had in mind. Hernán Cortés' outburst, used as the epigraph for this section of the chapter, was characteristic. This was a matter in which the Spanish government was deeply interested, and with good reason. By the time Mexico and Peru were invaded, Emperor Charles V found himself increasingly involved in European responsibilities which were as expensive as they were extensive. The affirmation of Spanish power, the maintenance of the imperial authority in Germany, the defense of the Catholic faith against the Protestant offensive—all these things demanded that Charles' treasury should be constantly replenished. The crown, then, had as direct an interest in stimulating the mining of precious metals as did the settlers themselves, for the crown's rake-off, as we shall see, was considerable. Everything conspired to make the quest for gold and silver, and the subsequent mining of those coveted commodities, one of the major determinants of the pattern of Spanish imperialism in America.

Spanish expansion through the Caribbean islands and across the American mainland, then, obeyed several primary impulses: territorial aggrandizement, evangelistic zeal and, not least, the desire for gold and silver. What we can certainly deduce—even before considering the nature of the collision between Spain and the indigenous civilizations of America—is that the Spanish colonizers themselves had no particular desire to establish the modest, somewhat egalitarian, self-helping farming settlements which other colonizers later set up in other parts of the world, not least in North America. Their national tradition was a crusading and conquering tradition; their priorities were those of subjugation and, not to put too fine a point on it, open plunder. They arrived in America not as disaffected emigrants eager to build a new way of life for themselves, but as triumphant conquerors, the proud and confident servants of an empire with a divine mission.

But these particular predispositions were greatly aggravated by the situation which already existed in the American continent. Both in the West Indian islands and on the mainland, the invaders found well-established, sizable, sedentary populations. They were presented with a golden opportunity to become aristocratic overlords of a subservient and exploitable mass of men. The wealth was there to be won, and everything predisposed the Spaniards to win it. The distribution of the Inca treasures after the fall of Cuzco was perhaps the most completely symbolic event in the conquest of America. It epitomized the nature and purpose of the invasion. Dozens of further expeditions set out across the mountains and into the jungles to find more Cuzcos; as it happened, no more Cuzcos were forthcoming. This hardly mattered. Even when the relatively limited opportunities for direct plundering were exhausted, there were still mines to be opened up and exploited; for those unable to become miners there were still lands to be turned into farms and ranches, and, above all, there were still the Indians. In the new social and economic order that emerged after the initial cataclysm of the conquest, the Indians were assigned the unenviable role of supplying all that the conquerors needed in the way of manpower; they were required, quite simply, to become the basis of the colonial labor force. What this sometimes meant in practice we shall see in the next section. For the moment, it is sufficient to note that as a conquered people, the Indians were doubly at a disadvantage in dealing with their new overlords.

The edifice of the Spanish domination of America as it developed after the conquest rested essentially on three pillars: (1) direct control of the Indian labor force through the encomienda system; (2) the sharing out of land and, in particular, the appropriation of Indian lands; and (3) the ownership and exploitation of the copious mineral resources which were found in Mexico and Peru. These social and economic arrangements were very rapidly placed within a solid framework of law and administration provided by an imperial government whose main priorities were strict centralized control and the enhancement of its own revenues. Each of these aspects deserves a brief mention here.

The important institution of the encomienda, the earliest major instrument of direct control over the subjugated natives, has been mentioned twice already in this book, for it became a major issue in the early management of the empire in connection with the fortunes of the Indian population. It is necessary to stress once again than an encomienda was not in any sense a feudal grant of *land*. It was a grant of Indians, whom the encomendero was expected to civilize and Christianize in the general interests of the empire. In return, he had the right of accepting tribute from his Indian charges and, if tribute was not forthcoming, their services in the form of labor.[1] As we have seen, the abuses which followed from this apparently simple arrangement were tremendous, and caused prolonged controversy in official circles. The debate reached its climax in the 1540s and was resolved in a compromise. Well before the end of the sixteenth century the encomienda was already on the decline as the main means of mobilizing the Indian labor force; its main value to the encomendero was, thereafter, as a source of tribute. For its

[1] During the reconquest in Spain the encomienda was a grant of land and people, and the holder was given feudal jurisdiction over its inhabitants; in theory (though not always in practice) the American version did not imply jurisdiction.

part, the crown pursued a very gradual policy of limiting the conditions under which encomiendas could be held. In the early eighteenth century, a series of laws abolished the institution except in a few out-lying areas. It is clear that one reason for the crown's persistent attempts to regulate and limit the use of the encomienda was the fear of allowing a strong and coherent class of encomenderos to consolidate itself. A powerful group of American feudal magnates capable of challenging the central government had to be avoided at all costs.

In general, very large grants of land—with or without encomiendas— were fairly uncommon in the opening phases of colonial rule. Hernán Cortés, it is true, was given considerable tracts of land in various parts of Mexico (notably in Oaxaca), together with more than twenty Indian townships and upward of one hundred thousand Indians. At the beginning of the nineteenth century, the conqueror's descendants were still landlords for more than one hundred and fifty thousand people. But Cortés' case—the case which perhaps most closely resembles a truly feudal grant of land and vassals—was exceptional.[1] Often, of course, a Spanish settler merely moved into the position previously occupied by an Aztec or Inca landowner, and even if he was theo-retically no more than an encomendero, he was frequently able to assume de facto ownership of the land in question. It is difficult to say how often this happened. Quite apart from all the various "unofficial" expedients which the settlers might have employed in order to secure themselves lands, there were straightforward grants by the government. For the foot soldier of the conquering expedition, there would be a *peonía*, approximately 100 acres in size, capable of supporting a family. For a cavalryman, a *caballería* of roughly five hundred acres was deemed appropriate. In theory, Indian lands were to be respected when grants of this sort were made; in practice, there seems little doubt that this stipulation was often (perhaps even usually) ignored.

In the earliest decades of the American empire, the land situation can fairly be described as confused. Many different interests clashed over the ownership of particular stretches of land. The crown itself, the settlers, the Church (which, as we shall see, became a major owner of land in colonial times), and sometimes the Indians—all of these found themselves involved in continuous disputes. Rights were jealously asserted; Spanish-American lawyers began to develop a fondness for litigation on property matters which has lasted from that day to this. In 1571, partly as a means of raising revenue, the crown issued legal

[1] Cortés' personal fortune was probably the largest in the Indies; moreover he proved an extremely enterprising proprietor, whose ranches, farms, and sugar mills were admirably productive.

titles to all lands in a specific area; the landowners who benefited from this regularization of their position paid the crown a suitable fee. As part of the deal, the crown then agreed that there were no further unclaimed lands in the area in question. This expedient was repeated on several occasions later on. Indian lands vacated when the Indian population was "regrouped" were also occupied by the settlers. Within half a century of the conquest, many individuals had built up substantial holdings; the outlines of the future system of great estates—which shall be mentioned in the next section—had already become visible. But in addition to individual holdings, it should also be remembered that the Church very quickly acquired lands on a large scale despite several attempts by the crown to stop this; and the growing colonial cities were awarded stretches of common land, as municipalities were in Spain.

As a result of the acquisition of land by the settlers, the pattern of American agriculture was very largely transformed. New crops and new livestock were introduced from Europe from Columbus' second voyage onward. The new pattern was clearly discernible in the Caribbean islands before the advance onto the mainland: the growing of wheat and cotton was common, and pigs and cattle spread rapidly through the island colonies. In part, of course, these familiar activities existed to satisfy the settlers' tastes; several items, however, were exported back to Spain in reasonable quantities, notably sugar and cattle hides. When the Spanish empire reached the mainland, the pattern was very similar, though the traditional agriculture of the Indians was badly disrupted by the disturbing arrival of cattle. In Mexico, Indian resistance to these menacing beasts was sufficiently stubborn to shift most ranching activity away from the center of the country.

Father José de Acosta, the Jesuit author of the first truly comprehensive account of the Spanish Indies, gives us an interesting and amusing catalogue of what was to be found on the farms of Spanish America within a few decades of the original conquest:

There is at the Indies every good thing that Spain brings foorth; in some places it is better, in some worse, as wheate, barley, herbes, and all kinds of pulses; also lettuce, cabbage, radishes, onion, garlike, parsley, turnips, parsnips, nightshade, or apples of love; siccorie, beetes, spinach, pease, beanes, vetches; and finally, whatsoever groweth heere of any profits, so as all that have voyaged thither, have been curious to carry seedes of all sorts, and all have grown. . . . As for those trees that have most abundantly fructified, be orange trees, limons, citrons, and others of that sort. In some parts there are at this day, as it were, whole woods and forests of orange trees; the which seeming strange unto mee, I asked who had planted the fields with so many orange trees? they made mee answer, that it did come by chaunce, for that oranges being fallen to the ground, and rotten, their seeds did spring, and of this which the water had carried away into diverse partes, these woods grew so thicke, which seemed to me to be a very good reason.[1]

The traffic in new produce was by no means one-way. If Europeans brought in wheat and barley, Americans too had a number of things to offer in return. The conquerors adopted maize, the great pre-Columbian staple crop, themselves; and the taste-buds of the Old World were in due course titillated, and eventually captivated, by such novel items as the tomato, chocolate, and the humble potato.

The development of mining in the earliest decades of colonial rule was, in contrast, somewhat disappointing, though later (as we shall see) it was to become the most productive of all colonial activities. For the first twenty years or so, when colonization was confined to the islands, most of the gold produced came from Hispaniola, and the quantities involved were relatively small. It was the shift to the mainland which brought the first real upsurge of mining activity; but even there, it was some time before the most spectacular finds were made. The emphasis altered now from gold to silver, which was far more abundant on the mainland. The first mining boom only got underway after the 1540s and 1550s, with the important discoveries at Potosí (Upper Peru) in 1545, and at Zacatecas and Guanajuato in Mexico (1548 and 1558 respectively). These three places immediately became major centers of population. In Mexico, where some smaller silver mines had opened up in the 1520s, production rose rapidly after the middle of the century: between 1551 and 1575 it was something like seven times greater than it had been between 1522 and 1550. In Peru the first dramatic rise in production occurred slightly later.

One of the principal factors in boosting silver production was the introduction, around 1560, of the *patio* process of extraction, the separating out of silver by mercury. With the more difficult ores, the older method of smelting still had to be used, but the patio process, with a number of modifications, soon spread. Mercury became an extremely important commodity, and control of its supply a useful mechanism for regulating the mining industry; from 1559 it was made

[1] *The Natural and Moral History of the Indies*, trans. Edward Grimston, ed. C. R. Markham, 2 vols. (London, 1880), I, 265. On the next page Acosta tells us that the "conserve of oranges" (i.e., marmalade) made in the Caribbean islands was the best he had ever tasted. Acosta was in America between 1570 and 1587. His book was published in 1590.

a government monopoly. When the mercury deposits at Huancavelica (Peru) were discovered in 1563, the crown "nationalized" the mine, which thereafter provided a reasonably regular supply for Peru; Mexico, throughout colonial times, was supplied from Almadén in Spain. The control of the mercury supply, however, was only one aspect of state intervention in the industry. Mining was for the most part organized by individual capitalists (often quite substantial capitalists), but it was the crown, which legally owned the subsoil, which awarded and revoked the concessions, which dictated the privileges and the responsibilities of the miners, and which also took a considerable royalty—after some initial variations, the royal *quinto*, or fifth.

It is difficult to overestimate the importance of the growth of large-scale mining in the midcentury period. From the viewpoint of the Spanish state, it amply compensated for the increased responsibilities and expenses incurred in the conquest and administration of the new American empire. Since most of the silver was exported to Spain, the pattern of trade was greatly altered and the volume of trade greatly increased; the convoy system described in Chapter 2 was now given the shape and form it was to retain until the eighteenth century; new centers of prosperity were created in America itself, the mining towns becoming important new markets. Agriculture was immensely stimulated: food had to be provided for the miners, mules for the mines. New wealth flowed into the pockets of fortunate individuals and into the coffers of Church and state alike; and while much of this wealth returned to Europe, some of it remained in America, to finance the building and embellishment of cities. The solidity and splendor of the viceregal capitals which so impressed visitors from Europe in the following century was based very largely on the labor of the great mining zones.

Although the Spanish colonization of America was overwhelmingly the work of private individuals, we have already seen that they acted only with the approval of—and in a contractual relationship with—the central government. The Spanish state proved more than a little suspicious of its own agents of conquest. It showed concern, almost from the start, to bring the growing American empire under centralized, bureaucratic control. The conquistadores were not permitted to carve out their own fiefs in the New World; they were fairly quickly set aside, to make way for the introduction of regular organs of government. The outline of settled administration was there from the beginning, from the end of the 1490s. Well before the mid-sixteenth century, zealous royal officials were filling in the details both in Spain and in the colonies themselves. An imperial bureaucracy—small by today's standards, large by the standards of its time—soon began to undertake the endless task of adjusting the disorderly and often puzzling human reality of the Indies to the requirements of official policy. Trade was regulated and controlled from the earliest moments of the advance into the Caribbean. A network of governorships and presently viceroyalties, of Royal Audiencias and treasury offices, of local magistrates and law courts, was brought into existence. A conquistador and his followers might very well be the first men into a particular territory; but the next would undoubtedly include a lawyer, a treasury official, a priest. For in addition to the officers of civil government, the Church contributed its priests and missionaries to complement the physical subjugation of America with its spiritual conquest.[1] Church and state alike set up the rigid framework within which Spanish-American life was to be lived for three centuries.

The spectacle of the rapid imposition of settled institutions in Spanish America was in some ways an impressive one. The Portuguese colonization of Brazil was altogether slower and less systematic. Portuguese motivations were far more straightforwardly commercial than those of the Spaniards, and with a growing mercantile empire in the East the crown proved relatively indifferent to the progress of the American territory which fell to it under the Tordesillas Treaty. For the first thirty years of the sixteenth century the chief American commodity which interested Portugal was brazilwood, the red dyewood which gave the transatlantic colony its name. The tiny trading posts set up by the *brasileiros* along the South American coast were the only signs of Portuguese colonization until the 1530s. Due in part to strategic reasons, the crown then divided Brazil into fifteen captaincies, which were handed over to some twelve *donatários*, or concessionaires; these were in effect feudal vassals charged with colonizing the captaincies at their own expense. The captaincy system was a failure; only two of the colonies prospered. From 1549 onward the crown itself stepped in, providing a somewhat loose framework of official administration for the territory.

The basis of the infant Brazilian economy was sugar, which had long been cultivated on the Portuguese Atlantic islands, notably Madeira. Portuguese merchants knew the European markets well; competition from the Spanish West Indies fell off when Spanish energies were turned to silvermining; and, as a result, Brazil became the first really important sugar colony in the New World. The self-contained plantation, with its extensive fields of sugar cane and its *engenho* (mill) powered by water or by oxen, quickly became the characteristic feature of Brazilian life. The plantation was the nucleus of Portuguese settlement in Brazil; its sugar was produced almost entirely for immediate export

[1] The first American bishoprics were established as early as 1504.

to Europe; other agricultural activities existed only because sugar existed. But sugar needed laborers. Brazil lacked the sedentary population which was to be found in Mexico or Peru; the enslavement of the local Indians proved unsatisfactory; and the dilemma was resolved by the early introduction of Negro slavery. The social organization of the colony was, therefore, highly patriarchal. A small class of plantation owners soon came to dominate colonial life, and the institutional framework within which they operated was markedly less tight than in the Spanish empire.

By the year 1580 it was clear that the Spanish invasions and the Portuguese settlement of America had succeeded in imposing a radically new way of life on large tracts of the continent. Judged by purely economic standards, many of the changes brought about can be seen as positive. As Professor William Glade rightly puts it: "New crops and crop technologies, medieval European mining techniques, new arts and crafts, wheeled vehicles, livestock and draught animals—all these were brought in by the Iberians and increased the potential economic capacity of the Western Hemisphere."[1] At the same time, the existence of large native populations available for exploitation as sweated, or forced, labor certainly accentuated the more "parasitic" predispositions of the Spanish settlers; while the Brazilian planters' widespread reliance on slavery had much the same effect in the more commercial environment of the Portuguese empire. Normal social divisions of the kind which were universal in Europe at that period were harshened by the difference of race and culture between the conquerors and the conquered, between the Brazilian planters and their slaves. The remaining two centuries or so of colonial rule did little to modify this state of affairs, and a great deal to reinforce it.

If the impact of Europe on America was vital to the way in which the New World was to develop in the future, the impact of America on Europe was also profound, both intellectually and economically. The revelation of exotic new territories, of old-established civilizations suddenly overthrown by Spanish arms, of mineral resources on a scale hitherto unimaginable was in many ways a drastic one. At the end of the Middle Ages, Western Europe had developed an outward urge sufficient to embrace the newly discovered continent. American silver, and the American trade, may well have accelerated the European expansion which followed. In some sense at least, the New World was called into existence to speed the progress of the Old.[2]

[1] William P. Glade, *The Latin American Economies* (New York, 1969), p. 54.
[2] For a recent discussion on this point, see J. H. Elliott, *The Old World and the New* (New York, 1970), Chap. 3.

Aspects of Colonial Life

And therefore in my Opinion, it is the most absurd thing in the World for the King to make those parts a Treasury to supply Him with Gold & Silver only, and not rather with men; seeing that these latter are, of the two, of much the greater value.

TOMMASO CAMPANELLA (1598)

Although it is impossible here to give more than the merest and most superficial impression of the immensely rich and variegated panorama of colonial Latin American life, some of its more important aspects must nonetheless be discussed. The main aspects on which we shall concentrate here are five in number, although the first naturally embraces a whole host of subordinate issues. (1) The basic economic activities of the period—mining and agriculture above all, but especially the latter—were responsible for fixing the Latin American social order in molds which are easier to describe than (as modern politicians have found) to remove. How was this so? Here we must look in particular at the development and persistence of the fundamental agrarian institution of Latin America, the *latifundio*[1] or great estate. Here, too, I must try to indicate what became of the immense wealth generated in mining zone and countryside alike. What became of the considerable profits made by miners and landowners? Where and how did they spend their money? (2) This leads one on logically to a discussion of the role of the city, which was peculiarly important in Spanish America, though not in Brazil. Colonial Spanish America was highly *urban*, though not highly *urbanized*. What were the consequences of this preference for city life? (3) What, too, of the all-pervading influence of the Catholic Church? Its priests and missionaries, its diocesan organization and its religious orders were present in Latin America from the very first. It became not only a main instrument for influencing the colonial psychology but also an economic factor of prime importance. (4) Clearly, we must also attempt to assess the role of the state. The Spanish empire was, by the standards of the time, a highly organized empire; this was less true of Portuguese Brazil, although similar attitudes may be attributed to the Portuguese government, even if they were less rigidly translated into official policy. How far was the state interventionist in character? How far was it a vital influence which regularly impinged on the lives of the colonial populations? How far was it a help or a hindrance to the growth of prosperity? (5) Finally, what kind of social order did all these things create? How divided was it, in terms of wealth

[1] The Spanish word derives from the Latin, *latifundium*, "large estate."

173

and opportunity? Did it contain the seeds of future progress? I hope to suggest some tentative answers to some of these questions.

Tommaso Campanella, the Neapolitan writer, saw the Spanish Indies as essentially a "Treasury" supplying the Spanish monarchy and motherland with an unceasing flow of precious metals. His observation was a correct one, as far as it went, for had there been no silver mines in Mexico and Peru the history of America would certainly have been profoundly different.

Silver predominated throughout, from the middle of the sixteenth century to the end of colonial times. Silvermining, as we saw in the previous section, developed most rapidly and most spectacularly in Mexico and Peru, and it remained concentrated in those two places. Of the two, Peru produced more silver than Mexico until around 1680, after which date the positions were reversed; Mexico maintained production much more successfully thereafter, although the sheer amounts of Peruvian silver probably proved greater if the colonial period is taken as a whole. The most famous single mining center in the Peruvian viceroyalty was, of course, Potosí, situated at thirteen thousand feet above sea level in what is today Bolivia. Its great age lasted from the 1570s to the 1630s—a relatively short period of time. But during that time, its mines were by far the most productive in America. From 1660 or so onward it was outstripped by the rest of Peru; the important deposits of Pasco had opened up in the 1630s. In its day, Potosí is supposed to have contributed half the world's supply of silver. In Mexico, the most important mines—accounting for over half the total Mexican production—were at Guanajuato, Zacatecas, and San Luis Potosí. Guanajuato was the most successful of all over the whole colonial period, yielding more silver than any other mine in America.

Outside the two main viceroyalties, there were three areas of lesser importance as far as mining was concerned. New Granada and Chile both accounted in their time for respectable quantities of precious metals, though in comparison with Mexico or Peru neither of them could be said to be more than marginal. New Granada was Spanish America's chief producer of gold. Most of it came from placer deposits in the province of Antioquía, the Cauca valley, and the Chocó, the greater part in the eighteenth century. The remoter captaincy-general of Chile possessed a number of silver mines, and also produced copper in reasonable quantities, though not for export to Europe. Both these metals were to become important for Chile after independence. Outside the Spanish empire altogether, colonial Brazil's eighteenth century mining boom proved more dramatic: more gold was mined there in seventy years or so than in the whole of Spanish America in three hundred. Brazilian diamond production in the eighteenth century was also of some significance.

There must inevitably be considerable curiosity about the total production of precious metals in colonial times. Whether final and completely trustworthy figures can ever be arrived at is very doubtful, but it may be useful to reproduce the careful estimate of the value of precious metals mined which Alexander von Humboldt prepared at the start of the nineteenth century:

Production of Precious Metals 1492–1803

	Pesos
Mexico	2,028,000,000
Peru and Buenos Aires*	2,410,200,000
New Granada	275,000,000
Chile	138,000,000
Portuguese colonies	855,500,000
Total:	5,706,700,000

* After 1776 Upper Peru, with its rich mining areas, was transferred to the viceroyalty of the River Plate.

At the very least, Humboldt's figures give us some indication as to the relative importance of the different areas involved; and the commanding position of Peru and Mexico can be very easily appreciated. It should not be supposed, however, that gold and silver production was either wholly steady or invariably on the increase. I can only indicate the general trend here. The boom which began with the major discoveries of the 1540s and 1550s lasted for roughly a century, but by the start of the eighteenth century there was a noticeable fall-off in production, particularly in Peru. Later in the eighteenth century—as we shall see—the Spanish government was obliged to take steps to improve mining technology and to stimulate production once again. The Brazilian gold mines were, similarly, most productive during their earlier stage, rising to a peak around 1760, after which they declined in importance. These various fluctuations had a significant effect, as was only natural, on the economic history of the colonies.

Some of the silver and gold mined in America remained there, but for the most part it was exported in bullion or coin to Spain and Portugal. In the second half of the sixteenth century, silver accounted for eighty percent and more of all Spanish American exports. In the course of the seventeenth century the growth of contraband made it difficult to know how much silver actually reached Europe, but legally or illegally the quantity remained substantial. In 1637, at Portobelo on the Panama isthmus, that extraordinary Englishman Thomas Gage— whose vivid impressions of seventeenth-century colonial life will be quoted more than once in this section—marveled, as well he might, at the trains of "mules which came thither from Panama, laden with wedges of silver; in one day I told two hundred mules laden with nothing else, which were unladen in the public market place, so that there the heaps of silver wedges lay like heaps of stones in the street."[1] Year by year the Spanish treasure convoys made their laborious way across the Atlantic; only once (1628) was the silver fleet captured. In Spain the silver was finally dispersed. The government's sizable share went into the royal treasury—and out again, to pay, among other things, for the nation's foreign wars. The remainder went into private hands in Spain, or, increasingly in the seventeenth century, to the rest of Europe. Its effects on the European economy have been long debated, but its part in the price revolution of the period is indisputable.

Mining enterprise in America was for the most part private, and the mineowners themselves were often capitalists on a large scale, employing a large labor force. In the heyday of the great Potosí mines, in the first years of the seventeenth century, it is estimated that some eighty mineowners were responsible for silver production. They were accompanied by nearly three hundred *mayordomos* or managers, thirteen thousand Indian mitayos, and forty thousand free Indian day-laborers. The pattern was similar elsewhere. The mita/repartimiento system of drafted Indian labor remained in use until the end of colonial times (and probably beyond); it is probably true that mining could not have survived without it. In Mexico, by the end of the eighteenth century, free wage labor had replaced the repartimiento in most mines; the persistence of the old system was more notable in Peru. The availability of forced labor in this way was one cause of the relative sluggishness of mining management in colonial times. There was little incentive for the

---

[1] Thomas Gage, *The English-American: A New Survey of the West Indies*, ed. A. P. Newton (London, 1928), p. 368. Gage's Catholic father sent him in 1612 to study with the Jesuits in Spain, but he later joined the Dominicans. He spent the years 1625 to 1637 in Mexico and Central America, arriving illegally there with the intention of traveling on to the Philippines. Abandoning this plan, he went first to Chiapas and later to Guatemala, where he lived for a while among the Indians. He returned to Spain in 1637 via Panama. Soon afterward his conversion to Protestantism caused him to settle in his native country, where he married and became a minister of the Church of England. The English Civil War found him a supporter of the parliamentarians, and he later accompanied the expedition sent by Cromwell to the West Indies. Gage died in Jamaica in 1656, soon after the capture of the island. His *English-American*, an outstanding and vivid account of his American travels, though somewhat colored by recently acquired Protestant prejudice, was published in 1648. Most of it makes excellent reading.

mineowner to experiment with new techniques or to innovate, for there was never a serious shortage of manpower; and indeed, when innovation came in the eighteenth century, it was sponsored not by the mineowners themselves but by the government.

The constant emphasis on mining, it has frequently been argued, was Spain's chief disservice to colonial Latin America. Some historians have even seen it as a sophisticated form of plunder, an expression on an imperial scale of the conquistador mentality. Tommaso Campanella's observation does not seem wholly irrelevant here. Quite apart from the silver directly appropriated by the crown, it is clear that much of the profits derived from mining ended up in Spain and other European countries rather than America, particularly in the earlier part of the colonial period. Nevertheless, this is by no means the whole story. The income which accrued to the crown was used in part to provide the American colonies with their administrative structure, in addition to paying for wars in Europe. The prosperous mining communities themselves attracted a flow of goods and services which would not otherwise have grown up. The Potosí market, in its day, was the most important in Peru. Furthermore, the needs of the mining communities fostered the growth of agriculture in those areas which were geographically able to supply what was needed. Towns were founded, fields cultivated, new trade routes developed, in order that miners should be fed and clothed. Whole regions in the colonies came to owe their livelihood to the existence of the mines.

A good case in point is the interior and northwest of Argentina—a modest enough region in colonial times, although more important in terms of wealth and population than the backward littoral of Buenos Aires until the eighteenth century. The towns and estates of the interior were essentially geared to the demands of the Upper Peruvian mining area. The early development of the interior—Córdoba was even able to support a university from the 1620s onward—testifies to the immense influence of Upper Peruvian mining, and shows how it became the main motive force for whole areas of the colonial economy.

Although mining represented the decisive economic element in colonial Latin America, we should not forget that it absorbed only a fraction of the labor force, and that the overwhelming majority of the people lived on the land. This was to remain true until the twentieth century. With the important exception of the Brazilian sugar plantations, most farms and ranches in colonial times were in business to supply the local market or a neighboring colony rather than to export to Europe, although this altered to some extent toward the end of the colonial period. The Spanish settlers' preference for urban life and the consequent proliferation of colonial cities meant that there was always a steady demand for the products of the countryside. Indeed, the earliest stimulus to agriculture and livestock-raising on the American mainland was the existence of the cities. These were provisioned more or less successfully throughout the colonial period, though there were occasional food shortages, and the crown kept a constant and very watchful eye on the situation.

It would be an endless task to list the different agricultural and pastoral activities which came to characterize the various regions of the Spanish-American empire; the paragraph from Father Acosta quoted earlier (pp. 168-9) shows that most European crops and trees were transplanted at an early date, while familiar European animals—cattle, sheep, horses, pigs, asses, etc.—quickly adapted themselves to life in the New World. Crops which were originally American were often taken over and continued by the Spaniards and Portuguese: maize, tobacco, potatoes, and so forth. Geography was the ultimate determinant of what was grown and where. Access to and from the cities and mining zones was a further factor. Sometimes, too, the strict regulation of economic activity by the state played a part in dictating production. Peru and Chile, for instance, were permitted to cultivate the grape and to provide South America with wines; Mexico and the Caribbean, by contrast, were kept supplied from Spain in order to protect the interests of the Spanish wine-producers.[1]

The fortunes of colonial Brazil, as we have seen, were largely built on one crop: sugar. Except for a short period in the eighteenth century, when precious metals came to the fore, sugar remained by far the most important commodity exported from the colony; it was supplanted by coffee soon after independence. Already by the 1620s, sugar cultivation was sufficiently remunerative to entice the Dutch into a serious effort to take over the Brazilian northeast. After the eventual Dutch withdrawal, sugar experienced a short-lived boom, but thereafter quickly went into decline due to the competition which followed the opening up of sugar plantations in the Caribbean island-colonies. By this stage, the sugar industry had triggered off ranching on a large scale along the São Francisco valley, just as ranching in the southernmost provinces of Brazil accompanied the eighteenth-century mining boom in Minas Gerais. But although mining and ranching diversified the colonial economy in a significant way, the sugar plantation had already stamped a distinctive and fundamental aspect on the Brazilian social order.

[1] There were a number of prohibitions directed against Peruvian wines in the colonial period, but these were ignored in practice. The crown's main concern seems to have been to protect the Spanish producers from unhealthy competition from Peru.

By far the most notable feature of the sixteenth- and seventeenth-century Latin American countryside was the formation and development of the great estate. It is important to distinguish the three main types of estate which came into existence at this stage, for all of them remained important throughout Latin America until the twentieth century and in most countries have remained important until the present day. The hacienda, the plantation, and the ranch were the three basic types. They were marked by significant differences. Of the three, the plantation was the most definitely commercial, very often geared to export on a fairly large scale, usually noted for its ruthless use of labor—which in Brazil and the Caribbean more often than not meant slave labor. Ranching, especially cattle-ranching, bred a more open way of life. Given the nature of the work itself, even the most autocratically inclined rancher was obliged to make some concessions to his cowboys and laborers, who were often stubborn and independent men. The hacienda, by contrast, was markedly less commercial than the plantation and markedly less open than the ranch. It bore a superficial resemblance to the medieval European manor; the condition of the tied peasantry who inhabited it was close in some ways to serfdom, and shall be briefly discussed in a moment.

Despite the differences, however, the three types of great estate were all of a piece in other respects. They were all characterized by sheer size; they dominated the countryside, not merely in the sense that they took the best land, but also because other landholdings of smaller size, which shall be mentioned presently, were in one way or another subordinated to the latifundio. Finally, they conferred upon their owners a considerable degree of wealth and, very often, the power of life and death over their tenants and laborers. The most important social group in colonial Latin America, and in the Creole republics that followed in the nineteenth century, was a fairly cohesive class of Creoles and peninsular Spaniards or Portuguese which grounded both their economic power and their social prestige in the bedrock of latifundio-ownership.

The origins of the latifundio—and in particular the hacienda—are to be sought not in the institution of the encomienda (as was once assumed by many historians) but in a much more complex process. This process started with the earliest grants of land to the Iberian settlers (mentioned in the previous section), and its development involved encroachment on Indian lands, the sale of public lands by the government, and, not least, the need to reorganize agricultural labor as a consequence of the abrupt decline in the indigenous population. In Brazil, the setting up of the sugar plantations was less complicated, and the most difficult process to disentangle, inevitably, is the one which occurred in the densely populated Indian regions, most notably Mexico and Peru. It was there that the hacienda system became most deeply rooted.

Although the latifundio did not grow directly out of the encomienda, there is nonetheless an important connection between the two institutions: for there can be no doubt that encomenderos often made use of their position to acquire lands of their own, sometimes conveniently blurring the distinction between the Indians "commended" to their care and the land on which those same Indians lived and worked. But there were numerous other methods by which land could be appropriated: direct seizure, unlawful occupation, straightforward purchase from the Indians, long-term lease, the amalgamation of peonías and caballerías granted soon after the conquest, matrimonial alliances between powerful families, and so on. By the end of the sixteenth century, as we saw in the previous section, the crown was prepared to regularize the legal position of properties which had come into existence in all of these ways. It was also quite willing to sell off public lands as a means of increasing its own income. The consolidation of great estates was probably irreversible, given the continued demand for food in the colonial cities and the increasing inability of native Indian agriculture to meet this demand.

The last factor was probably decisive in pushing the latifundio—in particular the hacienda—beyond the point of no return. By the early seventeenth century, the drastic decline of the Indian population caused Spanish and Creole employers of labor to seek ways and means of heightening its availability and efficiency. The masters of the new estates found themselves increasingly dissatisfied with the supply of labor through the repartimiento or mita system, which proved cumbersome and unreliable for their purposes. The alternative was to attract Indians from their own communities and to persuade them to take up permanent residence on the estate. Mestizos as well as Indians soon found a place on the great estates as laborers or often as tenant-laborers. The landowner could guarantee the newcomer a small plot of land for his own subsistence, a modest wage, and plentiful credit. The practical effect of these arrangements was to bind the Indian, or mestizo peón as he became known, to the latifundio. The estate itself provided the peón with food, clothing, and perhaps implements—and as part of the deal plunged him into debt, a debt which could be transmitted from one generation to the next.

Debt-peonage of this kind became basic to the Spanish-American agrarian economy during the seventeenth century, after which the earlier device of drafted, forced labor survived only for mining and for public works. The new system applied not only in agriculture but also in mining and manufacturing—although its most serious and permanent effects were undoubtedly felt on the land. The hacienda became the fundamental unit of landholding in the Spanish-American countryside, just as the plantation did in colonial Brazil. Its owner was a Creole or a Spaniard, sometimes a successful trader or miner who had acquired land for reasons of prestige as well as profit. If, as very frequently occurred, the owner was absent in the city for large parts of the year, the practical management of the estate was in the hands of a mayordomo, or overseer-manager. The Indian or mestizo peóns, often with their own small parcels of land, made up the remainder of the hacienda population, together with a fluctuating and irregular number of casual or seasonal laborers. Where the peón possessed his own plot of land, he was almost certainly bound to contribute several days a week in labor for the hacienda, devoting the rest of his time to cultivating his own plot. There were, naturally enough, considerable variations as between different regions of Spanish America in the way this system actually operated. Sometimes the peón might discharge his obligation to the landowner in the form of produce; elsewhere he often accepted the responsibility of supplying a set number of laborers, drawn usually from the members of his own family, for a set number of days' work.

Very often, the hacienda was in effect a self-contained economic unit, producing not only its own food, but also its own clothing, pottery, implements, and (such as it was) domestic furniture. It was difficult, though not impossible, for the average peón to move from one hacienda to another. If he abandoned the hacienda altogether, his chances of avoiding a wandering life of vagabondage were slim. Indebted peóns who fled from an estate were subject to the sanction of law—for official policy held, and the colonial authorities agreed, that debt-peonage was a more desirable and efficient institution than forced labor, and lent full support to the land-owning class. But in any case, the peón may well have perceived the hacienda as the best of all possible worlds—or rather, of the worlds immediately available to him. The fact of moving to an estate, and mixing there with mestizos and Creoles, quickly cut him off from his Indian roots. The Indian communities—perpetually subject to the demands of the forced-labor system and to the unscrupulous exactions of the corregidores—would hardly have exerted a particularly magnetic attraction on him any more. Life on the hacienda may often have been back-breaking, but the peón was certainly better off in most respects than a plantation slave, and he may even have come to develop feelings of respect and personal affection for the landowner, who protected as well as exploited him. The monotonous routine of agricultural labor was, after all, interrupted from time to time by festivities organized by the hacienda itself—a visit by the landowner, for instance, might be the pretext for prolonged bucolic jollifications and the dispensing of largesse. One should certainly beware of idealizing the hacienda, as some historians have done,[1] for it can hardly be defended on either humanitarian or economic grounds, but equally one should not embrace the opposite extreme by assuming that its internal arrangements were wholly intolerable and oppressive.

It has often been asserted that the hacienda was basically "feudal" in character, and the term "feudal" has been used more than most in denunciations of landowners in Latin America from the time of independence onward. There were, however, important differences between the medieval European manor—insofar as one can safely generalize about its nature—and the colonial estate. The Latin American landowner had none of the military or political obligations which characterized his medieval European counterpart. Furthermore, the wealth derived from the hacienda was, for the most part, put to use well away from the area which had produced it. The *hacendado*'s local investment was minimal. Even the *casa grande*, the big house which stood at the heart of the estate, was less sumptuous, even in the eighteenth century, than its European equivalent. The Spanish-American propensity for urban life meant the massive transfer of hacienda wealth to the cities, where it underpinned an upper-class style of life modeled on that of Spain. The Spanish-American landowner spent relatively little time on his estates; for many of his peóns he must often have been a somewhat remote and mysterious figure. Unlike many of the feudal lords of Europe, he took his pleasures not among his tenants and laborers, but away from the estate; his interests and preoccupations were focused elsewhere. At best the hacienda was a "semi-feudal" institution, at worst a debased kind of feudalism. Since it depended on a captive and semiservile labor force, it was in no real sense "capitalist" either. A truly appropriate adjective has still to be suggested. Too much, then, should not be made of the resemblances between colonial Latin America and medieval Europe.

The significance of the spread of the great haciendas in colonial times cannot easily be overestimated. It stamped colonial society with ineradicable marks of deep immobility, economic conservatism, and rigid class differences. The hacienda insulated the enormous mass of the tied peasants and servile laborers from any real contact with the outside world. There was little chance that the hacienda population—which by the end of colonial times must have amounted to a consider-

[1] Particularly those of a strongly pro-Hispanic cast of mind. But "Merry Latin America" is even less convincing than "Merry England" as a vision of the past.

able proportion of the colonial population as a whole—could form part of a wider economy than that of the estate itself; the system effectively hampered the flow of goods and products which might have developed in a more open and equitable agrarian social order. In short, the hacienda sealed off vast numbers of people from the "normal" operations of the market, not merely by isolating them in self-contained units but also by perpetuating deplorably low standards of living. By capturing and fixing the agrarian population, the great estate also barred the way to pioneering processes of settlement.

If the hacienda deprived the peón of opportunity, it also deprived the landowner of any stimulus to make his estates more efficient or productive. He had a large labor force permanently at his disposition, a labor force, moreover, which was easily able to fulfill the tasks of the hacienda in an unchanging and inefficient manner. This probably did a great deal to further accentuate the somewhat parasitic inclinations of the Creole landowners. There were few pressures which might have given the hacendado's psychology an economic or, more specifically, an entrepreneurial cast. His estate was never in real danger of being overwhelmed by competition. In fact, most of the pressures were in the other direction, the direction of consolidation and conservatism. The law enabled the landowner to perpetuate his control over the land and to hand it down to the generations which followed him. In Spanish America, as in Spain, the *mayorazgo*, or strict entail, was a common device, inherited from medieval Castile, by which this could be accomplished. Once a mayorazgo had been instituted, the estate concerned could pass only to the landowner's eldest son or the next in line in the family; it could not be subdivided.

For most of the colonial period, and well beyond, being a landowner was regarded as the most clearly desirable condition for an upper-class Creole. Land became the basis of his social prestige as well as of his wealth. It was looked on as an ideal form of permanent investment, and Creoles who did well for themselves in trade or in mining usually aspired to an estate before anything else. In a world which was still predominantly agrarian, this was to some extent inevitable. Nonetheless, it tended to reinforce the more conservative and parasitic inclinations in the Creole psychology and to limit interest in innovation or general economic opportunity.

Although the hacienda spread nearly everywhere in colonial Latin America—there were approximately five thousand (including ranches) in Mexico alone by 1800 or so—other units of land did manage to survive in uneasy coexistence alongside. In isolated and untypical areas such as Costa Rica in Central America, or Antioquía in New Granada, the small or medium-sized Spanish or Creole property came to predominate, and such properties were to be found everywhere else, even if overshadowed by the latifundio. The Indian communities, too, retained such lands—still a very sizable amount at the end of colonial times—as had remained intact through the long process of European occupation and encroachment. At the opposite extreme from the latifundio stood the tiny independent plot of land worked by a single family, the type of microscopic smallholding often referred to as the *minifundio*. If not actually a part of the hacienda itself, a minifundio was very often dependent on it in one way or another; otherwise it was to be found in remote and infertile areas where its existence mattered to nobody, except the poverty-stricken mestizo or Indian who ran it.

So far, I have laid stress on both mining and agriculture as the two basic aspects of the colonial economy—mining because of its profound effect on the general development of the colonies, and agriculture because of its impact on the lives of the great majority of the population. A word or two should be said here on the subject of manufacturing. As in all preindustrial social orders, manufacturing in colonial times was essentially the "processing of the harvest" and the working of metals from the mines. The import of European manufactured goods for personal and domestic use was confined to the richer classes, and colonial Latin America was therefore obliged to develop a full range of manufactures, arts, and crafts to supply the remainder of the population. Clothing was an obvious first necessity, and textile mills put in an early appearance. (In Mexico a fairly large-scale silk industry actually grew up in the 1530s, only to decline in the 1580s when the Philippine trade brought in silks from China.) When, in 1569, Viceroy Francisco de Toledo was ordered to close down the Peruvian textile workshops competing with imports from Spain, he discovered that local demand simply could not be met in this way, and ignored the order. However much the Spanish government might wish to limit colonial production, the exigencies of the situation across the Atlantic usually nullified this.

Textile mills very quickly became universal in the Indies; no province was without them. The larger workshops, known as *obrajes*, soon gained a particularly bad reputation for their ruthless exploitation of Indian labor, and the Spanish crown made numerous attempts to regulate them. In the cities, a full range of arts and crafts could be found as soon as the cities themselves had achieved a reasonable size, and some places became associated with particular products: Puebla's hats were famous, as were Arequipa's bells, and Quito's leatherwork. On the coasts, in particular the Pacific coast, several shipbuilding centers emerged, to serve local, coastal shipping requirements. At Guayaquil, for instance, warships with up to sixty cannon were built, and a whole host of ancillary activities developed—from Guatemalan pitch and tar to Chilean rope fibres.

Urban artisans and craftsmen were generally placed under the supervision of the municipal authorities, and were organized in guilds (*gremios*) on the European pattern—craft guilds survived in America long after their decline in Spain itself. It is difficult to say whether industrial development was held back in any way by this particular scheme of organization, but it is clear that the government's insistence on its right to regulate (if necessary by impeding) manufacturing, combined with the general Creole unwillingness to invest heavily in this activity, made anything approaching an "industrial revolution" wholly unlikely. Colonial manufacturing *could* no doubt have been transformed, had the government been interested and had the Creole population been given some genuine incentive to transform it. As it was, independence gravely weakened many of the arts and crafts which had flourished in colonial days.

All the economic activities I have so far mentioned, together with trade, created wealth, often very considerable wealth. What became of it? Some of it, of course, was appropriated by the government which, in the Spanish empire, as we saw, took a fifth of all silver produced and which also imposed a wide variety of taxes on the colonial population. Government also benefited from the various monopolies which it ran (which I shall mention presently) and from the sale of both public lands and public offices. The Catholic Church, too, sucked in a good deal of wealth from donations, benefactions, and bequests—an expression of Creole piety which the Church did nothing to discourage and plenty to foster. Wealth that remained in private hands was confined, for the most part, to landowners, miners, and merchants. Given the styles of life favored by these groups, the city benefited far more than the countryside. Wealth was thus concentrated not only in terms of social class but also in terms of geography—and so began the great Latin American contrast between town and country that forms so large a part of the economic and social history of the region.

Although the colonial upper classes derived great wealth from mining, land, and trade, they never developed habits of saving or investment which would have turned their wealth to the long-term advantage of the great majority of the population. Much has been made of the patterns of "conspicuous consumption" which prevailed among landowners, miners, and traders, and there can be little doubt that a great deal of money was spent simply on maintaining a suitably opulent way of life. This characteristic was by no means exclusively Latin

American at that period, and its influence on the general progress of the region may have been less profound than is sometimes supposed. Nonetheless, it did contribute something to the perpetuation of the psychology which had itself created it—a psychology which involved a notable absence of the more sophisticated and adventurous kinds of economic motivation. It helped, too, to maintain the predominance of the city over the countryside—for the city was the place to which wealth was immediately transferred and the place where much of it was dissipated.

The Spanish-American city—the remarks which follow cannot in any sense be applied to Brazil—was an achievement that deserves attention. It failed to compare, probably, with the great European cities of the time, though Mexico City was perhaps the most populous town in the Spanish-speaking world. Colonial society was always somewhat dowdier and arguably more conservative than metropolitan society. But even so, no other overseas colonies possessed such towns! Even within a century of the conquest, foreign visitors found themselves highly impressed by the scale and luxury of places like Mexico City and Lima. Thomas Gage, who passed through Mexico City in the 1620s, wrote at length on his impressions of the city. Some of his observations are worth quoting here.

Mexico [is] now one of the greatest cities in the world in extension of the situation for Spanish and Indian houses. . . . Almost all Mexico [is] new built with very fair and spacious houses with gardens of recreation. Their buildings are with stone, and brick very strong, but not high, by reason of the many earthquakes. . . . The streets are very broad, in the narrowest of them three coaches may go, and in the broader six may go in the breadth of them. . . . It is a by-word that at Mexico there are four things fair, that is to say, the women, the apparel, the horses, and the streets. But to this I may add the beauty of some of the coaches of the gentry, which do exceed in cost the best of the Court of Madrid and other parts of Christendom. . . . The streets of Christendom must not compare with those in breadth and cleanness, but especially in the riches of the shops which do adorn them. Above all the goldsmiths' shops and works are to be admired. . . . [The] churches and chapels, cloisters and nunneries, and parish churches . . . are the fairest that ever my eyes beheld, the roofs and beams being in many of them all daubed with gold, and many altars with sundry marble pillars, and others with brazil-wood stays standing one above another with tabernacles for several saints richly wrought with golden colours, so that twenty thousand ducats is a common

price for many of them. . . . The gallants of this city shew themselves
daily, some on horseback, and most in coaches, about four of the
clock in the afternoon, in a pleasant shady field called *la Alameda* . . .
where do meet as constantly as the merchants upon our exchange
about two thousand coaches, full of gallants, ladies and citizens, to see
and to be seen, to court and to be courted, the gentlemen having their
train of blackamoor slaves, some a dozen, some half a dozen waiting
on them, in brave and gallant liveries, heavy with gold and silver lace,
with silk stockings on their black legs, and roses on their feet, and
swords by their sides. . . . There is nothing in Mexico and about it
wanting which may make a city happy; and certainly had those that
have so much extolled with their pens the parts of Granada in Spain,
Lombardy or Florence in Italy, making them the earthly paradise,
had they been acquainted with the New World and with Mexico,
they would have recanted their untruths.[1]

Throughout colonial times Mexico City led Spanish America in urban
splendor and domestic wealth, but a score of other cities displayed, on a
smaller scale, the same municipal aspirations and triumphs.

A common design—the gridiron plan—was stamped on the colonial
cities from the start. It was an import from Europe. Relatively little can
be known about the cities of pre-Columbian America. It does not seem
particularly likely that they were laid out in the same way. The main
square of Aztec Tenochtitlán was approached on at least three sides by
straight causeways. Similarly four highways (to the "four directions"
of the empire) led out of the main square in Inca Cuzco. But whether
the remainder of these two important capitals was planned in accordance
with a regular and symmetrical design is impossible to say. Neither was
the gridiron plan known in medieval Spain. The decision to lay cities
out in this style was due to the peculiar conditions of their foundation—
it was, after all, a commonsense way of dividing a given area into easily
distributable properties. Furthermore, it seems likely that the Spaniards
of the period were aware of, and influenced by, Greek and Roman
precedents and in particular the recommendations of the Roman
architect Vitruvius.[2] At all events, the gridiron plan became the standard
for the Spanish-American city. Right up until the end of colonial times,
new towns were required to adopt this same basic design.

The focus of each city was the central *plaza de armas*—huge and
magnificent in Mexico or Lima, smaller and more intimate in the lesser

[1] Gage, *op. cit.*, pp. 81–96. The Alameda is still there.
[2] See Dan Stanislawski, "Early Spanish Town Planning in the New World,"
Geographical Review, XXXVII (New York, 1947), 94.

centers of imperial power. The modern visitor to the Zócalo in Mexico City, for instance, can derive a partial impression of the general scheme of things. The square was surrounded by the outward and visible signs of empire: the palace of the viceroy or governor, the cathedral, the municipality, the prison, perhaps a barracks—in short, the main administrative and religious buildings were to be found there, or at any rate within a block or two away. The plaza became a focus for certain key aspects of social life—the evening *paseo* inherited from peninsular practice, bullfights, executions, and the solemn ceremonies attending religious holidays, the births of royal princes and princesses, peace treaties, and the accessions and deaths of monarchs. From the plaza, the regular pattern of city blocks—each block conforming to the stipulated size—spread out in all directions, eventually merging into the poorer districts and finally the countryside. Relatively few cities were ever fortified, except in the Caribbean.

It is important to remember that the affluence—both public and private—of the Spanish-American city was far from accidental. The city had been the essential nucleus of Spanish colonization in America. It had been planted there at the very beginning; there was no question of settling the countryside first and allowing the city to grow up naturally and spontaneously—as happened, say, in the English thirteen colonies of North America. There is a real sense in which the Spanish-American city can be said to have preceded the Spanish-American countryside, in time as well as in importance. The countryside was colonized *from* the city: the city was in no sense the *result* of the countryside. In medieval Europe, the towns had to some extent grown up in the interstices of the feudal order; they had played a leading part in the revival of trade and manufacturing that followed the Dark Ages; their burgesses had acquired a role in society different from, and sometimes opposed to, that of the land-owning magnates of the countryside. In colonial Spanish America, by contrast, the city stood at the heart of the social order; its municipal government was in the hands of the landowners themselves; no specifically and distinctively urban interests could therefore crystallize, for there was nothing against which they could measure or assert their difference.

In any colonial Latin American town, the most sumptuous building was invariably the church; its tower, dome, or spire always overtopped the other buildings. Spread out across the Indies, a multitude of cathedrals, churches, and monasteries testified to the immense influence of a key institution. In some ways, the Catholic Church was almost a branch of government, for the Iberian monarchies possessed extensive control over the ecclesiastical establishment. In the Spanish empire, a series of generous grants of authority from the Papacy enabled the crown to exercise even greater supervision in America than in Spain. Without the crown's permission no priest could travel to the New World, no church or monastery could be founded, no Papal Bull could circulate unless its text had been looked over by the Council of the Indies. A separate ecclesiastical hierarchy was set up in the colonies within twenty years of Columbus' first voyage, and in 1545, with the creation of the archdioceses of Mexico, Lima, and Santo Domingo, it became fully independent of the metropolitan establishment. The religious orders, too, moved into America on a fairly large scale, to organize the "spiritual conquest" of the native populations. The Spanish Inquisition (which had tribunals in the two viceroyalties from 1569 and a third at Cartagena from 1610) was similarly present, though it was less energetic in the New World than in the Old.[1] (In Brazil the Holy Office never established a permanent branch.)

Although the colonial Church produced its share of truly saintly men, there can be little doubt that its representatives shared more than a few of the propensities which marked the conquerors and settlers of the region. There is plenty of evidence to show that many priests and members of the orders showed no very great attachment to the ideals of poverty, chastity, or even obedience. On his arrival in Vera Cruz in 1625, Thomas Gage lodged at the local Dominican establishment, and was astonished at the sumptuous style in which the prior's chamber was furnished. Such opulence produced two different reactions among the members of the party of religious with which Gage was traveling.

> This sight seemed to the zealous friars of our Mission most vain, and unbeseeming a poor and mendicant friar; to the others, whose end in coming from Spain to these parts was liberty, and looseness, and covetousness of riches, this sight was pleasing and gave them great encouragement to enter further into that country, where soon a mendicant Lazarus might become a proud and wealthy Dives.[2]

In Mexico City, Gage felt strongly that the lives of the clergy and religious cried "up to Heaven for vengeance, judgement and destruction."[3]

An insight into the behavior of the Peruvian clergy a hundred years later can be drawn from the famous confidential report on conditions

---

[1] The American tribunals dealt with approximately six thousand cases in their time, which lasted until independence. Some one hundred of their victims were burned at the stake; many more died in prison or under torture.

[2] Gage, *op. cit.*, pp. 33–34.

[3] *Ibid.*, p. 89. We should remember that Gage had become a Protestant by the time he wrote this.

in the colony which was written by the Spanish naval officers Jorge Juan and Antonio de Ulloa. They found the regular clergy to be more scandalously guilty of decidedly irregular behavior than their secular counterparts. In "the perverted customs of their disordered lives," Juan and Ulloa tell us, they surpassed all other sections of society. Concubinage was universal, and in many Peruvian parishes the priest considered it a point of honor to keep a woman. In some towns the monasteries were little better than "public brothels," and in the larger cities they frequently became a "theatre for unheard of abominations and execrable vices." Religious houses, according to this report, often arranged dances, at which "no abominable sin goes uncommitted and no indecency unpractised."[1]

To Juan and Ulloa the explanation for this pattern of clerical behavior seemed fairly simple: the Church was too rich. Its great wealth, they believed, should be cut down; and on the whole the Bourbon monarchs of the eighteenth century agreed with this view. The Church derived its wealth from parochial income (tithes were collected for the Church by the state), from a wide variety of benefactions, and from the accumulation of property. Although the government was less than enthusiastic about the way in which ecclesiastical properties multiplied, there seemed little it could do about it. The process was irreversible. The religious orders proved peculiarly adept at increasing their ownership of land, both in the countryside and in the town. By the 1570s there were already some two hundred religious houses in Mexico alone; by the mid-seventeenth century, something in the neighborhood of eight hundred could be found scattered across the Spanish Indies. By European standards the populations of monasteries and convents in America were fairly small; this did not prevent them from acquiring an immense amount of property. Governors and municipal councils alike sometimes expressed the fear that the religious orders would eventually own everything.[2] By the end of colonial times, certainly, there were provinces in Mexico where (so Humboldt assures us) the Church owned four fifths of the land.

The wealth of the Church was put to a variety of uses. Most of what would nowadays be regarded as "social services" were the effective responsibility of the Church, which built such hospitals as existed in

[1] Jorge Juan and Antonio de Ulloa, *Noticias secretas de América* (London, 1826), pp. 490, 494–95, 501.

[2] In 1578 the cabildo of Mexico City claimed that the Augustinians and Dominicans owned the best properties in the town; in 1644 the same cabildo petitioned Philip IV to prohibit new monasteries on the grounds that, otherwise, the Church would get everything. In 1632 the bishop of Santiago (Chile) asserted that the orders would one day possess everything unless quickly checked.

colonial times. Education, too, was for the most part an ecclesiastical preserve—a fact which did much to stamp the various educational institutions in the Indies with a markedly traditional and theological bias. The result of this was to discourage the reception of new philosophical currents or the promotion, through education, of the kind of technical skills which could conceivably have had an effect on the colonial economy. It is true that in the eighteenth century at least, traces of the European Enlightenment were to be found in some of the colonial universities, and that a handful of eminent Creoles developed a taste for science in quite an impressive way; foreign visitors sought them out and learned a great deal from them. But it is difficult not to see these cases as somewhat exceptional.

As an economic institution, the Church did little to encourage innovation or efficiency. For the most part its lands were rented out to private individuals, and the rents charged do not seem to have been particularly high. The Church, like the private Creole hacendado, was constrained by the massive availability of cheap labor and by a decided lack of interest in making its estates more productive. Its role as a financier was affected by similar considerations. In a time and place where relatively few private moneylenders or bankers existed, the Church became the most important single source of capital. Yet although its lending was widespread, its lending habits were indiscriminate, and were of a kind which confirmed and reinforced the colonial social and economic order rather than of a kind which might have created new forms of economic enterprise or activity. A *safe* return on its investment was what the Church wanted; it was not especially interested in either a quick return or a high one.

Visiting Europeans were less concerned with these particular aspects of the Church's role than with the more conspicuous irregularities of clerical behavior already mentioned. But one religious order, the Society of Jesus, enjoyed an exemplary reputation. Its members displayed a notably godly, righteous, and sober manner of living. Its religious and educational duties were carried out with punctiliousness and care. Its pioneering ventures on the outlying fringes of the empires —particularly its chain of Indian reductions in Paraguay—were justly famous. Whatever they did and wherever they went, the Jesuits were true to the hard-working and intensely disciplined tradition of their order.[1] In the often somewhat indolent atmosphere of the Indies, their

[1] The extent to which the Jesuits felt themselves to be under an absolute discipline as soldiers of the Church is well illustrated in a famous anecdote from the life of the order's founder, St. Ignatius Loyola. Asked what the effect on him would be if the Pope were to decree the abolition of his beloved Society, he replied: "Half an hour's mental prayer, and I would think no more about it."

example was a powerful one—admired, envied, and hardly ever imitated.

The economic activities of the Jesuits were very widespread and have often been studied. Well before they were expelled from the Iberian colonies, they had built up a far-flung chain of profitable enterprises—plantations, estates, workshops, vineyards, commercial depots, shipyards—all of which were managed with commendable zeal and something approaching genuine business acumen. The profits went toward the upkeep of their schools, colleges, and Indian missions, and in contributions to the central organization of the order. The French historian François Chevalier has written, of their work in seventeenth-century Mexico, that "their understanding of economics, their business sense, and their efficient exploitation of landed property struck a relatively new and discordant note in the Indies, where so many hidalgos and cattle barons were disdainful of economics."[1] This was equally true in other parts of the colonies. It is interesting to speculate how far the history of colonial Latin America would have been altered had the other religious orders, and the rest of the Church, been similar in outlook and behavior to the Society of Jesus. Such a development was, however, wholly unlikely. Even for the Jesuits, economic concerns were never the most important, never the supreme object of their zealous activity. The Church's mission was a supernatural one, and all its works were in the last analysis dedicated *ad majorem gloriam Dei*.

The Catholic Church was, as I have already indicated, in some sense a branch of the state. That the government regarded it as such is clear from the way in which its affairs were so minutely and constantly supervised and regulated. The Church was expected to inculcate the habits of obedience and loyalty to the transatlantic monarchs and to make a place in its teaching for the doctrine of divine right by which those monarchs justified their position on earth. The role of the Church in influencing the political and social outlook of the colonial population cannot, therefore, be easily underestimated or undervalued. How far it went toward fostering and perpetuating generally "noneconomic" values is more debatable, but it is more than probable that it went some way in this direction.

No description of the Spanish-American empire or even the somewhat less rigidly governed Brazilian colony would be remotely comprehensive without a proper reference to the commanding position of the state. That government plays an important part even in situations where the greatest latitude is given to individual enterprise goes without saying; otherwise it would hardly exist. But in situations where (as in the

[1] F. Chevalier, *Land and Society in Colonial Mexico* (Berkeley and Los Angeles, 1970), p. 250.

Iberian colonies) relatively little was left, theoretically at least, to individual or private initiative, the role of government was of outstanding significance. Here we must consider the principal ways it intervened in the colonial social and economic orders.

The first point to remember is that the state invariably assumed overall responsibility for the shape and direction of the colonial economies. The private enterprise of mine, plantation, and workshop was subordinated to the fundamental purposes of the state, placed within a relatively inflexible framework of rules and regulations, and stimulated or depressed in accordance with official policy. The trade system was, as we shall see, regulated and controlled with considerable strictness. Furthermore, the crown took a direct hand in organizing the labor force. In Spanish America, as we have seen, the enslavement of Indians was prohibited at a very early date, but the crown legalized and controlled the import and use of African slaves, it arranged and supervised the forced-labor institutions of repartimiento and mita, and it sanctioned and enforced debt-peonage. Over and above this, the state made evident efforts to rationalize colonial production—limiting or fostering a particular line in a particular area so as to benefit other areas. A good case in point, and one which I have already mentioned, was the Peruvian production of wines, which it was not permitted to export to Mexico or the Caribbean.

The Spanish state did occasionally take a direct hand in the running of certain specific enterprises. There were always a small number of straightforward government monopolies, usually run under license: these included (at different periods) playing cards, salt, gunpowder, pepper, tobacco, stamped paper (for legal documents), and snow.[1] Monopolies, however, were probably viewed more as money-raisers than as a particularly important form of state intervention for the sake of state intervention. For the most part, it was assumed that private individuals would actually carry the responsibility of running (and benefiting from) most of the enterprises in the colonies, although necessarily within—and limited by—the general framework prescribed by the state. Officials of the treasury, or indirect representatives of the crown, were ubiquitously on hand to collect the multitude of taxes which the crown saw fit to impose. Most fiscal revenue, in the Spanish case, was derived from mining and commerce, though a number of other expedients were used as well, ranging from the standard Indian tribute (which grew in importance with the decline of the encomienda) to what in effect were forced loans from the richer inhabitants of the colonies.

[1] In both Mexico City and Lima snow was brought down from the mountains for use as a primitive form of refrigeration.

In no sphere, perhaps, was state regulation and control more apparent than in trade. Like all other European imperial powers at that period, Spain and Portugal operated on the basic assumption that commercial activity should, as far as the colonies were concerned, be conducted exclusively *within* the empire; foreign trade was regarded as the prerogative of the metropolis. Until the eighteenth century, Spanish-American trade (more than the Brazilian trade) wore a somewhat medieval look, though a medieval look adapted to vastly increased distances. It was conducted essentially on the basis of a major supervisory agency in Spain, merchant guilds, regular fairs, and transatlantic convoys, all of which were carefully and constantly controlled (and in the case of the fairs and convoys, scheduled) by the government. (See pp. 89–90 for an outline of the Spanish system of convoys.) All trade to and from Spanish America was minutely regulated and supervised by the Casa de Contratación (Trade House) at Seville, one of the earliest specifically imperial institutions to be created—it opened in 1503. The merchant guilds which chiefly concern us for the moment were those of Seville (organized in 1543), and Mexico City and Lima (formed in 1594 and 1613 respectively). The great merchant houses which belonged to these organizations—which were known as *Consulados*—effectively monopolized the trade of the Spanish-American empire. (Their position was paralleled by that of the Lisbon merchants in the Portuguese empire though transatlantic trade was a state monopoly.) As pressure groups, the merchants of the Consulados were among the most powerful in the empire, adept at maintaining their own privileges, and acutely aware that the crown was dependent on them not only for ensuring the maintenance of the transatlantic trade but also for the occasional much-needed loan. The most influential Consulado was that of Seville.

The somewhat cumbersome and unwieldy nature of the imperial commercial system lent itself, as might be expected, to evasion. Neither Spain nor Portugal could wholly isolate itself from the rest of the world, and increasingly in the seventeenth century, the subjects of foreign powers found that smuggling goods in and out of the Iberian empires was big business. There is absolutely no way of assessing how much trade was carried on in this illegal and irregular way, but the constant preoccupation of the authorities with the prevention of smuggling is a good indication that the volume of trade involved was fairly considerable. On the rare occasions when foreign powers were granted specific trading or maritime privileges by Spain, such privileges were invariably and profitably abused. In 1701, when French vessels were accorded the right to take on provisions in Spanish-American ports, a short-lived smuggling boom very rapidly developed. The British, after receiving the asiento in 1713, were frequently accused of using the concession to introduce a wide variety of illegal goods. There can be little doubt that the Creole aristocracies—not to mention more than a few colonial merchants—were sometimes involved in such operations up to their eyebrows.

The extent of state regulation in the Iberian commercial systems has often been presented as one of the main causes of the relative economic backwardness of the American colonial empires. Would a more open and flexible commercial system have led to greatly increased trade? Would the absence of the powerful Consulados and their monopoly have contributed to the same end? We do not know. It is entirely possible that the trade that was actually conducted, combined with the illegal trade carried on by foreign contrabandists, represented the total commercial activity that was conceivable at that period. It is significant that when international trade did show marked signs of growing, in the eighteenth century, the Spanish and Portuguese monarchies embarked on policies of substantial reform in order to liberalize the system, with results which we shall see in the next section. On the traditional commercial system, which operated for two of the three centuries of colonial rule, one can do no more than submit an open verdict.

An outline of the Latin American social order as it existed toward the end of colonial times should already have become at least vaguely clear to the reader. It may be helpful, before finishing the present section, to summarize some of the main characteristics. It was, first, a social order where deep inequalities of both wealth and the opportunity to acquire wealth prevailed. For this, the original circumstances of conquest and colonization must be held ultimately responsible; to talk of the "original sin" of the conquest, as does one modern sociologist,[1] does not seem unduly fanciful. The dominant position in society was held by a small upper class which consisted of a Creole land-owning aristocracy, the mineowners, the leading merchants (often Europeans by birth), and the transient representatives of the imperial state. For the most part this upper class enjoyed considerable wealth, the opportunity to acquire an education and, at any rate occasionally, the chance to travel. Below it in the social hierarchy was a small colonial middle class—minor bureaucrats, the owners of the smaller Creole properties referred to, the better-off artisans and craftsmen, and so forth. Nearly all of these passed for and were regarded as Creoles, even if many of them were in fact mestizos.

The social order of colonial Latin America may be conceived of as a

[1] Stanislav Andreski, *Parasitism and Subversion: The Case of Latin America* (London, 1966), pp. 23–27.

shallow pyramid tapering up into a tall, thin tower, whose narrow summit was placed far above the base of the structure. Its ample base was enormous; it was, simply, the great majority of the population. The peón of the hacienda, the free laborer of farm or mine, the Indian subjected to the mita, the African plantation slave—these were some of the more characteristic types to be found there. It is impossible to generalize about the conditions under which all of them lived, for there were, no doubt, substantial regional and occupational variations. Let us take—as an example of what sometimes befell the Indian population —the description of conditions in the Peruvian obrajes drawn up by Juan and Ulloa in the eighteenth century. (Debt-peonage was as common in the obrajes as it was on the hacienda.) Work there began at first light. The Indians were locked into their different workshops and left there (apart from a short lunch-break) until dusk. Failure to complete the required tasks brought severe punishments; flogging was very common. The best idea which their readers could form of an obraje, Juan and Ulloa tell us, was to envisage it as a galley which never ceased to sail along but which never actually got anywhere, even though its oarsmen made superhuman efforts. To be sent to the obrajes was a punishment which filled Indians with terror, and yet it was (in Peru at least) a common one. On the roads of the viceroyalty, Indians could often be seen on their way to this particular form of purgatory—their hair tied to the horse's tail. Conditions of labor in the textile mills were paralleled, Juan and Ulloa found, on the land and elsewhere. The lives of the Indians, they wrote, could be epitomized as "constant poverty, interminable oppression, and exorbitant punishment."[1]

It is true, of course, that considerable inequalities of wealth, status, and opportunity were common to all European nations (not to mention other parts of the world) at the period Juan and Ulloa made these observations. Were conditions so very much worse in Latin America? In many instances, probably not. Yet the American historians Stanley J. Stein, and Barbara his wife, are certainly right to pose some rhetorical questions on this subject:

Were west Europeans forced into mines and kept there in the seventeenth century without surfacing from Monday to Saturday? Was there in operation in western Europe an annual labor draft which forced unwilling laborers to move hundreds of miles to pitheads along with their families, supplies and pack animals? To change the scene, were there west European occupations in which employers

[1] Juan and Ulloa, op. cit., pp. 275–79, 292. Juan and Ulloa denounced debt-peonage as a form of slavery.

could calculate with frightening accuracy that a worker's life would be no longer than five to ten years in their employment—which the Brazilian planters calculated for Negro slaves on sugar plantations in the first half of the seventeenth century?[1]

Whatever the condition of the lower classes as a whole, there can be small doubt that in several of the expedients adopted by miners and planters to satisfy their labor needs in colonial times we can see exploitation and human degradation at its most naked and most fearful. We should not forget, either, that the state took an active hand in organizing and regulating such expedients.

The accentuation of social divisions as a result of conquest and (particularly in the Brazilian case) the use of slavery was perhaps the most serious characteristic which the colonial period bequeathed to later times. There were, however, others which were bound to play a part in the way Latin America would develop when the colonial period was over. As colonial dependencies, Spanish America and Brazil were deliberately isolated from the rest of the world, in accordance with the official philosophy of the state. By and large, this isolation was maintained with remarkable success by the Iberian governments. The stability of the colonial social order was, therefore, guaranteed. No disturbing influences came to remold Creole habits of thought or to galvanize the colonial economy. There were no contacts with foreign nations to provoke either disdain or emulation. (The rivalry between the Spanish colonies and Portuguese Brazil was sporadic and confined for the most part to a remote corner of the American continent.) Nor did the exigencies of warfare ever play a part in stimulating local progress. The Caribbean, it is true, became an arena of international conflict on more than one occasion, but the colonies never found themselves in a position where they had to gear their resources to large-scale war. The net result of this significant degree of isolation—fostered by geography itself and confirmed by imperial policy—was to perpetuate a climate of indolent conservatism, and a solidification of the existing social order.

This particular climate was itself encouraged, as we have seen, by some of the internal characteristics of the colonial social order: especially the availability at all times of a vast reserve of labor. Economic activity was never drastically threatened by shortage of manpower. There were invariably plenty of Indians, mestizos, or Negroes to work the estates, the mines, the workshops—and, not least, as domestic servants, to provide the Creole aristocracy with a comfortable way of

[1] Stanley J. and Barbara H. Stein, *The Colonial Heritage of Latin America* (New York, 1970), p. 79.

life. In Brazil the plantation system and the heavy importation of slaves created a similar state of affairs, despite the superficially more commercial atmosphere of the colony.

The pervasive role of the imperial state, too, left its mark on subsequent generations. In its determination to maintain centralized control over the colonies, the state was distrustful of local or independent initiative. Spontaneous and private organizations—whether they were dissenting churches, rudimentary political associations, or societies for advancing knowledge—were not permitted to develop. Nonconformity in any shape or form was absent; it smacked too much of heresy. Local initiative had little chance of success unless it was immediately tied in some way to the state. Since the state regulated economic activity, it became at least as important for the would-be entrepreneur to secure the favor of the viceroy or intendant as it was for him to further the fortunes of the enterprise in question. The state was a vital and permanent element in the calculations of miners, landowners, and traders, to be taken into account at all times. Any initiative for the renewal or reform of the colonial economy would, therefore, have to come from the state rather than from energetic and public-spirited individuals on the spot.

The patterns of behavior which this situation stimulated became deeply engraved on the Creole psychology. Already by the eighteenth century, the Iberian colonies in America were strangely old-fashioned and immobile compared with many parts of Western Europe, though the glitter of their wealth still attracted the rapacious attention of foreigners. No new and disturbing breezes ruffled the surface of that wide and stagnant pool, with its beautiful water plants and its fetid depths. The Protestant Reformation was, of course, religiously excluded. The scientific revolution of the seventeenth century was barely noticed. The great currents of the Enlightenment seeped only slowly and partially into Latin America. None of these immense influences, which were slowly but steadily transforming the life of Europe, encountered more than a superficial reception in the Iberian colonies. The tasks which faced the Creole leaders after independence were greater than they could appreciate. But before they were faced at all, the Iberian empires were to undergo a brief but striking period of renewal, which, if it did not seriously modify the fundamental characteristics hinted at here, nonetheless gave the end of colonial times a distinctly different atmosphere from that of the earliest decades.

Late-Colonial Changes

. . . the commendable idea of adjusting this great kingdom [New Spain] and

making its political and economic system uniform with that of the metro-polis ...

KING CHARLES III OF SPAIN (1765)

Up until the eighteenth century, the dominant economic interest of the Spanish crown in its American dominions had been concerned primarily with the extraction of precious metals. In the final decades of the colonial period—not that the crown or anyone else knew they were to be final—the traditional emphasis on silver and gold was supplemented by a somewhat novel interest in agriculture as a source of wealth. Ironically enough, at the moment when the Spanish empire was discovering the potential of agriculture, the Portuguese colony in Brazil underwent an important shift in the direction of mining.

These changes of direction were in many ways the most significant in the closing years of the colonial period. But it is important to set them in perspective. Both for Spain and Portugal, the eighteenth century brought an acute awareness of national decline. Spain was no longer the awesome great power she had been under Philip II; the War of the Spanish Succession presented her with the depressing spectacle of half the powers of Europe contending for what they confidently presumed to be her corpse. Extinction or adaptation—these seemed to be the alternatives for eighteenth-century Spain. She chose the latter course of action. The outcome was a series of reforms put in hand by the new Bourbon dynasty, especially in the reign of King Charles III (1759–88). In Portugal, the virtual dictatorship of Pombal (1750–77) fulfilled a not dissimilar task, though it did less, perhaps, to offset the general decline of the nation.

In all these plans for reform and renewal the American empires formed a key element. Spanish and Portuguese statesmen came to believe that a successful program of national regeneration had to be based on a more efficient exploitation of colonial resources. The colonies were to be tied more closely to the metropolis; in the Spanish case, the old reliance on precious metals was to be supplemented by a new interest in agriculture; the commercial system was to be remodeled in order to counteract the impact of smuggling. Enlightened despotism in its Iberian form possessed many of the same impulses that characterized it in other parts of Europe: rationalization, centralization, administrative reform—these were some of the keynotes. Unlike Frederick the Great or Turgot, Catherine of Russia or Joseph II, Charles III and Pombal had vast imperial canvases on which to paint their pictures of reform.

In essence, the commercial reforms of the Spanish Bourbons concentrated on breaking down traditional monopolies and (sometimes by establishing new ones) on widening the scope of commercial activity. Already by the end of the seventeenth century, it was apparent that the convoy system was in decline. From 1740 onward, the Cartagena and Panama convoy was abandoned, with ships now being permitted to sail to Peru around Cape Horn. The Panama isthmus, long a key point on one of the most important of imperial trade routes, rapidly declined in importance and prosperity. The Mexican convoy survived for slightly longer, on a somewhat irregular basis, and was only finally abolished in 1789. Long before that date, the individual licensed vessel had become the standard means of maritime transport in the Spanish empire.

The merchants' guilds were also gradually deprived of the monopoly position they had enjoyed for so long. Seville—because of the silting up of the River Guadalquivir—was no longer suitable to fulfill its role as the focal point of the Spanish end of the American trade, and from 1680 Cadiz became the monopoly port. In 1717 both the Casa de Contratación and the Seville Consulado were shifted to Cadiz. This, of course, merely constituted moving the monopoly from one place to another. The traders involved remained the same. Other Spanish trading communities, however, were eager to take a share in a commerce which was now conspicuously growing, and the 1760s and 1770s saw the abandonment of the system of monopoly ports. Every part of Spain was now able to trade with most parts of the Indies. In the colonies themselves, the two Consulados of Mexico City and Lima were joined by as many as eight new companions[1] in the middle years of the 1790s. The commercial oligarchy of Andalusia continued, as might be expected, to maintain a predominant position in imperial trade; but following these various measures of liberalization it was increasingly under challenge.

A second way in which the old Seville–Cadiz monopoly was cut down was the creation of chartered trading corporations of a type long familiar in the British, French, and Dutch empires. Of these the most important was the Real Compañía Guipuzcoana de Caracas (Royal Guipuzcoan Company of Caracas) set up in 1728—it was, in fact, the only such company to achieve any lasting kind of success. The Caracas Company, as it is usually known, was granted a monopoly of trade with Venezuela, a somewhat backward province whose coasts were only too accessible to Dutch contrabandists. Not only did the company greatly reduce Dutch smuggling, it also greatly increased Venezuela's production of

---

[1] Vera Cruz and Guadalajara in Mexico, Havana in Cuba, Guatemala in Central America, and Cartagena, Caracas, Buenos Aires, and Santiago in South America. All of these were set up in 1793–95.

cacao and introduced a number of other export lines into the colony—
notably tobacco, coffee, and indigo. The effect of these changes was to
bring Venezuela to a previously unknown pitch of prosperity. In 1785
the company was reorganized and given a monopoly on trade with the
Philippines. The privileged chartered corporation, with which the
Portuguese had previously had experience, was a vital part in Pombal's
plans for the growth of Brazil's contribution to the Portuguese economy.
He established two of them: one trading with Pará and Maranhão, the
other trading with Pernambuco and Paraíba. Neither of these was
anything like as long-lasting as the Caracas Company.

In the River Plate region, too, the last decades of the colonial era
brought great changes. The traditional importance of the area was
described by an English Jesuit in a book printed in 1774:

> This country affords little for exportation to Europe, except bull and
> cow hides, and some tobacco, which grows very well in Paraguay;
> but it is of the greatest importance to the Spaniards, because all the
> mules, or the greatest part of them, which are used in Peru, come
> from Buenos Ayres and Cordova, and some from Mendoza; without
> which they would be totally disabled from carrying on any traffic, or
> having any communication with the neighbouring countries.[1]

"Except bull and cow hides . . ." Even at the time the book was published, cattle hides were booming as an export commodity. Demand
for leather in Europe was rising rapidly, with the beginnings of what
was very soon to become the industrial revolution. The littoral of
Buenos Aires had always exported hides in a small way—perhaps to
the tune of around twenty thousand per year during the seventeenth
century. By the mid-eighteenth century the annual total had risen to
one hundred and fifty thousand, by 1800 to a million. Buenos Aires,
now the capital of the newest viceroyalty of the empire, became a
bustling (though still somewhat modest) commercial city.

One further Spanish-American province which presented a new face
to the world at the close of the eighteenth century should be mentioned:
Cuba. The occupation of Havana by the British in 1762–63 was a deeply
traumatic experience for the Spanish government, and a significant
commercial moral could be drawn from the fact that more than seven
hundred ships had put into port during the British tenure of the city,
while previously no more than fifteen a year had been seen there. In
the closing decades of the century, Cuba quickly became the biggest
sugar-producing colony in the Spanish empire, a role enhanced and
reinforced when the French sugar colony of Saint Domingue was

[1] Thomas Falkner, *A Description of Patagonia* (Hereford, 1774), p. 48.

removed from the commercial arena by the slave revolt of the 1790s.

The new developments which I have mentioned all point to a growing interest in agricultural and pastoral activities as a source of wealth— an interest sometimes actively fostered by the "enlightened" Sociedades económicas de amigos del país (Economic Societies of Friends of the Country) which came into being in various colonial cities, as in Spain, toward the end of the eighteenth century.[1] But more traditional sources of wealth were by no means ignored. Silver production, particularly in Mexico, was once again on the increase, and the crown took an active hand in reorganizing mining activity by setting up a new miners' guild in Mexico and by enacting (1783) a notable code of mining law. To foster technical improvements in the industry, teams of experts (German or German-trained) were sent to America. Fausto de Elhuyar (the German-educated Spanish scientist who discovered tungsten) was sent in 1786 to take charge of the Mexican mines, while his subordinate, Baron Thaddaeus von Nordenflicht, went to Peru. Elhuyar's outstanding achievement in Mexico was the foundation, in 1792, of an excellent School of Mines which won the applause, a few years later, of Alexander von Humboldt. Neither Elhuyar nor Nordenflicht met with especially helpful attitudes on the part of the colonial miners, whose generally conservative outlook made them suspicious of attempts at innovation. Despite this, the production of silver at the end of colonial times had never been greater.

It should, of course, be borne in mind that the basic assumptions of the two Iberian powers in relation to their American colonies were still firmly mercantilist in nature. The increased colonial trade, it was supposed, was still to be conducted *within* the empire, while foreign trade as such was to be reserved to the motherland. Nonetheless, there were a number of occasions when this rule was relaxed, particularly when, in the 1790s and 1800s, warfare once again disrupted maritime communications across the Atlantic. Already in 1782 the newly acquired Spanish province of Louisiana, which had a predominantly French population, was permitted to trade with any port in France where a Spanish consul was to be found. In 1797 permission was given to vessels belonging to neutral powers to trade with the Spanish colonies, and although this provision was suspended in 1799, it reappeared in 1805. The Spanish government had no particular liking for such expedients, but deemed them necessary in the emergency conditions that prevailed after the outbreak of the French revolutionary wars.

Colonial rule in the Indies, then, ended on a note of greater prosperity, greater activity, greater achievement. The cities flourished as

[1] The total membership of these societies in the colonies was around seven hundred.

never before, embellished by new buildings—many of the new churches in the ornate Spanish late-baroque style—and by the paving and lighting of the streets. The glittering society of the colonies had never been gayer. Civilization (something more than a mere veneer) extended its influence: in the universities and literary *tertulias* of the Indies, some of the latest ideas from "enlightened" Europe were digested; the latest music from Germany and Austria was played; a handful of Creoles speculated on the vast changes being set in motion by the American and French revolutions. In one way or another, colonial horizons were beginning to open up, revealing new possibilities of life and action at least to a few sensitive Creole spirits.

What was the impact of all these various changes on the social and economic order of the colonies? As always in history, some of the effects were unintended. With the breakdown of the older, stricter pattern of trade, a new type of peninsular merchant put in an appearance in the colonies. Often something of a *parvenu*, he affronted the sense of propriety of the somewhat staid Creole aristocrat and the older sort of Creole or peninsular merchant—and thus contributed more than a little, probably, to the rise in tension between Creoles and Europeans that seems to have occurred in the eighteenth century. Similarly, the opening up of new areas of the empires to trade made older vested interests rather resentful. The Consulado of Lima, for example, could hardly feel especially happy when it lost its long battle to prevent the expansion of commerce in the River Plate. The new mercantile groups which now formed in several of the colonies, by vigorously advocating the claims of local progress, sometimes promoted intercolonial rivalries which were later to solidify, after independence, into national rivalries. A case in point was the long-standing commercial squabble between Peru and its subordinate captaincy-general of Chile. In ways such as these the heightening of commercial activity, though designed to draw the Spanish empire closer to the motherland, may well have contributed to loosening traditional ties not merely between Spain and America but also among the American colonies themselves.

The neo-mercantilist upsurge of the eighteenth century also raised a number of issues which would ultimately call for action by the imperial state. The Iberian powers had never been able to pretend that colonies and motherland together formed a self-sufficient economic unit, independent of external influences and interests. Foreign powers had always had a stake in the American colonial trade *through* the motherlands. British trading interests, for instance, had long enjoyed a privileged position in Lisbon. In Spain, too, several foreign countries gained what amounted to a semilegal position in transatlantic commerce. There were several ways in which foreigners could operate: they could use Spanish trading enterprises as "façades" for their own interests; they could enter into partnerships with Spaniards; they could maintain Spanish agents to act on their behalf. None of this might have mattered if the Spanish economy, and in particular Spanish manufacturing, had been able to supply colonial needs, but despite the considerable Bourbon effort to promote a more dynamic economy, this was never the case. Spain was to some extent a middleman; it is not unnatural that a few Creoles may have begun to think in terms of a trade which would eliminate the middleman. Farming and ranching interests in the New World—most notably, perhaps, in Venezuela, and the River Plate—began to question the imperial prohibitions on extra-imperial trade. Mariano Moreno's celebrated *Representación* of 1809, arguing in favor of allowing British trade in the River Plate, was perhaps the most eloquent document to formulate this point of view. His initiative was hotly opposed, needless to say, by the local representative of the Cadiz monopoly. The numerous if modest colonial manufacturers, on the other hand, saw things differently. They appreciated that if Latin America was to be opened to foreign trade, then their own activities would be undermined by new and powerful competition. There was, therefore, no universal or uniform demand for breaking down the imperial monopoly at the close of the colonial era. All that can safely be said on this subject is that *some* Creole interests were aware of the advantages an end to the monopoly might bring.

What the long-term impact of these late-colonial reforms and changes might have been we can never know. It can certainly be argued that the basic design which lay behind them—the rationalization and harmonization of the imperial economies—was misconceived, that the separate provinces of the American empires were in any case growing apart economically and socially as well as, in some sense, psychologically. But we assume too often that because things turned out in a particular way they were *bound* to do so. In the case of late-colonial Latin America, the reforming activities of successive monarchs and ministers were never given a chance to show their worth over a really long period of time. The events of 1807–8 intervened too soon, and, with the coming of independence, a radically new set of circumstances began to prevail. For together with the viceroys and captains-general there vanished many of the basic assumptions which for better or for worse had held Latin America together for three hundred years.

Independence

We occupied ourselves, on this occasion, in ascertaining the sentiments of the peasantry. At first we were rather disappointed with their calmness, and wondered to hear them speaking with so little enthusiasm, and in terms so little vindictive, of the Spaniards; while we remarked that the upper classes, in the same town, were filled with animation whenever the subject was mentioned. . . . It must, however, be remembered that, with regard to the effects of this Revolution, the upper and lower classes are differently circumstanced. The peasant's station in society had not been materially changed by the subversion of the Spanish authority; while that of his land-lord was essentially altered in every point. . . . In Chili, while the peasant remains nearly as before, his superior has gained many advantages. He has obtained political independence; he is free, and secure in his person and property; for the first time in his life he has a share in the government of his country.

CAPTAIN BASIL HALL, ROYAL NAVY (1820)

Some historians have gone so far as to deny any special significance to the independence period, maintaining that the essential shape and form of the Latin American social order remained unaltered. Such a view is somewhat exaggerated. As a direct consequence of independence, new external influences began to exert their sway over the region; certain internal characteristics were reinforced and even solidified; and, not least, what may be called the geographical distribution of economic vitality was markedly changed. All of these things meant that although Latin America continued to wear a decidedly "colonial" look for several decades after independence, the region now began to undergo a series of subtle, and sometimes not so subtle, changes of direction. These we will try to identify in this section.

The immediate and short-term effects can be dealt with in a paragraph. The wars of independence themselves dislocated economic life to some extent, although for the most part they were fought with rather small armies by European standards. In areas where the fighting was prolonged, however, warfare proved little short of catastrophic. The trade between Upper Peru and the north of Argentina, for instance, declined abruptly and drastically. In Venezuela and parts of New Granada, and to some extent in the Banda Oriental as well, the promising developments of late-colonial days were cut short as populations fled, cattle were destroyed, and crops uprooted.[1] But areas like these were fairly exceptional. Elsewhere, farming and ranching continued as before, and in some places expanded. Mining, on the other hand, was

---

[1] The most destructive fighting probably occurred in Venezuela, where the population may have declined by as much as an eighth in this period, and where a good deal of livestock was destroyed.

hard-hit in its traditional centers, in ways which we shall see presently. Trade increased notably in a number of major ports, and quickly settled into a new pattern.

From the 1820s onward, Latin American social and economic history acquired, in one important respect, a radically new setting. The political fragmentation of Spanish America meant that, in place of a series of imperial provinces, there were now several independent republics, taking on the attributes of nation-states and behaving in accordance with this new status. In the long term, the consequences of this were serious, for political fragmentation was bound to carry with it the possibility of economic fragmentation. It is possible, of course, to exaggerate the degree to which the old provinces of the Spanish empire had been economically integrated; nevertheless, some degree of integration within the empire had certainly existed. With the emergence of the new republics, this was abandoned. Each of the new states preferred to trade directly with the maritime nations of the outside world rather than to concentrate its commercial efforts on its immediate neighbors. Within a generation of independence, trade between the different areas of Latin America was lower, in proportion to the total volume of Latin American trade, than it had been in colonial times.

Such a state of affairs would never have arisen—*could* never have arisen—without the immense expansion of Latin America's commercial horizons that now occurred. As independent states, the Latin American countries could trade with anybody they liked. The ports were flung open to the vessels of any country whose merchants cared to send them. In Spanish America, political revulsion cast a shadow over the traditional commercial links with Spain; there was all the more reason, then, why the new republics should turn to other trading partners.

Of all the foreign powers eager to move into the space so recently monopolized by Spain, none was better placed than Great Britain. During the long Napoleonic wars, she established her maritime supremacy beyond all doubt. Her navy, the most powerful in the world, was able to give due protection to a vast and competent merchant fleet. (A South American squadron was established by the Royal Navy in 1808; from 1812 it operated in the Pacific as well as the Atlantic.) British manufactures, too, enormously stimulated by the growing industrial revolution, needed markets; and during the Napoleonic blockade of the British Isles, most of the potential markets lay outside Europe. The first and most notable example of the new commercial penetration occurred in Brazil, whose ports were thrown open to international trade in 1808, just after the arrival of the royal family; two years later, in a series of treaties, Brazil conferred highly favorable trade privileges on Great Britain. The country was immediately flooded with manufactured goods, although for the time being she exported relatively little in return.

In the aftermath of independence, foreign trading communities began to establish themselves in all the major Latin American ports, the British well to the fore among the newcomers. In the course of time, their position was ratified in the several commercial treaties concluded between the states of Latin America and Europe. The ports and the capital cities of the new republics became more cosmopolitan than at any previous stage of their history. For the most part, the foreign traders were welcomed; their presence was seen by many Creoles as practical proof of the new internationalism that prevailed in Latin America. Many British traders, moreover, lent financial and moral support to the independence movements—a posture that did them no harm at all and often did them good. By the middle of the 1820s, it has been estimated, there were perhaps as many as a hundred British trading concerns established in Spanish America, not to mention those set up in Brazil; and other European countries sent their merchants as well. There were, however, two or three places where the foreign presence was especially noticeable. Of these, Buenos Aires was perhaps the outstanding example: by the end of the 1820s, four million pesos' worth of exports passed through the port; the British community there was three thousand strong by this time. Valparaíso in Chile grew at an astonishing pace from a somewhat miserable village into a flourishing and bustling commercial center; from that day to this its business district has always retained a faintly British air. Rio de Janeiro, too, grew rapidly thanks to the boom in foreign trade. Other ports lagged behind these three, but the impact of new traders and new business was felt everywhere, in ports and capitals alike.

The biggest effect of the reorientation of foreign trade on the internal economy of the region was in the field of agriculture and livestock-raising. In Brazil, to take a first example, coffee had been increasingly cultivated from the mid-eighteenth century, spreading from Bahia to Rio de Janeiro, from Rio de Janeiro to Paraíba and southern Minas Gerais, and finally into São Paulo. Four fifths of all coffee exported up to the year 1822 was exported in the years after 1812—an eloquent witness to the new power of foreign trade. By 1830 or so, Brazil supplied about forty percent of the world's coffee; it had supplanted sugar as the country's leading export. For Buenos Aires meanwhile, the late-colonial boom in the export of cattle hides continued and accelerated. It was accompanied by a new boom in another pastoral commodity: salted meat. There was a market for this on the slave plantations of the

Caribbean, though not much interest or demand in Europe. The first *saladeros*, or salting plants, were installed in the River Plate not long before independence; one of their most active promoters was no less a person than Juan Manuel Rosas. In the island of Cuba (which had remained a Spanish colony though with the benefits of international trade) the rise in sugar production which had set in toward the close of the eighteenth century continued apace, especially in the 1830s. Another example was Chilean wheat. The Creole landowners who had supplied the Peruvian market in late-colonial times now took advantage of their country's position as the only significant wheat-growing area on the west coast. In a remarkable though short-lived burst of activity, they supplied the new markets created by the Californian gold rush at the end of the 1840s and the Australian gold rush of the 1850s.[1] In general, there was a heightened demand abroad for dyewoods, skins, drugs, coffee, etc., all of which increased production after independence. Latin American cotton, however, was unable to compete effectively with the massive United States cotton export. European agriculture sometimes set up a demand for Latin American products, as in the singular case of Peruvian guano, intensively exported as fertilizer in the middle years of the century.

There were a number of factors—absent in colonial times—which now had the effect of strengthening and consolidating the hold of the latifundio in the Latin American countryside, and it is proper to mention these here, even though some of the developments to be mentioned in the next chapter played a part as well. In those areas where royalist property was confiscated, or merely vacated by owners who were *peninsulares* and who now returned to Spain, a certain amount of land passed into the hands of Creoles who were thus able to augment their own holdings. The total amount of land affected in this way was probably not very sizable. Church property, too, became an obvious target for expropriation and redistribution when governments of an anticlerical cast of mind assumed office; and we may surmise that the idealistic struggle against clerical obscurantism sometimes masked the most shameless rapacity. In several of the new republics, the decades following independence saw a discernible transfer of ecclesiastical lands to private ownership—often, no doubt, benefiting landowners whose holdings were already large. Mexico in the years of the *Reforma* was perhaps the most outstanding example of this diminution of the

---

[1] Chilean exports to California and Australia lasted only a very few years and disappeared when Californians and Australians alike developed their own agriculture; but the experience gained helped Chilean producers to send wheat to the British market later in the century.

economic power of the Church. Finally, we should not ignore the opportunities which were opened up to Creole hacendados with the ending of the legislation protecting the Indian communities. Ineffective as such legislation had often been in colonial times, it nevertheless managed to guarantee the continued existence of a substantial amount of Indian community land. In the strongly Indian areas of Mexico and the Andean highlands, the process of encroachment and usurpation was renewed (if it had ever really been abandoned), and with greater force than before. In Mexico, toward the end of the nineteenth century, the Indian communities were ruthlessly deprived of their lands, yet this was perhaps no more than the most flagrant example of a more general trend in all those countries where the Indian population was numerous. More and more Indians now found themselves as peóns living on the great haciendas, bound to their new masters by inescapable obligations of debt and labor. The period of independence, then, served to open the way to a marked consolidation of the hacienda system whose effects on the social order were outlined earlier (see pp. 182–83).

If agriculture survived and (in some areas) prospered as a consequence of independence, the fortunes of mining were far less favorable. In the two great traditional silvermining centers, Mexico and Peru, the wars of independence brought what can only be described as disaster. As we have seen, silvermining had never been more productive than at the end of colonial times. Twenty years later, a scene of pitiful desolation confronted visitors to the most famous Mexican and Peruvian mines. In the intervening period, an abrupt decline in activity had set in. The colonial mechanism of credit had seized up; the dislocations caused by the wars of independence had cut off the supply of mercury; in many cases the abandoned mines had flooded and become completely water-logged. It was clear that, if silvermining were to revive, a massive injection of capital was needed. Where could such capital be raised? Local money was not available in sufficient quantities. But there was now at least one foreign country whose thrifty citizens had money to spare for investment abroad—Great Britain. For generations, the mineral wealth of Spanish America had been legendary; the writings of Alexander von Humboldt, then appearing, gave an optimistic and sanguine impression of its continuing potential. In the mid-1820s, some twenty-six Latin American mining ventures were established in London, with an authorized capital of twenty-four million pounds sterling (although less than four million pounds was paid in). Nearly all of them were failures. The problems of inspecting the mines and arranging their technical rehabilitation proved insurmountable. It was several decades before mining revived on a large scale in either Mexico or Peru. Here, then, the consequences of independence were catastrophic.

However, this is by no means the whole story. If some traditionally important mining areas went into decline, others now emerged into the full light of day. In Chile, for instance, the new vein of silver struck at Chañarcillo in 1832 brought immediate prosperity to the mining interests, while copper, a metal relatively despised in colonial times, was extracted and exported on an unprecedented scale. A British estimate at the time indicated that between 1803 and 1811, roughly seventeen thousand quintales (one quintal is just over one hundred pounds) of copper had been produced each year; by the mid-1820s, some sixty thousand quintales were being produced. The distinctive Chilean climate of political stability did much to foster economic activity, and not least by local entrepreneurs, for both copper and silver were exploited by Chilean rather than foreign capitalists. Chilean foreign trade trebled between 1845 and 1860.

The opening of Latin American ports to new currents of foreign trade had one further consequence which it is important to mention: the decline of domestic manufacturing. The craftsmen of the cities were particularly hard-hit by foreign competition. Within a few years of the breakdown of the Iberian empires, British textiles, for instance, were selling everywhere in Latin America, effectively driving out of business many of the local weavers. Other lines, such as the wines of the Argentine interior, were faced with severe competition from foreign imports. Although it is dangerous to generalize on this point, it is clear that the tariff policies of the new governments failed, in the long run, to protect domestic manufactures against the impact of international trade. Sometimes, the mercantile interests of the ports tended almost to forget that they were part of the same country as the inland cities where manufacturing was concentrated. In the Argentine case, for instance, it now became possible to import a wide range of items from Europe which were of better quality than the locally produced equivalents; it was cheaper to bring them across the Atlantic than to have them transported from the cities of the interior. At the same time there were several attempts by public-spirited Creoles or foreigners to introduce more modern manufacturing industries. Most of these ventures, however, ran into considerable difficulties and failed fairly rapidly.

International trade, agricultural expansion, the decline in mining, a menacing situation for local craftsmen—some of the changes brought about by independence were substantial enough. Yet it is evident that many of the more familiar aspects of the social and economic life of Latin America were hardly touched by these developments. The basic arrangement of the different social classes was modified only in rather subtle ways; it was not profoundly disturbed. For the Creole aristocracies, admittedly, the removal of the complex structure of imperial government constituted a decisive change for the better. In colonial times, they had possessed economic power while being barred from wielding effective political power. This anomaly (as they saw it) was now put right. In each of the newly established republics, the Creole aristocracy became the governing class. In the empire of Brazil, the most powerful landowners formed the most solid support for the throne. From the time of independence on, in fact, it becomes possible to regard these landed aristocracies as oligarchies—the term has been much used in political invective since that time. The Creole aristocracies now controlled the state, although sometimes they were fairly firmly disciplined by an executive power which conceived itself as the guardian of national as opposed to merely aristocratic interests—as, for instance, in Chile after 1830 or in the empire of Brazil.

Although the other social classes and groups in Latin America were for the most part unaffected by the winning of freedom, it is likely that there was now a shift in the general direction of greater social fluidity. The colonial system of castes, which had greatly complicated ordinary social distinctions, was now dismantled by the new patriot governments. The legal disabilities under which mestizos, mulattoes, Indians and Negroes had labored were no longer recognized. The abolition of slavery by most of the new regimes (except in Brazil and the Spanish colony of Cuba) doubtless benefited a substantial number of Negroes. The removal of the protective legislation of colonial times had a more chequered effect on the Indian population, as was mentioned in Chapter 3. But, taken all in all, measures such as these *did* probably open up a limited number of new opportunities to Indians, Negroes, and "the castes" alike. Bolívar's armies contained several Negro and mulatto officers of high rank; and for the first time in Latin American history we see mestizos and mulattoes—a few of them—making their way in politics, trade, or the armed forces.

It would be difficult to argue that changes such as these were mor than of marginal importance, or that they notably altered the prevailing psychology of the different social groups of the region. True, the adoption of political liberalism instilled into many Creoles the desire for progress, and the number of public-spirited individuals who tried to devise ways and means of stimulating progress was higher now than before independence. But too many of the old conditions remained: the latifundio was untouched or strengthened; the availability of a vast labor reserve was undiminished; the circumstances which had helped to perpetuate parasitic inclinations from the sixteenth century onward were still omnipresent; the arrival of foreign traders was seen less as a challenge than as a convenient and easy help to making money. Foreign (especially British) visitors frequently remarked on the apparently noncommercial ethos of the region. Francis Bond Head, who visited southern South America in the 1820s, wrote, in a series of notes on the practicability of mining ventures in the area, a summary of what he found in this respect: "The richer class of people in the provinces unaccustomed to business.—The poorer class unwilling to work.—Both perfectly destitute of the idea of a contract, of punctuality, or of the value of time."[1] In the ports and capitals, it is true, visiting traders and consuls found a more congenial climate, but the trading communities were still something of an exotic growth—rendered more exotic by the fact that many of the traders who composed them were themselves foreigners.

In general, the old landmarks of Latin American life remained intact. The Church retained its widespread influence, even when the new republican governments found themselves entangled (as they sometimes did) in acrimonious negotiations with the Papacy. Foreign observers at this period, particularly those with a Protestant background, nearly always remarked on the pervasive sway exercised by the Church. Two impressions of Latin American life in the 1820s and 1830s may be mentioned here—and I do not apologize for quoting them at some length, for they present an interesting reflection of the "feel" of the situation. The first concerns the Chile of the 1820s. Francis Bond Head's travels took him, among other places, to Santiago.

> The town is full of priests—the people are consequently indolent and immoral; and I certainly never saw more sad examples of the effects of bad education, or a state of society more deplorable. The streets are crowded with a set of lazy, indolent, bloated monks and priests. . . . The men all touch their hats to these drones, who are also to be seen in the houses, leaning over the backs of their chairs, and talking to women who are evidently of the most abandoned class of society. The number of people of this description at Santiago is quite extraordinary. . . . The power of the priests has diminished very much since the Revolution. They are not respected; they have almost all families, and lead most disreputable lives. Still, the hold they have on society is quite surprising.[2]

[1] F. B. Head, *Rough Notes taken during some Rapid Journeys across the Pampa and among the Andes* (London, 1826), p. 279. Head was later governor of Upper Canada during the troubles of 1837.

[2] Head, *op. cit.*, pp. 190–92.

The second impression, couched in somewhat more romantic language, is of Mexico at the end of the 1830s, seen through the eyes of Mrs. Frances Calderón, the Scottish-born wife of the Spanish minister to the new republic. At one point in her lively account of Mexican life, she forms an interesting contrast between Mexico and New England, and the Church is at the heart of the comparison.

> Travelling in New England . . . we arrive at a small and flourishing village. We see four new churches, proclaiming four different sects; religion suited to all customers. . . . Hard by is a tavern with a green paling, as clean and new as the churches, and there are also various smart *stores* and neat dwelling-houses. . . . The whole has a cheerful, trim and flourishing aspect. . . . Everything proclaims prosperity, equality, consistency. . . .
>
> Transport yourself in imagination from this New England village to that of ——, it matters not which, not far from Mexico. . . . The Indian huts, with their half naked inmates, and little gardens full of flowers; the huts themselves either built of clay or the half-ruined *beaux gestes* of some stone building. . . . There, rising in the midst of old faithful-looking trees, the church, gray and ancient, but strong as if designed for eternity; with its saints and virgins, its martyrs and relics, its gold and silver and precious stones, whose value would buy up all the spare lots in the New England village; the lépero [beggar] with scarce a rag to cover him, kneeling on that marble pavement. . . . And that Gothic pile of building, that stands in hoary majesty, surmounted by the lofty mountains, whose cloud-enveloped summits, tinged by the evening sun, rise behind it; what could so noble a building be but the monastery, perhaps of the Carmelites, because of its exceeding rich garden, and well-chosen site, for they, of all monks, are richest in this world's goods. Also we may see the reverend old prior riding slowly from under the arched gate up the village lanes, the Indians coming from their huts to do him lowly reverence as he passes. Here, everything reminds us of the past; of the conquering Spaniards, who seemed to build for eternity; impressing each work with their own solid, grave and religious character. . . . It is the present that seems like a dream, a pale reflection of the past.[1]

Due allowances should, of course, be made. Francis Bond Head's "sample" may not have been very representative; Mrs. Calderón may

[1] Frances Calderón de la Barca, *Life in Mexico* (London, 1960), pp. 355–57. Mrs. Calderón's book was first published in 1843, the same year as Prescott's *Conquest of Mexico*, and was a bestseller.

have been unduly concerned with the "picturesqueness" of the Mexican countryside. But both of them, in their different ways, point to the undeniable fact that the Catholic Church was still firmly in place in postcolonial Latin America. For the time being, at least, it continued to enjoy a preponderant influence in education, and to affect in countless intimate ways the psychology of the people.

The Church had, as we have seen, been one of the salient features of the colonial organization of Latin America. So, too, had been the state. What became of the state after independence? In the Spanish-American case, of course, the imperial state was replaced by a multiplicity of national states, each controlled in the last analysis by the local, national aristocracy rather than by a complex imperial bureaucracy dependent on a transatlantic monarch. Following independence, the state was no longer the somewhat impersonal authority of colonial times; it fell directly within the grasp of the Creole aristocracies. It is hardly surprising, then, that they came to look on the state as an instrument of their enrichment: the pursuit of power became a principal means of pursuing prosperity. This may well have helped to divert Creole attention from the possibilities of securing influence and status through directly *economic* activities.

Two things, however, made the state a less efficient instrument of intervention in economic matters than before. The first of these was a new predisposition in favor of liberal economics. This should certainly not be exaggerated. Many of the Creole statesmen of the first decades after independence maintained a distinctly neo-mercantilist cast of mind and were determined to preserve the role of the state in the regulation of the economy. But at the same time there tended to grow up a generalized belief—imported from Europe—in the desirability of freer trading arrangements and in the notion that, where possible, governments should withdraw from an excessively active role in economic management.

Second, and perhaps more important, the state itself became rather less effective as a machine. Peninsular bureaucrats sometimes left Latin America altogether, or at the very least retired from the public adminstration. The various checks on bureaucratic conduct which had been a feature of colonial administrative practice now disappeared, and public posts rapidly became part of a locally based "spoils system" operated by successful Creole politicians. A position in the bureaucracy came to be regarded as a means of enjoying an income at the expense of the general public. There were, naturally enough, exceptional cases. In the Chile of the 1830s, Diego Portales eliminated sinecures, set new standards of behavior for government officials, and brought into existence a small but conscientious civil service. Even in Chile, however, public jobs formed part of a "spoils system," however much their holders were required to behave properly.

A decline in the quality of public administration was clearly related to the fiscal problems which confronted most of the new states. The collection of taxes at this period was in many respects much less efficient than in colonial times. There was little capital available for public investment, and yet many Creole governments were anxious to rehabilitate their countries after the wars of independence, to put in hand improvements in transport and education, and—often a costly item— to maintain reasonably respectable armies and navies. Their own income was minimal; domestic capital in general was probably flowing out of the region rather than accumulating locally; and government after government felt obliged to turn to the London money market for loans. In 1822 there were four issues of Latin American government bonds in London; in 1824–25 there were ten more. In all, their nominal value came to £21,129,000. Only three countries—Bolivia, Haiti, and Paraguay—did not float loans in London at this period. The story of these loans is, in most respects, a sad and sorry one. Most of the governments concerned received little more than half the money they had contracted for; and the loans were spent either on paying off previously incurred debts (not least to the British merchant communities) or on increasing the military establishment. Furthermore, the Creole governments rapidly found themselves unable to service the loans; by the end of 1827, all payments of interest had ceased. This experience, coupled with the failure of the mining ventures mentioned earlier, made the British investor understandably chary of putting money into Latin America—a chariness that lasted several decades. Moreover, it did nothing to sort out the early fiscal and monetary problems of the new republics.

From what has been said so far, it will be apparent that the social and economic problems of the new Latin American governments were considerable. The fragmentation of the region into countries which in many cases were small and powerless, undermotivated aristocracies with a noncommercial outlook, the persistence of an agrarian system which impeded any real widening of the internal market, a state now regarded as an instrument of enrichment, Creole traders forced gradually to yield place to their more efficient foreign competitors, a severe threat to local manufacturing—these conditions made it doubly difficult to promote what might be thought of as genuinely autonomous economic progress. Difficult—but not impossible, except perhaps for the smaller countries. This is a point to which we shall inevitably return in the next chapter. For the moment it is perhaps important to return to one of the opening themes of the present section, and to stress once again the expanding horizons which greeted Latin Americans in their new dawn of freedom. For the outside world was changing—and the region's new commercial connections were visible proof of this.

Already within twenty or thirty years of independence, the new links with Western Europe had done much to create new contrasts in Latin America. There were two contrasts of note. One was between the sea-ports and the capital cities on the one hand, and the countryside and provincial towns of the interior on the other. In the ports and the capitals, the impulse of foreign trade and a cosmopolitan population brought new life and new currents of civilization—ideas, fashions, books, music, furniture, new manners, new aspirations, and so forth. The provinces of the interior remained somewhat sleepy and traditional by comparison. Foreign influences penetrated late or not at all.

Beyond this contrast there lay another, in some ways more striking. The measure of this second contrast can most easily be gauged by a simple comparison of the areas most frequently mentioned in this section with those mentioned in previous sections. Brazil, Argentina, Chile—these three countries have been the ones which have sprung most naturally to mind in illustrating the changes that occurred as a consequence of independence. None of them figured as prominently in the descriptions of the colonial period. There, the two great viceroyalties, with their mineral wealth and their Indian populations, stood out head and shoulders above all other parts of the two Iberian empires. Yet for the first few decades after independence, neither Peru nor Mexico seemed particularly close to the heart of such progress as was occurring in Latin America. The scene had shifted to the territories whose colonial experience had been one of backwardness and neglect, but for whom independence had given new opportunities. Chile, Brazil, Argentina—these countries were to enjoy a leading position in nineteenth-century Latin America. For this, their connections with the outside world were very largely responsible. Independence, then, brought a real shift in what we may loosely think of as the Latin American balance of power.

Chapter 5

SOCIAL AND ECONOMIC DEVELOPMENT
SINCE 1860

The International Economy

What is the force that is at the back of this progress? Sirs, it is British capital. . . . Truly, sirs, British capital is a great anonymous personality, whose history has not yet been written.

BARTOLOMÉ MITRE (1861)

Ever since the first discoveries of the fifteenth-century Portuguese, the growth of international and indeed intercontinental trade had been continuous. Plainly, the faint outlines of something approaching an "international economy" were already present in the sixteenth and seventeenth centuries. The English poet John Dryden foresaw the outlines growing thicker.

> Instructed ships shall sail to rich commerce,
> By which remotest regions are allied;
> Which makes one city of the universe,
> Where some may gain, and all may be supplied.[1]

It was an accurate forecast, and it fell to the nineteenth century to make the dream come true. Increasingly after the 1860s—Mitre asked his rhetorical question at the opening of an Argentine railway in 1861—Latin America found itself tied into an economy more truly international than anything which had previously been seen in history. At first, the advantages of this arrangement seemed a good deal more obvious than any disadvantages the future might bring.

The industrial revolution in Great Britain and in the main continental states of Europe enormously stimulated international trade. The European market for non-European primary products was greatly

[1] "Annus Mirabilis" (1666).

enlarged, due to a rising population whose living standards were also rising. The industrial nations, for their part, sought new and profitable markets overseas. They proffered surplus capital for investment all around the world. The lines of communication for this new, worldwide economy were made speedier and more efficient by the steamship and the electric telegraph. At the center of this complex web of economic forces stood Great Britain, the first industrial nation, whose capital city assumed the role of financial capital of the world. London became the main bestower of capital, shipping services, insurance, and commercial intelligence to the extent that it "became easier for Chile to pay a bill in Peru by means of a draft on London than to pay direct."[1]

It is certainly no accident that I refer to Great Britain as the "center" of the new international economic network, for it is clear that the world did now become divided—paradoxically because of the very degree to which it had become united—into a "center" and a "periphery," to use the terminology of the ECLA economists (see p. 66). The effective measure of the difference between center and periphery lay in the degree of industrialization. The countries of the center were becoming increasingly industrialized; whatever the initial miseries of industrialization, their populations were coming to enjoy a higher standard of living, greater educational opportunities, better levels of health, and so on. The countries of the periphery, by contrast, were still heavily dependent either on agriculture or on mining; the well-being of their populations—or at least large sections of their populations —grew less rapidly or not at all. There was, in effect, a kind of unofficial international division of labor, the center pouring out factory-produced manufactured goods and the periphery supplying the primary materials to help feed and clothe the populations of the industrial nations and to maintain their industrial output. If we accept the ECLA terminology, Latin America's role in this de facto division of labor was clearly peripheral rather than central, as we shall see presently.

Because of the industrial revolution and the revolution in maritime transport, the sheer *scale* of economic activity increased dramatically. Between the 1820s and World War I, the value of international trade is estimated to have shown a *twenty-sevenfold* increase. The tonnage of the world's merchant fleets rose from just under 7 million in 1840 to 43 million in 1913. Between 1860 and 1914, industrial production more than quadrupled. That there was something wholly novel and spectacular in nineteenth-century progress was apparent to many Europeans well before the middle of the century. "What earlier century had even a presentiment that such productive forces slumbered in the lap of

[1] Frank A. Vanderlip, *What Happened to Europe* (New York, 1919), p. 158.

social labour?"[1] So wrote the two sternest critics of nineteenth-century European capitalism, paying a perfectly conscious tribute to its achievements.

The international economic system with which Latin America now began to find herself increasingly associated came effectively into being in the mid-nineteenth century and lasted more or less intact until 1914. After World War I, strenuous efforts were made by those most intimately concerned to reconstruct prewar conditions as far as was possible, but the depression which set in after the great crash of 1929 ended them once and for all. What were some of the principal characteristics of the period? It was, of course, a time of considerable progress in technology—an uninterrupted progress which for better or worse has continued since. Technical improvements all around led to a great increase in productivity both in industry and in agriculture. At the same time, many of the old restrictions on commercial activity were abolished; Great Britain reached complete free trade in 1860–61; and it was at that period that "the world attained the greatest degree of freedom in international trade that it has ever known."[2] The rises in tariffs that occurred later in the century offset this to some extent, but down to 1914 trade was still remarkably unrestricted throughout the world. These things, moreover, developed against a backcloth of international peace and stability; not until 1914 was this backcloth torn to pieces.

The most notable and serious effect of the international economy on Latin America was the way local economic activity now became geared to the production of a limited number of primary commodities, both mineral and pastoral–agricultural, which were extracted or grown or raised on an unprecedented scale. (Mexico produced more silver between 1851 and 1915 than during the *entire colonial period*.) At the end of this "gearing" process, the Latin American republics fell into three basic types: (1) those which exported pastoral products and temperate crops, Argentina and Uruguay being the two main cases; (2) those which exported tropical agricultural products such as coffee, sugar, or tobacco; Brazil, Ecuador, Colombia, and most of Central America and the Caribbean fell into this category; (3) mining and oil-producing countries, such as Chile, Bolivia, Mexico and, later, Venezuela. All of these countries now tended to specialize in one or more primary products for export.

[1] K. Marx and F. Engels, *The Communist Manifesto* (1848).
[2] Sanford A. Mosk, "Latin America and the World Economy," *Inter-American Economic Affairs*, II (1948), 62. Mosk's article, on which I have leaned heavily in these paragraphs, is a brilliant summary of the period.

A brief list of the most important of these commodities is probably in order at this stage, for they remained (and some still remain) basic to the economies of the region well beyond the period under review here.

Copper: Coppermining centered, as always, on Chile, though one or two other countries also produced smaller quantities.

Tin: Bolivian tinmining, afterward so important to the country's economy, opened up just before the turn of the century. Production in 1897 was 3,750 metric tons; by 1913 this had risen to 44,590.

Nitrate: The output of sodium nitrate (the world's best natural fertilizer) in the northern deserts of Chile soared after the War of the Pacific, when Chile conquered the main nitrate-producing areas.

Petroleum: Oil was increasingly in demand after the turn of the century, with the rise of the internal combustion engine. Prior to 1900 Peru was the leading producer; the torch soon passed to Mexico, then in the final years of the Porfiriato; Mexico was eclipsed by Venezuela in the 1920s.

Meat: The export of cattle-on-the-hoof or refrigerated meat came increasingly to characterize the Argentine economy after 1880. Most of it was destined for the British market.

Cereals: Once again, Argentina led the field. Early in the twentieth century, the country became one of the world's great granaries.

Coffee: Toward the end of the nineteenth century, Brazilian coffee production finally centered itself on the state of São Paulo. By 1900 the country produced between two thirds and three quarters of the world's supply and was already meeting with serious crises of over-production. One or two other countries supplied alternative brands, notably Colombia, where production rose from 23,000 bags in 1845 to over a million in 1915.

Sugar: Cuban production greatly expanded during this period. The first million-ton *zafra* (sugar crop) occurred in 1894. After 1903, by which time the island had recovered from the war of independence, harvests were consistently over the million-ton mark.

Bananas: These became the staple product for several of the small republics of Central America, where production boomed after the turn of the century.

Rubber: Another commodity much in demand with the spreading predominance of the motor vehicle, rubber derived from the tree known as *Hevea brasiliensis* growing in the Amazon basin. Brazil's brief but spectacular rubber boom set in in the 1880s, and by 1910 the country accounted for eighty-eight percent of the world supply.

It will be seen that I have listed ten key commodities here. Others could certainly be mentioned, for a very large number of natural resources were now exploited either for the first time or very much more efficiently than in the past. The ten commodities named, however, came to occupy a peculiarly vital position in the economic life of Latin America. Nearly all of the twenty republics were in one way or another dependent on the export of one or more of these commodities by the 1920s.

The second way in which the international economy affected the progress of the region was in the considerable inflow of foreign capital which now developed. By 1913, it has been estimated,[1] foreign investments in the region totaled somewhere in the region of $8,500 million (£1,700 million). Some $5,000 million of this was British in origin, the remainder being accounted for by France, Germany, the United States, and a number of smaller countries (notably Italy, Belgium, Spain, and Switzerland). The commanding position of Great Britain can be very easily appreciated here; by the time of the outbreak of World War I, one fifth of all her overseas investment was concentrated in Latin America. But the contributions made by other countries were respectable enough. Much of this investment occurred from the turn of the century onward: the British stake doubled between 1900 and 1914; the French stake tripled; and the United States' contribution rose fivefold between 1897 and 1914. Where did all this capital go? A substantial proportion of the foreign money invested went into government bonds or railways, each of which accounted for roughly a third of the total; the remaining third was distributed over specific enterprises, with a marked preference for public utilities. American investment, however, departed from this pattern to some extent, showing a greater interest in the exploitation of raw materials for export to the United States than in public bonds, rails, or utilities.

Foreign investment was by no means evenly distributed throughout Latin America. Although every republic received something, the lion's share (about four fifths) went to Argentina, Brazil, Chile, and Mexico. Argentina alone took about a third of the total. We shall examine these four cases presently.

The gearing of local production to the world market, and the import of substantial quantities of foreign capital—these two developments brought about social and economic changes on a bigger scale than anything since the sixteenth century. In describing these changes, it is

[1] I have here followed the figures given in Glade, *op. cit.*, pp. 216-24. There is always a certain amount of guesswork involved in calculating foreign investment totals in this period.

FROM CORTÉS TO CASTRO

perhaps useful to bear in mind an argument which was advanced in the 1820s to justify British investment in the ill-fated mining enterprises of the period. A young English pamphleteer summarized the benefits which would accrue both to Great Britain and to Latin America from the mining associations in the following terms: "To England, they will primarily afford considerable profit. To America, they will yield all those advantages, which result from the circulation of a large quantity of capital."[1] The pamphleteer later became more famous in other connections; his name was Benjamin Disraeli. The British side to his argument need not concern us here, though it is by no means certain that British investments in Latin America after 1860 or so were especially profitable.[2] What, we may ask, were the advantages for Latin America? If there were advantages, were there not disadvantages as well?

In the first place, the gearing of the local economies to export and the inflow of foreign capital undoubtedly contributed a great deal to the "modernization" of the region, or at any rate part of it. However unsatisfactory some of its aspects may have been, there *was* a revolution in transport in the latter part of the nineteenth century. Latin American cities were able to benefit from the latest technical inventions: gas-lighting appeared in the 1850s, usually installed by British concerns, and electric street-lighting began to replace it from the 1880s onward; electric tramways spread rapidly in the 1890s and 1900s; though in the more general uses of electricity Latin America lagged behind both Europe and the United States. The year 1881 saw the first telephones installed in Rio de Janeiro, Buenos Aires, and Valparaíso; other major cities rapidly followed suit.[3] (By 1914 Latin America had approximately two hundred and fifty thousand telephones, roughly half as many as Europe.) Numerous technical improvements in mining and agriculture from the industrial nations were domesticated, and none of the great increases in production already referred to would have been possible without them. Here, it might be thought, Latin America derived some solid advantages.

Moreover, the presence of foreign traders, foreign capitalists, foreign

---

[1] [B. Disraeli], *An Inquiry into the Plans, Progress and Policy of the American Mining Companies*, 3rd ed. (London, 1825), p. 78.

[2] On balance it would seem that British investment in Latin America was never as profitable as investment either in the British empire or in the United States, where the economic "climate" was more stable. See, on this point, J. Fred Rippy, *British Investments in Latin America 1822–1949* (Minneapolis, 1959).

[3] The telephone was, of course, pioneered in North America, and it was usually introduced by American companies; but British or other European interests often managed to secure control of the enterprises.

immigrants, and foreign companies did at least something to reorder and to dynamize the extremely sclerotic arrangements which had hitherto prevailed in credit, banking, and commercial organization. In the aftermath of independence, one of the few reliable sources of credit had been the trading communities, where the foreign presence was particularly noticeable. Significantly, most of the earliest banking houses in the region grew out of the import/export communities or were sponsored by foreigners, for the most part in the 1860s. (The first British bank in the River Plate was set up in 1862.) Over and above this, the patterns of commercial organization favored by the foreign new-comers lent themselves to imitation, though more than a few Latin American presidents had occasion to lament that "the spirit of association," as it was often called, seemed to take time in becoming rooted among the richer classes. Very often, of course, foreign enter-prises, including banks, became an integral part of the local economy concerned and for most practical purposes ceased to be foreign. This was not so much the case with mines or certain types of plantation—which tended to be subsidiaries of foreign-based companies—but it *was* particularly true of ventures backed by immigrants; though they might retain strong emotional connections with their homelands, and even pass these links on to subsequent generations, they were nevertheless deeply committed to the country of their adoption. Many of them married locally, and founded families which achieved a leading position in society. The contribution of such people in late-nineteenth- and early-twentieth-century Latin America was considerable. Some of them became formidable entrepreneurs, created sizable industries, and ended up as millionaires.[1]

It was in the newer kinds of economic activity that the immigrants tended to do well. In distribution and retailing, for instance, their influence spread away from the seaports and capitals and into the interior. Their role in the growth of manufacturing industry was especially notable, for large-scale industry, when it came, did not develop out of the artisans' workshops which had come down from colonial times, but was started from scratch by immigrants or foreigners, or, occasionally, local Creole entrepreneurs.

On the whole, however, Creole imitation of foreign entrepreneurship was not particularly widespread. There were, as always, exceptional cases. Nineteenth-century Chile, for instance, produced more than a handful of admirably enterprising and dynamic miners, bankers, and

---

[1] The role of local immigrant "solidarity" should not be minimized. In Argentina, Torcuato di Tella began his career as a manufacturer with local Italian backing, and the same was true of Francisco Matarazzo in Brazil.

agriculturalists; prior to the War of the Pacific, nearly all the pioneering of nitrates in the Bolivian-owned Atacama Desert and a substantial part of the production in the Peruvian deserts of Tarapacá, was the work of Chileans. Some mention, too, has to be made of the extraordinary case of Irineu Evangelista da Sousa, Viscount Mauá, one of the most notable personalities of the Brazilian empire. Mauá planned and financed and organized railways, steamer lines, canals, an iron foundry, textile mills, and even (in 1874) the famous submarine cable to Europe. This was a remarkable achievement, but its underlying importance lies precisely in the fact that it *was* remarkable.[1] Had there been a thousand Mauás the modern history of Brazil might have been very different, but at no time did it seem very probable that anything like a thousand Mauás would spring from the ground. Whatever progress the international economy brought Latin America, it certainly did not stimulate the formation of an energetic class of local capitalists, capable of influencing the policies of governments.

The Creole land-owning aristocrats, meanwhile, had never had it so good. This was in some respects their golden age. Their style of life became more comfortably opulent than ever before. Trips to Europe grew more frequent, society weddings more sumptuous. Frivolity did not reign entirely supreme. Some aristocrats became immensely cultured, and contributed truly invaluable services to the jurisprudence and the historiography of the region. But as owners of haciendas, ranches, and plantations which had never been more profitable, there was little need for them to seek new wealth or to foster novel kinds of economic enterprise; wealth was already theirs, in full abundance. Law and politics ranked high in their esteem as professions for their sons; trade and manufacturing did not.

Furthermore, the public policies pursued by the governments of the period did much to favor the land-owning interest, as was perhaps only natural. Public investment for economic (as opposed to purely ostentatious or military) purposes tended to flow into such things as improved port facilities or the occasional railway—creating an "infrastructure" which benefited the exporter rather than anyone else. Governments did much to expand and consolidate the hold of the hacienda or ranch in the countryside: during the Porfiriato in Mexico, for instance, the final, ruthless encroachment on Indian community lands which occurred was amply backed by the administration. In Argentina, where General Roca's "conquest of the desert" opened up vast tracts of public land,

---

[1] Significantly, Mauá started his career as an employee of a British trading house. He went bankrupt after his bank failed in 1875, an indirect consequence of the Paraguayan war.

much of this passed directly into the hands of the Creole aristocracy from the 1880s onward. With amiably disposed governments, new wealth flowing in from greatly increased exports, and a complete lack of competition from new interests, it was small wonder that the opening decades of the twentieth century found the position of the land-owning aristocracies stronger and more entrenched than ever.

The traditional predominance of the city was also maintained during this period. Indeed, it was reasserted, for there was once again a good deal of public investment in urban improvements. Most capital cities spent handsome sums of money on programs of beautification. In the Chile of the early 1870s, the energetic Intendant of Santiago, Benjamín Vicuña Mackenna, transformed an ugly and derelict hill in the city center into one of the most delightful urban parks in Latin America (if not the world). In Mexico City, Porfirio Díaz added to the municipal improvements sponsored earlier by Emperor Maximilian. Lima was substantially embellished in the later 1890s, under President Nicolás de Piérola. In the early years of the twentieth century Pereira Pássos, the brilliant prefect of Rio de Janeiro, gave that hitherto fetid city a much-needed face-lift. A thousand miles up the Amazon, at the height of the rubber boom, the city of Manaus endowed itself with a sumptuous opera house. The most astonishing transformation, however, took place in Buenos Aires. The rather disagreeable, colonial-style town soon blossomed into a splendid and proud metropolis, with spacious avenues, leafy parks, monumental squares, magnificent railway termini, the world's largest opera house, and the first underground railway in Latin America. Here, too, the predispositions of colonial times were reinforced rather than modified.

Despite this, the considerable increase in economic activity which set in after 1860 *did* begin to alter the social order in a number of ways. In numerical terms alone, the middle classes—and we shall later have occasion to ask what is meant by "middle classes" in Latin America— now began to blossom in a handful of countries, notably those of southern South America. The immense lower class, too, started to show several new faces. Railways, ports, nitrate *oficinas*, meat-packing plants, efficiently exploited mines—these required labor of a new and sometimes more sophisticated type, and nuclei of a concentrated (and potentially organizable) working class were observable throughout the region before the end of the nineteenth century. Labor agitation of a modern-looking kind—strikes, demonstrations, etc.—put in its first real appearance in the 1890s, and was usually repressed with brutal severity. These new developments were to become especially significant later on, and they will be dealt with in the section that follows.

225

In the genuinely internationalist commercial climate which prevailed during this period, some of the new dilemmas which now confronted the Latin American countries went largely unappreciated. Latin American national sentiment, where it developed, failed for the most part to show a distinctively economic aspect. Yet foreign influence in the local economies was notable enough. Foreigners had come to dominate the import/export trade in the main ports and capitals. The fact that many businesses were owned or run by immigrants mattered less; they were in the process of becoming Latin Americans anyway. But the foreign ownership of railways, for instance, was considerable. And a number of foreign concerns (e.g., the British-run Peruvian Corporation) did come to exercise what might be thought to be an improper degree of influence in specific republics. A very high proportion of Latin America's imports and exports was carried in foreign vessels, the British taking the lion's share everywhere south of the Caribbean, where United States ships were soon tending to lead the field.[1] More serious still, perhaps, was a growing tendency for foreign concerns to gain control of some of the vital natural resources of the region. This was especially true in mining and oil. Here foreign enterprise was given a chance to intervene on a large scale. Increasingly after the turn of the century this meant American rather than European enterprise. As one American economic historian has written, "by the 1930s, the bulk of the productive mineral resources of Hispanic America was owned by capitalists from the United States."[2]

In times of general prosperity, of course, Latin American governments could easily persuade themselves that by concentrating their country's efforts on "monoproduction" (i.e., specialization in one particular commodity) they would guarantee themselves a decent flow of revenue. Most of them relied heavily on duties levied on exports. But monoproduction brought its dangers too. A market might suddenly become depressed, and if alternative markets were not available, then the outlook became serious, for there would be no means of paying for the normal heavy import of capital and consumer goods from the industrial nations. But was there any need to worry? For the most part the geese went on laying the golden eggs. Economic orthodoxy held that

[1] Of the ships entering the port of Buenos Aires in 1900, 51.1 percent were British, 14.9 percent German, 11.5 percent Italian, 11 percent French, 4.6 percent Spanish or Portuguese, and 0.8 percent American. In Valparaíso the same year 65 percent of the ships were British, 28.3 percent German. In Vera Cruz in 1901, 29.2 percent were British, 25.6 percent American, 20.3 percent Spanish, 8.2 percent German, and 7 percent French. In Havana in 1912, however, 74.9 percent were American and only 17.4 percent British. See Robert G. Albion, "British Shipping and Latin America 1806-1914," *Journal of Economic History*, Vol. I (1951).

[2] J. Fred Rippy, *Latin America and the Industrial Age* (New York, 1944), p. 194.

in the course of time the benefits of free trade would be distributed evenly across the world, that local industries would spring up spontaneously, and that archaic social conditions would be gradually overcome. Alternative doctrines of an economic nationalism based on high protectionist tariffs were occasionally assimilated (by the Chilean president Balmaceda, for example) but failed nearly everywhere to undermine the conventional wisdom.

By the early years of the twentieth century, a few Latin Americans were becoming increasingly aware of some of these issues, and beginning to see them in a different light. In a very interesting book published in 1913, the Peruvian Francisco García Calderón wrote:

To sum up, the new continent, politically free, is economically a vassal. This dependence is inevitable; without European capital there would have been no railways, no ports, and no stable government in America. But the disorder which prevails in the finances of the country changes into a real servitude what might otherwise have been a beneficial relation.[1]

A few years later, in the 1920s, the Chilean writer Joaquín Edwards Bello (who himself came from a distinguished immigrant family of the sort referred to earlier) interpreted the situation of his own country in rather more embittered terms:

The trans-Andine railway, the most expensive in the world, is English. By boarding a tramcar, talking on the telephone, eating breakfast, buying in a shop, turning on the light, the Chilean is contributing to the admirable life of an English capitalist who takes his tea or plays his polo in the British Isles. . . . Harrods, the best shop in Santiago, is English. The sheep ranches of Magallanes are in the hands of Englishmen, which means they pay miserable export duties, because they naturally pay lawyers who are influential in government.[2]

Awareness of the disadvantages of monoproduction and of foreign control of local resources and enterprises was, as we shall see, to become

[1] F. García Calderón, *Latin America, Its Rise and Progress* (London, 1913), p. 382.
[2] Joaquín Edwards Bello, *Nacionalismo continental* (Santiago, 1968), p. 51. British capital played a big part in opening up the southerly province of Magallanes (including Tierra del Fuego) to sheep-raising. In the 1890s the two largest enterprises concerned (one of which was 66 percent British-owned, the other just over 50 percent) successfully evaded the Chilean government's requirement that 80 percent of the operating capital should be Chilean. The growth of the province entailed the brutal elimination of some of the primitive local Indian tribes (e.g., the Tehuelches and Onas) by agents of the companies, sometimes with the connivance of the governor of the territory.

a principal issue in Latin America after 1914 and even more so after 1930.

How inevitable was this particular effect of the international economy? The nineteenth century and the early twentieth yielded two notable examples of countries which escaped from a "peripheral" condition and arrived either at the center of the international economy or somewhere near it: the United States and Japan. Space precludes a serious discussion of how this occurred, but both these examples should certainly be mentioned in passing. In the case of the United States, which was heavily dependent on European capital right up to World War I, much was owed to the antecedent colonial order, which permitted the growth of an extremely strong entrepreneurial class in the nineteenth century. No deeply traditional landed aristocracy (except in the South) stood in the way of progress; landowners were for the most part industrious, self-reliant, and go-ahead. Judicious government action (not least in the sphere of protectionist tariffs) encouraged the growth of trade and industry, an efficient agriculture, and an educational system with a suitably technical strand to it. All of these measures were animated by a clear sense of national purpose which included a definite economic dimension, with an eye to establishing the country in an independent and leading position. Already by the 1870s the United States was one of the main industrial nations, still relying to a marked degree on foreign capital, but able to turn this to her own advantage. The case of Japan was perhaps even more striking, although industrialization did not reach European levels until after World War I. The transformation of this island empire into an industrial state, after a long period of extreme isolation from the rest of the world, depended in a high degree on the national discipline imposed by the monarchy, the most traditional institution in the land. The Japanese emperor had the good fortune to be a god, which made it easier for aristocrat and peasant alike to obey him and to adapt their lives to the changes brought in by foreign technicians.

In the Latin American case, some of the legacies of colonial times have already been noted. It is strikingly apparent that the Creole republics inherited a very different social order from the one which grew up in the United States. The Japanese example, too, was impossible to follow; although many of them held an excessively high opinion of their own merits, it did not occur to Latin American presidents to try to establish a claim to divine status. They were not gods; and they were often not obeyed. In the United States the international economy strengthened and (as a result) transformed the characteristics which had been present in colonial times. In Japan the international economy (though *not* European technical knowledge) was barred from penetrating the country too deeply. In both these respects the experience of Latin America was profoundly different. The local impact of the international economy solidified the position the aristocracies had inherited from colonial days; the international economy was accepted, welcomed, and encouraged precisely (we may surmise) because it would *not* transform traditional habits and mentalities. It fortified, all too often, those parasitic predispositions which the leaders of society had embraced and cultivated since the earliest days of Iberian colonization. In short, the fostering of exports suited too many people in powerful positions in Latin America, and although it led to unquestionable progress in many spheres, it did not lead—and was purposefully not *made* to lead—to a diversification of economic activity. Too many previously existing arrangements were left intact.

Nor did the region experience any of those abrupt shocks which have been known to affect the lives of other nations in vital ways. The connection between warfare and social reform in the European case is an indisputable one. But no major war really disturbed the even tenor of Latin American life, and the effects of the two substantial international conflicts which occurred in the region between 1864 and 1883 were negligible—though here is a subject on which little research has been carried out. No Latin American state was systematically and permanently geared to aggression during this (or any other) period. No government ever seriously felt the need to disturb some aspects of the social order, to discipline its aristocracy, or to conciliate the poorer classes in order to win their support for the purposes of waging war. Here again, one might think, was a major influence which kept things in their place and did not rearrange them.

By no means all of the generalizations made so far in this section hold good in equal measure for all the different countries of the region. There were significant local variations, sometimes fairly striking ones. A brief look at four of the republics chiefly affected by the international economy seems indicated here. Argentina, Brazil, Chile, and Mexico— these were by any standards the leading states of Latin America at the turn of the century. What had become of each of them?

ARGENTINA

In Argentina progress was most rapid and affected the majority of the population. A large and empty country, endowed with a rich soil and easy access from the sea, Argentina had no large proportion of her population sealed off by the hacienda system. Indeed, her total population was small—less than two million in 1869. In place of the extreme availability of cheap labor which was to be found elsewhere in Latin

America, Argentina suffered from a relative scarcity of manpower—and her labor requirements were only met, in fact, by a massive influx of migrants from Europe. Once the era of Rosas and the gaucho hordes had been left behind, successive liberal administrations adopted policies which were highly favorable to growth.

Pastoral activities had long formed the basis of such prosperity as was enjoyed by the River Plate region, whose *estancias* had kept up a continuous export of cattle hides and salted meat since before independence. Now, with the growth of an enormous new market for beef in Great Britain, hides and salted meat yielded place in the export lists to live cattle, and (from the 1880s) chilled or frozen meat; *Le Frigorifique*, a French vessel specially fitted out to show the possibilities of refrigeration, made an experimental voyage to Argentina in 1876, and from 1883 a regular service of such ships plied between the River Plate and England. From the 1880s, *frigoríficos* (meat-packing plants) multiplied along the shoreline of the River Plate. Argentine *estancieros* gradually improved the quality of their cattle, adapting their meat to the taste of the English customer. Argentine beef soon attained what was conceivably the highest quality in the world.[1] Alongside this tremendous expansion of cattle raising went a more surprising development: the growth of a flourishing commercial agriculture. Starting in Santa Fe and drifting from there into the province of Buenos Aires itself, crop cultivation spread apace, underwritten by an influx of immigrants without precedent in Argentine (or Latin American) history.

The wealth generated by this extraordinary boom in exports was, of course, prodigious. Some of it flowed into the pockets of the foreign investors who had supplied most of the capital for the economic miracle. More, perhaps, passed into the hands of the powerful estancieros who owned the pampa. Their cattle and their wheat were in constant demand; their land never ceased to appreciate in value; their pseudo-renaissance palaces and English-style mansions proliferated across the great green plain. Some of them, at least, placed their sons in English public schools. They traveled, too. *Riche comme un argentin* ("rich as an Argentine")—so ran a familiar French phrase in the golden years before World War I. And while the estanciero class became supremely affluent, the remainder of the population soon found its living standards at a higher level than those of its counterparts elsewhere in Latin America. Illiteracy was down to thirty-five percent by 1914.

At the foundation of this economic miracle lay Argentina's connection with the British market. It was a connection which the estanciero aristocracy and the governments of the day (the latter drawing their

[1] Only Scottish beef fetched higher prices at Smithfield during this period.

key personnel from the former) both accepted and stimulated. That they failed, for the most part, to use the wealth derived from this connection to promote internal industrial growth has sometimes been held against them by subsequent generations. It does not seem to have preoccupied them very much at the time. Should it have? There was certainly no deep-rooted British conspiracy to maintain Argentina's dependence on agrarian products. It need not be supposed, either, that the long Anglo-Argentine relationship necessarily benefited Great Britain more than Argentina. Argentina had an effect on Great Britain, just as Great Britain had an effect on Argentina. As Professor H. S. Ferns has put it:

> Any agricultural landlord or farmer in Britain between the years 1890 and 1939 could argue that Argentina was a factor in their fate, and a very adverse one. Derelict fields in Cambridgeshire existed in part because fields in the Argentine Republic were heavy with cheap cereals, and Argentine *estancieros* have wintered on the Riviera while herdsmen in Shropshire went bankrupt. These are facts which make nonsense of myths about British imperialism and Argentina as a semi-colony of a great and powerful state.[1]

Myths, however, are often more enduring than facts. And it remains true that the wealth created by the export boom was not used to promote industrialization or economic diversification. In the last analysis, this was due to a conscious and rational calculation on the part of the Argentine governing classes; they were the only people in a position to do anything about it, and they chose not to.

BRAZIL

The empire of Brazil was, in fact, the first Latin American state to receive substantial amounts of foreign investment, slightly preceding Argentina; this was due partly to the strength of the trading connection established with the country by the British from 1810 onward, but also, no doubt, to the climate of political stability reached (particularly from the early 1840s) under the auspices of the imperial monarchy. Roughly at the time of independence, the coffee *fazenda* replaced the sugar plantation and the mine as the focal point of Brazilian progress. For most of the nineteenth century, world demand favored this activity, and prices were good. In the early decades of the coffee boom, Negro slavery was still the standard means of filling labor

[1] H. S. Ferns, *Britain and Argentina in the Nineteenth Century* (Oxford, 1960) pp. 488–89.

requirements, but the end of the slave trade reduced the supply, created manpower shortages, and caused many *fazendeiros* to reflect on the advantages of free labor. With the abolition of slavery, European immigrants began to flood into southern Brazil, creating a situation not entirely dissimilar to that which prevailed in the River Plate—the bulk of the population well inside a modern, money economy, and a solid commercial agriculture giving rise to considerable prosperity. By the early years of the twentieth century, São Paulo was unquestionably the richest and most developed area of Brazil.

The fortunes of Brazilian coffee, even so, illustrate a not unfamiliar Latin American dilemma stemming from monoproduction. Increasingly after 1890 or so, Brazilian coffee began to suffer periodic crises of overproduction, while world prices began to fluctuate alarmingly. Brazil was quite simply producing too much coffee; the world did not need it all. What was the remedy? At Taubaté (São Paulo) in 1906, representatives from the three main coffee states (São Paulo, Minas Gerais, and Rio de Janeiro) set up a coffee "valorization" scheme. The state governments agreed to buy up a large part of the harvest, and hold it back from the market until prices had risen to a suitable level, though they were obliged to borrow money abroad to cover the cost of their purchases of coffee. At the same time, no new coffee fazendas were to begin operations. The Taubaté agreement and a similar agreement which followed it after World War I seemed to work fairly well. In 1924 the federal government itself intervened with a similar scheme. Production was, however, still too high. In the mid-1920s São Paulo alone was in a position to supply the whole of the world's demand for coffee. The depression brought problems of greater magnitude than before. There was, indeed, an awful lot of coffee in Brazil.

Southern Brazil, with its substantial commercial progress based on coffee, was by no means the whole country. The northeast was still highly dependent on sugar. Indeed, the actual volume of sugar exports in the nineteenth century was greater than in colonial times, even though the European demand fell off with the rise of beet sugar in Europe itself, and there was plenty of competition from the Caribbean. After 1900, in fact, much Brazilian sugar production was for the domestic market, not least in the expanding south. There were a number of changes in the direction of modernization in the sugar industry at the close of the nineteenth century and afterward: railways (in which the government took a considerable interest) permitted sugar processing to take place further from the sea than before, while the old *engenho* (mill) yielded place to the much more efficient *usina* ("factory"), one of which could do the work of fifty engenhos. Unfortunately, despite the continued production of sugar, and a great expansion of both cacao and tobacco in the Bahia area, the northeast presented a remarkably different aspect from that of the booming south. Its development in colonial times as the major focus of sugar production had left the region with a large population, predominantly Negro and mulatto in composition. This population continued to grow, but there was no corresponding rise in either the area of land cultivated or agricultural efficiency. The abolition of slavery did nothing to raise the income or the standard of living of the plantation laborers. Away from the plantations, subsistence agriculture was common. Stark poverty prevailed over large areas. In periods of drought, the inhabitants of the *sertão* flocked to the already overcrowded coast, complicating a situation which was already serious. Throughout the nineteenth century, in fact, the northeast wore something of the look of a "depressed area"—and the twentieth century only served to exacerbate its problems.

Thus the impact of the international economy on Brazil was a good deal less homogeneous than it was in Argentina. In the River Plate, no such region as the Brazilian northeast existed; the old northwest declined, but was in any case an area whose population and importance was falling all the time. In the age-old struggle between Buenos Aires and the interior, the triumph of Buenos Aires was overwhelming. In Brazil, by contrast, regional disparities were severely accentuated. A "modern," open, and dynamic south contrasted dramatically with a "traditional" and stagnant northeast. Some of the enormous problems which Brazil faced in later years stemmed directly from this contrast.

CHILE

Much of the proud nineteenth-century record of the smallest of the four republics under discussion here was due to a pattern of economic success which compared favorably with that of any other Latin American state in the period. Politically, the country was extraordinarily stable. In this particular climate, foreign trade expanded and domestic entrepreneurship seems to have developed more than it did elsewhere in Latin America. The state took an active hand in the economic progress of the nation. It reserved, until 1849 at least,[1] the coasting trade to Chilean vessels; it contracted loans to build railways; it greatly stimulated education. Far-sighted statesmen like Portales in the 1830s or Montt in the 1850s seemed to be pursuing a vision of national progress and national greatness. According to their lights, and in nineteenth-century Latin American terms, they surely succeeded.

---

[1] The date is significant; the gold rush had attracted Chilean merchant vessels en masse to California, leaving the coast denuded of shipping.

The country's economic fortunes rested on the solid foundations of mining and agriculture. In mining, silver and copper predominated until the 1870s, when silver production declined. In the 1880s nitrates headed the export lists. Nitrate oficinas multiplied across the northern deserts, so recently won from Bolivia and Peru by Chilean arms. Now, for the first time, there was a substantial foreign stake in one of the country's richest natural resources. British interests—most notably those of John Thomas North—owned nearly half the nitrate lands being exploited, and accounted for some sixty percent of output in the year 1890. Many Chilean politicians were unworried. The nitrate companies —foreign and Chilean alike—paid a hefty export tax, which boosted public revenues throughout the 1880s. "Let the *gringos* work away in the nitrate fields," President Domingo Santa María (1881–86) is reputed to have said; "I shall be waiting for them at the door." Santa María's successor in the presidency, José Manuel Balmaceda, was more preoccupied by what he saw as a potential "industrial dictatorship" on the part of the British nitrate interests in Tarapacá. He proposed a prohibition on further British acquisitions in the north, and an end to the British monopoly of railways in the nitrate zones.[1] In the meantime he himself made use of the very considerable revenues from export taxes to sponsor a program of public works without precedent in Chilean history, and to give encouragement to domestic manufacturing. Further developments were cut short, however, by Balmaceda's defeat in the civil war of 1891.

Nitrate exports continued to provide successive Chilean governments with their chief source of income for three further decades, but production went into a critical decline following the invention of synthetic nitrate by the German scientist Fritz Haber during World War I.[2] By this stage, however, copper mining was entering a new and much more productive phase. New mines of considerably greater size were now opened up, owned and exploited by American interests, and Chile soon came to be associated with copper in the way she had previously been associated with nitrates. Despite their contribution to the national wealth, the nitrate and copper zones never had the effect of "develop-

[1] Balmaceda did not advocate the expropriation of the British nitrate interests, but he was extremely concerned by the extent to which North's enterprises were coming to constitute a state within a state. "We cannot" he told Congress in June 1889, "shut the door on free competition in nitrate production in Tarapacá, neither can we consent to that vast and wealthy region becoming a simple foreign factory."

[2] Chilean capital remained important in nitrates. In 1910 the Chilean investment amounted to around £10.4 million, the British at £10.7 million. In 1911–12, Chilean interests were responsible for 38.5 percent of nitrate exports, the British for 37 percent. Third place was occupied by German capital.

ing" large areas of the country. Isolated for the most part in the arid and underpopulated north, they were little more than enclaves. Only a fraction of the Chilean population found employment there, although enough to make the desert the birthplace of the Chilean labor movement.

Chilean agriculture during the same period offered a somewhat deceptive picture of vitality and progress. As I mentioned in the previous chapter, Chilean wheatgrowers succeeded in exploiting the short-lived Californian and Australian markets in the later 1840s and mid-1850s, and they also exported grain in sizable quantities to Great Britain—but an important factor in this later development was the absence of competition from the major wheat-producing countries (Argentina, Australia, Canada) which had not yet got into their stride. Chilean grain exports reached their peak in 1875. No truly substantial changes flowed from these essentially temporary export booms. The Chilean hacendado merely took on extra labor—there was always plenty available—and cultivated some of the normally unused land on his estate. The immobility of the traditional hacienda system remained stamped on the face of the Central Valley.

After 1900 or so, a mood of doubt began to take hold in intellectual circles in Chile. The country's progress no longer seemed as promising as it had for most of the nineteenth century. By some it was held that government and aristocracy alike, corrupted by easy wealth, were rapidly degenerating. The rise in population was coupled with no comparable rise in agricultural productivity; before the new century was very old, Chile was resorting to the occasional imports of food which later became a permanent feature of the scene. The mounting "social question" combined with a nagging sense of national decline made the future seem less hopeful than many Chileans of the 1870s and 1880s—let alone Portales or Montt—would have believed possible.

MEXICO

Unlike Argentina, an "empty" land, or Brazil, where late-nineteenth-century progress affected different regions unequally, Mexico was a nation which had received the full inheritance of Spanish colonial rule. Its social order bore the familiar marks of a parasitically inclined aristocracy and a widespread hacienda system, to which had been added in the course of the nineteenth century the disadvantages of political chaos and fiscal disorder. The mid-century developments of the Reforma, however, did much to consolidate the power of the land-owning class; many thousands of properties passed from the Catholic Church into the hands of private landlords. The hacienda continued to expand during the long dictatorship of Porfirio Díaz, who rigorously insisted on applying the provisions of the Lerdo Law to the Indian communities, now debarred, as "corporations," from holding common land. Public lands were given away to private companies and individuals in rich profusion.

The Porfiriato saw a massive increase in foreign investment, and its policies were extremely favorable to this process. Local commercial law was reformed; the last remnants of the old internal customs barriers were demolished; the budget was balanced and the reserves built up; the Mexican government soon acquired an unfamiliar reputation for financial probity and competence. Mexico's proximity to the United States, combined with the fact that by the time of the Porfiriato the United States was in a position to export large amounts of capital, meant that American enterprise and finance soon acquired a leading position. By 1910 approximately $1,000 million (£200 million) of American money was invested in Mexico; the British investment in the same year stood at £77 million. At the end of the Porfiriato, three quarters of all Mexico's exports went to the United States.

Foreign interest in the country since colonial days had traditionally been concerned with mining. This was now renewed and revived. Díaz handed out mining concessions to foreign concerns with gay abandon, failing to safeguard Mexican interests by insisting on the training of Mexican technicians or in the other ways which were open to him. Perhaps the most extraordinary example of his policy in this respect was the sale of the Tampico oilfields in 1900 at a price of around a dollar an acre. These rapidly passed into the hands of British and American interests, who were permitted to export oil without paying tax to the Mexican government.

It was on the land, however, that the consequences of the dictatorship's determination to domesticate the international economy were most disastrous. The assault on the Indian villages, the extension of debt-peonage, the concentration of landownership—these combined to produce an ultimately explosive situation. The expansion of the hacienda was not by any means paralleled by an expansion in efficiency. Indeed, although the haciendas were responsible for the bulk of Mexican food production, they failed to fulfill the task of maintaining it at a proper level; the government eventually had to import food. Meanwhile the traditional patterns of life on the land were greatly fortified. Absentee landlordism, under-use of land on the great estates, soil erosion that went unchecked, and a wholly deplorable state of poverty for the great majority of peóns—these were the standard characteristics. A sordid and inhuman pattern of misery lay beneath the glittering surface of Díaz' vulgar "success story."

Taking the four cases sketched here, it is apparent that the most striking contrast is the one between Mexico and Argentina. In simple terms of economic statistics, both countries seemed to offer a picture of sustained progress between 1860 and 1910 or so. Yet it is clear that progress was far more genuine and widespread in the Argentine case than in the Mexican. Argentine development occurred in a country where a frontier could be pushed back and the land opened up—in great part by a stream of immigrant newcomers who staked their own future on the country's. In many respects, the growth of Argentina was somewhat comparable to that of Canada, Australia, or New Zealand. The comparison should not, perhaps, be pressed all the way, but it is a legitimate and interesting comparison nonetheless. In Mexico, by contrast, economic progress was essentially superimposed, often brutally, on a situation where the shadow of the past still hung heavily over the present. The outcome in Argentina was a degree of prosperity unusual in Latin America. In Mexico the outcome was a revolutionary disaster.

Is it possible to sum up the ultimate effect of the international economy on Latin America as it existed prior to 1930? The period was in some ways as formative as the era of the original Iberian conquest. On the one hand, it brought undeniable progress. On the other, its impact was assessed perhaps in a rather short-sighted way by the various Latin American governments of the day, who failed to turn it to their advantage from the viewpoint of autonomous growth. Many aspects of the traditional social order were in fact consolidated rather than rearranged. No radically new domestic interests took the field. And so a state of initial dependence which (as García Calderón argued) was in some ways beneficial was allowed to continue unchecked. We should not, however, cast too many stones. Latin Americans were by no means the only people who assumed that nineteenth-century progress would continue indefinitely, and that its benefits would eventually rub off on everyone everywhere. They were not to see that after 1914, when European civilization released its own pent-up forces of barbarism, and again after 1930, when the depression cast its sinister shadow across the region, they would be obliged to turn their attention to the more questionable and debatable features of their own social and economic condition.

Changes and Constants

*The ideal of peoples whose economic condition is dependence is naturally
autonomy; without it all liberty is precarious.*

FRANCISCO GARCÍA CALDERÓN (1913)

As we approach the present, the problems in presenting even the
sketchiest of outlines of social and economic developments in Latin
America grow greater. It is manifestly impossible to present a general
outline which does not oversimplify many issues. All I can hope to do
is to indicate some of the main changes which have affected the region
since the international economy in its classical form broke down, and
at the same time to suggest the principal elements in the situation
which have remained strikingly unchanged. For Latin America in its
most recent half-century—rather less than one ninth of its whole history
—has displayed an interesting pattern of both changes and constants.

The guns which boomed so hideously in Europe in August 1914
reverberated far beyond the confines of the Old World. In Europe,
civilization was shaken to its foundations. In Latin America, the age
of innocence, ended. The international economy as described in the
previous section was now disrupted at its very core. For the next four
years the industrial nations devoted their best energies to destroying
each other; to put an army in the field in the center was more important than to increase the export of manufactured goods to the
periphery. True, the general attempts at "reconstruction" when
World War I was over proved partially successful. The 1920s may be
considered as a kind of epilogue to the pre-1914 period. More than a
few of the Latin American states (most notably Argentina) basked once
more in the sunshine of a renewed prosperity based on exports. But it
was essentially a false dawn. After 1930 the depression abruptly halted
the precarious recovery that had taken place: Latin American exports
to Europe, to take one measure of what now occurred, fell in value by
well over half between 1929 and 1932. Even more than 1914, perhaps,
the start of the depression opened up a period when few (if any) of the
basic assumptions about the international economy as it had previously
existed could be taken for granted.

In terms of international trade, the keynote of the new period was
uncertainty. New uncertainties would probably have risen anyway, even
without the general disruption of trade caused by two world wars and
the depression. In the course of the twentieth century, partly under the
stress of war, many industries in the nations of the center became
markedly more efficient in their use of raw materials imported from the

countries of the periphery, and sometimes needed less. The advance of technology provided substitutes for metals and other materials; in many of its uses, for instance, copper could be replaced by aluminum, while Haber's discovery of synthetic nitrate removed the need to take Chilean exports of the real thing, thus forcing the Chilean nitrate industry into a tragic decline. As far as Latin America was concerned, several mono-productive export lines found themselves under heavy competition from other parts of the world. The rubber of Southeast Asia, for example, destroyed the Brazilian export for good and brought to an end the glittering fortunes of the Amazon city of Manaus. Copper was now mined in the Congo and in Northern Rhodesia (now Zambia). In Europe itself, sugar-beet production continued to lessen the need to buy from Brazil or the Caribbean.

Additional competition was aggravated by a new tendency for world prices to fluctuate alarmingly. One can certainly exaggerate the extent to which prices had remained stable in the classical period of the international economy, but the twentieth-century variations were far more severe than any that had been seen previously. Often now there were fluctuations of up to twenty percent a year. Markets were no longer certain; production became difficult to plan; many Latin American interests found themselves exposed to economic breezes which often seemed unpredictable and even whimsical. A vague sense of powerlessness began to take root. Governments began to appreciate the need for a more intelligent and forward-looking export strategy. There were, of course, several short-term gains. During both the world wars, the belligerent Allied powers (though neither the Central Powers in World War I nor the Axis in the second war) bought Latin American foodstuffs and strategic raw materials at favorable prices, enabling many Latin American countries to build up handsome sterling or dollar balances in London or New York. But these conditions were essentially temporary, and on both occasions peacetime brought a return to the new tradition of uncertainty.

The new period also brought with it a notable retreat from the free-trading assumptions of the nineteenth century. Brick by brick, new tariff walls rose to grimly imposing heights. Nations everywhere sought to protect themselves from the economic blizzards and hurricanes that now blew so fiercely. Great Britain, whose role in the international economy had been so crucial, abandoned free trade in 1931–32 and sought new security in a program of imperial preference, turning, in the Ottawa agreements of 1932, to the nations of the empire and the commonwealth for her food and raw materials. Argentina was the Latin American state most seriously affected by this collapse of the British economy. In the belief that the British connection had to be maintained at all costs, the conservative Argentine government of the day sent its vice-president to London to negotiate an agreement which would do this. The resultant Roca–Runciman Pact (1933) ensured the continuation of meat exports to Great Britain; in return, British goods were given preference in the Argentine market.[1] In the new and desperate circumstances of the 1930s, bilateral agreements of this sort made sense—but they were a fair reflection of what had happened to international trade.

From the Latin American viewpoint, the most serious immediate effect of the two wars and the depression was the sudden decline in the availability of capital goods and in manufactures generally. In World War I, which gave Latin America a first taste of this new shortage, British industries were less concerned with supplying export markets than with contributing to the war effort. Shipping was reduced—partly through danger, partly because it was needed elsewhere—and Germany, under blockade, was no longer in a position to supply those states which remained neutral. Even when Latin American countries had money to pay for European manufactured goods, these were not forthcoming. Similar considerations can be applied to the 1930s and to World War II. Deprived of a regular or consistent flow of the products of industrial Europe, Latin America was obliged to do one of two things: encourage domestic industries, or buy from elsewhere. As we shall see presently, the world crisis of 1914–45 compelled the Latin American governments to look more closely at the problem of industrialization. Indeed, the history of Latin American industry very largely begins with World War I. At the same time, there was a substantial redirection of the region's foreign trade.

The chief beneficiary of this redirection, inevitably, was the United States. Well before World War I, American capital in significant amounts had flowed into the Caribbean and, to a lesser extent, South America. The United States had bought appreciable quantities of raw materials and was a principal market for Brazilian coffee. Now, with European competition either temporarily eliminated or at a general disadvantage, Americans began to buy from and sell to Latin America on a greatly increased scale. It is entirely probable that this development would have occurred anyway, but events after 1914 enormously accelerated the process. Not until the recovery of Western Europe after World War II, and the growth of new economic groupings in Latin America itself in the 1960s, was the general tendency of the region's foreign trade to move into the orbit of the United States even partially

[1] The Roca-Runciman Pact was renewed in 1936.

modified. The following two tables give a fair indication of the extent of the commercial relations between Latin America and the United States in recent decades:

Latin American–United States Trade*

Year	% of Latin American Exports Going to U.S.	% of Latin American Imports Coming from U.S.
1913	30.8	25.0
1928	31.5	36.7
1938	33.2	33.4
1948	37.2	57.7
1962	42.1	41.1

Year	% of U.S. Exports Going to Latin America	% of U.S. Imports Coming from Latin America
1913	14.4	26.0
1928	16.0	23.1
1938	16.1	23.1
1948	24.7	35.5
1962	15.3	20.7

* Wendell C. Gordon, *The Political Economy of Latin America* (New York, 1965), p. 301.

From these figures it will be seen that Latin America's dependence on the United States as a market between 1913 and 1962 was considerably greater than the American dependence on Latin America. (This is not the whole story. Something, ideally, should be said about the *nature* of the goods exchanged, since some are obviously more vital to both parties than others. Nevertheless, the general affirmation holds good.) The twentieth-century United States has been a good deal less sensitive to foreign trade than nineteenth-century Great Britain. Endowed with an immense domestic market and with plentiful natural resources, and shielded by a greater measure of protectionism, the industrial progress of the United States has depended far less on relations with foreign primary-producing countries than was the case with Great Britain. The commercial opportunities for Latin American exporters, therefore, are more circumscribed today than they were before 1914.

Clearly connected with this redirection of foreign trade were a number of changes in the way foreign capital flowed into Latin America. At times, of course, it hardly flowed at all, as in the 1930s. When it did flow, it came from the United States rather than from the older sources. During World War I, American capital in Latin America increased by around fifty percent, while British capital remained at its previous level. In the 1920s the British investment rose slightly, but the American investment doubled. By 1930 the United States had supplanted Great Britain as the chief supplier of foreign capital to the region. The depression and World War II saw a drastic decline in the British stake: between 1939 and 1949 the British investment was halved. Not until well after the war did Western European capital again enter the region in substantial quantities. The predominance of the United States went largely unchallenged. The precise amount of capital invested in the region by American interests since 1945 has varied considerably, not least because of recurrent political uncertainties. In the 1940s and 1950s, the inflow of capital was very rapid, but the Cuban revolution (which appropriated some one thousand million dollars from American investors) acted as something of a brake. In 1962, it is estimated, direct private American investment south of the Rio Grande totaled close on nine thousand million dollars.[1]

Two points of importance connected with the inflow of American funds should be noted here. British investment in the pre-1914 period, as we saw, tended to gravitate toward government loans, railways, and public utilities. This was very much less true of the new American investment, which displayed a notably greater interest in the exploitation of raw materials and (more recently) in manufacturing industry. Venezuelan oil and Chilean copper, for instance, received a major share. Railways and utilities were neglected. The private investor was no longer interested, either, in supplying funds to Latin American governments; this became increasingly a matter for the government of the United States, which, as mentioned on p. 53, set up the Export-Import Bank for this very purpose in 1934. In later years the World Bank and the Inter-American Development Bank (particularly the latter) also played a substantial role in the external financing of the region. Private investment in governments was thus gradually replaced by public aid, though the distinction between "investment" and "aid" sometimes proved difficult to draw.

That the various changes on the international scene which I have described were bound to have a profound impact on Latin America cannot reasonably be doubted. The region as a whole, and in particular

[1] The British investment in Latin America stood at £164 million at the end of 1962 (compared with around £750 million in 1914). The German investment at the end of 1964 was DM 1,514 million. It is worth mentioning that American capital in Latin America in the 1960s grew at a snail's pace compared with American capital in other parts of the world.

its governments, discovered some of the disadvantages of its general position. The orthodox assumptions which underlay the old international economy were severely challenged by events themselves. Politicians of most shades of opinion became conscious of certain fundamental needs, needs which had to be satisfied if Latin America were ever to protect itself adequately against the hazards of international economic life and, by the same token, to promote internal progress. This new awareness did not come overnight, and in some respects it had already dawned before 1914. A new tone in economic and social criticism had become visible in a handful of Latin American writings before the close of the nineteenth century; after the turn of the century, such writings became more frequent, and after 1914 much more frequent. The basic priorities demanded by the new situation gradually took shape in the minds of politicians, businessmen, intellectuals, and men-in-the-street. The economies of Latin America, it was now increasingly felt, had to be diversified, since monoproduction for overseas markets (the eggs-in-one-basket tendency) was altogether too risky. The traditional reliance on imported manufactured goods had to be counteracted by a vigorous promotion of domestic industries. The very considerable foreign stake in the Latin American economy had to be regulated and controlled. The state, which had to some extent withdrawn from the economic arena in the nineteenth century, now had to be prepared to move nearer the center of the stage once again, in order to promote these desirable changes of emphasis.

In the public policies adopted to further economic progress in the twentieth century, two general approaches can be identified. (A third has put in an appearance in more recent times, and will be mentioned at the end of this section.) It may be useful to outline these two general attitudes at this point.[1]

It was always possible, of course, to pretend that the disruption of the international economy was only temporary; this pretense was to some extent encouraged by the brief recovery of the 1920s. Latin Americans could always assume that the two wars and the depression were ephemeral aberrations, and that things would one day return to "normal." By 1950 or so, when the disruption had gone on for the better part of forty years, it was perhaps less easy to make this case convincing. Even so, more than a few governments continued to base their assumptions on the view that stable markets and freer trading arrangements would eventually return. The policies which they adopted, in

[1] Professor William Glade terms these two approaches "Orthodox" and "Neo-orthodox": see Glade, *op. cit.*, pp. 376–482. I have referred extensively to his interesting and illuminating discussion of the issues in writing these paragraphs.

accordance with the first approach I mentioned, were designed to stimulate the production of primary products for export, to create a suitable climate for further infusions of foreign capital, and to put their own house in order by modernizing transport and communications, education, the public administration, and taxation. Industrialization as such, it was expected, would somehow emerge "naturally" and spontaneously from "export-led growth." The temptation to follow this approach was perhaps greatest in the smaller republics (e.g., those of Central America), where the absence of a large domestic market made vast and ambitious plans for industrialization look somewhat ridiculous.

It would be tedious to make a complete list of the governments which tried to put this particular approach into practice: the Odría government in Peru could certainly be cited as an example, as could the Gómez regime in Venezuela, the National Front administrations in Colombia, and some of the Argentine governments which followed the era of General Perón. (Traces of the approach could also be found in the post-1964 governments of Brazil.) By the 1960s, it was apparent that many of the good intentions of the protagonists of this approach had been frustrated. Public administrations proved less easy to reform and modernize than had been supposed; the taxation systems of most of the countries concerned were never overhauled in a truly realistic way; education did not expand particularly fast; agriculture did not become outstandingly more productive or efficient.

In its reforms of certain public institutions, however, the approach made a definite contribution to the twentieth-century shape of Latin America. Nowhere was this truer than in the sphere of central banking: by the 1960s all the Latin American republics had central banks, with the exception of Panama and Haiti. Central banking institutions had existed in Uruguay since 1896 and in Bolivia since 1914, but it was the twenty years after 1923 that saw the multiplication of such authorities. They were usually set up with foreign (either British or American) advice and assistance: the Banco Central de la República Argentina, for instance, owed much to the British financial experts F. F. J. Powell and Sir Otto Niemeyer, and, under its first director, Raúl Prebisch, adopted a successful and pragmatic line of action reminiscent of that of the Bank of England.[1]

The second and more interventionist approach which concerns us here was based on a somewhat different set of assumptions. In due course, the economists of the UN Economic Commission for Latin

---

[1] Central banks were set up as follows: Colombia, 1923; Chile, Guatemala, Mexico, 1925; Argentina, El Salvador, 1934; Costa Rica, 1936; Venezuela, 1939; Nicaragua, 1941. The only bank wholly uninfluenced by foreign advice was that of Mexico.

America (ECLA) provided this second approach (which tended to coincide with its own) with considerable theoretical backing, although the approach as such can be seen in action well before the foundation of ECLA. The starting point for the second approach was to be found in the view that the countries of the periphery were at a permanent disadvantage in relation to those of the center. Several basic "asymmetries," it was thought, combined to worsen the periphery's trading position. The center, for instance, demanded *less* from the periphery as technology became more sophisticated; at the same time, the periphery tended to demand *more* from the center as its economies became more complex. Latin America's terms of trade, it was now believed, were unlikely to improve. Export-led growth, then, seemed a more and more dubious strategy.

The second approach held that the key to genuinely autonomous progress in Latin America was to be found in industrialization. Imports of manufactured goods should, in fact, be held down to appropriate levels in order to promote domestic industries and to improve the general trading position of the region. Foreign capital, while welcome in certain fields, was not to be assigned the principal role envisaged for it in the first approach. Indeed, there was now a generalized belief that external financing, when needed, should be arranged in the form of loans negotiated and agreed between governments rather than in the form of private investment. A variety of devices was suggested for the regulation and control of foreign trade: quotas, tariffs, permits, licenses, differential exchange rates, etc. A vital role was now reserved to the state. Government itself was to become directly involved in specific enterprises. It is useful at this point to quote some of Professor Glade's words on this particular subject:

The nationalization of railways and other public utilities, the creation of government banks, the organization of public enterprises in the petroleum and electric power fields, the initiation of state-owned steel mills, and, in fact, the general disposition to use public investment to foster the development of pivotal or basic industries—all of these widespread efforts to domesticate the key sectors of the economy and to use the instrument of government to fill the gaps in national production and resource patterns have had at their core one essential rationale. . . . [The] social decision was taken to abridge or suspend the market mechanism by organizing resources through the major public institution that stands most independently above the market: the state.[1]

[1] Glade, *op. cit.*, p. 409.

It is not altogether fanciful to see, in the second approach, the beginnings of a gradual return to a kind of mercantilist attitude—an attitude which had certainly been in retreat in the period before 1914.

While the influence of the second approach can be traced in specific policies throughout the twenty republics, there were several countries where it was adopted to a greater extent than elsewhere. In Uruguay, for instance, the presidencies of Batlle y Ordóñez ushered in a period when many of the concerns mentioned occupied a major position on the agenda of successive governments. Argentina, across the estuary, showed signs of developing similar policies under the radical administrations of 1916–30 and the conservative regimes of 1930–43; under Perón, however, economic progress was very vigorously stimulated in accordance with the main principles of this approach. A third case which could be mentioned was that of Brazil under Getúlio Vargas and, indeed, the governments which followed up till 1964. But it was probably in Chile that the emphases of the second approach were most widely imprinted on the national scene. From the 1920 presidential election onward, many aspects of Chilean public policy can be seen to have moved in the new direction; and the process gained considerable momentum during the fourteen years of Radical Party ascendancy between 1938 and 1952. Other countries and governments could, certainly, be included in this list. Both the Mexican and Bolivian revolutions gave rise to regimes which displayed many of the characteristics associated with the second approach, but in these two cases the second approach began to shade imperceptibly into a third, which will be mentioned in its proper place later in this section.

In considering the main impact of these two approaches on recent social and economic developments in Latin America, it is useful to start by recalling some of the characteristics which the "classical" international economy—not to mention the colonial era—had left with the region. How did things look in, say, 1914? The contrasts were formidable. In the vast majority of the twenty republics the hacienda system maintained its ancestral hold over what was still a very substantial proportion of the population, effectively sealing it off from the more modern sectors of the economy. The ownership of land was still concentrated in the hands of an aristocracy whose main concerns were parasitic rather than productive. The owners of the estates might change; the estates themselves did not. Nearer the main cities and the ports, however, the impact of the international economy had brought into existence a much more modern situation: a money economy, capitalist enterprises, excellent links with the outside world, etc. It is easy to see how a "dual society" theory of Latin American development became so widespread and popular; the contrasts between old and new, traditional and modern, seemed to many foreign visitors the most interesting feature they found in the region.

Many traditional attitudes and outlooks persisted in the Latin America of 1914, even in the cities and ports. Governments and aristocracies alike tended to invest in ostentation rather than production. Opera houses, battleships, or trips to Europe seemed worthier objects of attention than factories, rural schools, or local libraries. It was quite simply easier to put capital into the export sector of the economy than to put it elsewhere, and in times of uncertainty, even before 1914, it was often considered safer to build up handsome-looking bank accounts abroad. This latter practice among the upper classes was still to be found at the start of the 1970s.

Despite this persistence of traditional habits and attitudes, the international economy had nonetheless brought certain changes of a novel kind, particularly in those countries where its impact had been greatest. The cities and ports, through which the vastly increased trade of the period was obliged to move, developed fairly rapidly as sizable markets. The region, especially southern South America, was gradually becoming more urbanized. Trade itself demanded the services of an ever-increasing number of white-collar employees. In those countries where literacy was growing and where the most serious educational expansion was to be found, schoolteachers and journalists, government officials and clerks now proliferated. Together with the owners of smaller-scale farms, and with the small industrialists now to be found in several countries, these new groups came to constitute a section of society which, in terms of its income and status, was clearly distinct from the aristocracy. Numerically significant after 1900, the Latin American middle classes were quietly (and sometimes not so quietly) entering the scene. Educated, often articulate, sometimes vocal, they were eager to win themselves a place in the sun. The political developments associated with the names of Batlle, Irigoyen, and Alessandri (however much their importance may have been exaggerated) indicated very clearly that the middle classes were making their voices heard.

So, too, were the small industrial working classes—the railwaymen and the stevedores, the operatives of the frigorificos, the growing number of factory workers. Their trade unions, some of which grew out of the mutualist friendly societies which had abounded in the towns of nineteenth-century Latin America, were at this stage small and weak. But in spite of a generally unfavorable bargaining position, they now began to stake a claim for attention which few governments could entirely ignore. The organization of labor in unions was nearly everywhere confined to the city. In the countryside, the wage earners of the ranches and plantations, the tied peasantry of the haciendas, and the poverty-stricken cultivators of the minifundio remained largely unaffected by the trade unionism which was growing up in the towns. Outside the countries of southern South America and Mexico (now undergoing the tumultuous experience of the revolution) these new actors in the Latin American drama—middle classes and trade unions alike—were in any case to remain a somewhat fragile and exotic growth for several more decades.

Although there had been little deliberate effort to foster its growth, industry in the Latin America of 1914 was already showing a few signs of vitality. As yet, the scale was still modest enough. But the expansion of urban markets toward the end of the nineteenth century had given the would-be small industrialist new opportunities. Associations of manufacturers had been set up in a number of countries well before the turn of the century, a good case being the Chilean Sociedad de Fomento Fabril (Manufacturing Development Society) of 1883. Immigrant entrepreneurs, as we have seen, often played a notable part in establishing factories; capital for these new enterprises came less from the landed aristocracies than from the flourishing trading houses of the ports, which often had money to spare. The earliest industrial effort, as might be expected, went into the production of nondurable consumer goods for the local market and of materials for the building trade. Cement, glass, furniture, textiles, beer, cigarettes—all of these lines were widespread. Heavy industry had developed to a much slighter extent, although in a number of places the specialized needs of the railways or of mining had called into existence metalworking plants and engineering workshops capable of turning out rolling stock or the occasional piece of machinery. The process was most advanced in Argentina, where the third national census in 1914 revealed a total of more than four hundred thousand industrial workers.

After 1914 and still more after 1930, industrialization became one of the dominant themes in the increasingly dissonant symphony of Latin American life. World War I gave a considerable boost to local industrialists, though some of the impetus was lost when imports of manufactured goods were resumed in the 1920s; industrial production grew relatively slowly, if at all, during that decade. The much longer disruption of the depression and World War II presented industrialists with further opportunities; by this time, a number of governments were actively interested in stimulating domestic industrial growth. The year 1930, in fact, may be taken as the point of departure for all serious attempts to endow the region with a solid industrial base.

At the risk of being overschematic, it can be said that the pattern of Latin American industrialization in the four decades after 1930 centered on a considerable effort in the field of "import substitution" backed up by a determined drive (usually on the part of the state) to provide those basic industries—steel, oil, electric power—without which manufacturing could not have expanded. Import-substitution began, as was inevitable, in the field of nondurable consumer goods, and proceeded through "light" consumer-durables to capital goods. In no case, by 1970, had import-substitution fully embraced the two final categories,[1] for the provision of which Latin America continued to rely on imports from the more industrialized nations. In the larger Latin American states, what has sometimes been called the "easy" phase of import-substitution was complete well before 1970. It is impossible here to give a detailed account of the different phases of industrialization, for these varied from country to country; the following table shows the percentage increases in industrial production in the five countries chiefly affected between 1929 and 1957:

Percentage Increases in Industrial Production*

	1929–37	1937–47	1947–57	1929–57
Argentina	23	73	50	220
Mexico	46	86	98	407
Brazil	42	82	123	475
Chile	16	9	58	100
Colombia	90	110	130	830

* Celso Furtado, *Economic Development of Latin America* (Cambridge, 1970), p. 88.

The striking performance of Colombia during this period is partly explained by the low level which her industrialization process had reached in 1929 as compared with the other four countries, and partly by a number of unusually favorable internal conditions.

While a high proportion of manufacturing industry was set up by private interests and remained in private hands—either domestic or foreign—the role of the state should not be underestimated. By imposing protectionist tariffs and limitations on imports, by using such devices as multiple exchange rates and fiscal incentives, the state did much to create a propitious climate for industrialization. But it often went further than this, taking the initiative in setting up development corporations,

[1] By "nondurable consumer goods" is meant such items as beer, cigarettes, foods, etc. "Consumer-durables" (or "durable consumer goods") are things like cars, washing machines, radios, gas or electric ovens, etc. "Light" consumer-durables are things like washing machines or radios. "Capital goods" are simply definable as goods used to produce other goods, e.g., machinery of one kind or another.

public or mixed enterprises, and (less frequently) state trading agencies. The state development corporation (CORFO) established by the Popular Front government in Chile in 1939 was the first of its type; it later served as a model for other countries in the region. Governments showed particular concern to build up steel production and to secure control of energy. The steelworks set up in the 1940s at Volta Redonda in Brazil and at Huachipato in Chile were visible proofs of Latin America's new aspiration to possess autonomous national steel industries. The care shown by successive governments in Mexico, Brazil, Argentina, and Chile to develop publicly owned petroleum and electricity industries was a further proof, if proof were needed, of a new determination to control the basis of industrial growth. Other factors sometimes played a part as well. In the Argentina of Perón, for instance, industrial progress was partially tied to military requirements.

The years between 1930 and 1970, then, seriously modified the traditional picture of Latin America as a predominantly agrarian region. Argentina, Brazil, Mexico, and Chile had all taken giant strides along the road to becoming fully industrial countries, and the growth of industry in all but the smallest republics had become a truly notable feature of the region's life. In Brazil, Mexico, and Argentina, industry contributed more than thirty percent to the gross domestic product by the start of the 1960s.[1] Yet it was still logical to describe Latin America as semiindustrial rather than industrial, if by "industrial" was meant the condition attained by the United States, Europe, Russia, or Japan. There was still some way to go before imports of certain consumer-durables and capital goods could be dispensed with, although Latin Americans could certainly claim that as a result of the substitution process most of their imports were now essential rather than frivolous. There was an even greater distance to travel before Latin America could contemplate a native computer industry, for instance, or the production of jet aircraft, or the building of a nuclear power station. Moreover, by the 1960s it was everywhere apparent that industrialization as such was making less of an impact on the living standards of the Latin American population than might have been expected. This was in some ways a rather curious phenomenon, given the experience of the older industrial nations, where the spread of industry had done much to eliminate the grinding poverty of the preindustrial social order. There were, in fact, a number of anomalous aspects of the way in which the region was industrializing.

For the production of the most modern and sophisticated kinds of

[1] In the later 1960s manufacturing accounted for 23 percent of the total Latin American GDP and about 14 percent of the labor force.

capital goods in particular, vast outlays of capital were often necessary —capital which all too frequently could not be mobilized locally. Nor could a suitable variety of up-to-date technical skills be found in the Latin American countries, due in part to the persistence of traditional, "noneconomic" biases in most of the region's education systems. The result of this was a certain tendency for key sectors of modern industry to come into existence under *foreign* auspices. After 1945 in particular, American, European, or (increasingly) "multinational" corporations set up their subsidiaries in many Latin American states. In the major Latin American countries, especially in the 1950s and 1960s, industry gradually became divided into three main sections: (1) a fairly old "national" private section, owned and operated by Latin American capitalists organized in a somewhat traditional way, i.e., with family interests predominant; (2) a "national" public section, consisting of those basic industries owned and operated by the state; and (3) a foreign private section controlled and frequently operated (at the managerial level at least) by the citizens of foreign countries. Industries in the first section were concerned, essentially, with the production of textiles, food and drink, building materials, and so forth. Those belonging to the second section generally produced steel or oil or electricity. It was the third section that contained many of the newest and most dynamic industrial enterprises, supplying the latest in consumer goods as well as capital goods.

One of the chief characteristics of these newer, often foreign-controlled industries was that they were capital-intensive: their high productivity was based on a sophisticated use of modern technology and on a labor force which was small in relation to the amount of capital invested. Older industries had tended to be labor-intensive: they required a large and on the whole less skilled labor force. The expansion of new industries in the 1950s and 1960s, therefore, did less than might have been expected to open up new opportunities for employment. It did not create jobs on anything like the scale that would have been needed to counteract the labor surplus that existed in most of the countries concerned. Short of a radical reorganization of manufacturing, there was no reason to suppose that Latin American industrialization would ever draw large sections of the population into its vortex. Yet, as we shall see in a moment, there was a growing and urgent demand for employment in many of the Latin American countries. The cities were now expanding at an unprecedented rate; the traditional pattern of life in the countryside was beginning to break up; and the population explosion bade fair to transform a tragic and serious situation into a catastrophic one.

251

A second anomalous aspect of Latin American industrialization which disturbed some observers in the 1950s and 1960s was the problem of markets. Since colonial times, as we have seen, the Latin American social order had been characterized by very marked disparities of income and by the immense numerical size of the poorer classes. For various reasons (some of which I shall attempt to identify presently) the twentieth century saw a continuation of this pattern. Around 1960 the distribution of income in the region followed the sort of pattern indicated by the following table:

Income Distribution*

Category	Percentage of Population	Percentage of Total Income
I	50	16
II	45	51
III	3	14
IV	2	10

* ECLA, *El desarrollo económico de América Latina en la postguerra* (New York, 1963), p. 68. It should be stressed however, that this table was based on data from only four countries, viz., Chile, Ecuador, Mexico, and Venezuela. There were naturally considerable variations within categories.

From this it will be seen that the top five percent of the population at that period was very well off indeed, while fully half of the population was very poor. The general lack of purchasing power on the part of a majority of the population meant that the domestic markets for consumer goods were often rather tightly constricted. Furthermore, the expensive tastes of the richer classes continued to dictate industrial diversification of the sort already mentioned, i.e., capital-intensive enterprises turning out a wide range of sophisticated consumer goods. But given the relatively small size of the upper classes (which included the better-off sections of the middle class) the available markets in that particular direction were soon saturated. Latin American industry now had to search for alternative markets, and this may legitimately be seen as one reason for the considerable interest in "integration" which was shown by businessmen in the 1960s. But since most Latin American republics possessed similar problems relating to size of markets, it could reasonably be doubted whether "integration" was a long-term answer. Other possibilities included an increased Latin American export to non-Latin American markets, not least those offered by the industrial nations. Some industrial nations, it was believed, might find it cheaper to import Latin American manufactured goods than to produce the same goods themselves.[1]

Forty years after the economic crisis of 1930, it was apparent to many that Latin American industrialization, while often achieving impressive rates of growth, had manifestly failed to diffuse prosperity or even an acceptable standard of life to a significant proportion of the population. But it had certainly expanded the "modern" sector of society to some extent. Most Latin American cities now came to have fairly extensive districts which bore an appreciable resemblance to the more affluent suburbs of Europe or North America. With their comfortable houses and country clubs, their private schools and fashionable boutiques, their supermarkets and service centers, such districts might well convince a foreign visitor of the existence of a large and prosperous middle class. He would in fact be right to be so convinced. But he would (especially if he came from Western Europe) observe, too, that these middle-class people lived rather better than their counterparts in Great Britain, Germany, or France, not to mention the Soviet Union; he would notice that in some respects (not least in the availability of domestic servants) they lived more comfortably than comparable groups of people in the United States or Canada. If, however, this hypothetical foreign observer were to extend his investigations a little further, he would quickly discover some additionally interesting differences between the middle classes of Latin America and those of the industrial nations.

He would first establish that there were very considerable problems involved in defining the nature and function of the Latin American middle classes and that some sociologists had gone so far as to deny their existence.[2] Their size around, say, 1960, varied substantially from country to country. According to one fairly generous estimate, they accounted for perhaps as much as thirty-five percent of the population of Argentina and for thirty percent in Chile and Uruguay; in Mexico or Brazil they represented about fifteen percent of the

---

[1] Given the proximity of the American market, a good test case for this in the future will be Mexico.

[2] The problem of defining the nature and role of the different social classes in Latin America is one which has lent itself to an enormous amount of confusion, mostly because of the uncritical transplanting of European presuppositions about what social classes *ought* to look like, behave as, etc. A convincing case for regarding many Latin American countries as divided into two "sectors," an upper and a lower, is made by Richard N. Adams, "Political Power and Social Structures," in C. Véliz, ed., *Politics of Conformity in Latin America* (London, 1967). Most of what are generally referred to as "middle classes" fit into the upper sector. Within the upper sector, however, there is obviously what might be called an "upper-upper" sector, identifiable as an "oligarchy." In view of this, the retention of the term "middle class" is probably useful, provided it is clear what is being talked about.

nation.[1] These were fairly impressive proportions. A glance back into recent history, however, would tell our foreign visitor that these Latin American middle classes, however numerous, had not played a particularly notable part in the process of industrialization. A small entrepreneurial middle class (in which the presence of immigrant talent was especially prominent) had played, it is true, an important role in establishing the earliest Latin American industries. But it never developed into a powerful, insistent, aggressive or triumphant body capable of overriding the interests of the aristocracy or the state. Very often, indeed, its most successful representatives were incorporated into the ranks of the aristocracy. As we have seen, it was the state itself, and later on, foreign interests, which became the leading protagonists of industrial progress. In many countries economic power, as reflected in the ownership of land and in the control of banking and industrial concerns, had remained concentrated to an astonishing degree. In more than a handful of the Latin American republics, the traditional land-owning aristocracy had successfully extended its grip to many spheres outside agriculture, and was still somewhere near the center of the stage. There was little room for a powerful entrepreneurial group of industrialists drawn from the middle classes, even if such a group had arisen.

The Latin American middle classes, then, failed for the most part to take a particularly striking lead in modernizing their countries; they did not attempt to establish themselves in the role which their counterparts in Western Europe or North America often developed. They included an entrepreneurial and commercial element, certainly; but this was hardly the element which counted. The middle classes came to be predominantly professional or bureaucratic, or made their living in a wide variety of white-collar occupations. The liberal professions expanded considerably from the close of the nineteenth century onward; the growth in the influence of the state entailed the creation of a large number of posts in bureaucracies which were often artificially inflated. The traditional Hispanic *empleomanía* (mania for public jobs) now found a multitude of new outlets. In southern South America at least, the middle classes were large enough and vocal enough to win themselves access to government in the first three decades of the twentieth century. To say, as do some writers, that since then the middle classes have been "in power" is probably to misread the situation—for in many countries a tightly knit network of rich, aristocratic families still occupy the main positions at the summit of society long after the political changes usually associated with the "rise of the middle sectors."

[1] See John J. Johnson, *Political Change in Latin America: The Emergence of the Middle Sectors* (Stanford, Calif., 1958), p. 2.

Representatives of the middle classes may well have entered government, and governments may have become markedly more responsive to middle-class interests, most notably, perhaps, in the increased provision of government jobs; this did not mean, however, that the principal redoubts of the aristocracy were attacked or even undermined, even when vocally antiaristocratic governments were in office.

That the Latin American middle classes quickly developed the psychological predispositions which habitually characterized the region's aristocracies seems certain. Unlike their counterparts in Victorian Britain or modern America, they failed to idolize the virtue of thrift, and devoted themselves with singleminded zeal to conspicuous consumption. Often, indeed, they lived beyond their means, but declined to draw the appropriate Micawberish conclusion. It is difficult to resist the supposition that the somewhat parasitic outlook of the traditional aristocracy was transmitted more or less intact to the middle classes (and quite possibly to everyone else). Certainly the middle classes devoted a great deal of time and energy to reproducing what they conceived to be aristocratic patterns of living, even if on a necessarily reduced scale. When possible, they patronized private schools. Most of them were unable to spend several months traveling in stately fashion to Europe; but more than a few *were* able to fit in the occasional shopping excursion by airplane to Miami. As with the aristocracy, they invested their money, when they invested at all, less in productive activities than in land or urban property—and in countries often afflicted by chronic inflation, this made good sense.

Foreign experts, notably in the United States, often saluted the Latin American middle classes in the 1950s and 1960s as a truly "new" element in the situation, viewing them, with misplaced optimism, as the harbingers of reform, modernization, and all the other desiderata of life in the affluent northern half of the hemisphere. Yet in many respects, the middle classes preserved both a traditional outlook and a traditional role: their function, even when outwardly entrepreneurial or commercial, was often heavily dependent on the action of the state. They represented less a new theme than a set of variations on an old one. But, as suggested earlier in this section, the middle classes were by no means the only new twentieth-century actors in the Latin American drama. The urban working classes, already present to a limited extent in 1914, were enormously strengthened by the growth of industry, although by European standards they were still relatively small even in the 1960s, representing approximately one seventh of the labor force in Latin America. Nevertheless, trade union activity was bound to become more prominent with the progress of industry; and it did. Once again, however, Latin American trade unions played a rather different part from that of their North American or European counterparts. These undoubtedly stimulated production by increasing the purchasing power of the working class and by encouraging capitalists to plow their profits back into industry rather than spend them on purely ostentatious purposes. In both Europe and North America, in fact, trade unions became powerful instruments of economic improvement—though not without some notable struggles in their early years. In Latin America, such a development was from the first rather improbable. Several factors militated against the growth of a large-scale and independent union movement with mass memberships.

A trade union's bargaining position is immensely enhanced when labor is scarce; but, except to some extent in Argentina, such a condition has never been found in Latin America, where labor has invariably been only too plentiful. This contributed in the twentieth century to the relative weakness of such trade unions as were organized, and made them look less to their own independent strength than to some powerful protector—which in practice meant the state. In the early years of the century, the state represented the interests of the employers with considerable faithfulness, and tended to repress (and often savagely repress) the labor movement. Later, however, a number of regimes came to look on the unions as a useful source of support. In the very special circumstances of the Mexican revolution, for instance, the unions came to occupy an influential position both politically and socially; they became a key element in the postrevolutionary "establishment." Elsewhere, "populist" dictators such as Vargas and Perón tended to build up the union movement as one of the instruments of their power, which gave it prestige and influence at the expense of being fairly heavily dependent on the state. In the Argentine case, trade unions had already reached a reasonably strong position prior to the advent of Perón, and his period of office left them with what by Latin American standards was a unique place in the national life. In Brazil, by contrast, the unions failed to develop so strongly after Vargas had left the scene.[1]

By the 1960s the most substantial labor movements in Latin America were to be found in the countries I have already mentioned together with Chile. Leaving aside the special case of Cuba, where the unions were totally subordinated to the state after 1960, it could be said that the organized movements of urban labor in other countries were still small, rather weak, and often legally restricted in their scope for action.

[1] Trade unions played an important part in the Bolivian revolution of 1952. The tin-miners' and peasants' unions were a power in the land thereafter, though the regimes after 1964 tended to assert strict government control over their activities.

Except in Mexico and Bolivia, unionization of the peasantry was almost unheard of until the 1960s. Unions in key sections of industry, it is true, were able to win reasonable pay and conditions for their members, and these became (in some cases) a kind of "labor aristocracy" more concerned with defending its own position than with agitating for more general improvements which would benefit the less fortunate (and more numerous) remainder of the urban lower class. Here once again was a reason why the living standards of the great mass of the population were unaffected by the changes brought about by industrialization.

The rise of industry, the enlargement of the middle classes, the delicate growth of trade unions—all of these twentieth-century developments were essentially urban in nature. As so often in the past, the city provided the main location for such progress as occurred. In the countryside many of the familiar landmarks of colonial times and the nineteenth century still survived intact. The latifundio or great estate and its polar opposite, the minifundio, continued to maintain their predominant position in the pattern of land tenure. One estimate of how land was distributed in the region around 1950 gives the following picture:

Land Distribution—1950s*

Size of Farm (Hectares)	Percent of Farms	Percent of Land Area
0–20	72.6	3.7
20–100	18.0	8.4
100–1,000	7.9	23.0
Over 1,000	1.5	64.9

* Thomas F. Carroll, "The Land Reform Issue in Latin America," in Albert O. Hirschman, ed., *Latin American Issues* (New York, 1961), p. 165.

Nearly two thirds of the land, then, was owned by less than two percent of all landowners, while at the other end of the scale nearly three quarters of all "landowners" (using the term somewhat ironically) farmed rather less than four percent of the land. Medium-sized properties accounted for the remaining third or so. The concentration of landownership in Latin America around 1950, therefore, could still be said to be extreme. Its effects in colonial times and in the subsequent period have been mentioned more than once in this and the previous chapter. As we have seen, it encouraged the persistence of a pattern of widespread and unalleviated poverty in the countryside, and a decidedly noneconomic, not to say parasitic, psychology among the landowners themselves. Honorable exceptions there always were; but however honorable, they were always exceptional.

Some of the events of the twentieth century brought important changes—some of them gradual and barely perceptible, others very drastic—to the Latin American countryside. In three republics (Mexico, Bolivia, Cuba) the traditional agrarian system was violently overhauled and in some ways transformed. (By the end of the 1960s two other countries—Chile and Peru—were also undergoing substantial agrarian reforms.) These cases will be briefly examined in their due place; for the moment, it is important to mention some of the ways in which the "traditional" and "unreformed" pattern of rural life began to break up in the twentieth century, with serious consequences for the Latin American social order.

The dominant agrarian institution, the latifundio, whether ranch, plantation, or hacienda, had existed untouched since colonial times. The nineteenth century, as we saw, strengthened its hold over the countryside. Ranches and plantations had always been somewhat more efficient than the traditional hacienda—but all three varieties of latifundio were obliged to heighten their productivity in the twentieth century, due to the expansion of the urban market and, of course, to the region's continued dependence on the export of agricultural or pastoral produce. Though generalizations on this subject are dangerous, it seems fairly certain that a major twentieth-century tendency was for a growing number of estates to specialize, increasingly, in a single crop for a particular market, and to "rationalize" production accordingly. In many cases, estates encroached still further on lands cultivated by the Indian communities (particularly in the Andean countries) and also on the minifundio. Sometimes, too, sections of the old tied peasantry, subject to debt-peonage, were transformed into a more conventional wage-earning labor force.

As part and parcel of these changes in the countryside, peasants and laborers now began to leave the land in increasing numbers. Often enough, conditions there no longer seemed even minimally bearable. Even when not actually dispossessed of their plots or minifundios, peasants found it more and more difficult to make a living on the land. A rising population, combined with the cumulative effect of the frequent subdivisions of minifundios after inheritance, forced many thousands of them to seek new opportunities. Specific local disasters— the prolonged violencia in Colombia, or the recurrent droughts of the sertão of the northeast of Brazil—were also sometimes responsible for migratory movements. And while the miseries of the countryside helped to extrude population, the cities acted as a powerful magnet drawing people into their field of force. Most of the opportunities for industrial employment were concentrated in the cities. Such welfare services as operated were far more effective in urban than in rural areas. And with the advent of the bus and the lorry, transport was now easier and perhaps cheaper than before. The notable migrations from country-side to city which occurred were, therefore, the result of several forces which "pushed" and several which "pulled."

The consequence of the drift away from the countryside can be summarized in two words: accelerated urbanization. Here we come to one of the most dramatic changes of recent decades. From the earliest decades of colonial times, as we have seen, Latin America (with the partial exception of colonial Brazil) had been in many important senses an *urban* region; it now became an increasingly *urbanized* region as well. The population of the cities and towns swelled enormously; several of the national capitals, for instance, became cities with several million inhabitants. By the 1960s Latin America could boast (if it were a boasting matter) three "giant" conurbations: Buenos Aires, Mexico City, and São Paulo. A dozen other cities had populations of between one and four million. Roughly one Argentine in three lived in Greater Buenos Aires, one Uruguayan in three in Montevideo, one Chilean in four in Santiago, one Peruvian in five in Lima, and one Mexican in seven in Mexico City. There were difficulties, it is true, in assessing what precisely constituted an "urban" population in Latin America. Some calculations, for instance, were based on the dubious (if general) assumption that anybody who lived in a settlement of more than two thousand people could be counted as an urban creature. On this basis, approximately fifty-four percent of Latin Americans were living in towns by 1970. If a population of fifty thousand were taken as a more realistic basis for what constituted an urban area, then the average proportion was more like one third, rising to around a half in the River Plate area.[1]

Whatever measure was chosen by the experts, however, there could be little doubt at all that Latin America was gradually ceasing to be a predominantly agrarian region. This did not mean that urbanization was necessarily proceeding very harmoniously. Indeed, there were many respects in which it was not. In Western Europe or the United States, the growth of the towns had been intimately associated with the rise of industry. The factories had absorbed the workers who had left the

[1] In the early 1940s, according to one estimate, roughly fifteen percent of the Latin American population lived in cities of more than one hundred thousand inhabitants, making the region approximately half as urbanized as the United States. See Francis Violich, *Cities of Latin America* (New York, 1944), p. 42.

land, and whatever their initial miseries, their standard of living had risen, certainly in the long term and possibly in the short term as well. Given the pattern of industrialization in Latin America, no such process occurred. The migrations to the city took place at a time when, as we have seen, industries were becoming more capital-intensive, and hence unable to absorb all of the job-hungry migrants from the country-side. Many of the newcomers to the city were obliged to find employ-ment in "service" occupations of one kind or another. They were often chronically underemployed or quite simply unemployed. (Many "ser-vice" occupations could in fact be considered as little more than a disguised form of unemployment.) The great number of bootblacks, lottery-ticket sellers, domestic servants, newspaper-kiosk proprietors, stallholders, messenger-boys, fruit vendors, shop assistants, and so forth to be found in most Latin American cities was visible proof of a tragic inability on the part of migrants from the countryside to find work in industry, or, often enough, any kind of permanent employment at all.

The Latin American city, traditionally important as a focus of govern-ment and economic power, had always possessed its poorer districts. Which city in the world did not? But with the ever-mounting flow of people from the countryside, a new and disturbing phenomenon gradually crystallized: the growth of shanty-towns. Practically unknown before World War II, these ramshackle and insanitary settlements quickly came to disfigure the outskirts and interstices of many Latin American cities. The names given to shanty-towns varied from country to country. In Brazil they were called *favelas*, in Peru *barriadas*, in Chile *callampas*, in Argentina *villas miseria*—but the reality behind these different names was essentially and depressingly similar. They often lacked the most minimal attention from the authorities. Few doctors served their needs, which were manifold. Electricity and water were often absent, or at the very least painfully slow in being provided. The shanties themselves were constructed of wood, cardboard, or any material that came to hand. Dogs, children, and rats roamed indis-criminately through dusty "streets" which turned instantly to mud if rain fell. Chronic sickness and malnutrition compounded the miserable situation of the inhabitants. Settlements of this type housed (if that is the right word) perhaps a quarter of the population of the major urban centers of Latin America in the 1960s, placing an immense strain on the resources of those governments which actively set out to improve the situation. Sociologists described the inhabitants of the shanty-towns as "marginal": "marginality" was, in fact, little more than a euphemism for one of the grossest forms of human poverty and degradation. Ironically enough, however, many of the people most affected by "marginality" regarded their new urban existence as superior to the life they had left behind them in the countryside. Would their children think the same? That remained (and remains) an open question.

One feature of the Latin American scene which exacerbated all these problems in the 1950s and 1960s—and will go on exacerbating them in the future unless something is done about it—was in itself the most explosive problem of all: the rise in the population. It is difficult to exaggerate the seriousness of this phenomenon. The Latin American population in 1900 was around sixty million. It passed two hundred million at the end of the 1950s and is expected to pass three hundred million sometime in the mid-1970s. Its rate of growth in the intervening period was the highest in the world. One of the main consequences of this was that by the middle of the 1960s nearly half the population of the region was less than fifteen years old.

This great and rapid expansion of the population, combined with its increasing juvenescence, placed the Latin American social order under what was clearly a potentially immense strain. Sheer pressure of numbers tended to nullify the impact of such economic progress (often far from negligible) as was being made. The exceptionally high rates of growth in the Mexican GNP between 1940 and 1970, for instance, combined with the efforts of the socially conscious governments which emerged from the revolution, could have been expected to eliminate most forms of poverty. They did not. It is impossible to deny that one of the chief culprits was, simply, the population explosion. The tremendous growth in numbers—particularly severe outside southern South America—meant more mouths to feed, more houses to build, more jobs to be created, more medical clinics to be paid for, more schools to be constructed, and so on ad infinitum. It also meant that while the *proportion* of illiterates in Latin America continued to fall (from forty-two percent in 1950 to thirty-six percent in 1960) the total *number* of actual illiterates was rising in many areas. The list of consequences could be extended indefinitely. Pressure of numbers was bound, above all, to enlarge the growing class of "marginal" people, with future results which any reasonably well-endowed imagination could easily foresee. The problems facing most Latin American governments by the end of the 1960s were heartrending in their extent, and indeed in their complexity. Economic growth had to be stimulated at the same time that urgent social needs were satisfied. To many this seemed an impossible task and one for which a miracle or some kind of magic was needed.

The growing problem of urban "marginality" and the evident

persistence of rural poverty combined in the 1950s and 1960s to suggest to many Latin Americans that the two policy approaches I mentioned earlier suffered from serious inadequacies. A third approach began to take shape in a number of intelligent Latin American minds. It was most frequently expressed in a growing demand for what were often called "structural" reforms, reforms which would be concerned essentially with what were conceived to be barriers or bottlenecks in the structure of the social order. The automatic targets for such reforms, it was increasingly felt, were such matters as the unequal distribution of income, the concentration of landownership, or the educational backwardness of much of the region. The need for a fundamental agrarian reform—either through the redistribution of land or through direct state control of the land—was widely stressed.

This third approach implied a general reorganization of the social order which would certainly entail damaging a number of interests, especially those of the richest sections of the community. What was evidently needed from now onward was a more truly conscientious effort to renovate the social order and to remove the most obviously sclerotic arrangements within it. There was no precise agreement on how this was to be done. It was clear, however, that the main concerns of the protagonists of this new approach were related to the three main practical experiences of drastic social reorganization which had occurred in twentieth-century Latin America: the Mexican, Bolivian and Cuban revolutions.[1] (In the 1960s, for obvious reasons, the Cuban case attracted a good deal of attention.) What lessons, if any, could be deduced from the example of these three revolutions?

The *Mexican revolution* was by far the most violent upheaval of the most recent sixty years of Latin American history. It was a turbulent, confused, and often highly contradictory process, with decidedly mixed results. (This last feature is one it has in common with most historical processes.) Its most significant features, perhaps, were a serious attack on the latifundio system, the consolidation of a powerful but flexible postrevolutionary state, and a dynamic emphasis on industrialization. The Mexican hacienda, as we saw in the previous section, reached its apogee under Porfirio Díaz, and it was the reaction of the landless Indians and mestizos against this which transformed the essentially political movement of 1910 into a major social convulsion. The years between 1910 and 1940 witnessed a substantial redistribution of land

---

[1] Guatemala (1944–54) and Argentina (1945–55) have sometimes been considered as "frustrated" and "partial" revolutions respectively. Limitations of space prevent me from examining these two cases.

which effectively demolished the former predominance of the hacienda. Most of the land which was distributed was organized in the form of *ejidos*—communal property usually divided into individual plots—of which there were around twenty thousand in 1960. New lands brought under cultivation through irrigation projects were also organized in this manner. Private estates continued to exist, but they were now very often under new ownership and tended to operate on a far more commercial basis than before the revolution, partly because of the permanent possibility of expropriation—a sword of Damocles which the post-Cárdenas governments suspended over the landowners' heads (and occasionally dropped). The creation of the ejido in itself did relatively little, perhaps, to raise the living standards of the Mexican peasant but it did give him a stake in the land which he had not possessed under the Porfiriato, and a much greater confidence in the future.[1] It also kept a high proportion of the rural population on the land.

The second result of the Mexican revolution which many observers found significant was the gradual emergence of a strong central government backed by a large and well-articulated political party (from 1946 onward styled, eloquently enough, the Institutional Revolutionary Party) which was itself a coalition of peasants' organizations, trade unions, and other important sections of the community. The government tolerated the formation of rival political movements, but its own party invariably led the field in elections, making the presidential succession a matter for decision within the councils of the party rather than at the polls. After 1940, successive Mexican governments increasingly emphasized industrialization as the key to progress, but by no means neglected the agricultural sector, whose efficiency was constantly being heightened. Numerous irrigation schemes, in particular, were now sponsored throughout the countryside. The state itself acted as entrepreneur in a number of important enterprises (oil, electricity, and steel, for instance), and deliberately stimulated private investment as well. More than most Latin American countries, Mexico by the 1960s possessed a confident and energetic capitalist class, though a capitalist class that was highly dependent on the good will of the state. Whether this formula could be successfully applied in the future, with many of the familiar Latin American problems crowding in on the Mexican people, remained to be seen.

On the *Bolivian revolution* it can only be said that the MNR (National

---

[1] The private sector, rather than the ejidos, contributed most to the increase in Mexican agricultural production. Between 1940 and 1960 Mexico tripled her output of maize and sugar and septupled her output of cotton. These were only a few of the achievements of the country's agriculture during that period.

Revolutionary Movement) governments from 1952 to 1964 were obliged to cope with almost insurmountable difficulties, which derived from a singularly unpropitious geographical and historical background. That they accomplished anything at all might seem to be something of a miracle. As it was, the most important single development they sponsored was an agrarian reform whose effects went a long way toward destroying the traditional hacienda and also toward setting up a more diversified and efficient pattern of agriculture. Most of the peasants on the altiplano now became proprietors of independent minifundios, though consuming far more of their own produce than before, with the inevitable result that food production for the cities dropped. Although the vast majority of her population still lived on the altiplano, Bolivia was able to look toward her underpopulated eastern lowlands, where, in the course of the 1950s and 1960s, agricultural colonization proceeded at a modest but steady pace. This offered encouraging long-term prospects, even though the country's general level of development was still appallingly low. Moreover, as the events after 1964 revealed only too sadly, the Bolivian revolution failed to "institutionalize" itself as effectively as the Mexican revolution had done.

The *Cuban revolution*, even after a full decade of Dr. Castro's government, presented many features which were difficult to interpret. The imposition of totalitarian rule, combined with strenuous attempts to "mobilize" the population, created a situation in which plans for economic progress could be pushed ahead at great speed. Cuba's economy, as we have seen, had been geared to the export of sugar since the end of the eighteenth century; it was far more "capitalist" than the Mexican or Bolivian economies had been; it had also been more extensively penetrated by American interests than any comparable Latin American economy. After 1960 Dr. Castro quite simply eliminated the richer classes, either drastically limiting their income or allowing them to emigrate; he also cut all links with the United States. Welfare schemes, housing developments, and the abolition of many forms of privilege all helped to raise the living standards of the poor, though consumption was held down (often through a system of rationing) while the state accumulated capital for the purpose of financing social and economic improvements; public investment in development was soon far higher in Cuba than in any other Latin American state. A genuine and much-needed attempt was now made to promote science and technology and to apply these to economic needs. Indeed, a greatly increased educational effort was one of the revolution's most important features, even if some branches of education were heavily impregnated with the systematized

264

mumbo-jumbo of "dialectical materialism." Despite (or perhaps because of) the rigors of a somewhat spartan existence, the average Cuban's sense of pride in his country was greatly increased and intensified.

The earliest efforts of Dr. Castro's government were devoted, somewhat chaotically, to rapid industrialization. This reduced Cuba's capacity to import, and from 1963 onward there was a renewed emphasis on sugar. A ten-million-ton zafra was planned for 1970, and the eight-and-a-half-million tons actually achieved in that year was a very respectable total. In the organization of the economy, much was heard of the need to foster "moral" incentives in place of the "material" incentives common in Russia and the Communist countries of Eastern Europe; a selfless sense of civic duty was to replace the desire for individual economic improvement as the main motive force in Cuban society. This particular emphasis, peculiar to the Cuban revolution,[1] derived from the distinctive ethical and moral predispositions of the revolutionary leadership, which were remarkably uncompromising. A dozen years after Dr. Castro's descent from the Sierra Maestra, it still remained an open question whether this approach could lead successfully to long-term economic progress.[2] But part of the groundwork for such progress had undoubtedly been established in Cuba as a result of the years of revolution.

The concrete achievements of the Cuban revolution and the example of the Mexican and Bolivian revolutions before it, served to convince many Latin Americans of the urgent need for "structural" reforms. The daily spectacle of poverty, with all that poverty implied in terms of wasted lives, made an impact on a growing number of people who themselves were by no means poor. In too many areas, stagnation rather than progress seemed to be the rule. Even at the end of the 1960s, the combined gross domestic products of the Latin American countries were still less than one fifth of the gross domestic product of the United States. In the year 1966 some thirty thousand computers were at work in the United States; in Latin America, the number was around a hundred.[3] Millions of Latin Americans still lived in squalid housing,

---

[1] In Latin America, that is. Interesting comparisons could no doubt be made with Mao Tse-tung's China.

[2] Attempts to assess the effects of moral incentives have been few and far between. One observer has concluded that the policy as applied up to 1970 did not succeed in transforming the "consciousness of the masses," and could well have contributed to a fall-off in production, especially in agriculture. See Carmelo Mesa-Lago, "El problema de los incent ivos en Cuba," *Aportes*, No. 20 (April 1971).

[3] Some eight thousand were in use that year in Western Europe.

still suffered from the evil effects of an unbalanced or inadequate diet, still failed to receive even a minimal education, and still found their way barred to greater economic opportunities. In terms of living standards there were, naturally enough, considerable variations as between different countries. Argentina was furthest away from the Latin American "average" in one direction, Haiti furthest away in the other. The average itself, however, was still shockingly low.

The ideal of economic autonomy seemed as remote as ever. This seemed peculiarly galling in a century when, for better or worse, nationalist ideals were sweeping the world. Latin America as a whole still remained substantially dependent on the export of agrarian or mineral products and the import of technology. There seemed no immediate or dramatic way this dependence could be lessened.

More than a few of the political developments of the 1960s stemmed from a contemplation of these disturbing facts. The reform programs of Frei and Allende in Chile, of Beláunde and Velasco Alvarado in Peru, and of a dozen other political leaders up and down the subcontinent, were affected, influenced, and (in some cases) galvanized by the new demand for "structural" changes. But even at the start of the 1970s it was still difficult to see whether any genuinely new social forces were emerging in Latin America—forces capable of giving a vital impulse to progress in the region. Where were the key groups of men waiting in the wings for their chance to act? Where were the "modernizing elites"?

There *were* a number of groups whose future behavior bore watching, if no more. They were drawn from the region's various armed forces, from the ranks of the Catholic Church, from the predominantly middle-class universities, and from the *técnicos*, or technical-professional men, to be found in many countries. A few tentative points can be made about these four groups—all of which were seen, by different observers, to be potential contenders for power with a view to reform.

The Latin American armies, noted in some republics for their frequent interventions in politics, occupied a somewhat special position in the social order. Their organization was genuinely nationwide and relatively speaking more efficient (in a significant number of countries) than that of the official bureaucracy. They often seemed to symbolize the "nation" more effectively than civilian politicians. It was hardly surprising, therefore, that army officers should begin to ponder their role rather carefully. The 1960s saw a series of military interventions (Brazil in 1964, Argentina in 1966, Peru in 1968) which seemed at first sight to be somewhat different from the previous patterns of interference in politics: the armed forces *as an institution* rather than as the instrument of a particular *caudillo* or clique of officers now assumed the responsibilities of government. Here was one tendency which seemed significant for the future, though just *how* significant remains to be seen.

In the Catholic Church, too, there was increasing ferment in the course of the 1960s, due in part to the *aggiornamento* ("updating") of the Church presided over by Pope John XXIII, who was extraordinarily popular among the faithful (and not only the faithful) in Latin America. The papal approval of programs of social reform, expressed in such important documents as Pope Paul VI's encyclical *Populorum progressio* (March 1967), struck a responsive chord among several sections of the Latin American clergy. This was in many ways a very interesting development. The Church, as we saw, had occupied a privileged position during colonial times; even when under attack from nineteenth-century anticlericals it retained a remarkably widespread influence. Insofar as it had a political and social attitude, this tended to be somewhat conservative. Even in the 1960s several Latin American hierarchies maintained this particular cast of mind. But there was now a growing tendency in the direction of reform.

To many foreign observers, the hundred and fifty or so Latin American universities[1] seemed a certain breeding-ground for groups which manifestly wished to contend for political power. The universities had long been noted as a focus of political ferment. Their campuses in the 1960s often resembled ideological supermarkets where the latest fashionable outlooks imported from Paris or Peking were bought and sold with an almost commercial fervor. "Critical"—though hardly self-critical—thought was much in vogue. This was sometimes the expression of a genuine and profound dissatisfaction with the injustices and anomalies of Latin American society. It may also have masked the more practical frustration of groups which saw little immediate possibility of an outlet for their energies, for the universities were tending to overproduce graduates, whose employment opportunities were none too secure. The interest of a significant minority of Latin American university students in insurgent movements in the 1960s could not be denied; and among such students a discernible effort to "go to the people," as they put it, marked them off from previous generations. Hitherto, any genuine sympathy with the sufferings of the poor had been conspicuous by its absence—no tradition such as that of the Russian Narodniks of the 1870s ever found a place among the Latin American upper classes. Even in the 1960s, attempts to "go to the people" were still somewhat limited in scope.

[1] Perhaps a third of these were rather small in size, with less than one thousand registered students.

The final group which should be mentioned is more difficult to define and trace. In many Latin American countries, especially the medium-sized and larger ones, groups of *técnicos* may well have begun to crystal-lize in the 1950s and 1960s.[1] Often trained abroad and acquainted with recent technical, economic, or managerial theories, their outlook made them impatient with what they viewed as the more archaic aspects of Latin American life. Their aim, insofar as it was coherent at all, was to "modernize" their countries in accordance with a pragmatic and flexible scheme of action. Many of them were somewhat skeptical of the easily assembled ideologies which found favor among university students, whose qualifications were often inferior to their own. In countries where the armed forces assumed power during the 1960s, more than a few técnicos assisted them in the tasks of government. Whether they might one day wish to exercise power directly and in their own right remained (and remains) an open question.

Whatever the future might hold for groups such as these, one thing was abundantly clear in the Latin America of the 1960s. Control of the state was a necessary precondition for the progress of the region—if such progress were to be furthered by these new contenders for power or others who contended with them. And the state itself was changing. There was a growing awareness that it needed to become something more than what it too often seemed to be—a means of satisfying the richer classes' built-in empleomanía. In the absence of "modernizing elites" the state seemed the only instrument which could be used to effect social and economic changes thought to be desirable. In the years after 1914, as we have seen, the functions of the state in many Latin American countries were greatly enlarged, particularly in the economic sphere. (The Cuban revolution took this remorselessly to its logical conclusion.) Some writers believed, rightly or wrongly, that the tentative withdrawal of the state from the economic arena during the classical period of the international economy was now being reversed, and that the most recent era of Latin American history was increasingly characterized by a return to an older and in many ways more traditional pattern, the pattern of mercantilism and centralized economic direction. A perceptive Chilean scholar, writing in 1967, suggested that this might be an almost subconscious response to a baffling situation:

Latin America stands now on the frontiers of ideology; none of those systems based on the European experience of the industrial revolution

[1] *Técnico* cannot be translated as "technician," which has different connotations in English; it would be equally misleading, at present, to use "technocrat." "Technical-professional men" would be closer.

—including classical radicalism, socialism, liberalism, communism and the like—seems to apply to a situation which excludes the social and political concomitants of industrialization. . . . In such a situation, perhaps displaying a greater pragmatic capacity than is generally acknowledged, Latin America has gradually returned to her own essential traditions of centralism.[1]

But was centralized government the only answer? Was it an answer at all? Whether at the frontiers of ideology or not—and the writer was certainly correct in implying that many of Latin America's problems were *sui generis*—the region's commanding imperative at the start of the 1970s was the imperative of progress. This is a history book, and so far I have written this chapter in the past tense. But it will be apparent that most of the changes and constants I have mentioned in this section are very much part of the present, whose boundaries with the past are always somewhat indefinite. In discussing some of the issues which the past has bequeathed to the Latin America of today and tomorrow, I must briefly shift into the present tense.

Some Contemporary Dilemmas

Latin America is an active volcano.
PRESIDENT SALVADOR ALLENDE OF CHILE (1971)

The Latin America of the 1970s is a region of profound contrasts and profound problems. The problems, at least, are all concerned with what is today called development and what used to be called progress. Yet there is no single direction which progress takes. There is no universal agreement on the matter, and it is difficult to see how there can be. Politics invariably raises its ugly head. A set of aims which is regarded as highly praiseworthy by one political movement may well be considered anathema by another. Anyone studying the various recipes for progress which exist should certainly devote a good deal of time to analyzing the *political* presuppositions of their authors. Nevertheless, I must obviously make an attempt at identifying at least some of the main dilemmas which face contemporary Latin America.

To do so I shall have to make an arbitrary assumption about the essential goals of economic and social progress. *Not* to progress is to condemn many millions of Latin Americans to abject poverty. Given the continuing rise in population, as we have seen, such poverty is likely to become *more abject* rather than less. The fundamental goal of pro-

[1] Claudio Véliz, "An Historical Introduction," in C. Véliz, ed., *Latin America and the Caribbean: A Handbook* (London, 1968), p. xxiv.

gress, then, is bound to be *abundance for all*, through an increased production and supply of goods and services. Only in this way can the large-scale and heartbreaking poverty which prevails in so many parts of Latin America be eliminated, even though we should bear in mind that the complete abolition of all forms of poverty is not something which, as yet, has been achieved in any country on earth—what has been done in the sturdy and democratic monarchies of Scandinavia perhaps comes closest to that ideal.

Abundance and the elimination of poverty—here, I suggest, is the basic aim on which all would probably be agreed. It is, of course, agreeably vague. A European has no particular right to suggest to his Latin American friends that they should adopt one blueprint rather than another. But he may perhaps be within his rights in pointing out that it is easier to draw up a blueprint than to carry the design into production, and that at the start of the 1970s, despite the best intentions of governments and sociologists alike, the old dilemmas remain in place, stubborn and apparently immovable.

The dilemma from which all other dilemmas spring can be expressed quite simply. In order to begin to achieve the goal I suggested as appropriate, Latin America needs to promote both economic *and* social progress simultaneously. Economic growth must be at least faster than the growth of the population, otherwise living conditions inevitably fall below their *present* inadequate levels. At the same time, an increased *social* investment is urgently needed if the most distressing aspects of Latin American poverty—ill-health, squalid housing, malnutrition, illiteracy—are to be even partially counteracted. Progress, therefore, is not enough; *rapid progress* is what is essential. *Si volumus non redire, currendum est:* if we want *not* to go backward, it is necessary to run. Pelagius' dictum may aptly be applied to the situation. This fundamental dilemma is not exclusive to Latin America. Roughly two thirds of mankind are in the same boat. In general, Latin American levels of development are considerably higher than those of South and Southeast Asia or most parts of Africa, but they are still appreciably lower than those of the main industrial nations of the northern hemisphere or of such isolated southern hemisphere countries as Australia and New Zealand.

In the course of the last twenty years or so, the continued underdevelopment of so large a portion of the human family has begun to arouse emotions ranging from mild concern to savage indignation in an increasing number of people of many different kinds in the industrial nations. It is clear that from the most elementary moral considerations it is the duty of the richer nations of the world to help the poorer ones overcome their poverty and to try to make certain that their own continued prosperity is not achieved at the expense of the poorer countries. It is their duty even out of enlightened self-interest, by no means the least worthy of motives.

In view of the human race's proven capacity for preferring short-term gains at the expense of long-term benefits, a good deal of skepticism must be expressed on the possibility of a really vast program of aid materializing in the next few years. It may never be realized at all, in which case some kind of global shipwreck may confidently be predicted at some stage in the not-so-distant future. Massively increased financial aid and technical help, however, would by no means be a panacea for all Latin American ailments. It would serve no real purpose at all unless it were so planned and directed as to sow the seeds of future prosperity in the region.[1] And in order for these seeds to germinate, the soil would necessarily have to be plowed and watered beforehand. This plowing and watering, it can be argued, should take place whatever happens.

No list of the dilemmas confronting Latin America could possibly hope to be exhaustive—nor do I have the space to tackle the more detailed kinds of problem, such as the particular ways in which education might be expanded or inflation contained. There is, however, a *cluster of central issues* which bears examination. The best-laid schemes of reform are certain to go adrift unless these particular issues are squarely faced by the reformer concerned.

THE POPULATION EXPLOSION

Whatever may have been asserted to the contrary by both Catholic and Communist interests, no program of social and economic reorganization can hope to achieve more than marginal success if the problem of *numbers* is not given due care and attention. It is, quite simply, irresponsible to pretend otherwise. Yet it is surprising how often the whole question is ignored by Latin American social scientists, who are otherwise very prolific in recipes for development. It would, of course, be absurd to accuse them of a conspiracy of silence on the matter—but silence, for the most part, there has been. To some extent the need for a definite population policy *has* been less appreciated in Latin America than in some other areas of the world, partly because the region *is* rather sparsely populated in relation to its own size, and this has fostered the illusion that the population can continue to expand without causing too much trouble. Such a view might conceivably be justified in countries whose general levels of prosperity were rising continuously and where the majority of the population had left the

---

[1] I am leaving out of account the obvious desirability of *emergency aid* for the victims of famines, earthquakes, etc.

grosser forms of poverty behind for good.[1] It cannot easily be justified in Latin America, where very considerable problems of structural unemployment and urban marginality have been growing steadily in the present century, and where the rise in population merely serves to exacerbate an already tragic situation.

And yet this view *is* often justified in Latin America, sometimes on the grounds of religious doctrine and sometimes through a misplaced sense of nationalistic pride. Even within the past ten years there have been more than a handful of attacks, in the press and in the legislatures of Latin America, on programs designed to foster family planning. When such programs are associated with foreign advice, and in particular American advice, they can only too easily be denounced as unwarranted interference in the internal affairs of the region. Denunciations of this sort are a cheap way of securing short-term political support. There are undoubtedly a number of factors which militate against the easy acceptance of birth control in Latin America. Their force should certainly not be underestimated. The important role assigned to the *extended family*, for instance, or the apparent preference for *large* nuclear families—these things are extremely difficult to change, for they lie close to the heart of the complex of allegiances and values which helps to underpin the social order in general. Nevertheless, it is the manifest duty of Latin American governments to adopt effective measures to bring the rising birth rate under control, which would have as one of its chief effects a diminution in the size of families.

And it should not be thought that birth control on its own can be regarded as in any sense an excuse for not doing other things or as a substitute for parallel reforms in public health, housing, and education which are also needed if it is to be a success. Even if large-scale, widespread programs of family planning were put into effect tomorrow, their effects on the social situation would not be felt for a generation. Whether we like it or not, the increasing juvenescence of the Latin American population is bound to exacerbate social tensions in the near future and to create considerable problems in the proper provision of employment and social welfare. If these tensions and problems are to be even partly counteracted for the generation-after-this, then massive action is needed immediately.

A number of specific steps *have* been taken in recent years in the direction of setting up birth-control schemes. In general, however, it

---

[1] Recent debates on population growth in both Great Britain and the United States show that it is by no means automatically justified even in these circumstances. Perhaps Australia, New Zealand, and Canada are the only English-speaking countries which can positively justify this view.

can be said that the various Latin American efforts in this field have been discreet and relatively small-scale. The revolutionary government in Cuba, for instance, has evidently failed to place a population policy particularly high on its list of social priorities; despite the availability of birth-control devices in the island, the general public has shown few signs of wishing to limit the size of families, and no real pressure has been exerted in this direction. In this respect, Cuban policy can be unfavorably compared to that of Japan, which in the 1950s succeeded in drastically reducing the increase in her birth rate.[1] It should be stressed time and time again that Latin American governments, of whatever political complexion, cannot afford to wait for social and economic improvements to bring about the kind of spontaneous limitation of the population which occurred in many of the industrial nations. Birth control is certainly not a panacea: but it *is* a demonstrably necessary component in any process of accelerated development, and without it such a process must inevitably be frustrated.

THE AGRARIAN QUESTION

The issues raised by the agrarian situation in most of the Latin American countries are complex and profound, and a very great deal of attention has been lavished on them in the course of the past twenty years or so. As usual, the basic problem is both social and economic. In the mid-1960s it was estimated that some seventy million Latin American country-dwellers received an annual income of *less than seventy dollars*. Economically, it remains true that Latin American agriculture is woefully underproductive and is not able to meet all of the food requirements of the different countries of the region. An ECLA survey of the mid-1960s sums up the general situation most eloquently:

> The bulk of the rural population has no surplus income and not even enough land to permit an increase in investment, while those who own most of the land and income are seldom interested in developing their own property, stepping up production, and raising productivity, or have the capacity to do so. The profits made on large estates are hardly ever ploughed back into the land; instead they are spent on urban investment and luxury consumption, or sent out of the country.[2]

[1] See Hugh Thomas, *Cuba or the Pursuit of Freedom* (London, 1971), p. 427. Communist countries have traditionally maintained a somewhat ambiguous attitude toward birth-control programs. In Russia they do not seem to have been much encouraged, although China now appears to be making efforts to bring down her birth rate.

[2] Economic Commission for Latin America, *Economic Survey of Latin America 1966* (United Nations, New York, 1968), p. 312.

The double aim of an agrarian reform, therefore, must be to heighten the efficiency and productivity of agriculture while at the same time guaranteeing greater opportunities to the peasants and laborers of the rural areas. The core of the problem is the continued existence of the latifundio and in particular the traditional hacienda —whose abiding social and economic effects have already been mentioned.

The historical roots of the problem go very deep. From early colonial times onward, the Latin American countryside has been an underprivileged and for the most part neglected area in comparison with the city. As we saw, the great majority of aristocratic landowners developed essentially urban preoccupations and failed to acquire even the most minimal interest in rural improvements. There were honorable exceptions to this rule, especially from the later eighteenth century onward, but in general Latin American landowners have never been noted for a deep affection for the countryside and its people. In this respect, the emphasis on rural issues in both the Mexican and the Cuban revolutions can be seen as an encouraging innovation. Dr. Castro's almost obsessive and much publicized enthusiasm for livestock, for instance, could profitably be imitated by other Latin American politicians. What is needed, quite apart from anything else, is some kind of Latin American Physiocratic movement—which would follow eighteenth-century precedent by fostering a suitable mystique of the countryside, promoting the foundation of agricultural academies, and reversing the time-honored Latin American tradition which allows wealth to accumulate while men decay.

The need for an agrarian reform which would eliminate the latifundio has been widely accepted, at least in theory. As we have seen, far-reaching reforms on the land were set in motion by the Mexican Bolivian and Cuban revolutions, and in very recent years Chile[1] and Peru[2] have also embarked on such a course of action, and in what appears to be a serious way. Elsewhere, despite a plethora of much-trumpeted laws, plans, congressional reports, and good intentions, agrarian reform has made very little substantial progress or has been confined to small-scale colonization schemes (about which we shall say

[1] The Chilean agrarian reform (1967) aimed at giving some one hundred thousand families land within five years; at the close of the Frei administration in November 1970 between twenty thousand and thirty thousand families had benefited. Under Allende the process was greatly speeded up, though at the cost of some confusion. By mid-1972 some 60 percent of the land was under direct or indirect government control.

[2] It is too early to evaluate the success or otherwise of the agrarian reform decreed by the military government in mid-1969.

more presently). The dangers involved in reorganizing the countryside are considerable, though they almost certainly do not outweigh the dangers of *not* acting at all. A reform which simply subdivides the latifundio into a series of tiny small-holdings may do little to give the peasant or the landless laborer greater economic opportunities. This was the case in Haiti at the start of the nineteenth century, when the sugar plantations were broken up; and the condition of the Haitian peasantry today can hardly be described as spectacular. In some areas, too, it is simply not practical to distribute land to all the landless laborers who might want it; either there is too little land or too many such laborers. A further problem is that agrarian reform may actually reduce production, at least in the short term, since any drastic reorganization of the land tenure system is likely to cause temporary dislocation and confusion.

None of these problems should deter governments from going ahead. The main issue is *land tenure*: and the initial questions to be asked here concern possible exemptions from a reform and the amount and form of compensation for the owners of expropriated estates. Should there be exemptions? Should landowners be compensated? Plainly, there *should* be estates which are exempt from expropriation on the grounds of efficiency, and the danger here is that a doctrinaire antilatifundism might sweep out of existence not merely those properties which are badly run, but also those which are well run. With the nutritional needs of Latin America (not to mention Asia and Africa) already so poorly satisfied, no truly efficient agricultural concern should be dislocated for purely ideological reasons. On compensation, there might seem to be a case for making this fairly slight: many hacendados have done relatively little to raise production, to improve the living conditions of their peasants, or (often enough) to pay the usually rather light taxation which is due from them. If an agrarian reform is large-scale, it may often be impossibly expensive to give immediate compensation to landowners, in which case the best solution is probably to indemnify them in the form of government bonds redeemable over a period of twenty or thirty years.

In any agrarian reform program, very serious thought has to be given to the system or systems of land tenure that are to replace the "unreformed" arrangements. Many writers favor widespread cooperative arrangements embracing a multitude of small or medium-sized individual family or communal holdings. It is clear that to import foreign models wholesale is often wholly inappropriate. It would be difficult if not impossible to try to spread an English or Danish type of agriculture—capital-intensive, highly mechanized, with minimal labor

—to a situation where, because of the rise in population, labor-extensive farming will be a social need for at least another generation.[1] Mexico and Bolivia, as we have seen, developed fairly flexible arrangements following their attack on the hacienda; communal or semicommunal holdings coexist with private farms of varying sizes. Cuban agriculture, by contrast, has been largely collectivized along Russian lines—the sugar plantations passing directly from private ownership to state control. Private latifundism was, in effect, turned into state latifundism. Whether collectivization of this kind is a proper answer to the agrarian question in the rest of Latin America is at least debatable. The main argument against collectivization on the Russian model is that in many circumstances it alienates those whom it is supposed to benefit, and the whole purpose of an agrarian reform is to enable people to work more effectively rather than with a bad grace.

Whatever system of land tenure is envisaged, there are several further points which should (and do) preoccupy agrarian planners in Latin America. Given the already existing labor surplus on the land, there is no sense in attempting to go for a full-scale mechanization *tout court*, as this would free too many peasants for the drift to the cities. In many cases what is often called an "intermediate" agrarian technology is needed. This would do a great deal to heighten productivity, while keeping most of the agricultural labor force on the land. There is no reason at all why yields should not be greatly improved, even where a multitude of small-holdings has replaced the latifundio. Given proper organization, for instance, much can be expected from the new "miracle" strains of wheat and maize which have been perfected in the so-called "green revolution" of recent years. If an agrarian reform is to succeed, however, it cannot stop short when the redistributive phase is complete: credit, education, technical help, and constant encouragement must be supplied in increasing amounts to the peasants.

It is sometimes suggested that "colonization" schemes are a substitute for agrarian reform. (The settlement of peasants on public land on a fairly large scale was, in fact, a main feature of the Venezuelan agrarian reform of the 1960s.) It would be idle to deny that in any moderately happy future, the colonization of public lands which at present lie empty would play an increasingly important part in Latin American agricultural progress. Some areas (e.g., the eastern lowlands of Bolivia) offer excellent possibilities. But in general, geographical factors combined with the depressed condition of the Latin American countryside prevent widespread movements of population into unoccupied terri-

[1] This is being optimistic and depends on the implementation of birth-control measures.

tories. Any truly substantial "frontier" movement in Latin America, therefore, would probably *follow* rather than parallel an agrarian reform, as the Bolivian experience tends to indicate.[1] The lesson cannot be stressed too often: for both social and economic reasons, the improvement of agriculture has to be effected in the areas farmed at present.

In a few areas of Latin America, it is not wholly impossible that an alternative approach—the proper taxation of land—might yield results similar to those of a full-scale agrarian reform. (In Argentina, a country with an honorable agrarian tradition, the whole notion of an agrarian *reform* would need careful thought, since for the most part the traditional hacienda is not to be found there.) If a prohibitive tax could be imposed on land which was under-used, then owners might be obliged to take steps to improve their efficiency or to sell the property in question. But while lip service has often been paid to the ideal of land taxation, no Latin American government has ever imposed more than a negligible tax on landowners. In the last analysis this becomes a political question, since in many countries landowners have successfully remained close to political power for so long; and have doubtless seen it in their interest to resist land taxation, not to mention agrarian reform itself.

It should never be forgotten that the main aim of an agrarian reform should be to create a new and essentially positive relationship *between man and the land*. In eighteenth-century Peru, the Spaniards Juan and Ulloa noticed that those fortunate Indians who owned their own land cultivated it with great application. They drew from this the moral that nobody would make an effort to work more efficiently "without the incentive of some advancement."[2] In Latin American agriculture, the moral still holds good today. It is probably true to say that a successful solution to the agrarian question is the essential key to any long-term and really substantial progress Latin America is likely to enjoy in the future.

THE DISTRIBUTION OF WEALTH

In Latin American history the distribution of land has been intimately associated with the distribution of wealth. The extreme disparities of income which characterize most of the twenty republics have a number of unfortunate effects, which help to perpetuate—and nowadays to

[1] It is only fair to mention, however, that a strong case *has* been made for the opening up of the interior of South America as the key to development, though not as a substitute for reforms in the "coastal" areas where settlement has so far been concentrated: see Carlos Matus, "El desarrollo del interior de América Latina: ¿tesis fantasiosa o interrogante fundamental?" in *Dos polémicas sobre el desarrollo de América Latina* (Santiago, 1970).

[2] Juan and Ulloa, *op. cit.*, p. 286.

exacerbate—the social and economic problems of the region. There are reasons for supposing, therefore, that rapid progress of the sort urgently needed in Latin America cannot be achieved unless measures are taken to raise the levels of income of the poorer classes—which constitute the majority of the population in most countries.

Some of the more obvious effects of the severe maldistribution of wealth which is to be found in Latin America have already been touched on in this chapter. What may be considered as the excessive income of the top five percent or so of the population creates an anomalous pattern of industrial diversification, given the fact that the tastes of the upper classes need to be satisfied in a European or an American manner. Meanwhile, the excessive poverty of millions of the upper classes' less-favored fellow citizens prevents the growth of a large domestic market on which domestic industry could feed. Any government which aspires to make rapid progress must take account of this basic fact. Yet the internal pressures making for redistribution of income are not really in evidence. The trade unions, for instance, have been hampered in their demands for higher wages by the continued existence of a vast labor surplus. (This has been less true in Argentina, and in certain key sectors of industry elsewhere.) The unionization of the peasants—except in the countries where an agrarian reform has taken place—has proceeded very slowly if at all. In the present situation, therefore, only the state is really in a position to take a suitable initiative.

It is probably true that high income disparities can be justified if the richer classes put their higher income to productive use. This has never occurred on the necessary scale in Latin America, though this does not mean that it will never occur in the future. All the indications are that when he is not actually spending it, the Latin American investor prefers to put his money into landed or urban property, or to send it abroad. Furthermore, the amount of money he tends to invest is by no means large in proportion to what he spends on conspicuous consumption. This tendency can be explained in many different ways. It is due in part to the psychology which history has bequeathed to the region; it can be seen, in more recent times, as a defense against the chronic inflation from which some countries have suffered; and it can also be regarded as a response to political uncertainty. Whatever the explanation, the tendency *has* existed and *does* exist. Unless it can be counteracted, and unless thriftier habits can be encouraged among the more fortunate Latin Americans, then it would seem likely that the state will have to assume the responsibility of reordering patterns of expenditure and consumption.

In the industrial nations, governments have long imposed a wide variety of fairly heavy taxes on personal income and on personal consumption; direct income tax, and such devices as purchase tax, sales tax or (more recently) the value-added tax of the European Common Market, have been widespread. Such measures have enabled governments to spend more on social welfare, on education, on housing and similar benefits, all of which have raised living standards and contributed to economic efficiency. In Latin America, the levels of direct income tax are generally very low indeed compared with those of the industrial nations, and the extensive use of indirect taxation does nothing, of course, to raise the income of the poor. Income tax is very widely evaded in many countries. A good deal of lip service is paid to the ideal of taxation reform—as with agrarian reform—but nothing very substantial is actually *done*.[1]

It is sometimes assumed—if only because this was in part the experience of the older industrial nations—that *increased* inequality is a condition of progress, that entrepreneurship and higher investment can be induced in this way only. This argument is highly dubious in the Latin American case, in view of the spending habits of the richer classes already mentioned. Given the need to augment the size of the internal market, what in fact is needed is greater equality. A serious agrarian reform could do much to bring this about, as would a truly resolute reform of taxation.

ALLEGIANCES AND VALUES

In every social order, the formal institutions and arrangements established by law and by convention are paralleled by an informal complex of customs, allegiances, values, and so forth, which can be described in anthropological language as the "culture" of the society concerned. In Latin America, there is some reason to believe that this informal complex is in some respects stronger than the formal network of institutions. How far this is due to the heritage of the traditional Iberian psychology sketched in Chapter 3, and how far it is the outcome of social and economic factors deriving from colonial times, must remain matters for speculation and research. But the strength of a Latin American's individual and family allegiances and values need not be doubted.

Even bearing in mind the changes brought about by industrialization, Latin America remains a rather *patriarchal* region, many of whose people bear the traces of a somewhat deferential cast of mind. This characteristic stems to a large extent from the organization of the latifundio, where the *patrón* (boss) exercised (and in many areas still

---

[1] Against this, it has to be admitted that tax *collecting* proved rather more effective in the 1960s than in earlier decades.

exercises) considerable authority, and where the peasant came to look upon the patrón as a kind of protector, a strong man to whom allegiance could be given. Traces of this attitude, and the paternalism which is the other side of the coin, can be found in many situations in Latin American life, not merely on the hacienda. It can be found in industry, especially in the smaller factories, but also to some extent in large business concerns as well. Studies of Latin American business organizations tend to reveal that more authority is conventionally focused on the man at the top than is common in, say, the United States; there is greater *personal control* and less *delegation of authority*. At a distinctly different level of society, similar values can be found among the country-dwellers who migrate to the shanty-towns surrounding the cities. Politically, this sometimes expresses itself in widespread support, among the "marginal" population, for "populist" caudillos or politicians who, rightly or wrongly, give an impression of strength. The loyalty shown by the inhabitants of the barriadas of Lima toward General Odría was a commonly noted fact a few years ago. Comparable groups in Colombia have shown considerable enthusiasm for another ex-dictator, General Gustavo Rojas Pinilla. Examples like this could be multiplied. The strongly "personalist" character of much of Latin American political life seems to derive from this particular kind of deferential response to paternal authority.

It has often been noted that Latin Americans tend to place a high value on individualism. This is true, but it should not be taken to mean that Latin American styles of individualism are necessarily the same as those which are commonly associated with the English-speaking world, though they may have more than a little in common with those to be found in the Latin countries of Europe. Anglo-Saxon individualism tends to be measured against or at any rate in relation to a group. It is collaborative rather than defiant, associative rather than assertive. "The spirit of association," whose absence was so lamented by several nineteenth-century Latin American statesmen, has never been as deeply rooted in the twenty republics as in some other parts of the world. This may be due, in the last analysis, to the hostile attitude shown by the Iberian monarchies toward independent initiatives and organizations during colonial times.

For the average Latin American (if there is such a creature) three allegiances usually seem of paramount importance: allegiance to his family, to his *compadres*, and to his friends. The family, usually the extended family, is an institution whose hold over Latin American life is extraordinarily tenacious. The family comes first: its members must be protected, helped, fixed up with jobs, allocated property. Nepotism in both politics and business is often widespread, and regarded as perfectly natural. The relationship of *compadrazgo* (in Brazil, *compadresco*) possesses a very similar importance for many Latin Americans. In many cases compadrazgo is virtually a means of uniting two separate families in a formal alliance. It is a personal treaty of allegiance which can be concluded between people of very different social standing or between those who are equals—in either case it implies a very firm loyalty and a de facto equality between those who adopt the relationship.[1] A third major allegiance is given to friendships, which often seem to involve a greater degree of willingness to do favors than is normally the case in the English-speaking world. Relatives, compadres, friends—these are the people with whom a Latin American establishes his strongest working links. More impersonal but equally confident kinds of relationship based on commercial or professional links seem to be less common in the Latin American context. How does this complex of allegiances and values affect economic life? An American historian concludes that:

Comparatively the Latin American complex: 1) sacrifices rigorous economically directed effort, or profit maximization, to family interests; 2) places social and personal emotional interests ahead of business obligations; 3) impedes mergers and other changes in ownership desirable for higher levels of technological efficiency and better adjustment to markets; 4) fosters nepotism to a degree harmful to continuously able top-management; 5) hinders the building up of a supply of competent and cooperative middle managers; 6) makes managers and workers less amenable to constructive criticism; 7) creates barriers of disinterest in the flow of technological communication; and 8) lessens the urge for expansion and risk-taking. These Latin qualities are not necessarily detriments to the good life, perhaps just the opposite, but they are hindrances to material progress under the Anglo-American concepts of a market-oriented capitalist economy.[2]

Many of these distinctive Latin American predispositions may be thought to reflect the traditional priorities of an agrarian social order dominated by a landed aristocracy. Their survival has been impressive. They will *probably* disappear almost automatically with the spread of

---

[1] *Compadrazgo* can override political differences, which are usually ignored in such a relationship.

[2] T. B. Cochran, "Cultural Factors in Economic Growth," *Journal of Economic History*, XX (1960), 529–30.

industrialization, when the older forms of paternalism and individual self-assertion and the present valuations placed on the family, compadrazgo, and friendship will—or should—at the very least be subtly modified.

THE EFFICACY OF THE STATE

In view of much said so far in this chapter, it is apparent that the role of the state in Latin America is likely to become an increasingly important one. What sort of instrument *is* the state? How easily can it be used to bring about desirable social and economic reforms? It is difficult to escape the conclusion that in many respects the countries of Latin America are, to use the expression of the Swedish economist Gunnar Myrdal, "soft states." Their "softness" is evidenced in the frequently encountered gap between legislative intention and law enforcement, in a marked tolerance of corruption, and in a general failure to lay down what may be thought of as the rules of the game. It would no doubt be possible to devise a scale which measured the extent of "softness" in the different Latin American republics: some are plainly "harder" than others. Mexico since the revolution, for instance, seems to have become notably less "soft" in many respects, although widespread corruption has by no means been eliminated there; Chile, Uruguay, and Costa Rica have never been noted for administrative corruption, although other aspects of softness are to be found in those agreeable lands; the totalitarian regime in Cuba has certainly abolished corruption (at least of the grosser and more damaging sort) and may well end up by producing a "hard" state. Oddly enough, military dictatorships tend to be no different, as far as softness is concerned, from other types of government, though they may be very hard indeed toward their oppositions.

This particular characteristic of the state in Latin America may well have its roots in colonial times, but can more easily be traced to what occurred following the wars of independence. For many of the more powerful Latin Americans, the state then became a *means of enrichment*, an object of plunder, worth conquering and worth retaining. The public administration was regarded as a legitimate field for augmenting personal income by often highly questionable means. Public jobs were looked upon as suitable for distribution to political supporters, members of a president's family, or the clients of a particular aristocratic clique. In the twentieth century, with the emergence of the middle classes, public administrations were expanded to satisfy a rising demand for jobs. Throughout most of the period since independence, therefore, to win control of the state has been an easier way of acquiring wealth and status than to channel energies into other activities such as business or commerce.

In some republics, corruption has long enjoyed a favorable position in the political system. Edward Gibbon once described corruption as an "infallible symptom of constitutional liberty"—but that incomparable ironist might well have lost his normal composure had he contemplated the extent of corruption in some of the Latin American states. Dictators, and even constitutionally elected presidents, have massively embezzled the public treasury, handed out lucrative contracts to relatives and friends, connived at profitable evasions of the laws they themselves have enacted, and salted away their ill-gotten gains in Switzerland or the United States.[1] This kind of behavior is duplicated at lower levels of the government and public administration. Bureaucrats, customs officers, and policemen quite frequently accept bribes. Many Latin American bureaucracies, moreover, are overstaffed; often enough, the bureaucrats themselves are ill-paid and have little conception of "public service"—both of these conditions need to be altered before a "hard" state can even begin to emerge.

Two consequences of this situation—one practical, one moral— seem of particular importance. The first concerns the sheer efficacy of the state as an instrument of public betterment. Laws may well be enacted; but this is a very different thing from saying that they will be put into effect. A tax may be decreed; but this is no guarantee that it will be adequately collected. The social welfare legislation which is to be found on the statute books of nearly all the twenty republics is often admirable—on paper. But in real life, it is extraordinarily difficult for minimum wage levels, stipulations about conditions of work, or un- employment payments to be actually enforced. Since independence, Latin American governments have proved remarkably efficient at exiling, imprisoning, or executing members of the opposition, and at bolstering up the privileges and incomes of their own supporters; their efficiency in other directions has rarely been outstanding.

The moral effects of the "softness" of most Latin American states are equally unfortunate. The credibility of governments is much reduced. Nothing is more demoralizing than to see a government flagrantly breaking its own rules. If public office is no more than a means of enrichment, what is the sense of adopting an attitude of public- spiritedness? It is probably no accident that public-spirited men and women have been more numerous in those republics which have

[1] The countries mentioned earlier should certainly be excepted from these general- izations. In Chile, for instance, it is a common belief among the public that a president leaves office poorer than when he enters it.

managed to curtail corruption to some extent than in those which have not. In general, the persistence of corruption and administrative inefficiency undermines public morale and leads to a widespread and often bitter skepticism about the good intentions of governments.

A well-known Argentine journalist wrote recently that "In our part of the world the left fails as well as the right. What is lacking is something to do with the rigour, the seriousness, the perseverance of the political systems, and with the rule of authority."[1] It is impossible to disagree with this verdict. But the difficulties facing Latin Americans in attempting to "harden" their administrative and political systems are especially formidable. In most of the older industrial nations, many aspects of "softness" prevailed until well into the nineteenth century, and were successfully counteracted at a period when the role of the state was limited by the philosophy of laissez-faire. Public administrations at that time were relatively small, and could be reformed fairly rapidly; the spirit of dispassionate public service then spread automatically to new branches of the administration when the powers of the state were once again increased in the course of the twentieth century. No such process is possible in Latin America. If the role of the state in the Latin America of the near future is to enlarge still further, as seems at least possible, then the public administration will necessarily continue to be sizable. This implies problems on a far greater scale than those which confronted the nations of nineteenth-century Europe.

ECONOMIC DEPENDENCE

The countries of Latin America can be said to be economically dependent on countries *outside* Latin America in three main ways: (1) Foreign markets are needed for the Latin American primary products whose sale provides the region with funds to buy imported goods. (2) Foreign technology and foreign technical skill—not to mention foreign money—are needed in the process of industrialization, which is seen as the key to the future prosperity and economic independence of the region. (3) Foreign (particularly American and multinational) enterprises control some of the natural resources and—over the past few decades—an increasing proportion of the manufacturing industry of the region.

It is possible, though not necessarily desirable, for Latin American governments to eliminate (3) as a cause of dependence; this occurred in Cuba in 1960. Assuming that rapid progress is the fundamental aim, however, it is practically impossible to eliminate both (1) and (2). What measures can be taken to offset the more questionable effects of economic dependence? This is a complex and many-sided subject, and

[1] Mario Grondona, "Hacia la izquierda," *Visión*, November 6, 1970, p. 43.

it will not be possible to do more than suggest a few of the dilemmas involved.

As we saw in the preceding section, Latin American exports have been constantly threatened in the twentieth century by diminishing markets, increased competition from other areas of the world, fluctuating prices, and periods of uncertainty. The situation is made somewhat more difficult by the fact that many Latin American republics remain dependent on the export of *one* crop or mineral product, which makes it impossible for them to gain on the roundabouts what they lose on the swings. Latin America's share of world trade has fallen appreciably since World War II, but at the same time the region's need to *import* goods has been increasing. The principal problem for the Latin American countries, therefore, is to secure adequate and stable markets abroad, together with better and less variable prices for their commodities.

There are several ways in which this problem can be tackled. Bilateral arrangements can sometimes assure favorable market and price conditions, at least in the short term. This was the case, for instance, with the Roca–Runciman agreement concluded between Argentina and Great Britain in 1933, or, more recently, the Cuba–Soviet sugar agreements of the 1960s under which Russia provided Cuba with a guaranteed market for her sugar and arranged to pay prices which were well above the world average. Something, too, can be done through international commodity agreements. Brazil, which in the 1960s continued to supply about forty percent of the world's coffee, has played a considerable role in the international Coffee Council, which works to secure a better position for all coffee-producing countries.

The diversification of exports—in terms of both commodities and markets—is a further approach which can yield results. Relatively few major export lines have supplemented the staples mentioned in the first section (see p. 220), although Peruvian fishmeal underwent a prodigious expansion in the early 1960s. Much depends, here, on the changing pattern of world demand, and how quickly Latin American exporters can seize—or indeed, stimulate—new opportunities. Any major expansion in coffee exports, for instance, would require new habits on the part of consumers in the industrial nations. Could the Japanese be persuaded to become coffee-drinkers on a large scale? Could more of the British or the Russians be weaned from their national affection for tea? Leaving aside primary products, it is probably also true that Latin American manufactured or semimanufactured goods could find suitable markets abroad—if only the trade policies of the major industrial powers were satisfactorily geared to this, which they are not.

Any long-term improvement of Latin America's trading position probably depends on much stiffer negotiations with the industrial nations, carried out in conjunction with countries in Africa and Asia who are affected by problems of a similar nature. It is interesting to note in this context that the Latin American countries played a leading part in the establishment of the United Nations Conference on Trade and Development (UNCTAD) in the 1960s. Neither the first session of this body (Geneva, 1964) nor the second (New Delhi, 1968), nor the third (Santiago, 1972) yielded very much in the way of concessions from the industrial nations, which have so far shown a less than adequate degree of interest in improving the commercial position of the poorer two thirds of the world. Some kind of serious international agreement, however, remains vitally necessary, for the problems which the first three UNCTADs failed to resolve will by no means disappear, however much the industrial nations would like them to. The object of such an agreement must be to secure a genuine measure of equitable *interdependence* rather than the present system of unequal dependence.

A poor trading position is one symptom of dependence; the "technology gap" is another. In attempting to accelerate the pace of industrial progress, Latin America has to rely heavily on imported technology and technical skills. These can only come from the industrial nations, and there is certainly a sense in which this is an advantage for Latin America: modern industrial processes can, in fact, be transplanted without the Latin American nations having to go to the immense trouble of inventing them separately. Nevertheless, the fact that the region's independent technological base is somewhat fragile does tend to highlight its dependence on the outside world. This is to some extent inevitable— for ever since the beginnings of industrialization, countries have borrowed technical knowledge and technical skills from other countries which were further advanced on the path of industrial progress. The vital thing is for such knowledge and such skills to be quickly domesticated in their new environment—as they were, for instance, in Japan or Russia. In Latin America, however, the process of domestication is hampered by a number of factors: technical education has not been developed to the necessary extent; relatively little national effort has gone into building up facilities for scientific research; and, not least, many of the foreign-controlled industries in the region depend on research centers in North America or Europe rather than in Latin America itself.[1]

[1] An important exception here is medicine. It is notable that Latin American hospitals were able to carry out heart transplants very soon after Dr. Christiaan Barnard pioneered the technique in South Africa.

An essential element in any process of faster economic progress must be a truly serious Latin American effort to increase the scale and the quality of scientific and technical education, and to foster the region's scientific research. (It has been estimated that in 1966 the United States devoted 3.4 percent of its GNP to scientific research; in the same year Latin America devoted around 0.2 percent of its combined GNPs to the same end.) A key role here must be reserved to the universities, where at present there is relatively little post-graduate or doctoral work in the sciences. It is clear that throughout Latin American history, educational biases have been markedly non-scientific, and although a number of universities in the region possess excellent medical and engineering faculties, a great deal has to be done to correct the traditional predispositions of many Latin American students. On almost any analysis, Latin America needs more chemists, agronomists, engineers, and doctors, and far fewer lawyers and sociologists. A definite change in educational priorities is indicated.

It may be useful at this point to say something about foreign aid. It is clear that from the viewpoint of rapid progress, outside assistance, both technical and financial, is an obvious desideratum. The amount of foreign aid—most of it American, under the Alliance for Progress—which went into Latin America in the 1960s was by no means negligible, and numerous specific improvements in the region have been carried out as a result. Nevertheless, a number of observations on the way in which the aid programs have functioned seem in order. Going on the experience of the 1960s, it can be said that most aid is tied to exports from the country which puts up the money: an American loan to Colombia, say, can only be used to buy American goods. This may not necessarily suit Colombia; the goods concerned may be less desirable than alternatives available in, say, Western Europe. Most other countries follow American practice in this respect. It is also clear that aid can be said to be tied *politically*, that American aid programs, for instance, have been designed to prevent countries from falling into the hands of anti-American political forces. It would be foolish to pretend that this is incomprehensible, and the practice is by no means confined to the United States. (The very considerable Russian aid to Cuba, for instance, might well dwindle rather rapidly if Dr. Castro suddenly discovered an overwhelming affection for the Chinese.) Both these habits—attaching political as well as economic strings to disbursements of aid—probably affect the efficacy of the aid itself. A solution here would be for the governments concerned to channel their aid to Latin America through the the United Nations and its various agencies, not excluding the World Bank.

A second major problem associated with foreign aid concerns the form in which it is given. Money is usually *loaned* rather than *granted* outright. This involves the countries which receive aid in frequent repayment difficulties. Often enough, new loans are provided merely to enable such difficulties to be overcome—at the cost, of course, of incurring new obligations. American practice in this respect contrasts sharply with the tremendous and generous outpouring of United States aid to Europe in the postwar period. It may be recalled that under the Marshall Plan, some thirty thousand million dollars was disbursed for the purposes of European reconstruction, and that approximately twenty-thousand million of this was in the form of outright grants. If some kind of crash program of aid is ever devised for Latin America, then there would be much to be said for following this striking and noble precedent.

The third aspect of economic dependence which I have chosen to underline—the foreign control of Latin American natural resources and manufacturing industry—presents peculiarly delicate dilemmas. The foreign ownership and exploitation of Latin American mineral wealth has been a main target for economically nationalist governments over recent decades. President Cárdenas' expropriation of the British and American oil companies in Mexico in 1938 was the first truly notable action taken by a Latin American government in this respect; the most recent examples have been the Peruvian and Chilean nationalizations of American oil and copper interests in 1968 and 1971 respectively. Governments preoccupied with the issue of economic independence can pursue two course of action in relation to foreign mining or petroleum concerns: they can either nationalize, or they can adopt a policy of extracting heavy royalties from the companies concerned. Nationalization carries with it the danger of long and acerbic diplomatic wrangling and the possibility of short-term disorganization in the mines or oilfields or whatever may have been nationalized. The taxation of foreign enterprises, by contrast, may not satisfy the domestic aspiration toward economic autonomy.

The precise *extent* of foreign control of Latin American manufacturing industry is difficult to determine, but it can safely be assumed to be considerable. An American historian, writing of one of the major industrial areas of Latin America, concludes that:

By the early 1960s perhaps half the industrial capital in São Paulo's private sector, excluding craft shops, was foreign-owned or controlled. Few of the largest Paulista firms had succumbed, but whole new lines had arisen in foreign hands: automobiles, pharmaceuticals, tobacco, construction equipment, tires and electronics.[1]

[1] Warren Dean, *The Industrialization of São Paulo* (Austin, Texas, 1969), p. 237.

In countries where the original industrial base was smaller than São Paulo's, the proportion of manufacturing industry in foreign or multinational hands may well be greater than half. The implications of this situation are easy to see. Quite apart from the profits which may or may not be sent out of the country rather than reinvested locally, foreign enterprises in the newer sections of industry are, in the last analysis, dependent on decisions taken *abroad*, by their head office, and their contribution to the country in which they happen to be operating *may* be curtailed or otherwise affected for reasons which have nothing to do with the country concerned. This is especially true, perhaps, of the multinational corporations, whose operations span the world. A factory belonging to such a corporation may be closed down in country X merely in order to spur on the performance of a similar factory in country Y. In such a case, country X has no power to intervene.

There is an argument which favors the complete elimination of foreign private investment, and it is this:

The Communist countries, rigidly excluding foreign venture capital, have made relatively more progress toward industrialization in recent years than have most of the less developed capitalist countries that have welcomed foreign investment. Even in the non-Communist world, the most remarkable progress in the past half century has been made by Japan, which has followed a policy of excluding foreign capital only slightly less rigid than Soviet Russia's.[1]

Against this, it can certainly be argued that the exclusion of foreign capital and foreign enterprise is no *automatic* guarantee of industrial progress. Furthermore, foreign and multinational enterprises *do* play a crucial role in the transmission of the more sophisticated modern technologies to Latin America, and measures to "phase out" foreign investment in local industry would have to include alternative arrangements for the introduction of those same technologies.

Several means have been suggested to reduce the extent of foreign control while retaining the technological advantages of allowing foreign enterprises to operate on Latin American soil. Mixed ventures, for instance, might be a way out of some circumstances: governments or local capitalists might associate themselves with foreign enterprises *on terms of equality*, which would increase their decision-making power.

[1] C. S. Burchill, "The Multinational Corporations," *Queens Quarterly*, Vol. LXXVII, No. 1 (Kingston, Ontario, 1970), p. 6. Western investment in several Communist countries has, however, been on the increase in the past few years.

A somewhat different approach is offered by the idea of the "management contract"—though this has so far scarcely been tried in Latin America. Under such a contract, a foreign company could agree to establish a factory or plant for a limited period of time. During that time, the company could undertake to train nationals of the country concerned to take over the running of the enterprise on the expiry of the contract, at which point the host country would assume ownership of the enterprise. During the operation of the contract, the company would receive a fee and also any profits it made. Such an arrangement could be useful to the host country and to the company alike.

The basic problem which faces a Latin American government bent on economic autonomy is, when it comes down to it, quite simple. Ways and means have to be found whereby foreign enterprises, if admitted at all, can be more effectively harnessed to the domestic industrial progress of the nation in question. Mixed ventures and management contracts are only two possible methods. There are no doubt many others.

The whole question of economic dependence is undoubtedly aggravated, in the Latin American case, by the starkly obvious fact that much of the region is overwhelmingly tied, economically speaking, to *one* foreign country, the United States. This undoubtedly inflames the whole issue and provides Latin American nationalists with a single target at which to aim their arrows of wrath. Surveying the pattern of economic relations which has grown up in the twentieth century between Latin America and the United States, it is easy to agree with Salvador de Madariaga's conclusion that

> The power of the North is so huge compared to that of the South that, like a machine or a monster, it paralyses and devours the nearly defenseless South, so that all that remains free and independent there might be said to owe its freedom and independence less to its own exertions than to the moderation and wisdom of the North.[1]

It is wholly understandable that for many Latin Americans an immensely tenacious political myth, based on a firmly held belief in the malevolent designs of American Imperialism,[2] should have crystallized

[1] Madariaga, *Latin America Between the Eagle and the Bear* (London, 1962), p. 84.
[2] The word "imperialism," like many others, has acquired connotations which are by no means universally recognized or accepted. As used by a number of political movements in Latin America (and elsewhere)—and they are as entitled as anyone else to use what jargon they please—it means, in essence, *economic* penetration, influence, domination, or control. Military and political penetration, influence, etc.—the traditional forms of empire-building throughout the ages—are regarded as essentially

at the heart of more than one political ideology. The facts have very often lent themselves—and continue to lend themselves—to such an interpretation. American companies have by no means been guiltless of shady practices in their dealings with some Latin American governments; more than ten thousand million dollars of American money is currently invested in the region; a high proportion of Latin American imports and exports come from or go to the United States on terms which are not necessarily favorable to Latin America; some American concerns have undoubtedly enjoyed very high profits when operating in the region; the American government has often shown what Latin Americans could interpret as an excessive degree of support for American enterprises; many of the Latin American economies may justifiably be said to be extensively penetrated by American interests. Clearly, foreign or multinational companies *do* behave in rather arrogant ways on occasions. The most notorious instance of this in recent times was the affair of ITT, the giant American conglomerate, which offered a million dollars to the Central Intelligence Agency in 1970 to prevent or impede the election of Dr. Salvador Allende as President of Chile. (The offer, which one might have thought less than adequate to the purpose, was refused.) It is not to be wondered at that the region has to some extent acquired "a self-conscious colonial mentality."[1] American economic penetration in Europe can justifiably be regarded as a *challenge*; in Latin America, where the domestic industrial base is far weaker than in Europe, it is not unnatural that it should be seen as a *menace*. It is inevitable, therefore, that any assertion of a will toward economic autonomy is bound to bring Latin America and the United States into some kind of conflict. But it is important to set this in perspective. A complete severance of economic links between the two regions would probably do Latin America more harm than it would the United States. As a former American ambassador to Brazil puts it:

> In her relations with Latin America, the United States has an alternative. She can work in the Northern hemisphere and do extremely well at it. . . . Her choice, of course, has thus far been to stay

---

complementary or "formal," if they occur at all. Thus the huge American investment in Canada and the presence of American companies in Europe are examples of imperialism; the Russian occupation of the Baltic states in 1940 and the Chinese invasion of Tibet in 1950 are not. This is a narrow and profoundly unhistorical formula. In this book at least, the term is used in its wider sense—the building and running of empires. It should be recognized, however, that the word in its narrow sense is common in Latin American political discourse.

[1] Glade, *op. cit.*, p. 354.

in and with the Latin American region. But if either she or the Latin American region were to choose otherwise, it would not be any unmanageable strain on the economic life of the United States.[1]

This may properly be called economic sabre-rattling, although Mr. Berle's main point is almost certainly accurate. Individual enterprises within the United States might well receive an unpleasant jolt from such a turn of events; the American economy as a whole could readjust without too much trouble.

There is much to be said, therefore, for reordering the economic links which currently exist between the United States and Latin America so as to ensure that they work to the benefit of Latin America. It is fairly easy to demonstrate that, on balance, this is not wholly the case at present. The problems involved are no doubt forbidding in both scale and complexity—but they will eventually have to be faced by both parties. A complete severance of all links, as in the Cuban case, leads to unnecessary difficulties—whether they like it or not, the United States and the countries of Latin America *do* share the same hemisphere and *are* natural trading partners. But the nationalization of some foreign-owned concerns, the laying down of enforceable ground rules for foreign private investment, and an insistence that public loans or grants should be used in the way Latin American government and planners want—these are realistic objectives for Latin America. Whether they are achieved by patient discussion and rational acceptance, or by acerbic quarrels and quixotic posturings (on both sides) remains to be seen. History has already provided examples of both procedures.

In the world of today—and even more, perhaps, in the world of the future—independence can never be total for any country, not even the superpowers. Complete autarky, even on the basis of regions or blocs, does not seem a particularly desirable aim on any grounds. In the nineteenth century, the most "independent" Latin American state was probably the Paraguay of Dr. Francia; in the twentieth century, Haiti at various moments of the Duvalier dictatorship occupied a similar position—but it is not often that one hears Haiti exalted as a shining model of social or economic (or any other kind of) progress. In this matter, as in so many others, a balance has to be struck. Canada, to take a non-Latin American example, is "dependent" on the United States to an extent undreamed of in most Latin American countries, yet the Canadian standard of living is as high as that of its powerful neighbor, the Canadian government is able to enforce legislation affecting American companies, and the country pursues a foreign policy

[1] Adolf A. Berle, *Latin America: Diplomacy and Reality* (New York, 1962), pp. 9-10.

which differs in several important respects from the kind of foreign policy traditionally popular in Washington.[1]

A LATIN AMERICAN COMMONWEALTH?

One of the most marked contrasts between Latin America and the United States is to be found in the sphere of political organization. The United States is in fact what its name proclaims: *united*. It is a single, though federal, nation-state. Latin America, by contrast, consists of no less than twenty nation-states, only three of which bear comparison (in terms of population) with the main nation-states of Western Europe. It is legitimate to ask, therefore, whether Latin America has any real chance of promoting her own economic autonomy except on a basis of regional union. "Integration" has become a catchphrase in the last ten years—and in many ways this must be regarded as a healthy sign that the dilemma has been recognized. Politically, as we shall see in Chapter 7, the dream of union has been a powerful and recurrent one since the sundering of the Iberian empires, though never sufficiently powerful to override the rise of strong national sentiment in each of the twenty republics. Since the wars of independence, the social and economic history of the region has been cast in a mold of national division and (sometimes) national rivalry. Given the impulse of foreign trade and the international economy, these divisions and rivalries were accentuated in the course of the nineteenth century, most Latin American countries preferring to trade with Western Europe and later the United States than with their own immediate neighbors. This procedure did little to strengthen the economic autonomy of any single country, and a good deal, perhaps, to weaken the economic autonomy of the region as a whole.

Leaving aside Brazil, Mexico, and Argentina as possible exceptions, the Latin American republics are, quite simply, too small to develop large-scale industry on the basis of their own potential internal market, and their bargaining position, in negotiations with the United States or any other industrial power, is far from satisfactory. The creation of a single Latin American market—or at any rate a series of wider markets based on groups of countries within the region—seems a necessary condition for long-term industrial progress. Moreover, if Latin America as a whole could speak with a united voice in commercial negotiations

[1] This is not ignore the fact that several currents of opinion in Canada are disturbed by the extent of the Dominion's economic links with the United States. The *Toronto Daily Star* published, on March 30, 1970, the findings of a Gallup Poll which showed that fifty percent of the population believed that Canadian dependence on the United States had increased since 1960. In 1961 forty-three percent had believed that dependence was increasing.

with the outside world, somewhat greater attention would be paid to the region's point of view. The 1960s saw the establishment of three Latin American groupings designed to further the cause of economic integration: the Latin American Free Trade Area, the Central American Common Market, and (more recently) the Andean Group. The meeting of the American Presidents in 1967 agreed to aim for a full Latin American Common Market by 1985. Two years later the exclusively Latin American "Consensus of Viña del Mar" (which shall be referred to in Chapter 7) contained what has been realistically described as "the most comprehensive summation ever set forth of Latin America's position on the demands of development in the twentieth century."[1] The Consensus, in fact, was a clear statement of a common regional position vis-à-vis the outside world in general and the United States in particular.

It would be unfair to pronounce more than the most tentative of verdicts on the experience of the three economic groupings which emerged in the 1960s in Latin America, if only because their life has so far been very short. The Central American Common Market set up in 1960 displayed a record of success for most of the 1960s: trade between the member states rose by almost eightfold between 1960 and 1968. The immediate future of the grouping was placed in doubt in mid-1969 with the brief "football war" between El Salvador and Honduras,[2] and at the time of writing the prospects seem at the very least uncertain. The much larger Latin American Free Trade Area (ALALC) established under the Treaty of Montevideo (1960) produced an initial increase of trade between the member countries, but by the mid-1960s it was evident that progress in many directions was slower than had been expected: this was particularly true in the field of tariff negotiations. Fears were expressed in some of the medium-sized republics that ALALC would automatically foster the industrial predominance of the bigger states, particularly Argentina and Brazil.

It was partly in response to these difficulties that special interest was shown, after the mid-point of the 1960s, in regional groupings *within* ALALC—groupings designed to prepare the ground for a more effective measure of integration at a later stage. Two minor examples of this can be mentioned. In the later 1960s the Brazilian government attempted to stimulate the integration of the countries sharing the Amazon Basin by (among other things) declaring the city of Manaus a free port. In April 1969, too, the countries sharing the basin of the

[1] Federico G. Gil, *Latin American–United States Relations* (New York, 1971), p. 272.
[2] Salvadorean troops began advancing into Honduras following a controversial football match between the two countries. The root cause of the conflict, which was speedily ended under OAS pressure, was the somewhat resented presence of three hundred thousand Salvadorean workers in Honduras.

River Plate (Brazil, Argentina, Uruguay, Paraguay, and Bolivia) signed a separate agreement to promote the integration of that particular area. By far the most notable move in this direction, however, was the setting up of the Andean Group—"the union of the middleweights," as it has been called. The Andean Pact, signed in May 1969 by Bolivia, Chile, Colombia, Ecuador, and Peru, provides for a customs union with a common external tariff by the year 1980. The Andean Group has taken significant steps toward creating genuinely supranational organizations to oversee the process of integration. Its Development Corporation, moreover, is financed entirely by the countries concerned. The future development of this particular grouping should be watched with great interest.

The problems to be overcome before regional integration can be reached are very considerable. The existing transport systems do not link the different countries of Latin America in a very efficient way. The different levels of economic (and in particular industrial) progress to be found in the region are a further hindrance. The chief difficulty, however, is probably political in nature: schemes of economic integration can succeed only if there exists a *political will* to make them succeed. It is entirely possible that this political will is now gradually crystallizing in Latin America, and the evident determination of the west coast republics to further the progress of the Andean Group is an encouraging augury.[1] Even if a United States of Latin America is difficult to foresee in the near future, there is no reason why a Latin American Commonwealth of Nations should not soon take its place on the political map of the world.

Before ending this section, I shall make some general comments on two important issues which are sometimes regarded as urgent dilemmas: (1) the shape and form of the *future social order* toward which progress should (ideally) be made, and (2) the much-discussed question of *reform and revolution*.

As I said at the outset, it is not incumbent on a European—or, indeed, a North American, a Russian, an African, or an Eskimo for that matter —to become excessively concerned with the debate on specific "blueprints" for the future of Latin America. Since these will in any case be worked out by Latin Americans themselves, there is little point in becoming concerned. Nevertheless, it is perhaps useful to devote some attention to the problem of the labels which are often attached to blueprints. Terms such as "capitalism," "socialism," "feudalism," "Communism," etc. are never more than fairly vague approximations. We

[1] The Chilean government of Dr. Salvador Allende made it clear, on assuming office, that Chile would remain an enthusiastic partner in the work of the Group.

may agree, certainly, that Western Europe civilization in the nineteenth and twentieth centuries has been "capitalist" in the sense that private enterprise has played an important part in its economies, both national and international. We may, equally, regard it as being fairly convenient to define, say, twelfth-century Europe as "feudal," even though twelfth-century Europeans did not appreciate that they were living under feudalism. "Socialism" and "Communism," however, were terms devised at a period when no social order on earth approximated, even remotely, to either.[1] They were essentially descriptions of a *future* ideal. After the Bolshevik revolution, the Soviet government claimed to be establishing a "socialist" order, though many Western socialists regarded this with a certain amount of skepticism; nevertheless, after 1917 it was no longer possible to claim that some approximation to "socialism" did not exist—and by the end of the 1960s, with the emergence of other "socialist" states in Asia and Africa (not to mention the Russian-style "People's Democracies" of Eastern Europe) there were clearly several different approximations, whose respective advocates often vied with each other in their pretensions to revolutionary purity.

For the most part, rightly or wrongly, "capitalism" and "socialism" seem to be the main contemporary alternatives toward which a political leader can steer. But, in practice, how absolute is the contrast between them? Are they, in fact, the only alternatives? It is perhaps useful to quote an observation of Arnold Toynbee's on this subject:

In real life, every social system that can be observed at first hand or reconstructed from records in a mixed system, lying at some point between undiluted socialism and undiluted free enterprise. The statesman's task is to strike that note in the gamut that tunes in with the particular social circumstances of his time and place; to find the right mixture between free enterprise and socialism for driving his truck of state on the particular gradient on which it happens to be travelling at the moment. What the world needs above all now [1948] is to get the issue of free enterprise versus socialism off its ideological pedestal and to treat it, not as a matter of semi-religious faith and fanaticism, but as a commonsense, practical question of trial and error, of, more or less, circumstance and adapatation.[2]

[1] The term "socialist" to describe a particular type of thinker seems to have been first used, in Latin, in the mid-eighteenth century; "socialism" with more or less its modern connotations came into use in the 1820s in both England and France.

[2] Toynbee, *Civilization on Trial* (London, 1948), p. 148. It is worth remarking that even the Soviet Union, where large-scale capitalism was abolished in the 1920s, still relies for some of its food supply on the primitive capitalism of the collective-farm worker selling private produce in the local urban market.

So far so good. But Toynbee's view, unfortunately, runs counter to common human practice. Political and social issues *are* very often treated in Latin America as matters of semireligious faith, and it could certainly be argued that politicians and peoples need to be sustained by some kind of vision of the future toward which they hope their activities will lead. Some, indeed. would argue that a kind of Sorelian "myth" is needed, particularly when accelerated economic development is on the national agenda. But myths can be highly dangerous as well as highly useful. Here, once again, a balance has to be struck, and it is no easy task to strike one.

It should be reasonably apparent from a reading of the present chapter that the social and economic development of Latin America has been strikingly different in many respects from that of Western Europe or the United States. The region was never "feudal" in the European sense, and has never been "capitalist" in the American sense. What adjectives can, in fact, be used to help classify the Latin American social and economic order? It would be foolish to suppose that all countries fit easily into simple schemes of classification. How, for instance, would one label the social and economic order of the Byzantine empire? Latin America is in a not dissimilar position. Its historical development has defied many of the "rules" laid down by social theorists. There is no reason to suppose, therefore, that the future development of Latin America will resemble that of other parts of the world—indeed, it would be surprising if it did. "Very possibly," writes an American, Adolf Berle, "we shall see social systems emerging in some parts of Latin America . . . completely strange to our own institutions and ways of thinking."[1] A Mexican writer, Professor Abelardo de Villegas, considers it likely that Latin America "will trace a number of paths intermediate between absolute socialism and capitalism."[2] We find a former Peruvian guerrilla leader, Héctor Béjar, urging Latin American left-wingers in 1971 to support the building of a new social order and to "struggle to see that it is neither the dehumanized capitalism of the present day nor the rigid bureaucratic dogmatism . . . which people have tried to palm off on us as the sole model of socialism."[3] The quest for distinctively Latin American forms of social and economic organization is likely to be more penetrating in the future. A Chilean writer may be allowed to have the last word on this subject:

It is indispensable to find a Latin American way to development, something autochthonous, our own, which responds to the character-

[1] Berle, *op. cit.*, p. 23.
[2] N. Calder, ed., *The World in 1984*, II (Penguin Books, 1965), 57.
[3] *Síntesis Latinoamericana*, No. 84, April 14, 1971, p. 18.

istics and ways of life of the region. . . . It is conceivable that some countries should develop on the basis of capitalist or neocapitalist structures, that others should base themselves on Marxist principles of varying tendencies, and that a third group should adapt formulas which come from neither of these sources. . . . Latin America must discover new schemes of economic organization, implant new forms of democracy, develop new attitudes in international relations, imagine new patterns for work in its societies. . . .[1]

It is certainly to be hoped that the Latin America of the future will include variety as well as progress.

It is sometimes affirmed that the "only" solution to Latin American dilemmas is by inducing a revolution (assuming that this is possible) and reconstructing the political and social order from the ground up. The exponents of this view, some of whom we shall meet in Chapter 6, usually assume that "revolution" and "reform" are different things, and they reserve a good deal of opprobrium for the latter term. The distinction is less real than apparent. What we may think of as a "genuine" or "serious" social revolution is, in fact, a series of reforms, drastic or mild depending on the circumstances, and administered rapidly and (often) brutally. The most drastic reforms so far carried out in a very short space of time in Latin America have been those of the revolutionary government in Cuba since 1959. It is certainly fair to ask, in the Cuban case, whether the game has been entirely worth the candle and whether a less uncompromising approach could have effectively promoted economic progress and national independence more firmly. The basic question all revolutionaries must face (though most of them do not) is concerned with the relationship of ends to means, and, in particular, whether the end is not very largely *conditioned* by the means to achieve it. Is violent upheaval[2] the most efficient means of achieving the end of a reconstructed social order? That major revolutions introduce a considerable element of uncertainty and unpredictability into the life of a nation is fairly obvious. They may introduce a great deal else besides. The point was well expressed, at the start of the 1950s, by the British writer Sir Denis Brogan:

It may well be that in any society a time may come when the necessary adjustments can only be made by force. The question then is, will the force produce the adjustments and, if it does, will the profits of

---

[1] Juan Somavía, "Del sistema interamericano al sistema latino-americano," in Carlos Naudón, ed., *América 70* (Santiago, 1970), p. 53.

[2] Considered as an armed conflict the Cuban revolution was tiny, as violent upheavals go, compared with the Mexican.

the adjustments cover the losses that the use of violence will most certainly impose? For we know enough today to know that no revolution ever carries out the programme on which it is sold to the public. It may do more; it may do less; it will certainly do many things its promoters do not promise and do not want. If it is really long-drawn-out and really violent, it will give magnificent opportunities to knaves, fools and monsters.[1]

In many parts of Latin America the dilemmas at the start of the 1970s are (or at any rate give a convincing impression of being) a good deal more acute and serious than they were in the Europe of the early 1950s, but the same principle should certainly be applied.

A comment like this, however, is clearly based on certain historically derived notions about what revolutions are like, and in particular what they have been like in Europe, where they have tended to take on a sanguinary and oppressive form. The American political scientist Charles W. Anderson rightly reminds us that " 'Revolution' in Latin America need not imply catastrophe. The term is part of the political culture of the area, and its implications are most ambiguous."[2] As we have seen, Latin American history is peppered with *revoluciones* of one kind or another; even though most of them have been little more than palace revolutions or mild skirmishes in the main squares of tropical cities, the *concept itself* forms part of the Latin American approach to politics in a way it has never really done in Europe or even —despite 1776—the United States. There is much to be said, therefore, for looking beneath the vivid and stirring rhetoric in which many Latin American governments (not to mention oppositions) have indulged, and trying to establish the real substance of what is going on.

It should be clear from what I have suggested in this section that drastic social reforms may very well be needed if Latin America is to intensify the pace of progress. Some would argue that the social and economic difficulties of the region are so great that the sort of government required to provide solutions would have to be extremely draconian.[3] One thing is quite obvious in the Latin American case: whether revolution is called for or not, there *is* a crying need for *resolution*.

---

[1] Brogan, *The Price of Revolution* (London, 1951), pp. 266–67.

[2] Anderson, *Politics and Economic Change in Latin America* (Princeton, N.J., 1967), p. 380.

[3] It is probably true that the code of laws established by Draco, archon of Athens nearly two thousand six hundred years ago, was a good deal less draconian than many codes of law in the twentieth-century world. I point this out in fairness to the memory of that half-forgotten magistrate, who should certainly not be compared with Hitler, Stalin, Trujillo, or Duvalier.

Are "genuine" or "serious" revolutions to be looked for in the Latin America of the future? "Indeed, all Latin American revolutions now begin to look serious," wrote the historian Crane Brinton in 1964.[1] Many Latin American governments in the 1970s do undoubtedly face the extraordinarily difficult task of steering their ships of state on a course between the Scylla of continued immobility and increasing poverty, and the Charybdis of violent and possibly very destructive upheaval. It *may* be the case that the problems are nowadays so huge, in some countries at least, that eventual shipwreck is unavoidable—in which case it can only be hoped that the survivors will be successful in finding a happier way of life for themselves on whatever desolate island they reach, and in building, in the fullness of time, a new and more seaworthy vessel that will carry them on a straighter course into calmer seas. It may equally be the case that some countries will manage to avoid foundering and will find smoother waters sooner than we are justified in thinking at present; the unexpected can never be entirely ruled out in human affairs. Alternatively, the present situation may drag on for a long period, characterized by occasional explosions of anomic violence, repression, and tragic passivity. Latin America *is*, as President Allende of Chile has said, an active volcano. This does not necessarily mean that an imminent eruption is to be expected. Active volcanoes can lapse into quiescence.

In the past two decades or so, countless well-paid Cassandras have foretold imminent doom for the states of Latin America. As with the original Cassandra, their tales of warning and woe have not been given due attention by those in a position to do something to alter the situation. The original Cassandra was proved right; her modern successors have yet to be proved wrong. Some governments would perhaps do well to remember a point crisply enunciated by Francis Bacon the better part of four centuries ago: "the surest way to prevent seditions (if the times do bear it) is to take away the matter of them." Perhaps the gravest question in contemporary Latin America is whether the times do indeed bear such a course of action, or whether the possibilities of an appropriate *via media* have finally been exhausted.

These particular considerations have taken me right over the threshold of politics. This is perfectly natural and understandable, for all of the questions I have raised in this section are in the last analysis political questions. It is the politicians' job to find the answers.

---

[1] Brinton, *Anatomy of Revolution*, new ed. (New York, 1965), p. 265.

Chapter 6

POLITICAL TRADITIONS

The Imperial Framework

I have marvelled sometimes at Spain, how they clasp and contain so large dominions with so few natural Spaniards.

FRANCIS BACON

For impressionable historians the most remarkable thing about the two Iberian empires in America was their duration. As empires, they remained intact for three centuries, and no other modern empires of comparable size have lasted half as long. If staying-power is a criterion of political success, then Spain and Portugal were outstandingly successful in America. As we have seen in previous chapters, much of the modern fabric of Latin American life—particularly the ethnic and social materials which have built it up—derive from colonial times. In sketching some of the distinctive political traditions of the region, it is therefore valuable to glance briefly at the institutions and practices of the colonial period. How were the empires organized politically? How were they governed? What patterns of political behavior were formed?

The political history of Latin America displays at least one "great divide," the wars of independence. Superficially at least, the Creole governments which emerged after independence rejected the colonial past in its entirety. They imported a brand-new political philosophy and attempted, often without very much success, to implant the institutions and practices of nineteenth-century liberalism. But the past is not defeated easily, and it would not be surprising if a number of colonial practices, habits of mind, and instincts were carried over, perhaps imperceptibly, into the new era. Any discussion of Latin American politics, then, must start in the colonial period.

The Iberian monarchies were authoritarian and absolute—absolute in theory and to a large extent in practice. This absolutism (notably in the case of Spain) was being achieved precisely at the period of the colonization of America. America offered a virgin territory where a

301

highly centralized and highly controlled administrative organization could be put into practice. In America there were no powerful feudal magnates disposed to challenge the authority of the crown; there were no traditional medieval liberties which had to be respected or dismantled; the majority of the population consisted of subjugated Indians, whose "protection" also implied control. It is hardly surprising that, given the aims and priorities of the sixteenth-century Spanish state, the American dominions should have been ascribed a political framework which was tight, bureaucratic, centralized, and hierarchical. In dealing with colonial politics, however, it is important to remember the differences between the Spanish dominions and Portuguese Brazil; the Portuguese monarchy was as absolute as that of its neighbor, but in practice its administrative arrangements as applied to Brazil were never as extensive or as effective. On paper at least, more than a few of the institutions which were to be found in the Spanish American empire were duplicated in Brazil. In real life, the organization of the colony was more shadowy. The effective Portuguese attitude to Brazil lay about halfway between the constant supervision Spain applied to her colonies and the "salutary neglect" which the British allowed to their possessions in North America. In the present section, we shall mostly be concerned with the more elaborate and interesting Spanish-American case.

The government of the Spanish-American empire was rigidly hierarchical and, by the standards of the period, remarkably bureaucratic. (The mountains of paper stored at the Archive of the Indies in Seville to this day testify eloquently enough to the ample activities of the vast imperial bureaucracy.) Enthroned at the apex of the hierarchy sat the monarch himself: the focus of all authority and power, the dispenser of all justice, the wielder of immense patronage. The king, it was universally believed, ruled by divine right. He demanded, and received, unquestioning obedience, ceremonial homage, and fervent loyalty. The majesty of his office was the focus of a cult assiduously fostered in public ceremonies and private observances. In the remotest corners of the empire his portrait was revered and his authority respected. In such a system, much depended on the qualities of the monarch. Under vigorous and expansionist kings such as Charles V (I) or Philip II, or under reformers like Charles III, the whole empire could breathe an atmosphere of confidence or (in Charles III's case) reinvigoration. An indolent or indecisive monarch could, through his indolence or indecision, adversely affect the morale which prevailed throughout the huge administrative machine. But the machine itself survived even the worst monarchs.

A Spanish monarch, however mediocre or decrepit, was obliged to oversee the affairs of his American empire in very considerable detail. Often, indeed, the most minute issues were submitted to his personal judgement. Naturally enough, the king needed both advice and assistance, and from 1524 onward this was provided by the Royal and Supreme Council of the Indies—a body which, together with the king, was the effective government of the American empire. The Council of the Indies was initially a fairly small body, consisting of four or five members; under the later Hapsburgs, it was enlarged to twenty or more. Its functions were similar to those of the other great territorial councils of the Spanish monarchy, the most important of which was the prestigious and powerful Council of Castile.[1] It framed all laws and decrees; it supervised the administration of the colonies; it watched over ecclesiastical affairs; it censored books; it dispensed patronage and took charge of military and naval matters—though both of these latter functions it eventually delegated to specialized committees. In the eighteenth century, during the period of the Bourbon reforms, the Council's work was reassigned to newly established ministries, and the Council itself lost a good deal of its former influence though less, perhaps, of its former prestige; it was finally abolished only in 1834.

Both the monarch and his councillors operated in Spain; no Spanish king ever visited the American continent. The colonial territories themselves were organized as a series of provinces—usually viceroyalties or captaincies-general—whose chief distinguishing mark was that they each possessed a viceroy or governor and a Royal Audiencia. Four viceroyalties were created in Spanish America, two in the sixteenth century, two more in the eighteenth. In addition to these there were one or two independent captaincies-general. Throughout colonial times, however, the main viceroyalties—supreme in wealth and importance—were those of Mexico and Peru, although Peru lost substantial portions of her territory to New Granada and the River Plate in the course of the eighteenth century.

Responsibility for the government and administration of each province was shared by the viceroy (or governor) and the Royal Audiencia. The viceroy (or governor) was the direct local representative of the transatlantic monarch. He was invested with considerable prestige, though his power was to some extent constrained by his local Audiencia, by the right which many of his subordinate officials had to correspond directly with the Council of the Indies, and, not least, by his own

[1] The other territorial councils, toward the end of Philip II's reign, were those of Aragon, Portugal, Italy, and Flanders. A number of specialized councils also played a part in government. The Council of Finance, for instance was given joint responsibility (after 1557) with the Council of the Indies for the financial administration of the empire.

immediate dependence on the will of the king. While in practice a viceroy was able to administer his province without day-to-day interference
(thanks chiefly to geography), all major decisions had to be referred back
to Spain. Viceroys were very often drawn from the ranks of the Spanish
aristocracy, often from the oldest and most reputable families. Their
term of office was supposed to last three years, but in practice was
longer. (Sixty-two viceroys governed in Mexico during the colonial
period, forty-one in Peru.)

The power of the viceroy (or governor) was complemented and to
some extent checked by the *óidores* (judges) of the Royal Audiencia, of
which he was president. In medieval Spain, Audiencias had been purely
judicial bodies; in the American colonies, they took on political and
administrative functions as well, advising the viceroy or governor in the
running of the territory in question. Legally, an Audiencia was the
supreme court of appeal for the colony in criminal cases; civil cases
could sometimes be taken higher, to the Council of the Indies in Spain.
There can be little doubt that in general the colonial Audiencias were
conscientious bodies, which performed their tasks soberly and well.
Viceroys and governors were ephemeral creatures; the Audiencias, by
contrast, were a permanent fixture, and were able to build up a strong
corporate spirit and a valuable knowledge of the province concerned
from one generation of óidores to the next. Ideally, the Audiencia was
expected to work in harmony with the viceroy, but conflicts occasionally
sprang up between them, and although the viceroy's position was, in the
ultimate analysis, the stronger of the two, an Audiencia sometimes
managed to secure the viceroy's deposition or recall. The importance of
the Audiencias is difficult to exaggerate, for the boundaries of their
areas of jurisdiction tended to become the boundaries of the new
Creole republics in the nineteenth century.[1]

Local administration within each of the main American provinces
was organized on the basis of districts of irregular size, each of which
was governed directly by a governor or magistrate responsible to the
viceroy (or governor) and Audiencia. These subordinate officials were
given a number of different titles, the most familiar of which was that
of *corregidor* (magistrate); Indian districts were governed by a *corregidor
de indios* (Indians' magistrate). It was probably at this level of the public
administration that the more scandalous malpractices were most
common. There is abundant evidence of corruption, extortion and

[1] The Audiencias established in Spanish America were: Santo Domingo, Mexico,
New Galicia, Guatemala, Lima, New Granada, Quito, Charcas, Chile, Caracas,
Buenos Aires, and Cuzco. The last was Cuzco, set up in 1787 in the aftermath of the
Túpac Amaru rebellion.

exploitation on the part of provincial corregidores: those who governed Indian districts (especially in Peru) were notorious for such activities. The petty tyranny exercised by the corregidores in the highland areas of Peru was a principal cause of the insurrection of Túpac Amaru. By that time, however, the old system was rapidly being replaced by a new one designed to set higher standards of efficiency and probity. The corregidores and other local governors disappeared. Their place was taken by a new breed of colonial officials, the Intendants. These were more professional, better remunerated, appointed for longer periods, and given authority over wider areas. The new system of Intendancies was introduced in Havana in 1764, in Buenos Aires in 1782, in Mexico and Chile in 1786, and in the remainder of the empire in 1790.

The government of the Spanish-American empire, therefore, was based on a strict chain of command which ran from the king and the Council of the Indies at the highest level, through the viceroy (or governor) in the colonies themselves, down to the corregidores and later the Intendants at the district level. There were also two parallel chains of command which, on American soil at least, were independent of the main administrative structure. The royal treasury maintained its own largely separate organization, and the ecclesiastical hierarchy was similarly subject to its own internal arrangements. Given the considerable power of the Church in colonial times, it is hardly surprising that jurisdictional conflicts sometimes arose between the archbishop or bishop of a given territory and the local viceroy or Audiencia. Such conflicts usually had to be resolved at the highest level, the level of king and Council.

To some extent the division of authority among viceroy, Audiencias, and bishop acted as a check on bad government and the abuse of power. A viceroy who aspired to become a local tyrant could be restrained by his Audiencia or by complaints sent to the Council of the Indies by the local bishop or archbishop. But there were two formal judicial arrangements which supplied a more direct control on the activities of colonial officials: the *residencia* and the *visita*, the first a judicial postmortem on an official's conduct, the second (as its name implied) an inspection while the man concerned was still holding office. Residencias were generally taken very seriously. A special judge set up a tribunal, collected evidence, and finally reached a verdict. If an official were found to be guilty of malfeasance, he could be fined or even imprisoned. Visitas ranged from wholesale inspections of entire provinces by powerful Spaniards to minor investigations of corrupt corregidores. The most important Visitors sometimes virtually assumed the functions of government during their inspection: a good example is the famous visita to New Spain carried out by José de Gálvez between 1765 and 1771; a few years later, another notable Visitor, José Antonio de Areche, took charge of the repression of Túpac Amaru's insurrection in Peru.

As has been stressed on several previous occasions in this book, the highest positions in the colonial administration—viceroys, óidores, bishops, etc.—were in the great majority of cases reserved for European Spaniards. Creoles, for the most part, were able to find (or to buy) employment in only the more humdrum branches of the administration and in subordinate positions. (Many of the corregidores, for instance, were Creoles, and the introduction of the Intendancy system at the end of colonial times damaged their interests fairly markedly, since most of the new Intendants were Europeans.) There was one political institution, however, where Creoles were able to play an important part, and that was the cabildo, or municipal council. The cabildo in Spanish America knew two heroic ages, both of them short: the era of colonization, and the era of independence. The formation of a municipality and municipal council was the most characteristic and symbolic event in the march of sixteenth-century Spanish colonization; the city, as we have seen, became the original nucleus of each colonial settlement, and its council effectively governed the territory in the very early years; similarly at the very end of colonial times, it was the cabildos of Spanish America which took the political initiative and established the autonomous Creole governments.

Within the structure of the imperial administration, the cabildo was a good deal less powerful and influential than the viceroy or Audiencia. Its members, drawn from the *vecinos* of the city—the better-off Creoles and resident European Spaniards—were selected by the governor, the viceroy or (sometimes) the king, though in some cases the cabildo itself had a decisive voice in appointments. From the reign of Philip II onward, councillorships (like many other public offices) were bought and sold, and in many cases municipal office became hereditary, passing from one generation to the next. There was no real element of democracy in these arrangements, even though one or two individual cabildos did manage to secure the right to elect their own members. (The cabildo of Buenos Aires, for example, elected the majority of its councillors and obliged them to serve; this was due to the remoteness and backwardness of the colony, for councillorships were not as ardently sought after there as in the more prosperous parts of the empire.) The chief significance of the cabildo as an institution was that it provided the Creole community with a partial political outlet; Creole landowners may have been barred from high office, but they *could* deliberate together to some extent in the cabildo.

The kind of political life which developed in the Spanish-American empire was effectively confined to the rigid framework of institutions described here. A political career was inseparable from an administrative career, as is also true, for instance, in the modern U.S.S.R. An ambitious Spaniard—or much less frequently an ambitious Creole—was obliged to win the favor and patronage of a viceroy or of the Council of the Indies or of the king himself. Everything depended on a favorable hearing at court; friendships and contacts had to be sought in order for a particular petition or request to be brought to the attention of a councillor or minister; anyone who aspired to high office in the colonies was well advised to discover which particular clique had the ear of the king. Politics, then were essentially *court politics*. There were no independent political *bases* from which would-be politicians could spring to power. No parties could be formed, even in the limited sense in which they were formed in, say, eighteenth-century England. There was, indeed, no such thing as an electorate. Every organization within the empire had to be connected in one way or another with the main administrative structure.

The main administrative structure itself was, as we have seen, somewhat cumbersome and heavily bureaucratic. The central government, by setting up mechanisms which checked the activities of the highest executive officials in the colonies, made sure that no such official could become too powerful. The authoritarian principle which animated the empire had to be preserved; excessive local initiative was to be distrusted. Yet this should not be made to imply that *all* local initiative was prevented. Geography alone saw to it that in practice a viceroy could act vigorously if occasion so demanded. He was well advised, however, to cultivate a sixth sense as to what was likely to be approved and what was not.

Despite the impressive degree of control exerted by the Spanish crown over its colonial officials, and despite the truly monumental legislation that was formally enacted for the American dominions, there is a good deal of evidence to suggest that the colonial population itself —not to mention quite a few of the officials—disregarded the law on many occasions. Laws which a viceroy deemed imprudent to enforce could always be returned to Spain for further consideration by the Council of the Indies: *Obedezco pero no cumplo* ("I obey but do not carry out") became a standard formula in the Spanish empire. It was a revealing expression of the freedom which colonial officials often enjoyed in practical matters, even though it would never have occurred to them to challenge the authoritarian principle which underlay the imperial government. It is by no means impossible that the disregard for laws which characterized Latin America after independence stemmed from this discrepancy between what was ordained and what was actually executed in colonial times.

The authoritarian legacy of the Spanish-American empire—the "viceregal tradition," as it has sometimes been called—was to influence political behavior throughout the nineteenth century and beyond. But it was by no means the only legacy. The tradition of bureaucracy—the remorseless Spanish-American mania for paperwork and proper documentation, which has proved so useful for later generations of historians —survived beyond the fall of the empire. So, too, did a particular approach to public office: the view that public office was in itself an *economic* opportunity. The sale of office in colonial times was widespread; introduced mostly in order to increase the royal revenues, it became a standard practice. It should not in itself be regarded as a sign of corruption—it was by no means exclusive to the Spanish empire, and was no more and no less than a means of staffing the public administration at a minimal cost to the government. But those who bought public jobs were not necessarily satisfied by the prestige and power this gave them; they often expected a return on their investment —and this undoubtedly stimulated the spread of corrupt practices. Although the sale of office was generally abolished by the republican governments of the nineteenth century, something of the old approach survived.

Dissidence and opposition in the Spanish empire could take only two forms: petitioning through the normal legal channels or open rebellion. A great deal of effort and time was spent on campaigning for specific concessions or privileges, usually through the main administrative structure, and very often the interested parties got what they wanted. If all else failed, however, rebellion was the only alternative course left open. The long-standing Latin American tradition of revolt derives at least as much from the colonial period as from the turbulent nineteenth century. Revolts against unpopular or tyrannical governors or viceroys, against excessive taxation, against corrupt or arbitrary magistrates— these occasionally interrupted the otherwise even tenor of colonial life; at least fifty such revolts occurred in colonial times, and this figure takes no account of Indian and Negro rebellions. Straightforward repression was by no means the only response made by the authorities on these occasions. An accommodation with the aggrieved rebels was quite frequently possible; unpopular governors *were* recalled, arbitrary privileges *were* suspended, hated taxes *were* reduced or even abolished. With very few exceptions, the pattern of colonial revolts was identical: rebellion against the monarchy as such was unthinkable, and the target for the rebels' darts of wrath was invariably a particular official or a particular institution. The cry of "Long live the king, and death to bad government," heard so frequently in colonial times, was eloquent proof of the distinction drawn in the Spanish-American mind between the king himself and the unworthy and deficient agents who carried out his wishes. Revolts with the more fundamental purpose of over-throwing the political system as a whole, or of removing a given territory from the Spanish empire, were extremely rare. Even the momentous insurrection of Túpac Amaru was somewhat confused on this point, for although Túpac Amaru himself gave clear signs of his willingness to found a new state in the Peruvian highlands, he never-theless protested his fervent loyalty to King Charles III at the same time.

Only in the final two decades or so of colonial rule, as we saw in Chapter 1, did revolutionary movements actually attempt to undermine the foundations of the political order in Latin America—and without the earth-shaking assistance given to them by Napoleon, they would not have succeeded. Until the 1780s it was difficult, if not impossible, for an intelligent Spanish American or Brazilian to contemplate any alternative political system. Political heterodoxy could only be ex-pressed, for most people, by transferring allegiance from one royal house to another, and for the most part this was inconceivable. The American and French revolutions altered this situation. The enduring principles of colonial obedience and absolute monarchy were now successfully challenged—a point that did not go unnoticed by the more acute Creoles. The alternative political system had presented itself. Despite this, it can hardly be denied that the Spanish crown had struck deep roots of loyalty among the colonial populations. The efforts of the separatists of the 1790s and early 1800s were pitiful, and failed to win widespread approval in the colonies. It was the cataclysm of 1807–8 in the Iberian peninsula itself that forced Latin Americans to launch themselves on to the unexpected (and, for many, unwelcome) course of becoming revolutionaries.

The Impact of Liberalism

Legislators! Duty summons you to resist the shock of two monstrous enemies who fight between themselves and attack you at the same time: tyranny *and* anarchy *form an immense ocean of oppression surrounding a tiny island of freedom battered perpetually by the violence of waves and hurricanes.*

SIMÓN BOLÍVAR (1826)

Toward the close of the eighteenth century, as we have seen, "enlightened" ideas from Europe began to spread through Latin America, finding a congenial home in the minds of a handful of Creole intellectuals and aristocrats. A few of these plotted (not very effectively) in the 1790s to liberate the colonies and set up new republics. After 1810, they moved fully into the political limelight. For these discontented Creoles, there was one unequivocal and shining precedent: the anticolonial revolution of the English thirteen colonies in North America. Colonies, it seems, *could* emancipate themselves, *could* be governed without authoritarianism and without a transatlantic monarchy. The French revolution did not inspire Latin America in quite the same way. Many Creoles seem to have been horrified by the excesses of the Girondin and Jacobin Terror and by the anticlericalism of the most prominent French leaders of the 1790s. But many of the underlying political concepts, not to mention superficial attitudes, of the revolution exercised a deep fascination. The early national anthems of the new states tended to be composed in tones faintly (and sometimes not so faintly) reminiscent of the *Marseillaise*.[1]

The revolutions for independence marked an extremely radical shift in the framework of Latin American politics, and nowhere was this truer than in the sphere of political theory. Hitherto, the doctrine of absolute monarchy underpinned by divine right had prevailed almost unchallenged—and those who, like the Jesuits, showed signs of challenging it, were speedily brought to heel. The political philosophy which underlay the struggle for independence and the attempts at nation-building which followed was *liberalism*, whether cautious and conservative or radical and utopian. The basic outline of this new philosophy was fairly easy to grasp. Governments, it was held by liberals, derived their authority from the consent of the governed. Sovereignty belonged to the people, or, as the French put it, to the nation. This sovereignty could (and in real life had to) be delegated to a government, but this government was accountable to the people in many important respects. Furthermore, a government had to be *seen* to derive its powers from the people; it should, in fact, be elected *by* the people. At the same time, however, governments had a built-in tendency to become overbearing and tyrannical if they were too strong—as Creoles thought the absolute monarchies had been. It was therefore

[1] Much could be written on the considerable impact of Napoleon Bonaparte on nineteenth-century Latin American dictators, many of whom saw themselves as worthy successors to the Corsican adventurer. The creation of a Brazilian *empire* rather than kingdom in 1822 was largely due to the French precedent. An empire was considered more democratic.

necessary to separate and balance the three essential powers which, liberals believed, were inherent in government: the legislative, executive, and judicial powers. (This insistence on the separation of powers was derived, of course, from the United States, which derived it from a mistaken interpretation of the "classical" British constitution.) Government, in short, had to be weakened lest it become a threat to liberty. There were always, too, certain things which a government could not touch. Man was invested with certain natural and inherent rights, conferred on him by the Law of Nature itself and hence extremely sacred. What were these natural rights?[1] There were four which chiefly mattered to the Creole liberals. There was the fundamental right to *liberty*—freedom of behavior provided this did not endanger the rights of others, freedom of expression, and (rather less certainly in the Latin American case) freedom of religious worship. The right of *equality* did not carry any particular implication of social or economic equality; it meant equality before the law, and an insistence that equal punishments should be applied to offenders irrespective of their social background. The right of *security* entailed the establishment of strict guarantees against arbitrary and illegal government action. The fourth right, the right of *property*, needs no explanatory comment. It was, needless to say, greatly emphasized by the new generation of Creole politicians that assumed power after independence. Since many of them were prosperous landowners this was hardly surprising.

The new political philosophy of liberalism was accompanied by several further shifts in the Creole outlook, all of which were historically associated with the rise of liberalism itself. The first of these was a gradual domestication of the idea of *progress*. This had, perhaps, been prefigured to some extent in the writings and actions of those eighteenth-century Spaniards and Creoles who were influenced by the Enlightenment. But the hope of progress now became a regular theme in Creole political oratory and journalism. It was widely believed that what was needed for the new republics to advance speedily along the path of progress was a correct set of liberal institutions, the elimination of as many economic restraints as was possible without ruining government revenues, and a powerful emphasis on education. Once these things were accomplished, the future was certain to be bright. The Creole writers of the time vied with each other in producing lyrical and utopian visions of the future progress of their countries; and the essential

[1] At the time of the Latin American independence movements, of course, some currents of liberalism were abandoning the traditional "natural rights" arguments. Bentham, it will be remembered, dismissed the French Declaration of the Rights of Man (1789) as "mere bawling on paper." But the theory enjoyed a long popularity in nineteenth-century Latin America.

ingredient in all such visions was material prosperity, spreading to as many people as possible.

A second shift in the Creole outlook was in the direction of nationalism. Progress, it was felt, was to be achieved within the framework of the *nation-state*; patriotic feelings, sometimes remarkably intense, abounded in the writings of the independence period.

A third noteworthy change of emphasis after independence was to be found in the political models to which many Creole politicians turned for inspiration. Spain (and to a lesser extent Portugal) were now universally condemned as oppressive and backward nations. By contrast the United States, Great Britain, and France were looked upon as advanced countries whose political institutions deserved imitation. Bolívar, at Angostura in 1819, recommended the members of his Congress to study the British constitution, and described the United States as "unique in the history of the human race." The American prototype was frequently copied when it came to designing suitable constitutions for the new republics. The more fervent Creole liberals found much to admire in the republican tradition of France; the 1848 revolution later drove many of them into transports of delight. Great Britain, too, seemed to present a worthy picture of liberalism in action, and it was certainly no accident that the main political movements of nineteenth-century Latin America often chose to style themselves "conservative" and "liberal."

It is easy—far too easy—to smile at the political pretensions of the early Creole leaders in Latin America, and to accuse them of irresponsible optimism in the way they interpreted the situation in their new republics. Their problems were immense; the colonial legacies were far stronger than they believed; they forgot the important principle that laws had to be enforced as well as enacted. Nevertheless, their belief in the desirability of representative government was sincerely held, and despite the thousand disappointments which they and their successors experienced over the next hundred and fifty years, it became far more deeply rooted than is often assumed. The circumstances of the period, however, obliged Creole liberals to face cruel dilemmas for which their newly imported philosophy left them largely unprepared.

One problem, for instance, was the franchise. In a representative system, there had to be elections, but who could vote? No country at that time, however liberal, enjoyed the benefits of universal suffrage, and it was hardly to be expected that Latin American liberals would attempt an experiment that was regarded even in England as somewhat foolhardy. In populations with a high degree of illiteracy and poverty, a rapid extension of voting rights was deemed unpractical. The new

Creole republics therefore adopted a very limited franchise, often with a stiff property qualification attached. It would probably be unfair to imagine that the attainment of universal suffrage was regarded in the way the Catholic Church regards the Second Coming—as an event set in an immeasurably remote future. Some liberals were confident that it could be reached fairly quickly. Virtually none of them, however, believed that it would come overnight. When elections were held at all in the decades immediately after independence in Latin America, an insignificant proportion of the population actually voted.

A second difficulty concerned the extent to which the Creoles themselves were able to operate a system of representative government. Much stress was placed, in the writings of patriot leaders, on the need for "republican virtue" in the new states. Virtue—what we might nowadays call "experience"—was regarded as an essential attribute in a properly functioning liberal republic. Now experience, as Oscar Wilde once wrote, is the name we give to our mistakes. In terms of making mistakes, the Creoles were singularly fortunate; they had never made any. They had never had the chance. Their ancestors had never been members of an elected colonial assembly, had never debated the rights and wrongs of a given tax or law, had never learned how to organize themselves in political parties or factions. Freedom, for them, had come very suddenly; it had certainly not broadened down from precedent to precedent. Their political inheritance was authoritarian in character, as we have seen. They were instinctively used to an ultimate authority to which they could appeal and which fixed the permanent and stable administrative structure through which they were obliged to work. Both the ultimate authority and the administrative structure were now removed. There now existed what can best be described as a political vacuum, which liberal theory alone was not able to fill.

The pattern of political *behavior* which developed after independence, therefore, did not by any means correspond to the imported liberal political philosophy embraced so ardently by so many Creole leaders. The shadow of the caudillo fell quickly across the Latin American scene; constitutions and legislatures were swept aside, restored, swept aside again; the armies of the Creole republics flexed their new-found muscles; generals "pronounced" and presidents went into exile; many of the new republics, in short, suffered from intermittent violence and prolonged dictatorship. It is one of the major ironies of Latin American history that the wars of independence, which were fought to rid the colonies of "arbitrary" and "despotic" government, had as their direct outcome the creation of governments which were often far more arbitrary and despotic than the imperial monarchy had ever

313

been—and infinitely more grotesque. Which colonial viceroy could have compared to Rosas, Santa Anna, or García Moreno? The difficulties of establishing stable liberal institutions were apparent to the more sensitive Creole spirits very early, within a year or two of the outbreak of the campaigns for independence. Simón Bolívar in his Cartagena Manifesto of 1812, asserted baldly that "Our fellow citizens are not capable of widely exercising their rights by themselves; they lack the political virtues which characterize the true republican."[1] Nearly twenty years later, at the end of his life, the Liberator came to a still more disillusioned conclusion: "America is ungovernable."

What was the solution to this problem? It is useful to refer briefly to Bolívar's own ideas on the subject. Bolívar advocated very strong executive government and, in parallel with this, a conscious, state-directed effort to foster republican virtue. The idea of a strong executive power occupied a key place in Bolívar's political thinking. As a temporary measure, at least, he believed that the executive should be freed from the restraining power of the legislature; otherwise it could hardly cope with the turbulent conditions of the period. He therefore urged the creation of extremely powerful presidencies; in his Bolivian constitution of 1826, for instance, he recommended presidencies-for-life, the holders being allowed to name their own successors.

But a strong executive, in Bolívar's view, was only one side of the coin. The other was the inculcation of political virtue. Bolívar believed that special institutions should be entrusted with this particular task. He found admirable precedents in the world of classical antiquity. In his famous Angostura speech of 1819, he elaborated on this notion:

> From Athens let us take her Areopagus and her guardians of customs and the Laws; from Rome let us take her censors and her domestic tribunals; . . . from Sparta let us take her austere institutions, and . . . let us give to our Republic a Fourth power with dominion over the infancy and the hearts of men, over public spirit, over good customs, and over Republican morality. Let us so constitute this Areopagus that it watches over the education of children . . . , that it purifies what is corrupt in the Republic.[2]

The interesting idea of a Fourth power in the state received its most precise constitutional application in the Bolivian constitution of 1826, which many consider to have been Bolívar's political masterpiece. Here the Liberator invented a tricameral legislature, whose third

---

[1] V. Lecuna, ed., *Proclamas y discursos del Libertador* (Caracas, 1939), pp. 15–16.
[2] *Ibid.*, p. 228.

chamber, the Chamber of Censors, was to possess the exact functions of moral supervision already mentioned. But Bolivia was unpromising territory for such an experiment, and the constitution soon broke down.[1]

Leaving aside Bolívar, a number of other Creole liberators and politicians saw the answer to the problem of authority in the establishment of monarchies. At the time of Latin American independence, monarchy (whether absolute or constitutional) was still the standard form of government in most parts of the world, not least the Euro-American world. Even in revolutionary France, Napoleon found it necessary to acquire an imperial crown. Monarchism had several powerful advocates in Spanish America; of these San Martín was the greatest. Some of the early Argentine congresses were quite prepared to import a Bourbon prince to sit on the throne of the River Plate, while San Martín himself conceived of a Pacific Coast empire based on Lima with a European prince at its head.

The failure of these early schemes to establish Latin American monarchies was total. There were several good reasons for this. The intellectual opposition to monarchy was too strong; republicanism seemed the automatic accompaniment to independence and the liberal political philosophy, and here the American precedent was probably a powerful one. Furthermore, no suitably blue-blooded European prince could be found to assume the responsibility of governing the River Plate, Peru, or Colombia. Even if such a prince could have been persuaded—an unlikely possibility—he might not have long tolerated the contentious Creole politicians who would have surrounded him. He might well have found the court facilities in, say, Buenos Aires somewhat rudimentary. The alternative was for a Creole liberator to set himself up as a crowned head, but the experience of Agustín de Iturbide in Mexico was a sobering one and it may well have deterred Bolívar, for instance, from attempting the experiment; ultimately, no Creole, however eminent, could supply himself with the majestic aura of legitimacy which the Spanish monarchy had previously possessed.

History must occasionally concern itself with lost opportunities, and it is interesting to speculate whether the history of nineteenth-century Latin America would have been much altered by the adoption of constitutional monarchy as a form of government. It is entirely possible that in some instances at least the state would have become

[1] A Chilean writer of the independence period, Juan Egaña, held similar views to Bolívar on the need for a Fourth or Moral power in the state and incorporated the idea into the short-lived Chilean constitution of 1823.

much less of a focus for corruption and easy moneymaking than in practice it did. The example of the empire of Brazil—where the problem of "legitimacy" was solved by the continued presence of the House of Braganza—is perhaps an instructive one. Not for nothing did the President of Venezuela characterize the fall of the empire in 1889 as the disappearance of the "only true republic" in Latin America.

Strong and effective monarchies in, say, four or five groupings of the former colonies might possibly have averted some of the chronic political difficulties which the nineteenth-century Creole republics experienced. But this was not to be. With the solitary exception of Brazil, the new states turned themselves into republics. This in itself was a striking proof of the extent to which the liberal philosophy had become rooted in Latin American minds. It remains now for us to outline some of the particular ways in which liberal and constitutional governments actually operated in Latin America during the remainder of the nineteenth century—bearing in mind that the twentieth century, too, has tended to perpetuate these particular traditions.

A very important point to be borne in mind is that the tradition of constitutional government was never—save for one or two exceptional instances—uninterrupted or continuous. The rival and parallel tradition of violence and dictatorship, which will be considered in the section that follows, asserted itself only too regularly, wrecking the orderly continuity of republican institutions time and time again. Nevertheless, we should certainly take note of those cases where a continuous constitutional tradition *was* implanted. As we have seen, more than a few Latin American countries succeeded in maintaining regular, legal government over substantial periods of time: Argentina between 1862 and 1930, Mexico after the revolution, Colombia for much of the twentieth century, Venezuela after 1958—all these are good cases in point. But only three Latin American republics managed to win themselves a more or less permanent reputation for continuous respect for constitutional legality. These were Chile, Uruguay, and Costa Rica, countries which are nearly always bracketed together in general discussions of Latin American politics.

Of the three, the case of Chile is by far the most striking. After an initial period of mild confusion in the 1820s, the republic acquired a considerable measure of institutional stability in the 1830s, and the regular march of presidential terms of office and congressional elections continued, uninterrupted, until the civil war of 1891. Following that tragic episode, it resumed immediately, only to be interrupted for a second time between 1924 and 1932. Since 1932, however, no further upheavals have disturbed the steady operations of the constitution. The

Chilean record of political stability, therefore, is one which relatively few European nations can rival—let alone most of Chile's Latin American friends and neighbors. How is this stability to be explained? Chile was fortunate in being geographically compact; her land-owning aristocracy was extremely cohesive; no really disastrous ethnic or regional divisions disfigured the scene; and she fell into the hands of a very remarkable Creole statesman, Diego Portales, whose personal priorities were somewhat different from those of the more characteristic Latin American caudillos of the age.

The essence of Portales' thinking on politics is to be found in a letter he wrote in 1822, nearly ten years before he himself assumed power in Chile.

> *Democracy* . . . is an absurdity in countries like those of America, which are full of vices, and whose citizens fully lack the virtue necessary for a true *Republic*. Nor is *Monarchy* the American ideal: if we come out of one terrible monarchy merely to go into another, what do we gain? The *Republic* is the system we must adopt; but do you know how I conceive it for these countries?—a strong, centralizing Government, whose members are genuine examples of virtue and patriotism, and thus set the citizens on the straight path of order and the virtues. When they have attained a degree of morality, then we can have the completely liberal sort of Government, free and full of ideals, in which all the citizens can take part.[1]

Whether the political system that emerged in Chile in the 1830s answered to Portales' recommendations is not a question that need detain us here; but it certainly ushered in the remarkable political stability for which Chile was noted thereafter.

How did the Chileans make it work? In the first place, the president was given extremely wide powers. Congress was by no means rendered impotent, but the executive (until 1891 at least) was effectively pre-dominant. The central government made skilful use of the electoral machinery to secure compliant legislatures; not to put too fine a point on it, all Chilean elections between 1830 and 1891 were "fixed." The two attempts by an opposition to overthrow the government by force (in 1851 and 1859) were rigorously suppressed; with the general relaxation that occurred in the 1860s and 1870s, dissident politicians

---

[1] E. de la Cruz and G. Eeliu Cruz, eds., *Epistolario de don Diego Portales*, 3 vols. (Santiago, 1937), I, 177. The reference to monarchy is probably explained by the fact that Portales wrote this letter in Lima, where San Martín's monarchist schemes were being widely discussed at the time.

found themselves a place in the sun *within* the political system; laws were enforced to an extent which was uncommon in nineteenth-century Latin America. Most significantly of all, perhaps, successive Chilean governments managed to foster a deep sense of pride in the nation's achievements—a sense which was greatly enhanced by the Chilean victories in the wars of 1836–39 and 1879–83. The Chilean population gradually acquired what amounted to a feeling of superiority—for Chile could justifiably be contrasted with the unruly "tropical" republics in other parts of Latin America. It can scarcely be denied, then, that the nineteenth-century experience conditioned the marked respect for constitutional forms which has remained a characteristic of Chilean life for most of the twentieth century.

The cases of Uruguay and Costa Rica show a somewhat different pattern of development. Neither republic acquired its constitutional tradition anything like as early as Chile; for most of the nineteenth century Uruguay was plagued with civil strife and the rule of successive caudillos, while Costa Rica settled into constitutional routines only toward the end of the century—and both countries have experienced brief dictatorial interruptions once or twice in the twentieth century, but these have been as markedly out of character as was the short period of disorder and dictatorship in Chile between 1924 and 1932. Uruguay's relative immunity to the diseases of arbitrariness and military intervention owes much to the considerable educational effort made toward the end of the nineteenth century and to the remarkable welfare legislation put in hand by José Batlle y Ordóñez and his successors. Costa Rica's ethnic homogeneity and the relatively equitable distribution of land in that temperate and pleasant republic have been similarly favorable.

Chile, Uruguay, Costa Rica—all three countries, interesting as they most certainly are in their own right, must be considered as exceptions. Over the remainder of Latin America, a more familiar pattern of political life developed, a pattern whose main characteristic was (and is) the alternation of civilian and constitutional forms of government with dictatorial and arbitrary forms, often military in nature. This alternation of two distinctive traditions persisted into the twentieth century, and can still be observed at the present day. It is, however, by no means the whole story, for newer forms of government have emerged in the course of the past few decades, and whether these can be regarded as developments from previous traditions or as original creations is a question to which we shall return later in this chapter. For the moment, some concluding generalizations are evidently needed in assessing the liberal and constitutional interludes in Latin American history.

These interludes have, of course, been very numerous. Indeed, judged by the number of constituent assemblies they have summoned, the Latin American republics might justifiably be supposed to have developed an almost excessive affection for constitutional forms. The republic of Ecuador, for instance, drafted in 1967 her sixteenth constitution since 1830; many other republics could rival the Ecuadorian record. Latin American constitutions, with one or two honorable exceptions—the 1833 document in Chile or the 1853 one in Argentina, for instance—have never been noted for their longevity. But this is slightly misleading. Very often, what is presented as a "new" constitution is no more than an old one embellished with a few important amendments. Nevertheless in those countries where the alternation of civil and dictatorial rule has been most marked, the drafting of a new constitution has come to be regarded as the indispensable sign of a return to what the optimists conceive of as "normality."

It is plainly impossible to generalize about the specific constitutional arrangements which have tended to prevail in Latin America, for these have often varied considerably from one country to another. One or two definite trends can certainly be observed. Although the Latin American republics failed, for the most part, to adopt Bolívar's ideas on government, most of them *did* eventually accord the executive considerable authority in their various constitutions. The nineteenth-century Chilean emphasis on strong presidential government was very far from unique. Few Latin American presidents have ever been as effectively checked by their legislatures as the president of the United States. Most presidents, moreover, have been endowed with handsome emergency or "special" powers, within the constitution. Presidential terms of office have (on paper at least) tended to be long rather than short: six years is a fairly common period, though a number of countries (Bolivia, Colombia, and Costa Rica, for instance) have copied American practice in this respect. In very nearly all the twenty republics, however, a president has been denied the right of immediate re-election. Indeed, Mexico, which began its revolution with the famous slogan of "No re-election!" bars a president from re-election at any stage after his term has ended.

The typical Latin American presidency, then, has been a powerful office; the typical Latin American legislature, by contrast, has rarely succeeded in winning predominance within the political system. This is not to say that legislatures have never been able to harass the executive or to delay the enactment of laws; but on the whole they have never tended to occupy the central position in political life that the Congress of the United States, for instance, very clearly occupies, to the frequent chagrin of American presidents. In their formal organization, most Latin American legislatures have been bicameral, i.e., divided into a

Senate and a Chamber of Deputies; the unicameral form has been adopted only in small countries, notably those of Central America.[1]

Despite the long federalist–centralist struggles of the nineteenth century, no Latin American government has devolved very much authority on the provinces. Even in countries with nominally federalist constitutions (e.g., Argentina or Mexico), the central government usually possesses very considerable powers of "intervention" in provincial affairs. Nothing approaching the federal systems of Switzerland or the United States has ever appeared in Latin America.

As in other parts of the world, representative government in Latin America has increasingly rested on a widening franchise and on the growth of a wide range of political parties. As mentioned earlier, the initial problem of the franchise was solved in Latin America by a stringent limitation of voting rights, and an extensive use of property qualifications. Such devices were not uncommon in other parts of the world at that period, and in general it can be said that the Latin American republics moved toward universal suffrage at a reasonably respectable pace; the widening of electoral rights became part and parcel of the political programs of Liberal and Radical parties in several countries. Virtually all the twenty republics had adopted something approaching universal suffrage by the 1960s, together with secret voting, votes for women, and various systems of proportional representation. One important qualification has to be made to this statement: in many republics, literacy is still a necessary condition for voting, and in countries where illiteracy rates are still high the size of the electorate is thus considerably reduced.

It is no easy task to determine how far electoral practices in the Latin American countries are corrupt or fraudulent. The issue is complicated by the propensity of many politicians to allege fraud or corruption when they themselves are defeated. Whatever the truth about the normal run of elections in Latin America—and in some countries they are as clean, open, and honest as anywhere else in the world—it can hardly be doubted that pressures of a dubiously legal kind have often been exerted on individual voters or on groups of voters, and that a limpid expression of the will of the people has thus been thwarted on many occasions. Some of the more traditional devices for preventing the people's voice from making itself heard have undoubtedly been in decline during the twentieth century, though it would be foolish to suppose that they do not still survive, particularly in rural areas and in

[1] The program on which Dr. Salvador Allende campaigned in Chile in 1970 contained a plan for a unicameral legislature, though this was not reckoned to be high on the new president's list of priorities, and was not introduced.

the less-developed republics. Until fairly recent times, it was common in many parts of Latin America for a landowner to "mobilize" his own tenants and employees in the cause of his local Liberal or Conservative Party, and the electoral strength of these two parties (still maintained in some countries) depended heavily on such practices. A modern parallel may perhaps be found in the use which political agents in the cities sometimes make of newly arrived migrants from the countryside, providing them with various appropriate services in exchange for the promise of their vote.

In most Latin American republics (not to mention Spain and Portugal) the working of representative government has tended to become enmeshed with a network of political "bosses" at the local level. (This was certainly true for much of the nineteenth century and it has remained true for much of the twentieth although the growing urbanization of Latin America has done much to alter political patterns in this particular respect.) The political boss was known in many parts of Spanish America as the *cacique*, in Brazil as the *coronel*.[1] Caciques and coronels may have been landowners or local businessmen, or sometimes even government officials. Their basic qualification was that they possessed an intimate knowledge of their own particular locality; in many cases this was not particularly difficult since they often owned most of their own locality anyway. Their main task was to "organize" the area politically—making sure that votes went a certain way at election time, and generally ensuring local support for a particular government or party. This network of caciques or coronels was an indispensable political aid to many governments, but it also hampered any government which wished to override local vested interests in pursuit of reform. The bosses had to be "squared" constantly; they had to be handed economic concessions of various sorts, public jobs for their families and compadres, the odd seat in congress, and so on. The golden age of the political boss may well be over in Latin America, but the tradition still survives.

Since the independence period, the twenty republics have seen a steady growth of political activity as measured in the organization of *political parties*. It may be helpful to outline one or two general characteristics of party activity at this point. The earliest political movements in the region, were largely divided along liberal/conservative or federalist/centralist lines. This remained true for much of the remainder of the nineteenth century. With the expansion of the franchise and the emergence of sizable middle classes and urban working classes, parties

---

[1] *Cacique* means Indian chieftain; *coronel*, colonel. Usually, however, political bosses were neither.

very rapidly increased both in number and in outlook. From the 1920s onward, a wide variety of political parties, ranging right across the ideological spectrum, has played a decisive part in Latin American politics (see pp. 340–71).

The parties with which I am chiefly concerned here are those parties which are obliged to *compete for votes*. Parties which have come into existence as organs of government in "one-party states" (whether "open" as in the Mexican case or "closed" as in Cuba) clearly belong to a rather different category, which we shall consider later in this chapter. Competitive parties in Latin America tend to exhibit a number of common features. They seem, for instance, to be unusually prone to fissiparous tendencies; parties generate other parties, or divide in two; their life is often very short. Even in a more or less "stable" party system like that of Chile, the number of different parties can multiply very rapidly on occasion; some *thirty-six* (twenty-four of them newly registered) contested the Chilean congressional elections of 1953, though many of these, having failed to elect their candidates to congress, promptly disappeared.[1] Whatever their experience with blades of grass may have been, Latin Americans have long since discovered the secret of making two political parties grow where only one grew before. Despite these observations, it must also be recognized that many of the party splits and divisions in Latin American political life occur on the *fringes* of parties or movements, and that a fair number of political parties have enjoyed remarkably long lives. The once glorious Chilean Radical Party, for instance, has endured for more than a century.[2]

A second notable characteristic of party activity in Latin America is its frequent *personalism.* In the past, parties have very often been formed to supply the necessary electoral backing for an ambitious political leader, and in such cases the retirement or death of the leader concerned usually brings the life of the party to an end. When a party falls under the dominance of a powerful figure, or is actually created by him, it is sometimes difficult to sort out whether the party is "personalist" in this sense or whether it exists as an independent force in its own right. Cases of apparently personalist parties surviving the downfall or death of their creators can certainly be found in Latin America. The two parties hastily assembled by Getúlio Vargas at the close of his dictatorship in Brazil played a major part in national politics until the coup d'état of 1964. A still more notable example is

[1] Admittedly, this was somewhat exceptional. Chilean politics in the past twenty or thirty years has essentially been the interplay of five or six major parties.

[2] Nonradical Chileans were heard to remark, at the time of the party's centenary, that this disproved the old proverb *No hay mal que dure cien años* ("There's no ill that lasts a hundred years").

the fate of the *Peronista* movement in Argentina, which retained a permanent hold on roughly a third of the electorate during the decade after Perón's downfall, and which may be expected to enact an important role in Argentine national life in the future.

Given the multiplicity of political parties in Latin America, patterns of coalition politics are more common than the regular alternation of a government and opposition in office. One or two countries, however, have lived for many years in what might be called a two-party system. In Uruguay, for instance, the age-old rivalry of Blancos (conservatives) and Colorados (liberals) has continued into modern times, although both of the parties are divided into smaller factions, which enjoy legal status and run separate candidates at election time. Costa Rica has tended to develop a pattern of two-party rivalry in recent years, the main contenders being the conservative Unificacion Nacional party and the center-left Liberacion Nacional party headed by José Figueres. Perhaps the most remarkable example of a two-party system, however, is Colombia, although both the Liberal and Conservative parties have shown, over the past decade, the kind of internal divisions which are to be found in the two Uruguayan parties.

The German writer Max Weber distinguished two ideal types of political party: (1) the *Amtspatronagepartei,* whose raison d'être is the winning of power in order to exercise patronage, and (2) the *Weltanschauungspartei,* which seeks to govern in accordance with specific policies based on abstract ideas. It is by no means easy to apply this distinction to Latin American political parties. Politics in the region has always been markedly "ideological" on the one hand, and intimately related, on the other, to the satisfaction of the richer classes' empleomanía. Parties which have proved remarkably adept at providing their supporters with public jobs have nevertheless regarded themselves as furthering the noble cause of some ideological crusade. Similarly, parties or movements which start by proclaiming their passionate adherence to some great reforming principle often end up by sharing out the spoils of office as intelligently as their predecessors. These considerations can be applied as much to movements of the left as to movements of the center or right.

Soon after the start of the present century, a distinguished English visitor to South America set down his impressions of its political life in some notable paragraphs. He concluded that, of the countries through which he had traveled, both Chile and Argentina were "*bona fide* republics." In Chile, he observed, "Government . . . is carried on with the same spirit and by the same methods as it was in England during the eighteenth century." Argentina, too, could be said to be

323

"a constitutional republic, whose defects, whatever they may be are the defects of a republic, not of a despotism disguised under republican forms." The promising examples of Chile and Argentina, he thought, showed

> that with favouring conditions the true constitutional spirit can be more and more infused into constitutional forms and the old habits of violence eradicated. The case of Argentina in particular suggests the process by which we may expect that other Latin-American states will, by degrees, advance towards a more settled and genuinely legal government.[1]

The bland optimism of 1912 was a long way from being justified by the events of the years that followed. Yet I cannot bring myself to believe that it was altogether foolish. It can hardly be denied that, on almost any analysis, the impact of liberalism in Latin America was a profound one. Over the decades, the franchise *did* widen, the political game *was* opened to larger sections of the population, the organization of political parties *did* increase. That Latin American republics have time and time again *returned* to constitutional forms, that even the most sanguinary dictators should often have taken the trouble to pay lip service to the notion of representative government—these are indications that the initial liberal impulse cannot easily be eradicated. A tradition alien to Latin America a hundred and fifty years ago has survived, and in some soils it has taken root. It is certainly no longer alien.

But neither is it the only tradition.

Dictators and Dictatorships

I believe that programmes . . . should not be announced, but simply carried out.

COL. JUAN DOMINGO PERÓN (1944)

Give me a balcony, and I will win the country!

ATTRIBUTED TO DR. JOSÉ MARIA VELASCO IBARRA,
PRESIDENT OF ECUADOR 1934–35, 1944–47,
1952–56, 1960–61, 1968–72

Two incidents from the very earliest phase of independence gave eloquent proof that the liberal and constitutionalist tradition in Latin

[1] James Bryce, *South America: Observations and Impressions* (London, 1912), pp. 543–46.

America was to be flanked (and often outflanked) by an alternative and equally tenacious tradition. It is said that Dr. Francia, then a member of the Paraguayan national junta set up in 1811, once strode into a meeting where the Paraguayan attitude to King Ferdinand VII was being discussed, carrying a pair of loaded pistols. Putting them on the table, he declared: "I have two arguments against the sovereignty of King Ferdinand VII, and here are both of them!" At about the same period a Chilean army officer, José Miguel Carrera, was conversing with a member of one of the most influential Chilean families, who was happily boasting that his various relatives now occupied all the senior positions in the patriot government—one was president of the congress, another president of the junta, a third president of the new supreme court, and so on. This did not amuse Carrera. "But who," he asked bluntly, "is the president of the bayonets?" Within a few weeks of that conversation, Carrera staged the first of the very few coups d'état in Chilean history, thus proving that *he* was.

Over the next century and a half, Latin Americans learned to live with thousands of arguments like Dr. Francia's; presidents of the bayonets—and tanks and aircraft—have abounded. Many explanations have been given for this Latin American propensity for violence and dictatorship, and it is certainly possible to point to a series of factors which must be regarded as essential elements in any comprehensive elucidation of the problem. Much has been made, for instance, of Creole "inexperience" in managing constitutional forms of government. A great deal, too, could be said of the various legacies of the colonial period: first, the authoritarian tradition, which accustomed men to a fixed, immutable chain of command rising hierarchically to a single focus; second, an approach to public office which viewed the state as the vital instrument of economic advancement and hence as something which it was desirable to capture. Equally, there were specific circumstances arising out of the struggle for independence itself which made settled government next to impossible: the breakdown of royal authority in many areas gave ample opportunity to local "strong men" to assume power over provincial and even national populations; furthermore, the wars of independence effectively "militarized" extensive portions of Spanish America by calling into existence small but powerful armies which could be used, when peace returned, for political rather than military purposes.

Conditions such as these certainly helped to foster a political atmosphere which violence and dictatorship would find congenial. Thus the cabinet maneuver, the election campaign, the formation of party coalitions, and so on were quickly supplemented, as fundamental techniques of political action in Latin America, by the violent revolt, the coup d'état, the palace revolution, the armed intervention. The outcome was a long and often melancholy chronicle of dictators and dictatorships. The features of this chronicle which most stand out are four in number: (1) personalism, (2) a frequent resort to violence, (3) militarism, sometimes referred to as praetorianism, and (4) dictatorial government. We shall consider each of these aspects in turn, and conclude by noting the ways in which the pattern as a whole has been changing—or may have been changing—in the middle decades of the twentieth century.

PERSONALISM

As a phenomenon personalism enters into the constitutional as well as the dictatorial tradition of Latin American politics; and a caudillo can as easily attain power through an election as through an armed revolt. Taken by and large, however, the link between personalism, and more specifically the caudillo tradition, and dictatorship has been a strong one. The appeal of the caudillo has been extraordinarily widespread in Latin America, and it is tempting to explain so persistent a phenomenon in terms of some deep-seated psychological tendency, of a pattern of allegiances and values which positively *welcomes* paternal and even patriarchal authority. But other factors must certainly be considered: above all, perhaps, the allure of the state as an institution from which to extract *economic* advantage. As a general rule, caudillos flourish not because they themselves are strong, but because the institutional and "cultural" barriers to their rise are in some sense inadequate.

What is a caudillo? The eminent Spanish writer Salvador de Madariaga has divided Latin American politicians into two basic types: "doctors" (who are essentially civilian politicians deeply fascinated by abstract ideas) and "generals." Most (though not all) caudillos have been drawn from the ranks of "generals"—which in practice may be said to include colonels, junior officers, or even mere civilians, some of who have misleadingly borne the title of "doctor."

> The general is not interested in principles. . . . He is, in the American phrase, a go-getter. His aim is power, and he feels no qualms as to the ways and means to attain it, or indeed to retain it. He may be an officer with a certain level of technical military training and education, but, not infrequently, will be a self-made general, having reached the top of the military ladder by unorthodox ways, and a self-taught man, more self than taught. His knowledge of the roots of the country, the village square, pond, drink shop and police station, will be

326

concrete and extensive. He will often be of mixed blood in countries rich in Indian stock. He will be quite astute, ruthless, and, if need be, cruel.[1]

It is quite clear that this admirable description fits the great majority of nineteenth- and even twentieth-century caudillos. Many of the most notable representatives of the breed may have had relatively modest origins; but this in itself has never been a necessary qualification. General Páez in Venezuela began his rise to power, in the wars of independence, as an illiterate cowboy; General Rosas in Buenos Aires, despite his very considerable skill on horseback and with the gaucho lasso, was nonetheless the scion of one of the great ranching families of the provinces, and his relatives did extremely well out of his regime. Both were, however, self-made and self-taught in Madariaga's sense. It was as easy for Fulgencio Batista, the son of a poor sugar worker, to learn the rules of the game as it was for Dr. Fidel Castro, whose father was a prosperous planter. In some ways it was easier—for the university-trained Latin American generally gains smoother access to ordinary, "civilian" political circles than a roughneck from the countryside.

The essential element in any caudillo's career is the emotional link which he is able to form with his followers, whether these be a group of army officers or the national population as a whole. Such a link can be assiduously fostered, as it was by Perón in 1943–45, when he carefully courted the Argentine trade unions. It can arise almost spontaneously, as it did when Dr. Fidel Castro made his triumphal journey from Santiago to Havana in January 1959. It is difficult to say whether a caudillo's appeal to the public inevitably depends on the possession of certain specific qualities. Some caudillos have been admired for their personal austerity, others for just the opposite; but physical courage and (where appropriate) military prowess are essential ingredients in a caudillo's makeup, as are a readiness to speak plainly (if not brusquely) and to demonstrate a virile approach to the problems of domestic government and foreign relations. Most Latin Americans respond positively to the discovery that their own particular caudillo "has got trousers," to use a common Spanish-American expression.

Apologists for individual caudillos or, indeed, for the caudillo tradition as a whole have never been lacking in Latin America. One of the most famous of these was the Venezuelan, Laureano Valenilla Lanz. His book *Cesarismo democrático* ("Democratic Caesarism") was published (by the Venezuelan government) in 1929. It contained an

[1] S. de Madariaga, *Latin America between the Eagle and the Bear* (London, 1962), p. 10.

327

eloquent and intelligent defense of the caudillo tradition in Venezuela, a tradition currently being exemplified in the regime of Juan Vicente Gómez. The book considered dictatorship as the only appropriate form of government for the conditions which prevailed in Latin America. Constitutions, elections, congresses, liberal ideas—these, Valenilla Lanz argued, were essentially alien to Latin American ways of feeling and doing things. What the region needed was "democratic Caesars," powerful individuals who themselves personified the collective will of the community.[1]

Is the caudillo on the decline in contemporary Latin America? There are many Latin Americans who would like to think so, but there is little evidence to suggest that their optimism is justified. Some patterns of political life in the region have remained remarkably tenacious from the time of the Spanish conquest onward: even in the days of empire, men who looked suspiciously like more recent caudillos could occasionally be found at the head of movements of revolt. When Gonzalo Pizarro returned to Lima after the battle of Añaquitos in 1546, he was acclaimed as "Liberator and Protector" by the citizenry, thus curiously anticipating both Bolívar and San Martín, not to mention the dozens of caudillos later hailed as liberators, restorers, pacifiers, benefactors, or maximum leaders. Not until the nineteenth century, of course, could a caudillo emerge as ruler of the state; and his golden age was, beyond all question, the several decades which followed the struggle for independence.

During the twentieth century, by and large, the more traditional kind of caudillo has been confined to the smaller republics; Trujillo and Somoza may perhaps be regarded as the outstanding modern representative of the breed. At the start of the 1970s, only General Alfredo Stroessner, the dictator of Paraguay since 1954, seems cast in the former mold.[2] But this is not to suggest that the caudillo is dead, merely that he has assumed new coloring. The political and social environment in which Colonel Perón climbed to power was certainly a great deal more sophisticated and complex than the one in which Juan Manuel Rosas, for instance, exercised his baleful authority. But there are sufficient similarities between the two regimes to enable the observer to see them as falling within the boundaries of a common tradition.

Of all the caudillos who have arisen in more recent times in Latin America, Dr. Fidel Castro is surely the most surprising and extraordinary. He does not appear to have been even partially motivated by

---

[1] Valenilla Lanz' book was widely acclaimed in Italy, where the author was looked upon as a sort of honorary Fascist.

[2] For General Stroessner's career, see Richard Bourne, *Political Leaders of Latin America* (Penguin Books, 1969), pp. 98–130.

economic ambition; it is most unlikely that he has salted away as much as a single peso in a Swiss bank account. Although doubtless much influenced by a desire for personal glory, he nonetheless possesses ethical predispositions which, whatever may be thought of their realism, place him in a rare category among Latin American dictators. He answers to all the requirements of a classically "charismatic" leader. To make these observations is not to cast doubts on the nature of the Cuban revolution, which was clearly Communist in a real sense as well as being a nationalist revolution deriving as much from Martí as from Marx; but it seems difficult to deny that a dominant factor in *the way it became* a Communist revolution was, simply, the will of its caudillo. A distinguished Nicaraguan poet was told in Cuba in 1970 that the Cuban people were only superficially Marxist in outlook; what Cubans really were was *"fidelista* and if Fidel were to declare that Marxism is bad in Cuba, all the Cubans would cease to be Marxists."[1] No political leader could ask for more. Whatever else the Cuban revolution may or may not have done, it has certainly reasserted—to an almost incredible degree—the tradition of the caudillo.

VIOLENCE

It has been in the nature of most caudillos to win power by means of violence, to rule thereafter by force, and (very often) to fall as the result of further violence. Much has been written on the "roots of violence" in Latin America; once again, deep-seated psychological tendencies have been invoked as an explanation. But violence is a universal problem, and no doubt stems from an innate biological impulse common to all men. It is certainly arguable whether Latin America, as a region, is any *more* violent than anywhere else: in terms of international conflict Latin America's record does not even begin to compare with that of Europe, while for large-scale brutality to his own people no Latin American dictator can yet be compared with Stalin. Latin American political violence owes much to the weakness of the institutional *barriers* to violence. If it is possible, for whatever reason, to overthrow a government by force, then it will tend to be done, or at least attempted. And in some countries it has been done or attempted very frequently indeed: between 1825 and 1971 Bolivia experienced no less than 187 "irregular" occurrences of this sort.

The most frequent expression of political violence in Latin American history has been the coup d'état. Paradoxically, a coup can often be

---

[1] Ernesto Cardenal, interview with *La Prensa* (Managua, Nicaragua) reproduced in *SEUL* (duplicated bulletin of the Servicio Europeo de Universitarios Latino-americanos), No. 22, February 1971.

virtually nonviolent; tanks surround the presidential palace, a dramatic interview is held between the insurgent officers and the president they are about to throw out, a few arrests are made, the new junta or caudillo is sworn in, and life goes on as normal in the city streets. On other occasions, the takeover is more complicated and perhaps more sanguinary: some army units may remain loyal to the outgoing president, civilian organizations may be involved, the air force may be required to buzz or strafe the presidential palace, the navy may even have to threaten to bombard a port, and a certain amount of unpleasant street-fighting may take place. These procedures are most common when a civilian president is being dislodged in favor of a military government. When a military president is in power, coups d'état can be simpler: the matter can often be decided inside the high command—in fact, such abrupt changes as those which occurred in Argentina in 1970 and 1971 (when Levingston replaced Onganía and Lanusse replaced Levingston) hardly rank as coups at all.

The Latin American armed forces, however, by no means hold a monopoly on violence, though they are better-equipped for it than most other people. Civilians themselves sometimes find it necessary to strike, to riot, to organize armed revolts, even to conduct full-scale civil wars in pursuit of political ends. A well-entrenched dictator, of course, is more difficult to dislodge than a civilian president, and the transition from dictatorial to constitutional rule is usually less smooth than the opposite process. The Colombian and Venezuelan revolts against Rojas Pinilla and Pérez Jiménez in 1957–58 are good examples, nonetheless, of how it can be done. In both cases, a wave of strikes and demonstrations was coupled with dissaffection in the armed forces, which deserted their caudillos and stepped in to "hold the ring" while a new pattern of civilian politics was being established.

The most serious kinds of armed revolt, whether organized by civilian elements or by disaffected groups within the armed forces, sometimes culminate in full-scale civil war. This was perhaps more common in the nineteenth century, when a number of Latin American republics (Argentina, Mexico, and Colombia in particular) were plagued with intermittent but far-reaching civil strife. Civil war can begin in a specific region and later spread to the rest of the country concerned; it can be sparked off by a caudillo or military clique seizing control of a provincial garrison; it can take the form of guerrilla organizations confronting the regular army; it can involve rival political parties (e.g., the Colombian liberals and conservatives) arming their followers and setting them at each other's throats. None of these time-honored techniques automatically guarantees success. Coups probably fail more often than not; demonstrations are often ineffectual; guerrilla campaigns (as in the 1960s) can prove quixotic and disastrous; civil wars do not necessarily end in the victory of the rebels. Violence on its own is often useless; many conditions are needed before a forcible overthrow of a government can be regarded as a practical possibility, including the widespread unpopularity of the government in question. Some Latin American dictatorships, as we have seen, last a very long time—Rosas, Porfirio Diaz, Gómez, Trujillo, Somoza, to name but five, all exercised power for two or even three decades. Of these five, Rosas and Diaz were only dislodged by massive revolts, Trujillo and Somoza were assassinated, and Gómez experienced the peaceful fate—unusual for an incumbent Latin American dictator—of dying in his bed.

The recurrent use of violence in Latin American politics poses some difficult but important questions about the underlying political stability of the region. The techniques of the coup and the palace revolution, the armed insurrection and the civil war, have been so widespread in the hundred and fifty years since independence that some political scientists have asked, justifiably enough, whether they really constitute examples of genuine political *instability*. Such methods could easily be regarded as an integral part of the Latin American "political system," which, as a system, has remained remarkably stable over the years. But it is important to remember that the coup and the revolution were never perceived by the *outside world* as signs of an underlying stability— quite the contrary. Latin America's traditional reputation for revolutions and comic-opera generals was the outcome of these foreign perceptions. It is hardly an accident that those countries where "political stability" as understood in Europe prevailed were the countries which developed the fastest and which received the heaviest foreign investment: Brazil and Chile at the start, Argentina and Mexico later on. Individual entrepreneurs might find rich profits in Ecuador or Bolivia, but the vast majority of foreign capitalists preferred the more conventional security of the "stable" countries.

MILITARISM

The phenomenon of the caudillo has been accompanied, traditionally, by the phenomenon of militarism or, as it is sometimes called, prae-torianism. This latter term is a reminder of the influence enjoyed by the army during the Roman empire. In A.D. 193, the Praetorian Guards (the well-paid imperial bodyguards) murdered the emperor, Pertinax, and proceeded to auction off the empire to the highest bidder.[1]

[1] See Edward Gibbon, *Decline and Fall of the Roman Empire*, Chaps. 4 and 5.

Throughout the tumultuous third century, it was the army that made and unmade emperors, though not usually as picturesquely or as shamelessly. No Latin American army has quite gone as far as the Roman soldiers who killed Pertinax, but presidents have been made and unmade by the military as regularly and as firmly as emperors were in the days of Rome's protracted decline and fall.

Militarism in this form has been a constant in human history, though it has played a much more prominent part in Latin American politics than it has in either Western Europe or the United States, where military activity has been directed *outward* rather than *inward*. True parallels for the Latin American experience can best be found, perhaps, in Eastern Europe in the interwar period, and in Asia and Africa since 1950 or so. The persistence of this phenomenon in Latin America has aroused a great deal of comment; as with the propensity to caudillo rule and the use of force, any explanation must center on the inadequacy of normal institutional restraints. It is significant that Chile, where strong civil institutions and political parties emerged at an early stage after independence, has seen very little in the way of military intervention. This is also true of twentieth-century Uruguay and Costa Rica. Military intervention has also been exceptional in modern Colombia. The postrevolutionary regimes in Mexico managed to tame and domesticate the armed forces in a very singular and successful manner.

The roots of militarism are to be found in the independence period. The presence of Spain and Portugal in the New World in colonial times was not in any real sense a military presence. Soldiers there certainly were, but usually to defend the imperial frontiers in places—the Caribbean, the River Plate, the south of Chile—where a foreign (or indeed native) power menaced the territorial integrity of the empires. But such cases apart, their military organization of their Iberian empires was far less notable than the administrative organization.

Toward the end of colonial times, Creole militias were established, giving many Creole aristocrats the "feel" of military rank and the legal privileges which went with it, and this may be seen as part of the background to the extensive "militarization" of Latin America (especially Spanish America) at the time of independence, when the new Creole states organized their own armies, equipped them with weapons, and sent them into action. For the most part these Creole armies were small, poorly equipped, and often prone to large-scale desertion. Nonetheless, they provided an ambitious caudillo with a perfectly adequate instrument with which to capture control of the state. With rare exceptions, standing armies were kept in being when the wars of

332

independence were over. Some of the leaders of the struggle for independence quickly saw the dangers. San Martín warned his compatriots that the presence of victorious generals in new states was by no means an unmixed blessing; President Santander told Colombians that although arms had given them independence, only laws could give them liberty. The advice of these eminent men went unheeded. The tiger was already out of its cage. The expensive tastes of generals had to be satisfied; attempts by civilian politicians to cut down the army budget or the size of the military establishment were more often than not a signal for military insurrection; only in a very few instances was it necessary for the Latin American armies to do anything as energetic as fight a foreign foe.

The close of the nineteenth century brought a new phase of Latin American military history. The rough, undisciplined rabbles of former times now gave way to better-equipped, better-trained bodies of men. A discernible process of military professionalization set in; Prussian and French missions arrived to advise the Latin American governments; staff colleges were founded; a military career became a recognized and even respectable activity for the sons of aristocratic and (especially) middle-class families. But professionalization, despite early hopes, did not imply a withdrawal from the political arena. Indeed, some countries which had long been immune now developed the disease. In Brazil, the opening years of the republic were characterized by a very strong military presence in politics, and thereafter (right down to 1964) the Brazilian armed forces seemed almost to arrogate to themselves the "moderative power" once exercised by the emperor. In Argentina, the sixty-year interlude of constitutional government was brought to an end by the military intervention of 1930, a year which saw a notable resurgence of army caudillos throughout Latin America. In the Argentine case the armed forces have remained within striking distance of the presidential palace, if not actually in it, ever since.

It is possible to distinguish three main types of military intervention in Latin American history: (1) The armed forces are used by a particular caudillo (often an officer) to win power and to keep it thereafter; the armed forces may themselves generate a caudillo in order to secure higher pay or better equipment. (2) The armed forces as an institution take over the government for a brief period, usually with a view to returning it to civilian control at an early opportunity. (3) The armed forces as an institution take over the government on a long-term basis and use it to carry through specific reforms. (Whether such reforms are left-wing or right-wing, and whether they work or not, is beside the point.) Types (1) and (2) were common in the nineteenth century

333

and have occurred frequently in more recent times as well. Type (3) is confined to the 1960s, though it may, of course, recur in the future. It is not generally associated with the rule of a particular caudillo.

The motives for military intervention vary greatly, and range from the purely predatory to the genuinely reformist. The average Latin American officer corps is invariably conscious of its power, and is acutely interested in its own economic position. More than one Latin American coup has occurred simply because officers were badly paid. Loftier causes, however, are quite capable of engaging the support of the armed forces. When civilian politicians are more than usually indecisive or opportunistic, a high command may feel impelled to take power if only to restore "order" and "morality"—words which recur with some frequency in the proclamations of newly arrived military governments, though on occasion they are far from unjustified.[1] There is a sense, then, in which the armed forces feel ultimately responsible for the national honor, and this can be combined with a determination to rout out "foreign" political philosophies which threaten to undermine the fabric of national life.

Since 1960 or so, much attention has been lavished on what observers have seen as a distinctively *new* current of militarism: "Nasserist" or "technocratic" militarism. The basic assumption here is that the armed forces as an institution are capable of taking a hand in large-scale social and economic reform, as they are popularly supposed to have done in Egypt after 1952. Clearly, the most interesting case of this kind of militarism, if it exists at all, is to be found in Peru. For several years prior to their decisive intervention in Peruvian politics in 1968, the Peruvian armed forces had shown a marked inclination toward reforming activity: their notable Center for Higher Military Studies (CAEM) had briefed officers on such important military and strategic matters as urban planning and agrarian reform. The record of the Velasco Alvarado government after 1968 indicated that these reforming proclivities could speedily be translated into action. The Peruvian military leadership is known to contemplate a very long period in power— thirty years has even been mentioned as the time it will take to create

[1] The provocations *are* sometimes considerable. In July 1963 the Ecuadorian armed forces overthrew the constitutional president, Carlos Julio Arosemena, who, at a reception the previous night, had drunkenly insulted the American ambassador, vomited, and (according to one news report) "committed still more indecorous actions." (What these were was not specified.) The incoming military junta issued a statement affirming that the ex-president "was frequently drunk" (which was true), that "he stained the national honour" (a matter of interpretation) and that "he sympathized with the communists" (a dubious assertion).

"genuine democracy" in the country. Since the start of the military revolution, other Latin American high commands have shown considerable interest in the Peruvian example.

DICTATORSHIP

We need say relatively little on dictatorship *per se*, since the main outlines of this recurrent Latin American phenomenon will by this stage have come more or less into focus. It may be helpful, nevertheless, to attempt to describe some of the main characteristics of the different types of dictatorship which have been observable in the region over the past century and a half. No classification could pretend to be exhaustive. Some kinds of dictatorship do, however, stand out more than others, and these I shall mention here.

a) The first type which springs automatically to mind is the *predatory, personal* dictatorship, of which there have been many, especially in the smaller republics. The most normal course of events in such a dictatorship is very simple. An ambitious caudillo seizes the state, retains it by force, and "milks" it to the advantage—sometimes to the quite spectacular advantage—of himself, his family, and his friends and henchmen. The most obvious examples of this sort of dictatorship are, as has been suggested, to be found in the histories of the smaller republics. Confining ourselves to the twentieth century it is fairly easy to identify the long reign of the Somoza dynasty in Nicaragua or of Generalissimo Trujillo in the Dominican Republic as classic cases in point. Neither the original Somoza nor the Dominican Benefactor were able to enjoy the fruits of their tenure of office in old age, but a more fortunate dictator, Fulgencio Batista of Cuba, left office with a personal fortune estimated at three hundred million dollars. It may please predatory dictators of this kind to render lip service to constitutional ideals, by allowing puppet congresses to meet from time to time or even by governing through a succession of figureheads; these expedients, however, have rarely been known to fool anyone.

b) What may appropriately be described as dictatorships *of order* have also been common. Here a caudillo is less interested in enriching himself (though he *may* do so) than in staving off what he conceives to be national disaster at the hands of incompetent or opportunistic civilian politicians. Not infrequently such dictatorships have been characterized by fairly simple nationalist ideals, by a very orthodox social and economic outlook, and, not least, by programs of public works. Reforms in the direction of "efficiency" or "morality" are by no means absent under such governments. The regime of General Carlos Ibáñez del Campo, one of the very few dictators who have managed to climb to power in Chile, falls clearly into this class; the government of General Rojas Pinilla, which came to power at a period of acute and damaging civil strife in Colombia, can be considered as a further example. Dictators of this type are usually less flamboyant and less acquisitive than those in the first category.

c) *Transitional* dictatorships have been extremely frequent in some Latin American countries. These tend to be short-lived, for obvious reasons; they are designed to "hold the ring" for a while in periods of political stress or to pave the way from a long period of caudillo rule into a restored constitutional regime. The immediate post-Perón governments in Argentina (1955–58), the regime of Admiral Wolfgang Larrázabal in Venezuela (1958) and the Peruvian military junta of 1962–63 are some of the more characteristic examples of recent years. The transitional dictatorship, when it occurs, is rarely associated with any particular caudillo; very often, indeed, it is a reaction against caudillo rule, and it may therefore be run collectively by a junta—sometimes a purely military junta, and sometimes a mixed military-civilian body.

d) In the twentieth century in particular a number of dictatorships clearly qualify for the description of *reforming*. The long regime of Getúlio Vargas in Brazil and the decade of Peronist rule in Argentina,[1] represented periods of considerable change for the peoples of those two countries. More recently, the Peruvian military dictatorship set up in 1968 has adopted a sharply reforming set of politics. In each of these cases, the fundamental impulse behind the dictatorship seems to have been the impulse of modernization—modernization geared (especially in Perón's case) to dreams of national glory. Reforming dictatorships, insofar as they come into collision with powerful vested interests, are bound to seek support from outside the ranks of the armed forces: thus Vargas, though heavily dependent on the Brazilian armed forces (especially after his coup in 1937), sought links with business and organized labor. The Perón regime was underpinned by a coalition of both the armed forces and the trade unions. Attempts may be made by reforming dictatorships to "mobilize" the citizens of the country concerned, sometimes through a specially created political party. Perón adopted this technique; Vargas did not.

e) All dictatorships are by definition authoritarian in nature, but in the twentieth-century world some have gone further than this and have

---

[1] Here it should be recalled that Vargas' dictatorship proper began in 1937, and that Perón was elected president in perfectly fair elections; by the end of his government, however, Perón was clearly a dictator.

become what is often called *totalitarian*, i.e., they aspire to a total control of the life of the country concerned. Some of the predatory, personal dictatorships in Latin American history have prefigured totalitarianism to a marked extent—the Trujillo regime, for instance.[1] But the only unequivocally totalitarian dictatorship in Latin America (so far) has been the "dictatorship of the proletariat" established in Cuba by Dr. Fidel Castro. Here the technique of "mobilization" has been pushed much further than it was, for instance, in Perón's Argentina, although the main instrument of mobilization is less the newly fashioned Cuban Communist Party (which seems to enjoy markedly less power than its opposite numbers in Russia or the Eastern European satellites) than the dense network of Committees for the Defense of the Revolution, which, block by block and street by street, drum up support for the regime and generally supervise the spare-time activities of the population.

None of the five types of dictatorships suggested here should necessarily be regarded as "pure." What has been described as a dictatorship of order can easily turn into something more obviously predatory or personal, and predatory elements are by no means absent from some reforming dictatorships, as is evidenced in the large-scale corruption which accompanied the later stages of the Perón regime. If a government has genuine reforms to its credit, however, these predatory characteristics may be forgotten or forgiven by the dictator's followers.

> *Ladrón o no ladrón,*
> *Queremos a Perón!*
>
> Whether a thief or not,
> We still want Perón!

was a cry occasionally raised by Perón's supporters in the years which followed his downfall. The Argentine elections of 1973 revealed how powerful this sentiment remained nearly two decades later.

Looking at the hundred and fifty or so years since independence, the most remarkable feature of Latin American politics has undoubtedly been the sheer persistence of the two principal traditions described in this chapter: the tradition of liberalism and constitutionalism, and the tradition of violence and dictatorship. Nevertheless, it is only fair to

---

[1] Some nineteenth-century dictatorships, e.g., those of Rosas or Francisco Solano Lopez, clearly constitute prefigurations of totalitarianism; but in both cases the apparatus of the modern state, and in particular the pervasive influence of the mass media, were lacking. Totalitarianism can best be considered as a genuinely twentieth-century phenomenon.

337

emphasize that both traditions have changed and developed over the years. The constitutional tradition has witnessed a constant widening of the franchise and a growth in political parties, so that popular participation in politics (as expressed in voting) can certainly be said to have increased. The tradition of dictatorship, which was overwhelmingly personal and predatory for much of the nineteenth century, has moved decisively into the sphere of social and economic reform. In the 1960s, as we have seen, military intervention took on new forms, and a wholly new kind of dictatorship was established in Cuba. Further developments along these lines can undoubtedly be expected in the future.

In the course of the twentieth century, one Latin American country has succeeded in combining the two main traditions, at least to some extent. The type of government which has developed in postrevolutionary Mexico can only be described as *sui generis*, and it deserves close study. The essence of the "free one-party system" as it has operated in Mexico since the 1930s is the control of the state by the PRI (Institutional Revolutionary Party), as it is now known. The PRI has won every election since its formation, though opposition parties are permitted to organize and even to flourish. The president of the republic is invariably a senior member of the party, and his election to the presidency has been a foregone conclusion in every such contest since 1934; this does not exempt him from the duty of conducting a vigorous (and exhausting) election campaign up and down the country. The PRI itself is a protean organization formally divided into "sectors": there were originally four of these—agrarian, labor, popular, and military—but the sector representing the armed forces was dissolved in 1940. The agrarian sector contains peasant organizations; the labor sector embraces the trade unions; and the so-called popular sector is an umbrella for a wide variety of interests and organizations, though in practice it is said to represent the bureaucracy. With all its faults, the PRI constitutes a reasonably well-oiled machine for the articulation of many different interests within the Mexican nation. It is, in many senses, an authoritarian government, but is capable of great flexibility.

Increasingly in the past two decades or so, the imperatives of social and economic progress in Latin America have prompted a good deal of speculation on the subject of forms of government. Development has become a *political* issue. Is there a *kind* of government which is especially favorable to economic development? Are traditional forms of government outmoded? Is electoral democracy a farce? Is totalitarian dictatorship or military rule the only answer? Questions like these have been put with great frequency in academic debate and in popular disputation. As was suggested in Chapter 5 (pp. 282–84), the key problem is less concerned with *forms* of government than with the *efficacy of the state* as a machine or instrument of social betterment. In general the state in Latin America has been "soft" rather than "hard"—even when the utmost harshness has been employed against political oppositions. This point has to be borne in mind by all Latin American rulers—whether elected presidents, military dictators, or charismatic leaders.

Three definite types of government are usually mentioned in discussions relating to the problem of development: (1) totalitarian dictatorship which "mobilizes" the population, (2) reforming military dictatorship, and (3) more vigorous kinds of constitutional democracy. Each of these suffers from decided disadvantages. Totalitarianism (whose advocates do not refer to it as such) can certainly eliminate or at least disregard traditional vested interests, but it carries with it many uncertainties. It is not clear, for instance, how long "mobilization" can actually last in practice, though it can undoubtedly achieve great things while it lasts. José Ortega y Gasset once remarked that revolutions last only fifteen years, and some historians would regard this as being generous. Certainly, the initial spasm of enthusiasm which a revolutionary government is often capable of generating does not seem capable of enduring indefinitely; the idea of "permanent revolution" has (so far in human history) proved an illusion. Furthermore, the sheer concentration of power which occurs in a totalitarian system poses very serious problems. Lord Acton's view that all power tends to corrupt and that absolute power corrupts absolutely has yet to be proved wrong in practice, while the centralization which seems inseparable from totalitarian arrangements is no guarantee, in itself, of efficient government. The stifling of criticism which invariably accompanies the imposition of totalitarian rule (however "mobilized," however "mass-based") can often help to perpetuate the most glaring social and economic stupidities.

In countries where militarism has flourished in the past, it is not wholly impossible that reforming military dictatorships could give a decisive impetus to progress; but a necessary condition for this would be the elimination of the predatory characteristics which have often been found in the various officer corps in Latin America. The spoils of office are sometimes very tempting indeed. Nevertheless, the development of nationalist and reforming currents of opinion within the Latin American armed forces should clearly be watched with interest. Armies, to put it crudely, possess the fire-power to enforce political decisions; they may in some cases be better organized than a civil service or political party; and, as the recent cases of Argentina, Brazil, and Peru tend to indicate, they are less touchy about social and economic criticism—and

339

perhaps more open to constructive suggestions—than is often supposed.[1]

Among Latin Americans who like to consider themselves as radicals, no form of government is less popular than constitutional democracy. It is widely believed in such circles that constitutions and congresses have invariably been the plaything of oligarchic groups uninterested in the welfare of the great majority of the population. Clearly, however, popular political movements *can* win power through elections (as occurred in Chile in 1964 and again in 1970) and can use that power to introduce the reforms in which they believe. It may be argued that of the present range of political parties in Latin America, most are insufficiently reform-minded, that they tend to "sell out" once in power, or that they are incapable of decisive action. These criticisms carry a ring of truth; but the fault lies less with the system as such than with the parties themselves and, not least, their leaders. In some countries, constitutional arrangements *may* conceivably restrict swift and decisive legislation, but in most cases the degree to which a vigorous president can take the initiative, if he so desires, is very striking.

A sense of perspective is useful in contemplating the political expedients which have been adopted in Latin America in the past and which are likely to be adopted in the future. Lord Acton, whose liberal credentials can scarcely be placed in doubt, wrote in 1877:

> The purchase of judicial appointments is manifestly indefensible; yet in the old French monarchy that monstrous practice created the only corporation able to resist the king. Official corruption which would ruin a commonwealth, serves in Russia as a salutary relief from the pressure of absolutism. There are conditions in which it is scarcely a hyperbole to say that slavery itself is a stage on the road to freedom.[2]

Whether we accept Acton's assumptions or not (and we could certainly do a lot worse) the relevance of this to modern Latin America should be readily apparent.

Movements and Programs

We shall conclude the present chapter with a short survey of the main parties, political outlooks, and ideologies which have been found in the

[1] The Argentine and Brazilian regimes of the 1960s cannot be said to have imposed really stringent prohibitions on the expression of dissident political or economic thought. Military governments of this sort are in a real sense less "ideological" than, say, Communist or Fascist dictatorships would be, and hence see no overwhelming need to stifle heterodox opinion. Attacks on the "honor" of the armed forces, however, represent a degree of heterodoxy which is *not* permitted.

[2] Lord Acton, "The History of Freedom in Antiquity," in *Essays on Freedom and Power* (London, 1956), p. 55.

recent history of Latin America and which, in most cases, continue to be found in the region today. One or two general observations are in order at the outset. Political parties or movements are often classified in terms of their position in some hypothetical "political spectrum" ranging from right to left, terms which derive from the seating arrangements adopted in the French national assemblies of the 1790s. There are few safe rules for allocating a particular position to a particular party.

For present purposes, let us make the assumption that the most useful criterion, at least for developments since 1920 or so in Latin America, is the attitude adopted by a party or movement toward *state intervention in the economy*. Let us further assume that for the most part right-wing forces fight shy of excessive state intervention and are pledged to maintain and perhaps to expand the role of capitalism in the economy. Left-wing forces, on the other hand, are interested in extending the scope of state intervention in what they conceive to be the interest of the community in general.[1] Communist parties, for instance, are clearly left-wing, and indeed on the extreme left, because of their ultimate goal of a wholly state-owned and state-operated economy and the abolition of most forms of private property. One must admit, of course, that some political movements are very difficult to "place" in a position in the political spectrum if it is conceived in these terms. *Anarchism*, for instance, rejects the state altogether and has no interest in establishing collectivist economic forms. *Fascism* and *National Socialism* are two further cases which must be regarded as difficult; they are sometimes considered to be on the extreme right, but their opposition to capitalism and "bourgeois" parliamentary institutions means that they have more in common with the revolutionary left than it is usually tactful to admit. (This is for the most part an academic question in Latin America, although the term "fascist" is frequently used there, as elsewhere, as a rather meaningless piece of political invective.) *Nationalism* as a political tendency can ally itself with any of the ideologies and outlooks to be mentioned in this section, and has often done so in the past few decades.

It may be helpful, at this stage, to illustrate the positions of some of the main parties and movements mentioned in this chapter in the form of a diagram. The reader must forgive me if he finds his favorite party too far to the left or right.

One further distinction is perhaps in order. As noted on several

[1] In this sense, of course, most governments in the world have moved a long way to the left in the past hundred years. Consider the ten key measures recommended by Marx and Engels in the *Communist Manifesto* for what they called the "most advanced" countries; all of them have been wholly or partly implemented in Western Europe by governments, some of them right-wing, which have rejected Marxism.

Latin American Political Spectrum, Late 1960s

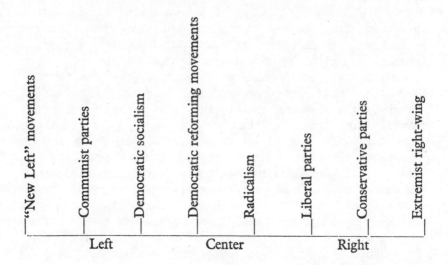

previous occasions in this book, the terms "revolution" and "revolutionary" have always been common in Latin American political life, and
this is truer than ever today. It is very difficult to discover an altogether
suitable criterion by which to decide whether a movement is revolutionary or not. The mere invocation of the words "revolution" or
"social change" cannot be regarded as a very useful touchstone, for
right-wing movements sometimes claim to be "revolutionary"[1] and
any coherent social and economic policy brings with it "social change"
in one direction or another. Again, the attitude of parties or movements
toward the use of violence is a somewhat dubious criterion, for most
political forces in Latin America have either advocated the use of
violence or actually used it at one time or another. Unsatisfactory as this
may be, it seems important to draw a distinction between "democratic"
outlooks, which provide for some degree of respect for individual rights
and constitutional legality, and "revolutionary" outlooks, which are

[1] Both the Brazilian and Argentine military coups of 1964 and 1966 ushered in
revolutions, according to the generals who carried them through. In the Chilean
presidential election of 1970 all three candidates were revolutionaries, for even the
right-winger, Don Jorge Alessandri, was occasionally referred to by his followers as a
"true" or "constructive" revolutionary. (His supporters even issued a gramophone
record of "positive protest songs.") In plain fact, all three candidates expressed the
utmost respect for the forms of the constitution; so none of them was revolutionary in
any real sense at all. Latin American politicians, like those in other parts of the world,
are always to some extent prisoners of their own rhetoric.

based on the view that such things cannot be allowed to stand in the way of whatever social and economic improvements are being advocated; and it should be clear that revolutionary movements, understood in this sense, *are* extremely interested in drastic social and economic reform. It should be recognized here that I am referring, essentially, to *outlooks* and *programs* rather than what may or may not happen, in practice, under a given regime.

I. THE RIGHT. The classic division of political opinion in nineteenth-century Latin America was between liberalism and conservatism. It is difficult to generalize about the nature of the difference between the two movements. In some countries the federalist/centralist split complicated the issue; but even in the Argentine case, for example, it is possible to regard Rosas and the provincial caudillos who supported him as conservatives, while the opposition to his rule was led by men who were happy and proud to look upon themselves (and label themselves) liberals. The liberal and conservative parties of the nineteenth century were not parties in the modern sense; they lacked rigorous organization; their membership, drawn entirely from the educated upper classes, was extremely variable and often inert; politicians changed sides with great frequency. In countries where political stability of the conventional sort prevailed—e.g., Chile and Brazil —parties assumed somewhat more coherent forms. Indeed, Chile developed a taste for party political battles at a relatively early stage,[1] and this taste has never lost its hold on ordinary Chilean people. Conservatism, in the nineteenth century, tended to emphasize the "traditional" side to Latin American life. It was very attached to the hacienda as a "natural" form of land-holding. It was usually very proclerical. It stood, very often at least, for centralized government as opposed to federalism. In economic policy, conservatives were more likely to be protectionist than free-trading. It is by no means true however, that *all* conservative elements idealized the traditional social order or insisted dogmatically on upholding its every feature. Examples of vigorously innovative conservative politicians and statesmen are easy to find: Lucas Alamán in Mexico or President Manuel Montt in Chile are a couple of excellent cases in point. Nevertheless, conservatives were clearly in favor of a social order in which the power of landed property was respected, in which welfare for the poor was best left to the charitable initiatives of private individuals or the Church, and in which the authority of the central government was *felt*—though not in too fundamental a way in the economic sphere.

[1] Party politics gained ascendancy following the split in the ruling conservative party in the second presidency of Manuel Montt (1856–61).

Nineteenth-century liberals, by contrast, regarded themselves, and wished to be regarded, as innovators and progressives. They often affected a marked distaste for the "feudal" and Hispanic aspects of the social order which surrounded them. Far more than the conservatives, they were open to foreign (i.e., European or American) ideas. The 1848 revolution in France fascinated them, as did the *risorgimento* in Italy.[1] Some of them looked to Great Britain for inspiration, although admiration for the English political system was probably more a conservative characteristic; for many liberals the United States was the great model on which future progress should be based. In Argentina, for instance, Sarmiento positively rejected the example of Western Europe, which he saw as decadent, and turned with great enthusiasm to the lessons he thought could be derived from the history of the young and vigorous American republic.

In economic matters, liberal parties tended to be antiprotectionist and positively to welcome the impulse of the international economy. In domestic politics, they were often in the forefront of the struggle for a widened franchise and a reduction in the political and economic power of the Church. Their anticlericalism, however, was less doctrinal than political: even when pressing for the confiscation of ecclesiastical property, many of them remained good Catholics. An old and revealing Colombian definition of the difference between liberals and conservatives may be cited here: "conservatives pray in public and drink in private; liberals drink in public and pray in private."

The struggle between those men whose praying and drinking habits were so different was a profound one, often overflowing into ferocious civil wars; but it flourished at a period when political activity was still exclusively the preserve—one might almost say the game—of the upper classes, and in particular the landed aristocracies. The social changes brought about by the impact of the international economy toward the end of the nineteenth century were sufficient, in some cases, to throw the traditional political movements onto the defensive. From the opening years of the twentieth century onward, liberals and conservatives alike could reasonably be identified as part of the political right. In many republics they increasingly came to work in harmony in electoral alliances and government coalitions, and in some cases actually merged. This process was certainly assisted by the decline in importance of some of the traditional issues which had previously divided the parties, in particular the issue of the Church. In some republics, the separation of Church and state was accomplished without excessively bitter feelings

[1] The more clerically minded conservatives tended to sympathize with the Papacy after 1870, when the Pope became the "prisoner of the Vatican."

344

being aroused; elsewhere the Church remained "established" without provoking political tempests; everywhere, ecclesiastical issues were overshadowed by the "social question."

Conservative and liberal parties survive, under a wide variety of different labels, in most Latin American republics. In both Colombia and Uruguay, where political life is still to some extent focused on the rivalry between the two traditional movements, the liberal or (in the Uruguayan case) Colorado parties have shifted their ground. In Colombia, movements within the liberal party have veered toward the left, while the Uruguayan Colorados, under Batlle's auspices, became in the early twentieth century what can properly be described as a pioneering example of a democratic reforming movement. Elsewhere, liberals and conservatives have remained firmly on the right, and have usually been noted for their tenacious resistance to agrarian reform whenever this has been proposed, for their hostility to welfare legislation, and for their ability to mobilize substantial sections of the rural vote—though this final characteristic is a good deal less noticeable than it used to be. The standard emphasis in right-wing speeches, manifestos, and propaganda are on "order," "work," "traditional values," and so forth—and these themes can often appeal to electorates who are tired of perpetual *politiquería* (shameless politicking), even though the right-wing politicians who espouse such themes may be as opportunistic as everybody else, and indeed usually are.

Even in countries where powerful reforming or left-wing forces have come to the fore in recent years, the right is by no means dead. In Chile, for instance, the National Party (a fusion of the old liberal and conservative parties arranged in 1965) won twenty percent of the popular vote in the congressional elections of 1969, and the right-wing candidate came close to winning the presidential contest of 1970.[1] Approximately two tendencies can be found in the right-wing movements of the past thirty years or so: (1) a strictly speaking "reactionary" trend, emphasizing, tradition, Catholicism, and (not infrequently) the Hispanic antecedents of Latin American life, somewhat idealized; and (2) an outwardly more "modern" trend, emphasizing the importance of business efficiency, limited government, and the need to stimulate rather than to depress capitalist incentives. The "reactionary" trend reached its fiercest expression in recent years in the career of Laureano Gómez, conservative president of Colombia from 1950–53. Gómez did not disguise his considerable admiration for the Spain of General Franco, to whom he extended moral support during the Civil War. In

[1] In the congressional elections of 1973, the National Party received twenty-one percent of the vote.

a speech delivered in 1937, Gómez pronounced the following extra-ordinary sentences:

> Spain, marching forward as the sole defender of Christian civilization, leads the Western nations in the reconstruction of the empire of Hispanidad, and we inscribe our names in the roster of its phalanxes with unutterable satisfaction. . . . We bless God who has permitted us to live in this era of unforeseen transformations, and who has given it to us to utter, with a cry that springs from the very depths of our heart: "Up Catholic, Imperial Spain!"[1]

It would be grossly unfair to present Gómez' views as typical of the Latin American right, though they deserve to be remembered. Many right-wingers would dismiss Gómez as a political dinosaur and his exaggerated Hispanism as a quixotic absurdity; his priorities are certainly not those of most right-wing parties in the 1970s.

Whether the right in Latin America, at present uneasily poised between a diehard defense of traditional vested interests and the adoption of a reforming capitalist impulse, can be successfully renovated in order to play a part in the political life of the future is one of the more fascinating questions of the 1970s; a current of serious, vigorous, and innovative conservatism could arguably be of great benefit in some Latin American republics. It would, however, be obliged to devise a clear-sighted strategy to deal with all the social and economic dilemmas described in Chapter 5. Whether or not this is a real possibility is very much an open question. But in one way or another the right is certain to play some kind of part in Latin America in the years ahead.

2. RADICALISM. In two Latin American countries—Chile and Argentina—the first organized political challenge to the traditional liberal and conservative parties came from Radicalism, a political tendency which has been largely confined to southern South America.[2] The history of the Chilean and Argentine Radical parties has been a long one and for that reason alone they deserve a place in this survey. In Chile, the Radical Party emerged in the 1860s; its first cabinet was appointed in 1875; by the 1930s it had established itself as the biggest single political movement in Chile; it governed the country between 1938 and 1952; thereafter public esteem for the party tended to decline. Argentine radicalism dates from the organization, in 1890, of the opposition Civic

---

[1] Germán Arciniegas, *The State of Latin America* (London, 1953), p. 163.
[2] The Uruguayan Colorado Party under Batlle may be said to have taken on something of a radical coloring, and in social and economic matters went further to the left than the Chilean and Argentine radical parties of that period.

Union; when this split a year or two later the adjective "radical" was added to the section of the movement which remained in opposition; the Radical Civic Union (commonly known as the Radical Party) governed the country between 1916 and 1930; in 1957 the party split in two, "intransigent" radicals parting company with "people's" radicals; the first of these contributed Arturo Frondizi, the second Arturo Illía, to the presidency in the period between the fall of Perón and the rise of Onganía. In both Chile and Argentina, radicalism has traditionally been associated with the middle classes.

In its early decades, the Chilean Radical Party was mostly preoccupied with the question of electoral freedom and the limitation of the power of the Church; many of its leaders were also freemasons, and displayed a *doctrinal* hostility toward Catholicism which had been absent from liberal anticlericalism. If there was one key issue for the radicals of the period it was the secularization and state control of education. After the turn of the century, the "social question" tended to predominate in the party's deliberations. At the party's notable Third Convention (1906) two tendencies, "individualist" and "socialist" respectively, fought for supremacy in the course of a superb series of debates, the "socialist" tendency just winning. Since the early 1930s, the Chilean Radical Party has consistently defined its doctrine in terms of "state socialism," although in practice its leadership has veered as sharply to the right as to the left: there were radical ministers in the right-wing government of Jorge Alessandri at the start of the 1960s, just as there were radical ministers in the cabinet of the Marxist president, Dr. Salvador Allende, at the start of the 1970s.[1] In the last few years, however, the party has commanded less than fifteen percent of the popular vote.

Argentine radicalism, like its Chilean counterpart, was initially concerned with the winning of electoral freedom; its social and economic position at the time Irigoyen was elected to power in 1916 was not particularly coherent. Irigoyen himself believed that the state should at least "acquire . . . a position of greater authority in the industrial enterprises that provide public services,"[2] while the program presented by Arturo Frondizi in his election campaign of 1958 looked in some respects to be an attempt at stealing some of the clothes from Peronism. This left-wing and nationalist program was not, however, carried out

[1] In 1969 the Chilean Radicals split over the question of support for the left. The "official" Radicals, part of Dr. Salvador Allende's coalition, suffered a further split in mid-1971. Three Radical parties fought the congressional elections of 1973; all of them did badly.

[2] José Luis Romero, *A History of Argentine Political Thought* (Stanford, Calif., 1963), p. 221.

wehn Frondizi became president. The radical outlook in Argentina has always been somewhat further to the right than Frondizi's program would suggest. Moderate doses of state intervention, moderate economic nationalism, and a strong insistence on the advantages of electoral democracy—these have been the classic characteristics of the movement. It may safely be assumed (insofar as anything can safely be assumed) that in the next few years in Argentina, the Radicals will continue to enjoy the support at the polls of a substantial section of the electorate. In March 1973 they won twenty-one percent.

3. DEMOCRATIC REFORMING MOVEMENTS. If radicalism is a phenomenon confined to southern South America, no such regional limitation can be applied to the cluster of "democratic reforming movements" which have appeared in the course of the last half-century. It should be squarely admitted at the outset that the term "democratic reforming movement" is not a very satisfactory one; but then neither are any of the other labels—"social democratic" and "populist" are among the most common—which have habitually been attached to the parties and movements concerned.

Despite the difficulty of supplying an adequate label, there can be no doubt whatever as to the historical importance of the parties and movements in question. They can be said to occupy a left-of-center position in the political spectrum, though some are perhaps nearer the center than others. The four most famous examples are: APRA (Peru); MNR (Bolivia); Acción Democrática (Venezuela); Liberación Nacional (Costa Rica). Even bearing in mind the very different circumstances of its origin, and the obvious fact that it has never had to contend for power in the same way, the Mexican PRI should probably be associated with this group of parties. In more recent years, a number of similar movements, basing themselves on apparently somewhat different ideological foundations, have also emerged: the chief of these is Christian Democracy.

Common to these movements are several key elements: a degree of economic nationalism, expressed in the nationalization of foreign concerns or the higher taxation of such concerns; a decided interest (where appropriate) in the incorporation of the Indian communities into the life of the nation in question; a strong belief in programs of social welfare; a vocal dismissal of right-wing oligarchies and "the established order"; and an emphasis on political democracy. When democratic reforming movements have been in power, they have often been criticized, from their left; this, however, has not usually rescued them from the bitter enmity of the right or saved them from brutal persecution from the same quarter.

348

a) APRA. APRA has never enjoyed power,[1] but its influence on other Latin American movements has been very considerable. In one sense, APRA could be classified as a "former revolutionary party" rather than as a democratic reforming movement, for its general approach to social and economic questions and to the issue of Latin American relationships with the United States has become markedly less astringent over the years. The ideological foundations of APRA were provided by Haya de la Torre, who was much influenced in his youth by Marxist–Leninist theory and the example of the Mexican revolution. The initial program of APRA was very much a reflection of these influences. Haya asserted that the orthodox Communist emphasis on the urban working class as a revolutionary force was a palpable absurdity in Latin America, which hardly possessed one. He advocated the formation of a *multiclass* alliance against what he styled foreign imperialism, and, as an integral part of the struggle, the unification of Latin America. The APRA attitude to political democracy at this period was at best ambiguous. The movement's propaganda basically emphasized the need to set up anti-imperialist, anti-oligarchic governments; there was no insistence whatever that this had to be done by peaceful means.

Even in the 1920s, however, Haya distinguished between different kinds of foreign (i.e., imperialist) capital. He took Lenin's hypothesis that imperialism was the last stage of capitalism and, in effect, turned it on its head. For the industrial nations, Haya affirmed, imperialism might well be the last stage of capitalism; for the less-developed, "colonial" countries of the world, it was manifestly the *first stage* of capitalism. If history were to move according to the progression suggested by Marx, then the capitalist phase had to be accepted as necessary, and hence imperialism (in Lenin's or Haya's sense) had a part to play in the development of Latin America. It had to be prevented from abridging the economic autonomy of Latin America, but providing this was done, foreign capital could be welcomed. In domestic policy, a key place in APRA theory was occupied by the need for an agrarian reform which would successfully integrate the Indian communities into the life of the Peruvian nation. APRA's extremely strong "Indianist" emphasis was responsible for the movement's adoption of the term "Indo-America" in place of "Latin America," a convention *Aprista* writers have retained.

Many of these particular emphases remained a standard part of the

[1] In the 1962 and 1963 Peruvian presidential elections APRA secured about one third of the vote and at that period its membership may have been as high as five hundred thousand.

APRA outlook, but a number of changes occurred as the years went by. Haya de la Torre himself, nothing if not an eclectic thinker, drew on influences as different as Einstein—whose theory of relativity inspired Haya's abstruse conception of "Historic Space-Time"—and Toynbee in order to refine, indeed to redefine, his political philosophy. His originally rather fierce anti-Americanism softened toward the close of the 1930s, as a result of the rise of Nazism in Europe and the development of the Good Neighbor policy by President Roosevelt. (Haya asserted that it was Yankee imperialism, rather than his own theories, which had changed direction.) APRA now became firmly committed, in theory at least, to the idea of effective political democracy. From its beginnings APRA had consistently opposed Communism on both theoretical and practical grounds. In the 1950s, Haya de la Torre argued that the only countries which had given "a positive, creative and realistic answer to Communism"[1] were those in which democratic socialist parties were in power—and he urged Latin Americans to follow the example set by Scandinavia.

It might seem a somewhat hopeless task to transform a Peru into a Sweden, and by no means everyone would think this wholly desirable even if it were possible. Nevertheless, whatever APRA's day-to-day political performance may have been like in practice in Peru, the movement's place in history is very secure: it undoubtedly helped to set the style for a number of similarly-inclined movements; it contributed a great deal to the common stock of Latin American ideals in the 20th century; and (whatever may be thought of the solutions it offered) it remained faithful to the notion that distinctively Latin American solutions had to be sought for Latin American dilemmas. Only the most dogmatic and ungenerous anti-Aprista would fail to concede the very high place which Haya de la Torre has occupied in the development of the political thought of twentieth-century Latin America.

b) "APRA-style" Movements and the PRI. Of the several movements which have so often been dubbed "APRA-style," the closest to APRA itself has probably been the Bolivian MNR, or Nationalist Revolutionary Movement, associated from its earliest years with the career of Victor Paz Estenssoro. The Venezuelan Acción Democrática (Democratic Action) and Costa Rican Liberación Nacional (National Liberation) movements originated, for their part, in countries where there was little need for the strong "Indian" emphasis of APRA or the MNR.

---

[1] V. R. Haya de la Torre, *Mensaje de la Europa nórdica* (Buenos Aires, 1956), p. 11. One of Haya's complaints in this particular collection of articles (some of which are very stimulating) was that the sources of information available to Latin Americans neglected "the Europe of social democracy."

These three movements are also marked to some extent by divergent ideological backgrounds; the MNR, for instance, was often accused in its early days of sympathy for National Socialism. These differences are no doubt important ones, but they should not blind us to the considerable similarities which exist between these various tendencies. Unlike APRA, the APRA-style parties have all enjoyed power, so that it is possible to assess their historical role in terms of achievements as well as theoretical programs. What have been the common features of these various movements?

All of them have displayed a common preoccupation in the social and economic spheres with moving away from laissez-faire doctrines and with asserting the right of the state not merely to intervene generally in the economy but also to act, where necessary, as an entrepreneur in its own right. Each of the three movements mentioned, when in power, sponsored nationalization measures or insisted that foreign concerns should pay greatly increased royalties: Paz Estenssoro's expropriation of the "Big Three" tin companies and the British-owned railways in Bolivia, Betancourt's policy toward the American oil companies, or Figueres' dealings with the United Fruit Company could be mentioned here. State intervention and control, however, has not been seen as part of a general drive against private property or even capitalism as such. In the 1960s, the program of Acción Democrática in Venezuela distinguished between what it called the "nonproductive" or "parasitic" capitalist class and the "productive" capitalist class, and granted, with some reservations, that the latter group could play a "progressive" role in Venezuelan society.[1]

In the political field, the APRA-style parties have generally been firmly attached to the principles of electoral democracy and representative government; and this is not very surprising in view of the political circumstances in which they were born. All of them have had to struggle against dictatorships of one kind or another. Seen in this light, Rómulo Betancourt's pride in being the first constitutionally elected Venezuelan president to complete his term of office acquires additional significance.

A third important characteristic of these parties has been their clear desire to remain free from foreign ideological pressures. When in

---

[1] The nonproductive "capitalist class" or "bourgeoisie" were to be regarded as the "oligarchy"; the "productive bourgeoisie" was distinguished from "the middle classes," defined as a heterogeneous group consisting of many different interests and professions; the "peasantry" and "working class" were to be found at the bottom of the scale. Acción Democrática was defined as an "organic alliance of exploited classes," i.e., the peasantry, the working class, and the "democratic" middle class; this alliance was said to have a "positive" attitude toward the "productive bourgeoisie."

power between 1952 and 1964, the MNR insisted time and time again that its outlook was essentially Bolivian and Latin American. In an essay written several years before the movement reached power, Paz Estenssoro expressed the hope that his movement would lead to an eventually "socialist" regime but made it clear that "It is not possible to apply to Bolivia . . . principles applicable or already applied to other people in other countries. Here social phenomena are of a different nature. . . ."[1] Speaking at an Acción Democrática banquet in March 1964, at the end of his term of office as president of Venezuela, Rómulo Betancourt insisted on his movement's basic ideological independence; AD's ideology, he said, was "national revolutionary, not traced from foreign molds. . . . It has not been, and nor is it, an organization enclosed in the straitjacket of reverently worshipped theoretical dogmas formulated by men and political movements in socio-economic circumstances very different from our own."[2] With the development of the Cuban revolution in the 1960s, the leaders of the APRA-style movements tended to adopt a hostile—in Betancourt's case, very hostile—attitude toward the Castro regime.

This is, perhaps, the place to mention the somewhat different case o the PRI, the ruling party of Mexico. It would clearly be nonsensical to classify the PRI as an "APRA-style" party: its own particular outlook stemmed entirely from the turbulent circumstances of the Mexican revolution, and it should certainly not be forgotten that Haya de la Torre, and hence APRA, derived some of their inspiration from the example of that revolution. Nevertheless, the officially declared aims of the PRI, as it has developed over the years, seem to correspond in several important respects to those of the parties mentioned here. Following President Cárdenas' reorganization of the ruling party in 1938, it issued an interesting declaration of principles, part of which may be quoted here:

1. The party . . . accepts, absolutely and without reservations, the democratic system and the form of government established by the Political Constitution (of Mexico). . . . 3. It recognizes the existence of the class struggle as a phenomenon inherent in the capitalist regime of production, and upholds *the right of the workers to contend for public power in order to use it for their betterment*. The diverse manifestations of the class struggle, manifestations subject to the

---

[1] Quoted in Robert J. Alexander, *Prophets of the Revolution* (New York, 1962), p. 201.

[2] R. Betancourt, *La revolución democrática en Venezuela*, 4 vols. (Caracas, 1968), IV, 368–69.

different periods of its dialectical development, *will be attuned to the peculiarities of the Mexican environment.* (Italics added.)

The fourth article of this declaration announced that one of the fundamental objectives of the party was "the preparation of the people for the imposition of a workers' democracy and for arriving at a socialist regime."[1]

The Mexican revolutionary ideology did not exist prior to the revolution itself; it grew up spontaneously, was given different emphases by different interests and personalities, was fed by the occasional foreign influence, and crystallized somewhat slowly. It has never been surrounded by what Betancourt called a "straightjacket of reverently worshiped dogmas." Nevertheless, the historical experience of the revolution itself *does* come close to being reverently worshiped in Mexico. Efforts are made by the PRI to depict the progress of the Mexican nation as part and parcel of a *continuing* revolution. Since revolutions do not last indefinitely, and as it is now sixty years since the revolt against Porfirio Díaz, this can hardly be accepted as a particularly convincing claim; at best it is a useful political myth.

As an indication of some of the main positions adopted by the PRI as Mexico moved into the 1970s, I shall quote at some length from the inaugural address delivered in December 1970 by Luis Echeverría, the sixth "party" president to take office since the retirement of Cárdenas in 1940.

Through our Revolution, we have affirmed individual liberty, internal peace, uninterrupted growth, and our capacity for self-determination before the world. Nevertheless, there still exist grave deficiencies and injustices that could endanger our achievements. . . . We cannot expect the firmness of our institutions and the expansion of our wealth alone to solve our problems. *It would be denying the best of our heritage if we were to encourage the conservative trends that have developed out of a long period of stability.* To preserve the strength of the Revolution, we must rather reject conformity and accelerate overall growth. . . .

Our basic philosophy is true solidarity among Mexicans. We want internal peace to be the fruit of the nation's dynamic and constructive forces and not merely a precarious adjustment to routines, interests, and unproductive selfishness. . . . The program to be carried out will

[1] Ernesto de la Torre Villar, Moisés González Navarro, and Stanley Ross, eds., *Historia documental de Mexico*, II, (Mexico DF, 1964), 500-1.

continue in force until the very poorest have attained an adequate standard of living. . . .

Being a revolutionary means accepting a permanent responsibility that excludes pursuit of profit, ambition for power, and destructive impulses. *Today's revolutionary is the incorruptible public servant, the loyal soldier and the honest leader, the industrious farmer and worker, the teacher, the scientist, the artist and the student, all unselfishly devoted to their tasks. He is also the entrepreneur who is a patriot and, at the same time, has social vision.* He is not, however, the impostor and dreamer of revolutions, the anarchist, the *agent provocateur*, the turncoat impelled by forces and interests alien to us, whom we Mexicans know well. . . .

In Mexico, *we do not accept that the means of production should be managed entirely by public agencies;* at the same time, we have outgrown the theories that would leave promotion of the economy entirely to private efforts. Experience has taught us that growth of capital alone is not sufficient if we are unable to apply it properly. Investment must be channeled to where it is most needed: to agriculture, to infrastructure, for the purchase of capital goods, and labor-intensive enterprises. . . .

Foreign investment should not displace Mexican capital but complement it through association when this is considered useful. Mexican capital, in any case, should handle such association *with discernment, dignity and patriotism*, and use this capital to modernize its plants. . . .

Agrarian redistribution has not ended. I reaffirm my solemn commitment: I will not rest a single day of my administration from the task of promoting the betterment of the farmers and the improvement of our rural areas. . . . We shall strengthen the *ejido* to transform it into an active component of democracy and make it highly productive. . . . of technology, we shall force farming out of its traditional immobility. . . .

We shall strengthen our ties of cooperation and brotherhood with the nations of the *Indian–Latin community of the American continent.* . . . A new era, more aggressive and mature at the same time, is beginning for our nations. This is evident in the identity of purpose with which we act and in the dynamic drive to transform anachronistic structures within our countries and in our foreign relations. . . .

The path a country chooses to follow is worthy of respect. *Our own Revolution was not imported nor have we tried to export it.* Countries that seek to impose their solutions on others violate the basic principles of the international community. . . .

I believe in *the doctrine of the Mexican Revolution,* and I have been trained in the discipline of public office. . . . The Mexican people were never daunted by the grave challenges of history. On this day, I call upon them to reaffirm the staunchness of their principles and to live to the full the rich philosophy of the Constitution of 1917.[1] (Italics added.)

c) Democratic Socialism. Despite several respects in which the "APRA-style" parties can be said to resemble European social-democratic movements, very few significant examples of what may be thought of as "pure" democratic socialist tendencies can be found in modern Latin America. Quite a number of political parties expressing these tendencies have been founded in the region from time to time, but, almost without exception, they have never succeeded in establishing themselves as serious political forces. It is more for the purposes of record than for any other reason that I mention, at this point, the distinguished Socialist Party of Argentina.[2] It was born in the mid-1890s, more or less at the same time as the Argentine Radical Party, but it at no time came within striking distance of winning power, it failed to mount an effective challenge to the Radicals, and its greatest successes were already in the past by the time Perón took over the destinies of the Argentine nation. Strongly opposed to Peronism, it nonetheless survived into the 1950s and 1960s though only as a shadow of its former self.

The Argentine Socialist Party combined a strong belief in socialism with an equally firm attachment to political democracy. Its leaders—Juan Bautista Justo, Alfredo Palacios,[3] Nicolás Repetto, and others—were strongly influenced by the revisionist currents of Marxism then flowing in Europe and by the example of the powerful Social-Democratic Party of Germany. The Bolshevik revolution in Russia confronted the party with the kind of dilemma then common in socialist circles in Europe; the majority of Argentine socialists rejected Bolshevism as fanatical and undemocratic. Twenty years later, the rise of Perón provoked similar hostility from the Socialist Party, which regarded him

[1] Translation from *Mexico 1970–1976. Presidential Inauguration* (Mexico Business Council pamphlet), pp. 6–23.

[2] It may seem odd that I do not include the powerful Chilean Socialist Party in this category. The difficulty with the Chilean Socialists is that while many of them could certainly claim to be included as individuals, the party as a whole, to judge from its recent programs, has now adopted a much more revolutionary line than in the past. The appointment in 1971 of Senator Carlos Altamirano as secretary of the party would seem to confirm this trend: he is a noted advocate of the "guerrilla way."

[3] Whom John Gunther in 1941 called "probably the single most vivid personality in Argentine political life": *Inside Latin America* (London, 1942), p. 226.

355

as self-evidently fascist. In a book published in 1950, the socialist leader Américo Ghioldi wrote: "The true conflict of our age is between democracy and totalitarianism. . . . Socialism will be democratic and liberal or it will not be anything."[1]

d) Christian Democracy. All the democratic reforming movements mentioned so far have been clearly *secular* in outlook. It was perhaps inevitable that in an essentially Catholic region such as Latin America, social reform movements with a distinctively Catholic or "social-Christian" coloring should eventually arise. Christian Democratic parties of varying sizes were to be found nearly everywhere in Latin America by the 1960s. In Chile in 1964 and in Venezuela in 1968 Christian Democrat presidents—Eduardo Frei and Rafael Caldera—were elected to power, in the Chilean case with an overwhelming mandate. A popular jingle heard at Christian Democrat rallies in the early 1960s.

> *Con Frei, Cornejo y Caldera*
> *Está la América entera,*[2]

> The whole of Latin America
> Is with Frei, Cornejo and Caldera.

indicated that the movement believed itself to be on the brink of great successes. But despite the Chilean and Venezuelan cases, most Christian Democrat parties by the end of the decade were still very small and weak.[3]

The position which the various Christian Democrat parties occupy in the political spectrum tends to alter according to the country. The Venezuelan party, COPEI, is generally admitted to be somewhat to the right of the Chilean party. The intellectual roots of Christian Democracy—and I am referring especially to the Chilean variety—are to be found in the great papal encyclicals dealing with social and economic questions, Leo XIII's *Rerum novarum* (1891) and Pius XI's *Quadragesimo anno* (1931) in particular, and in the ideas of a number of outstanding modern Catholic thinkers, the most notable of whom was the late Jacques Maritain. A deep opposition to what are considered the "dehumanizing" features of capitalism has long characterized Christian Democrat philosophy. Capitalism, which (according to this view) denies Christian brotherhood and exalts the profit motive, should be replaced —Christian Democrats believe—by a more humane system of social

[1] Quoted in George I. Blanksten, *Peron's Argentina* (Chicago, 1953), p. 383.

[2] Héctor Cornejo Chávez is a prominent Peruvian Christian Democrat.

[3] At the start of the 1970s the Venezuelan COPEI leads the government coalition in Venezuela; elsewhere the best prospects for Christian Democracy seem to be in Guatemala and El Salvador.

and economic organization, to which the label "communitarianism" is sometimes attached. The intellectual debates which occurred during the period 1964–70, when the Christian Democrats were in power, showed serious differences of opinion within the party as to the nature of "communitarianism." Those on the left tended to regard it as a democratic variety of socialism, while the right-wingers advocated what seemed in essence to be a much-reformed capitalism with a strong element of worker participation in the management of enterprises.[1] For most Christian Democrats, however, a communitarian society probably represents a "third way" of development, excelling and surpassing both capitalism and socialism.

Together with their profound belief in social reform, Christian Democrats have remained passionately attached to pluralism (a favorite word of theirs) and political democracy. It was a basic concern of the Frei administration in Chile to stimulate popular participation and the formation of new and active pressure groups. An insight into Frei's thinking on this question can be derived from an interview he gave two days after his election in 1964:

It will clearly be very difficult to stimulate the creation of an organic popular basis for our democracy without the active participation of the state. In Chile there does not exist a vigorous basic structure. Consequently, for the first stage at least, the state must give an impetus to this vast movement whose goal is to make the country democratic. Given this end, the best conditions of development are those of an interplay of tension and collaboration between the state and the pressure groups. On the one hand, the state will foster the consolidation of these groups; on the other hand, they will be given legal status so that they can come to have an existence of their own, independent of the state's direct intervention. Our conception of social democracy tends to make the higher organisms of the state a product of the basic popular organizations. What is essential in this policy is to avoid the formation of paternalist or *étatiste* structures.[2]

How far the Christian Democrat government between 1964 and 1970 succeeded in avoiding "paternalist" approaches is a matter of dispute; what cannot be disputed is that it *did* tackle the problem in a way which no Chilean government had done before.

[1] See Paul E. Sigmund, ed., *Models of Political Change in Latin America* (New York, 1970), pp. 310–15.
[2] Luis Mercier Vega, *Roads to Power in Latin America* (London, 1969), p. 159.

357

Like APRA before it, Christian Democracy in Chile (and elsewhere) has attached "particular importance" (to quote the party's 1957 declaration of principles) to the economic and political integration of Latin America. The impulse which the Frei administration gave to this idea in its foreign policy was remarkable. As an example of this emphasis on integration which also displays something of the European inspiration of the Christian Democrat attitude on this issue, I shall quote a few sentences from a speech made by Radomiro Tomic at an international Christian Democrat Conference held in Santiago, Chile, in July 1961.

Men who were Christian Democrats discovered, in this generation, in our own time, a new material and a new architecture with which to render the homage which the Christian owes to God. First it was a word. A word which shook the immobile air of two thousand years. A rather disconcerting word, enclosed by a vague and magical sense: Benelux. Later, scarcely seven years ago, it was the European Coal and Steel Community. . . . Two years ago it was the European Economic Community, the Common Market, overcoming the accumulated barriers of two thousand years of antagonism, rivalries and wars. . . . I do not know if anything deeper, purer, more beautiful in the eyes of God has been created by the human spirit in many centuries than this Coal and Steel Community, this economic union of Europe, this common European destiny after so much division, so many hatreds. These are the new Cathedrals which God demands from the reason and the heart of contemporary man! . . . These new Cathedrals are rising meter by meter beneath the skies of Europe, and tomorrow—supreme justification for Christian Democrats!— they will rise too in Latin America![1] (Italics added.)

In their fervent desire for reform, their attachment to pluralism and democracy, and their belief in integration, Latin American Christian Democrats contributed much to the political debate of the 1960s. Some kind of further role—perhaps a major one—undoubtedly awaits the movement during the rest of the 1970s.

4. REVOLUTIONARY MOVEMENTS. (a) *Fascism.* Latin American fascism, such as it was, is now mostly of historical interest; the "pure" fascist parties, such as Plinio Salgado's Integralistas in Brazil or the Chilean Nacistas declined and fell even before Mussolini and Hitler did. Neither the Integralistas nor the Nacistas ever came close to winning power, though their parades and occasional military actions enlivened (and sometimes bloodied) Brazilian and Chilean life in the 1930s. Much

[1] R. Tomic et al., *Con Los Pobres de América* (Lima, 1962), pp. 36–38.

358

more serious than either of these movements were the governments of Getúlio Vargas and Juan Domingo Perón, to which the adjective "fascist" was frequently applied at the time by those who opposed them. How fascist were they?

Vargas' 1937 coup d'état in Brazil effectively set up the outline of a totalitarian system, but it was never more than an outline. A number of what must be considered as essential fascist attributes were always missing. Vargas' own political philosophy was never very rigorously definable. It used to be said that it could be summed up in the words *Deixa como está para ver como fica* ("Leave things as they are to see how they will turn out"), hardly an attitude that would have commended itself to either Hitler or Mussolini. Furthermore, Vargas never proceeded to form a political party ready to exercise a monopoly on power; the Brazilian *Estado Novo* produced no "movement" in the Nazi or Fascist (or Communist) sense. While political opposition remained hazardous and at times downright dangerous under Vargas' rule, it can hardly be maintained that he was an inflexible or ruthless character or that the nature of his government was particularly draconian. Vargas' regime may have vaguely aspired to become fascist in some sense; it drew some of its inspiration, certainly, from the quasi-fascist authoritarianism of Dr. Salazar in Portugal; but it was in no ultimate sense a fascist regime. Vargas' extensive commercial relations with Germany and his occasionally favorable references to the Reich in speeches can best be seen as a means of winning concessions from the United States.

With Argentine Peronism we are in altogether deeper water. Corporativist ideas circulated fairly extensively in the Argentine armed forces well before Perón came on the scene. (General Uriburu, the leader of the military coup of 1930, was fascinated by the possibility of creating a corporate state in Argentina, although he was prevailed upon to abandon the scheme.) Perón himself, a rising young officer who took part in the 1930 coup, was sent to Italy as military attaché in 1938. Deeply impressed by Mussolini's brand of balcony politics and by the symptoms of national regeneration which he saw around him, the young Argentine officer returned to his country with definite notions of reproducing his Italian experiences in the River Plate, and with little doubt as to whom he should cast in the role of Duce. Soon afterward, he helped to organize a military lodge or secret society, the GOU,[1] dedicated to spreading fascist ideas in the army.

In May 1943 the GOU issued a secret manifesto, or memorandum,

[1] GOU stands for Grupo de Oficiales Unidos (United Officers' Group), whose motto was *Government, Order, Unity.*

359

which deserves to be quoted here at some length, for it displays most admirably the intellectual background to the regime of General Perón.

The era of the nation is gradually being replaced by the era of the continent and the largest and best prepared nation will rule the destiny of that continent in the new organization. *In Europe that country is Germany. . . .* In North America the United States will be the monitor nation for the time being. But in South America there has not yet emerged one nation whose superiority is so manifest that its leadership can be accepted without discussion. There are only two nations qualified for that leadership: Argentina and Brazil. OUR MISSION IS TO BRING ABOUT OUR INDISPUTABLE PREDOMINANCE. The task is immense and the sacrifices are many. But nations are formed only through total sacrifice. The great leaders of our independence sacrificed their fortunes and their lives. *In our own time, Germany has given life a heroic meaning.* These will be our examples. . . . Once we have acquired all internal power, our mission will be to be strong, stronger than all the rest of the countries combined. We must arm despite all internal or external difficulties. *Hitler's struggle in peace and war will be our guiding star.* . . . A mirage? Utopia? *Consider the case of Germany.* Defeated in war, in 1919 she was forced to sign the Treaty of Versailles, which placed her under the Allied yoke at the level of a secondary nation for at least fifty years. But in less than twenty years Germany staged a fantastic march to recovery. . . . *Our government will be an inflexible dictatorship,* though at first it will make those outward concessions which are necessary to form alliances. We must win the people to us, but they must of necessity *work, sacrifice and obey.* Only in this way will we be able to carry out the armament programme that is indispensable to *our conquest of the continent. As in Germany, we will use the radio and the schools to inculcate in the people the spirit that will impel them along the heroic road they must travel.* Only in this way will they renounce the comfortable existence they now lead. Ours will be a generation sacrificed in the name of a higher ideal: the Argentine nation, which one day will shine with unmatched brilliance to the greater good of the continent and all mankind.[1] (Italics added.)

It is perfectly clear that more than a few of the obsessions revealed in this manifesto found a place in the program of the Perón government. Perón never lost sight of the GOU's evident aspiration to lead the South American continent. By the time he fell from power in 1955, he had also gone some way in the direction of imposing totalitarian govern-

[1] Quoted in Arciniegas, *op. cit.*, pp. 52–54.

ment—although "corporativist" notions played no real part in his plans, and the prominent role given to the trade unions bore only a little resemblance to the position of these bodies in the systems established by Hitler and Mussolini. Unfortunately for Perón, the international situation very quickly rendered the fascist aspirations of his regime irrelevant. After 1945 it was no longer particularly prudent or useful to express admiration for dictators whose policies had brought such momentous disasters to their countries, and Argentina could obviously no longer be connected to an international fascist bloc. (Had Germany won the war, things would doubtless have been very different.)

But despite the disappearance of old friends, Perón undoubtedly felt that a distinctive ideology was needed for his regime, and in 1949 he discovered the concept of "Justicialism"; an imposing philosophical edifice was soon constructed around this term, though a number of malicious observers quickly decided that this was no more than opportunistic mumbo-jumbo. Justicialism, as expounded by Perón and various official philosophers, rested on the hypothesis that there were four basic forces which molded human history: materialism, idealism, individualism, and collectivism. Each of these in an extreme and unchecked form, led to tyranny. Three further forms of tyranny were produced by combinations of these forces. Materialism and collectivism generated Communism; idealism and collectivism resulted in Nazism or Fascism (no longer the *beau idéal* of Peronism); materialism and individualism, by contrast, produced capitalism. Justicialism, defined as a "third position" (though in view of the foregoing it was in fact an *eighth* position!), was brought into existence when the four basic forces were in perfect equilibrium.[1] Perón was insistent that this philosophy occupied no particular place in the political spectrum, and in fact boasted of its admirable flexibility.

It is difficult to generalize about the ways in which Peronist ideology has developed since the fall of the dictator in 1955. The movement itself is more interesting than any ideology it possesses or does not possess, as the case may be. It would certainly be absurd to regard it as "fascist" in any real sense—though it may have a few fascist overtones left—nor is there much evidence to suggest that "Justicialism" is taken particularly seriously by the bulk of the trade unionists who, in effect, *are* the Peronist movement as it is nowadays. In terms of its outlook and practical program, the majority of the movement can probably be classified as "democratic reforming": the drive toward a better deal for the working class, and a privileged position for the trade unions, the emphasis on economic independence, and the belief in an internationally

[1] Blanksten, *op. cit.*, pp. 283–90.

respected Argentina—these are the aspects of the Perón regime chiefly recalled (and recalled with pleasure) by those who call themselves *Peronistas*. But the movement remains a capacious one, and on its fringes, both to left and right, elements espousing ferocious anti-Semitism and ultra-nationalism on the one hand, and a fervent admiration for the Cuban revolution on the other, continue to add variety to the Argentine political scene.

The unexpected resurgence of Peronism in the Argentina of 1973 was the work of a Justicialist Liberation Front (FREJULI) incorporating a wide variety of opinions of the kinds just indicated. Perón himself, perhaps, was the only real unifying force behind the coalition. His views had not gained much in precision over the years. In an interview given to the Italian newspaper *La Stampa* before his return to Buenos Aires in November 1972, he seemed to be advocating a political course similar to that of the military revolution in Peru. Dr. Allende's Chile, he said, was too far to the left; the generals' Brazil was too far to the right. This statement at least had the merit of allowing the new Peronist administration a wide area for maneuver.

b) Communism. Before discussing the historical role of the Latin American Communist parties, it may perhaps be useful to say something about the considerable influence Marxism has enjoyed in the region in the twentieth century.[1] It has appeared in many different forms: as a vague propensity to think in terms of "class" or economic determinism, as a method of providing explanations (sometimes over-simplified, sometimes highly sophisticated) for Latin America's social and economic predicaments, and (particularly Marxism–Leninism) as what amounts, in effect, to a political religion guaranteeing that most precious of all human possessions, certainty. As a philosophy with which people are proud to associate themselves, it has been very widespread in intellectual circles, far more so than in comparable circles in the English-speaking world.

Over and above this, Latin American intellectuals have tended to adopt far more favorable evaluations of the ostensibly Marxist-based development of the Soviet Union than have been common in, say, Western Europe. It would probably be true to say that for a large number of Latin American intellectuals a less-than-critical approach to Soviet achievements has been widely accepted. In particular, the

[1] Marx and Engels, ironically enough, knew very little about (and were almost wholly uninterested in) Latin America, and their attitude to the region, such as it was, bore all the marks of a European superiority complex. Engels believed that the imposition of United States' tutelage over Mexico (and by implication the rest of Latin America) was highly desirable in the interests of progress: see *Marx-Engels Werke*, XXIX (Berlin, 1963), 280.

industrial base which Russia already possessed in 1917 tends to be disregarded, while information on the period of the Stalin terror, for instance, is frequently dismissed as "imperialist propaganda."

Prior to the Bolshevik revolution in 1917, Marxism as a political creed (as opposed to a philosophical tradition) was largely transmitted to Latin America in the revisionist, evolutionary shape it had acquired at the hands of the great Western European socialist parties, but its impact was not especially profound. After the creation of the Soviet state, Marxism—to be more precise Marxism–Leninism—once again acquired an overtly revolutionary flavor, and in Latin America as elsewhere, Communist parties were soon established to spread the new doctrines. In essence the newly established parties in Latin America accepted the Marxist hypothesis of the inevitable progression of history from stage to stage, adopted the distinctive Leninist belief in the necessity for a revolutionary elite or "vanguard," and looked forward to a day when a "dictatorship of the proletariat" could be established, after which the "building of socialism" and, subsequently, the "building of communism" could be undertaken under the leadership of the Communist parties.

Almost from the first, Latin American Communist parties were affiliated to the Third (Communist) International, or Comintern; some eight parties from the region were represented at the Sixth Congress of this body in 1928. Communist tactics at this period—and, indeed, afterward—were largely dictated by what was thought appropriate in the U.S.S.R. Until the mid-1930s, most parties followed a very intransigent line, rejecting alliances with other political forces and generally attempting to lay the groundwork for an eventual seizure of power. This early period saw the only two armed Communist insurrections in recent Latin American history. In 1932 the Communist movement in El Salvador succeeded in organizing a peasant-based revolt against the dictatorship of General Maximiliano Hernández Martínez;[1] it was crushed with considerable ferocity by the dictator. Three years later the Brazilian Communists, under Luis Carlos Prestes, rose in revolt against Getúlio Vargas; they were defeated, although not as bloodily as in El Salvador.

From the mid-1930s, with the growing menace of Nazism in Europe, Communist parties switched to a policy of collaboration with other left-wing forces and, if necessary, with movements they regarded as "bourgeois." Only in Chile did this new tactic pay off, with the election to power in 1938 of the Radical-dominated and Communist-backed

[1] Dictator from 1931 to 1944; a vegetarian interested in theosophy and the occult. About ten thousand people were killed during the repression of the revolt.

Popular Front, although the Communist Party itself declined to participate in the government. In 1946, with the election of the Radical president Gabriel González Videla, the Communists accepted three places in the cabinet,[1] but González Videla's subsequent break with the party brought this happy association to an abrupt end. The "cold war" period after 1945 brought lean years to several Communist parties; some were illegalized. In Guatemala, where Communist influence rose steadily during the Arévalo and Arbenz governments, the CIA-backed rebellion of Castillo Armas brought a further sharp setback. In most of the twenty republics, Communist parties remained small, weak, and inclined to cliquishness, although these disadvantages were to some extent offset by their undoubted capacity for organization and hard work. Only in Chile did the party regularly obtain more than ten percent of the popular vote in elections during the 1960s.

The situation for Latin American Communists was complicated in no small degree by the emergence, after 1960 or so, of rival revolutionary movements on the extreme left. The Sino-Soviet quarrel, for instance, had discernible repercussions in Latin America, with the defection of a number of militants and the formation of pro-Chinese Communist parties in several republics. A more serious problem was created by the development of the Cuban revolution. Dr. Fidel Castro, as we have seen, turned to the Cuban Communist Party for help in administering his social revolution but, in doing so, effectively transformed the party into his own personal instrument.[2] Furthermore, Dr. Castro's advocacy of immediate, violent revolution throughout the Western hemisphere sharply conflicted with the official position which the Soviet Union now adhered to on these matters and with the line taken by most Communist parties on the Latin American mainland. To many Communists, conscious of the difficulties of assessing whether their countries were in a "revolutionary situation" or not, Dr. Castro's views smacked of what Lenin had once described as the "infantile disease" of uncontrolled left-wing revolutioneering.

The relations between Dr. Castro and the Latin American Communist parties during the 1960s were generally fairly cordial and correct

[1] It was the second time this had occurred in Latin America; Communist ministers had been present in the Cuban cabinet during the government of President Fulgencio Batista (1940–44).

[2] Dr. Castro successfully challenged the "old guard" Cuban Communists in 1962, when he denounced their "sectarianism." The party itself was fused with other organizations, an amalgam which in 1965 became the "new" Cuban Communist Party. In 1968 a further "old guard" conspiracy, headed by a "microfaction" which sought Russian support against Dr. Castro, was nipped in the bud. The leader of the "microfaction," Anibal Escalante, who had been the chief victim of Dr. Castro's 1962 denunciations, was sentenced to fifteen years in prison.

—with one or two exceptions—but the militantly pro-Cuban revolutionary movements that now began to spring up felt themselves under no particular obligation to be polite to the Communists (or, indeed, to anyone else). The Communist parties now found themselves under attack from groups which claimed to be further to the left and more revolutionary; in reply, they stigmatized such groups as "bourgeois" and "adventurist." The main point at issue between the Communist parties and these "New Left" movements during the 1960s was a tactical one rather than anything else. Should true revolutionaries take to the hills or the streets or the jungles or the shanty-towns and thus try to *induce* a "revolutionary situation," or should they patiently organize, consolidate an appropriate working-class or trade-union base, collaborate where necessary with like-minded political forces, and use nonviolent, constitutional methods of winning power? The "New Left" sympathized with the first notion, the Communists with the second. In Chile, where the Communist Party had traditionally been strong for many years, the victory of Dr. Allende's coalition in 1970 seemed to indicate that the Communist strategy was a sound one, and that power *could* actually be won through the much-despised framework of bourgeois legality. But Chile, it could plausibly be argued, was rather a special case. The debate continues.

Since it seems likely that the various Latin American Communist parties pay some attention to Soviet ideas on the development of the Third World, it may be useful to give some indication as to what these are. The fundamental Russian assumption of recent years is that a "noncapitalist road to development" can enable an underdeveloped country to bypass the "capitalist stage" of history, although it is impossible for the "socialist stage" to be reached immediately. The first step on this "noncapitalist road" is to establish a "national democracy" based on an alliance of social classes which, while it will certainly contain the proletariat, may well include elements of the bourgeoisie and "progressive" army officers. There should be no drastic rupture of relations with the United States or other Western countries, but national policy should certainly be redirected toward "anti-imperialism." Among specific measures which a "national democratic" regime should undertake are an agrarian reform, the consolidation of a strong public sector in the economy, control of the mass media so as to educate the mass of the people, the diffusion of the ideas of "scientific socialism" (i.e., Marxism–Leninism), and the building up of a "vanguard party" capable, eventually, of taking over and leading the nation concerned toward the goal of socialism.

In practice, even when the terminology used is somewhat different, most Latin American Communist parties look to this particular scheme or something rather like it as a guide to future action. The program on which Dr. Allende was elected to power in Chile in 1970 shows interesting similarities of approach.

c) *"New Left" Movements*. "Castroist," "Guevarist," "ultra-revolutionary"—these adjectives, and many more, some of them far from complimentary, have been applied to the cluster of revolutionary movements and organizations which arose in Latin America following the triumph of, and inspired by, the Cuban revolution. They can best be referred to, I think, as "New Left" movements,[1] for they invoke the Marxist–Leninist tradition, which places them on the extreme left of the political spectrum, and some of their emphases *are* clearly new. The main features of these movements have been: an uncompromisingly black-and-white vision of contemporary history, a strong emphasis on "the armed struggle" as the main means of winning power, and a relative indifference to organized or established Communist parties as the "vanguard" of the revolution. The "New Left" has revived the time-honored Latin American tradition of guerrilla warfare, and by his death in Bolivia in 1967, Ernesto "Che" Guevara became its supreme martyr as well as its supreme hero and mentor.

Perhaps the best summary of the "New Left" interpretation of contemporary history is to be found in the Second Declaration of Havana, issued in February 1962. This presented a somewhat simplified Marxist picture of Latin America (and indeed world) history and called for a vast "anti-feudal" and "anti-imperialist" struggle based on a peasantry mobilized by "the workers and revolutionary intellectuals" of the region. "Sectarianism" and "dogmatism" (i.e., the attitudes of the orthodox Communist parties) were condemned as impediments to the formation of broad movements embracing everyone from "the old militant Marxist to the sincere Catholic who has no love for the Yankee monopolies and the feudal landowners." American imperialism was identified as the enemy; by defeating it, Latin American revolutionaries would "perform an even greater service for humanity" than did the insurgents of the early nineteenth century in defeating Spain. The Declaration stated a theme which quickly became the leitmotif of "New Left" pronouncements in the 1960s: *"The duty of every revolutionary is to make the revolution."*

---

[1] I place quotation marks around the term "New Left," not because I wish to cast doubts on the seriousness of the movements concerned, but because it is not, at the present time, the sort of expression which has acquired that relative durability which historians tend to think of as "permanence." In ten years' time it may be possible to discard the quotation marks, though by that stage the adjective "new" will have to be called in question.

The exhortation was taken literally. All over Latin America, small groups of genuine or would-be revolutionaries banded together in movements with a bewildering variety of names—though "National Liberation" or "Revolutionary Left" were fairly standard ingredients. Mesmerized by the Cuban example, they quickly established "guerrilla fronts" in rural areas of several republics, most notably Venezuela, Colombia, Guatemala, and Peru. Nowhere did this tactic succeed in bringing down a government, and the failure in 1967 of the Bolivian campaign headed by no less a person than Che Guevara prompted widespread heart-searchings and a reassessment of the position of the countryside and the peasantry as the focal points of guerrilla strategy. After 1967 new attention was paid to the possibilities of revolutionary action in the cities; "Urban guerrilla" movements began to appear in several countries; and the more audacious exploits of such movements quickly caught the attention of the world's press. In Uruguay the imaginatively led *Tupamaro* group seriously exacerbated an already difficult political situation; elsewhere, urban guerrilla activities were at the very least an embarrassment to several governments.[1]

As far as aims are concerned, most "New Left" movements would probably concur with the Uruguayan Tupamaros, who issued a "program of government" in March 1971. It contained six main points: (1) expropriation of big estates and ranches; (2) nationalization of all large factories; (3) state control and operation of foreign trade; (4) state control of banking and credit; (5) expropriation without compensation of all foreign-owned industries, banks, etc., (6) confiscation of luxury houses for use as cultural centers.[2] The "New Left" is discernibly less reverent toward the Soviet Union than are the orthodox Communist parties, and Cuban ideas of "moral incentives" and the creation of the "new man" play an important part in its vision of the postrevolutionary future. A somewhat vague approach to the specific institutional arrangements that may be expected in a country ruled by the "New Left" is probably derived, at any rate in part, from the belief that hard-and-fast

[1] Some of the more notable achievements of these movements can be mentioned here. In August 1970 the Tupamaros captured and killed an American adviser to the Uruguayan police; in January 1971 they kidnapped the British ambassador, Mr. Geoffrey Jackson. In 1969 the American ambassador to Brazil was kidnapped and later exchanged for a number of imprisoned revolutionaries—a tactic used with other diplomats elsewhere. In Argentina, "revolutionary Peronists" kidnapped and killed the former president, General Pedro Aramburu (July 1970). Guatemalan urban guerrillas killed the American ambassador (1968) and the West German ambassador (1970). One of the main "theorists" of urban guerrilla action was the Brazilian Carlos Marighella, whose *Minimanual of the Urban Guerrilla* contains a series of coldblooded practical recommendations. Marighella himself was ambushed and shot by the Brazilian police in 1969.

[2] *Síntesis Latinoamericana*, No. 79, March 25, 1971.

institutions can get in the way of the authentic freedom to which, it is confidently supposed, the revolution will eventually lead. Che Guevara's comment on the relative lack of conventional institutions in the new Cuba should perhaps be remembered here:

> We are seeking something new that will allow *a perfect identification between the government and the community as a whole,* adapted to the special conditions of the building of socialism, and avoiding to the utmost the *commonplaces of bourgeois democracy* (such as legislative houses, for example). . . . We have been greatly restrained by the fear that any formal aspect might make us lose sight of *the ultimate and most important revolutionary aspiration:* to see man freed from alienation.[1] (Italics added.)

The idea of a perfect identification between government and community can be traced back, perhaps, to the concept of popular sovereignty as crystallized in the French revolution.[2] The emphasis on freedom from "alienation," however, places Guevara in a more contemporary tradition, one which derives from the "rediscovery" of the early writings of Marx.

The Latin American "New Left" is peculiarly insistent that violence is inevitable and necessary in the pursuit of power. Guevara himself, it will be recalled, viewed the creation of "two, three or many Vietnams" as something to be looked forward to in the struggle against imperialism; at the time of the Cuban missile crisis of 1962 he evidently wrote "we must proceed along the path of liberation even if this costs millions of atomic victims."[3] Critics of the "New Left" accuse the movement of glorifying violence. If this is true it certainly differentiates this particular current of opinion from classical Marxism, and even from the Marxism–Leninism of the Communist parties—where violence is never ruled out but *is* regarded as at best a somewhat regrettable necessity, as the "midwife of history."

A further characteristic of the "New Left" is its relative indifference to established or organized Communist parties as the "vanguard" of the revolution. Whoever makes the revolution automatically *becomes* the vanguard: this is the standard doctrine, and a doctrine blessed on many occasions by Dr. Castro. It is clear that this vanguard is obliged to

[1] "Man and Socialism in Cuba," in John Gerassi, ed., *Venceremos! The Speeches and Writings of Ernesto Che Guevara* (London, Panther Books, 1969), p. 544.

[2] It is difficult to see what connection this idea has with any specifically *Marxist* tradition. Hitler and Mussolini, to name but two modern dictators, would have been happy to subscribe to it.

[3] Quoted in Hugh Thomas, *Cuba, or the Pursuit of Freedom* (London, 1971), p. 1417.

occupy the key position in the postrevolutionary order. It will inevitably have to take dictatorial powers in order to refashion the social and economic systems. As Guevara put it,

> The vanguard group is ideologically more advanced than the mass; the latter is acquainted with the new values, but insufficiently. While in the former a qualitative change takes place which permits them to make sacrifices as a function of their vanguard character, the latter see only by halves and must be subjected to incentives and pressures of some intensity; it is the dictatorship of the proletariat being exercised not only upon the defeated class but also individually upon the victorious class.[1]

Some Latin Americans in the 1960s argued that the various movements of the "New Left" were very small and that although their nuisance value might be considerable they nonetheless lacked real political weight. There is some truth in this. The nucleus of each of these movements in the 1960s consisted essentially of "intellectuals, professional people and students"[2] and it was by no means clear whether they always bore in mind Lenin's famous dictum that serious politics begin "not where there are thousands, but where there are millions."[3] Nevertheless, great things sometimes spring from very small beginnings. Until 1917 Lenin's Bolsheviks were an insignificant minority in the life of the Russian empire, a minority even among reforming and revolutionary groups. In the 1920s Hitler's National Socialists could safely be dismissed as an unimportant nuisance in German politics. The "New Left" in Latin America has shown itself capable of a fair degree of self-discipline and occasional ruthlessness, and these qualities would—if history is a reliable guide—serve it well if circumstances brought the millions, as opposed to the thousands, onto its side.

d) Catholic Revolutionism. Closely associated with the "New Left"— indeed, in some respects part of it—are a number of distinctively Catholic revolutionary movements in which members of both clergy and laity play a part. They criticize Christian Democrat or "social-Christian" movements rather in the way "New Left" movements criticize the orthodox Communist parties. The roots of Catholic revolutionism are to be found in the intellectual ferment in the Catholic

---

[1] "Man and Socialism in Cuba," *loc. cit.*, pp. 543-44. Gerassi describes this essay as "One of the great documents of the history of socialism" (*ibid.*, p. 13). One wonders what Marx or Engels would have made of this.

[2] Luis Mercier Vega, *Guerrillas in Latin America: The Technique of the Counter-State* (London, 1969), p. 68.

[3] V. I. Lenin, *Selected Works*, VII (London, 1937), p. 295. Lenin made the observation in 1918.

Church which accompanied and followed the Second Vatican Council. Many Catholics in Latin America, as elsewhere, came to believe that the "post-Conciliar" Church should re-examine its social and economic attitudes fairly radically. In 1968 the Second Episcopal Assembly of the Church in Latin America, held at Medellín, Colombia, gave a decisive impulse to currents of Catholic opinion which favored drastic social reform. The Assembly's opening session was held in the presence of Pope Paul VI, then on a flying visit to Colombia. Among other things, the Medellín conference applied the expression "institutionalized violence" to the economic and social injustices prevailing in Latin America, and accepted that the Church was required to fulfil a "creative task in the process of development."

During the 1960s several prominent Latin American churchmen publicized the plight of the poor and advocated radical cures for the social infirmities of the region. Of these churchmen none was more notable than Dom Helder Câmara, Archbishop of Recife, a fierce opponent of the military regimes in Brazil after 1964. (The Pope is once believed to have referred to Dom Helder as "my Communist arch-bishop.") While personally repudiating violence as an appropriate political tactic, Dom Helder nevertheless indicated a certain sympathy for those who felt obliged to resort to it.

Pope Paul VI's encyclical *Populorum progressio* (1967) affirmed by implication the right of rebellion against "manifest, long-standing tyranny." Some priests went a good deal further than this in the later 1960s, and proclaimed what amounted to a generalized right of revolution. A few, renouncing the cloth, had already joined guerrilla movements of the "New Left." Perhaps the most famous of these was the Colombian priest, Camilo Torres, a man of upper-class extraction who was killed by Colombian counterinsurgency forces in February 1966. Torres explained his adherence to a revolutionary political position in a "Message to Christians" which he issued in August 1965. He wrote:

It is necessary to take power away from the privileged minorities in order to give it to the poor majorities. This, if done rapidly, is the essence of a revolution. The Revolution can be peaceful if the minorities do not violently resist. . . . *The Revolution is not only permissible but obligatory for Christians who see in it the only efficacious way of realizing love toward all men.*[1] (Italics added.)

For Catholic revolutionaries, Torres' name is venerated in the way Guevara's is by the "New Left." Various movements have, in fact, been named after him, and his stock stands high in Havana.

[1] Camilo Torres, *Liberación o muerte* (Havana, 1967), pp. 37–38.

It is perhaps important to distinguish here between revolutionary movements which (in part, at least) aspire to renovate the Church in the "post-Conciliar" era, and movements composed of Catholic members who work entirely "in the world," outside the Church. Of the latter, the "Golconda" group can be taken as reasonably representative.[1] It originated in 1969, and its "Buenaventura Manifesto," signed by (among others) the local bishop, declared the movement to be in favor of "a socialist type of society," affirmed a commitment to "the various forms of revolutionary action against imperialism," and stated as an aim "the displacement of the governing classes." The Catholic revolutionaries' vision of contemporary history is in many respects indistinguishable from that of the "New Left," and although they reject the "cosmic vision" implied in Marxism, they nonetheless tend to look upon Marxism as a useful "theory" of political action. They probably place somewhat greater emphasis than the "New Left" on the political education—usually called *concientización* ("consciencization")—of the poor. It is conceivable that in this respect they are closer to the example of nineteenth-century Russian Narodniks than other Latin American revolutionaries; and, if they are priests, their practical experience with ordinary folk may well make them more aware of everyday realities.

Some observers have seen in Catholic political movements, whether democratic or revolutionary, a sinister "neo-clerical" design to maintain and perpetuate the hold traditionally enjoyed by the Catholic Church over the peoples of Latin America. Others have seen in the insistence of certain revolutionary clerics that capitalism is a sin—an assertion which, in the Latin American context, begs far too many questions for it to be taken seriously—a reversion to the medieval European attitude toward economic activity. Still others regard the emergence of these movements as the first real sign that the Church is beginning to abandon her traditional alliance with governments and privileged classes, an alliance which began more than sixteen centuries ago with Emperor Constantine. Up to the present, Catholic revolutionary movements have been supported by only a small minority of priests and laymen. They have been outnumbered by Catholic reforming movements with more modest aims in view, and these in their turn have probably been far outnumbered by Catholics of a much more traditional and conservative cast of mind. Several Latin American hierarchies have adopted a hard line in relation to Catholic revolutionism.

The turbulent priest is by no means the least interesting of the new actors who have taken their place on the stage of Latin American history.

[1] The name was taken from the place where, in August 1969, some sixty priests met to elaborate a common revolutionary attitude.

Chapter 7

LATIN AMERICA, THE WEST,
AND THE WORLD

*Most sovereign Lord: the greatest thing since the creation of the world,
with the exception of the incarnation and death of Him who created it,
is the discovery of the Indies.*

FRANCISCO LÓPEZ DE GOMARA (1552)

The freedom of the New World is the hope of the earth.

SIMÓN BOLÍVAR (1824)

*America is therefore the land of the future, where, in the ages that lie
before us, the burden of the World's History shall reveal itself—perhaps
in a contest between North and South America. . . . It is for America to
abandon the ground on which hitherto the History of the World has
developed itself.*

GEORG WILHELM FRIEDRICH HEGEL (1830)

*I believe that there are sufficient valid reasons for being dissatisfied with
the terms in which the relations between Latin America, the United States
of America and other great powers have developed. This is not only due
to others; to a very decisive extent the responsibility for these terms lies
with us, because we have failed to define, state and defend our principles
and rights with clarity, force and in a united manner.*

PRESIDENT EDUARDO FREI OF CHILE (1969)

What, so far, has been the place of Latin America in world history?
What have been the main relationships which Latin America has
enjoyed (or endured) with other parts of the globe? In seeking to
examine these questions, I must remind the reader of one underlying
fact. Latin America was the first, and for that reason remains the oldest,

of the permanent offshoots of Western European civilization. The "planetary rhythm" to human history mentioned in the first paragraph of this book was largely set in motion by the maritime nations of Western Europe's seaboard. Between 1450 and, say, 1940, a handful of these nations effectively seized control of much, indeed the greater part, of the planet. In Asia and Africa, the local populations eventually repulsed the foreigner, sometimes bloodily, sometimes with the foreigner's own consent. His viceroys and armies withdrew. What has been described as the "era of Vasco da Gama" in world history came to an abrupt end. In the American continent the story was different. At a somewhat earlier period, Western Europeans there were repulsed by other Western Europeans who had become natives of the continent which they themselves, or at any rate their forefathers, had previously invaded. In contrast to what occurred in Asia and Africa, Western man left permanent offshoots of his civilization in the New World, and these offshoots remain: the extraordinary civilization of North America, and the equally distinctive "Latin" civilization of the Caribbean and South America.

For about nineteen twentieths of the period indicated, Latin America's most important relationships with the rest of the world have undoubtedly been with Western Europe or with its own companion-offshoot to the north. In the new system of international politics that began to take shape after 1945, it was no longer certain that this would always remain the case. The 1960s saw the unprecedented spectacle of a Latin American republic, Cuba, developing intimate and tenacious links with one of the new, non-Western centers of power in the modern world: Soviet Russia. As shall be suggested toward the end of this short chapter, other possible relationships between Latin America and non-Western powers may well grow up in the future. It would be arrogant for a European to suggest that there is anything irregular or undesirable in this. Whatever happens, however, it is clear that most of Latin American history so far *has* taken place in an "Atlantic" or Western framework, and that future developments can hardly alter the fundamentally Western character of the region. The Latin American countries are—as we have seen—very different in many respects from either Western Europe or North America, and have had a very different history; but they are in the family.

The Colonial Period

In the extraordinary European expansion that began in the mid-fifteenth century, Mexico, the Caribbean islands, and South America were the first areas to bear the full brunt of conquest and colonization.

A Pan American Airways advertisement in 1966 referred to South America as "the last of the unspoiled continents" of the world. How peculiarly ironic! In simple fact, it was the first continent to be spoiled, or at any rate *de*spoiled, by Western European man. The process was, as has been repeatedly stressed in previous chapters, a singularly cruel one. It raised moral questions of the most profound importance—not least to some of the Spaniards who observed at first hand the atrocities that accompanied the subjection of the Amerindian population. Nevertheless, the outcome was clear. Spain and Portugal were not dislodged by the indigenous inhabitants of the continent. They imposed their religion, their language, and many aspects of their culture; and the civilization of the Iberian peninsula took root amid the remote and exotic surroundings of America.

The conquest of America, followed soon afterward by the union of the two Iberian empires, brought the Spanish monarchy to its highest peak of greatness. To Tommaso Campanella, as to others, this seemed to be the visible fulfilment of a vast and inevitable scheme of history, for had not the course of empire always moved westwards?

> The Universal Monarchy of the World, beginning from the East and so coming at length to the West, having passed through the hands of the Assyrians, Medes, Persians, Greeks and Romans (who were divided by the Imperial Eagle into Three Heads), is at length come down to the Spaniards, upon whom, after so long Slavery, and Division, it is wholly conferred by Fate: and that with greater splendour than on any of his Predecessors.[1]

There must have been many Spaniards, particularly Castilians, who felt something like this about their immensely powerful monarchy. Philip II, like Charles V before him, was unquestionably the most awesome potentate in Europe. There seemed little that Spain could not do, no part of the world which could escape from her influence. And yet the dream of universal empire failed, and failed more rapidly than Campanella could have foreseen. Throughout the unhappy seventeenth century Spain and Portugal declined; their economies languished; their armies met with defeat. By 1700 the Iberian peninsula was no longer the dynamic force in European politics it had so recently been. At the time of the Treaty of Utrecht, to use the sobering phrase of J. H. Parry, Spain "appeared to retain its American empire through the forbearance of the rest of Europe."[2]

---

[1] T. Campanella, *A Discourse Touching the Spanish Monarchy* (London, 1654), preface.

[2] J. H. Parry, *The Spanish Seaborne Empire* (London, 1966), p. 292.

Yet both Spain and Portugal and their overseas empires survived. In the Spanish case, as we have seen, the Bourbon dynasty attempted, not altogether without success, to refashion the empire and its organization. The attempt failed—partly because the central initiative required was not forthcoming from the supine Charles IV, and partly because, by the end of the eighteenth century, a wave of international revolution was breaking on both sides of the Atlantic. Quite unintentionally, Napoleon Bonaparte succeeded in accomplishing what generations of rapacious foreign marauders had signally failed to accomplish: the dismemberment of the Iberian empires. It was, perhaps, his single most permanent achievement.

It is in the nature of colonies to be dependent, politically and economically, on their metropolis. Colonial Latin America was no exception. The region's connection with the Iberian peninsula was not questioned until the very end of colonial times. Loyalty to a transatlantic monarch seemed, to the overwhelming majority of Latin Americans who thought about such things at all, to be part of the natural order of things. The Creole aristocrats of Mexico or Peru might occasionally feel disgruntled at the commercial predominance of the merchant oligarchy of Andalusia; but it did not occur to them to doubt the need for both monarchy and empire. The American colonies grew up in splendid isolation from all parts of the world except the Iberian peninsula. The fierce Catholicism espoused by the Iberian monarchies inculcated the view that contact with the outside world was dangerous from the viewpoint of morality and faith. Dependence and isolation, then, were the key features of colonial Latin America's place in the world.

In any empire, however, tensions inevitably arise between the metropolis and the colonies, and these tensions are generally exacerbated when great expanses of ocean separate the component parts of the empire in question.[1] It can hardly be denied that the Spanish and Portuguese record in containing such tensions was a very successful one, but they were bound, perhaps inevitably, to rise to the surface more frequently with the passing of the years. The American populations, especially the Creole populations, gradually became aware of their distinctiveness. As mentioned in Chapter 3, the familiar regional rivalries of peninsular Spain were transmitted intact to the New World, and were, in the course of time, eclipsed by a newer pattern of regionalisms based on the attachment which the Creoles came to feel for their own particular provinces. In the eighteenth century, in the brief era

---

[1] Empires whose provinces are geographically contiguous, e.g., Rome or Russia, seem to have an easier time in this respect.

of enlightened despotism, a number of intelligent and well-read Creoles developed markedly optimistic evaluations of their own ability and of the economic potential of their provinces. Several literary works composed at that period reveal a growing delight in the specifically local and American features of colonial life.

This mounting Creole admiration for America as opposed to the Iberian peninsula was reinforced by several factors. The decline of Spain and Portugal was apparent to many Creole visitors to those countries. But the colonies themselves were by no means in a state of decline. Business had never been better than it was in the later eighteenth century. Might it not be possible that Spain and Portugal needed the colonies more than the colonies needed Spain and Portugal? A few Creoles, at least, had read Montesquieu: "The Indies and Spain are two powers under the same master; but the Indies are the principal power, and Spain is no more than the accessory. It is a vain policy to wish to bring the principal power to the accessory; the Indies will always draw Spain to themselves."[1] The example of the American revolution proved that it was possible for colonies to rule themselves. But, as we have seen, it took something more than mere example to persuade the Creoles to become revolutionaries.

This is not the place to sketch the impact of colonial Latin America on the intellectual history of Europe; but the region was certainly a source of considerable fascination to scores of "enlightened writers." Some of these—Jan Cornelius de Pauw for instance—aroused Creole hostility with their theories of the inherent inferiority of American man, while others contemplated the New World through decidedly rose-colored spectacles and discovered noble savages, virtuous and courageous Indians, and even exemplary Creoles. *"L'Américain, farouche en sa simplicité,/Nous égale en courage, et nous passe en bonté,"* says one of the characters in Voltaire's "Peruvian" drama, *Alzire*. ("The American, fierce in his simplicity,/Equals us in courage, and surpasses us in goodness.")

In general, European writers found what they wanted to find in America, and since most of them never went there this was relatively easy to do. (This tendency can still be found among Western European intellectuals today.) One or two of them looked to the Creoles as potential agents of a regeneration of the human race. Abbé Raynal gave voice to this feeling in a well-known (and far-fetched) speculation:

But if they [the Creoles] once ceased to have negroes for slaves, and kings who live at a distance from them for masters, they, perhaps,

[1] *De l'Esprit des Lois*, Book XXI, Chap. 22.

would become the most astonishing people that ever appeared on earth. The spirit of liberty which they would imbibe from their earliest infancy, the understanding and abilities which they would inherit from Europe; the activity, which the necessity of repelling numerous enemies would inspire; the large colonies they would have to form; the rich commerce they would have to found on an immense cultivation; the ranks and societies they would have to create; and the maxims, laws and manners they would have to establish on the principles of reason: all these springs of action would, perhaps, make of an equivocal and miscellaneous people the most flourishing nation that philosophy and humanity could wish for the happiness of the world. If ever any fortunate revolution should take place in the world, it will begin in America. After having experienced such devastation, this new world must flourish in its turn, and, perhaps, command the old.[1]

It is not surprising that Raynal's book was banned in the Spanish dominions. Those few Creoles who managed to read it were no doubt flattered by his estimate of their role in future events, an estimate which may well have contributed something to the optimistic mood in which the new Latin American governments of the early nineteenth century tackled the task of nation-building.

To describe Latin America's role in world affairs in colonial times as purely passive would be a grievous misunderstanding of the real situation. The region was certainly dependent on the Iberian peninsula, and effectively isolated from other parts of the world. Nevertheless, its gold and silver and commerce had an active impact on the growth of the economy of the Old World; and, as we have just seen, its very existence became a source of intellectual speculation, of poetry and drama in eighteenth-century Europe. There *was* an important sense, however, in which Latin Americans (as distinct from Latin America) could play no real part whatever in relation to the outside world: as long as they remained part of an empire, their foreign relations were inevitably decided for them in Madrid or Lisbon. To acquire a political personality of their own, and the means to mold their own economic future, Latin Americans needed independence. Only then could the region be said to have stepped onto the stage of history as an actor in its own right. Its initial entrance, in fact, was somewhat timid and rather confused.

[1] G. T. Raynal, *A Philosophical and Political History of the Settlements and Trade of the Europeans in the East and West Indies*, trans. J. Justamond, 4 vols. (London, 1776), III, 197.

Independence and Balkanization

The term "balkanization" may seem a trifle inappropriate, since Latin America was in fact "balkanized" several decades before the Balkans; nevertheless, it is a more than adequate expression of what occurred in Latin America during and after the wars of independence. Some Latin American writers have seen fit to explain the political fragmentation which occurred in the Spanish empire as the result of a sinister design on the part of foreign "imperialist" powers, notably Great Britain. An assertion such as this runs clean counter to common sense and historical probability. Great Britain had no diplomatic representatives in Spanish America until the middle of the 1820s, by which time political fragmentation was an established fact; the British trading communities in the region did little which could be construed as interference in politics, unless lending money to governments is regarded as such; the records of the Royal Navy reveal no irregular interference in the political life of the newly established states; and the only British diplomatic intervention of consequence in what we loosely think of as the independence period was the mediation between Argentina and Brazil which resulted in the creation of the Republic of Uruguay.

The root causes of the balkanization of Latin—or rather Spanish—America were unrelated to whether a politically fragmented continent was more "convenient" to the great powers than one which was politically united. The most likely explanation for the breakup of the former Spanish colonies into a series of independent republics is the strength of Creole regionalism, which itself was mostly the product of geography. Furthermore, it should not be forgotten that whereas the thirteen colonies of North America had conducted a *common* revolutionary offensive against Great Britain, the Spanish-American colonies launched a series of separate and unconnected assaults on the imperial authority. The 1810 revolutions in Caracas and Buenos Aires occurred almost simultaneously, and while the example of these movements may have influenced the course of events in New Granada and Chile, there is no evidence that it was the decisive factor involved. Father Hidalgo's insurrection in Mexico owed nothing to South American precedents. What is undeniable, of course, is that all these changes were set in motion by events in Spain, and the establishment of governing juntas in 1810 stemmed directly from the example of the juntas established by the Spaniards in their heroic struggle against Napoleon.

As we have seen, the peculiar circumstances of Brazilian independence allowed at least one substantial section of the South American continent to emerge as a single nation-state. Mexico, too, contrived to hold together as a sizable country. But elsewhere, Spanish America entered international life not as a single and potentially powerful unit, but as a series of small, weak and badly organized republics. From the start, Creole opinion was divided as to whether this was a desirable state of affairs or not. To judge from the considerable enthusiasm with which the new states quickly adopted the apparatus of separate nationhood—flags, currencies, coats-of-arms, customs posts, armies and navies, diplomatic services, national anthems—it might be thought that most Creoles accepted that regional feeling had now crystallized as *national* feeling. Some, certainly, accepted political fragmentation as inevitable. Mariano Moreno, for instance, writing in the *Gaceta de Buenos Aires* at the end of 1810, rejected the idea that it was possible to confederate or otherwise unify the colonies which were emerging from Spanish rule. Differences of geography, race, and custom between the different viceroyalties and captaincies-general seemed to him to be overwhelming. It was perfectly true, of course, that even by the end of the colonial period Argentina presented a somewhat different social aspect from, say, Peru or Mexico. Elsewhere, Chileans' memories of their previous commercial subordination to Peru may have played a part in dampening the desire for unity; similar rivalries further north were not unknown. Incipient nationalism could feed on all such differences, and did.

Nevertheless, even granting the strength of regional feelings, the notion of creating a solid political alliance—and perhaps some stronger form of union—between the new states was a common one, and by nobody was it taken more seriously than Simón Bolívar. His ideas on the subject are worth examining briefly. They were not wholly consistent. Once or twice in his career, for instance, he openly advocated the formation of *one* Spanish-American nation, "one country for all Americans" as he put it. But in the letter to Andrés Santa Cruz (1826) quoted above (p. 131), the Liberator seemed to surrender completely to the view that a Creole's native land or *patria* should take precedence over everything else. And in his "Jamaica Letter" (1815) he admitted that a *single* Spanish-American nation was an impossibility—"climatic differences, geographic diversity, conflicting interests and dissimilar circumstances"[1] prevented it. Bolívar was drawn by the parallel which he affected to see between the Spanish-American situation and the fall of the Roman empire and subsequent formation of new nations. Despite his acceptance of this somewhat dubious parallel, he was eager to contemplate schemes for offsetting the mounting political fragmentation of the region. Some kind of loose political association, he felt, was in order.

[1] Vicente Lecuna and Harold A. Bierck, eds., *Selected Writings of Bolívar*, 2 vols. (New York, 1951), I, 116.

This might take the form of a confederation, alliance, or league; the Amphictyonic League of ancient Greece might provide a suitable precedent.

The basic principle of Bolívar's internationalist schemes was fairly simple and logical. Each Latin American state would continue to enjoy full freedom as to its own internal affairs; but some sort of international treaty or pact would regulate the relations between the states and the relations between the league or confederation with the outside world. Bolívar appreciated more clearly than most of his contemporaries the *international* dangers of remaining disunited. It was essential, he thought, for Latin America to speak with a united voice, to settle its own disputes peacefully and amicably, to devise common commercial policies and to negotiate with foreign powers from a position of relative strength. Occasionally Bolívar's ideas on this subject grew somewhat utopian. In 1826, for instance, at the time of the Congress of Panama, he jotted down some of his hopes for the outcome of that ill-fated conference. Great Britain, he wanted to think, could be persuaded to join the Latin American confederation which was to be established; a close association with Great Britain would, in the course of time, enable Latin Americans to acquire British characteristics, which Bolívar thought was highly desirable.

None of Bolívar's international plans ever came to very much. The Congress of Panama was poorly attended and only Bolívar's own republic, Colombia, ratified its "federal" agreement. The grandiose scheme mooted in 1826–27 for an "Andean Union" (Colombia, Peru, and Bolivia), with Bolívar as president-for-life, never gained universal acceptance. Even the Liberator's original federation, Colombia itself, disintegrated in 1830. A picture of failure? Certainly the years since Bolívar's death have done much to confirm his fears of what disunity might bring in its train. The majority of Latin American nations have never been able to negotiate from a position of strength; the region as a whole can be said to have been weaker, internationally, than it would have been had Bolívar's ideas been put into practice. But at the same time, an ideal was born in the 1820s which has never been forgotten since, the ideal of Latin American unity. Today, under the name of "integration," it seems somewhat less utopian and somewhat less foolish than it did in Bolívar's time.

The New World and the Old

It was, then, a fragmented and balkanized Latin America that took its place in what the Chilean declaration of independence (1818) referred to as "the great confederation of the human race." It was several years,

however, before the new states were recognized as juridically independent by the great powers of Europe. There was no lack of sympathy
for the Latin American cause in Europe or in the United States; and
thousands of foreign volunteers, men of many different nationalities
with the British contingent leading the field, flocked to the assistance
of Bolívar and San Martín. But their presence in South America during
the campaigns of liberation in 1817–21 was unofficial if not actually
illegal, for the great powers were either neutral toward Latin America
or, alternatively, actually allied with Spain. It fell to the United States,
rather than any of the great powers, to take the first steps toward
diplomatic recognition. As early as 1810–12 the American government
made some tentative moves in this direction, but its impetus was
checked by the outbreak of the War of 1812 and also by its persistent
desire to round off the Louisiana Purchase by acquiring Florida from
Spain. The Spanish government agreed to cede Florida in 1819, but did
not ratify the treaty until 1821. Only then was the United States free to
act. Congress authorized recognition of the Latin American states in
May 1822, and President James Monroe accredited consuls and
ministers to Mexico, Colombia, Argentina, and Chile within the next
year.[1]

Of greater practical importance was the attitude of Great Britain.
Until the mid-1820s British policy toward the emergent Latin republics
was based on the hope of an accommodation between the colonial rebels
and their motherland or, failing that, the establishment of monarchies
in Latin America. Neither of these ideas came to anything, but recognition was unavoidable: British commercial interests, and a substantial
section of enlightened public opinion, were determined to support the
cause of the new republics for reasons both of self-interest and of
genuine liberal idealism. There was an additional diplomatic factor of
great importance: the apparent intention of the reactionary Holy
Alliance in Europe to help Spain reconquer America. Historians have
since cast doubt on the seriousness of this intention—but the threat
seemed real enough in the early 1820s. If Spain reconquered America,
and if Spain (as seemed likely) was in the pocket of France, then the
equilibrium of Europe would be gravely disturbed. It was necessary for
Great Britain "to call the New World into existence to redress the
balance of the Old." It was the British foreign secretary, George
Canning, the coiner of that famous phrase, who in October 1823 persuaded the French ambassador in London, Polignac, to commit France
(the power in the Holy Alliance most intimately concerned with Spanish
affairs) to a policy of noninterference (either directly or by lending

[1] Brazil and Central America were recognized in 1824, Peru in 1825.

support to Spain) in the New World. The threat, real or imaginary, from the Holy Alliance was thus thwarted, and British recognition of the new republics came soon afterward. Commercial treaties were concluded with Argentina and Colombia (1825) and with Mexico (1826), though it was several years before a number of other countries, Chile and Peru, for instance, were recognized by Great Britain. Canning himself remained deeply interested in the fortunes of the new states and enthusiastic about the commercial advantages which Great Britain could obtain there. "Spanish America is free," he wrote, "and if we do not mismanage our affairs sadly, she is English."

When the American colonies of Great Britain revolted against the motherland in the 1770s, the quarrel, fierce as it was, did not leave permanent scars on the relations between the two countries. Indeed, Great Britain recognized the independence of the United States as soon as the successful rebellion was over. A similar attitude was adopted by Portugal in relation to Brazil—the old kingdom and the new empire established diplomatic relations in 1825, only three years after the break between them. No such generosity (or realism) was favored by the Spanish government in the case of its former colonies. Not until 1836 was Mexico recognized as an independent republic, and most of the remaining Spanish-American countries had to wait a good deal longer, some of them until late in the nineteenth century.

George Canning had originally intended that the United States should be associated with Great Britain in a joint maneuver to resist the supposed American pretensions of the Holy Alliance. President Monroe was by no means wholly averse to the idea, but several particular circumstances—not least a hostile note from the Czar of Russia,[1] and his awareness of Canning's desire to weaken the American position in Latin America—compelled him to take a separate diplomatic stand of his own. Before doing so, he consulted (among others) the ancient Thomas Jefferson, then in peaceful retirement at Monticello. Jefferson wrote:

Our first and fundamental maxim should be, never to entangle ourselves in the broils of Europe. Our second, never to suffer Europe to intermeddle with cis-Atlantic affairs. America, North and South, has a set of interests distinct from those of Europe, and peculiarly her own. *She should therefore have a system of her own, separate and apart from that of Europe.* While the last is laboring to become the

[1] The czar informed Monroe that Russia had no intention of recognizing the new states; Monroe also had to bear in mind the Russian claims to the west coast of North America.

domicile of despotism, our endeavors should surely be, to make our Hemisphere that of freedom.[1] (Italics added.)

In his message to Congress on December 2, 1823, Monroe included a statement of policy that was to echo and re-echo through the years ahead. The European powers, said the President, had no right to "extend their system" to the New World; although the United States would make no effort to intervene in those European possessions which still remained in the Western Hemisphere (e.g., Cuba), she would none-theless veto any European attempt to regain colonies which had been lost. The United States, in effect, told the Old World, in no uncertain terms, that the Western hemisphere intended to remain master in its own home.

Two observations should be made on Monroe's pronouncement—which from the 1850s onward was usually referred to as the Monroe Doctrine. In the first place, it did not prohibit *American* interference in Latin American affairs. This was tactful, for more than a few Americans at that time were confident that the Spanish colony of Cuba, to take but one example, would eventually come to form part of the United States, rather in the way a ripe apple falls from a tree. Second, the United States, with only a small navy, was powerless to *enforce* the Monroe Doctrine. Fortunately, Great Britain was equally eager to guarantee the independence of Latin America, and was able to do so since the Royal Navy was the strongest in the world. It was, in fact, Great Britain rather than the United States which kept intact the embryonic "American system" implied by Monroe's statement. This also meant, of course, that Great Britain could ignore the Monroe Doctrine in practice—and, in the years which followed, minor British interventions in the affairs of Latin America were not uncommon. Great Britain applied coercion to Brazil in an effort to end the slave trade; she occupied the Falkland Islands off the coast of Argentina in 1833; in the 1840s she seized strongholds on both the Atlantic and Pacific coasts of Nicaragua; she blockaded Rosas in Argentina. Moreover, Great Britain did little or nothing to prevent a number of interventions by other great powers. Spain's brief Mexican adventure in 1829, the French expedition to Mexico nine years later, the French blockade in the River Plate, and, most notably of all, the setting up of the Franco-Hapsburg empire in Mexico—the British role on these occasions was one of acquiescence.[2]

The Latin American republics' entry into international politics was

[1] Jefferson to Monroe, October 24, 1823.
[2] The British pressure on France to withdraw from the River Plate in 1840 had less to do with Argentina than with the Franco-British disagreement over Mehemet Ali.

thus complicated from the start by the emergence of two distinctive diplomatic ideals: the ideal of Latin American unity (Bolívar's dream of an association of Latin American countries working in harmony) and what was later to be called the "inter-American" ideal (Monroe's notion that there should be a separate Western hemisphere system of international relations, associating the United States and Latin America but excluding the Old World). These two ideals were by no means mutually exclusive; there was no need for them to conflict; and yet it can hardly be pretended that they have ever been harmonious ideals. The one has often seemed to endanger the other. This tension has formed an important strand in the weave of Latin America's relations with the outside world.

The Era of the *Pax Britannica*

The century following the Latin American wars of independence was, as centuries go, a peaceful one. No major international conflagration disturbed the growth of trade. Relations between states were, for the most part, conducted by civilized men in a civilized manner. The warships of the Royal Navy guaranteed the freedom of the seas. This era, the era of the *Pax Britannica*, saw the different parts of the world increasingly knit together in a complex network of economic forces whose center was, in fact, Great Britain. During this period, Latin America's main relationships were with the great powers of the Old World; the Iberian peninsula was rejected as the main focus of Latin American attention; but the growing giant in North America soon commanded a degree of attention that could not be denied.

The ideal of Latin American unity—the tradition of the Congress of Panama—was twice brought to the fore during this period. On both occasions, the reason was a turn of events which seemed to constitute a threat to the territorial integrity of the region. When, in the mid-1840s, the exiled Ecuadorian politician, Juan José Flores, started to organize an expedition in England, with the intention of invading his homeland and establishing a European-protected monarchy, the Peruvian government took the initiative and summoned a conference of American states to Lima. The idea was received with enthusiasm by a number of countries, although only five (Bolivia, Chile, Ecuador, Peru, and Colombia) sent representatives. The conference met between December 1847 and March 1848 and drafted a series of international agreements on trade and navigation, the arbitration of frontier disputes, military collaboration, and so forth. None of these agreements was ever ratified by any of the five republics which took part in the Lima conference. Another chance came in the 1860s. Following the Spanish seizure of the

Chincha Islands off the Peruvian coast, a second Lima conference was convened. This time seven governments (those of Bolivia, Colombia, Chile, Ecuador, Peru, El Salvador, and Venezuela) were represented. Once again, several major agreements were concluded; the two most important concerned the arbitration of disputes between Latin American states and the formation of a defensive military alliance. As on the previous occasion, none of these agreements was ever ratified.

The two Lima congresses represented the peak of the movement toward Latin American unity in the nineteenth century, and, as we have seen, neither was a conspicuous success. The aspiration to unity was, in fact, contradicted at every turn by the growth of nationalism in the individual Latin American states. Often enough, we may surmise, national consciousness was confined only to a section of the population. It was strongest in the cities and ports, weakest in the countryside, weakest of all, perhaps, in those areas with large Indian populations. But it existed. It existed most of all among politicians and in the minds of governments. The outcome was a pattern of rivalries: rivalries over frontiers, over commercial arrangements, over the maltreatment of citizens. Only on relatively few occasions did these rivalries take the form of serious fighting between states. The tradition of internal, political violence in Latin America has been a strong one; violence between countries has been altogether less frequent than in any comparable area of the world.

In the contest between unity and diversity, then, diversity won. Though they rarely resorted to fighting each other, the Latin American states faced the outside world as distinctive entities, unwilling to band together to protect interests that one might have thought they held in common. The development of the international economy reinforced this trend. Each state found it easier and more profitable to trade with Western Europe or (later) the United States than to foster commercial links with its immediate neighbors. Occasional voices were raised in Latin America to combat this process. A Chilean conservative, Antonio García Reyes, argued in the mid-1840s in favor of an "American Commercial League": "it is extremely important" he wrote, "for the American Republics to grant mutual favours to each other in order to free their industry from the European yoke."[1] But voices such as García Reyes' cried in the wilderness.

For most of the period in question, by far the most important foreign power for most Latin American countries was Great Britain. As Canning had foreseen, the region became "English" in many significant respects.

[1] V. Letelier, ed., *Sesiones de los cuerpos legislativos de la República de Chile*, 38 vols. (Santiago, 1887–1908), XXXIV, 663.

The British economic embrace was tight. Yet British influence was by no means confined to the economic sphere. The British political system was widely admired in Latin America; Disraeli and Gladstone were revered by many Latin American politicians; aspiring Liberal or Conservative statesmen followed the debates in the House of Commons with interest. In matters of business and sport, the British reigned supreme. The punctiliousness and honesty of British traders and businessmen—not to mention their punctuality—won applause, even if the Creole environment proved impenetrable to other social conventions imported by the *gringo*. Expressions such as *palabra de inglés* ("an Englishman's word") and *hora inglesa* ("on the dot") became part of the Spanish language. Aristocratic gentlemen's clubs comparable to those of Pall Mall sprang up in most Latin American capital cities. We should not forget, either, that one of the most deeply rooted modern manias in Latin American life was originally introduced from Great Britain. I refer, of course, to football.

British influence in Latin America was never all-pervading, important as it was. British governments, as opposed to specific British commercial interests, had little interest in the region. At a period when the British empire was expanding to its greatest extent, there was no particular wish to acquire territories in South America or the Caribbean. Such direct political interventions as occurred were invariably of a rather minor sort. The Lion's tail twitched only sporadically in Latin America, and never very energetically. No Latin American government was ever dispossessed of office as a result of British interference. There were, it is true, the blockades and expeditions I have already mentioned, but the most notable of these, Great Britain's attempt to coerce Rosas, ended in humiliating failure. Occasionally, too, the conflicts between Latin American states provoked attempts on the part of Great Britain to mediate. In June 1880, for instance, Mr. Gladstone tried to secure a joint intervention by the European powers to put an end to the War of the Pacific; the scheme was blocked by the resistance of the German chancellor, Bismarck.

A second factor which mitigated British influence in Latin America was the extensive attraction exerted by France. The British may have dictated business conventions and (to some extent) social and sporting fashion; but the French radiated *culture*. Politically, the French record was, if anything, rather more interventionist than that of the British. In the years following the wars of independence, France was a member of the Holy Alliance and her political stance was, in consequence, somewhat repugnant to the Latin American republics. Later, the Mexican episode of 1838, and the more tragic events of the reign of

Maximilian and Carlota, did little to restore France's reputation. This scarcely mattered. The strength of the Creole attachment to French culture was not diminished by political disapproval. French literature supplied most of the models for nineteenth- and early-twentieth-century Latin American novelists and poets; French philosophy enjoyed a considerable vogue. Positivism, for example, swept through the intellectual circles of several Latin American republics like a brush-fire. It inspired the revolt of the Brazilian army in 1889, the historical speculations of earnest Chileans, and the educational reforms of the Juárez period in Mexico. No European capital city inspired enthusiasm and affection in more Creoles than did Paris. By the early years of the twentieth century, thousands of them were living there, living off the income from their estates and savoring the solid delights of the *Belle Epoque*. The souls of good Argentines, it was widely believed, migrated to Paris when they died.

Toward the United States, Latin American attitudes were always somewhat more ambivalent. At the end of his life, Bolívar told the British envoy in Colombia that the United States was "destined by providence to plague America with torments in the name of freedom."[1] Plainly, the heady expansion of the North American republic, its rapid march across the continent, its extraordinary increase in population, and its prodigious economic progress were causes for trepidation as well as admiration. Both emotions were, in fact, common during the nineteenth century in Latin America. The political democracy and social egalitarianism of the United States aroused feelings of sincere respect, and some Latin Americans saw these things as a model to be imitated; at the same time, there existed a more or less persistent awareness that the sheer growth and power of the United States might constitute a future hazard for the "Dis-united States" of Latin America. "A country . . . continually developing and growing in its power and wealth . . .," wrote the foreign minister of Chile in 1882, "a country of such faculties and such exceptional conditions must possess an irresistible tendency toward expansion."[2]

These two characteristic attitudes—admiration shading into imitation, and trepidation shading into hostility—went hand in hand in nineteenth-century Latin America. The first was well exemplified in the career of Domingo Faustino Sarmiento, the Argentine statesman. Sarmiento— as any reader of his masterpiece, *Facundo*, will remember—started out with a deep reverence for Europe, for him the source of all enlightenment

[1] Lecuna and Bierck, *op. cit.*, II, 732.
[2] Robert N. Burr and Roland D. Hussey, eds., *Documents on Inter-American Co-operation*, 2 vols. (Philadelphia, 1955), II, 32.

and progress. This attitude did not survive his visit to the Old World in 1845–47. Before returning to South America, Sarmiento visited the United States and fell in love with the social and economic patterns he saw there. Europe, Sarmiento concluded, was decadent, senescent, corrupt, and backward in comparison with the vigorous and progressive democracy of North America. The Latin American countries who wished to progress, Sarmiento asserted from then onward, could only do so if they followed the American example. Like Jefferson, Sarmiento wanted the whole of the Western hemisphere to be the hemisphere of freedom. Sarmiento's compatriot Juan Bautista Alberdi and scores of lesser Latin American figures held very similar opinions about the rising Colossus of the North.

Such views were easier for an Argentine to accept than, say, a Mexican or a Central American. United States influence in southern South America was minimal, and was destined to remain minimal for many more years. In the Caribbean, however, the United States was a next-door neighbor. In the 1840s its government deprived Mexico of half her territory; in the 1850s its filibustering citizens made life in Central America even more turbulent than it was normally. When the Civil War broke out in the United States, most Latin Americans lent enthusiastic moral support to Lincoln's efforts to save the union and abolish slavery—but one or two appreciated that a victory for the south might be a blessing in disguise. The Guatemalan, Antonio José de Irisarri, wrote from the United States in 1861:

> For my part I do not believe that universal policy or the cause of humanity would lose much—indeed, I think they would gain a great deal—if two or more independent Republics were to be formed out of the States which up to now have composed this Union. For the Union had reached a degree of power which threatened the existence of the other small republics of the American continent.[1]

The defeat of the Confederacy spelled an immediate end to hopes such as these.

Between 1865, the year the second Lima Congress closed, and the mid-1880s, Latin America was mostly preoccupied with the two most serious international conflicts of the nineteenth century, the War of the Triple Alliance and the War of the Pacific. The climate was no longer

---

[1] Diplomatic dispatch to the Guatemalan government, August 20, 1851, quoted in John D. Browning, "Los Estados Unidos vistos por un observador centro-americano del siglo pasado," in *El ensayo y la crítica literaria en Iberoamérica* (Toronto, 1970), p. 45.

propitious for attempts at fostering Latin American unity. It was at this period that the United States sponsored, in 1889–90, the first of those inter-American meetings that were later referred to as Pan-American Conferences. It was held in Washington and attended by all the Latin American states except the Dominican Republic; its deliberations were conducted in an atmosphere of considerable good will. In practical terms, however, the conference achieved very little. American attempts to secure agreement on an inter-American customs union were doomed to failure by the obdurate attitude adopted by the Argentine delegation, an attitude supported by a majority of the other Latin delegations. James G. Blaine, the U.S. Secretary of State, who was elected president of the conference, dwelt on the theme of "America for the Americans" in advocating a customs union. One of the Argentine delegates, Roque Sáenz Peña, in a vigorous speech, extolled South America's extensive links with Europe and defended a wider concept:

Let the century of America, as the 20th century is already called, behold our trade with all the nations of the earth free, witnessing the noble duel of untrammelled labour in which it has truly been said God measures the ground, equalizes the weapons, and apportions the light. Let America be for Humanity![1]

The "inter-American" ideal, then, did not flourish unchallenged. Pan-American conferences continued to meet, and even managed to conclude useful agreements on a number of technical matters, but genuine collaboration between the United States and Latin America was hampered by political developments in the Caribbean. The Spanish-American War, the creation of Panama, the enunciation of the Roosevelt corollary to the Monroe Doctrine—these important events immediately cast their shadow over the "Pan-American" aspiration.

By the 1890s, in fact, the United States had entered the ranks of the great powers. It now rivaled, and in some respects already surpassed, the main nations of the Old World in industrial strength. The Spanish-American War was, in an important sense, a signal that the American nation had "arrived." Many of the most characteristic American pronouncements of the period revealed a growing awareness of well-earned power, and in some cases a belief in American superiority. In 1895, when Great Britain and Venezuela were locked in a dispute over the boundary of British Guiana, the U.S. Secretary of State, Richard Olney,

[1] Thomas F. McGann, "Argentina at the First Pan-American Conference," *Inter-American Economic Affairs*, I (1947), 49–50.

took it upon himself to remind the British of the existence of the Monroe Doctrine. His reminder has been much-quoted. "Today," he wrote, "the United States is practically sovereign on this continent, and its fiat is law upon the subjects to which it confines its interposition." An acute crisis in Anglo-American relations developed; rumors of war went the rounds on both sides of the Atlantic; but the British government eventually gave in to American pressure and agreed to go to arbitration in the Venezuelan affair. It was a sign of the times. The mightiest empire in the world had been obliged to admit a moral defeat. The *Pax Britannica* no longer prevailed in the Caribbean.

For Latin America, the changes of the 1890s were especially significant. The United States, in the course of a century, had transformed itself from a somewhat modest agrarian republic into a tremendous industrial power with strongly expansionist impulses. The dilemmas for Latin America which flowed from that fact were manifold. Admiration and trepidation continued to walk hand in hand, but the latter emotion was now somewhat more pronounced. Some Latin American nations might still wish to follow the United States in her manner of achieving economic progress. At the start of the twentieth century some writers assumed, a little too readily perhaps, that Argentina, for instance, would soon become a kind of Spanish-speaking replica of the United States in the southern hemisphere.[1] But the very *extent* of American power was bound to increase, and sharply increase, Latin American forebodings. Was not the "Pan-American" ideal, for instance, a "cover" for American economic penetration south of the Rio Grande? Did not the slogan "America for the Americans" *really* mean "*Latin* America for the Americans"? Questions such as these were asked repeatedly in Latin America in the early years of the twentieth century, and the American replies were not very reassuring. Even when the Argentine foreign minister Luis María Drago proposed to give real substance to the shadowy "inter-American system" by multilateralizing the Monroe Doctrine (1902), his efforts were rebuffed in Washington.[2]

By 1910 or so, the relationship between Latin America and the United States had come to occupy a leading position in the general pattern of Latin America's relationships with the outside world. But

[1] Lord Bryce, one of the most intelligent foreign observers of the period, declared quite flatly: "Argentina is like Western North America. . . . It is the United States of the Southern Hemisphere." (*South America. Observations and Impressions* [London, 1912], p. 315.)

[2] Drago's proposal was made as a result of an Anglo–German–Italian debt-collecting expedition to Venezuela at the end of 1902. He argued that the Monroe Doctrine should be enforced by the American states acting together rather than by the United States alone.

except in the Caribbean, the region's principal connections—economic, political, and emotional—were still with Great Britain and France. But new links were being forged, not all of them equally welcome. Spain, much reviled by Spanish-Americans for most of the nineteenth century, was now readmitted emotionally and politically to the region. This, being fairly innocuous, *was* welcome. As the shadow of the Protestant United States loomed larger to the north, the Spanish-American countries began to rediscover their Catholic, Iberian background and to take pride in it. Many Spanish-Americans, perhaps most, supported the Spanish cause in 1898. Pan-Americanism was countered by Pan-Hispanism, a "movement" which expressed itself mainly in the organization of conferences and scholarships, the standardization of spelling conventions in the Spanish language, and in the introduction of such sacred observances as the *día de la Raza* or "day of the Race" —an annual commemoration of Columbus' arrival in the West Indies designed to exalt the traditional and common virtues of the Hispanic peoples on both sides of the ocean.

The possibility of German expansion into Latin America—which presented itself in this period—was a good deal less welcome. Indeed, it was actively feared by many Latin Americans. Germany, a latecomer to the ranks of the European great powers, saw no reason why she should be denied an expansionist role in the world. The German economic stake in Latin America grew fast after the turn of the century; several countries professionalized their armed forces with German help. A few currents of opinion within the Reich actually favored the acquisition of territories in South America.[1] The "German peril" may not, as it turned out, have been very real, but it certainly existed in the minds of a number of Latin American writers and politicians. The more imaginative of these detected a "Japanese peril" as well. The virulently anti-Yankee Argentine writer Manuel Ugarte wondered whether this particular "peril" could not be turned to useful account by Latin America; a connection with the Japanese empire might, he thought, offset the southward expansion of the United States. Such were the speculations of intelligent Latin Americans as they contemplated their republics' place in the world at the start of the twentieth century—a century whose course was so soon to be transformed by the hammer-blows of two gigantic conflicts.

[1] In his book *Gross Deutschland* (Greater Germany) published in Leipzig in 1911, Otto Richard Tannenberg argued that southern South America, i.e., southern Brazil, Argentina, Chile, Uruguay, Paraguay, and part of Bolivia, should become German. Chile and Argentina were to be permitted a degree of autonomy and would retain their own language, although German would become an obligatory second language in their schools.

Echoes of War

The uninterrupted progress of the Western European nations, with which Latin America had been so intimately linked, came to an abrupt and tragic halt in August 1914. The outbreak of war had discernible effects on the economic life of Latin America but, these apart, the region was largely untouched. Two epic naval battles were fought off South American coasts: in November 1914 warships of the German navy defeated a British force near Coronel, in Chile, and a month later the British had their revenge off the Falkland Islands. With this exception, the tides of war flowed far away—watched with horrified fascination in the Latin American capitals. Following the entry of the United States into the war in 1917, eight Latin republics followed suit. Seven of them were in Central America or the Caribbean, where American influence was naturally strongest. The eighth, Brazil, the only state of any importance to declare war, had long been noted for a strongly pro-American foreign policy, and some of her ships had been torpedoed by German U-boats. A number of countries broke off diplomatic relations with the Central Powers, but Argentina, Chile, Colombia, Mexico, Paraguay, and Venezuela remained neutral throughout the war.

World War I weakened the economic links which existed between Latin America and Europe, and enormously strengthened the position of the United States. The *Pax Britannica* no longer existed. The U.S. Navy was now by far the most powerful in the Western hemisphere, and the Washington Naval Conference of 1921–22 (part of the postwar peace settlement) ratified the predominance of the United States in the waters around the American continent. Great Britain continued, it is true, to enjoy commercial and diplomatic hegemony in southern South America, but this was increasingly challenged everywhere save in the River Plate. The accentuation of American influence did nothing to reduce Latin American forebodings. On the contrary, it heightened them. One event after another tended to confirm these traditional fears. American intervention in the Caribbean and Central America was at its peak; nothing, it seemed, could stop the southward march of the Colossus.

The advance of American interests and American influence provoked two basic reactions, which were sometimes intertwined. The first of these was a literary attitude more than anything else. Whatever the *material* achievements of the United States, it could be claimed, Latin America possessed moral and spiritual qualities which were decidedly superior to those of the boorish and uncultured Yankee. The Uruguayan writer José Enrique Rodó, author of the classic essay *Ariel* (1900), came to be regarded as the chief exponent of this view, not altogether accurately.[1] It was held, in one form or another, by numerous Latin American intellectuals in the early years of the twentieth century—and its roots are sunk deeply into the nineteenth.

A second reaction, whether combined with the first or not, was more clearly political. It was prefigured most sharply by the Cuban patriot and writer José Martí, who knew North America well. Martí enormously admired the United States as perhaps the freest country in the world, but feared that American materialism, combined with the obvious expansionist urge of the time, would place the independence of his native Cuba in jeopardy. Martí died in 1895, but the events of the years that followed confirmed some of his fears. The thirty years after the Spanish-American War saw the rise of a distinctively anti-Yankee literature throughout Latin America. "Yankee imperialism," "Wall Street imperialism," "dollar imperialism"—these and many similar phrases became part of the standard political vocabulary of the region. The United States, according to this interpretation, was a materialistic plutocracy bent on dominating Latin America and quite possibly the entire world. Several influential writers of the period from 1900 to 1930 took up this theme: the Argentine Manuel Ugarte, the Venezuelans Rufino and Horacio Blanco-Fombona, the Mexican Carlos Pereyra were but four among many. Ugarte's book *El destino de un continente* ("The Destiny of a Continent"), published in 1923, was perhaps the most unequivocal expression of the anti-American viewpoint; it was very widely read.

It was in these circumstances that a new emphasis began to be placed on the old ideal of Latin American unity, a unity now conceived as necessary to sheer survival. Menaced by the overwhelming power of the United States, Latin America's only realistic response was to build a solid defensive union. Roque Sáenz Peña, the Argentine statesman, proposed the formation of a Latin American League. His distinguished compatriot José Ingenieros called for the fostering of a new Latin American consciousness springing from the joint action of peoples rather than governments. Unity was a key feature, too, in the political program of Haya de la Torre's APRA. Many other examples could be mentioned. It is true that several prominent Latin Americans—the Chilean jurist Alejandro Alvarez or the Uruguyan president Baltasar Brum, for instance—continued to place their faith in hopes of a genuinely

---

[1] The widely accepted equation of Ariel with Latin America and of Caliban with the United States cannot reasonably be drawn from what Rodó actually wrote, although it has been. See the illuminating introduction by Gordon Brotherston to his edition of *Ariel* (New York, 1967).

"inter-American" system, underpinned by a "multilateralized" Monroe Doctrine, but such ideas found less of a real echo.

Lying somewhere near the heart of the new aspiration to Latin American unity was a growing feeling of dissatisfaction at the way the region had remained "marginal" to world history for so long. Some writers detected a serious failure on the part of the governing classes. Latin America's progress, it was felt, had been inadequate and partial. The region as a whole made no real mark on the world. The Chilean writer Edwards Bello lamented the fact that the Spanish-American republics, "with a hundred years of independent life, neutral in war, go on begging for loans and hoping that civilization will come to seek them out. They contribute nothing, apart from primary materials, to industry; nothing to science."[1] The indictment was a serious one. What was the remedy? It was hopeless to assume that twenty separate republics could defend their interests against rapacious foreign powers in general and the United States in particular. Some kind of "continental nationalism" was the only answer.

After World War I, Latin America was, in fact, slightly more involved in international politics than at any previous period. Her delegates took part, sometimes very actively, in the work of the League of Nations at Geneva. Indeed, the League was seen by many Latin American diplomats as an altogether more important forum than the various assemblies of the discredited "inter-American system," and as a possible counterweight to the predominance of the United States in the Western hemisphere. These hopes were speedily disappointed. But by now Latin America was being drawn far more fully into the international scene. Once again, the possibility of German expansion aroused the fears of Latin Americans. And for some of them it aroused hope: for the rising power of the Third Reich could be looked upon as a useful alternative focus of attention for Latin American nationalists eager to reduce American influence in the region. For the United States, Latin America suddenly acquired a much greater political and strategic importance than at any stage in the past. "Hemisphere solidarity"— the watchword of the 1930s and early 1940s—was indispensable if the contagion of National Socialism was to be prevented from spreading to the New World.

World War II impinged far more directly on Latin America than did the first war. All of the twenty republics eventually declared war on the Axis powers and joined the alliance of the United Nations. Chile and Argentina it is true, proved somewhat dilatory in throwing their support behind the Allied cause. Chile felt understandably nervous

[1] J. Edwards Bello, *Nacionalismo continental* (Santiago, 1928), p. 48.

about the vulnerability of her long and unprotected coastline to a Japanese invasion. Argentina had a government which scarcely bothered to conceal its underlying sympathy for the Axis. But, leaving aside the equivocal position adopted by the Argentines, sympathy for the "inter-American" ideal had never been stronger in Latin America than during the early 1940s. Optimists like the Mexican foreign minister Ezequiel Padilla believed that Pan-Americanism could become a great instrument of collaboration between the Western hemisphere nations, an instrument which could lift the Latin American economies into the modern world. It would be untrue to say that all Latin Americans shared Padilla's views or suddenly became ardent "Pan-Americanists," but his sanguine hopes for the future struck the dominant note in the region at the time when the death of Adolf Hitler, the evil genius of modern European history, and the mushroom clouds over Hiroshima and Nagasaki, brought into existence the world we know today.

The Age of the Superpowers

The outcome of World War II produced changes in the balance of power within the Western world and the world as a whole which were so far-reaching that we must briefly pause to take some stock of them here. The scholars of the future may well consider 1945 as one of the most crucially important dates in world history. Western Europe, devastated for a second time by its own internecine conflicts, was no longer a credible counterweight to the United States. Indeed, the world had suddenly passed from an age of great-power rivalries of the traditional kind into a period in which two gigantic "superpowers," as they came to be known, became the ultimate arbiters of the fate of mankind. Armed with overwhelming nuclear and thermonuclear might, they now stood head and shoulders above all other possible contenders. Europeans did not need to be reminded of this decisive change, for the eastern part of their continent now fell firmly within the sphere of influence of the enigmatic colossus whose territory spanned the Eurasian landmass—Soviet Russia, whose armies had played so conspicuous a part in the defeat of Hitler's short-lived Reich. Like the United States, she now appeared in the full light of day as a superpower and, as a consequence, was almost certainly bound to challenge the United States for leadership of the world. This, at least, was how it appeared in the years which immediately followed 1945.

What was the nature of this new superpower? For centuries, Russia had been a huge but relatively little-known empire on the eastern fringe of European civilization—an empire, moreover, which had spread across to the remotest confines of Asia. Her relations with the West had always been somewhat ambiguous. At times her rulers had seemed anxious to "westernize" as fast and as uncompromisingly as possible, but at no time, it is fair to say, had Russia become fully incorporated into Western civilization or wholly associated with the Western tradition.

After the Bolshevik revolution of 1917, however, the old Russian empire was reordered in quite extraordinarily drastic and brutal fashion. Its headlong accumulation of military and industrial power astonished the world. But the growth of the Eastern superpower had a still more novel aspect. The leaders of the new Soviet Union claimed to be putting into practice the doctrines of Karl Marx and to be building a socialist order, which, guided by the mysterious dynamic of historical materialism, would eventually give way to a communist order and the consummation of human progress. The immense increase in Russian power and the modernization of that vast country clearly constituted an ideological challenge of formidable proportions, particularly in those parts of the world which lagged behind Western Europe and the United States in economic progress. Latin America was no longer bound to conceive of her future development in exclusively Western European or North American terms. A few Latin Americans had, as we have seen, maintained this from the 1920s onward; with the emergence of Russia as a superpower, there were strong reasons for this view to spread. Furthermore, it was now possible for Latin American nationalists to invoke Soviet support in any tussle with their own neighboring superpower. But other changes soon occurred as well. The collapse of the old European colonial empires, the growth of new states in Asia and Africa alike, the impressive recovery of Japan and, not least, the resurgence of China under Communist leadership after 1949, meant that the cold-war rivalry of the United States and the U.S.S.R. was to be conducted against a much more multicolored planetary backcloth than might have been expected. Indeed, their rivalry itself was never to be quite as simple as some writers of the late 1940s imagined. Western Europe— not least Germany—rose yet again from the ashes of war, grew prosperous once more, and began to pursue the elusive ideal of unity. China and Russia, far from constituting a "monolithic" Communist bloc, developed an increasingly bitter rivalry, amounting to what was almost a second cold war, and reaching a climax in border clashes along the Ussuri River in 1969. The remainder of the world became urgently concerned with the problems of economic progress.

The contemporary world—the world that has taken shape since the momentous events of 1945—no longer presents a simple picture to the observer, if it ever did in the past. Latin America—and here we return to the main theme—can no longer be regarded exclusively as a kind of third element in an Atlantic and Western world, inevitably bound to maintain permanent economic and political links with the other two elements. Nor should the other two elements be considered as unchanging and fixed; this is an important point to which I shall return presently.

The years immediately after World War II found the Latin American countries more closely connected to the United States than ever before. Politically, the setting up of the Organization of American States (1948) as a regional organization of the United Nations seemed to set the crown on long years of activity for the Pan-American movement; the "inter-American system" was now apparently on firmer foundations than ever before. Economically, there was a renewed flow of American capital into the region; and, for the time being at least, Western Europe seemed incapable of providing an alternative supply of funds, while nobody as yet dreamed that the Soviet Union would invest heavily in Latin America. The closeness of the connection with the United States, however, emphasized and accentuated the Latin American feeling of dependence. Some Latin American politicians accepted the need for a close association with the United States. Haya de la Torre, for instance, was convinced of the need for hemispheric partnership and American aid. Others were more cautious, at least in their long-term aspirations. Still others regarded the United States as wholly and malignly imperialist, and desired complete emancipation from what they thought of as her baleful and sinister influence. All these various attitudes were sharpened by the overwhelming but simple fact that the United States was now a superpower.

Two things made matters worse. In the first place, the new superpower no longer showed particular interest in Latin America; the problems of Europe and of Asia seemed more urgent and pressing in Washington. And second, such American policy as there was toward Latin America seemed unduly influenced by somewhat crude considerations of cold-war strategy. The events which occurred in Guatemala in 1954 confirmed the more lurid assessments of American aims. To many Latin Americans in the 1950s the threat of Communist penetration was less real than the threat to national liberty posed by the engineering of the downfall of President Arbenz. Ten years after the end of the war, the relations between Latin America and the United States were at their lowest ebb since the 1920s. But except in Argentina, where Perón had proclaimed an independent position in international affairs, these dissatisfactions were not reflected in Latin American foreign policies. Whatever lay below the surface, the sea itself remained tranquil. Then, like a tropical hurricane, Dr. Fidel Castro broke the calm.

The Cuban revolution may be said to have had an impact in Latin America comparable in some ways to that of France in the Europe of the 1790s. The parallel should certainly not be pressed too far. France in the 1790s was the most populous (and in many senses the leading) nation in Western Europe, and the energies released by her revolution were eventually harnessed to the task of conquering and reforming half the continent. Cuba, a midget of a country in the 1960s, was in no position to send a Grand Army through the mainland of America. Her influence was, and indeed had to be, a moral one; the practical assistance that could be given to the various "guerrilla fronts" that appeared in the 1960s was negligible in comparison with the ideological effect of the revolution. And whatever the failures and troubles of the revolution in Cuba as it gets older—Dr. Castro's speech on July 26, 1970 indicated that these were considerable—its influence is likely to remain significant for a long time to come.

For the Cuban revolution represented in an extreme form the general aspiration to independence that was growing up in Latin America. Those who contemplated the island's experience dispassionately—and perhaps there were relatively few who could do this—might well have come to the conclusion that to exchange one form of dependence for another rather different form was by no means the best way of promoting national independence. But Cuba *did* succeed in escaping from the all-pervading influence of the Colossus. She proved that it could be done. There were, no doubt, disadvantages in the way she chose to do it. By the start of the 1970s Cuba was probably in debt to Russia to the tune of one thousand five hundred million dollars and as dependent on the good will of Soviet politicians and commercial planners as she had previously been on the variations of the American market. When all is said and done, increased independence may lie more in the diversification of foreign economic links than in exchanging one set of links for another. Even so, the intransigent stand taken toward the United States by the Castro regime—and the fact that the regime actually survived—greatly encouraged and perhaps accelerated the Latin American drive toward greater autonomy.

The Cuban eruption undoubtedly placed new strains on the "inter-American system," whose reorganization at Bogotá in 1948 had never quite achieved the results hoped for by optimistic Pan-Americanists. The United States managed to secure the diplomatic isolation of the Castro regime, and there was a good deal of Latin American support for President John F. Kennedy's quarantine of Cuba during the missile crisis of October 1962. But events such as the American intervention in the Dominican Republic in 1965, and the difficulties of infusing life into the Alliance for Progress, made an increasing number of Latin American governments question the usefulness of the "inter-American system." The anomalous aspects of the system were apparent to everyone. Cuban propaganda jeered at the Organization of American States (OAS), describing it as no more than the United States' "Ministry of Colonies." Even a stouthearted friend of the United States such as the Spanish writer Salvador de Madariaga found the Organization to be in need of substantial reform. At the start of the 1960s Madariaga wrote:

> The O.A.S. should be thoroughly recast. There is a fundamental make-believe in it, in that it is supposed to be a meeting of equal partners on equal terms, while in fact the U.S.A. dominates the whole. . . . While Latin America remains dispersed as a dust of weak nations, none of which can compare even in mere order of magnitude with the United States, the O.A.S. can hardly claim to be more than a decorous shield to veil the supremacy of the one over the many without altogether hiding it.[1]

Madariaga suggested that, ideally at least, the OAS should consist of only two members: Latin America as a whole and the United States.

Latin American awareness of American supremacy in the Western Hemisphere was perhaps never more nagging than in the 1960s. The economic relationship referred to in Chapter 5 was coming more and more to be seen as unsatisfactory from the Latin American viewpoint. In the political sphere, the influence of the Colossus seemed excessively pervasive. Military assistance pacts, discreet hints from American ambassadors, a considerable propaganda effort, and, not least, the relatively unpublicized activities of the Central Intelligence Agency— all of these things aroused suspicion south of the Rio Grande. The United States provided highly efficient counterinsurgency training for a number of Latin American armies. The U.S. Army sponsored in 1965 a social science research project on political attitudes in Chile—the notorious Camelot Plan. A strident outcry in Chile, where the affair quickly became a scandal of the first magnitude, prevented the project from being carried out.

Phenomena such as these have been interpreted as clear evidence of the malevolent designs of American imperialism, and they do contribute useful ammunition for those who think in such black-and-white terms,

[1] Madariaga, *Latin America between the Eagle and the Bear* (London, 1962), pp. 178–79.

of whom there are a fair number in Latin America.[1] Whether the United States is seeking to control an "empire" or whether she is attempting to maintain what has traditionally been thought of as a "sphere of influence" is, perhaps, of small importance, though such shibboleths are significant in Latin American political life. The basic problem is really a simple one. Ever since the United States became a great power, and still more since she became a superpower, the position of the smaller states of the Western hemisphere inevitably became somewhat equivocal. As the late Professor Alfred Cobban pointed out in a valuable study of the question of national self-determination, "small nations that lie in the shadow of great powers are liable to come under their influence to a degree which raises the question of national independence, even in the absence of annexation."[2] The parallel between Latin America and Eastern Europe which is sometimes drawn is perhaps somewhat misleading: leaving aside the special cases of the Panama Canal Zone and the Guantánamo naval base, the United States does not maintain large numbers of troops on Latin American soil and, as the Playa Girón fiasco of 1961 revealed, there are evident limits beyond which the American government does not seem prepared to go in defending its position in Latin America, for there can be small doubt that a full-scale American invasion of Cuba on that occasion would have brought about the end of the Castro government, though no doubt very bloodily. (Some Cuban Communists are said to have wanted this to occur, so as to produce a Western "Hungary.") But, these considerations apart, the fact that Latin America lives in the penumbra of a superpower raises problems of unusual acuteness, not only for Latin America but also for the United States. These problems will not simply go away, and they are likely to become more serious in the course of the 1970s.

Stated quite simply, the main interest of the United States lies in having *nonhostile* states on her doorstep. Even superpowers have the right to survive. The Cuban case shows clearly that there are profound strategic objections to permitting a strong Russian military presence in

[1] And not only in Latin America. In June 1969, as part of the Holland Festival, an "opera" entitled *Reconstruction* was put on at the Carré Theater, Amsterdam. It was ostensibly an attempt to reconstruct Mozart's *Don Giovanni* "in terms of the death of Che Guevara." Don Juan personified American Imperialism; his female conquests were Latin American republics, whom he raped on a bed shaped like the South American continent. During the course of the "opera," stage hands gradually erected a forty-foot statue of Guevara, who thus became the Stone Guest who frightened Don Juan in the closing scene. (William Mann, "Opera for the Big Top," *The Times*, London, June 30, 1969, p. 6.) This extraordinary performance probably tells us more about the state of the so-called "avant-garde" in Europe than anything it might reveal about the realities of Latin American life.

[2] Cobban, *The Nation State and National Self-Determination* (London, 1969), p. 170.

the Western hemisphere. The establishment of a militantly pro-Russian or pro-Chinese regime in Latin America would plainly present peculiar dangers from the viewpoint of international stability, and all people everywhere, not just Latin Americans, have—or should have—a fundamental interest in seeing that peace is preserved. But could the United States reasonably object to "neutralist" regimes in Latin America? It would be perfectly possible, in fact, for the United States to accept the existence of "socialist" republics in the region, providing these did not offer military facilities to powers which were ill-disposed toward the United States. The world can ill afford too many Cuban-style missile crises.

From the Latin American viewpoint, there are, perhaps, only two ways in which American supremacy can be made to weigh less heavily. First, intimate connections *can* be sought with alternative centers of power in the world, which is what some Latin American nationalists would like to have done with the Third Reich, and which the Cuban government *has* done with the Soviet Union. This tactic, as I have suggested, is likely to provoke American trepidation and a positively hostile American reaction. The second way in which American supremacy can be offset is by seeking Latin American unity—and I shall presently mention one or two recent moves in this direction. Ultimately, truly harmonious relations within the Western hemisphere can be achieved only when both parties—Latin America and the United States —speak to each other from positions of equality, or at any rate much nearer to equality than is possible at the moment. To approach the Colossus of the North without mistrust, Latin America must aspire more notably to become a Colossus of the South. Juan José Arévalo's popular fable of the shark and the sardines can be relegated to the lumber-room of the past only when the sardines transmogrify themselves into a second shark. This does not mean, of course, that Latin America should feverishly attempt to build nuclear weapons[1] or raise a crack marine corps; but my metaphor need not imply those qualities traditionally associated with sharks—for some kinds of shark are actually vegetarians.

Today and Tomorrow

At the start of the 1960s the establishment of a Communist regime in Cuba brought the Soviet Union into the Western hemisphere and very nearly touched off a third world war in the process. By the time the 1960s ended and the 1970s began, events elsewhere in the world suggested very

[1] In 1967, in fact, twenty-one Latin American and Caribbean states signed the Treaty of Tlatelolco, which makes the region a denuclearized zone.

strongly that a new and somewhat more fluid international situation was gradually replacing the hard-and-fast political landscapes of the cold war. These particular events are still in process; but it is not too early to hazard the supposition that Latin America may benefit from their effects.

The United States since the middle of the 1960s has been the scene of unusual, paradoxical, and at times tragic excitements. Its internal commotions have been noisier than at any time since the Civil War. The aspirations of the Negro community, race riots, massive protests against the merciless and suspect war in Southeast Asia, revelations of government misconduct on a vast scale, unease over problems of environmental pollution and urban decay, the widespread use (or rather abuse) of drugs, the apparent disaffection and parasitic hedonism of a significant minority of the younger generation[1]—the American people in recent years has been confronted with a whole host of puzzling, stubborn, and at times infuriating issues. Whatever the outcome of these recent discontents within the United States, it seems at least likely that a substantial reordering of American priorities is slowly occurring. The determination of the administration of President Richard Nixon to avoid embarrassing foreign entanglements can be regarded as a case in point. The moderate American reaction to the nationalist policies pursued by Peru and Chile in 1968–71 is, in part at least, the product of this attitude. To present a "low profile" is the order of the day.

In Western Europe, meanwhile, the movement toward economic (and more tentatively toward political) unity has shown some signs of strengthening since the commanding figure of General de Gaulle withdrew from French politics in 1969. The enlargement of the Common Market as a result of the entry of Great Britain and other states in 1973 will naturally entail renewed speculation, and perhaps action, on the question of devising a new shape for Western Europe. For most of its short life, the Common Market has been based on somewhat conservative assumptions—understandable and even praiseworthy in view of Europe's proven capacity for self-destruction in the past. The mixed economies of the postwar period have done their work well; the Western nations of the Old World have become more prosperous than at any previous period of their history. But the 1970s may see an alteration in this pattern: we should not forget that "the lesson of European history is that Europe is never settled, but always restless and uneasy."[2] The

---

[1] Particularly the better-off members of the younger generation.
[2] H. A. L. Fisher, *A History of Europe from the Beginning of the 18th century to 1937* (London, 1952), p. 742.

question "What *kind* of Europe?" seems more and more likely to be debated in the future. That a united (or relatively united) Europe should be "outward-looking" rather than "inward-looking" is arguably of great importance for Latin America. There are, conceivably, many ways in which the Old World can be called in to redress the balance of the New.

In recent years European interest in Latin America has shown considerable signs of reviving. Various European heads of state and politicians have paid official visits to the region. In 1964 President de Gaulle, whose mildly anti-American policies made him something of a hero to nationalist currents of opinion, visited several Latin American republics. In 1968 Her Majesty Queen Elizabeth II toured Brazil and Chile; her reception in both countries was extraordinary and brilliant It was the first time a reigning British monarch had set foot on Latin American soil.[1]

Outside the Western world, the panorama of the last few years has been equally changeable. The Soviet Union's alliance with Cuba has not prevented her from concluding commercial agreements or collaborating in other ways with a number of Latin American countries whose governments are far from pro-Cuban. Further east, Japan bids fair to become the world's second industrial power by the end of the 1970s, and the influence of the great Japanese economic interests is likely to be felt in Latin America, as elsewhere. Japanese trade with the region has risen considerably in the last ten years, and Japanese capital may well find a useful role there in the future. The onward march of China to an eventual superpower status seems assured, though the direction this spartan and inscrutable power will take when the next generation of leaders takes over is impossible to guess.[2] Chinese influence in Latin America so far has been ideological rather than economic—and in any case very small-scale.

It is against this changing backcloth that the most recent events in Latin America—and those which are likely to occur over the next few years—should be set. One important feature of this new situation should be mentioned, and indeed underlined, at this point. North America, Western Europe, Russia, and China are all, in the last analysis, what might be termed "centripetal" powers. None of them need *depend* on international trade; all can be economically self-sufficient with a bit

[1] The first state visit by a Latin American president to Great Britain took place in 1965: Eduardo Frei of Chile was the distinguished visitor.

[2] At the time of writing it is too early to estimate the consequences of the détente between China and the United States which began in mid-1971. The very existence of Sino-American contacts, however, indicates the continuing fluidity of the international scene.

of effort if the need arises. The only significant "centrifugal" power remaining is Japan. Any accentuation of the "centripetal" character of the regions mentioned *might* seriously prejudice the commercial prospects of Latin America, and this should clearly be avoided. But at the same time, an unfavorable change of direction in world trade—or even such events as the dollar crisis of 1971—might have the salutary effect of turning Latin American attention toward the problem of unity.

The ideal of Latin American unity in the past decade or so seems, on the one hand, to have been obscured by the political tensions generated by the Cuban revolution, and yet, at the same time, paradoxically enough, to have shown certain underlying signs of re-emergence. It is on the latter aspect that attention should be concentrated. There is no need for me to recapitulate here the various ways in which the cause of Latin American economic integration has been furthered in the years since the formation of the Central American Common Market and the signing of the Treaty of Montevideo, not forgetting the subsequent creation of the Andean Group. The ease with which these ambitious plans can be brought to fulfilment should certainly not be exaggerated. Nonetheless, it is clear that they have been animated from the start by a long-range vision of Latin American unity; their progress, however chequered, has fostered a new awareness of the potential splendor of Bolívar's dream. It would be invidious to single out the countries which have most actively promoted this process, but the foreign policy of Chile between 1964 and 1970 should certainly be mentioned as having been decisively geared to the ideal of unity.

In May 1969, at the Chilean seaside resort of Viña del Mar, the Special Latin American Co-ordinating Committee, bestknown by its Spanish acronym, CECLA,[1] produced what future historians may possibly regard as one of the most interesting and important collective pronouncements of the Latin American nations in many years. This document, known as the Consensus of Viña del Mar, set out a common Latin American position on the question of development, particularly insofar as relations with the United States were concerned. The signatories of the Consensus asked the Chilean foreign minister, Gabriel Valdés, to deliver a copy to President Nixon. This he duly did on June 11, 1969, summarizing the contents of the CECLA document in a speech to the American president. Among other things, he told Mr. Nixon:

[1] This body, created at the suggestion of the Brazilian government, was asked by the "Group of the 77," a joint committee of seventy-seven underdeveloped countries, to prepare a statement on Latin American objectives for UNCTAD.

... the present interests of development in Latin America are not identical to those of the United States. They even tend to become progressively contradictory in many aspects. ... The emergence of *a growing continental nationalism that seeks an affirmation of Latin American personality*, with conceptions, values and patterns of organizations of its own, must be accepted as *legitimate and irreversible.* (Italics added.)

It was easy for critics and cynics to dismiss the Consensus of Viña del Mar as yet another exercise in idealistic rhetoric, as a meaningless symbolic gesture, or as a misconceived theory espoused by the "Latin American bourgeoisies," whatever they may be. It would, of course, be unreasonable to take it as a glorious culmination of the movement toward Latin American unity—but it might possibly be fair to look on it as an "end of the beginning," and something more than just an expression of pious hopes. The document did, after all, present clear evidence that a spirit of "continental nationalism"—to use the phrase adopted by Valdés—was springing up. It reflected a growing determination to abandon fatalism and to place Latin American destinies more firmly in Latin American hands. Its harshest critics could hardly do more—if asked to replace it with another document—than express the same aspirations in very similar terms.

The new moves in the direction of Latin American unity in the 1960s were the most significant to be taken since the independence period and the failure of Bolívar's dreams of confederation. They were certainly more realistic—and actually *did* more—than the plans debated in the two Lima conferences of the mid-nineteenth century. But within Latin America itself, writers and politicians alike were, by the start of the 1970s, considering a variety of different possible arrangements which might smooth the way for, complement, or (under other circumstances) actually reverse the trend toward unity. A case in point—an important case—was the formation, already mentioned several times, of the Andean group of countries, which pledged themselves to common plans for development and growth. The Central American Common Market, too, had by 1970 shown an impressive record of achievement, though how far this can be continued remains to be seen. Both of these experiments affected groups of states *within* Latin America rather than the region as a whole. And in certain circles, too, there was a growing belief that those nations which bordered on the Pacific Ocean should capitalize on the fact that they faced toward such highly developed countries as Japan and Australia, and toward such potentially considerable markets as China and Indonesia. In September 1970 at Viña del

Mar an academic conference considered ways and means in which Latin America could turn her attention to the Pacific basin. Those who took part included representatives not only from Latin America but also from New Zealand, Australia, Singapore, and Japan. The conference, I repeat, was an academic rather than a political occasion,[1] and whether this Pacific aspiration could be translated into practical policies is very much a question for the future—but the idea itself seems an interesting one, and full of fruitful possibilities for the west coast republics.

Is there any need for *all* the Latin American states to join in the formation of a distinctive bloc? Bolívar's dream—in one version at least—included them all. Yet might it not be better, for instance, for Mexico to seek closer economic relations with the United States or for Chile and Peru, say, to develop the trans-Pacific links I have already mentioned? It is, of course, perfectly legitimate to assume that the Latin America of the future could very well turn out to be somewhat polymorphous—after all, we should not forget that Canada figures as part of the North American civilization as well as the United States, and the fact that Canada possesses different national interests from those of the United States has not (so far, at least) impeded good-neighborly collaboration on many issues, especially defense and the easy movement of people across a wholly undefended border. It may well be that if in the future a united Latin American bloc comes into existence, some Latin American states may wish to assume a Canadian-style position in relation to the states included in the bloc. And why not?

It is impossible, then, to assume that the rounded shape and form of Latin American unity is easily or safely predictable. The Viña Consensus, the common hopes of the Andean group, the contemplation of new commercial opportunities across the Pacific—these things may best be regarded, perhaps, as straws in a wind whose ultimate direction, at the start of the 1970s, is still difficult to chart. One thing does seem increasingly clear, however. The weathervane may shift from side to side; the wind itself may be gusty and steady by turns; but the wind may also be blowing away some of the cobwebs that have obscured the Latin American vision for so long. For a greater self-confidence is in the air. Latin Americans of many kinds now seem to appreciate once again that the impetus to progress has to spring from within, and that there is no need to accept or adopt a fatalistic attitude toward the future or to the outside world. The elusive quality of *confidence*—which lies midway between apathetic underconfidence and brash overconfidence

---

[1] The conference was held under the auspices of the Institute of International Affairs of the University of Chile, whose public-spirited director, Dr. Claudio Véliz, was a notable advocate of trans-Pacific contacts. Véliz is now in Australia.

—is the root of all achievement. If it can be increasingly harnessed in the Latin America of the next few years, then there is no reason why the region, through its own progress, should not make a substantially greater impact on the rest of the world than has been common in the past. Latin Americans often claim that they have been "marginal" to the main processes of the history of mankind in the last five hundred years, and it is difficult to disagree altogether, but need this remain true indefinitely? The only people who can answer that are the Latin Americans themselves.

Ever since its discovery, Latin America has exercised an exotic and potent attraction on the imagination of Europe. Abbé Raynal's belief that the Creoles would contribute "a fortunate revolution" to the world was far from being an isolated fantasy. "I am often inclined to think," wrote an English pamphleteer in 1830, "that this best part of the New World has, perhaps, been reserved to carry liberalism to its greatest extent."[1] Hegel, in the sentence used as one of the epigraphs for this chapter, looked on the New World as the place where the burden of world history would be revealed—though, being Hegel, he saw this revelation in terms of conflict rather than peace or friendship. The habit of projecting optimistic and even utopian hopes onto the remote and mysterious screen so conveniently provided by Latin America is not easily lost. In 1960 two English observers saluted the Cuban revolution as nothing less than "a fresh invention of man in society."[2]

In all such visions, the future plays a dominant role. The exiled German writer Stefan Zweig, contemplating the immense geographical extent of the country in which he took refuge in 1939, wrote: "Where there is space, there is not only time but also the future. And in Brazil one can feel the strong rustling of its wings."[3] The English novelist Christopher Isherwood compared the effervescent surface of South American life which he observed on a visit in 1947–48 to the bubbles on the water of a pot:

What is cooking in there, with such ominous sounds, nobody now alive will ever know. A new race and a new culture, certainly. Perhaps an entirely different kind of sensibility, an original approach to life, expressed in other terms, another language. But whatever it may be, it *is* cooking.[4]

[1] Anonymous, *On the Disturbances in South America* (London, 1830), p. 44.

[2] P. Anderson and R. Blackburn, "Cuba, Free Territory of America," *The New University*, No. 4 (Oxford, December 1960), p. 23.

[3] *Brazil, Land of the Future*, 2nd ed. (London, 1942), p. 133.

[4] Isherwood, *The Condor and the Cows* (London, 1949), p. 195.

Who knows? Such visions may one day come true, and the agonies and misfortunes of Latin American history described in this book may be looked back on as half-forgotten nightmares, as the outward signs of a barbarous epoch left behind for good. I suspect, however, that even when utopia is finally reached, Plato's ghost will still be on hand to ask, with Yeats, "What then?" But at this point history shades into metahistory, poetic fantasy, and sheer hallucination. And here, too, my account must come to an end, for in the very nature of things it cannot deal with those unknown regions of future time for which there is no known chart, compass, or lodestar.

A Note on Further Reading

The historical literature on Latin America is enormous and it is growing substantially every year. Readers who are interested in making a serious or more specialized study of a particular period or aspect of Latin American history are strongly advised to consult one of the following two bibliographical guides:

R. A. Humphreys, *Latin American History. A Guide to the Literature in English* (London, 1958)
Charles C. Griffin (ed.), *Latin America. A Guide to the Historical Literature* (Austin, Texas, 1971)

Beyond this, the serious reader is recommended to look at the history sections of the annually published *Handbook of Latin American Studies* (Cambridge, Mass., 1936–51, and Gainesville, Florida, 1951 onwards).

Footnotes and references have been kept to a minimum in this book, but the reader may find many of the works referred to or cited to be of interest in exploring the subject further.

Index

Abascal, José Fernando de, 14
Acosta, Father José de, 126, 168–9, 178
Acton, Lord, 339, 340
Africans, *see* Negroes, Slave trade, Slavery
Agrarian reform, 273–7
Agriculture, 39, 83–4, 168–9, 171–2, 177, 178, 180–2, 184, 199, 201, 205, 207, 219, 244, 257, 258, 273–7
see also Specific countries
Aguirre, Francisco de, 147
Aguirre Cerda, Pedro, 48
Airlines, 96, 98–100
ALALC, *see* Latin American Free Trade Area
Alamán, Lucas, 343
Alberdi, Juan Bautista, 388
Alvarez, Alejandro, 393
Alessandri, Arturo, 45, 48
Alessandri, Jorge, 69, 70, 342n., 347
Alexander VI (Pope), 2, 119n.
Allegiances and values and development, 279–82
Allende, Dr. Salvador, xiv, 70–1, 274n., 291, 295n., 300, 320n., 347, 365, 366
Alliance for Progress, 67, 287, 399
Altamirano, Carlos, 355n.
Alvear, Marcelo, 45
Amazon River, 81–2
American People's Revolutionary Alliance, *see* APRA
Amerindians, *see* Indians
Ancón Treaty (1883), 31
Andean Common Market, 67, 295
Andean Group, 97, 294–5, 404
Andean Pact, 295
Anderson, Charles W., 299
Andes Mountains, 78–80, 86, 93–4
Anglo-Spanish Treaty (1604), 6

APRA (American People's Revolutionary Alliance), 47, 56, 67, 116, 348, 349–50, 393
Aranda, Count, 130
Araucanian Indians, 103, 112, 114, 148
Arawak Indians, 3, 102–3, 110
Arbenz, Lt.-Col. Jacobo, 59, 364, 397
Areche, José Antonio de, 306
Arévalo, Juan José, 59, 364, 401
Argentina
  agriculture, 207–8, 219, 220, 230
  in ALALC, 66n.
  British expeditions to, 10–11
  under Cámpora, 73, 362
  under Juárez Celman, 35
  colony of Spain, 4, 7, 177, 305, 306
  "de-Peronization," 59
  in Depression, 240
  descamisados, 58, 59
  estancieros, 230–1
  European immigration, 132, 153–5, 156, 157, 159, 230
  under Frondizi, 72, 347–8
  geography, 75, 76, 78, 81, 82–3
  under Illía, 73, 347
  independence from Spain, 12, 13–14, 205, 378
  Indians, 35, 114
  industrialization, 244, 246, 248, 249, 250
  international economy, 221, 229–31, 237, 238
  international relations, 381, 382, 383, 394, 395
  under Irigoyen, 43–5, 47, 347
  under Justo, 47
  under Lanusse, 73
  under Levingston, 73
  meat exports, 220, 230
  mestizos, 148

Argentina—*continued*
  middle class, 253
  under Mitre, 24, 28
  natural resources, 83, 84, 85
  under Onganía, 73, 330, 347
  under Perón, 57–9, 72, 100, 246,
    250, 256, 323, 327, 336, 337,
    359–62, 397
  political movements, 342n., 343,
    346, 347–8, 355–6, 359–62
  political traditions, 305, 320, 323–4,
    330, 331, 333, 336, 337, 339,
    340n.
  Radical Party, 43, 45, 47
  under Roca, 35, 114, 224–5
  Roca–Runciman Pact, 48, 240, 285
  under Rosas, 23, 24, 91, 153, 208,
    230, 327, 328, 337n., 343
  under Sáenz Peña, 43
  under Sarmiento, 24, 92, 343
  trade, 201, 207, 210
  trade unions, 256, 278, 361
  transport and communications, 87,
    88, 90, 91, 92, 93, 94, 95, 96,
    98n., 99, 100
  and United States, 73, 381
  urbanization, 259
  under Urquiza, 23–4
  War of the Triple Alliance, 26–9
  World War II, 53, 55, 57, 394, 395
Armed forces, 266–7, 282, 330, 336
  see also Caudillos, Militarism
Arosemena, Carlos Julio, 334n.
Artigas, José Gervasio, 13
Asiento, 8, 134, 135, 195
Asociación Latinoamericana de Ferro-
    carriles, 95
Atahualpa, 3
Audiencias, 109, 171, 303, 305, 306
Automobiles, 96–8
Avellaneda, Nicolás de, 24
Aztec Confederacy, 3, 104–5, 111,
    113, 187

Balboa, Vasco Núñez de, 2
Balkanization, 378–80
Balmaceda, José Manuel, 32, 227,
    234
Balta, President, 94
Banana production, 220
Bandeiras, 6–7

Banks, 244
Baquedano, Gen. Manuel, 31
Barreiro, General, 15
Barrientos, Gen. René, 61, 66
Batista, Fulgencio, 63, 327, 335,
    364n.
Batlle y Ordóñez, José, 43, 246, 345,
    346n.
Bautista, Juan, 113n.
Bay of Pigs invasion, 64, 400
Bazaine, General, 26
Béjar, Héctor, 297
Beláunde Terry, Fernando, 69, 97,
    116
Belgrano, Manuel, 112–13
Bello, Joaquin Edwards, 227, 394
Bentham, Jeremy, 311n.
Berle, Adolf A., 291–2, 297
Betancourt, Rómulo, 56, 63, 351, 352,
    353
Black Legend, 124
Blaine, James G., 389
Blanco-Fombona, Horacio, 393
Bolívar, Simón, 13, 15, 16, 17, 18,
    34n., 112, 113, 131, 141, 211,
    312, 314–15, 319, 379–80, 381,
    384, 387, 405, 406
Bolivia
  agriculture, 264, 274
  in Andean Common Market, 67
  under Barrientos, 61, 66
  Chaco War, 48, 49–51
  colony of Spain, 3
  constitution of 1826, 314, 315
  geography, 78–9, 82, 264
  Guevara in, 66, 367
  independence from Spain, 17–18
  Indians, 59, 114, 115–16, 117, 158
  Japanese immigration, 157
  mestizos, 158
  mining, 174, 219, 220
  MNR, 263–4, 348, 350–1, 352–5
  natural resources, 84–5
  under Paz Estenssoro, 61, 350, 351
  Peru–Bolivian Confederation, 21
  political movements, 348, 350–1,
    352, 367
  political traditions, 314–15, 319,
    329
  revolution, 263–4
  under Santa Cruz, 21

Bolivia—*continued*
  trade unions, 256n., 257
  transport and communications, 95, 97, 98–9
  War of the Pacific, 29–31, 220, 224, 386, 388
Bolognesi, Col. Francisco, 31
Bosch, Juan, 65
Boves, José Tomás, 13
Brasilia, 61, 71, 93, 97
Brazil
  agriculture, 171–2, 177, 178, 207, 219, 220, 231–3
  in ALALC, 66n.
  Brasilia, 61, 71, 93, 97
  "Brazilian miracle," 72
  under Castello Branco, 71
  castes, 151
  coffee production, 207, 219, 220, 231–2, 240, 285
  colony of Portugal, 2, 4–5, 6–7, 112, 123, 171–2, 201, 206–7
  under Costa e Silva, 72
  Creoles, 128n., 211
  under Deodoro da Fonseca, 33
  Depression, 47
  ethnic makeup, 132, 145, 149, 155–156, 157, 159, 232, 233
  under Garrastazú Médici, 72
  geography, 75, 76, 80, 81
  under Goulart, 71
  independence from Portugal, 9–10, 16–17, 211, 378, 382
  Indians, 103, 114, 116, 143–4, 172
  industrialization, 244, 249, 250
  Institutional Act, 71
  international economy, 221, 231–3, 239
  international relationships, 381, 382, 392
  under Kubitschek, 61, 71
  middle class, 253–4
  mining, 174–5, 178, 199
  under Morais, 33–4
  natural resources, 84, 85
  "New State," 51–2, 359
  under Pedro I, 17, 21
  under Pedro II, 21, 22, 28, 32, 93, 141
  under Peixoto, 33

  political movements, 342n., 343, 358–9, 363
  political traditions, 302, 309, 316, 321, 322, 331, 333, 336, 339, 340n.
  under Princess Isabel, 133
  under Quadros, 71
  regional disparities, 233
  republic, 33
  "Republic of Palmares," 33–4, 138
  revolution, 9–10, 21–2
  under Rio Branco, 32
  Second Reign, 22, 32, 141
  slavery, 32–3, 134, 136, 137–8, 139, 140, 141–2, 149–50, 155, 172, 179, 197, 198, 231–2
  transport and communications, 89, 91, 92–3, 94, 95, 97, 99, 100
  and United States, 72, 381n.
  under Vargas, 51–2, 55, 56, 61, 156, 246, 256, 322, 336, 359, 363
  War of the Triple Alliance, 26–9
  World War I, 392
  World War II, 55
Brinton, Crane, 300
Brogan, Sir Denis, 298–9
Brum, Baltasar, 393
Bryce, Lord, 390n.
Burton, Sir Richard, 142
Bustamante, José Luis, 56

Cabildo, 306
Cabral, Pedro Alvares, 2, 4, 163
"Caciques," 321
Caldera, Rafael, 68, 356
Calderón de la Barca, Mrs. Frances, 213
Calles, Plutarco Elías, 43, 52
Câmara, Dom Helder, 370
Camoens, Luis Vaz de, 123
Campanella, Tommaso, 174, 177, 374
Campomanes, Count, 130
Cámpora, Dr. Héctor, 73, 362
Canada, 293, 406
Canning, George, 381, 382, 385
Canterac, General, 17
Capitulaciones, 163, 170
Cárdenas, Gen. Lázaro, 52–3, 68, 115, 288, 352

Carib Indians, 3, 103, 110
Caribbean Islands, 3, 75–6, 103, 134, 135, 149, 168, 179, 219, 332, 388, 391, 392
   see also Cuba, Dominican Republic, Haiti, Hispaniola, West Indies
Carranza, Venustiano, 42, 43
Carrera, José Miguel, 325
Cartagena Manifesto, 314
Castello Branco, Gen. Humberto de Alencar, 71
Castes, 150–3, 211
Castillo, Bernal Díaz del, 164
Castillo, Ramon, 55
Castillo Armas, Col. Carlos, 59, 364
Castro, Gen. Cipríano, 34
Castro, Dr. Fidel, 63–5, 66, 68, 69, 264, 265, 274, 287, 327, 328–9, 364, 368, 398
Castro, Raúl, 63
Catholic Church, see Roman Catholic Church
Catholic revolutionism, 369–71
Caudillos, 19, 22, 23, 313, 326–9, 330, 331, 332, 334, 335, 343
   see also Dictatorships, Militarism
Caxias, Marshal, 28
CECLA, 404–5
Central America, 18, 40, 55, 57, 67, 75, 77–8, 90, 93, 97, 99, 101, 103, 138, 158, 183, 219, 220, 244, 320, 381n., 392
   see also Specific countries
Central American Common Market (MCCA), 67, 294, 404, 405
Central banks, 244
CEPAL, see ECLA
Cereals production, 220
Cervantes, Miguel de, 120, 127n.
Cervera, Admiral, 37
Chaco War, 48
Charles I (King of Spain), see Charles V
Charles III (King of Spain), 7, 8, 130, 199, 302, 309
Charles IV (King of Spain), 11, 152, 375
Charles V (Emperor), 3, 4, 7, 125, 127, 130, 134, 146, 165, 302, 374
Charrúas Indians, 114
Charter of Punta del Este, 67

Chartered trading corporations, 200–1
Chávez, Carlos, 43
Chevalier, François, 192
Chibcha Indians, 103, 110
Chile
   agriculture, 178, 208, 234, 235, 274
   under Aguirre Cerda, 48
   in ALALC, 66n., 67
   under Alessandri, 45, 48, 69, 347
   under Allende, 70–1, 274n., 291, 295n., 347, 365, 366
   Ancón Treaty, 31
   in Andean Common Market, 67, 295
   under Balmaceda, 32, 227, 234
   civil wars, 32, 316
   colony of Spain, 3, 14, 305
   Depression, 48
   ethnic makeup, 141, 147, 157, 159
   under Frei Montalva, 69, 274n., 356, 357, 358
   geography, 75, 76, 78, 79, 80
   under González Videla, 56, 364
   under Ibáñez del Campo, 48, 335–6
   independence from Spain, 12, 14–15, 211, 212, 214–15, 316–18, 380
   Indians, 103, 106, 112, 114
   industrialization, 185, 248, 249, 250
   international economy, 221, 233–5
   international relations, 381, 382, 394–5, 404–5
   middle class, 253
   mining, 174, 175, 210, 219, 220, 224, 234–5
   under Montt, 21, 233
   natural resources, 84, 85, 86, 220
   nitrate production, 29, 220, 224, 234–5, 239
   under O'Higgins, 20
   political movements, 343, 345, 346, 347, 355n., 357–8, 363–4, 365
   political traditions, 305, 316–18, 319, 322, 323, 324, 325, 331, 332, 335–6, 340
   under Portales, 20, 21, 214–15, 233, 317
   under Santa María, 234
   slavery, 141
   stability of government, 20–1, 316–318, 319, 322
   trade, 207

Chile—*continued*
trade unions, 256
transport and communications, 88, 90, 91, 92, 93, 94, 95, 96, 97, 99
and United States, 288, 381, 399, 402
urbanization, 259
War of the Pacific, 29–31, 220, 224, 386, 388
World War II, 55
Christian Democracy, 348, 356–8
Church, *see* Roman Catholic Church
Churchill, Winston S., 37n.
Científicos, 36
City, 173, 177–8, 182, 184, 185, 186–8, 194, 202–3, 216, 225, 246, 247, 248, 251, 253, 257, 258–61, 280, 306
see also Urbanization
Civil wars, 330, 331
Clemenceau, Georges, 155
Cobban, Alfred, 400
Cochrane, Lord Thomas, 15, 90
Coffee industry, 207, 219, 220, 231–2, 240, 285
Cold War, 55, 58, 364, 396, 402
Colombia
agriculture, 219
in ALALC, 66n.
in Andean Common Market, 67
Congress of Panama, 380
Depression, 48
under Gaitán, 56–7
geography, 81
under Gómez, 57, 345–6
independence from Spain, 12, 13, 15, 333
Indians, 103, 106, 110
industrialization, 244, 249
international relations, 381, 382
in Korean War, 55n.
Leticia Incident, 48
under López, 48
mestizos, 159
natural resources, 85
under Núñez, 34
under Pastrana, 67
political movements, 344, 345, 367
political traditions, 319, 323, 330, 332, 336
under Rojas Pinilla, 57, 63, 280, 336
under Santander, 333
Thousand Days' War, 34
transport and communications, 93, 97, 98, 100
and United States, 38, 381
Colonia, 8
Colonial government, 305–7
Colonial life
city in, 173, 177–8, 182, 184, 185, 186–8, 194, 202–3
hacienda, 179, 180, 181–3, 184, 209
latifundio, 173, 179–84, 208
minifundio, 184
peón, 180, 181, 209
plantations, 179, 181
ranching, 178, 179, 183
Roman Catholic Church, 173, 185, 188–92
social order, 173–4, 195
wealth, 185–6
Columbus, Christopher, 2, 101, 102, 120, 162, 163, 168, 189
Commodities, 220–1, 239, 285
Common market, *see* Central American Common Market, Latin American Free Trade Area
Communications, *see* Transport and Communications
Communist parties, 46–7, 56, 59, 64, 70, 271, 337, 341, 342, 362–6, 367
Concubinage, *see* Miscegenation
Condorcanqui, José Gabriel, *see* Túpac Amaru
Congress of Panama, 18, 380, 384
Conquistadores, 3, 4, 107, 121, 124, 131, 143, 146, 164, 170, 171
Consensus of Viña del Mar, 294, 404–5
Conservatism, *see* Right-wing movements
Consulados, 194, 195
Copper industry, 220, 234, 239
Córdoba Treaty (1821), 16
Cornejo Chávez, Hector, 356n.
"Coronels," 321
Corregidor, 304–5, 306
Corruption, 282–4, 304–5, 306, 308, 316, 321, 337
Cortés, Hernán, 3, 77, 104, 105, 115, 145, 165, 167
Cortés, Martín, 145n., 148
Costa e Silva, Marshal Artur, 72

Costa Rica
in Central American Common
Market, 67
civil war (1948), 57
ethnic makeup, 159
under Figueres, 57, 323
political movements, 348, 350
political traditions, 318, 319, 323,
332, 337, 338
transport and communications, 93
Cotegipe, Baron, 33
Council of the Indies, 4, 303, 304, 305,
307
Coups d'état, 329–31
Creoles
cabildo, 306
and castes, 151, 152
and colonial government, 304, 306
and economic development, 161,
179, 185, 195, 214, 223, 225, 228
and Europeans, 127–31, 376–77
French culture, 386, 387
after independence from Spain, 211,
214, 224, 311
and Indians, 112–14
and latifundio, 179, 181, 183, 184
nations, 18–39, 211–17, 228, 310–14,
316, 332–3
new nations, 131–3
Peninsular Spaniards, 128, 130, 151,
152, 179, 203, 208, 214
political behavior, 310–14, 316–18,
325, 332
rebellions, 9, 10, 12, 310
regionalism, 131, 375–6, 378, 379
social positions, 195, 197, 198, 203,
211, 214
Cromwell, Oliver, 6
Cuauhtémoc, 115
Cuba
agriculture, 208, 220, 264, 265, 276
under Batista, 63, 327, 364n.
Bay of Pigs invasion, 64, 400
under Castro, 63–5, 66, 68, 142,
242, 264–5, 273, 274, 282, 287,
327, 328–9, 337, 364, 398, 400
colony of Spain, 2, 8, 18, 37, 201,
305
in COMECON, 68
emigration, 157
ethnic makeup, 156, 157, 159

exporting revolution, 65, 66
First Declaration of Havana, 64
geography, 76, 78
independence from Spain, 37–8
Indians, 114
industrialization, 265
missile crisis, 65, 398
natural resources, 84
under Estrada Palma, 38–9
Platt Amendment, 38, 53
political movements, 364
political traditions, 305, 322, 335, 337
revolution of 1959, 63–5, 66, 68,
142, 242, 264–5, 298, 398
Second Declaration of Havana, 65,
366
slavery, 136, 139, 141, 142
and Soviet Union, 64, 285, 287,
364n., 373, 398, 403
Ten Years' War, 37
trade unions, 256
transportation and communications,
99
and United States, 37–8, 39, 52–3,
64–5, 68, 264, 398–9, 400

Daza, Hilarión, 29, 31
Declaration of Lima, 53
De Gaulle, Gen. Charles, 402, 403
Democratic reforming movements,
348–58
Democratic socialism, 355–6
Denmark, 6n., 135, 141n.
Deodoro da Fonseca, Marshal Manoel,
33
Depression, 48, 238, 239–40, 241, 243,
248
Descamisados, 58, 59
Dessalines, Jean Jacques, 10
Díaz, Adolfo, 45
Díaz, Bernal, 121
Díaz, Gen. Porfirio, 36, 39, 40, 114,
220, 224, 225, 236–7, 262–3, 331
Díaz Ordaz, Gustavo, 68
Dictatorships, 316, 318, 324–39
Dilemmas of contemporary Latin
America
agrarian question, 273–7
allegiances and values, 279–82
distribution of wealth, 252, 273,
277–9

Dilemmas of contemporary Latin America—*continued*
economic and social progress, 269–271
economic dependence, 284–93
future social order, 296–7
Latin American commonwealth, 293–300
population explosion, 271–3
reform and revolution, 295–6, 298–300
state and, 282–4
technology gap, 286–7
Disraeli, Benjamin, 222
Distribution of wealth, 252, 273, 277–279
Dominican Republic
under Bosch, 65
geography, 78
independence, 19, 26
mulattoes, 159
under Trujillo, 46, 335, 337
and United States, 38, 46, 65, 398–399
Drago, Luis María, 390
Drake, Sir Francis, 5
"Dual society," 246–7
Duvalier, Dr. François ("Papa Doc"), 46, 292

Echeverría, Luis, 68, 353
ECLA (Economic Commission for Latin America), 66, 218, 244–5, 252, 273
Economic dependence, 284–93
Economic development
capitulaciones, 163, 170
central banks, 244
colonial government, 193–5, 197, 198
"dual society," 246–7
foreign aid, 287–8
foreign-controlled industries, 251, 288–90
future developments, 266–9
governmental involvement, 245–6, 249–50, 256, 268, 278–9, 282–4
guilds, 185, 194, 200, 202
import-substitution, 249, 250
income distribution, 252
after independence, 205–16

manpower, 197–8, 256, 278
markets and, 252, 284, 285, 293
middle class, 225, 247, 252, 253–5
political aspects, 338–9
and population growth, 261
Roman Catholic Church and, 190–1, 192
"structural" reforms, 262, 265, 266
technology gap, 286–7
trade unions, 247–8, 256–7, 278
urbanization, 258–61
working class, 247, 255–6, 258–9
see also Agriculture, Industrialization, International economy, Mining, Ranching, Trade
Economic integration, 66–7, 252, 293–295
Economic Societies of Friends of the Country, 202
Ecuador, 18, 19–20, 34, 53–5, 66n., 67, 79, 84, 94, 95, 97, 114, 115n., 147–8, 150–1, 158, 219, 319, 334n.
Egaña, Juan, 315n.
Ejidos, 263
El Salvador, 93, 115n., 294, 356n., 363
El Supremo, 19
Electric telegraph, 92
Elhuyar, Fausto de, 202
Encomienda system, 107–8, 109, 110, 111, 125, 146, 166–7, 179–80, 193
Enríquez, Martin, 148
Escalante, Anibal, 364n.
Estancieros, 230–1
Estigarribia, Gen. José Félix, 49, 51n.
Estrada Palma, Tomás, 38, 39
Ethnic makeup
castes, 150–3, 211
Creoles, 127–33, 151, 152
"elite migratory groups," 155, 157
Europeans, 127–33, 153–7, 223, 230, 248
Iberians, 117–27
Indians, 101–17
mestizos, 110, 115, 132, 142, 145–149, 151, 158, 159, 180, 195, 211
miscegenation, 143, 144, 145–50
mulattoes, 149–50, 151, 159, 211
Negroes, 132–42, 145, 147, 149–50, 159, 211
non-Europeans, 157–8
prejudice, 151–3

Ethnic makeup—*continued*
  single main element, 158–9
  zambos, 150, 151
  see also Specific countries
European immigration, 127–33, 153–157, 159, 223, 230, 248
Export-Import Bank, 53, 242

Farquhar, Percival, 95
Fascism, 358–62
Faucett, Elmer J., 99
Feijóo, Fray Benito Jerónimo, 129
Ferdinand of Aragon, 2, 119–20
Ferdinand VII (King of Spain), 11, 12, 13, 325
Ferns, H. S., 231
Figueres, José ("Pepe"), 57, 323, 351
Flores, Gen. Juan José, 19, 384
Floridablanca, Count, 130
"Football war," 294
Forced labor, *see* Mita, Repartimento, Slavery
Foreign aid, 287–8
Foreign investment, 221–3, 226–8, 230–1, 234, 236, 240, 242, 291–2
  see also Great Britain, United States
France
  in Brazil, 5, 6
  French revolution, 10, 140, 202, 310, 368, 398
  Guadeloupe and Martinique, 6
  Haitian revolt, 10, 140, 241
  in Holy Alliance, 381–2, 386
  Mexican invasion, 25–6, 383, 386–7
  Paris Treaty (1762), 9
  relations with Latin America, 381–3, 386–7, 390
  Ryswick Treaty (1697), 6
  Saint Domingue, 136, 137, 140, 201–2
  Seven Years' War, 9
  slave trade, 135, 136, 140
  Versailles Treaty (1783), 9
  World War II, 53
  see also Napoleon Bonaparte
Francia, Dr. José Gaspar Rodriguez de, 19, 292, 325
Franco-Hapsburg empire in Mexico, 25–6, 383
Frei Montalva, Eduardo, 69, 70, 274n., 356, 357, 358, 403n.

Freyre, Gilberto, 143–4, 145, 150
Frondizi, Arturo, 72, 347–8

Gage, Thomas, 176, 186–7, 189
Gaitán, Jorge Eliécer, 56
Gálvez, José de, 306
Gama, Vasco da, 1, 119, 373
Gamarra, Gen. Agustín, 21, 141
Ganivet, Angel, 120, 123
García Calderón, Francisco, 227, 237
García Moreno, Gabriel, 19–20
García Reyes, Antonio, 385
Garcilaso de la Vega, Inca, 122n., 148
Garibaldi, Giuseppe, 22n.
Garrastazú Médici, Gen. Emilio, 72
Gasca, Pedro de la, 4, 144n., 146
Geography
  agriculture and, 178
  Amazon River, 81–2
  Andes Mountains, 78–80, 86, 93–4
  dimensions and position, 75–7
  lowlands, 81
  natural resources, 83–6
  pampa, 35, 82, 83
  plateau, 80–1
  regionalism and, 378, 379
  rivers, 79, 80, 81–2, 88
  surface configuration, 77–83
  volcanoes, 79, 80
  see also Specific countries
Germany, 242n., 391, 392, 394, 396
Ghioldi, Américo, 356
Gibbon, Edward, 283
Glade, William, 172, 221n., 243n., 245
Gladstone, William E., 386
"Golconda" group, 371
Gómez, Juan Vicente, 34, 96, 244, 328, 331
Gómez, Laureano, 48, 56, 57, 345–6
González Videla, Gabriel, 56, 364
"Good Neighbor" policy, 53, 350
GOU, 359–60
Goulart, João, 71, 72
Governor of colony, *see* Viceroy
Grancolombia, 34n.
Grau, Adm. Miguel, 31
Great Britain
  Anglo-Spanish Treaty, 6
  industrial revolution, 217–18

Great Britain—*continued*
  investment in Latin America, 221,
    222, 223, 226, 227, 230–1, 234,
    242, 378
  in Latin America, 5, 6, 10–11, 201,
    378, 383
  Paris Treaty, 9
  relations with Latin American
    states, 381, 382, 383, 385–6, 389–
    390, 391, 392, 403
  Roca-Runciman Pact, 48, 240, 285
  Seven Years' War, 9
  slave trade, 8, 135, 140, 141
  trade with Latin America, 206–7,
    208n., 209, 210, 215, 219, 240–1,
    378, 392
  Versailles Treaty, 9
  War of Jenkins' Ear, 8
Guadeloupe, 6
Guadalupe Hidalgo Treaty (1848), 25
Guaraní Indians, 8, 103
Guatemala, 59, 77, 85, 93, 103, 115,
  125, 158, 185, 356n., 364, 367,
  397
Guerrillas, 330, 331, 366, 367, 370,
  398
Guevara, Ernesto ("Che"), 63, 66,
  366, 367, 368, 369, 400n.
Guilds, 185, 194, 200, 202
Guzmán Blanco, Antonio, 19, 34

Hacienda, 179, 180, 181–3, 184, 209,
  224, 235, 246, 248, 258, 274, 276,
  280, 343
Haiti, 10, 19, 45, 46, 78, 136, 137,
  140–1, 159, 275, 292
Hawkins, John, 5
Haya de la Torre, Victor Raúl, 47, 56,
  69, 116, 349, 350, 352, 393, 397
Head, Francis Bond, 212
Henry the Navigator (Prince of
  Portugal), 119, 162
Hidalgo, Father Miguel, 12, 39, 113,
  378
Hispaniola, 2, 6, 19, 78, 138, 146, 169
  see also Dominican Republic, Haiti
Holy Alliance, 381–2, 386
Honduras, 78, 158, 294
Huayna Capac (Emperor), 106, 146n.,
  148
Huerta, Gen. Victoriano, 40–1, 45

Humboldt, Alexander von, 88–9, 130–
  131, 136, 139, 150, 152, 175, 190,
  202, 209

Ibáñez del Campo, Gen. Carlos, 45,
  48, 335–6
Iberians
  character, 120–3, 132
  conscience, 124–7
  Creole and European, 127–31
  medieval kingdoms, 117–20
  new Iberian nations, 131–3
Illía, Arturo, 73, 347
Import-substitution, 249, 250
Inca Empire, 3, 87, 105–7, 111, 187
Income distribution, 252, 273, 277–9
Independence of Latin American
  colonies, *see* Specific countries
Indians
  Araucanians, 103, 112, 114, 148
  Arawaks, 3, 102–3, 110
  Aztecs, 3, 104–5, 111, 113, 187
  before the conquest, 102–7, 122
  Black Legend, 124
  Caribs, 3, 103, 110
  Chibcha, 103, 110
  under colonial rule, 107–12, 166,
    167, 168, 176, 184, 374
  and conscience of the conquerors,
    124–7
  corregidor de indios, 304–5
  Creole attitude, 112–14
  encomienda system, 107–8, 109,
    110, 111, 125, 146, 166–7, 179–80,
    193
  Guaraní, 8, 103
  Inca Empire, 3, 87, 105–7, 111, 187
  after independence, 112–17, 209,
    211, 216, 224, 227n.
  Juzgado General de Indios, 109
  lands, 110–11, 113–14, 115, 166,
    168, 179–80, 184, 209, 224, 258
  and latifundio, 180, 181, 258
  Maya Empire, 103–4
  miscegenation, 145, 146–7, 148–9,
    151n., 152
  mita, 111, 113, 176, 180, 193, 196
  New Laws of the Indies, 4, 108–9,
    125
  obrajes, 196
  and political movements, 348, 349

Indians—*continued*
  population, 101–2, 110, 112, 115, 125, 134
  rebellions, 7, 9, 114
  "reductions," 8, 111, 191
  "regrouping," 109–10, 168
  Requerimiento, 124–5
  slavery, 107, 114, 124, 125, 176
  Toltec, 104
  Tupí, 103
  War of Castes, 114
  Yaqui, 114
  see also Mestizos, Specific countries, Zambos
Industrial revolution, 217–18
Industrialization, 181, 184, 193, 210, 223, 240, 243, 244, 245, 248–53, 260, 286
Ingenieros, José, 393
Inquisition, 189
Institutional Revolutionary Party, see PRI
"Integration," 55, 66–7, 252, 293–5, 380
  see also "Inter-American system," Unity
Intendancies, 305, 306
Inter-American Conference on Indian Life, 116
Inter-American Development Bank, 242
"Inter-American system," 55, 66–7, 252, 293–5, 388–9, 390, 394, 395, 397, 399
  see also "Integration," Unity
International economy
  commodities, 220–1, 239
  Depression, 238, 239–40, 241, 243, 248
  economic nationalism, 226, 227
  foreign investment in Latin America, 221–3, 226–8, 230–1, 234, 236, 240, 242, 291–2
  governmental policies, 224–5, 243–6
  impact on Latin America, 219–24, 226–9, 237, 246, 247, 385
  industrial revolution, 217–18
  monoproduction, 226, 227, 232, 239, 243, 285
  price fluctuation, 239, 285
  tariffs, 239, 245, 249, 294

World War I, 238, 239, 240, 243, 248
World War II, 240, 242
  see also Economic development, Specific countries
International relationships
  China, 396, 401, 403
  Cold War, 55, 58, 364, 396, 402
  colonial period, 373–7
  France, 381, 382–3, 386–7, 390
  Germany, 242n., 391, 392, 394
  Great Britain, 381, 382, 383, 385–6, 389–90, 391, 392, 403
  independence, 378–80
  Japan, 228–9, 391, 395, 396, 403
  nationalism, 379, 385
  Soviet Union, 64, 285, 287, 364n., 365, 367, 373, 395–6, 398, 400, 403
  Spain, 391
  and Superpowers, 395–401, 403
  United States, 381, 387–90, 391, 392–3, 394, 397–400, 401, 402
  Western Europe, 402–3
  World War I, 238, 239, 240, 243, 248, 392–4
  World War II, 53–5, 99–100, 240, 242, 243, 248, 394–5
  see also Specific countries
Investment in Latin America, *see* Foreign investment
Irala, Domingo Martínez de, 147
Irigoyen, Hipólito, 43, 45, 347
Irisarri, Antonio José de, 388
Irrigation, 83, 263
Isabel (Princess of Brazil), 33
Isabella of Castile, 2, 119–20
Isherwood, Christopher, 407
I.T.T., 291
Iturbide, Agustín de, 16, 24, 315

Jamaica, 6, 78, 163
Japan, 228–9, 391, 395, 396, 403, 404
Jefferson, Thomas, 382–3, 388
Jenkins, Robert, 8n.
Jesuits, 8, 145, 146, 150, 191–2, 310
Jiménez de Quesada, Gonzalo, 4
John III (King of Portugal), 4
John VI (King of Portugal), 17
Juan, Jorge, 112, 152, 190, 196, 277
Juárez, Benito, 25, 26, 36, 113, 387
Juárez Celman, Miguel, 35

July 26th Movement, 63, 64
Junot, Marshal, 11
Juntas, 11–12
Justo, Gen. Agustin, 47
Justo, Juan Bautista, 355
Juzgado General de Indios, 109

Kennedy, John F., 64, 65, 67, 398
Khrushchev, Nikita S., 65
Kipling, Rudyard, 121
Klinger, Gen. Bertholdo, 51
Korean War, 55
Kubitschek, Dr. Juscelino, 61, 71, 72
Kundt, Gen. Hans, 49

Lacerda, Carlos, 71, 72
Land distribution, 257–8, 273–7
Land grants, *see* Encomienda system
Land tenure, 275–6
Lanusse, Gen. Alejandro, 73
Larrázabal, Adm. Wolfgang, 63, 336
Las Casas, Fray Bartolomé de, 108, 125, 126, 134
Latifundio, 173, 179–84, 208, 257, 258, 274, 275, 276, 279–80
Latin American Free Trade Area (ALALC), 66–7, 95, 294
League of Nations, 394
Lecór, General, 13
Leguía, Augusto, 47, 96–7
Lehrer, Tom, 65
León, Pedro Lieza de, 145, 146
Leoni, Raúl, 68
Lerdo Law, 25, 36, 114, 236
Leticia Incident, 48, 53
Levingston, Gen. Roberto, 73, 330
Liberal movements, 342, 344, 345
Liberalism, 310–24
Lima Conferences of 1847–8, 384–5, 388
Lisboa, Antonio Francisco, 150
Lonardi, Gen. Eduardo, 58
López, Alfonso, 48
López, Carlos Antonio, 20
López, Francisco Solano, 20, 28–9

Maciel, Antonio, 33–4
McKinley, William, 37
Madariaga, Salvador de, 290, 326–7, 399
Madero, Francisco, 40

Madrid Treaty (1750), 8
Magellan, Ferdinand, 2, 3
Manrique, Jorge, 121
Manufacturing, *see* Industrialization
Marighella, Carlos, 367n.
Marina, Doña, 145
Maritain, Jacques, 356
Martí, José, 37, 393
Martínez, Gen. Maximilian Hernández, 363
Martinique, 6
Marxism, 349, 362–3, 365, 366, 368, 371, 396
Matarazzo, Francisco, 223n.
Matta, Filómeno, 36
Maua, Viscount, 92–3, 224
Maurice of Nassau, 6
Maurits, Johan, 6
Maximilian, Archduke Ferdinand, 26, 225, 387
Maya Empire, 103–4
Mayorazgo, 183
MCCA, *see* Central American Common Market
Meat production, 220, 230
Meiggs, Henry, 94, 97
Melgarejo, Mariano, 114
Mendoza, Pedro de, 4
Mestizos, 110, 115, 132, 142, 145–9, 151, 158, 159, 180, 195, 211
Mexico
  agriculture, 236–7, 263, 274
  in ALALC, 66n.
  under Cárdenas, 52–3, 115, 288, 352
  under Calles, 52
  under Carranza, 42
  Cientificos, 36
  civil war, 42
  colony of Spain, 3, 4, 5, 7, 166, 167, 303, 304, 305, 375
  Córdoba Treaty, 16
  Creoles in, 128n.
  under Díaz, 36, 39, 40, 114, 220, 224, 225, 236–7, 262–3
  under Díaz Ordaz, 68
  under Echeverría, 68, 353–5
  ejidos, 263
  expropriation of oil industry, 52–3, 288
  Franco-Hapsburg empire, 25–6, 383, 386–7

Mexico—*continued*
geography, 25, 77
Guadalupe Hidalgo Treaty, 25
hacienda, 235–6, 262
independence from Spain, 12, 16, 213, 378–9
Indians, 3, 103–5, 109, 110, 113, 114, 115, 117, 158–9, 167, 168, 180, 209, 224, 236, 262
industrialization, 184, 249, 250, 263
international economy, 221, 235–7
international relations, 381, 382, 383
under Juárez, 25–6, 387
Lerdo Law, 25, 36, 114, 236
under Madero, 40
mestizos, 146–7, 148, 158, 262
Mexico City, 185–7, 188, 225, 259
middle class, 253–4
mining, 166, 169, 170, 174, 175, 176, 202, 209, 219, 236
natural resources, 84, 85, 86, 166
under Obregón, 43
petroleum production, 220, 250
Plan of Iguala, 16
political movements, 348, 352–5
political traditions, 304, 305, 319, 322, 330, 331, 332, 338
Porfiriato, 36, 39, 40, 114, 220, 224, 225, 236–7, 262–3
PRI, 263, 338, 348, 352–5
Reforma, 25, 115, 208, 235
revolution, 40–2, 43, 115, 248, 256, 262–3, 298n., 319, 352
Roman Catholic Church, 189, 190, 213, 236
under Santa Anna, 24–5
slavery, 134, 141
Three Years' War, 25
trade unions, 257, 263
transport and communications, 87, 88, 89, 92, 93, 94, 95, 96, 99, 100
and United States, 24–5, 236, 381, 388
urbanization, 186–7, 188, 259
World War II, 55
Middle class, 225, 247, 252, 253–5, 282, 321
Militarism, 331–5, 339–40
Military Dictatorships, 331–5
Miller, Gen. William, 17
Minifundio, 184, 248, 257, 258

Mining, 84–5, 165–6, 169–70, 172, 174–7, 178, 184, 199, 202, 205, 209–10, 219, 220
Miranda, Francisco de, 11
Miscegenation, 143, 144, 145–50
Mita system, 111, 113, 176, 180, 193, 196
Mitre, Bartolomé, 24, 28, 32, 217
MNR (National Revolutionary Movement), 263–4, 348, 350–1, 352–5
"Modernizing elites," 266–9
Monarchism, 315–16, 317
Monoproduction economy, 226, 227, 232, 239, 243, 285
Monroe, James, 381, 383, 384
Monroe Doctrine, 383, 389, 390
Montalvo, Juan, 117
Montesinos, Fr. Antonio de, 108
Montevideo Treaty (1960), 66, 294, 404
Montezuma II (Aztec ruler), 104
Montt, Manuel, 21, 233, 343n.
Morais, Prudente de, 33
Morelos, Father José María, 12–13, 113
Moreno, Mariano, 204, 379
Morgan, Henry, 6
Morillo, Gen. Pablo, 13, 15
Morinigo, Higinio, 51n.
Motor vehicle transport, 96–8
Mulattoes, 149–50, 151, 159, 211
Mule, 87, 88, 92, 112, 176
Myrdal, Gunnar, 282

Napoleon Bonaparte, 10, 11–2, 141, 206, 309, 310n., 315, 375, 378
Napoleon III, 25–6
Nariño, Antonio, 10
Nationalism, 379, 385
Natural resources, 83–6
Nazi movement, 48n.
Negroes, 32–42, 145, 147, 149–50, 159, 211
see also Slave trade, Slavery
Nelson, Lord Horatio, 10
Neo-colonialism, 161
Neruda, Pablo, 56
Netherlands, 5, 6, 135, 178
New Granada, 4, 8n., 9, 13, 15, 34, 89, 107, 145, 152, 174, 175, 183, 205, 303
see also Colombia

New Laws of the Indies, 4, 108–9, 125
"New Left" movements, 365, 366–9, 370, 371
Nicaragua, 45, 46, 77, 78, 93, 335, 383
Niemeyer, Oscar, 61
Niemeyer, Sir Otto, 244
Nitrate industry, 220, 224, 234–5, 239
Nixon, Richard M., 402, 404
Nóbrega, Father Manoel de, 146, 149
Nordenflicht, Baron Thaddeus von, 202
North, John Thomas, 234
Núñez, Rafael, 34
Núñez de Vela, Blasco, 4

Obrajes, 196
Obregón, Alvaro, 42, 43, 52
"Ocatara incident," 94
O'Donojú, Gen. Juan, 16
Odría, Gen. Manuel, 56, 244, 280
O'Higgins, Ambrosio, 14n.
O'Higgins, Bernardo, 14, 15, 20
Óidores, 304, 306
Olney, Richard, 389–90
Onganía, Gen. Juan Carlos, 73, 330, 347
Order dictatorships, 335–6
Organization of American States (O.A.S.), 55, 294n., 397, 399
Orozco, José Clemente, 43
Ortega y Gasset, José, 339
Ouro Preto, Viscount, 33
Ovando, Governor (first Governor of Hispanida), 134, 146

Pacific aspirations, 405–6
Padilla, Ezequiel, 395
Páez, José Antonio, 19, 327
Palacios, Alfredo, 355
Palma, Estrada, 38, 39
Pampa, 35, 82, 83
Panama, 2, 38, 77, 87, 89–90, 98, 138, 176, 389
Panama Canal, 38, 47, 76, 77, 99
Pan-American Conferences, 1889, 95, 389; 1923, 46, 97; 1928, 46; 1938, 53; 1940, 53; 1942, 55; 1948, 55, 398; 1954, 59
Pan-American Highway System, 97–8
Pan-American Union, 38

Pan-Americanism, see "Integration," "Inter-American system," Unity
Pan-Hispanism, 391
Paraguay
  in ALALC, 66n.
  Chaco War, 48, 49–51
  colony of Spain, 4, 7, 8
  comuneros rebellion, 7
  under Francia, 19, 292
  Indians, 3, 103, 191
  Japanese immigration, 157–8
  under López, 20, 28–9
  mestizos, 147, 149, 159
  under Stroessner, 157–8, 328
  transport and communications, 95, 97
  War of the Triple Alliance, 26–9, 388
Paris Treaty (1762), 9
Parry, J. H., 374
Pássos, Pereira, 225
Pastrana, Misael, 67
Paternalism, 279–80
Paul III (Pope), 108
Paul VI (Pope), 370
Pauw, Jan Cornelius de, 376
Paz Estenssoro, Victor, 61, 350, 351, 352
Pedro I (Emperor of Brazil), 17, 21
Pedro II (Emperor of Brazil), 21, 22, 28, 32, 92, 93, 141
Peixoto, Marshal Floriana, 33
Peninsular Spaniards, 128, 130, 151, 152, 179, 203, 208, 214
Peón, 180, 181, 196, 209, 236, 258
Pereira, Juan Solórzano, 129
Pereyra, Carlos, 393
Pérez Jiménez, Marcos, 63, 330
Perón, Eva, 58
Perón, Juan Domingó, 57–9, 72, 73, 100, 246, 250, 256, 323, 327, 336, 337, 355, 359–62, 397
Personal dictatorships, 335
Personalism, 322–3, 326–9
Peru
  agriculture, 178, 208, 274
  in ALALC, 66n.
  Ancón Treaty, 31
  in Andean Common Market, 67
  APRA, 47, 56, 69, 116, 348, 349–50
  under Beláunde Terry, 69, 97, 116

Peru—*continued*
  under Bolívar, 18, 34n., 112, 113
  under Bustamente, 56
  colony of Spain, 3, 4, 5, 14, 166, 303, 304, 305, 375
  ethnic makeup, 145, 157
  under Gamarra, 21, 141
  geography, 78, 79, 80, 81-2
  under Haya de la Torre, 47, 56, 69, 116, 349-50
  independence from Spain, 14-15, 17, 205
  Indians, 3, 9, 87, 105-7, 109, 110, 111, 112, 113, 114, 115, 116, 126, 180, 196, 277, 305
  industrialization, 184, 193, 244
  international relations, 381n., 382, 384-5, 388
  under Leguía, 47, 96-97
  Leticia Incident, 48, 53
  Lima Conferences of 1847-8, 384-5, 388
  mining, 166, 169, 170, 174, 175, 176-7, 202, 209
  mita, 111, 113
  natural resources, 83, 84, 85, 86
  under Odría, 244, 280
  Peru-Bolivian Confederation, 21
  petroleum industry, 220
  under Piérola, 31, 225
  political movements, 348, 349-50, 367
  political traditions, 304, 305, 315, 334-5, 336, 339
  Roman Catholic Church, 189-90
  under Santa Cruz, 21
  slavery, 134, 139, 141
  transportation and communications, 87, 88, 89, 90, 92, 94, 96-97
  and United States, 288, 381n., 402
  urbanization, 187, 259
  under Velasco Alvarado, 69, 334-5
  War of the Pacific, 29-31, 220, 224, 386, 388
  war with Ecuador (1941), 53-5
Peru-Bolivian Confederation, 21
Petroleum industry, 85, 86, 220, 250
Philip II (King of Spain), 5, 7, 126, 199, 302, 306, 374
Philip IV (King of Spain), 190
Piérola, Nicolás de, 31, 225

Pizarro, Francisco, 3, 4, 122
Pizarro, Gonzalo, 4, 328
Plan of Iguala, 16
Plantation, 179, 181, 223, 258
Platt Amendment, 38, 53
Political movements
  Catholic revolutionism, 369-71
  Communism, 46-7, 56, 59, 64, 70, 271, 337, 341, 342, 362-6, 367
  democratic reform, 348-58
  fascism, 358-62
  liberal, 342, 344, 345
  Marxism, 349, 362-3, 365, 366, 368, 371
  "New Left" movements, 365, 366-369, 370, 371
  radicalism, 346-8
  revolutionary movements, 358-71
  right-wing, 342, 343-8, 358-62
  Roman Catholic Church and, 344-5, 347
  see also Specific countries
Political parties, 321-3, 330, 338
  see also Political movements, Political traditions, Specific parties
Political traditions
  authoritarian legacy, 301-2, 307-8, 325
  Bolívar on, 314-15
  bureaucracy, 170-1, 302, 307, 308
  caciques and coronels, 321
  civil wars, 330, 331
  in colonies, 301-9
  constitutional democracy, 316-21, 338, 339, 340
  corruption, 282-4, 304-5, 306, 308, 316, 321, 337
  coup d'etat, 329-31
  dictatorship, 316, 318, 324-37, 338, 339
  disregard for law, 307-8
  and economic development, 338
  electoral practices, 320-1
  legislature, 319-20
  liberalism, 310-24
  militarism, 331-5, 339-40
  monarchism, 315-16, 317
  movements and programs, 340-71
  personalism, 322-3, 326-9
  political parties, 321-3, 330, 338
  presidents, 319

Political Traditions—*continued*
  violence, 329–31, 332, 342, 368
  see also Creoles, Revolution, Specific countries
Pombal, Marquis of, 8, 199, 201
Population
  growth, 40, 66, 261, 269, 270
  Indian, 101–2, 110, 112, 115, 125
  nineteenth century, 130
  population explosion, 271–3
  sixteenth century, 127
  slave, 136
  twentieth century, 261
Porfiriato, *see* Díaz, Porfirio
Porres, Father Martín de, 150
Portales, Diego, 20, 21, 214–15, 233, 317
Portugal
  Colonia, 8
  colonies in Latin America, 1, 2, 4–5, 6–7, 123, 161, 163, 171, 302, 374–5, 382
  decline, 199, 376
  Iberian character, 120, 123
  imperial government in Brazil, 11
  Madrid Treaty, 8
  medieval kingdoms, 117, 118, 119
  migration to Brazil, 127
  San Ildefonso Treaty, 8, 10
  slave trade, 133, 134, 135, 138, 141
  Tordesillas Treaty, 2, 7, 171
  trade with colonies, 89, 90, 171–2, 175, 194, 195, 201, 202, 203–4
Poverty, 251, 252, 257, 260–2, 265–6, 269–70, 272, 278
Powell, F. F. J., 244
Praetorianism, *see* Militarism
Prat, Capt. Arturo, 29
Prebisch, Raúl, 244
Prescott, W. H., 111
Prestes, Luis Carlos, 363
Preto, Viscount Ouro, 33
PRI (Institutional Revolutionary Party), 263, 338, 348, 352–5
Puerto Rico, 2, 18, 37, 136, 141
Punta del Este Charter, 67

Quadros, Jânio, 71, 72
Quiroga, Vasco de, 111

Radicalism, 346–8
"Ragamuffins' revolution," 21–2

Railways, 92–6
Ranching, 178, 179, 183, 224, 230, 258
Raynal, Abbé, 376–7, 407
"Reductions," 8, 111, 191
Reforming dictatorships, 336, 339
"Regrouping" of Indians, 109–10, 168
Repartimiento, 176, 180, 193
Repetto, Nicholás, 355
"Republic of Palmares," 33–4, 138
Requerimiento, 124–5
Research, 287
Residencia, 305
Revolutionary movements
  Catholic revolutionism, 369–71
  Communism, 361–6
  fascism, 358–61
  "New Left" movements, 366–9
Revolutions
  colonial, 7–10, 12–18, 19, 20, 308–9
  comuneros, 7, 9
  independence, 9, 10, 12, 19, 20, 21–39
  Indians, 7, 8, 9
  "perpetual," 19, 20, 299, 308–9, 325, 342
  political parties and, 342–3
  reform and, 295–6, 298, 299
  of slaves, 138, 201–2
  see also Specific countries
Richelieu, Cardinal, 6
Right-wing movements, 342, 343–8
Rio Branco, Viscount, 32–4
Rio de Janeiro Treaty (1947), 55
Rivera, Diego, 43
Rivera, Gen. Fructuoso, 23
Rivers, 79, 80, 81–2, 88, 91, 92
Roads, 87–9, 92, 96–8
Roca, Gen. Julio, 35, 114, 224–5
Roca-Runciman Pact (1933), 48, 240, 285
Rocafuerte, Vicente, 19
Rodó, José Enrique, 392–3
Roehm, Ernst, 49n.
Rojas, Adm. Isaac, 58
Rojas Pinilla, Gen. Gustavo, 57, 63, 67, 280, 330, 336
Roman Catholic Church
  and capitulaciones, 163, 171
  Catholic revolutionism, 369–71
  and colonial government, 305
  in colonial life, 173, 185, 188–92

Roman Catholic Church—*continued*
  after independence, 208, 212, 213–214
  and Indians, 108, 109, 111, 124–5, 126
  Inquisition, 189
  Jesuits, 8, 145, 146, 150, 191–2, 310
  land acquisition, 167, 168
  Lerdo Law, 25, 36
  and miscegenation, 146, 147, 150
  political movements, 344–5, 347, 369–71
  and reform, 267
  and slavery, 138–9, 140, 150
Rondon, Gen. Cândido da Silva, 116
Roosevelt, Franklin D., 53, 350
Roosevelt, Theodore, 38, 45, 389
Rosas, Juan Manuel, 23, 24, 91, 153, 208, 230, 327, 328, 331, 337n., 343, 383, 386
Royal and Supreme Council of the Indies, *see* Council of the Indies
Rubber production, 220, 239
Ryswick Treaty (1697), 6

Sáenz Peña, Roque, 43, 389, 393
Saint Domingue, 136, 137, 140–1, 201–2
  see also Haiti
St. Peter Claver, 140
Salazar, Dr. Antonio Oliveira, 51, 359
Salgado, Plinio, 358
Sánchez Salazar, Gen. Leandro A., 132–3
San Ildefonso Treaty (1777), 8, 10
San Martin, Col. (later Gen.) José de, 14–15, 16, 17, 141, 315, 317n., 333, 381
Sandino, Augusto César, 46
Sandoval, Alonso de, 140
Santa Anna, Gen. Antonio López de, 24–5
Santa Cruz, Gen. Andrés, 21, 131, 379
Santa Cruz y Espejo, Francisco Eugenio, 150
Santa María, Domingo, 234
Santander, Francisca de Paula, 333
Santo Domingo, *see* Dominican Republic
Santos-Dumont, Alberto, 98

Sarmiento, Domingo, 22, 24, 92, 344, 387–8
Sauvy, Alfred, 66n.
Scientific research, 287
Scott, Gen. Winfield, 25
Sepúlveda, Juan Ginés, 125, 126
Serra de Laguisamo, Mancio, 122, 126–7
Seven Years' War, 9
Shanty-towns, 260, 280
Siqueiros, David Alfaro, 132–3
Slave trade, 133–7, 138, 141
Slavery
  asiento, 8, 134, 135, 195
  castes, 152, 211
  in colonies, 137–40, 207
  end of slavery, 139–42, 211, 232
  Indian, 107n., 114, 124, 125, 172
  legal position, 137, 139
  Negroes, 128n., 133–40, 193, 196
  population, 136
  revolts, 138, 201–2
  Roman Catholic Church and, 138–139, 140, 150
  treatment, 137–8, 140, 142
  see also Slave trade, Specific countries
Social order, 160–1, 173–4, 195–8, 210–11, 225, 258, 262
Social progress, 270
Society of Jesus, *see* Jesuits
Solano Lopez, Francisco, 337n.
Somavia, Juan, 297–8
Somoza, Anastasio, 46, 328, 331, 335
Sousa, Irineu Evangelista da, *see* Viscount Mauá
Sousa, Tomé de, 4–5
Soviet Union, 64, 285, 287, 364n., 365, 367, 373, 401, 403
Spain
  absolutism, 301–2
  Anglo-Spanish Treaty, 6
  attempted reacquisition of colonies, 26, 381–2, 384–5
  Black Legend, 124
  bureaucracy in colonies, 170–1, 302, 307, 308
  capitulaciones, 163, 170
  colonial government, 301–8
  colonial monopolies, 193, 194, 200
  colonial trade, 89–90, 168–9, 170,

Spain—*continued*
 171, 175–6, 193, 194–5, 200, 202–204
 colonies, 1–4, 5, 7, 8, 37, 87, 88, 89, 121–2, 161, 163, 184, 185, 332, 374–6
 Córdoba Treaty, 16
 Council of the Indies, 4, 303, 304, 305, 307
 and Creoles, 21–39, 128–31
 crown and colonies, 163, 165, 167–8, 170, 173, 176, 177, 178, 180, 184, 193, 199, 202, 301–3, 304, 305, 306, 307, 309
 decline, 199, 202–3, 376, 378
 Economic Societies of Friends of the Country, 202
 1820 revolution, 15
 Iberian character, 120–3, 132
 independence movements, 7–10, 12–18, 19, 20, 21–39, 308–9
 and Indians, 4, 107–12, 124–7, 374
 Madrid Treaty, 8
 medieval kingdoms, 117–20
 migration to New World, 127–8
 Napoleon and, 11–12
 New Laws of the Indies, 4, 108–9, 125
 Paris Treaty, 9
 Ryswick Treaty, 6
 San Ildefonso Treaty, 8, 10
 Seven Years' War, 9
 slave trade, 133–4, 135, 138, 141
 Spanish-American War, 37–8, 389
 Tordesillas Treaty, 2, 7, 171
 Versailles Treaty, 9
 War of Jenkins' Ear, 8
 War of the Spanish Succession, 7, 8, 199
 war with west coast South American republics, 26
 see also Specific countries
Spanish-American War, 37–8, 389
Special Latin American Co-ordinating Committee (CECLA), 404–5
Steamship, 90–2
Stein, Stanley J., 196–7
Stroessner, Alfredo, 51n., 157–8, 328
"Structural" reforms, 262, 265, 266
Suárez, Inés de, 144
Submarine cable, 92, 224

Sucre, Antonio José de, 15, 17–18
Sugar industry, 178, 201, 208, 219, 220, 232–3, 264, 265

Tannenbaum, Frank, 137
Tannenberg, Otto Richard, 39n.
Tariffs, 239, 245, 249, 294
Tavares, Antônio Raposo, 7
Taxes, 185, 193, 215, 244, 277, 278–9
Taylor, Gen. Zachary, 25
Técnicos, 268
Technology gap, 286–7
Telegraph, 92
Tella, Torcuato di, 223n.
Ten Years' War, 37
Textile industry, 184
Thousand Days' War, 34
Tin-mining, 220
Tiradentes, 9–10
Tlatelolco Treaty (1967), 401n.
Toledo, Francisco de, 126, 184
Toltec Indians, 104
Tomic, Radomiro, 70, 358
Tordesillas Treaty (1494), 2, 7, 171
Toro, Col. David, 49
Torres, Camilo, 370
Totalitarian dictatorships, 336–7, 339
Toussaint L'Ouverture, 10, 140–1
Toynbee, Arnold, 296, 297, 350
Trade, 89–90, 168–9, 170, 171, 175–6, 177, 193, 200–4, 206–7, 214, 238–241, 285–6, 385, 403, 404
 see also International economy, Specific countries
Trade unions, 247–8, 256–7, 278, 361
Transitional dictatorships, 336
Transport and communications
 airlines, 96, 98–100
 archaic phase, 87–90
 in cities, 259
 early modern phase, 90–6
 electric telegraph, 92
 maritime, 89–90, 96
 modern phase, 96–100, 259
 motor vehicle, 96–8, 259
 mules, 87, 88, 92, 176
 Pan-American Highway System, 97–8
 railway, 92–6
 rivers, 88, 91
 roads, 87–9, 92, 96–8

Transport—*continued*
steam navigation, 90–2
submarine cable, 92
Treaty of Ancón (1883), 31
Treaty of Córdoba (1821), 16
Treaty of Guadalupe Hidalgo (1848), 25
Treaty of Madrid (1750), 8
Treaty of Montevideo (1960), 66, 294, 404
Treaty of Paris (1762), 9
Treaty of Rio de Janeiro (1947), 55
Treaty of Ryswick (1697), 6
Treaty of San Ildefonso (1777), 8, 10
Treaty of Tlatelolco (1967), 401n.
Treaty of Tordesillas (1494), 2, 7, 171
Treaty of Utrecht (1700), 374
Treaty of Versailles (1783), 9, 130
Trinidad, 10, 79
Trujillo, Gen. Rafael Leonidas, 46, 65, 328, 331, 335, 337
Tucumán Congress, 112–13
Túpac Amaru, 9, 111, 112, 304n., 305, 306, 309
Tupamaros, 68, 367
Tupí Indians, 103

Ugarte, Manuel, 391, 393
Ulloa, Antonio de, 112, 152, 190, 196, 277
UNCTAD, 286, 404n.
United Nations, 55, 66, 244–5, 286, 287, 397
United States
aid to Latin America, 242
Alliance for Progress, 67, 287, 399
Civil War, 388
Cold War, 55, 396
economic development, 228, 241
European immigration, 153, 155
Export-Import Bank, 53, 242
"Good Neighbor" policy, 53, 350
Great Depression, 40
Guadalupe Hidalgo Treaty, 25
Inter-American Development Bank, 242
intervention in Latin America, 24–5, 45–6
investment in Latin America, 40, 221, 226, 236, 240, 242, 291–2
Korean War, 55
Louisiana Purchase, 10, 381
Mexican War, 24–5
Monroe Doctrine, 383, 398, 390
Panama Canal, 38, 47, 76, 77, 99
Platt Amendment, 38, 53
political traditions, 311, 315, 332, 344
recognition of Latin American states, 381
Spanish-American War, 37–8, 389
trade with Latin America, 240–1
Versailles Treaty, 9
War of 1812, 381
War of Independence, 9, 310, 376, 382
Washington Naval Conference, 392
World War I, 392
World War II, 53–5, 394
Yankee Imperialism, 45–6, 47, 290–291, 350, 392, 393, 399–400
see also International relations, Pan-American Conferences, Specific countries
Unity, 379–80, 384–5, 388–9, 393–4, 401, 404–8
see also "Integration," "Inter-American system"
Universities, 267, 287
Urban guerrillas, 68, 367
Urbanization, 258–61, 321
see also Cities
Uriburu, Gen. José, 47, 359
Urquiza, Justo José de, 23
Uruguay
agriculture, 219
in ALALC, 66n.
under Batlle y Ordóñez, 43, 246, 318, 345, 346n.
creation, 18, 378
Depression, 47
European immigration, 132, 153, 155, 157, 159
geography, 76
Indians, 114
under López, 28
middle class, 253
political movements, 345
political traditions, 318, 323, 332
under Rivera, 23, 114
transport and communications, 92, 95

Uruguay—*continued*
Tupamaros, 68, 367
urbanization, 259
War of the Triple Alliance, 26–9
Utrecht Treaty (1700), 374

Valcárcel, Luis, 116
Valdés, Gabriel, 404–5
Valdivia, Pedro de, 3, 144n.
Valenilla Lanz, Laureano, 327–8
Vargas, Getúlio, 51–2, 55, 56, 61, 156, 246, 256, 322, 336, 359, 363
Vasconcelos, José, 43
Velasco, López de, 150
Velasco Alvarado, Gen. Juan, 69, 334
Véliz, Claudio, 406n.
Venezuela
  Acción Democrática, 56, 63, 348, 350, 351, 352
  agrarian reform, 276
  under Betancourt, 56, 63, 351, 352
  under Caldera, 68, 356
  under Cipriano Castro, 34
  colony of Spain, 4, 200–1
  ethnic makeup, 156, 159
  geography, 79, 81
  under Gómez, 34, 96, 244, 328
  under Guzmán Blanco, 19, 34
  independence from Spain, 12, 13, 15, 205, 378
  Indians, 125
  industrialization, 219, 220
  international relations, 389–90
  under Pérez Jiménez, 63
  under Larrázabal, 336
  under Leoni, 68
  Miranda liberation attempt, 11
  natural resources, 84, 85
  under Páez, 19, 327
  political movements, 348, 350, 351, 352, 356, 367
  political traditions, 330, 336
  slavery, 139, 141
  transport and communications, 96, 97, 99
Versailles Treaty (1783), 9, 130
Viceroy of colony, 303–4, 305, 306, 307
Viceroyalties, 303, 379
Victoria (Queen of England), 33
Vicuña Mackenna, Benjamin, 225

Villa, Francisco ("Pancho"), 42
Villegas, Abelardo de, 297
Violence, 329–31, 332, 342, 368, 385
  see also Dictatorships, Revolutions
Virgin Islands, 6n.
Visitor, 9, 305–6
Vitoria, Francisco de, 126
Vitruvius, Pollio, 187
Voltaire, 376

War of Castes, 114
War of Jenkins' Ear, 8
War of the Austrian Succession, 8–9
War of the Pacific, 29–31, 220, 224, 386, 388
War of the Spanish Succession, 7, 8, 199
War of the Triple Alliance, 26–9, 388
Washington Naval Conference, 392
Weber, Max, 323
Wellington, First Duke of, 12
West Indies, 137, 138, 139, 163, 164, 168–9, 174, 184, 190, 202–3
Weyler, Gen. Valeriano, 37
Wheelright, William, 90, 92, 93
Wilberforce, William, 140
Wilson, Woodrow, 45
Wine industry, 178, 193, 210
Women, 144, 145
Wood, Gen. Leonard, 37, 38
Working class, 247, 251, 255–6, 258–9, 278, 321
World Bank, 242
World War I, 238, 239, 240, 243, 248, 392–4
World War II, 53–5, 99–100, 240, 242, 243, 248, 394–5

Xavier, Joaquim José da Silva, 9–10

Yankee Imperialism, 45–6, 47, 290–1, 350, 392, 393, 399–400
Yaqui Indians, 114
Yerex, Lowell, 99

Zambos, 150, 151
Zapata, Emiliano, 40, 42
Zumárraga, Bishop Juan de, 146–7
Zweig, Stefan, 407